CURTAIN TIMES:

THE NEW YORK THEATER: 1965–1987

by OTIS L. GUERNSEY JR.

Photographs by MARTHA SWOPE
Drawings by HIRSCHFELD

PART I: THE LATE SIXTIES
PART II: THE EARLY SEVENTIES
PART III: THE LATE SEVENTIES
PART IV: THE EIGHTIES

APPLAUSE
THEATRE BOOK PUBLISHERS

CURTAIN TIMES: THE NEW YORK THEATER: 1965–1987

Published by arrangement with Dodd, Mead & Company

LIBRARY OF CONGRESS CATALOGING-IN-PUBLICATION DATA

Library of Congress Cataloging-in-Publication Data

Guernsey, Otis L., 1918–
    Curtain times.

    Bibliography: p.
    Includes index.
    1. Theater--New York (N.Y.)--History--20th century.
I. Title.
PN2277.N5G8   1987   792'.09747'1   86-26536
ISBN 0-936839-24-4
ISBN 0-936839-23-6 (pbk.)

Martha Swope is represented exclusively by Martha Swope Photography, Inc., New York

Al Hirschfeld is represented exclusively by The Margo Feiden Galleries, New York

Applause Theatre Books
211 West 71st Street
New York, NY 10023
(212) 595-4735

First Applause Printing, 1987

CONTENTS

CREDITS

Drawings by HIRSCHFELD

Joel Grey as George M. Cohan in *George M*, p. 1
Zero Mostel as Leopold Bloom in *Ulysses in Nighttown*, p. 147
Jack Lemmon in *Tribute*, p. 295
Shirley MacLaine in *Shirley MacLaine on Broadway*, p. 413

Photographs by MARTHA SWOPE

Harvey Schmidt and Tom Jones with the cast of
    The Fantasticks, p. 2
Anthony Quayle and Philip Bosco in *Galileo*, p. 56
John Wood, Noel Craig and Brian Murray in *Rosencrantz and
    Guildenstern Are Dead*, p. 84
Howard Da Silva in *1776*, p. 118
Stacy Keach in *Indians*, p. 148
Alexis Smith in *Follies*, 178
William Hickey, Gene Fanning, Cherry Davis and Brad Sullivan in
    Small Craft Warnings, p. 206
Jack Albertson, Lewis J. Stadlen and Sam Levene in *The Sunshine Boys*,
    p. 238
Ed Flanders, Jason Robards and Colleen Dewhurst in *A Moon for the
    Misbegotten*, p. 268
Ellen Burstyn and Charles Grodin in *Same Time, Next Year*, p. 296
Peter Evans, Paul Rudd, Terry Alexander, Dolph Sweet and Kenneth
    McMillan in *Streamers*, p. 321
The Orphans in *Annie*, p. 344
Jessica Tandy and Hume Cronyn in *The Gin Game*, p. 366
Len Cariou and Angela Lansbury in *Sweeney Todd*, p. 388
Mickey Rooney and Ann Miller in *Sugar Babies*, p. 414
Lee Roy Reams and ensemble in *42nd Street*, p. 438
Roger Rees and David Threlfall in *Nicholas Nickleby*, p. 462
Anne Pitoniak and Kathy Bates in *'night, Mother*, p. 486
Gene Barry and George Hearn in *La Cage aux Folles*, p. 512
Brian Delate, Richard Chaves, Vincent Caristi and Jim Tracy in *Tracers*,
    p. 536
Linda Hunt and Kathryn Pogson in *Aunt Dan and Lemon*, p. 558

INTRODUCTION

Curtain Times is a uniquely comprehensive, uniquely detailed and uniquely *contemporaneous* history of the New York theater in the seasons from 1964–65 up to 1987. This isn't because the undersigned —who wrote these reports on the hundreds of Broadway and off-Broadway productions as they opened during these years—has special powers. *Curtain Times* enjoys this triple uniqueness because Glenn Young, publisher of Applause Theatre Books, had the special gumption to collect more than two decades of annual critical surveys (originally published in the *Best Plays* series of yearbooks) and present them here in a single volume. Each of these surveys is a report and criticism of a whole New York theater season: its hits and misses onstage and off, its esthetic innards. Each is a comprehensive overview which takes in every play, musical, specialty and revival, foreign and domestic, produced on and off Broadway during the 12 months between June 1 (the traditional beginning date of the theater season) of one year and May 31 of the next. So *Curtain Times* is as broad in grasp, complete in coverage and fresh in attitude as a whole library shelf of New York stage reviews.

The *Best Plays* series of theater yearbooks, from which this material comes, has been published by Dodd, Mead & Company, beginning with the season of 1919–20 and still going strong in its 68th year of continuous annual publication. The late Burns Mantle, drama critic of the New York *Daily News,* was its first editor; the undersigned is its fifth, the incumbent since 1964. Collected in *Curtain Times* with a collective index, these 1964–1987 season-by-season reports take on the added dimension of a two-decade historical record. And we hasten to emphasize that they aren't reflections recollected in cool, scholarly, long-range tranquility. On the contrary, they are reports from the immediate front of each theater year, with nerves still tingling and failures still smoking. They are a sort of critique of New York Theater in 1964–1987; a sort of journal of annual entries whose comments were directly pertinent to their immediate time and are unaltered in publication here (though we cut a small amount of obsolete material and added a few comments in 1987 perspective every five years in this collection); and yes, a sort of history, but not the kind that has all the trends and consequences neatly arranged to illustrate some historian's point of view. *Curtain Times* watches the theater go by, not through a tunnel of time, but from an aisle seat. It is history in the making as it is being made. And yet in perspective there is almost nothing (as we found in looking the material over for *Curtain Times* pub-

publication) that we'd wish to change or did change for this collection.

The *Best Plays* series takes its title from the selection of the ten best plays of each season, recording them with special prominence. So in the text of *Curtain Times*, the capitalized phrase "Best Play" refers to one of these selections, made solely by the editor—and there were many times over the years when we wished we could go beyond the traditional number ten (and did, sometimes, with special citations). But on looking through *Curtain Times*, there's nothing we'd want to change in the Best Plays selections, either. We have never identified what might have been our tenth choice in any season, and we must admit that the latter was always virtually equaled in quality by several of the distinguished "also-rans" described in detail in the course of this volume. Not one of the many published reviews of *Best Plays* has ever agreed entirely with our choice of the top ten, and that's as it should be in a world of individuals. But even in hindsight we stand proudly by our selections, while agreeing that some of them were merely first among equals.

Finally, we must emphasize that *Curtain Times* wouldn't have been possible without the cooperation and help of Jonathan Dodd of Dodd, Mead & Company, for which he supervises all the *Best Plays* volumes, and of the scores of men and women in the press departments of the New York producers who arrange for us to have a good seat at all the shows and did their best to make sure we reported them as accurately as possible, supplying all kinds of source material. And thanks to the generosity and supreme artistry of Martha Swope and her associates, Susan Cook and Carol Rosegg. We present examples of New York stage production season-by-season in their exceptionally fine photographs. We are also grateful to the late Howard Bay for his kind permission to illustrate an outstanding example of scenery and costume design with reproductions of his sketches for *"Man of La Mancha"* (and thanks to Henry Hewes for lending us one of these). And finally but heartily, we thank Al Hirschfeld for permission to use one of his drawings to illustrate each of our four half-title pages, selected by the artist himself from his work reproduced in *Best Plays*. As we all know, the theater at its best always looks like a Hirschfeld drawing—lucky for it, because it would have to change if it didn't.

Otis L. Guernsey, Jr.
Editor, Curtain Times *and* Best Plays

PART I: THE LATE SIXTIES

JOEL GREY AS GEORGE M. COHAN IN "GEORGE M!"

Harvey Schmidt and Tom Jones *in rear, at left and right of the banner,* authors of *The Fantasticks*—the three-decade musical, longest continuous run of record in the American theater—pictured with one of their many casts. As this *Curtain Times* record begins on June 1, 1964, *The Fantasticks* is already 2,000 performances old, and it will still be running as our record ends in the mid-1980s.

PHOTO BY MARTHA SWOPE

1964-65

IT WAS the worst of seasons, it was the best of seasons. On Broadway there were fewer productions of new plays than last year (47 to 52, counting new foreign plays in English), and fewer off Broadway too. At the same time, the Broadway theater racked up the highest year's gross in its history—more than fifty million dollars. Best or worst, it depended a lot on where you were sitting. If you happened to be watching the whole soggy mass of below-average comedies and musicals go by, then 1964-65 looked like one of the worst of seasons. But if you happened to have a fifth-row-center pair for *Fiddler on the Roof* (or a piece of *Baker Street* the week it played nine performances and grossed $103,210), then it looked like one of the best of seasons.

Call 1964-65 any dirty name you choose. Call it weak, call Broadway Philistine (if you are avant-garde), call off-Broadway sick (if you are conservative), call the whole season a failure and you may be right. But the one thing 1964-65 did *not* fail to do was touch the heights.

Certainly musical production was conspicuous for its six-figure flops (the most spectacular being *Kelly* which lasted only one performance on Broadway and cost $650,000), and for the march of wooden musicals through the winter months. But the wonderful *Fiddler on the Roof* balanced out a lot of dismal shows. Many seasons with a higher average quality produced no such nugget as *Fiddler*.

Certainly it was too bad that no new play "made it big" off Broadway—big, that is, in the sense of instant popularity and a long first run. But LeRoi Jones' *The Toilet* is a little giant of a one-acter which spoke with harsh clarity and should be heard again—and again and again. Certainly it was an unexpected displeasure that many highly-acclaimed London hits failed to whip up enthusiasm among New York audiences. The lack of support for *A Severed Head and Poor Bitos* and *The Physicists;* for *Oh What a Lovely War, Alfie* and *All in Good Time* (and with the decision still to come on *Half a Sixpence* and *The Roar of the Greasepaint—The Smell of the Crowd* which had only just arrived as the season ended) indicated that the reports about how exciting the London theater is are highly romanticized. Or maybe it indicates to Broadway's advantage and credit that whereas the London Stage specializes in giving its audiences a little something pleasurable, Broadway is in business to produce Something with a capital S.

Certainly it was regrettable that a managerial storm broke over the Repertory Theater of Lincoln Center, ending in the departure of the Messrs. Robert Whitehead and Elia Kazan from the premises. But the troupe contributed *Incident at Vichy* and an excellent *Tartuffe* to the season. And presumably Lincoln Center Rep will rise like a phoenix from its own ashes under the new direction of the Messrs. Herbert Blau and Jules Irving. And speaking of phoenixes, the one on East 74th Street that housed the Association of Producing Artists staged a very fine repertory season of its own.

Yes, the 1964-65 season ran like a roller-coaster from bottom to top and back again. In an overall statistical review of the year, *Variety* added up the

The 1964-65 Season on Broadway

PLAYS (25)

A Girl Could Get Lucky
Absence of a Cello
The Last Analysis
Beekman Place
Sign in Sidney Brustein's Window
INCIDENT AT VICHY
I Was Dancing
LUV
Conversation at Midnight
The Owl and the Pussycat
P.S. I Love You
SLOW DANCE ON THE KILLING GROUND
One By One
Poor Richard
Ready When You Are, C.B.!
Hughie
TINY ALICE
Peterpat
The Family Way
Diamond Orchid
Catch Me If You Can
THE ODD COUPLE
The Amen Corner
And Things That Go Bump In The Night
A Race of Hairy Men

MUSICALS (10)

FIDDLER ON THE ROOF
Golden Boy
Ben Franklin in Paris
Something More
Bajour
I Had a Ball
Kelly
Baker Street
Do I Hear a Waltz?
Flora, the Red Menace

REVUES (1)

The Committee

REVIVALS (9)

The Three Sisters
The King and I
The Merry Widow
The Changeling
Tartuffe
Brigadoon
Guys and Dolls
The Glass Menagerie
Kiss Me Kate

FOREIGN PLAYS IN ENGLISH (18)

Traveller Without Luggage
Oh What a Lovely War (revue)
Cambridge Circus (revue)
THE PHYSICISTS
A Severed Head
POOR BITOS
D'Oyly Carte (musical revivals)
Iolanthe
Trial by Jury
H.M.S. Pinafore
Pirates of Penzance
The Mikado
Ruddigore
Beyond the Fringe '65 (revival)
Alfie
Boeing-Boeing
All in Good Time
Half a Sixpence (musical)
Roar of Greasepaint, Smell of Crowd (musical)

SPECIALTIES (4)

Comedy in Music
This Was Burlesque
Maurice Chevalier at 77
Ken Murray's Hollywood

PRODUCTIONS BY FOREIGN-LANGUAGE TROUPES (14)

Folies Bergère
Laterna Magika
Prague Pantomime
Piraikon Theater
Medea
Electra
Wiener Blut
Zizi
Schiller Theater
Don Carlos
Capt. of Koepenick
Polish Mime
Moscow Art
Dead Souls
The Cherry Orchard
The Three Sisters
Kremlin Chimes

HOLDOVER SHOWS WHICH BECAME HITS DURING 1964-65

THE SUBJECT WAS ROSES
Funny Girl
Hello, Dolly
110 in the Shade

Plays listed in CAPITAL LETTERS have been designated Best Plays of 1964-65
Plays listed in bold face type were classified as hits in *Variety's* annual list of hits and flops.
Plays listed in *italics* were still running as of June 1, 1965.

total gross from June 1, 1964 to May 31, 1965 of all Broadway shows and found that it reached a record $50,462,765—far more than the previous record of $45,665,500 set in 1959-60. It's also significant that 1964-65 totalled up 1,250 playing weeks (if 10 shows run 10 weeks, that's 100 playing weeks), the second-highest total in theater history. The all-time record for playing weeks is 1,325 in 1947-48. In the high-grossing year of 1959-60 there were 1,156.

The reason for this remarkable numerical showing in 1964-65 was not, alas! the exceptionally high quality and appeal of the productions. The records were set partly because of an increased ticket price scale, with a $9.90 top for the biggest shows on preferred nights, and partly because of the tourist-visitors in town during the usually slack summer months, to see the New York World's Fair. As is the way of Broadway, much of the big year's gross piled up on the hits, with comparatively little sifting down to the lesser attractions. It should be noted, however, that on August 5, 1964 (just to pick a summer date at random) there were 21 shows running on Broadway. On the same day the previous summer there were only 11.

The 1964-65 season had hardly begun when the revival of *The Merry Widow* in the newly-opened New York State Theater at Lincoln Center registered New York's highest-known 8-performance week's theater gross: $98,-380. Before the season ended, *Baker Street* recorded the highest-known 8-performance week's theater gross in a regular house (the Broadway Theater): $95,293.96. And *Baker Street* pulled in $103,210 for the week in which it played an extra holiday performance.

So call 1964-65 anything you like; call it a record grosser or a major disappointment, it was the sum of many different, even contradictory, parts. Let's examine some of these parts individually, with particular attention to the hits; to the successes—the shows that more or less succeeded in their intention even though they weren't able to magnetize the box office; to the big repertory caper; to the season off Broadway; and to the major theater news developments during the period from June 1, 1964 to May 31, 1965.

Broadway

When you speak of a "hit" in the commercial, unsubsidized theater, you can mean only one kind of show: a show that got off the nut, that earned back its production cost and then some. In the theater as in life itself, there are many different kinds of success, some of which have nothing whatever to do with either money or popularity. But in Broadway parlance, there is no such thing as a "hit" that loses money.

Among the *new* works produced this season, there were 25 plays, 10 musicals, 1 revue and 11 imports, making a total of 47 new shows as compared with the previous year's 52. Padded out with revivals both domestic and foreign, and foreign-language productions, 1964-65 shows a grand total of 81 against 1963-64's 75.

A glance at the 1964-65 hit list discloses that two specialty shows and a foreign-language dance extravaganza did well. Victor Borge's *Comedy in Music, Opus 2* was the Danish comedian's second Broadway serving of smorgas-Borge, in an evening of dryly humorous chitchat and shreds of tunes delivered by a past master of the beautifully polished soft sell. Another solo-show charmer was seventy-seven-year-old Maurice Chevalier in his program of monologue and song. Another hit from France was Zizi Jeanmaire in the music hall dance revue *Zizi* staged by her husband, Roland Petit. *Zizi* played only 49 performances on Broadway but came in as a hit, having paid off its investment during the road tour.

The season's other hit revue was *The Committee,* brought to Broadway from San Francisco, where its topical material had originally been improvised by its young cast. This show was an in-and-out affair like most topical satirical commentaries, but it left 'em laughing with an ingenious finale in which each member of the cast was making a sound like a musical instrument, and the whole effect was a reasonable human facsimile of an orchestra.

Jean Kerr turned from the female of the species in *Mary, Mary* to the male in *Poor Richard,* with Alan Bates as a British poet sojourning in Greenwich Village. Miss Kerr's two comedies overlapped by a few weeks, *Richard* coming in with a new batch of her caustically charming witticisms before *Mary* closed after becoming Broadway's ninth longest-running play with 1,572 performances. *Poor Richard* never caught on with the theatergoers and had only a short run. It was the sale of the movie rights that put the show into the black.

And so we come to the meat of the 1964-65 hit list: *Fiddler on the Roof, Luv, The Owl and the Pussycat* and *The Odd Couple;* one musical and three American comedies. *Fiddler* was an enchanting production, one of those rare enterprises which, magically, brings out the best in everyone working on it. Joseph Stein based his book on Sholom Aleichem's stories about the Jewish peasant community of Anatevka in Russia in 1905. Stein's dramatization cherished each of the characters, from a knock-kneed tailor to a political agitator, so warmly that the whole show glowed. Jerry Bock's music for this Jewish folk tale sounded as though it had been written to be played on a ram's horn, and Sheldon Harnick's lyrics were zesty as sour cream. And Jerome Robbins staged the dances and the show itself like a family party. Its intimate celebrations, occasional fierce clashes of will and jolly private jokes become increasingly happier and louder until, suddenly, the whole jumping party is broken up by nasty neighbors (in this case the Russians, whose persecution of these people finally forces them away from their idyllic Anatevka to another paradise, America).

The Fiddler on the roof isn't the leading character; he's only a symbol of Anatevka, which continues to make lively music even while in some danger of falling and breaking its neck. The leading character here is Tevye the dairyman, torn between his Jewish traditions and the new enlightenment; just as Zero Mostel, who played Tevye brilliantly, was torn in his performance between precise craftsmanship and the impulse to make grand gestures and clown faces. He did a little of both. One of Tevye's problems is, he has five daughters (three of marriageable age) and the oldest chooses to love a poor nebbish tailor (played by Austin Pendleton as though he might be blown away by the next song number) instead of a rich butcher. Tevye's wife (Maria Karnilova) is a helpmeet who does exactly what she is told after she's decided it's the right thing. As the head of the family, Tevye is next to God and on speaking terms with Him. Tevye dares to believe that He could use a bit of advice from time to time—offered always with Mostel's small-boy smile.

Zero Mostel's lip-smacking, wheedling, bellowing performance was a gem of the modern musical stage; so ingratiating, in fact, that you could almost believe Somebody Up There was teasing Tevye, keeping him poor and making his horse go lame, just to hear Tevye complain. Mostel can use the soft pedal and break your heart at one moment, and next moment broadcast enough comic grandeur to fill Madison Square Garden. Sweating under a weary load here, lording it over the village there, Tevye was a larger-than-life-sized role, and Mostel was stretching its skin. With such acting of such material, under such direction as Jerome Robbins provided, no wonder *Fiddler on the Roof* was a smash hit; and no wonder it walked away with the New York Drama Critics' Circle award for the best musical of the season, with 14 out of a possible 19 votes.

Walter Kerr, drama critic of the New York *Herald Tribune,* led the first wave of enthusiasm for Murray Schisgal's comedy *Luv.* Kerr's review (a rave, like all of *Luv's* first night notices) was so perceptive of the play's content and intent that Mike Nichols, who had directed *Luv,* was moved to comment in a magazine article: "Walter Kerr said that *Luv* is about the fact that we have learned so much that we can no longer mean anything when we speak. I'm shocked by how quickly Kerr can find the essence of something and express it clearly. That is a really brilliant statement about the play which he found in one-half hour after seeing it."

Luv was Schisgal's Broadway debut; his short plays *The Typists* and *The Tiger* won awards off Broadway in 1963. According to Mike Nichols, the play satirizes the fact that expression has outstripped feeling, that a fetish is being made of suffering both in the theater and in life. After the first wave of raves there were a few ripples of dissent from those who reacted to *Luv's* tongue-in-cheek catalogue of despair as they might to a whining child. The play's three characters pretend that they are unhappy, that they are going to jump off a bridge or murder or love each other. Eli Wallach, Anne Jackson and Alan Arkin acted the archly satirical script and direction with such great skill that there wasn't a hollow laugh missing. But these characters are citizens of the soft underbelly of modern society, where it is fashionable to cry whether or not—and especially before—you are hurt, and to mistake discomfort or inconvenience for tragedy. These people have their thumbs in their mouths. Well, what's so funny about a man with his thumb in his mouth? That he might try to jump off a bridge, or that he might try to build one? *Luv* chose jumping, with the result that a lot of it—to use an old but handy expression—was as funny as a crutch.

Whatever any single subjective reaction to this play may have been, it must be conceded that it loomed large in its time and place and genre. *Luv* is European existentialism applied to the American Dream. It is a *comedie noire* with a yellow stripe up its back. At the very least it confirmed Schisgal (who, hopefully, will some day either cheer up or get mad) as a valuable new playwright and Mike Nichols as a leading director who was able to repeat his success of last season with *Barefoot in the Park* and *The Knack.* In fact, Nichols' average accumulation of exclamation points seems to be two per season. In 1964-65 he followed up *Luv* with the direction of another smash hit, Neil Simon's *The Odd Couple.*

In a season of sick jokes and sick problem plays, *The Odd Couple* brought a rosy flush of laughter to Broadway's sallow cheeks. While his *Barefoot in the Park* was still running to beat the band, Neil Simon delivered another strong and funny script, about a couple of divorced guys—a sloppy bear (Walter Matthau) and a finicking banty rooster (Art Carney)—trying to share an apartment in a more harmonious relationship than they were able to achieve with their wives. Of course they fail—that's the fun of it. Their quarrels over a burned roast begin to sound very much like a husband and wife getting on each other's nerves. There are no dark, twisting emotional meanings; this is only a joke, but an exceptionally good one, about the male animal torn between his urge for freedom and his need for domestic conformity. *The Odd Couple* acknowledges the irreconcilable enmity between messiness and neatness; the eternal conflict between the smoker and the ash tray emptier, regardless of sex. In it, Carney acted with the snap and speed of a bouncing golf ball, and Walter Matthau established himself as a top character man, straight man and comedian all in one and the same performance.

It should be noted that in the New York Drama Critics' Circle voting for the best play of 1964-65 (won by *The Subject Was Roses*) *Luv* and *The Odd Couple* tied for runner-up with 4 votes each. That can be counted as 8 votes for Mike Nichols, the director of the year.

Bill Manhoff's comedy *The Owl and the Pussycat* was also a hit; also a playwright's Broadway debut, and also a comedy about a couple trying to get along with each other in an apartment—but in this one, sex is a major means of communication. The Owl is a young writer; the Pussycat is a—well, an actress in TV commercials who has been thrown out of her own apartment for entertaining too many men there (and *he's* the one who lodged the complaint with her landlord).

Some of the interest in this play developed from the bi-racial casting of Diana Sands opposite Alan (son of Robert) Alda in a role written without color implications. The casting was a great success, and not only as a sample of casual integration onstage. Miss Sands is a charming and abundantly talented actress whose witty interpretation of her role was far more imaginative than the role itself. The script was routine boy-and-girl sex play, with all the usual jokes and rivalries, the little prides and passions. Miss Sands—and the ingratiating Mr. Alda, too—made a lot of it seem fresh and pleasant.

The long, uphill struggle of Frank D. Gilroy's *The Subject Was Roses*—first to survive, then to enter the hit column—was won this season. This play about a soldier's homecoming opened May 25, 1964, and played 8 performances before the new season began on June 1. Thus, statistically speaking, *The Subject Was Roses* is registered forever as a 1963-64 production. Yet all of its glass-slipper success story happened in 1964-65. It opened too late in the year for consideration for the major 1964 awards but won *both* of them in 1965: the Pulitzer Prize and the New York Drama Critics Circle award for the best play of the year (with a simple plurality of five votes against many competitors).

Yes, *Roses* was the year's Cinderella play, and in those 8 1963-64 performances Cinderella had not yet even *heard* about the ball. For all of these reasons (and making an exception, not setting a precedent), we hereby declare *The Subject Was Roses* an honorary member of the season of 1964-65.

Gilroy's only other play produced professionally in New York was *Who'll Save the Plowboy?* (1962, off Broadway). Now, in his Broadway debut, Gilroy was contemplating the American family unit as an emotional pressure cooker. The subject here is not roses, but thorns, as all the wounds resulting from family strife begin to bleed when a soldier (Martin Sheen) comes home to his parents (Jack Albertson and Irene Dailey). Gilroy is a master of his medium, a playmaker as well as a writer of dialogue hauntingly true to life. This couple has outwardly turned to stone after the many failures of understanding in a difficult marriage, but their son's homecoming breaks through their shells and exposes the suffering flesh, squeezes the marrow from the still-living bone underneath.

The Subject Was Roses opened to enthusiastic reviews in the daily newspapers; an advance sale of $165; professional shoulder-shrugging (even the second-nighters, who are supposed to love the theater were conspicuous in the number of absentees from the performance, including nineteen pairs of aisle vacancies), and general public apathy. Gilroy and the producers borrowed $10,000 above the original $40,000 investment to keep the show alive. Slowly, slowly attendance crept upward during the difficult summer weeks, until the grosses reached the play's very low break-even point and then passed it. It is now classified by *Variety* as a hit.

Any show still running on June 1, 1965 had a theoretical chance to pay off its investment and become a hit in the course of the following season. One of them, *Baker Street*—based on three of Sir Arthur Conan Doyle's Sherlock Holmes stories—was a late-opening powerhouse. Offered at a $9.90 top, it set new records for weekly grosses on Broadway and generally proved itself as a fresh and pleasant entertainment. Sherlock Holmes—played with panache by Fritz Weaver—seemed a little younger than he was when we saw him last. Here he's about James Bond's age and disposition. The stories chosen for the book of this musical were about the woman in his life, Irene Adler, and the arch-villain Professor Moriarty. The lyrics went with a satisfying lilt and crackle of wit, but the score was indifferent except for one romantic love song, "Finding Words for Spring." Holmes' detecting was accomplished with many disguises, and the show's other highlights included a Queen Victoria Jubilee Parade by the Bil Baird marionettes and a ballet of mugging and murder in the back alleys of gaslit London, with Jay Norman dancing the role of the victim.

Another musical, *Do I Hear a Waltz?*, was the occasion for a new Richard Rodgers score—and a new lyricist for Rodgers, Stephen Sondheim, whose many distinguished credits include the *West Side Story* lyrics for Leonard Bernstein and the *A Funny Thing Happened on the Way to the Forum* lyrics for his own score. The tone of this new show—whose book was written by Arthur Laurents from his play *The Time of the Cuckoo*—was romantic with bitter undertones and aftertaste, in the story of an American businesswoman's fling with a handsome shopkeeper in Venice. Mr. Laurents' star-spangled tourist, whose name is Leona Samish, is not really a nice girl after all—she's a self-centered, unsporting, unlovable and unloving creature much too bilious to make it as heroine of a musical. Everything in this show is muted, including the performances and the coppery Venice designs of Beni Montresor. The Rodgers-Sondheim effect was muted, too, with no deep passion or bliss or agony to sing about; just Leona Samish and her miseries. In this particular case, Rodgers and Sondheim seemed to be putting their flame to asbestos.

As of season's end, six other 1964-65 musicals were still running. *Golden Boy* featured a performance by Sammy Davis Jr. as the boxer in the Clifford Odets play, now adapted into a slow-footed musical whose only burst of speed was a resentfully ironic number called "Don't Forget 127th Street." *Bajour* was a tale of a gypsy swindle remarkable principally for the swing and sway of Chita Rivera's presence. *I Had a Ball* was an inventive show, in Onna White's meshing of the action with the musical numbers in "Can It Be Possible?" and "Fickle Finger of Fate," and in Buddy Hackett's portrayal of a Coney Island swami (performance after performance during the run, Hackett continued to improvise new comedy business and accents). *Half a Sixpence* was one of two British musicals which came in late when the 1964-65 show was almost over. With its musical numbers also staged by Onna White, and in art nouveau decor by Loudon Sainthill, it starred Tommy Steele, a young British music-hall talent of the old breezy, straw-hat-twirling school, smiling and dancing and singing his way through a very pleasant performance. This was a warm, appealing, old-fashioned musical set in 1900 and based on H. G. Wells' cockney rags-to-riches story *Kipps*. The other British latecomer was *The Roar of the Greasepaint—The Smell of the Crowd* with Anthony Newley as "Cocky" and Cyril Ritchard as "Sir" in a running musical commentary and battle between these human symbols of the "haves" and the "have-nots" (the two leads come on looking almost exactly like the master and slave in *Waiting for Godot*). It tried unsuccessfully to satirize every phase of authority all at once and at the top of its lungs, so that the temptation is strong to abbreviate the title *Roar and Smell*. It doesn't deserve that, though; it had one striking song number, "Who Can I Turn To," and some piercing ironies delivered by the Messrs. Newley and Ritchard. *Flora, the Red Menace* also concerned itself, somewhat more light-heartedly, with the haves and have-nots in a depression-years story kidding Communism. This show introduced to Broadway Judy Garland's daughter, Liza Minnelli, playing a budding fashion designer of the 1930s (and Miss Minnelli is more than good enough to keep). *Flora* was staged by George Abbott; it was his 105th Broadway show.

One of the straight plays surviving at season's end was *Catch Me If You Can,* with Dan Dailey as a vacationist whose wife has mysteriously disappeared, and Tom Bosley as the Catskill Mountains detective called in on the case. The trick ending in this whodunit is neat and surprising. Another straight play was James Baldwin's *The Amen Corner,* a powerful statement (but an indifferent drama) about a lady evangelist, portrayed by Bea Richards. *The Amen Corner* came to New York after a long run in Los Angeles. Still another play was the first-rate revival of Tennessee Williams' *The Glass Menagerie* in the fullness of its strength, with no time-loss of vitality since its first appearance twenty years ago on March 31, 1945, and with a fine cast: Maureen Stapleton, George Grizzard, Pat Hingle and Piper Laurie.

These were the hits and potential hits of the season in our commercial theater, where a success is not always a hit and a hit is not always a successful work of art. The public had money to spend and spent a lot of it in the theater, mostly on good laughs and good tunes and the splashy holdover hits from 1963-64. The public didn't support everything that was *good* during the season; it never does. But at least it can be said that the public didn't support anything cheap or tawdry; anything really *bad,* either.

Instant popularity isn't the only measure of success in the theater. Many shows succeed in their intention to some degree, even though they don't make it at the box office. Some plays (like *The Crucible* in 1953) are received with mixed reaction and have only a short first run but make a place for themselves in the long run of re-stagings here and abroad (Edward Albee's *Tiny Alice* may prove to be just such a work). Some plays are remarkable for a scene, or a performance, or an element of design—or an idea. Then there is the show like *Ben Franklin in Paris* with its star, Robert Preston (who shaved his head bald, rode in a stage balloon and did everything else he could to make this Sidney Michaels story of Ben in Versailles look alive); a show that succeeds in running from October to May and thus becomes a part of the background color and identity of the season, even though it never attracts a full audience.

Two of the above were translations of European scripts. Both were very well received in London productions and certainly deserve their places on the Best Plays list, even though they weren't able to attract large audiences on Broadway. The first, Friedrich Duerrenmatt's *The Physicists,* treated with biting irony the popular modern superstition that nuclear scientists may be somewhat out of their minds, because of the insanely destructive practical application of their researches.

In this latest version of the mad-scientist act, Duerrenmatt places three nuclear physicists in a comfortable Swiss sanatorium run by a most uncomfortably purposeful hunchbacked lady psychiatrist (played by Jessica Tandy). One of these geniuses (Hume Cronyn) apparently thinks he is Isaac Newton; another (George Voscovec) thinks he is Einstein; but in reality both are only *feigning* insanity in order to ferret secrets from the third mastermind (Robert Shaw). He's not really insane, either, and yet (here's the backspin on Duerrenmatt's humor) they are better off in the sanatarium. Insane, they are harmless; it is their reason which is dangerous, and to make this point the play opens with no one on stage but the corpse of a girl one of them has murdered—not, it turns out, from an insane whimsy, but from a rational motive. *The Physicists* was a wryly enjoyable *comedie noire*. It was handicapped as entertainment, perhaps, because its comic dismay at the potential results of scientific excellence was not a novelty, but an all too familiar part of everyday life in this nuclear era.

The other London hit on the Best Plays list, *Poor Bitos,* was a Jean Anouilh play translated by Lucienne Hill. Its action takes place ten years after World War II in a French provincial town, where a vengeful snob (portrayed by Charles D. Gray of the London company) organizes a wig party in his chateau in order to humiliate the officious, drab little public prosecutor Bitos (Donald Pleasence, who also played him in London) who has risen to some power in the area since the war. The guests at the chateau are to wear the wigs and assume the characteristics and attitudes of famous personalities of the French Revolution; for example, Bitos is to come as Robespierre.

Like last season's Anouilh play, *The Rehearsal,* which was notable for its seduction scene, *Poor Bitos* had a big scene—or, rather, a whole outstanding act. In its remarkable Act II, which was a major influence in the choice of *Poor Bitos* as a Best Play, the make-believe becomes real. The action flashes back to the French Revolution; now Bitos really *is* Robespierre. In these French Revolution vignettes, Anouilh pictured Robespierre as a man of ferocious pride; a wolverine whipped and scorned and passionately determined to avenge every slap with a blow of the guillotine; dedicated to the Revolution in hate and envy rather than in affection for the proletariat. Pleasence snapped and snarled through a precisely vicious characterization, in the season's strongest acting.

Poor Bitos was the second Anouilh play of the season—the first was *Traveller Without Luggage* (written by Anouilh in 1936, 20 years earlier than *Bitos*), with Ben Gazzara as an amnesiac who hates his cruel past when it is finally revealed to him with the help of his mother (Mildred Dunnock). These plays were samples of Anouilh's steady contribution to the American theater. *Poor Bitos* was the French author's thirteenth play produced on Broadway, making him the most-produced playwright of modern times (Tennessee Williams is runner-up with twelve).

William Hanley, like Murray Schisgal and Frank D. Gilroy, made the Best Plays list in his Broadway debut after one representation off Broadway (in 1963 with the two-play program *Mrs. Dally Has a Lover* and *Whisper Into My Good Ear*). His first work for Broadway was *Slow Dance on the Killing Ground,* an introspective drama developing its power in richness of character rather than in incident or situation. The "Killing Ground" of the title is the big wide violent world, and there is temporary sanctuary from it for three people in a small Brooklyn paper-and-soda store: the store's owner, Mr. Glas, a German refugee; Randall, a brilliant but eccentric Negro youth who—it is obvious—has done something horrible and is running from the police; and a homely lass looking for an abortionist. They are three actual or potential killers, but each has some comfort and reassurance to give the others in the course of their slow dance of character revelation. These are meaty roles, written to be supremely well acted (as they were) by George Rose, the noted Shakespearean clown, as Mr. Glas; and by Clarence Williams III and Carolan Daniels in their Broadway acting debuts under Joseph Anthony's painstaking direction.

Edward Albee's *Tiny Alice* never gained popular support, but it was the most-discussed play of the season. It was a horror play which finally speculated on the nature of God in a story about a lay brother (a tremulous devotee played by John Gielgud) seduced by a strange multi-billionairess in her castle, then made the victim of a ritual murder during which the strength and substance of his faith is severely tested. The discussions about *Tiny Alice* centered on its symbolism. What, in effect, did the play *mean?* What was it *about?* Irene Worth, as Miss Alice, wore blue (the color of the Virgin Mary) —was this a significant symbol? Was the whole play an allegory of Christ? Was it a parody of sainthood or a parody of *Alice in Wonderland?* Albee himself was finally drawn into the discussion in a press conference at the Billy Rose Theater, at which he stated that some of the critics were confusing the audience by reading too much symbolism into the play. Albee described his own work as a simple dramatization of a man's crisis of faith.

It's true that there was less intentional symbolism in *Tiny Alice* than met the critical eye. For example, Albee's published scripts contain detailed instructions by the playwright on every important element in the play; and nowhere does the *Tiny Alice* script specify that Miss Alice wear blue, though it does describe her boudoir as "Feminine, but not frilly. Blues instead of pinks." And it's also true that there was a chill wind of metaphysical mystery blowing through this play which was meant to be felt rather than to be analyzed. Like Henry James in *The Turn of the Screw,* Albee lets the nightmare world into his story without attempting to explain all its manifestations. The toy castle in the library of the big castle—what, or rather What, lives there? A mouse, maybe, Albee suggests, then roars with sardonic laughter. Which is the model and which the real world? And if you are dying; if you are locked in a dark attic closet (Albee asks), does it matter What comes to rescue you as long as Something comes? That was the nightmare question about the nature of Deity posed by *Tiny Alice;* and whatever hidden meanings it might have, its overt events and tone accomplished what, presumably, Albee meant it to accomplish. Whatever it meant, it gave you the creeps, inside and out.

Many other shows enjoyed some degree of prestige, notoriety, controversy, longevity or other form of success during the season of 1964-65. Revivals were a strong suit, beginning with Richard Burton's *Hamlet* which carried over from 1963-64 and set a new Broadway performance record (136) for that Shakespearean tragedy before it closed in August. The Actors Studio mounted a first-rate production of Chekhov's *The Three Sisters,* with Kim Stanley and Geraldine Page. The Music Theater of Lincoln Center (Richard Rodgers, president) took over the New York State Theater at Lincoln Center for its first summer season of musical revivals; two of them, presented for limited engagements of a month each. For its first summer program, the organization chose Rodgers' own *The King and I* (well, why not?) with Rise Stevens and Darren McGavin, and Franz Lehar's *The Merry Widow* (well, why?) with Patrice Munsel and Bob Wright. Both shows were as well-mounted as any commercial Rodgers production, and it wasn't long after the first one opened that all doubts about this programming were trampled to death in the rush for tickets. *The King and I* promptly surpassed *Jennie's* all-time record for a week's Broadway gross ($91,847) with a whopping $94,851. And then *The Merry Widow*—that unsophisticated choice for New York revival—took in $95,265 the first week (when a lot of the first and second-night audiences got in free) and eventually recorded $98,380. And speaking of revivals, the New York City Center Light Opera Company's *Brigadoon, Guys and Dolls* (with Alan King) and *Kiss Me Kate* (with Bob Wright and Patricia Morison) were most enthusiastically received.

Among the new shows, there were some partially interesting imports from London besides those already discussed in the preceding paragraphs. *Oh What a Lovely War* delivered a bitingly ironic commentary on the horrors of World War I, with mounting casualty figures projected in the background while in the foreground Victor Spinetti led his group of helmeted Harlequins through the glory songs and martial poses of the period. The revue, assembled and staged by Joan Greenwood from real war memoirs, wore out its one-note tune before the show ended, but it was good for at least one act and was runner-up in the Critics voting for best musical with 4 votes. Bill Naughton, a British playwright new to Broadway this season, tried twice: once with *Alfie,* an examination of a Cockney heel played by Terence Stamp, and again with *All in Good Time,* which in its best scenes was one of the year's strongest plays. The color of this comedy was gray, in a closeup of a working-class family whose son cannot consummate his marriage while he and his wife are forced to live under the same roof with domineering papa. *All in Good Time* brought Donald Wolfit out of his entrenched position in the classic theater to play the rough-edged, soft-centered modern father. Wolfit's excursion into modern theater was most successful. So was Marjorie Rhodes' portrayal of a British mother who specializes in deflation of her family's pretenses by means of sharply-pointed remarks.

The Iris Murdoch—J.B. Priestley comedy *A Severed Head* ran into production problems in transit from London to the New York stage and failed to get its best foot forward by opening night. Even so, the script was interesting as a bitter British stylistic equivalent of *Luv*. The prototypical scene in *A Severed Head* is the one in which an unfaithful husband pays a surprise visit to the house of a psychiatrist who has seduced his wife, only to find the bold doctor in bed with the doctor's own half-sister. The point is that when there is no longer any such thing as love and scarcely any such thing as sex, there is at least the possibility of outrage. A severed head is a naked outrage— that's the metaphor of the title—and the human metaphor of a severed head is Honor Klein, the half-sister played both in New York and London by Sheila Burrell. Honor is a naked outrage to every preconception of a stage heroine. She is a roll of barbed wire. She is muscular, tricky, cruel and—incredibly—at last desirable. That's the joke in *A Severed Head,* which was part of the cold, ironic humor of the red hot moment in the theater.

Among home-grown dramas there was the late Lorraine Hansberry's *The Sign in Sidney Brustein's Window,* about a Greenwich Village newspaperman and his hope for the future in the face of desperate people and events around him. Miss Hansberry's last stage work before her untimely death was more effective in certain scenes, with its strong sympathy for suffering but still-striving individuals, than it was as a whole. It opened to mixed notices and box office apathy. Partly because *The Sign in Sidney Brustein's Window* was clearly Miss Hansberry's last chance to speak, and partly because they felt the play deserved a hearing, theater people and others waged a battle to keep it open and attract audiences, forming an *ad hoc* committee to sustain it by any means possible, including discussion groups after the performances. With the help of a $5,000 donation and other smaller donations, *The Sign in Sidney Brustein's Window* stayed open until after Miss Hansberry's death, playing 101 performances to 70,000 people. Thus it won deserved attention and recognition, when without the special effort of its supporters it would have closed abruptly.

For a new playwright, notoriety can be classified as a form of success, and Terrence McNally acquired a fairly good-sized chunk of it with his late-season drama *And Things That Go Bump in the Night*. In it, a monstrous mother (Eileen Heckart) and her two monstrous children are living in a basement bomb shelter with "fa" and "grandfa," waiting for the monstrous thermonuclear end of the world. While waiting, they amuse themselves by luring in visitors and torturing them. The son entices a strange youth into an act of homosexuality and then drives the youth mad by showing him pictures of the event, in front of the other members of the family.

In the midst of this horrid stuff was the line "We will continue." More than one critic quoted it in reviews, in order to reply "Oh, no you won't"; and then a funny thing happened to *And Things That Go Bump in the Night* on the way to the warehouse. Instead of promptly closing the day after the Monday opening, the producers decided to run out the week and let the play be seen with all seats at $1. Only 700 turned up at the theater that Wednesday night, but for the rest of the week the violently-panned play sold out. It was decided to keep the play going the following week, too, keeping the $1 price except Friday and Saturday nights when they went to $2. Again, they played to about half a house through Wednesday and then sold out over the weekend.

Now, this $1-$2 gross, even in a sellout, was nowhere near enough to support this or any play on the scale to which all Broadway has made itself accustomed. *And Things* went bump and closed that second Saturday night, leaving behind an echo of its notoriety in the questions that still hung in the air. Is there an audience which would attend a Broadway play as casually as they attend a movie if it could be priced competitively? Was it only the lurid subject, or a combination of subject and low admission, that attracted people to this play? (Ordinarily, you can't *give* tickets away to a show that gets really bad notices.) Nobody knows the answers for sure, but *And Things That Go Bump in the Night* succeeded in raising the questions with its two-week experiment.

Noteworthy among the season's crowd of comedies was *Absence of a Cello*, by Ira Wallach. This one might have done better a few years ago with its satire of corporate conformity. In it, Fred Clark played a scientist trying to rearrange his casual, even sloppy life to fit a corporate image of orderliness as typified by Murray Hamilton as an executive screening the scientists for a job.

Susan Slade's *Ready When You Are, C.B.!* succeeded in providing Julie Harris with a role both eccentric and appealing—the role of an actress who is afraid to act and therefore devotes herself to renting out rooms in her West Side apartment. Her seduction by a handsome tenant—a Hollywood movie star played by Lou Antonio—was accomplished onstage with a good deal of charm, and it was a pleasantly healthy change from the sick sexuality in many other comedies and dramas.

Among other happenings of note (if not precisely of success) in the season's programming was the appearance on Broadway for the first time of two plays found in the *oeuvres* of distinguished American writers: Eugene O'Neill's *Hughie* and Edna St. Vincent Millay's *Conversation at Midnight*. The first was a boastful harangue spoken by Jason Robards Jr. as a guest reminiscing with the night clerk of a second rate hotel; and the second amounted to a series of verbal essays on various political and philosophical subjects. Both were disappointing. So were the first plays of the novelists Saul Bellow *(The Last Analysis)* and Edwin O'Connor *(I Was Dancing)*, in spite of yeoman service in the leading roles by Sam Levene in the former and Burgess Meredith in the latter.

Visiting foreign-language troupes created a little UN on the West Side in 1964-65. From France there was *Folies Bergère* (everybody knows what *that* is) and *Zizi*. From Czechoslovakia there was *Laterna Magika,* an experimental combination of live action and movie footage, with a hilarious sequence of a roller-skater's breakneck course through city traffic; and a miming troupe from the Prague Pantomime Theater. The Piraikon Theater of Athens sent over *Medea* and *Electra*. In German there was *Wiener Blut* and the Schiller Theater of West Berlin doing *Don Carlos* and *The Captain of Koepenick*. And there was the Polish Mime Theater and the Moscow Art Theater (on which subject more hereinunder).

The Repertory Caper

One day in early December after the fall of *The Changeling* as performed by the Repertory Theater of Lincoln Center down in the ANTA Washington Square Theater, Rudolph Bing of the Metropolitan Opera told the press that

William Schuman, president of Lincoln Center, was trying to persuade the Met's assistant manager, Herman Krawitz, to take over the direction of Lincoln Center Repertory.

That's how the story of the managerial mess at Lincoln Center broke—and that's how the Messrs. Whitehead and Kazan, co-directors of the company, found out that they were to be replaced (probably they had heard rumors but if so they had given little weight to them). "Wrongfully discharged" is the way Whitehead put it. They knew they were having problems with Lincoln Center management. There was dissatisfaction with some of their productions; *The Changeling* was clearly going to be an expensive failure even by the standards of subsidized repertory. But until the Krawitz story was made public, neither Whitehead nor Kazan realized just how cold was the winter of Lincoln's Center management's discontent with the results at the ANTA Washington Square Theater.

Lincoln Center's Whitehead-Kazan operations are now a matter of record —a record of which any producers might well be proud. They had three hits *(After the Fall, Incident at Vichy* and *Tartuffe),* one interesting failure *(Marco Millions)* and two flops *(But For Whom Charlie* and *The Changeling).* In the commercial theater, that's an astronomical average—and remember, these plays were by no means safe choices. Three were new plays and one *(The Changeling)* had never been done professionally in America as far as is known.

Lincoln Center Rep made the Best Plays list in 1963-64 with *After the Fall* and makes it again in 1964-65 with *Incident at Vichy,* both by Arthur Miller. The new drama has an old subject: the psychopathical cruelty of the Nazis to the Jews. But this play is also the work of an old pro who knows how to set up the kind of theatrical tension that breaks open each of his characters. Miller's setting is Vichy, France, during the German occupation. Here, among a dozen Jewish prisoners and their captors (the French police and Nazi officials), the playwright exposes every degree and nuance of guilt on a scale that runs from a pseudo-scientific master-racist German at one end, to a Jew who lets himself be saved by another's sacrifice at the other end. Harold Clurman, Lincoln Center's executive consultant, directed the play and helped the actors to bring out each character in sharp outlines, and yet maintain the teamwork which is the mark of a good repertory company. Each of the characters in *Incident at Vichy* has his moment of supreme importance, rather like those on *The Bridge of San Luis Rey.* Each had to be vividly realized without overbalancing the group as a whole; and in this production, each was. If there was any standout performance, it was that of David Wayne as a decent Austrian baron horrified to discover a form of guilt within his own personality.

Kazan's last directed play at Lincoln Center was *The Changeling,* a dark Jacobean (1622) play by Thomas Middleton and William Rowley. In it, Beatrice (Barbara Loden) hires De Flores (Barry Primus) to kill her fiance so she can marry another man; then, like a bird fascinated by a snake, she is seduced by the killer she hired. There's a madhouse subplot, and over David Hays' set brooded a skeletonized crucified Christ as a comment on the whole bloody business. *The Changeling* was a theatrical curiosity. Some of the performers hadn't yet learned to cope with the period style and some of Kazan's capering-madmen, gory-handed effects misfired. But some were very arresting indeed in a production which was uneven rather than downright bad (for example, Barry Primus' performance, David Hays' setting and Ben Edwards' costumes were among the best of the season). The loud critical outcry of derision against *The Changeling*—and corresponding apathy at the semi-subsidized box office—undoubtedly triggered the Lincoln Center board's moves against Whitehead and Kazan. Yet even this very production of *The Changeling* might have developed in repertory with more time and effort into a show well worth seeing. But apparently a modern American repertory company—even one so satisfactorily subsidized as Lincoln Center—cannot afford to carry a big financial flop, at least not in its early stages of organization.

The final production under Robert Whitehead's supervision was an excellent *Tartuffe*, with the company pulling together under William Ball's direction, and with Michael O'Sullivan in a marvellously spidery portrayal of Molière's rascal. The play was presented in rhymed couplets, in a new translation by Richard Wilbur. On opening night a special prologue, also in couplets, was spoken by Hal Holbrook. Its final rhyme was as follows:

". . . we're delighted
To dedicate this play to Robert Whitehead."

Certainly the old guard at Lincoln Center Rep did not fail to come up with popular fare; with *Tartuffe* and *Incident at Vichy* they clicked two out of three times in 1964-65. If there was an esthetic failure under their management, it was the failure to begin the growth, the seedling growth of a uniform policy or style or personality. They were unable, or unwilling, to begin a process of *becoming*. They were neither adopting a new American perspective on the classics nor refurbishing and storing American theater treasures. Perhaps it would have been unfair to require the Messrs. Whitehead and Kazan to make a beginning in so short a span as two seasons and six plays. In any case, they did not do it. After they left, the troupe was doing well with its three hits, but it had no trace of a specialty.

Meanwhile, the visiting Association of Producing Artists was showing aspiring repertory groups how to achieve success. The APA productions—all of them good-sized endeavors with large casts—were mounted under the artistic direction of Ellis Rabb at the Lydia Mendelssohn Theater at the University of Michigan in the fall, then brought to New York off Broadway at the Phoenix Theater, for the second straight season. This season the APA repertory specialized in stinging irony, in three familiar themes: Shaw's *Man and Superman* with the *Don Juan in Hell* scene included; a new stage version of Tolstoi's *War and Peace;* and an adaptation by John K. Savacool of Giraudoux' *Judith,* based on the Biblical quandary in which Judith found herself when, a virgin, she shared the invader Holofernes' bed to save Israel from conquest, and then slew him in the night. The whips and scorns in each of these stories were somewhat similar in tone, and they were cracked smartly by Rosemary Harris and the other members of the APA repertory cast.

In addition to APA, off Broadway enjoyed a windfall which managed to take root, temporarily at least, without any major declaration of purpose, no "Look Ma, I'm in repertory." Theodore Mann and Paul Libin of Circle in the Square brought Joseph Papp's Central Park *Othello*, starring James Earl Jones, indoors to the Martinique Theater where it played all season. In May it was joined by a production of *Baal*, Bertolt Brecht's first play, in which the Messrs. Mann and Libin managed to cast all 22 members of the *Othello* company. *Baal*—the drama of a degenerate who brings ruin to himself and others who come into contact with him—and *Othello* were alternating at season's end in a *de facto* repertory establishment.

Presumably the goal of any repertory group is to achieve perfection of performance within its chosen range of material. Once achieved, that perfection may be maintained (pickled would be a better word in some cases) for many years, as evidenced by the visits here of two perfect repertory troupes: the D'Oyly Carte of London and the Moscow Art Theater. The D'Oyly Carte was a wholly predictable delight in the latest of its tours in Gilbert & Sullivan operettas. The Moscow Art Theater was predictable, too, even though it had not visited New York since 1923-24 when it earned the city's admiration for its Stanislavskian realism and ensemble acting. 41 years later, it still deserved admiration—for its Stanislavskian realism and ensemble acting. Leaving aside *Dead Souls*—a heavy-handed sociological jape in which the actors get to show off individually—and *Kremlin Chimes*—in which the Communist mythology gets to show off—the Moscow Art Theater was as perfect as before in Chekhov's *The Three Sisters* and *The Cherry Orchard*, with the realistic, practised, teamed performing for which it is famous (Walter Kerr remarked in a review that he knew exactly what the characters were doing while they were offstage). The Moscow Art Theater was so perfect that we can expect another visit from them in a few decades—in *The Three Sisters* and *The Cherry Orchard*.

In comparison, our own fledgling experiments in repertory are hardly recognizable as potential swans. But growing up is a more creative process than growing old; and as we mature we should keep in mind that growth itself is admirable, and the point of perfection is very small in area.

Off Broadway

Uptown, downtown and across town from Broadway, 1964-65 was much as off-Broadway seasons have always been: arrogant, imaginative, physically uncomfortable on hard, narrow, sometimes tilted seats; with a mass of flops and a few very interesting successes.

There were fewer programs of new plays produced than in 1963-64 (33 as opposed to 38); fewer revivals (19 including the American Savoyards as opposed to 23), and fewer musicals (7 as opposed to 8). 8 cabaret-style musicals and revues, one specialty and 5 foreign-language shows brought the off-Broadway production total to 73 programs. Off Broadway, figures can be deceiving (even the ones just given), because the totals depend upon where the line is drawn to exclude purely experimental productions, and on various other problems of classification. But it is clear that the volume of production was down slightly off Broadway in 1964-65, a season in which producers were re-evaluating the rising cost of putting on plays and generally marking time. Specifically, 1964-65 was notable most of all for LeRoi Jones' moving one-acter *The Toilet,* a Best Play; for the APA repertory already described, and for the debuts of several playwrights-to-be-watched.

LeRoi Jones' *The Toilet* was presented on the same program with his *The Slave,* which latter was a mainstream black-supremacy polemic; a tirade against the whole white world and all its works, spoken by Lincoln Kilpatrick as the Negro leader of a future armed revolution. In highly favorable comparison, *The Toilet* is no mere harangue geared to the social ills of the moment. If it can be said that Jones wrote *The Slave* as a Negro protest, then it must be said that he wrote *The Toilet* as a human cry; as a man angry at squalor and cruelty but moved by the conviction that even down in the muddiest swamps of existence—the toilet of a boys' school, for example—the hardy wildflower of compassion grows.

There are no racial designations for the characters in the script of *The Toilet,* but as played off Broadway all but two were Negroes. A group of boys is going to gang up on a schoolmate (he is white) who has sent their leader (he is a Negro) a rather physical love letter. Some of these boys are twigs growing crooked with emotional sickness. All have fallen into the habit of brutality—brutal gestures and brutal, unimaginative language whose once-shocking epithets have grown meaningless from repetition, from over-use (and that is one of the effects which the Jones script achieves in over-using this language in the dialogue; as you hear the vulgar words repeated and repeated on the stage, they lose their shock).

There was a ballet-like quality in much of Leo Garen's staging of the off-Broadway production, notably in a scene in which the boys have a basketball roughhouse with a roll of toilet paper. These young characters, their attitudes and relationships, are uncomfortably real, as is Jones' lumpy dialogue. But *The Toilet* is no mere theater-of-despair caterwauling. Jones knows perfectly well that there is still plenty of hope for the human race. He expresses this instinctive optimism most eloquently in the final scene, when the Negro leader returns to comfort the white victim his gang has just beaten up. He has to sneak away from the others to perform this act of compassion; he'd rather not do it, but he can't help himself.

Elsewhere off Broadway, a great deal of interest was generated by playwrights in the debut or fledgling state. The Pulitzer Prize-winning poet Robert Lowell's first produced play, *The Old Glory,* was presented by the American Place Theater at St. Clement's Church in a fully-mounted production which justified earlier enthusiasm for it in a skeletal staging last year and won Lowell a Drama Desk-Vernon Rice Award for off-Broadway achievement. This program consisted of two one-act plays (three in the original version), of which the verse play *Benito Cereno,* based on a Herman Melville story, was the more effective. Its tale of a Yankee captain who puts down the rebellion of a Negro king on a Spanish slave ship makes nobody look good; but it does offer Lowell's poet's-eye-view of the kind of incident and emotional stress which underlie, historically, American race relations. The American Place Theater is the organization started two years ago as an experimental theater group at St. Clement's Church by Wynn Handman and the Rev. Sidney Lanier. Its effort to help new playwrights to develop, with *Benito Cereno* as its high point so far, has been outstanding, and it received a $225,000 grant from the Ford Foundation for the production of new scripts.

Herbert Lieberman made his New York debut with *Matty and the Moron and Madonna,* a drama which had won the University of Chicago Play Contest, judged by Kenneth Tynan. Grimly, but with great affection, this play tells the story of a boy whose father abandons him and whose crazed mother threatens him with an axe. The boy tries several avenues of escape, but finally, saintlike, he decides that his mission in life is to offer himself to his mother as a sacrifice, let come what may. Another grim—but undeniably promising—New York playwriting debut was Charles Nolte's *Do Not Pass Go,* about a smiling health faddist who cheerfully murders for kicks an old

The 1964-65 Season Off Broadway

PLAYS (28)

Kiss Mama
Shout From the Rooftops
My Kinsman, Major Molyneux & Benito Cereno
The Giants' Dance
Route 1 & Blastoma City
Helen
The Slave & THE TOILET
The Child Buyer
Play With a Tiger
All Women Are One
The Fourth Pig & The Fisherman
Say Nothing
The Great Western Union
The River, Passport & Mary Agnes Is 35
Theater 1965:
Up to Thursday, Balls & Home Free
Pigeons & Conerico Was Here to Stay
Hunting the Jingo Bird & Lovey
The Sweet Enemy
A Sound of Silence
The Day the Whores Came Out to Play Tennis & Sing to Me Through Open Windows
Matty and the Moron and Madonna
The Bitch of Waverly Place & The Blind Angel
Do Not Pass Go
Harry, Noon and Night
The Wives
Square in the Eye
The Exception and the Rule & The Prodigal Son
The Umbrella

FOREIGN PLAYS IN ENGLISH (5)

On the Necessity of Being Polygamous
The Room & A Slight Ache
Colombe
The Queen & The Rebels
Billy Liar

MUSICALS (7)

That Hat!
Gogo Loves You
Hang Down Your Head and Die
That 5 a.m. Jazz
The Secret Life of Walter Mitty
Babes in the Wood
The Wonderful World of Burlesque

FOREIGN-LANGUAGE PRODUCTIONS (5)

The Puppet Theater of Don Cristobal
The Shoemaker's Prodigious Wife
Good Luck
L'Annonce Faite a Marie
Enchanting Melody

SPECIALTY (1)

Worlds of Oscar Brown Jr.

REVUES (8)

A View From Under the Bridge
The Game Is Up
Bits and Pieces
Cambridge Circus
New Cambridge Circus
The Decline and Fall of the Entire World as Seen Through the Eyes of Cole Porter Revisited
Wet Paint
That Thing at the Cherry Lane

REVIVALS (19)

The Alchemist
The Tragical Historie of Doctor Faustus
Othello
Baal
The Cradle Will Rock
I Knock at the Door
Judith
In White America
American Savoyards:
Iolanthe
H.M.S. Pinafore
The Mikado
The Gondoliers
The Yeomen of the Guard
APA Phoenix:
Man and Superman
War and Peace
Pictures in the Hallway
Her Master's Voice
The Cat and the Canary
A View From the Bridge

Play listed in CAPITAL LETTERS has been designated a Best Play of 1964-65.
Plays listed in *italics* were still running on June 1, 1965.

man who works with him in the stockroom of a supermarket. Nolte, who played Billy Budd on Broadway, acted the role of the killer in his own script. A first play by Harold Willis, *A Sound of Silence,* won him a Drama Desk-Vernon Rice Award with its examination of people whose pretenses are exposed when a Negro minister visits the home of a scientist in a Northern Louisiana town. In Theater 65's New Playwrights Series, the best works were Frank Gagliano's *Conerico Was Here to Stay,* in which Jaime Sanchez' performance won a Clarence Derwent Award, and Joseph Morgenstern's *Lovey.* Sanchez acted in *Conerico* at the same time that he was acting Karolis in *The Toilet.* He had time enough to get across town from the St. Marks Playhouse to the Cherry Lane, out of one one-acter into another.

Harold Pinter managed to hold onto his franchise as an off-Broadway favorite with a program of two one-acters, one written originally for TV. Arthur Miller had a second success to his name during the 1964-65 season with a revival of *A View From the Bridge.* John Willard's thriller *The Cat and the Canary* enjoyed a popular revival. Among other items from the library shelves were plays by Ben Jonson, Christopher Marlowe (whose 400th anniversary year 1964 was, as well as Shakespeare's), Sean O'Casey, Jean Anouilh—and Bertolt Brecht, whose off-Broadway reputation was established by *The Threepenny Opera* and who is now enjoying an interest and a curiosity which amounts almost to a fad.

Musical expectations off Broadway turned into disappointments including *The Secret Life of Walter Mitty,* based on the James Thurber tale, and a revival of Marc Blitzstein's *The Cradle Will Rock* (short-lived as this was, a cast album was issued by MGM). The cabaret shows did better than the book musicals in 1964-65. These included the Second City productions; Julius Monk's show at Plaza 9; *The Game Is Up;* and *Cambridge Circus,* which opened first on Broadway and then moved downtown. A major cabaret curiosity of the season was called *The Decline and Fall of the Entire World as Seen Through the Eyes of Cole Porter Revisited.* It featured a clump of lesser-known Porter tunes from shows by the late composer, song numbers that never caught the public's fancy in their original presentation.

Viewed as a whole, 1964-65 was a tentative season off Broadway, with some floundering, without strong leadership, without new identity or an emergent trend among the new works. Off Broadway was marking time but continuing to develop new talent, not only at the APA, the American Place Theater, Theater 65 and in its regular playhouses, but also at small, unsung cafe theaters operating out of the limelight of reviews. The Cafe LaMama and Caffe Cino were putting on *a play a week,* from one-acters to full-length scripts, charging $1 admission and then passing the hat, serving free coffee. Obviously these cafes were a boon to new playwrights and their effect may become measurable in the future.

Offstage

As the 1964-65 season began, the new Codes of Ethics of the League of New York Theaters—together with the possibility of a Commissioner, or czar, to administer them—were very much in the news. These two Codes were drawn up during the winter of 1964 and made public in the spring. One of them dealt with the fiscal details of producing, the other with the handling of theater tickets. They covered some of the same ground as the new state legislation in these areas, which makes it a misdemeanor to scalp tickets and requires that producers file certain financial records with the state attorney-general's office.

At season's end there was still no czar; but the theater's financial and ethical problems were receiving attention from two sources. Attorney-General Louis J. Lefkowitz instituted actions (and got some convictions) against a few errant individuals in show business for such illegal and injurious practices as taking kickbacks for steering production contracts, and ticket-scalping (the selling of hit tickets at a premium above the legal limit). And John F. Wharton, a lawyer who helped organize and run the Playwrights Company, was named by the League (with the Shubert organization, which is not a League member, participating) to head a Legitimate Theater Industry Exploratory Commission. It was to make recommendations regarding the following: a new ticket policy adapted to modern conditions and designed to meet the needs of theatergoers; an up-to-date Code of Ethics; revision of laws which affect the theater; improvement of labor bargaining procedures; abolition of unfair taxes, and increasing the audience while improving theatergoing conditions.

Also on the agenda as the season began was the possibility of a special $25 ticket to the hits, to be placed on sale by licensed brokers 48 hours before curtain time, in order to satisfy legally the high-paying, last-minute demand for hit tickets in New York's expense-account society. It was hoped that such a ticket would retain the potential "ice" (illegal markup) for the legal benefit of legitimate show businessmen and artists. As a corollary to the de-icer ticket (which failed to become a reality in 1964-65) there was a suggestion by producer Alexander H. Cohen that a corresponding number of seats be marked *down* to bargain rates which might attract new audiences.

The sawbuck barrier held all during the season, with a $9.90 top, but there were rumblings that this barrier might soon be broken, as Alan J. Lerner announced his intention to offer his next musical, *On a Clear Day You Can See Forever,* at $11.90. And in another part of the Broadway forest, an effort was being made to straighten out and standardize the meanings of "loge," "mezzanine" and "balcony," which had a habit of varying from theater to theater.

One of the schemes to make the theater more appealing, institutionally, *did* come to pass. The law was amended to permit the installation of bars in the playhouses, and by season's end there were 3 such oases on Broadway. The high cost of a license and the relatively short drinking time discouraged a more widespread installation of this convenience.

Actors Equity staged a one-day strike on Sunday, June 7 (forcing cancellation of scheduled matinees of *Oliver* and *The Deputy*), to enforce its arguments in negotiating a new four-year contract. Both strike and contract were settled the following day. The weekly Broadway minimum for actors was raised from $117.50 to $125 and will rise to $170 during the four-year period of the contract. The 70-American-to-30-alien ratio for actors in any given cast was re-established. Off Broadway, Equity settled for a $10 raise to $60, a minimum which rises with the grosses on a sliding scale until it equals the Broadway minimum when an off-Broadway show grosses $9,000 a week or better.

Sidney Kingsley was named the new president of The Dramatists Guild, Inc., the organization of playwrights which as of October 1, 1964, became a corporation separate from the Authors League, of which it had formerly been a part and with which it continues to be affiliated. Ted Kalem of *Time* succeeded Howard Taubman of *The New York Times* as chairman of the New York Drama Critics Circle. Harold S. Prince was named president of the League of New York Theaters, then resigned this post as the season ended, in order to devote himself to his many other activities in the theater. Frederick O'Neal continued as president of Actors Equity. John Houseman was appointed to head the new Drama Division of the Julliard School when it moves to Lincoln Center in 1967.

Jerry Herman's song number "Hello, Dolly!" made it big in the Presidential election campaign, becoming "Hello, Lyndon!" for President Johnson's theme song. Throughout the year theater people participated as individuals in politics and social causes, but there was no strong institutional involvement in these matters. Plays relating to the Negro and integrated casts had long since become a commonplace. Broadway had reached the point at which it could be most helpful in the civil-rights situation by playing it cool, as in the raceless casting of Diana Sands in *The Owl and the Pussycat*. Artists continued to withhold their work, as a general rule and policy, from theaters and locales which still practise segregation. At one point Jerry Herman and Michael Stewart had considered allowing *Hello, Dolly!* to be produced in South Africa, in order to donate their royalties to Negro organizations there. They put it up to the N.A.A.C.P., which advised them against it. The boycott is worth more than the cash, the N.A.A.C.P. told them. "Artistic starvation" was expected to have a political effect, and so this plan to export *Hello, Dolly!* was dropped.

The managerial problems at Lincoln Center; the publication of the Rockefeller Panel Report *The Performing Arts: Problems and Prospects;* the establishment of the National Council on the Arts in Washington with Roger L. Stevens at its head; the bills to establish National Foundations on the arts and humanities to give encouragement and cash assistance—these and other 1964-65 developments brought the whole question of private and public subsidy of the theater into the limelight. The fate of *The Changeling* (16 of whose scheduled repertory performances were cancelled because of bad business after unfavorable reviews) illustrated the inadequacy of partial subsidy in a commercial-theater climate in which most shows are either complete hits or complete flops. The most sweeping generalizations on the subject of subsidy were made by the Rockefeller Panel (not one of whose 30 members was active on Broadway at the time of the report), which concluded that the best hope of the American theater lies in decentralization; in establishing, encouraging and subsidizing about 50 permanent professional theater groups from coast to coast.

Such was the season of June 1, 1964—May 31, 1965 in New York; a wide range of experience from exciting to despicable; denigrated by experts and encouraged by a $50,462,765 gross; reaching its peak in the emotions, the melodies and the humor of the Best Plays, and dipping to its nadir in the corrosive activities of a few furtive cheats hauled into court for scalping tickets. In 1964-65, there was no marked reversal of recent trends, either artistic or economic. New shows on and off Broadway were slightly fewer; costs and ticket prices and grosses were higher; help in the form of tighter organization within and subsidy without was still on the way rather than here. If there was any single outstanding characteristic of the 1964-65 season, it was this: never has the New York theater's capacity for survival, its knack of continuity, been more clearly defined. Beside Arthur Miller and Jean Anouilh and Friedrich Duerrenmatt and Tennessee Williams (in revival) stood Edward Albee and Neil Simon and LeRoi Jones and Harold Pinter; and beside them stood Frank D. Gilroy, William Hanley, Murray Schisgal, Bill Naughton and Iris Murdoch; yes, and beside them stood Bill Manhoff and Robert Lowell and Herbert Lieberman and Charles Nolte and Harold Willis. In 1964-65 the theater was in strong hands, many of them in their first grasp of Broadway, with still more strong hands reaching.

Sets and costumes begin as designer's sketches. *Above,* Howard Bay's design for *Man of La Mancha's* thrust stage. *Below,* Howard Bay-Patton Campbell costumes (Sancho, *left,* and Knight of the Mirrors, *right*) in that musical.

1965-66

"... THE THEATER was in strong hands, many of them in their first grasp of Broadway, with still more strong hands reaching."

That's the way our New York report ended in last year's *Best Plays* volume. As things turned out, it was prophetic. The new, 1965-66 theater season in New York was nowhere; it was headed for a disaster appalling in its unmitigated totality of mediocrity, when a funny thing happened—the new-reaching hands caught, took hold and gripped firm. When old hands faltered, scripts from brand new sources arrived in time to save the season.

In 1965-66 the playwriting "establishment" failed the theater on Broadway and off; yet in this same period audiences were treated to several fine musicals, two poetic dramas, a comedy mostly in verse disguised as prose, two hot comedies and other delectations. Where did they come from? You might as well say the stork brought them. Of the ten Best Plays in this volume, *eight* were either playwriting debuts in some sense or new territory for old practitioners, as follows: *Generation* was William Goodhart's first script produced on any stage; the book of *Man of La Mancha* was Dale Wasserman's first Broadway musical and Mitch Leigh's first Broadway score; *Cactus Flower* was Abe Burrows' first non-musical playwriting credit; *The Persecution and Assassination of Marat as Performed by the Inmates of the Asylum of Charenton Under the Direction of the Marquis de Sade* was Peter Weiss's American stage debut and *Philadelphia, Here I Come!* was Brian Friel's; *The Lion in Winter* was James Goldman's first Broadway effort solo, without a collaborator; the book of *"It's a Bird It's a Plane It's SUPERMAN"* was the professional playwriting debut of David Newman and Robert Benton, and *Hogan's Goat* was William Alfred's first professional production.

Any Broadway season is constructed from equal parts of talent, effort, hope and cash. The first varies from year to year with the winds of artistic chance. The last three flow more steadily, and they did so in 1965-66 as in previous years. Effort and hope (and money) went into a grand total of 76 shows this season, as compared with 81 last year and 75 the year before. Of these, 49 were new (counting new foreign plays in English). 1965-66 brought in the same number of new American plays—25—as in 1964-65 and one more musical—11. If you look for centers of gravity in the production list (see the one-page chart of the 1965-66 season accompanying this chapter) you will notice immediately that foreign authors had very much more than their share of success on both the top and second levels. And, among the 25 new American playscripts there continued an alarming preponderance of comedy over drama.

In the matter of money, *Variety* estimates that Broadway grossed a ring-tailed all-time-record $53,862,187, topping last year's record by more than three million. The number of playing weeks in 1965-66 (if ten shows play ten weeks, that's 100 playing weeks) reached 1,295—the second highest in theater history, second only to 1947-48's 1,325 and exceeding last season by 45 playing weeks. The record gross was attained with a top ticket price which

The 1965-66 Season on Broadway

PLAYS (25)

Mrs. Dally
A Very Rich Woman
GENERATION
Minor Miracle
The Impossible Years
Postmark Zero
Mating Dance
Xmas in Las Vegas
The Zulu and the Zayda (with music)
The Playroom
Me and Thee
CACTUS FLOWER
Ubu
Malcolm
The Wayward Stork
The Great Indoors
Wait Until Dark
Slapstick Tragedy
Nathan Weinstein, Mystic, Connecticut
First One Asleep, Whistle
Where's Daddy?
THE LION IN WINTER
3 Bags Full
Happily Never After
The Best Laid Plans

MUSICALS (11)

Drat! The Cat!
On a Clear Day You Can See Forever
Skyscraper
MAN OF LA MANCHA
Anya
The Yearling
Sweet Charity
Pousse-Café
SUPERMAN
A Time for Singing
Mame

REVIVALS (16)

South Pacific
The Music Man
Kismet
Carousel
The Saint of Bleecker Street
Street Scene
The Consul
Danton's Death
The Country Wife
You Can't Take It With You
Oklahoma
How to Succeed in Business Without Really Trying
Ivanov
The Most Happy Fella
Where's Charley?
Annie Get Your Gun

FOREIGN PLAYS IN ENGLISH (14)

Oliver (musical; return engagement)
Pickwick (musical)
Entertaining Mr. Sloane
The Right Honourable Gentleman
The Condemned of Altona
The Caucasian Chalk Circle
THE ROYAL HUNT OF THE SUN
The Devils
INADMISSIBLE EVIDENCE
La Grosse Valise (musical)
MARAT/SADE
PHILADELPHIA, HERE I COME!
Hostile Witness
Wait a Minim! (revue)

SPECIALTIES (4)

The World of Charles Aznavour
Marcel Marceau
Bunraku (puppet theater)
Mark Twain Tonight!

PRODUCTIONS BY FOREIGN LANGUAGE TROUPES (6)

The Comédie Française
L'Avare
Le Cid
La Reine Morte
Un Fil a la Patte
Bavarian State Theater
Woyzeck and Die Mitschuldigen
Die Ratten

HOLDOVER SHOW WHICH BECAME A HIT DURING 1965-66
The Roar of the Greasepaint—The Smell of the Crowd

Plays listed in CAPITAL LETTERS have been designated Best Plays of 1965-66.
Plays listed in **bold face type** were classified as hits in *Variety's* annual list of hits and flops as of June 22, 1966.
Plays listed in *italics* were still running on June 1, 1966.

broke the old sawbuck barrier ($9.90) and kept on inching upward: $11.90 for *On a Clear Day You Can See Forever* . . . $12 for *Superman* . . . ?

Of course, that $53,862,187 wasn't all profit—far from it. In 1965-66, average production costs had risen to $500,000 for a musical and $160,000 for a straight play (from $300,000 and $80,000 in the 1950s). There were five shows that were mounted but folded before their Broadway openings, and they cost their backers more than $750,000 (two of these, *Venus Is* and *The Office* folded in New York during previews). Five big musicals—*Drat! The Cat! Anya, The Yearling, La Grosse Valise* and *Pousse-Café*—died for $2,010,000. And that's not all. Seven of the holdover musicals from the 1964-65 season closed during 1965-66 at an estimated loss of $2,310,000.

On the other hand, *Fiddler on the Roof* holding over from 1964-65 has already earned an estimated $1,250,000, not including a film sale, and is still moving out. The fabulous *Hello, Dolly!* has long since passed the $3,000,000 mark. The arrival of *Sweet Charity* made it three high-grossers running concurrently on Broadway for Neil Simon. The other two, held over from past seasons, were *Barefoot in the Park* and *The Odd Couple*.

What kind of a season was it? Well, the new playwrights saved it from disaster, but not from its share of failures. In a broad sense it was a failure of American playwriting. Our authors came up with what, in my opinion, were the two best scripts of the year—*Hogan's Goat* and *Man of La Mancha*—but allowed the foreign authors to steal the bulk of the show both on and off Broadway, particularly over there on the dramatic, or "serious" side of the theatrical balance.

Black comedies darker than *Marat/Sade* fared almost as badly as sex comedies less adroit than *Cactus Flower*. Bear in mind, though—bear firmly in mind—that the important information conveyed in that sentence is not the fact of the several failures but the fact of the two successes. In a television documentary about Broadway a scene showed a bulldozer levelling masses of junked scenery on the Jersey Meadows, together with the comment that Broadway's major product is failure. This is a glaring fallacy, of course; but it's typical of a certain strain of criticism designed to be self-serving rather than public-serving, intended to make a mess that the critic can stamp around in and leave footprints calling attention to himself. Broadway's major product is fabulously successful shows that survive for years on the stages of the world, including our own regional theater stages. Broadway's major product is success, and its failures are merely a form of artistic waste; awkward and unsightly and even greater in bulk than the product itself, but of no more importance than a slag heap created by a gold mine.

John F. Wharton, who is consultant-director of the Legitimate Theater Industry Exploratory Commission, said that he has found a delightful and exciting new way to experience the theater. Ignoring the thud of flopping shows, he listens instead for the sound of success—the soaring melodies, the compelling language of good dramas, the relaxed laughter of good comedy. Did he hear such enjoyable sounds in 1965-66? He certainly did, and on a very broad scale from farce to drama. Mr. Wharton's attitude tells a clear truth about the theater, clear of the rubbish that often collects around it and obscures it. The truth is that if our theater brings forth exciting and entertaining shows, then it is serving its purpose no matter what other distressing things happen. Let those who get their kicks from the morbid contemplation of ugliness concentrate upon Broadway's slag heap of failure; I am for Mr. Wharton. 1965-66 brought forth its share of successes, and I prefer to scrutinize *them*. The quintessential truth is that there *was* a *Man of La Mancha*, a *Cactus Flower*, a *Hogan's Goat*, a *Marat/Sade* in New York this season—and lots more to make this an exciting year on and off Broadway. That is to say: whatever its failures, its degree of productivity or its "average," the 1965-66 season provided a group of shows that no theatergoer would want to have missed, or could ever forget.

Broadway

As usual, there were some special cases on the hit list. This year (as last year, with Victor Borge and Maurice Chevalier) there were two solo shows: Charles Aznavour with a repertory of songs, most of them in the French language; and *Mark Twain Tonight!*, Hal Holbrook's virtuoso performance of Mark Twain on the lecture platform, to which Holbrook has added new material since his first New York appearance off Broadway in 1959. This was his Mark Twain's Broadway debut in a limited engagement which became a triumph and received a special citation from the New York Drama Critics Circle. Another special case is the British musical *Pickwick*, with Harry Secombe, a popular grand opera tenor and musical comedy star, making his American debut as Charles Dickens' orotund traveller, philosopher and clubman. Imported to America after 18 months in London, *Pickwick* like Secombe himself was cheery, in good voice, but trying too hard to be droll, on too unsophisticated a level. The show was at its best in the quicksilver performance of Anton Rodgers as the rascally Mr. Jingle. *Pickwick* didn't do well on Broadway, but it didn't have to; David Merrick recouped its cost on a road tour before it ever faced Broadway's critics.

For some, the most satisfying kind of a hit may be the big-grossing Broadway musical with ice more than $25 thick on the tickets and a fat movie sale in the offing. For the genuine theater buff, though, the most satisfying hit is the one that coincides with artistic excellence. So it is a particular pleasure to note that four of this year's Best Plays achieved hit status at the box office: *Generation, Inadmissible Evidence, Marat/Sade* and *Cactus Flower*.

William Goodhart's *Generation* starred Henry Fonda as an advertising executive whose daughter has married a Greenwich Village photographer (married yesterday and the baby expected tomorrow). She and her devoted but arrogantly individualistic husband are determined to share the adventure of childbirth, without the help of doctors, in their studio-loft (designed by George Jenkins as the prototype of the militantly Bohemian pad: brick walls, exposed pipes, makeshift furniture). This comedy earned its place on the hit list and the Best Plays list not only by its expertise of timing in Fonda's smooth performance, or the lumpy humor of A. Larry Haines in the supporting role of a doctor brought in against the patient's will; it earned its place not just with gags about a man in a gray flannel suit confronting a beatnik son-in-law who sometimes likes to wear his wife's beads. Exploring the gulf between the generations, it finds and scrutinizes one of the real issues in today's running dispute between 20 and 40-year-olds.

Many of the most irritating contemporary youthful extravagancies are aimed (consciously or unconsciously) to penetrate and ridicule the false pretenses, the hypocrisies and mendacities of the previous generation, particularly in areas of moral and ethical judgment. Now, it isn't merely the father-in-law's preoccupation with making money in the advertising business that sets off the fireworks in *Generation*. What sends up the rockets is the father-in-law's pretense, even to himself, that he is not *really* like other advertising men but is "boring from within" to set higher standards of taste. It isn't his self-interest, but his euphemism, that invites scorn. It is this mendacity, the fact that he's kidding himself and others, this wanting to have his advertising cake and eat it too, that calls down the derision of his son-in-law (who may be kidding *himself* just a little, thinking that he's self-sufficient).

William Inge tried to work this same territory, this no-man's-land between the generations, in *Where's Daddy?*, also about a young married couple expecting a baby in the outrageous environment of a New York pad. Inge's play carried as many jokes under its arm as *Generation*, on somewhat the same general subject, but without a strong theme. It merely multiplied the character gags: the mother (Betty Field) who has decided to blink at nothing, however outrageous; a benign foster-father (Hiram Sherman); a hip Negro couple living next door. *Where's Daddy?* must be the kind of play people mean when they say that a Broadway season consists in "nothing but comedies." Inge's play was a nothing-but-comedy, whereas Goodhart's *Generation* went right to the heart of a very sensitive matter with almost every laugh.

The next (chronologically) of the Best Plays on the hit list was John Osborne's *Inadmissible Evidence*, which, taken together with *The Royal Hunt of the Sun, Marat/Sade* and *Philadelphia, Here I Come!*—all of them Best Plays which will be considered here as a group, though only two achieved formal hit status—brings up two subjects at once. The first and most problematical is the serious plight of serious plays in the Broadway theater. The second and more immediate is the prominence of foreign authors on Broadway in 1965-66.

Recent signs like the economic struggle for survival waged across two seasons (and finally won) by *The Subject Was Roses,* the failure last year of *Tiny Alice* and the continuing overwhelming preponderance of comedies on the production list, have led most observers to believe that the audience for so-called "serious" drama on Broadway is shrinking. (By "serious" I do not mean Sophoclean-serious, I mean serious on balance; scripts billed as "plays" rather than "comedies" and not played primarily for laughs. The borderline case is *Marat/Sade*.) Most dramatic scripts can't seem to get a grip on the audience, and it has been suggested that this alarming condition prevails simply because the plays haven't been strong enough. The scripts, it is argued, haven't managed to take a firm hold on the audience because they haven't managed to take a firm hold on their subject matter in our wildly upheaving, neurotic, stressful era.

This answer may be the right one. Maybe it *is* the plays and not the audience; because, this season, along came three on-balance-serious scripts from Europe (not counting *Marat/Sade*) which *did* find ways to harness the extremely complicated and powerful emotional forces of today; enough to attract an audience and run in glory and respect through the season, if not get off the nut at the box office. The first was Peter Shaffer's *The Royal Hunt of the Sun,* a spectacular confrontation both physically and philosophically between the Conquistador leader Pizarro and the great Inca Atahuallpa. This was a pageant of staging effects by John Dexter, costume and scenic effects (including a twelve-foot sunburst) by Michael Annals and setpiece language effects by Shaffer. David Carradine's physically stylized performance of the Inca man-God Atahuallpa became more and more effective as events approached closer and closer to Atahuallpa's murder. Here Pizarro, disillusioned with life's realities and admiring the Inca so much that he half-believes in his divinity (as Atahuallpa half-believes in Pizarro's divinity), puts Atahuallpa to death in the fervent hope that the Inca's father the Sun-God will revive him at dawn. In this murder Pizarro hopes to find the means for conquering death after a lifetime spent hating and fearing it. His last hope dies with the Inca's mortality.

Shaffer's play started slowly. It lumbered toward its climax through the bitter musings of Pizarro (Christopher Plummer) and the ironic reminiscences of a narrator (George Rose) about the adventures of the band of Conquistadors. But it built to an electrifying conclusion as Pizarro kills his Indian friend in an attempt to challenge death itself.

Another European on-balance-serious script that was good enough to attract audiences—and even to become a hit—was John Osborne's *Inadmissible Evidence*. It concerned itself with the corrosiveness of the mid-20th century. It studies and prods, prods and studies a middle-aged lawyer who senses that life is rolling over him, kicking down his values, placing him on trial for unavoidable errors of judgment, crushing him and moving on past him to a bright future he will never share. The lawyer positively festers onstage. His guilts and fears materialize in a dream trial and in rejections by those he loves and in devastating self-criticism. Each effort he makes to alleviate his condition by scratching at it makes it worse and loses him another friend, or another pound of self-respect, until he is all used up.

Osborne's script is a character revelation in thoughts spoken out loud; a form of theater that could be called a controlled tantrum. What's happening is, one man is coming apart, and the sound of it is piteous. The play vibrates, not with events, but with Osborne's gift for expression. It reaches its height of panicky emotion, not in any confrontation, but in a great overflowing of envy and admiration as the lawyer tries to explain himself one last time, reaching out for sympathy. And Nicol Williamson gave the season's best male straight-play performance as the lawyer. Nothing less than the best would have been adequate for a role so demanding that it required a gifted alternate, James Patterson, to play the matinee performances.

Inadmissible Evidence never ventures into way-out absurdism, but its tantrum construction is a far-out form of theater. Is a radical structure, then, the secret of success for modern dramatic material? Is a distortion of conventional form, touched up with a lick or two of sensation (as in a scene with a homosexual client in *Inadmissible Evidence* and the drooling madmen of *Marat/Sade*) necessary to the success of "serious" theater on Broadway?

No. A third European Best Play of 1965-66 (with a good chance of achieving hit status), Brian Friel's *Philadelphia, Here I Come!*, was conventional in structure and almost unfailingly modest in subject matter; yet it was the most powerful, the most poignant playscript of all the imports. As it begins, a young Irishman, son of a respected shop-owner in a small town, is going to his aunt's in Philadelphia to live and work. He hopes that his unresponsive father, whom he loves in spite of his callow mockery of the old man, will show some sign of regret at his departure. That's all it is: a simple little father-

and-son emotional estrangement which tears the feelings right out of your chest with the clarity and purity of its expression. It can be argued that, technically, *Philadelphia, Here I Come!* is a comedy; yet its subject and treatment are as severe as any drama could wish to be.

Philadelphia, Here I Come! has one eccentricity: the young man, Gar, is written to be played by two actors, one of whom represents Gar's external self and the other his secret thoughts—a device which cannot be said to be very new or very radical. Otherwise, there was very little mannerism in the concept or performance of this play. It isn't even written in the darlin' language of most scripts which are exported by the Dublin theater. This is a dour, North-of-Ireland work, spare and muscular in speech, weighing the words intended to describe a father and son who cannot reach each other in words, or by any other means. The play was fully realized in Hilton Edwards' fine staging, and it was brilliantly performed by a company in which the outstanding work was done by Mairin D. O'Sullivan as the elderly housekeeper who loves Gar and his father as she scolds them; and by Eamon Kelly as the inscrutible parent.

The urge to label Peter Weiss's *Marat/Sade* as a "serious" hit is strong but should be denied; *Marat/Sade* is a Best Play and certainly was a hit and won the New York Drama Critics award for the best foreign play of 1965-66 (in very strong competition), but it probably should be labeled a comedy despite its horrendous goings-on. The image on its advertising posters was holding out the masque of tragedy—but the masque of comedy was grinning underneath. It has been called a "black *Hellzapoppin.*" It was funny as a crutch, cheerful as a sick joke, a gargoyle play which enacted Marat's assassination (but that's not what it is really *about*) as staged by the Marquis de Sade and his group of amateur actors recruited from the drooling, crawling, gurgling, moaning, grimacing inmates of the madhouse at Charenton in France in the Napoleonic era. This script plays a strange game without much volleying. Instead, it is a series of brilliant vignettes, of historic poses presented almost as tableaux, pausing in the middle of each stroke to admire the form. Marat is seen as a single-minded, even bloody-minded man of the people and opposing him is the cynical, sensual, inner-seeking Marquis de Sade. Marat devotes himself to externals, to the people and revolution, to natural science, while de Sade believes only in self and in exploring every avenue of sensation. Their debate on inwardness vs. outwardness was never resolved in *The Persecution and Assassination of Marat as Performed by the Inmates of the Asylum of Charenton Under the Direction of the Marquis de Sade* (to give the play its full title for a change). But this debate was the inner circle of a show formed in concentric circles of ironic images and madmen's ravings.

As with many modern German scripts, Weiss's *Marat/Sade* has a built-in message about spreading and sharing guilt (i.e.: every civilization has its blood bath; the French had their "final solution" to the problem of the aristocrats—the guillotine—and followed it promptly with Napoleon's bloody and militaristic activities; *that's* what this play is about). But the message in this case is buried in vivid externals. There was shock value even in the costumes designed by Gunilla Palmstierna-Weiss (the playwright's wife). Peter Brook staged his madhouse scenes in a key of horrible fascination, in a *danse macabre* whose few formal paces among the spastic gestures and stampings were choreographed by Malcolm Goddard. This imported *Marat/Sade*—in an English version by Geoffrey Skelton adapted in verse by Adrian Mitchell—was one of the Royal Shakespeare Company's modern-play projects, so its cast was uniformly excellent, with a particular citation to Ian Richardson in the pivotal role of a paronoiac patient playing Marat and crying to the mob from his tin bathtub. (It should be emphasized that this show was acted on three levels: first, of madmen; second, of madmen playing historical figures amateurishly; third, of the historical figures fully realized.) During the New York engagement various members of the acting company stated publicly that the effort of performing *Marat/Sade* was almost too great, and that they would be glad when its limited engagement was ended. This complaint sounded strange to American ears: an actor who found his part so demanding that he wished his hit show would close? It sounded like a publicity gimmick because there is no real Broadway parallel to these performers' situation. They are members of a permanent repertory company, and they would go on acting, go on functioning after this too-exacting production closed. Some day, we hope, American actors will have complaints like that.

To make it on Broadway a serious play doesn't necessarily have to be perverted, or violent, or absurd, or camp, or existential enough, it just has to be *strong* enough to grip a contemporary audience with either a universal conflict (extrovert vs. introvert, father vs. son, civilized evil vs. savage evil, etc.) or an exceptionally timely one (modern man having the rug pulled out from under him). To succeed on Broadway, apparently, a serious play should have a strong underweave of black laughter—of sarcasm and irony—to indicate that this whole business of suffering may best be taken, after all, as a colossal joke. But as *Philadelphia, Here I Come!, Inadmissible Evidence, The Royal Hunt of the Sun* and *Hogan's Goat* off Broadway and maybe even *Marat/Sade* demonstrated this season, a script can tip its balance onto the dramatic side and still acquire eager listeners. It may be harder to write a strong drama in this era of cool, but once written it has an audience.

The fourth Best Play to make the hit list was *Cactus Flower,* the comedy smash which Abe Burrows adapted from a Paris (Europeans again!) hit entitled *Fleur de Cactus* by the comedy-writing team of Pierre Barillet and Jean-Pierre Gredy. It had the unmistakable look of a French farce in romantic convolutions in which the single theme of sexual attraction was played and replayed in as many variations as a Bach fugue. But everything else in it was 100 per cent Americanized and Burrows-ized: the successful young Park Avenue dentist, a philanderer in his boyish, clean-cut American way; his lanky and overly-efficient nurse who slowly develops into a long-stemmed American beauty as depicted in glorious living color and perfect comedy sense by Lauren Bacall; the luscious Greenwich Village good-time girl with a heart as big as all outdoors; plus an entertaining assortment of patients, rivals and night club types.

"*Cactus Flower* is maybe the first that has traveled this well since *Tovarich,*" Burrows commented of his work, and he believes a major reason for its success here is that he localized it so thoroughly that New York audiences identified with it perfectly. The characters, the jokes, the staging were all as Broadway as Abe Burrows; which is to say, they succeeded in creating uproarious laughter without really trying, with verbal and situation gags trained up to the easy manner and deep penetration of wit.

Another comedy on the hit list was *The Impossible Years,* the Broadway playwriting debut of Bob Fisher and Arthur Marx. In it, Alan King played a successful psychiatrist, a child-care expert, who can't manage his own teen-aged daughter. King is an actor-comedian, a caricaturist and monologist, who is accustomed to grabbing audiences and making them laugh, all by himself in some night club. He has a special gift of projecting both the underdog who may get up at any moment and win and the top dog whose position is shaky. Small wonder that he found the routine comic relationships of *The Impossible Years* adequate to his purpose of spending the season on Broadway. But no small admiration is due him for a splendid performance which put his play into the hit column.

Still another comedy hit was the Association of Producing Artists revival of *You Can't Take It With You.* In recent seasons APA repertory has been offered off Broadway by the Phoenix Theater with great distinction. Now, in moving to Broadway with a single production, the APA-Phoenix continued its success story, with an acting company that has developed into an ensemble (in *You Can't Take It With You* their star performer, Rosemary Harris, played the minor role of the ingenue) and with the Moss Hart-George S. Kaufman humor fully realized in Ellis Rabb's direction. The 30-year-old script about an eccentric family devoted to individualistic expression and yet inviting all comers to join in their zestful pursuit of happiness (except for the income tax man) proved to be even more appealing to modern audiences than scores of scripts written the day before yesterday.

The special dramatic category of thrillers was well represented on Broadway this season, and one of them made the hit list: Frederick Knott's *Wait Until Dark,* with Lee Remick as a blind girl victimized by a deadly insect of a villain (Robert Duvall) who has reason to believe that heroin is secreted somewhere in her apartment. In a climactic scene, as the plot thickened in a hushed theater, with the killer stalking the blind girl on a pitch-black-dark stage, there occurred a surprise that made the audience cry out aloud. The logic of *Wait Until Dark* was somewhat less than relentless in places, but a thriller has to get a pretty good grip on an audience to make it yelp.

Technically there were no American musical hits as of the end of 1965-66, but certainly wonderful *Man of La Mancha,* the musical play about Cervantes and his Don Quixote, would grace any season. It started slowly on the road to success, downtown at the ANTA Washington Square Theater (this musical has sometimes been called an off-Broadway show because of its geographical location, but it is not; its contracts with the authors, the actors, etc., are Broadway contracts). Even with good reviews it took a while for audiences to find it tucked away in its corner of the city. But finally they did, and *Man of La Mancha* became a hot ticket.* Among its many prizes and citations was the New York Drama Critics Circle award for the best musical of the season.

Man of La Mancha was produced by Albert W. Selden and Hal James, and it was one of those happy special cases in which many creative elements clustered into a solid success phenomenon. It had the best male performance in a musical in Richard Kiley's stringy, bony and finally heart-rending Don Quixote. It had top-notch singing support from Ray Middleton, Joan Diener and Robert Rounseville in a production staged with unfailing excitement by Albert

---

* According to a *Variety* estimate, it achieved formal hit status before the end of June, 1966.

Marre in the problematical area of the theater's thrust stage. Howard Bay's setting presented the play perfectly with an open-stage platform and a few props to represent plays-within-plays (Cervantes is in prison telling the story of Don Quixote to his fellow-prisoners and acting it out as he tells it). The set was versatile enough to contain the far-ranging imagined adventures of the knight of La Mancha and his squire Sancho Panza—all this without any cumbersome moving-about of scenery except for a ladder which descended into the prison set, ominously, to admit Inquisition characters. The musical had the best costumes (by Howard Bay and Patton Campbell), the best music and lyrics (by Mitch Leigh and Joe Darion), the best choreography (Jack Cole's) including the brutal rape of a serving-wench by lusty Muleteers, expressed in dance.

Man of La Mancha is an achievement of overall excellence, and in addition it opposes every modern theatrical fad and fashion except the fad of setting things to music. In recent years a trend has crept in like a trader rat to rob our drama of the bright things like anger and tragedy, leaving in their place dull despair and self-pity as though these were equal in emotion merely because they are equal in weight. *Man of La Mancha* treads heavily on this rat. It is musical drama that brought tears to the eyes of many in its audience; yet, lo and behold, it is theater of hope, drama of endurance, in angry revolt against all forms of despair. Don Quixote's dreams and knightly poses transcend any motive of mendacity; they achieve near-tragic stature in a hero whose goal is "To bear with unbearable sorrow, To fight the unbeatable foe"—and you can't get any farther from despair and surrender than that.

The Cervantes-Don Quixote character of *Man of La Mancha* is brother to the pipe dreamers of Eugene O'Neill's *The Iceman Cometh;* cousin to Willy Loman in *Death of a Salesman.* The show was out of (and, I think, above) its theatrical time in 1966 in the same way that Don Quixote was above *his* time in the 16th century. It may be, even, that some of the knight's aspirations are wholly incomprehensible, even as comic exaggerations, to the generation coming along. When the Mitch Leigh-Joe Darion song number "The Quest" was first recorded on a record for popular circulation, a line of the lyric expressing Don Quixote's ideals was changed from "To love, pure and chaste, from afar" to "To be better far than you are." Love like that they have never imagined, but being better they dig; especially in its meaning of being better off in a materialistic society.

No, the 1960s have no welcome mat out for plays of ideal and aspiration and courage; they are a time for plays about characters sitting in garbage cans complaining about what went wrong. If *Man of La Mancha* can't reverse the gravitation, maybe it can help to start a trend of its own. Dale Wasserman declares he knew he was working against the grain of the modern theater when he selected and organized the Cervantes-Don Quixote material. He was so admirably successful that maybe he will jog others out of the blue monotony of neurotic cynicism into an occasional appreciation of the human spirit in a larger-than-life phase.

Musically speaking, the season's first success was announced in the challenging trumpets of *Man of La Mancha;* then it rested on its laurels and made do with fair-to-middling shows until the last weeks, when it roused to the fanfare of *Superman* and *Mame.* Meanwhile, audiences subsisted on *Sweet Charity* and the musical musings of a couple of crazy, mixed-up kids named

Harris. In Alan Jay Lerner's *On a Clear Day You Can See Forever* Barbara Harris was just loaded with ESP (and talent, in an enchanting performance) as a lass who can read thoughts, make plants obey her orders to grow and, under hypnosis by a handsome psychiatrist, remember her previous incarnation. In *Skyscraper,* based on Elmer Rice's *Dream Girl,* Julie Harris is a dreamer whose romantic fantasies are acted out as she tries to choose among the men in her life, at the same time preventing the high-rise brigands next door from swallowing her little old New York house into their shiny new skyscraper project. There was a lot of handsome production designed by Robert Randolph in *Skyscraper* and a good tune in *On a Clear Day,* but it was the performing rather than the material that filled out these shows. The same was true of *Sweet Charity* even though it was Neil Simon himself who wrote the musical's book, based on the Italian movie *Nights of Cabiria.* In *Sweet Charity* (which opened at the refurbished Palace and brought that storied theater back to the legitimate stage), Simon's book about a dance hall hostess doesn't glitter as sharply as his two hit comedies that were concurrent with it, *Barefoot in the Park* and *The Odd Couple.* But an appealing song and dance performance by Gwen Verdon put the show over, with an important assist from Bob Fosse's choreography and staging.

Then Superman arrived in the nick of time to lift the season out of its musical lethargy. If our musical theater cannot create its own original material (and this year it cannibalized a comic strip, the novels *Don Quixote, Auntie Mame, The Yearling, How Green Was My Valley* and *Pickwick,* the movie *Nights of Cabiria* and the plays *Dream Girl* and *Anastasia*), then the next best thing is to find that the very choice of material adapted is a major part of the fun. So it was with the show whose official title was *"It's a Bird It's a Plane It's SUPERMAN,"* quotes and all, a Best Play, devoted faithfully and extremely cleverly to the comic strip on which it was based. It was not camped, but played as straight as possible in a good laugh at our secret longing for a hero who could solve all problems, defeat all enemies. The joke is not on Superman, as it is on TV's Batman. The joke is right where it should be—on us and our childish instincts. When something goes wrong in Metropolis, Clark Kent is there to fix it—meek Clark Kent, reporter on the *Daily Planet,* scorned as an underdog by his fellow-reporter Lois Lane until presto! he strips off his sober clothes and stands revealed, muscles bulging in his blue and red cape costume, the Superman of Lois's dreams. He is impersonated to the pen-and-ink life by Bob Holiday and directed in dead-pan style by Harold Prince (Superman is a straight man). This Man of Steel faces a foeman worthy of his invincible and indestructible mettle: a mad scientist, a gangling, threadpaper comic strip villain played by Michael O'Sullivan, who is furious because he's never won a Nobel Prize. He plots to draw attention to himself by destroying indestructible Superman. How? Physically Superman is invulnerable, but psychologically he is not; like mere mortals he needs to be loved, to have his good works appreciated. Taking dead aim at this vulnerable spot, the mad scientist pursues our hero through the musical's two lively acts; through an excellent, faintly rocky score by Charles Strouse and Lee Adams, waiting for him to alight from his flights through the air over Metropolis (by means, we assume, of a contraption of invisible wires); and finally penetrating Clark Kent's disguise with the help of a slippery newshawk played by Jack Cassidy.

The mad scientist nearly stages the upset of the century, but Superman wins out in the end (phew!). As a good guy, Superman is so square that it's too much to expect for him to be likeable. He is, though; this Superman is almost human. What is he but a knight-errant of the space age who can "fight the unbeatable foe" and win, who *can* "reach the unreachable star?" Superman is Don Quixote's dream come true; and Don Quixote's dream, though it may be laughable, is never ridiculous. The same goes for Superman in his welcome arrival in a stage version.

Following close upon the flowing cape of Superman was another musical whose heroine would no doubt have invited the Man of Steel to cocktails to feel his muscles—*Mame,* the life-loving subject of Patrick Dennis's novel *Auntie Mame* who (as Rosalind Russell) has already appeared in a play and a movie. Now (as Angela Lansbury) she appears in a musical version, sweeping all before her so that she may bring up her beloved nephew Patrick in the style to which he should be accustomed. He must learn to mix martinis, to tango in a speakeasy and, of course, to get along in a progressive school at which the little boys run around naked with the little girls. In wealth and in Depression, in foxhunting Georgia and in snobbish suburbia, Miss Lansbury's Mame was always equal to and a little bit ahead of the demands placed on her by a strenuous and all-embracing life, and so was the actress in her role. It was a delight to meet Mame's friends, too: Beatrice Arthur as a contralto musical comedy star ready at any moment to strike a heavy blow for her best friend or *against* her; Jane Connell as the mousy secretary who is sent forth to have some fun and comes back sadder, wiser and pregnant. It's also a pleasure to report that Jerry Herman's score is typical Jerry Herman: it bounces with singable songs for performers who want to expend a lot of energy, and his lyrics blend with the flow of the book adapted by Jerome Lawrence and Robert E. Lee from their own play. The William and Jean Eckart scenery and Robert Mackintosh costumes were both handsome and efficient, chic as could be but never overblown except for deliberate effect. *Mame,* the last new show of the year, put a real exclamation point on the 1965-66 season.

It's highly probable that *Mame* will achieve hit status; and so will *Sweet Charity* and *Man of La Mancha;* and so, very likely, will *Wait a Minim!* This revue from South Africa has been touring its own country and the world for more than four years; yet its young performers were still sassy and boisterous and proud of their material. The show was paced briskly by director-producer Leon Gluckman through efficient scenery made of sliding panels designed by Gluckman and Frank Rembach. A program note stated, "Coming from South Africa, where the political climate is hot and angry, it is inevitable that *Wait a Minim!* should have a point of view." This point of view punctuated the show in a repeated pantomime in which a white man makes friendly overtures to a Negro, then fires at him point-blank with a pistol. But as a whole the show had little to do with anger and much to do with melody and folk humor, with songs collected mostly from Africa but lightly salted with Asian and European numbers. The versatile young company not only performed all the satirical sketches, dances and songs but also played their own musical instruments—which in the case of *Wait a Minim!* was no mean accomplishment. Andrew Tracey played seventeen instruments onstage, including a sousaphone and a Chopi timbala (whatever that is); Paul Tracey played thirteen and Nigel Pegram ten.

Another musical, *A Time for Singing,* put forward Tessie O'Shea as the wife and mother of the coal-mining Morgans in an adaptation of Richard Llewellyn's *How Green Was My Valley*. Miss O'Shea has a friendly way with a song and a comedy line—which is more than could be said for her vehicle. It was a bulky but not very agile show—lots of good voices and songs, lots of romantic and sociological problems in the book, attractive and serviceable scenery by Ming Cho Lee, but not much beauty or inspiration, inner or outer, when all was said and done from its happy-family opening to its somber mine-accident conclusion. The built-in values of *How Green Was My Valley* did little to rescue *A Time for Singing;* nor could the built-in values of a book based on the play *Anastasia* and a score based on Rachmaninoff's music rescue *Anya;* nor could *La Grosse Valise,* with its built-in values of Robert Dhery humor, repeat the success of Dhery's previous revue from Paris, *La Plume de Ma Tante.* This was a season when very few sure-fire ideas worked out, and most reliable sources dried up, in musicals as well as elsewhere in the theater.

Turning to comedy, James Goldman's *The Lion in Winter,* about a roaring, clawing family gathering of Plantagenets and Capets in frosty Chinon at Christmas time, 1183, had only a short run—but this was the only respect in which it was the least of the Best Plays. It is a semi-historical, semi-dramatic comedy about succession to the crown of England. Henry II and his queen, Eleanor of Aquitaine, whom he holds imprisoned because of her several rebellions against him, have three sons: Richard (later King Richard the Lion-Hearted), Geoffrey and John (later King John who accepted the Magna Carta). All three sons are scheming for the crown in a day when primogeniture did not determine the succession. The script has hidden claws; it is printed out as prose, but much of it speaks and reads as pentameter. Its savage humor is offered in stylish irony by Rosemary Harris as Eleanor the scorned and scorning queen who plots keenly against her husband Henry for love of watching him suffer, and who is ready to eat him or love him, either one, alive and whole. Miss Harris's portrayal of Eleanor was realized in such depth that at one performance, as she delivered Eleanor's line about being able to express despair with a smile, the audience broke into applause of her acting. Robert Preston's performance, too, was among the season's best; a stylish, bearded, bristling lion of a Henry II who walks like a king and schemes like a Borgia but can't quite bring himself to destroy his own troublesome young. Outstanding supporting performances under Noel Willman's superior direction were given by Suzanne Grossmann as Alais the king's mistress and Christopher Walken as young King Philip of France. Will Steven Armstrong's costumes and scenery suggested the period without weighing down the actors or the play in ornament. His single set of pillars and arches, for example, represented all the many rooms of Chinon from bedroom to wine cellar, without shifting scenery, merely by moving in props like a tapestry or a table.

The failure of *The Lion in Winter* to attract a large enough audience to support it even modestly is one of those Broadway mysteries to which so many emphatic solutions are offered in sidewalk discussions. It was a period play, which is risky, but it was also a comedy, which is not. The deliberate use of anachronism in the script (wrapping up Christmas presents, etc.) has troubled some observers; others have praised it for helping modern audiences to identify closely with the characters. The powerful New York *Times* drama critic damned it with a who-cares attitude toward its subject matter, but plays have succeeded before over the dead body of *Times* opinion and will again. At the other end of the scale, Walter Kerr of the New York *Herald Tribune* praised Miss Harris's Eleanor as one of the ten or twelve best performances anyone might be likely to see in a lifetime of theatergoing, and many other journalists and show folk spread the good word about *The Lion in Winter* with the zeal of prophets. So why should *Lion* have failed? How could it have failed? No one knows for sure, but it is an outstanding script which must certainly have a long life before it in future productions. To its four producers—Eugene V. Wolsk, Walter A. Hyman, Alan King (in his second major contribution to this Broadway season) and Emanuel Azenberg—all credit for putting it on. To the Broadway theater, shame for its failure.

Elsewhere in comedy it was a rose-colored year. This season there was no special magic in the color black, even when laid on in great splashes. The blackest script played as a joke was *Entertaining Mr. Sloane,* the Broadway debut of its British author, Joe Orton. This was a play about a murderer who thinks he has found sanctuary with a family living in a house surrounded by a junkyard; but he finds that he is no match for this family, and the price of his security is to serve as lover to the middle-aged lady of the house *and* to her brother, both of whom enjoy being roughly handled. *Mr. Sloane* was relentlessly well acted by Dudley Sutton as the hapless murderer, Sheila Hancock and Lee Montague as his predators and George Turner as their whining father—but it seemed relentlessly forbidding.

The blackest American script of consequence was Edward Albee's short-lived adaptation of James Purdy's novel *Malcolm,* produced by Theater 1966. It was a low-camp charade of shining innocence eroded and degraded in the tale of a symbolically pure fifteen-year-old who vacates a symbolic golden throne to enter the world, where he is corrupted by friendship, luxury, art and love and destroyed in an orgiastic marriage with a pop singer. Estelle Parsons played a prostitute as the most overblown, slatternly, anti-feminine symbol to be invented for the stage in a long time, and Ruth White was outstanding as an all-consuming matron. But *Malcolm* succeeded only in proving that a little bit of camp goes a long way in the theater, and a lot of it was more than this play could bear. Like *Mr. Sloane, Malcolm* left an impression that was strong but unfavorable.

No, sick jokes didn't do especially well this season, even in the old reliable form of a clique for murdering the wrong sort of people in *UTBU,* a short-lived Tony Randall vehicle. Those who believe that the theater has a welcome mat out for neurotic sensationalism are thinking of a different time and place than Broadway in 1965-66. Here and now we had gentle comedies about a nice old Jewish grandpa and a friendly young Zulu; about a likeable old capitalist and family man juggling bags of diamonds with the parlormaid in his New York town house; about a rich Boston widow whose children are scheming to take her money away from her. The latter comedy was *A Very Rich Woman,* adapted by Ruth Gordon from a French script and played richly by her under the direction of her husband, Garson Kanin, with strong support from Ethel Griffies, Ernest Truex and Raymond Walburn as caricatures of the old Boston school, and with Diana Muldaur attractively in attendance as a nurse at the clinic in which the avaricious daughters imprison their indomitable mother. This play was acted as it was written, with relish, and it deserved a more enthusiastic response than it got.

So did Jerome Chodorov's *3 Bags Full,* in which Paul Ford played the abovementioned gent with the diamonds, bedeviled by his servants, his family and his business associate until he has no alternative but to stare out at the audience in an open-mouthed but silent plea for sympathy, in helpless resignation. Ford's performance was a show in itself, as was the art nouveau styling of Armstrong's setting and Freddy Wittop's costumes. *3 Bags Full* could have occupied a large place in the season, and it left a big hole when it closed. The other warm frivolity—*The Zulu and the Zayda*—lasted through most of the season with its story of a Jewish family living in South Africa and hiring a young Zulu (Louis Gossett) to look after their zayda, or grandfather (Menasha Skulnik), to keep him out of trouble. This script was the Broadway writing debut of the actor Howard Da Silva (in collaboration with Felix Leon). It concerned itself warm-heartedly—but fairly obviously—with interracial harmony, and it benefitted greatly from its production values: Dore Schary's gentle touch in the staging, the sets by William and Jean Eckart and eleven Harold Rome song numbers scattered through the play.

Sex was a highly successful subject for comedy—but only once, in *Cactus Flower.* In other plays indentifying themselves as comedies in the author's credit line ("A New Comedy by . . ."), sex was a flop this season—a one-performance flop in the cases of *Mating Dance* and *Me and Thee.* Jokes about artificial insemination (in *The Wayward Stork*) and marital and pre-marital relations (in *Happily Never After*) failed to get much of a laugh. To wrap up the subject of comedy on Broadway in 1965-66, some character ideas in plays which missed the mark were a horse-playing priest in *Minor Miracle,* a retired civil servant coping with a neurotic daughter in *Nathan Weinstein, Mystic, Connecticut* and a playwright posing as a beatnik in *The Best Laid Plans.*

In drama, the very best offerings were the plays described in the previous section, plus off-Broadway's *Hogan's Goat.* Next best were the thrillers, showing off (again) a foreign author in his (again) Broadway debut. This was Jack Roffey and his *Hostile Witness,* a coolly British cat-and-mouse game with a famous solicitor, played by Ray Milland, framed for murder and placed on trial before a wryly solemn judge (played in a memorably amusing vignette by Melville Cooper), and saved only at the very last second after every possibility of suspense had been squeezed dry under Reginald Denham's direction. More lurid games were played in the American thrillers: Frederick Knott's *Wait Until Dark,* described in the section on hits; and Mary Drayton's *The Playroom,* about a clique of pot-smoking teen-agers who kidnap a tot for spite and find that they may have to murder their victim in order to escape punishment for abducting her. *Wait Until Dark* succeeded in finding an audience for its screams-in-the-dark melodrama; *The Playroom* did not and closed early, although it was a script of quite considerable substance and just missed being one of the season's best.

Elsewhere in drama, the interesting failures were European, the sad disappointments, alas! American. Of course, American scripts on Broadway are usually raw and new, while European scripts were tested before being imported—somebody loved them enough to bring them over here. The late John Whiting's *The Devils,* based on Aldous Huxley's book, arrived in an excellent production by Alexander H. Cohen, in the magnificence of a lofty setting by Rouben Ter-Arutunian, and in the promise of bravura performing by Anne

Bancroft and Jason Robards in the grim story of a nun who hallucinates night-time visits from a handsome, libertine priest. She sends him to the gallows when she reveals publicly the supposed possession of herself and her sisters by this sacerdotal devil. Under the direction of Michael Cacoyannis, *The Devils* was less inward-searching than outwardly melodramatic (until scenes of the priest's growing self-knowledge in his painful demise), with Shepperd Strudwick alone finding the right key in which to perform, in his role of a disapproving bishop.

Michael Dyne's *The Right Honourable Gentleman* was also a point of some dramatic interest in the season, with its careful acting-out of a real Victorian political scandal. It was most expertly stylized under Frith Banbury's direction, with Charles D. Gray playing Sir Charles Dilke, whose reputation was destroyed in a messy divorce case just as eventual leadership of the party (Gladstone's) in Parliament seemed within his grasp. This was a good job expertly done but perhaps just a bit creaky in its theatrical joints as it played out its mannered expose.

A most conspicuous event was the seven-performance disappointment of the two Tennessee Williams one-acters, character portraits of aging and distressed women played by Margaret Leighton and Kate Reid under the portmanteau title *Slapstick Tragedy*. The news was bad for younger playwrights, too. William Hanley's full-length reworking of his one-acter *Mrs. Dally,* about a middle-aged woman's loneliness and frustration both in marriage and in a love affair with a young man, didn't quite fill out, even though Arlene Francis and Ralph Meeker were in excellent form as the married couple trying to console each other for what went wrong with their marriage. Jack Richardson missed with *Xmas in Las Vegas* (a cloud silver-lined with the fact that now, at least, we don't have to absorb that ugly abbreviation "Xmas" into the roster of enduring American play titles). *Postmark Zero* failed to dramatize successfully the World War II emotions of Stalingrad in letters from its participants; *The Great Indoors* grappled with problems of bias without accomplishment; and *First One Asleep, Whistle* closed after only one performance of its emotional problem of an unmarried mother and her 7-year-old daughter.

In revivals, a British production of Chekhov's *Ivanov*—the first major Broadway production of this play in modern times—brought John Gielgud and Vivian Leigh to New York for a limited engagement; theirs was a prime star attraction, if not exactly a Chekhovian triumph either from a standpoint of the play itself or its staging. Marcel Marceau returned to New York with his pantomime programs, including the Bip sketches and other routines which have retained all their charm and poignancy in the ten-year interval since their first presentation in New York, in 1955 off Broadway at the Phoenix Theater (Marceau appeared at the City Center, so that unlike his countryman, Charles Aznavour, Marceau's solo show wasn't under consideration for *Variety's* hit list; City Center shows never are). And not everything that happens in the theater district can be classified as a show to be recorded formally as "produced on Broadway." Among subsidiary activities was Vittorio Gassman's one-performance acting concert entitled *Game of Heroes,* the evening of February 21 at Lincoln Center. Then there was the visit of burlesque to the Times Square area in the spring, at the Hudson Theater, in a three-a-day form with programs changed weekly in the best grind-house tradition.

Individual successes of acting, direction, scene design, music and lyric writing, choreography, etc., have been mentioned along with their shows in this report. But there is an individual whose contribution to the American theater is so wide and *continuous* that he's in a class of achievement by himself. This season he (or his Arts Foundation) produced *Marat/Sade, Inadmissible Evidence* and *Philadelphia, Here I Come!;* he produced *Cactus Flower;* he produced *Pickwick* and the return engagement of *Oliver;* and just to avoid actually defying the gods (chutzpah, yes; hubris, no) he also co-produced a musical that folded out of town, *Hot September.* When he was not doing all this he was doing something else like annoying the *Times* drama critic. I refer of course to David Merrick, the man of this and every recent theater year. Merrick has elevated and enriched the American theater with his courage, taste and healthy avarice, and in turn it has quite properly elevated and enriched him. He livens things up generally, and it's a pleasure to have him around, not only for profit but also for fun.

It should be noted, too, that the scene designers provided an unusually interesting visual spectacle this season. It is almost an offense to pick out a "best" from among their outstanding work because only minor details of personal preference can make a distinction. The most conspicuous of the 1965-66 scenic successes were Howard's Bay's *Man of La Mancha,* the best design yet for that difficult stage downtown at ANTA Washington Square Theater; Jo Mielziner's *Danton's Death,* a first-time design for the new Vivian Beaumont Theater, and his *The Playroom;* Will Steven Armstrong's art nouveau *3 Bags Full* and his adaptable *The Lion in Winter;* Robert Randolph's *Skyscraper* and *Sweet Charity* and *Anya* AND *Superman;* Rouben Ter-Arutunian's *The Devils;* Michael Annals' *The Royal Hunt of the Sun;* William and Jean Eckart's *Mame,* and Ming Cho Lee's *A Time for Singing.*

The Repertory Caper

The effort to establish in New York City a subsidized resident repertory company within the Lincoln Center organization entered its second phase during the season of 1965-66. Following the two previous seasons downtown at ANTA Washington Square Theater under the direction of Robert Whitehead and Elia Kazan, the company was delivered over to the direction of Herbert Blau and Jules Irving and moved to its permanent home at the Vivian Beaumont Theater in Lincoln Center, where four productions were presented. The Messrs. Blau and Irving, recruited from the regional theater in San Francisco, where they had been operating a resident company called the Actor's Playhouse, inherited many problems from the old regime: dissension at the top, dissatisfaction in the company, deficit at the box office. They also inherited a certain amount of distinction from the two-year production record which included two *new* Best Plays (by Arthur Miller) and a couple of creditable revivals along with a couple of flops.

The Lincoln Center season's major distinction was its new environment and its stage designs. The Vivian Beaumont Theater (which finally cost $9,700,-000) is austerely beautiful, a highly efficient machine for putting on plays, with a machine's functional beauty. Outside, it has clean, squared lines of glass and travertine. Inside, its upholstery is bright red plush to stir the senses, and its walls and ceiling are a very dark brown so that they seem to disappear as the stage receives its lighting for the play. The stage itself is adaptable for radical thrust arrangements or proscenium openings of various sizes, and the auditorium seats 1,140 for proscenium-style plays and 1,083 when seats are removed to accommodate a thrust stage. The theater was designed by the late Eero Saarinen with Jo Mielziner. Mielziner's were the first sets to be used there, for *Danton's Death,* in a grand display of his and the theater's virtuosity, with a geometrical background of lines coming to a point in the distance, and with setpieces of scenery moved on and offstage, thrust forward and pulled back, comprising the major visual excitement and freedom of motion in an otherwise heavy and turgid play.

The Blau-Irving goal, if I understand it correctly, is to create a theater of loud involvement, with plays that have the "size" to fill their stage with modern social and emotional significance. This goal was exemplified in their choice of plays for Lincoln Center Repertory in 1965-66: *Danton's Death,* a ranting 19th century German play about the French Revolution and its tyranny disguised as public good; *The Country Wife,* a breather for the company, which had done it in San Francisco; *The Condemned of Altona,* another of those plays about widening the circle of German war and atrocity guilt, this one the American premiere of a 1959 Sartre script; and *The Caucasian Chalk Circle,* the New York premiere of an episodic Brecht work arranging human symbols (Chinese humans, each wearing his symbolic personality openly, in masks designed by James Hart Stearns) in the familiar message about the triumph of the honest peasant over wicked authority.

Certainly the first and last of these plays served what I understand to be the present purpose of Lincoln Center Rep. They were big enough to fill the Beaumont's stage, and loud enough to be heard clearly. But at the same time they were dull enough to be ignored easily. This was theater of harangue, and it raised doubt that its goal is worthwhile as compared, say, with a goal of perfecting an American repertory company in the ensemble presentation of a principally American repertory of plays. Blau and Irving chose *no* American play for their opening year's repertory.

It's no secret that while Lincoln Center Repertory has been fiddling, the Association of Producing Artists-Phoenix repertory has been burning with a bright blue flame of theater energy, bringing plays to New York which they mounted originally in Ann Arbor, Mich., under the sponsorship of the University of Michigan Professional Theater Program. Ellis Rabb is APA-Phoenix's director and his wife, Rosemary Harris, is its star performer. After a couple of seasons off Broadway, APA moved to Broadway this season; not in repertory but with a single production, a revival of the comedy *You Can't Take It With You,* a 30-year-old American script by a couple of commercial-theater fellows named Hart and Kaufman. Its success all year long in Broadway competition, and the success on Broadway last year of another group's revival of Tennessee Williams' *The Glass Menagerie* for 175 performances, leaves no doubt that there is plenty of juice in the body of American plays, plus a large New York audience for them when they are skillfully restaged. APA has announced its intention of playing a whole season on Broadway in 1966-67 in a repertory of seven plays including *You Can't Take It With You* and another work entitled *We Comrades Three* adapted from the writings of

Walt Whitman. While Lincoln Center is still deep in the experimental state after three years of experiment, APA is emerging as a full-blown Broadway fact.

The season's activity included visits from foreign troupes showing us what results may be achieved within the repertory system. The *Marat/Sade* brought to Broadway by David Merrick was a production by the Royal Shakespeare Company, a repertory group which is rooted in the performing traditions of its own country's greatest literary treasure and is employing these skills, stretching these muscles, in productions of new scripts. The Comédie Française polished like an old stone in the river of centuries, visited New York with Molière's *L'Avare,* Corneille's *Le Cid,* de Montherlant's *La Reine Morte* and Feydeau's *Un Fil a la Patte.* The Bavarian State Theater contrasted Büchner's *Woyzeck* with Goethe's *The Accomplice* on one program and offered Hauptmann's *Die Ratten* on another. The Japanese were represented by their Bunraku in an attractive repertory of puppet theater.

Off Broadway, the American Savoyards continued to offer Gilbert and Sullivan productions in seasons of repertory; and, musically speaking at least, the American stage heritage is living theater in New York. Three groups devote themselves to presenting again and again the great musical hits of the Broadway past. New York City Opera, a repertory company with guest stars, this year staged *The Saint of Bleecker Street, The Consul* and *Street Scene.* New York City Center Light Opera's one-by-one revivals in 1965-66 were *South Pacific, The Music Man* and *Oklahoma!,* together with a spring schedule of four Frank Loesser musicals: *How to Succeed in Business Without Really Trying, The Most Happy Fella* and *Where's Charley?,* to be followed by *Guys and Dolls.* The Music Theater of Lincoln Center's major one-at-a-time musicals, lavishly revived under the guidance of Richard Rodgers, were *Kismet* with Alfred Drake in his original role of Hajj, *Carousel* with John Raitt in his original role of Billy Bigelow and, on the last day of the season, *Annie Get Your Gun* with Ethel Merman in her original role of Annie Oakley.

This wealth of musical production is all to the good; now we need comparable showcases for our Broadway straight-play heritage, not instead of musical production, but to match it. New York is a city where a very rich man may walk up a street with a very poor man and turn into their doors at homes which are side by side. The extreme condition of each points up the extreme condition of the other, by contrast, and this same relationship exists between the two genres of American stage works. Our musicals are richly displayed, year after year, in revival and in repertory, while our straight plays subsist mainly upon spare print on the library shelves; unfleshed.

Off Broadway

There was apparent shrinkage off Broadway in 1965-66, blamed almost universally on rising production costs. This season there were 66 shows as compared with 73 a year ago. There were nine fewer shows, but one of them, William Alfred's *Hogan's Goat,* was the best straight playscript of the year in any part of the New York theater, in my opinion. There were fewer shows but more activity in what has become known as off-off-Broadway: the Cafe La Mama, the Judson Poets' Theater, etc. There were fewer shows, but produc-

The 1965-66 Season off Broadway

PLAYS (24)

Friends and Enemies
Swim Low Little Goldfish
The World of Ray Bradbury
Play That on Your Old Piano
Good Day and The Exhaustion of Our Son's Love
Kill the One-Eyed Man
HOGAN'S GOAT
Happy Ending and Day of Absence
Bugs and Veronica
An Impudent Wolf
The Parasite
The Pocket Watch
Rooms
Jonah
The Coop
Laughwind
Monopoly
Ludlow Fair and The Madness of Lady Bright
6 From La Mama (two programs of one-act plays)
The Journey of the Fifth Horse
Bohikee Creek
Fitz and Biscuit
Big Man

MUSICALS (3)

Hotel Passionato
Great Scot!
Hooray! It's a Glorious Day . . . and all that

REVUES (6)

The Game Is Up (cabaret)
Pick a Number XV (cabaret)
Just for Openers (cabaret)
New Cole Porter Revue (cabaret)
The Mad Show
Return of Second City (cabaret)

REVIVALS (17)

Krapp's Last Tape and The Zoo Story
New York Shakespeare
Love's Labor's Lost
Coriolanus
Troilus and Cressida
American Savoyards
The Yeomen of the Guard
Ruddigore
The Pirates of Penzance
Princess Ida
The Trojan Women (return engagement)
Happy Days (also performed in French)
Miss Julie and The Stronger
Medea
The White Devil
Winterset
Phèdre
The Deadly Game
When We Dead Awaken

FOREIGN PLAYS IN ENGLISH (7)

Troubled Waters
Live Like Pigs
The Trigon
Serjeant Musgrave's Dance
The World of Gunter Grass
Sunset
The Butterfly Dream

SPECIALTIES (6)

Mardi Gras (outdoor musical)
Leonard Bernstein's Theater Songs
An Evening's Frost
Woman
The Bernard Shaw Story
Half Horse Half Alligator

PRODUCTIONS BY FOREIGN-LANGUAGE TROUPES (3)

Hello Charlie (Yiddish musical)
The Fifth Commandment (Yiddish musical)
Who Do I Deserve This? (German revue)

Play listed in CAPITAL LETTERS has been designated a Best Play of 1965-66.
Plays listed in *italics* were still running on June 1, 1966.

tion of *new* playscripts held up pretty well (31 as compared with 33 last year), with most of the numerical drop-off taking place in the musical and revival categories.

There were no new Pinter, Becket, Genet or Ionesco plays and no clear evidence of any mould-breakers coming along behind them. Even Theater 1965-1966 marked time with *Krapp's Last Tape* and *The Zoo Story* and a revival of Beckett's *Happy Days* presented first in French, with Madeleine Renaud, and then in English, with Ruth White. The intellectual environment which produced the most interesting new playwright of the off-Broadway year was neither Houston Street nor King's Road, but Harvard. The season as a whole was overbalanced on the conventional side, no doubt about that.

The shining example of this off-Broadway year was *Hogan's Goat*, the first professional production of its author, William Alfred, a Harvard professor. His play is a verse drama about the first-generation Irish community in Brooklyn in 1890, zeroing in on a young political leader whose consuming ambition drives him to destruction.

Hogan's Goat is a fine play with a universal theme set in a background of American history—and if that sounds like an ideal qualification for the Pulitzer Prize, so much the more embarrassing. Once again in 1965-66, as in 1962-63 and 1963-64, the Pulitzer Prize givers withheld their award for theater. Trying to figure out no-award motives leads only to confusion; for example, when no award is given, is it because the prize is too important for the play? Does the prize go only to plays that are so obviously great and lasting that they will add to the luster of the prize—or is the prize intended to add to the luster of the play which, whatever its secondary faults, is the best of its season? Is a *Hogan's Goat* (for example) supposed to encourage the Pulitzer Prize and add to its distinction, or vice versa? I think we should get this all straight, somehow. Next time the Pulitzer Prize is offered perhaps the winning playwright should give some thought to whether he, in his turn, will *allow* the Pulitzer committee to distinguish itself with the great name of his play.

Hogan's goat of the title is one Matthew Stanton, immigrant and sometime fancy-boy of Agnes Hogan, a full-blooded creature who dies as the play begins (Alfred plans to dramatize the Agnes-Matt story one of these years). Hogan's Goat, as Stanton was once called to his chagrin, is now married to a woman whose indrawn nature is somewhat too delicate to endure the rough-and-tumble of Brooklyn politics. The Stantons have married secretly, in London, outside the Catholic Church; and this state of affairs is to them a guilty secret. The incumbent Mayor of Brooklyn is a crooked old wolf with long yellow teeth (this is the meatiest role, played by Tom Ahearne with seemingly total conviction that dishonesty is neither the best nor the worst but the only workable policy). As he maneuvers to snatch this office of Mayor from the old wolf, Stanton walks a tightrope between the Church's and the voters' anathema. He is destroyed as any tragic hero should be, totally, "down on my knees and all the world a desert," by his own temper, his own sinful past, his own overwhelming ambition.

Hogan's Goat was first produced by The American Place Theater, the group that has adapted St. Clements Church on West 46th Street for theater experimentation. Last year American Place produced Robert Lowell's *The Old Glory* including *Benito Cereno,* another poetic drama. Alfred's poetry is more theatrical than Lowell's; it is real spoken *language,* rich in the character and characteristics of the Irish community. Like Lowell's play, Alfred's ran its course at St. Clements and then was moved to another off-Broadway theater to make way for American Place's subscription program of three more productions. Its season which had begun so well with the year's best playscript continued with creditable work: *Jonah,* a play by Paul Goodman about facing commitments, with the Biblical character adopting a Yiddish accent; *The Journey of the Fifth Horse,* by Ronald Ribman based on a Turgenev story, which won an Obie Award; and *Doubles and Opposites,* a program of one-acters (and when one of the three didn't pan out, they dropped it and substituted some movie shorts).

If there were such a thing as a bandwagon off Broadway, it would be cut into two or three small, hinged segments. The program of one-acters, tightly connected or deliberately unconnected and contrasting, *is* off Broadway. American Place does them; Theater 1966 does them; Albee, Jones, Pinter and Ionesco made their New York stage reputations with them; of 1965-66's new-play programs off Broadway, fourteen were evenings of one-acters. Two of these were programs of experimental plays brought from off-off-Broadway's Cafe LaMama into more formal off-Broadway display for first-nighters and critics (who weren't especially impressed). Among 1965-66's single-play-wright programs of one-acters were those of Arkady Leokum, Ray Bradbury, Douglas Turner Ward, John White, Stanley Mann, Jerome Kass, Lanford Wilson, Robert Unger and Maxime Furlaud.

A season ago, LeRoi Jones' one-acter *The Toilet* emerged from one of these programs as a Best Play of its year. There was no such outstanding short work in 1965-66, but Jerome Kass's *Monopoly* was an especially interesting program of four intensely personal vignettes: a girl going to her first high school dance, a husband made to play dog for his wife, a middle-aged student in love with her young teacher, and an unhappy evening of Monopoly with two couples suffering emotional upheavals. Mr. Kass's proccupation is with human beings, not symbols, and he presents them with such understanding—such sympathy without excuses for their shortcomings—that his *Monopoly* was both a promise fulfilled and a promise of even better to come.

Ray Bradbury's evening of science-fiction one-acters deserved more attention than it received from New York audiences. Bradbury's technique is to comment on the present by projecting its characteristics into the future in immense blowups, exaggerations which might logically occur with the passage of time. For example, the villain of one of the short plays in *The World of Ray Bradbury* was a glorified TV apparatus that trapped and consumed its viewers—which is what may really happen some day if we fail to appreciate an entertainment phenomenon like Bradbury's imaginative view of externals, eloquently realized in this production by Eldon Elder's sets. Another deserving program that fared better was the actor Douglas Turner Ward's playwriting debut with the satirical sketches *Happy Ending* and *Day of Absence.* The first was a cynical joke about the valuable perquisites to be obtained in domestic service; the second was a Stepin Fetchit-like portrait of white Southern citizens who wake up one morning to find that all their town's Negroes have disappeared. Also, Arkady Leokum's *Friends* and *Enemies* commented forcefully on man's mistreatment of man in the relations between a meek waiter and a difficult customer, and a meek teacher and his tormenting pupil.

In some ways off Broadway always has been, and is becoming more and more, a Little Broadway. A conspicuous parallel in 1965-66 was the invasion by noteworthy foreign scripts. Certainly one of the most interesting new playwrights presented to New York audiences this season was John Arden, whose professional New York theater debut took place with the importation last summer of his *Live Like Pigs,* about a noisy, slovenly British family moving into a sedate housing project. A second, even more provocative Arden script followed in March: *Serjeant Musgrave's Dance,* a moody expression of pacifism set in Victorian days to let it speak for itself without contemporary bias. The script is paced like a dead march as it moves slowly toward its climax, with John Colicos as the "serjeant" who brings home a rotting corpse from the colonial wars to show the complacent citizenry what war *is.* Its slowness in coming to the point weakened the very suspense for which it strove so carefully, but it was a powerful play nevertheless.

Arthur Cantor's production and direction of *The Trigon* by James Broom Lynne was another high point of the season off Broadway. This was a British script about the fragile pretenses of two young men sharing a flat and the attentions of a girl; pretenses which are smashed cruelly, deliberately, by a stranger who seduces the girl and forces the two young men to look at themselves under the varnish. The relationships were most skillfully developed in Arthur Cantor's direction and in the acting, particularly in that of Jeremy Geidt in one of the season's top performances as the more effete of the young men. Another Cantor contribution to the off-Broadway year was the production of *The World of Gunter Grass,* selections in English from the work of the German novelist, adapted and staged by Dennis Rosa on a small but versatile set designed by Richard Seger.

There were some foreign failures, too. A translation of the Russian play *Sunset,* by Isaac Babel, didn't live up to expectations, nor did an adaptation of Ugo Betti's *Troubled Waters.* An adaptation of the classical Chinese *The Butterfly Dream* was merely a theatrical curio. And there was an adaptation of a Scandinavian script, *Break-Up,* that folded during previews, *before* opening night, just like an ill-starred Broadway venture.

The off-Broadway season's musical highlight was *The Mad Show,* a caper based on the comic viewpoint of *Mad Magazine,* conceived and staged by Steve Vinaver. The writing—a zany grab-bag of comments, portraits and sick jokes was another theater writing debut, that of Larry Siegel and Stan Hart, with Mary Rodgers supplying a spirited score played on piano and percussion. *The Mad Show* was a revue with comic-strip characters. Some of them, like Little Orphan Annie, were cut out of cardboard and stationed around the stage in some of the scenes. Others, like the members of a TV-crazed family or a group of football announcers, were portrayed by a small group of young and energetic actors. Stationary or in motion, it was fun—*Mad* fun.

The revue form seems to work as well in the off-Broadway context as the program of one-acters. Chicago's talented Second City returned with new material. In the cabarets, there was a new edition of Julius Monk's review at Plaza 9; another collection of Cole Porter songs, revisited; a new edition of *The Game Is Up* by Rod Warren, who also put on still another cabaret revue called *Just for Openers.* The phenomenally long run of *The Fantasticks* to the contrary (at season's end it had reached 2,538 performances and was still going strong), it seems to be the book musical that finds hard going off Broadway. Three tried this year and all failed: *Hotel Passionato* (sex and sin in hotel rooms), *Great Scot* (the life and times of the poet Robert Burns) and *Hooray! It's a Glorious Day . . . and all that* (love in a business office).

The flair and imagination of off Broadway's young stage artists enhanced a number of revivals in 1965-66, as in every previous season. The American Savoyards and the New York Shakespeare Festival were exploring their subjects as usual. There was a return engagement of *The Trojan Women* as staged by Michael Cacoyannis. There were revivals of Strindberg, Ibsen, Racine (in a new English version of *Phèdre* by William Packard), Maxwell Anderson (in a disappointing *Winterset*) and of James Yaffe's stage adaptation of Duerrenmatt's novel *The Deadly Game*. Gloria Foster gave an outstanding performance in the title role of Robinson Jeffers' *Medea*. Another standout was the Circle-in-the-Square production of *The White Devil*, John Webster's Elizabethan horror drama of seven murders staged by Jack Landau in modern dress.

The season's specialties included a program of Leonard Bernstein's theater songs and a program of Robert Frost's poetry and prose produced in the University of Michigan Professional Theater Program (same sponsorship as APA) and brought here for 132 performances. There were solo shows by Gale Sondergaard, Bramwell Fletcher and William Mooney. There were two shows produced for Yiddish-speaking audiences, and there was a German-language revue.

As conservatism set into the off-Broadway year in choice of plays and manner of production, the fringe activity increased. The moral of this 1965-66 theater story is that the process of ferment is persistent within the very lively New York stage. Many of those sparking bubbles at the top, on the starry stages of Broadway, are the end result of continuous yeasty ferment of imagination down on the bottom, where you can hardly see it taking place. Luckily for our theater, this process of generation persists no matter what sort of context is provided or withheld, or how many doors are closed against it. It persists in spite of rising costs and with or without subsidy; with the blessing of the theater establishment or in the face of its disapproval; if not on Broadway, then off; if not off Broadway then off-off-Broadway, wherever that happens to be.

Offstage

Offstage, 1965-66 was a year in which the Federal government dipped its toe into arts subsidy; a year in which drama critics were diminished (in number), criticized (by playwrights), changed (by the *Times*) and needled (by David Merrick); a year of strikes and rising costs and *Hello, Dolly!* in Vietnam.

In June, 1965, President Johnson signed the first bill setting up a program of Federal aid to the arts at a ceremony attended by many persons of national prominence in the arts (Arthur Miller refused his invitation in protest against foreign policy). This bill set up Federal arts-subsidy machinery which, like most government undertakings, sounds like a Rube Goldberg structure. Here is how the bureau pyramids: Congress established a National Foundation on the Arts and Humanities. Within this are two groups with the responsibility to disburse funds: the National Endowment for the Arts and the National Endowment for the Humanities. The Endowment chairmen (arts, Roger L. Stevens; humanities, Henry Allen Moe) are appointed by the President of the United States for four-year terms. Within each Endowment is a National Council composed of volunteers prominent in American arts who help the Endowment chairmen decide where the money is to go.

The National Endowment for the Arts received $5,000,000 on July 1, 1965. This has been spread around with the help of the National Council on the Arts, and there will be another $4,000,000 next year. In addition, $2,000,000 has been set aside to match funds for arts enterprises.

It was a rough year for the critics. The number of daily-paper first-night New York critics dropped from six to five with the merger of the *Herald Tribune,* the *World-Telegram and Sun* and the *Journal-American* into a single operating unit publishing one morning, one afternoon and one Sunday paper. John McClain was the odd man out, at his own request; Norman Nadel remained as drama critic of the merged evening papers. Walter Kerr remained at his morning paper post.

The playwrights' own privately-circulated journal, *The Dramatists Guild Quarterly* (of which this writer is the editor), looked closely at the work of the contemporary drama critics and rated it in various categories, in a poll conducted by the *Quarterly* among those playwrights, librettists, composers and lyricists whose work had been reviewed on or off Broadway during the 1964-65 season just past. In answer to the question, "Which critic wrote the most perceptive review of your 1964-65 work?" the dramatists picked Howard Taubman of the *Times,* Richard Watts Jr. of the *Post* and Walter Kerr of the *Herald Tribune,* in that order, by one-vote margins. Kerr was voted the critic whom the playwrights most enjoyed reading by two to one over his nearest rival (Watts), and Kerr also was the two-to-one choice as the critic who best understands playwriting, with Robert Brustein of the *New Republic* second and Richard Gilman of *Newsweek* third.

A substitution of major critics took place when Stanley Kauffmann took Howard Taubman's place on the *Times,* with Taubman moving on to roving, at-large comment on all the arts.

The critics were under continuous fire from David Merrick (he gives them no rest). In June he castigated the Messrs. Kerr and Taubman for their reviews of *The Roar of the Greasepaint—The Smell of the Crowd.* During the tryout run of *Cactus Flower* in Philadelphia, Merrick harassed a TV interviewer (Tom Snyder) sampling public opinion after a performance, in the following manner: Merrick and Harvey D. Sabinson, the show's press agent, joined those being questioned and, unrecognized by Snyder, told him on the air that the show was the greatest; then they gave the signal for another press agent, Robert Ullman, to cut the power line (which in fact he did), blacking out the TV program. In London, where Mary Martin's international touring company of *Hello, Dolly!* was received with less than enthusiasm by the London critics, Merrick advertised a rave review which Bernard Levin (at that time the *Daily Mail* critic) had written after seeing the New York *Dolly* a year or so previously. And, later on in a speech in Washington, D.C., Merrick delivered his Sunday punch against the London critics by declaring them worse than the New York critics.

Merrick's most conspicuous involvement with the business of play reviewing concerned Stanley Kauffmann and was triggered by the paid preview issue, which itself triggered more than one controversy this season. Paid previews came under new scrutiny after the late Dorothy Kilgallen reviewed a Broadway preview performance of *Skyscraper* in her *Journal-American* column on the grounds that it was a paid public performance and that her pre-opening night review could be evaluated by her readers as an appraisal of a not-quite-finished product in the same way as a *Variety* review of a show in its tryout tour. Many journalists agreed with her and applauded; most show folk did not.

When David Merrick was asked for his views on the preview-reviewing controversy, he said he didn't care what performance the critics attended, they wouldn't understand what they saw anyway. But when the final-preview tickets to Merrick's production of *Philadelphia, Here I Come!* arrived at the *Times* they were accompanied by a note "At your peril!" Coincidentally with Kauffmann's arrival at the Helen Hayes Theater to cover *Philadelphia*, it was discovered that the theater had "a rat in the generator." The lights went out, the performance was cancelled and the entire audience was given its money back and sent home. There was no show for Kauffmann to see and review.

Kauffmann had insisted from the beginning of the controversy that he was able to meet the stiff deadline if necessary, but he preferred the 24-hour review-at-leisure. Many theater folk were unkind enough to suggest that there never *really* was any rat in any generator; that Merrick went to considerable expense (and the innocent-bystanding preview audience to some inconvenience) to find out whether Kauffmann could meet the 80-minute deadline. Cancellation of this *Philadelphia* preview caused Kauffmann to review this show on opening night, and *Hostile Witness*, too, because *Witness's* last preview took place the night *Philadelphia* opened. And so now we know. Kauffmann *can* review in 80 minutes if he must (but when he finally saw *Philadelphia* he didn't much like it).

The critics troubled the theater by their absence as well as by their presence in 1965-66. There were two newspaper strikes, the first coinciding with the opening of the season. It began Sept. 16 and lasted twenty-four days, so that for the first two new plays, *Mrs. Dally* and *A Very Rich Woman*, there were only two reviews, by Kerr and Watts, whose papers weren't involved in the strike. *Generation* stayed out of town long enough so that all the critics were back on the job in time to review it when it finally opened.

The second strike, against the newly-merged *World Journal Tribune*, began April 24 and lasted through the end of the season, so that critics on these papers missed reviewing *Mame* and *A Time for Singing* and *The World of Gunter Grass* off Broadway. The absentees were sorely missed. Capable as the remaining critics may have been, the very smallness of their number (three: *Post, News, Times*) greatly increased that uneasy feeling in the New York theater that too much is riding on the judgments of too few.

The old tradition of "the show must go on" is more and more difficult to maintain in the face of complex modern catastrophes. On November 9 the lights went out—all the way out in the memorable East Coast power failure. Most shows managed to get back into business the following evening. Then the New York City transit strike of subway and bus workers on January 1 closed a production or two off Broadway for its duration. The Broadway shows stuck it out with two or three hits still playing to capacity but with others suffering for want of audiences.

The pricing and handling of theater tickets came often under discussion during the season, mostly centered upon the legally high-priced ticket rather than upon scalping—although there were reports in April of ice building up. Federal restrictions on the sale of theater tickets were repealed as of January 1, and efforts are continuing to have state and local restrictions relaxed, too. John F. Wharton recommended to the Legitimate Theater Industry Exploratory Commission that the theater work out a flexible-pricing policy in which last-minute tickets to the hits could be sold for as much as the traffic would bear up to $25. He also suggested that prices be lowered at mixed-review shows to stimulate sales, particularly among young audiences. In Wharton's opinion, the present rigid-price system fails to satisfy the affluent buyer unless he resorts to the black market, and it caters to the least desirable of the theater's customers, the one who wants last-minute cheap tickets to a hit and won't support a worthy flop. Wharton questioned the system in an article in Playbill: "Theater tickets are a perishable commodity. A Saturday night ticket is in great demand at 8 p.m. that night; at 11 p.m. it is worth nothing. A farmer who brings to market the only strawberries available that day will be paid everything the market will bear, and no one complains. Yet when the same principle is applied to theater tickets, outraged cries of 'black market' and 'robbery' go up. Why?"

For his musical *Superman*, Harold Prince edged the top tickets up to $12 and reduced his least expensive locations to $2. Tickets at both these prices sold well. The $9 and $3 locations sold last.

In housing, Broadway had a brief shortage of small, non-musical theaters at the peak of the season, but it was no great problem. New York gained the Vivian Beaumont (described in the section on repertory) and a refurbished Palace which was bought by James and Joseph Nederlander of Detroit. It was restored to some of its old glamor by Ralph Alswang (he stripped away the layers of "renovation" and uncovered ironwork and marble and a sculptured ceiling), and it was returned to legitimate theater use with the opening of *Sweet Charity*. The 54th Street Theater was renamed the George Abbott. Efforts to save the old Metropolitan Opera House were continuing as the season ended, with the opera company scheduled to begin performances in its new Lincoln Center home in the fall of 1966. Around the country these were some of the new theaters and/or cultural centers being constructed and planned during 1965-66: Theater Atlanta (Ga.); Saratoga (N.Y.) Performing Arts Center; 1,700-seat theater in La Jolla, Calif.; Studio Arena Theater, Buffalo; Scott Theater, Ft. Worth (Tex.); Cole Porter Theater, Los Angeles; Mechanic Theater, Baltimore; Houston (Tex.) Music Theater; Newark (N.J.) State College Theater for the Performing Arts; two Theater Group theaters at Los Angeles; Samaret (N.J.) Performing Arts Center; and of course the John F. Kennedy Center for the Performing Arts in Washington, D.C.

The 1965-66 New York theater revels now are ended; they took place with subsidy and fiscal reorganization under continuous discussion, while Broadway (and off Broadway) continued to get along as an old established permanent floating crap game of individual judgment and risk. There were problems and disappointments, but those who look to decentralization as the hope of the American theater of the future are looking for a short way home that leads over a cliff. The regional theater's playscripts are not *really* brought by the stork or even by the Rockefeller Foundation or the National Foundation on the Arts, they are gestated the hard way in New York. To change the metaphor a little, the regional theater is nursing lustily on Broadway and is a long, long way from being weaned. If New York goes dry, the regional theater must starve or worse; and by worse, I mean Ibsen and Chekhov.

Fortunately for *all* theater in America, Broadway continues to discharge its creative responsibility, even as it bears the weight of its own excesses. It is deceptively strong; it has no secret weaknesses, its weaknesses are all on the surface for any detracter to see. It is its strength that is hidden, like the power of a magnet. Every September the New York theater turns itself on and draws to itself every alloy of playwriting creativity until its minimum needs are filled. Even in a year like 1965-66, when usually reliable sources found themselves at a loss for the right words, the necessary inspiration took place. Somehow, the magnet drew in a musical based on a TV play, a verse drama from Harvard, a British repertory production of a German play, an adaptation of a French farce, just to name a few. Any one of these would have distinguished any season, and certainly they will distinguish future seasons in the regional theater and elsewhere, even in places where the taste and energy of the source is deprecated as the very plays that came from it are being revived.

This curious power of the New York stage may be magic; or it may be only the availability of a theater-oriented audience and the facilities to put on plays—in comfortable theaters and in uncomfortable ones; in coffee houses, in parks, in the streets. No. On second thought, it must be magic. The 1965-66 revels were summoned out of air, out of the thin air where fledglings fly, by some wizardry of inspiration. Most have served their purpose and are destined to vanish; but some are magically equipped to last on and on in new productions and fresh interpretations all over the country, all over the world and some, maybe, down through the years.

Anthony Quayle *top* and Philip Bosco in the Lincoln Center revival of *Galileo* by Bertolt Brecht.

PHOTO BY MARTHA SWOPE

1966-67

"THE BRITISH are coming, the British are coming!" the teen-agers warned us with their cries of rapture, and did we listen? No—most of us laughed when first the Beatles stepped off the boat, but soon it was too late to prevent the British from swarming all over the era with reinforcements like Tom Jones, James Bond, Vidal Sassoon, miniskirts and the Redgrave girls. Now they are here in strength, both feet planted in the center of American culture, not to be budged. Even the New York theater has fallen under their influence, their domination. The very best plays of the 1966-67 season in New York were written by Elizabethan playwrights—subjects of Queen Elizabeth II.

The year's best play was Harold Pinter's challenging *The Homecoming*. The year's best-*made* play was Frank Marcus's *The Killing of Sister George*. The year's funniest play was Peter Shaffer's *Black Comedy*. The best drama by far was John Wilson's *Hamp* off Broadway. Distinction in the area of the musical comedy/play continued to be a monopoly of American authors, who came up with *The Apple Tree, Cabaret* and (off Broadway) *You're a Good Man Charlie Brown* for the list of Best Plays. The excellent work of American authors in Edward Albee's *A Delicate Balance*, Robert Anderson's *You Know I Can't Hear You When the Water's Running* and (off Broadway) Jean-Claude van Itallie's *America Hurrah* was nevertheless overshadowed by the British presence.

1966-67 was the second dismal year in a row for American playwriting. Volume was off significantly, even alarmingly—19 new plays and 8 new musicals as compared with 25 and 11 in 1965-66 and 25 and 10 in 1964-65. American writers didn't even chalk up a significant record of disappointment. Most of our previously successful playwrights (I was going to say "well established," but there's no such thing as a well established playwright) were missing from the Broadway scene in 1966-67, so that the failure of Frank D. Gilroy's *That Summer—That Fall* after 12 performances stood out as an event. Foreign authors kept grabbing the limelight even in the matter of disappointment, notably with Peter Weiss's *The Investigation* (a financial success but a ponderous theatrical effort) and Brian Friel's *The Loves of Cass Mc-Guire,* both of which failed to stir up anything like the excitement of, respectively, the same authors' *Marat/Sade* and *Philadelphia, Here I Come!* of last season.

Paradoxically, there were about the same number of stage programs offered on Broadway—78 as compared with 76 last season and 81 the season before. But this total figure includes a huge number of revivals—32—exactly double the 16 revivals in 1965-66. With the Music Theater and the Repertory Theater of Lincoln Center, the City Center doing straight plays as well as musicals, visits from the D'Oyly Carte, the Bristol Old Vic, the National Repertory Theater and the APA-Phoenix, as well as other individual revival enterprises, it was a banner year for those who enjoy seeing the theatrical past evoked on the living stage.

Also paradoxically, business was tremendous, with record grosses on Broad-

The 1966-67 Season on Broadway

PLAYS (19)

A DELICATE BALANCE
We Have Always Lived in the Castle
Under the Weather
Don't Drink the Water
We Comrades Three
Those That Play the Clowns
My Sweet Charlie
Agatha Sue I love you
The Star-Spangled Girl
Come Live With Me
The Paisley Convertible
Love in E-flat
Of Love Remembered
The Natural Look
YOU KNOW I CAN'T HEAR YOU WHEN THE WATER'S RUNNING
That Summer—That Fall
A Warm Body
Little Murders
The Girl in the Freudian Slip

MUSICALS (8)

THE APPLE TREE
CABARET
Walking Happy
I Do! I Do!
A Joyful Noise
Sherry
Illya Darling
Hallelujah, Baby!

SPECIALTIES (4)

A Hand Is on the Gate
The Threepenny Opera
At the Drop of Another Hat
Hello, Solly!

REVIVALS (32)

Guys and Dolls
Show Boat
Annie Get Your Gun
Dinner at Eight
The Country Girl
The Rose Tattoo
Elizabeth the Queen
The Consul
Lincoln Center Rep:
The Alchemist
Yerma
Galileo
D'Oyly Carte:
The Pirates of Penzance
The Mikado
Ruddigore
H.M.S. Pinafore
Patience
APA-Phoenix:
The School for Scandal
Right You Are

The Wild Duck
You Can't Take It With You
War and Peace
Carousel
Marat/Sade
Bristol Old Vic:
Measure for Measure
Hamlet
Romeo and Juliet
Finian's Rainbow
The Sound of Music
Wonderful Town
National Repertory:
The Imaginary Invalid
A Touch of the Poet
Tonight at 8:30

FOREIGN PLAYS IN ENGLISH (10)

Help Stamp Out Marriage!
The Investigation
THE KILLING OF SISTER GEORGE
The Loves of Cass McGuire
The East Wind
How's the World Treating You?
Hail Scrawdyke!
THE HOMECOMING
The Astrakhan Coat
BLACK COMEDY and *White Lies*

FOREIGN-LANGUAGE PRODUCTIONS (5)

Gilbert Becaud on Broadway
Let's Sing Yiddish
The Apparition Theater of Prague
Les Ballets Africains
Sing Israel Sing

HOLDOVER SHOWS WHICH BECAME HITS DURING 1966-67

Man of La Mancha
Half a Sixpence
Mame
Philadelphia, Here I Come!
Sweet Charity
Wait a Minim!

Plays listed in CAPITAL LETTERS have been designated Best Plays of 1966-67.
Plays listed in bold face type were classified as hits in *Variety's* annual list of hits and flops publishd on June 7, 1967.
Plays listed in *italics* were still running on June 1, 1967.

way, and with attendance greatly improved off Broadway thanks to a large
number of fine shows. There were fewer new Broadway shows, but the holdovers were running longer. The new smash hits like *Cabaret* ($12 top) and
I Do! I Do! ($9.90 top) added their audience-pulling power to the many
popular holdovers: *Barefoot in the Park* (at a $6.75 top in its fourth year),
Cactus Flower ($7.50 in its second year), *Fiddler on the Roof* (third year,
$9.90), *Funny Girl* (fourth year, $9.60), *Hello, Dolly!* (fourth year, $9.90),
Mame (second year, $9.90), *Man of La Mancha* (second year, $8.50), *The
Odd Couple* (third year, $7.25) and *Sweet Charity* (second year, $9.50).

Into this theatrical supermarket the New York show-shopper poured a
total 1966-67 gross of $55,056,030 (according to *Variety* estimate), topping
the fifty million mark and breaking the record for the third straight year (previous records were set in 1964-65 with $50,462,765 and in 1965-66 with
$53,862,187). The number of playing weeks (if 10 shows run 10 weeks,
that's 100 playing weeks) in 1966-67 was 1,269, third-highest behind 1,295
in 1965-66 and 1,325 in 1947-48. In this statistic the fall-off in activity was
very slight, indicating that the reduced number of new productions is being
nearly balanced by the longer runs of the successes. It should also be noted
in passing by the box office that Christmas Week, 1966, brought in the highest
single week's gross in Broadway history: $1,519,636, the first such gross of
record (according to *Variety*) to go over the million-and-a-half mark. Touring Broadway shows also did exceptionally well at the box office ($43,572,-
116, more than $10 million better than last year) with a whopping increase
in activity to 916 playing weeks from 699 in 1965-66.

In 1966-67 Broadway was a Neil Simon festival. Simon came up with still
another comedy hit—*The Star-Spangled Girl*. Add this one to *Barefoot in the
Park, The Odd Couple* and *Sweet Charity,* and you reach the astonishing but
inescapable conclusion that Simon had *four* hit shows running simultaneously
on Broadway in 1966-67, and they were still running, *all of them,* at season's
end. Simon's best combined week's gross, it is estimated, topped $200,000.
Of course David Merrick, who does not write his shows himself, did better
than that. Merrick's weekly gross for *Hello, Dolly!, Cactus Flower, Don't
Drink the Water, I Do! I Do!* plus sundry holdovers and short-run new plays
that didn't make it ran as high as $325,000. Merrick's *Dolly* has already
passed the $30,000,000 level in worldwide grosses. Another big continuing
Broadway success story is that of *Fiddler on the Roof,* which has already
earned $2,580,000 in distributed profits and is still going strong—three reper-
tory companies, three, are doing the show in *Finland.*

Lots of cash at favored box offices, British playwrights, revivals, Neil Simon,
David Merrick—these were the peaks of the 1966-67 theater season. The
deepest valley was the fall-off in new-play production, and there were others,
notably the depressions dug by big musicals that failed to make it: *A Joyful
Noise* (closed after only 12 performances with a deficit of $500,000), or
Breakfast at Tiffany's which folded in previews leaving Merrick out $425,000.
The musical *Chu Chem* folded in tryout, as did three plays mounted in New
York for Broadway: *The Hemingway Hero, Two Weeks Somewhere Else* and
What Do You Really Know About Your Husband?

Stand far enough away from the 1966-67 season and you cannot help con-
cluding that it was as thin and gaunt in the creative department as it was fat
and sassy at the box office. It is hardly worth mentioning any more that the

volume of plays dealing in dramatic form with "serious" subjects is hardly worth mentioning. I say dramatic in *form* because there is much "serious" content and intent with the comic form of our theater. In fact, there are times when it seems that our trans-Atlantic theater is a soap box for those who feel certain that all Creation is a colossal joke on the human race, and who are striving to launch the newest, most acutely ironic laugh as the cosmos pulls the chair out from under yet another unfortunate, just-about-to-sit Job.

There is no lack of "serious" material in our theater, only of "serious" dramatic form. If *The Killing of Sister George*—in which the leading character is brought to practise mooing like a cow in order to survive—was for laughs alone, then who needs something to cry over? There's much to be said for conveying criticism and agony by indirection, and indeed the old definitions of "comedy," "drama" and "comedy-drama" are graying out in works like *A Delicate Balance* and *The Homecoming*.

It is argued that in the second half of the 20th century everything in general has become so uncomfortable, or at least so complex, that it can be faced *only* with laughter. Tears would be a kind of surrender. But even if all the special pleading is justified, and ours is indeed an especially trying age, you wouldn't guess it from the "serious" jokes in the Broadway comedies. Even if our festering problems of overpopulation, the bomb, the scientific adventure, etc., are ready to be sliced with satire and ridicule, that's not what's happening onstage, baby. What's happening—or what happened in 1966-67—was repetitious sardonic laughter in the time-traveled areas of sexual prowess, impotence and deviation. If the big kick is irony, the big hang-up is sex, not the state of the universe. The total annihilation of the human race may be the second-biggest joke in contemporary comedy, but if so it is running a very poor second.

The big best-seller among theater forms, however, remains the American musical comedy/play. Among the ten Best Plays of 1966-67, three are musicals, inevitably. As more and more creative effort is concentrated in this area a bigger proportion of our best theater work takes place within it. We have developed this form to the danger point of near-perfection where we can machine-make it—almost. Many of the musicals which turn up nowadays, even some of the most popular ones, are canned goods, taking some proven high-quality material from a novel or play and processing and packaging it in musical form. From a point of bias toward original creative forces, it's hard to decide whether in the long run it's better for the theater when this canning machinery works (as in *I Do! I Do!*, based on *The Fourposter*) or when it doesn't (as in *Sherry!*, based on *The Man Who Came to Dinner*). But canned or creative, the musical theater made still another strong season with the pulling power of new attractions and the staying power of the old ones; it is the equal of the ironic comedies in attracting attention and their superior in attracting audiences.

Broadway

At the Drop of Another Hat was a two-man performance by Michael Flanders and Donald Swann, British satirists in their second popular Broadway program of musical caricatures of animals, people and events. To a certain extent all British importations are special cases. Already mounted, cast, directed and rehearsed—or, at the very least, blocked out and perfected before London audiences—they cost relatively little in money and effort to bring to the point of a Broadway opening night, as compared with starting from scratch with a raw script. But the 1966-67 British plays were special cases of excellence, too, and it is a pleasure to note that they all approached hit level, with audiences attracted even to the perplexing mysteries of *The Homecoming.*

Harold Pinter consolidated his position as one of the world's leading playwrights of the absurdist or any other school with his much-debated *The Homecoming,* the year's best play and the Tony and Critics Award winner. Its setting (by John Bury) was the living room and hallway of a lower-middle-class London home; gray, drafty, the back wall knocked out to make a bigger archway, exposing the support beam and looking as though it had been raped and left for dead. Within this forbidding environment live a shouting, sometimes domineering father, his vapid brother who is a chauffeur, and his two sons. One of these sons is an indifferent boxer, and one is a pimp. Another is a Ph.D. (listen to the change in key), the eldest, a professor at a California university. He comes home for a visit, bringing his wife. After meeting her, the father and his two younger sons decide that they could use a woman around the house, for their sport and convenience. The Ph.D.'s wife would suit them very well, and she looks as though she could earn her own keep moonlighting as a prostitute in Greek Street (another change in key?). Calmly setting her own terms, the wife accepts this offer from her brothers and father-in-law to share their dubious hospitality (another change?). Her imperturbable teacher-husband departs for California, alone, never losing his cool, leaving his family competing and begging for his wife's favor (another?).

What does all this *mean?* audiences and critics have asked themselves. They also asked Pinter, who refused to elucidate, referring all questions back to the script. Two can play at that game. Before making any comment on *The Homecoming* I will present here the unedited notes which I scribbled in the dark during the performance. I am not a note-taker, and in the case of no other play during the 1966-67 season did I jot more than one or two words of reminder. But in the case of *The Homecoming* I found the following observations scrawled in my program:

> Corpses . . . cool . . . gallows humor but the trap never drops.
> Futile break in widepants cuffs.
> Fear in a cheese sandwich. Not a raised eyebrow but everything is sardonic.
> Utter destruction with injections of water and air.
> This may be the best playwriting there is.

Let Harold Pinter try to figure out what *that* means. Certainly I do not know what *The Homecoming* means any better than Pinter says he does, but I can tell from looking over these notes that it had a very strong impact upon me as it was taking place before my senses in the theater.

Pinter, I feel, was dramatizing simultaneously the conscious and the subconscious. He cannot pretend in external reality that the father of this family suddenly turns to his educated son and proposes that his wife become the family prostitute. What is happening—it seems to me—is that Pinter's characters begin a scene as people operating consciously in external reality; then in the course of the scene they blurt out and personify their subconscious drives, fears, longings. For example, the wife—played with fearful control by Pinter's own wife, Vivien Merchant, in this production—is at first merely the wife of a college professor, a bit ill at ease in the unfamiliar environment of her husband's boyhood home. But in the next beat (like a sudden change of key in a musical composition) she starts to personify everyone's sexual drives including her own.

This technique—or characteristic, if I am wrong about it being a deliberate effect by the playwright—is at times confusing and at times extremely effective. From the opening scene, dread underlies this play like a psychosis, dread often expressed in the characters' attitudes but never in their words. Finally this dread comes out into the open as though Pinter had slowly turned his characters inside out so that they begin acting not rationally but subconsciously, emotionally, atavistically. They hardly ever raise their voices, but they are on the gallows of life; there is fear even in their cheese sandwiches; the air they breathe, the water they drink, is destroying them. They are alive, and there is no greater peril than that.

After a London season in production by the Royal Shakespeare Company as directed by Peter Hall, *The Homecoming* arrived on Broadway perfect in performance and style. Paul Rogers, who played the father, was so caught up in his role that (he stated in an interview) he scrubbed up like a surgeon every night before going on because the old man (says the script) is fanatically neat. Ian Holm as the pimp-son cut a streak of cruelty through the play. The notation "futile break in widepants cuffs" refers to a telling wardrobe detail of John Normington as Sam, the chauffeur-brother, a perfect study in futility.

A second distinguished visitor (and a palpable hit) was *The Killing of Sister George* by Frank Marcus, the British drama critic and playwright, who made his Broadway debut with this comedy about an actress who plays a soap opera heroine: the ever-helpful visiting nurse "Sister George" in a BBC serial idealizing British country life. Now Sister George must be "killed" in the soap opera story in order to attract new public attention to the program. And in the play there is another "death" taking place at the same time that Sister George is being "killed." In the play's "real life," the actress who plays Sister George is a swaggering, cigar-smoking, take-charge type who lives with a pale young woman roommate she calls "Childie." Their private emotional relationship is being wracked and destroyed at the same time that the actress's role is being eliminated from the serial—leaving her, finally, alone on the stage, practising mooing. All she hopes to salvage from the wreck of her personal and professional life is the role of a cow in a forthcoming BBC idiocy.

In one of the season's top performances Beryl Reid portrayed the actress as a gallant creature; something of a bully who enjoys disciplining her weak-willed roommate; but standing up bravely to attempted bullying by a tailored woman executive from the BBC. In another standout performance Eileen Atkins became an angular symbol of arrested development and total selfishness as the babyish but not so innocent "Childie." The neurotic, doomed relationship between these two women may be part of the human comedy, but Marcus was not laughing *at* them in his excellent play. He has great sympathy for them in their emotional predicament; along with the laughter, his play both exposed and evoked strong feelings.

Last season Peter Shaffer was represented on the Best list by the philosophical-historical ironies of *The Royal Hunt of the Sun.* This season he was represented by the year's funniest play, the one with the punning title *Black Comedy,* a third jewel in Britain's triple-crown championship of Broadway.

Like *Charley's Aunt, Three Men on a Horse* and such, *Black Comedy* spins off from a single comic proposition, to wit: the fuses have blown so that the action takes place in pitch black darkness (but the reality of the lighting is reversed, so that when the setting appears blacked-out to the characters it appears brightly lighted to the audience). The characters are cardboard—designedly so—in a cutout situation. A fumbling young artist and his debutante fiancee have swiped the neighbor's elegant furniture to impress a millionaire who is coming to the studio to look at the artist's sculptures. The two-level setting designed by Alan Tagg (a stairway at right leads to a bedroom above) was deliberately cluttered to make it an obstacle course for characters in total "darkness" serving drinks, flirting and trying to sneak the furniture back while its rightful owner is in the room.

John Dexter's direction encouraged caricature in the acting of Michael Crawford as the harassed young artist, Lynn Redgrave as the waddling debutante, Peter Bull as her blowhard father, a colonel, and Donald Madden as the delicate young man who owns the furniture. In the dark, fears become exaggerated; secret repressions are secretly released (but the audience could see), in a very funny show which had all the earmarks of a comedy classic-to-be.

Black Comedy was commissioned by Britain's National Theater and was first performed by them (though not with this cast). Its action is continuous in a long one-act form, and Shaffer wrote a companion piece, the shorter *White Lies,* as a curtain-raiser for *Black Comedy* on the Broadway program. *White Lies* studied a fading fortune teller (Geraldine Page) victimized by a vicious young client; it was a little droplet of acid not quite so searing as its author had hoped. It suffered, too, from the handicap of standing in the deep shadow of its illustrious companion piece. Audiences came to the theater programmed by critical and word-of-mouth raves to laugh at *Black Comedy.* Sometimes they started laughing right away, as soon as the curtain rose (no point in not getting your full money's worth)—and often it took them a while to get over their preconceived *Black Comedy* notions before they could settle down to the rather more serious matter of *White Lies.*

The best American play of the Broadway year was Edward Albee's *A Delicate Balance* which was a hit and won Albee his first Pulitzer Prize. (A 1963 Pulitzer for *Who's Afraid of Virginia Woolf?* was voted by the jurors but withheld by the trustees.) Like *The Homecoming, A Delicate Balance* resists old definitions of theater. It is a comedy which coexists with nameless terror. Asked about his own definitions, Albee replied in an article in *Diplomat* magazine: "There's quite a difference between comedy and humor. *Virginia Woolf* was a comedy in the sense that everybody ended up with what they wanted (I'm being just slightly ironic). That's the definition of comedy: everybody ending up with what they want, or what they *think* they want. Now, serious theater must accomplish two things. The serious play has got to say something about the nature of the play as an art form itself; it has got to try to advance, to change that art form. It must also try to change the spectator in some fashion; alter his point of view, his view of reality, his view of the theater. This is the double responsibility of serious theater, and good intentions are never enough . . . I suppose *Virginia Woolf* was a serious comedy . . . Not everybody ends up with what they want, or what they think they want, in *A Delicate Balance*."

By this definition, it would be possible to regard Albee's *A Delicate Balance* as a drama; yet I would prefer to class it with *Virginia Woolf* as a "serious comedy" because, at the end, the delicate balance upset by the events of the play is restored. All is exactly as it was at the beginning of the play (almost). Albee ends *A Delicate Balance* with his unflappable suburban housewife resuming a conversation that was interrupted as the play began.

What happened in between certainly challenged the spectator to search himself with two questions: what obligations do we assume in accepting friendship and love? and what rights do we acquire in giving them? The arena for Albee's examination of these realities is a suburban household delicately balanced within all the proprieties: the husband Tobias (Hume Cronyn) toying with his after-dinner anisette, the wife Agnes (Jessica Tandy) exercising a delicately articulated control over all. The pressures in this household are controlled pressures, balanced pressures until a neighboring couple—Agnes' and Tobias' best friends—move right into the guest room without either invitation or explanation, seeking refuge from a fear they cannot describe or understand, a fear that descended on them suddenly as they were sitting at home in the void of their lives.

Seeking sanctuary at the same time is the daughter of the house, running home to mother after her fourth unsuccessful marriage. So here are two spearheads of need—friend and family—converging, clashing, competing for attention. How much consideration do Agnes and Tobias owe their friends in exchange for having enjoyed their friendship? These are friends who have nowhere else to go because they have no *other* best friends. And how much do Agnes and Tobias owe their daughter simply because she *is* their daughter? That is the tangle that Albee's play weaves and then unweaves, with tolerant Tobias and articulate Agnes acted with total comprehension by the Cronyn-Tandy husband-and-wife team. Like Albee's *Tiny Alice, A Delicate Balance* had a relatively short (132 performances) first run on Broadway. But *Tiny Alice* has since enjoyed several distinguished productions elsewhere; it is growing in stature with each appearance. *A Delicate Balance,* too, is a new root planted in the theater, and its continuing growth as part of the stage repertory of the 1960s seems inevitable.

The other three American playscripts hovering above or near the hit line were all comedies. Robert Anderson scored a hit with *You Know I Can't Hear You When the Water's Running,* a program of four one-acters, all on the periphery of sexual matters. It was directed by Alan Schneider (who also staged *A Delicate Balance*) so as to tune up the many ironic laughs in Anderson's script without tuning out his deep bass notes beneath the humor. The first playlet, *The Shock of Recognition,* presented a playwright who would show a naked man on the stage for all sorts of noble artistic reasons but is himself embarrassed by an eager actor stripping off his clothes in an attempt to grab the part. The second, *The Footsteps of Doves* exhibited a middle-aged married couple at the Rubicon of changing from a double to twin beds. The third, *I'll Be Home for Christmas,* was bitter fruit, as a middle-aged husband and wife expose the meaninglessness of their own marriage in discussing their children's sex problems: he with affection and understanding; she coldly and relentlessly "practical." The fourth playlet, *I'm Herbert,* is the muddled conversation of an old couple boasting of past love affairs but now unable to remember exactly who loved whom and when.

In his program of one-acters, Anderson was almost always laughing but not always joking. The characters were brilliantly served by an excellent cast: Martin Balsam as the eager-beaver actor and the middle-aged husbands; Eileen Heckart as the three wives, two middle-aged and one old; and George Grizzard as the playwright and the old roue. The Anderson plays were part of a banner one-act year in the New York theater, distinguished also by Peter Shaffer's long one-acter *Black Comedy,* Jerry Bock's and Sheldon Harnick's one-act musicals in *The Apple Tree,* Jean-Claude van Itallie's biting one-acters off Broadway in *America Hurrah,* together with Anderson's notably entertaining foursome.

In full-length and good-humored comedy, Neil Simon made the hit list again for the fourth straight time with his *The Star-Spangled Girl,* a bit of fluff about swinging young San Francisco intellectuals, and he did it in a season when it was very hard to sell love's young dream in wedlock, in flaming illicit romance or on twofers. In this one Simon presented two roommates (Anthony Perkins and Richard Benjamin, a young specialist at dead-pan comedy acting) editing a rebellious little magazine and competing for the beautiful girl (Connie Stevens) who moves in next door. The jokes and the sight gags flew thick and fast from Simon's supremely gifted imagination, almost hiding the fact that his comedy never got off the mark of its opening situation, and had nowhere much to go anyhow. *The Star-Spangled Girl* was witty (like all Simon scripts) and volatile (like all comedies directed by George Axelrod), but, finally, an incompleted sketch.

The third American comedy close to the hit line was Woody Allen's *Don't Drink the Water,* a heaping platter of corn buttered with one-liners in a script about a Newark caterer on a European vacation with his wife and daughter in an Iron Curtain country, wrongly suspected of being a spy and forced to take refuge in the American embassy, a Florida shirt among the morning coats. The play was just one big, overfed American folk joke; yet every year, it seems, Broadway has a "fluke" success like *Don't Drink the Water* (last season's was *The Impossible Years*). Nobody likes it but the audience. It appears to be merely a vehicle for some special performer (in this case Lou Jacobi, every feather indignantly ruffled as the bruised and innocent caterer). But the contemptible play runs on and on, defying all critical cliches and major casting changes. Obviously *Don't Drink the Water* was more than just a fluke; the character jokes about the impossible spy, the inept young American left to run the embassy in the ambassador's absence, momma in the embassy kitchen, the one-track-minded Communist policeman, etc., got plenty of laughs, an advantage that can't be laughed off so easily. A large segment of the regular Broadway theatergoing audience may feel a bit sheepish in their enjoyment of such fantasies as this. Never mind, *Don't Drink the Water* was a very funny situation comedy, and Allen richly deserved any success he could find with it.

Peter Weiss's *The Investigation* (English version by Jon Swan and Ulu Grosbard, who also directed the production) was remarkable as the only no-doubt-about-it-serious theater success of the Broadway season. It is a drama in the journalistic genre (like *The Deputy*) which not only contemplates a real event—the murder of 4,000,000 people in the German concentration camp at Auschwitz—but also borrows the words from reality to describe it. Weiss took the transcript of the Frankfurt trial of Auschwitz criminals and condensed it, adding nothing, but telescoping the testimony of accusers and accused, telescoping the people into composites, until there remained a highly distilled but uniformly factual account of a major horror. As a play (which, incidentally, was sold to NBC for about $450,000 for a color TV tape), *The Investigation* was not so much the experience of a tragedy as the examination of a tragedy after the fact, like an inquest held to fix responsibility for the death of Hamlet. It was grievous, but not challenging; terrible to contemplate but not dramatically terrible. *The Investigation* was bitter medicine which after all did nothing for our chronic illness, our continuing shock at this damnable turn of events in human history; nor did it much advance the cause of serious drama.

The steady stream of popular musicals upon which Broadway depends so heavily for both income and excitement continued, with *Cabaret* and *I Do! I Do!* approaching hit status and others not too far below it. *Cabaret* (orchestra $12 and $10 a seat; boxes $10; front mezzanine $7.90, $8.90 on Friday and Saturday nights; rear mezzanine $6.90, $5.90, $4 and $2) was a typical Broadway smash, high in price, popularity and quality. Also typically in the 1960s, it was cut from a pattern; it musicalized material from Christopher Isherwood stories about a young writer and a night-blooming girl who lives with him in hedonistic, pre-Hitler Berlin—material previously dramatized successfully in John van Druten's *I Am a Camera*. It has been converted successfully into a musical with flair and flavor in the adaptation, the score, the acting, the staging and the design.

The edge-of-darkness mood was deepest in the performance of Joel Grey as the Emcee, the compere of this sepulchral Berlin night spot, and by extension the symbol of the city's doom. He was a death-clown, hair plastered down, makeup emphasizing the skull behind the grin as he bids the customers "Willkommen" or suggests a new game in "Two Ladies." Joe Masteroff's book conjured up a Nazi bully who makes himself fairly unpleasant. But it isn't blows from the bully that shove this pleasure-seeking society over the cliff of the Nazi era, it is the soothing little nudges of the smirking Emcee. Grey combined his abilities as a mime, an actor and even as a makeup artist to produce an unforgettable negative of human nature.

Cabaret dipped love, hospitality, loyalty, patriotism in acid throughout its book, its Fred Ebb lyrics, its John Kander score, its staging and performances. Even the Boris Aronson settings contributed mightily to the irony—the cabaret "audience" was sometimes the theater's audience reflected in a huge trapezoidal mirror upstage. We were all in this *Cabaret*—or could have been, or could be again if we don't watch out. It was a good show about Berlin in 1929-30 in the full tradition of the American musical theater in 1966-67.

The season's second near-hit (as of May 31) musical was *I Do! I Do!* ($9.90), straight from the cannery and founding its popularity on musical and acting virtuosity. It was based on Jan de Hartog's *The Fourposter* about a marriage weathering the years and the storms. As a play and now as a musical this show had only two characters—no chorus line, no scene changes, no mirrors, nothing but a husband and wife and a double bed. It was still the same play, with holes cut out by Tom Jones and Harvey Schmidt for musical intervals, songs whose very titles form a precis of the plot: "I Do! I Do!", "I Love My Wife," "Something Has Happened," "Nobody's Perfect," "Flaming Agnes," "The Honeymoon Is Over," "When the Kids Get Married," "The Father of the Bride." With Robert Preston and Mary Martin playing the couple and singing the songs, the musical was the season's most attractive star turn. She can sing a little better than he can; he can act a little better than she can; they worked extremely well together, never exploiting an advantage, lending support over the rough spots. The Martin-Preston stint was a virtuoso duet, a show in itself.

Those were the hits, the almost-hits, the about-to-be-hits of 1966-67. Their number was small (11) but roughly the same as in other recent seasons. There is a steady appetite, it seems, for the best that is available in the theater in and around New York, either in vintage or non-vintage years.

The Apple Tree ($9.90) ran strongly all through the season. Certainly it was a triumph for Jerry Bock and Sheldon Harnick, a song writing team which came up not only with the best and wittiest score of the season but also, I believe, with its best book in their first try at writing a Broadway libretto themselves. *The Apple Tree* was not one musical, but three musicals, each a one-acter. The three playlets are based on two stories—Mark Twain's *The Diary of Adam and Eve* and Frank R. Stockton's *The Lady or the Tiger?* —and Jules Feiffer's cartoon story *Passionella*. The book material is of course second-hand; but here, at least, the stories consumed were of a different literary species, not cannibalized from the theater itself. They were adapted as though they were born in a trunk, however; and the three separate ideas— one of Adam and Eve discovering the world, one of clawing jealousy and one of Hollywood glamor—looked as though they were born triplets. One whispers *(Diary)* and one shouts *(Passionella);* one was plain *(Diary)* and one was fancy *(Lady or Tiger)*. But all three were played in much the same key of comic irony, with the last two items reshaped, somewhat, to match the Twain manner.

A high level of ironic comment was maintained in Mike Nichols' staging and in the caustic asides of a narrator (Larry Blyden). Between them, they never for a moment let any of the characters get away with an affectation, or the actors with a meaningless gesture. Barbara Harris's performance as Eve, Princess Barbára and Ella-Passionella was the season's musical best. The way she sang about wanting to be a mo-o-o-vie star may make it impossible for anyone to speak that word again without using at least three o's. Alan Alda, too, came on strong as Adam, Sanjar and Flip opposite Miss Harris's three poses. *The Apple Tree's* ups were high on the scale of musical entertainment. It was the season's best as a whole and in many of its parts—for example, Tony Walton's costumes, which solved the problem of clothing Adam and Eve by using some brown, nondescript fabric; then broke out into camp with Passionella's golden gown.

On the 1966-67 Broadway musical stage as a whole, there were 10 new shows mounted. Of these, one died in tryout—*Chu Chem,* about a Jewish family taking up Chen Buddhism. Another, *Breakfast at Tiffany's,* based on the Truman Capote novel, folded in New York previews after a change of titles (from *Holly Golightly*), directors, (from Abe Burrows to Joseph Anthony) and adapters (from Burrows to Edward Albee) in the course of production.

Two of the 10 musicals were almost-hits at press time, as previously noted. Of the remainder, the one that fared worst (only 12 performances) was *A Joyful Noise,* a show in folk-song style, based on a novel about a modern minstrel driven out of a Tennessee town by the father of the girl he loves, then making it big as a pop music idol. The show had a lively contemporary sound in the score by Oscar Brand and Paul Nassau and a brash contemporary air about it, but it was panned brown by the New York critics. John Raitt, in the leading role of the wandering minstrel, replied with an outstanding exhibition of gallantry under fire. On the second night, with all the wounds still fresh, Raitt nevertheless came out fighting in a solid, swinging performance. His show not only went on; it came on strong. Raitt's courage and professionalism seemed all the more admirable in a season when, all too frequently, the theater news carried announcements of fatigue, defection and other sighful disengagements on the part of Broadway performers.

One of the musical no-hitters, *Walking Happy* was this season's *Half a Sixpence.* Its book based on *Hobson's Choice* had a British flavor in its tale of a humble shoemaker's apprentice who marries the boss's daughter. *Walking Happy* became a vehicle for Norman Wisdom, the British comedian, a runty wizard of song and dance who filled every scene with his presence. And the Danny Daniels dances, expressing various stages of the apprentices's breakout, were one of the highlights of the season. Another shortlived musical, *Sherry!* was an amiable canning of the Moss Hart-George S. Kaufman comedy *The Man Who Came to Dinner,* with Clive Revill in the Monty Woolley role—pleasant enough both comically and musically but dated in its satire of the Alexander Woollcott-Harpo Marx-Gertrude Lawrence era.

A pair of musicals bearing stars and still running at the end of the season was *Illya Darling* and *Hallelujah, Baby! Illya* musicalized the movie *Never on Sunday,* with the shapely Greek actress Melina Mercouri in her celebrated performance of a congenial Piraeus prostitute (the material suffered in transition from screen to stage, but not Miss Mercouri). In *Hallelujah,* Leslie Uggams turned on her charm and her full singing voice for the story of a Negro girl determined to get out of the kitchen (in 1910), making it in show business (in the 1920s and 1930s), becoming civil-rights conscious (in the 1940s to 1960s). The years go by as indicated, but the characters do not age in this Arthur Laurents book (nor do they really come to fruition as personalities, that's one of the problems with the show). Laurents' work was remarkable, though, as the season's only original musical libretto. He deserves a special commendation and citation for keeping invention alive, for growing fresh material in a cannery year.

Turning to the so-called "serious" theater, drama had not disappeared entirely from Broadway in the season of 1966-67. But a home-grown attempt to tackle a pressing sociological problem onstage met with little success. David Westheimer's first Broadway play, *My Sweet Charlie,* was adapted from his own novel about a Negro lawyer (Louis Gossett) who has killed a man in a civil rights brawl, and a poor-white-trash girl (Bonnie Bedelia) who is pregnant and hopes to have her baby in secret. Both take refuge in an abandoned Gulf Coast summer cottage (one of the season's more effective designs, by Jo Mielziner). Their wary mutual mistrust at the beginning of the play works better in this script than their growing rapport and his final self-sacrifice to save her life. Another drama, *Of Love Remembered,* spanned two continents with its tale of a Scandinavian femme fatale migrating from Norway to Minnesota—but even with Ingrid Thulin in the lead it couldn't get its arms around the audience. *We Comrades Three* was an earnest effort by APA-Phoenix to present Walt Whitman and some of his works onstage, but even with Helen Hayes in the cast it lacked definition and force.

A most ambitious and highly respected effort of serious theater this season was Frank Gilroy's *That Summer—That Fall,* a transposition of the Phaedra tragedy to an Italian family in America today. Irene Pappas came over from Greece to play the darkly beautiful wife who develops a fatal passion for her husband's handsome young illegitimate son. Gilroy's dialogue was understated, almost coded; his characters flamed without losing their cool, if such a thing is possible—but perhaps it wasn't. It didn't work, but it was a worthy try in an admirable but generally unfelt example of serious drama (and here again, Mielziner's design was a standout).

Even in the form of thrillers, drama found hard going. Hugh Wheeler's adaptation of Shirley Jackson's novel *We Have Always Lived in the Castle,* about a teen-ager who has poisoned her family in a fit of rage, almost worked but not quite, though capably staged by Garson Kanin. A British thriller, *The Astrakhan Coat* by Pauline Macaulay, benefited from good performances by Brian Bedford (as an elegant young gang leader who steals and kills for kicks) and Roddy McDowall (as a numbskull waiter who is made the fall guy) under Donald McWhinnie's direction. But the play failed to stir up excitement, mostly because the victim was no match for his oppressor, and no object for strong sympathy.

With a scarcity of good new drama, the gray area between bright laughter and solemn agony became more eagerly explored, more populated with plays in the good-to-excellent class. This season, 12 new Broadway plays were billed in their programs as "comedies"; but I am not speaking only of them, or of black comedy, or camp, or other forms of cynical abrasion; nor does the expression "high comedy"—carrying as it does the comedy-of-manners image of a teacup slowly lowered to register severe shock—serve to encompass and include all this genre. I am speaking also of just-barely-comedy and perhaps-not-quite-comedy like this season's *The Homecoming* and *A Delicate Balance;* like last season's *Marat/Sade* and *Philadelphia, Here I Come!;* comedy that stings, that will do for serious drama until the drama snaps out of its doldrums; that will do perhaps *too* well because it offers the drama too much competition, like a too-competent understudy.

1966-67 brought a solid block of these gray plays from foreign sources (the foreign-play average tends to be high in comparison with American scripts, of course, because they are pre-tested on their home grounds; likewise the performances of foreign casts, who may have played together a year or more and are competing for "bests" with American actors who may just be getting the feel of the parts at award time). An interesting British entry (classified by its own author as a "comedy") was *How's the World Treating You?* in which a born loser (James Bolam) fails in the army, courtship and marriage and finally attempts suicide. It was a promising playwriting debut for Roger Milner, who made his West End and Broadway debuts with these caustic comments about how we fall victim to the whims and ambitions of others. A less auspicious British debut was David Halliwell's with *Hail Scrawdyke!* about a young painter who organizes an outrageous revolt. This play made a noise in Dublin and London (but lasted only 20 performances there) under the title *Little Malcolm and His Struggle Against the Eunuchs.* At least we were spared that title on a Broadway marquee. Renamed, recast and restaged by Alan Arkin, it lasted only 8 performances.

A couple of foreign plays in the just-barely-comedy category which did *not* enjoy the benefit of long previous practise were Brian Friel's *The Loves of Cass McGuire* and Leo Lehman's *The East Wind.* Both scripts were having their world premieres on Broadway, the first produced by the David Merrick Arts Foundation and the second by Lincoln Center Repertory. In *Cass McGuire,* as in last season's *Philadelphia, Here I Come!,* Friel was writing ruefully of family conflict. His Cass McGuire is an adventuress (a swagger role for Ruth Gordon under Hilton Edwards' direction) who has spent and misspent a full life in America, all the while sending money home to help her family. Returning home to Ireland, she is a disturbing influence on her family and is pushed off into a home for the aged, supported by her own money saved through the years by a family who didn't want it, either. This "You can't go home again" theme also turned up as part of *The East Wind,* also in its world premiere, the first new work offered by the Repertory Company of Lincoln Center in its Vivian Beaumont Theater. This was a human comedy played out by two refugees from the same small European town, one yearning for home and the other yearning to explore the world, winding up as partners in a London delicatessen. The homesick one returns for a visit and finds himself a stranger; the other never quite finds a home anywhere else. Both *The Loves of Cass McGuire* and *The East Wind* achieved moments of intense sympathy within unsatisfactory dramatic structures. They were songs rather than stories of pity.

On this side of the Atlantic, the cartoonist-satirist Jules Feiffer wrote a play, and instinctively his hand moved like a ouija-board platen into designs of black comedy. Feiffer's *Little Murders* was about a family headed by a fretful father (Heywood Hale Broun in an aggressive phase) who is worried. His son is effete, his daughter is marrying a hulking odd-ball pacifist, and people are shooting at him through the windows. The city has him surrounded (in Ming Cho Lee's brooding set) and eventually he and his family will feel the need to shoot back. There are a few whiplash vignettes, like the arrival of a psychedelic minister to perform the wedding ceremony. On the whole, though, seeing *Little Murders* was a bit like reading cartoon captions with your hand over the drawings. You got the impression that something fascinating might be taking place, but you were never entirely clear just what it was or what it meant.

Dark, too, was much of the humorous comment in Saul Bellow's program of three one-act plays—*Out From Under, The Wen* and *Orange Souffle*—which came to Broadway under the portmanteau title *Under the Weather* after previous stagings in Glasgow, Spoleto and London. There was no mystery about Bellow's subjects, however, in his second less-than-successful attempt to break out into the commercial theater. The first play was broadly farcical, about a widower's ruses to put off re-marriage. The weather clouds up in the second playlet about a Nobel Prize winner obsessed with a wen he once saw on an intimate part of a childhood playmate's body. The third, most carefully developed and longest of the one-acters, described the friendship of an 87-year-old industrialist and a prostitute—for ten years he's been visiting her, but when she finally tries to establish a close personal relationship, she fails.

Except for the hit and near-hit described previously, box office prospects were dark at the lighter end of the comedy scale. George Abbott staged his 107th and 108th shows to little avail. They were the British import *Help Stamp Out Marriage!*, a sex comedy with two couples, one married and one not, milling around the same apartment; and *Agatha Sue, I love you,* co-produced by Abbott's daughter Judith, the Broadway playwriting debut of a former stagehand, Abe Einhorn, in a farce about two gamblers and a pretty folk singer living cozily in a hotel.

Then there were the two doctor comedies about young interns, one married (in Harry Cauley's *The Paisley Convertible*) with tangled in-law problems, and one not (in Norman Krasna's *Love in E-flat*) but jealously monitoring each other's apartments with listening devices. Both plays were set on New York's East Side. The most remarkable feature of either of them was Donald Oenslager's two-level set for *Love in E-flat* with its dizzyingly high upstairs apartment, along whose naked striding edge the actors gamboled with seeming nonchalance.

Finally, in the sly romance department, not even the presence of TV comedian Soupy Sales in the leading role could save *Come Live With Me* from swift extinction, with its tale of a writer bedeviled in his London apartment by too many women including his wife—the Broadway debut of its authors, Lee Minoff and Stanley Price. William F. Brown's *The Girl in the Freudian Slip*, about psychiatrists and their personal sex problems, came along in late May as the caboose of the 1966-67 season but lasted only three performances. Two shows made an appearance of only one performance each: Lee Thuna's *The Natural Look,* her first Broadway effort, about a husband, a working wife and the advertising business; and Lonnie Coleman's *A Warm Body,* about a knowing archeologist in the apartment of a skeptical lady newspaperman for a night of chit-chat and other divertissements. This was a bad year also for at least one unusual idea around which Michael Stewart wrote his *Those That Play the Clowns*, starring Alfred Drake, but lasting only 4 performances In this one, a group of strolling players are interrupted in their routine procedures when they are asked to put on a very special performance —by a prince named Hamlet at a castle called Elsinore.

Among the year's specialty shows was *A Hand Is on the Gate,* a collection of prose excerpts, poems and songs by Negro authors in various keys from warm affection to outraged protest, representing various phases of American life and history. The ninety-five separate excerpts spoken and sung by a cast of eight are fully listed under this play's entry in the "Plays Produced on Broadway" section of this volume.

Among other specialties were two Yiddish musicals—*Let's Sing Yiddish* and *Sing Israel Sing*—and a revue facetiously entitled *Hello, Solly!* with occasional dialogue in English but with many Yiddish punch lines on the jokes.

Foreign specialties included the Republic of Guinea's *Les Ballets Africains;*
The Apparition Theater of Prague, a scenic illusion of free-floating, moving
objects carried by actors dressed in black and "invisible" against a black background; *Gilbert Becaud on Broadway* with a program of his own songs; and
the Stockholm Theater of Fantasy marionette version of *The Threepenny
Opera.* These marionettes were not puppets or any other kind of dolls. They
were living actors in costumes and masks who moved about the stage but
nevertheless did not speak or sing their own lines. The voices were done by
other performers.

Such were the new shows—19 American plays, 8 musicals, 10 foreign
plays in English, 5 foreign-language productions and 4 specialties—which
made up the 1966-67 Broadway season of 46 new works. Could anyone call
it a great year without blushing? Sure—Joel Grey could call it a great year,
and so could many other individuals who put their best foot forward. It was
the art itself that was out of step, not they, not the playwrights, actors, directors, designers, composers, lyricists, choreographers and others who did their
best work in 1966-67. No overall statistic, no sweeping critical evaluation can
take away from their achievement.

Revivals

There was a time when the Broadway theatergoer could complain that he
was being cheated of his heritage. The older glories evaporated from the scene
under the heat of the new productions massed in the playhouses. Well, in the
1966-67 season we enjoyed as liberal a helping of our theater heritage as anyone could readily absorb. Within what we term the "Broadway" theater, which
includes the two Centers, City and Lincoln, there were *five* repertory companies operating at one time or another, plus many one-shot revivals, bringing
the total of musicals and plays revived to 32—surely a modern Broadway
record.

This year found our local repertory group, the Repertory Company of Lincoln Center, still a long way from finding itself as an ensemble, or acquiring a
definite character within the New York theater's scheme of things. Its existence
had yet to be justified; it seemed to be waiting for a match to start a fire. Its
work was good but not exceptionally stimulating. It marked time with a production of Ben Jonson's *The Alchemist,* attractively designed and dressed by
James Hart Stearns and featuring yet another Michael O'Sullivan villain. It
pondered dark pools of marital hatred and frustration among Spanish peas-
ants in Lorca's *Yerma.* It came up with a new play—the aforementioned *The
East Wind* by Leo Lehman—its first under the Jules Irving-Herbert Blau management; unfortunately for the many American authors aching to be heard,
a foreign script, and an indifferent one.

Lincoln Center's revival of Bertolt Brecht's *Galileo* was its best work to
date. It provided a sturdy framework for a bravura performance by Anthony
Quayle of the 17th century astronomer (and for another fine display of design
and stagecraft in Lincoln Center's versatile play-machine). *Galileo* is a drama
of ideas (science vs. faith, the individual vs. the establishment, reason vs.
rote). It neglects the emotional, personal side of Galileo's confrontation with
Rome, in which he denied his own astronomical findings in order to escape
the Inquisitor's instruments of torture. The play does not much care how

Galileo felt when faced with this terror (the incident doesn't take place on the stage). It is interested in him principally as a symbol of truth. This *Galileo* was an adequate repertory item which nevertheless set no fires in this viewing.

No, Lincoln Center didn't find itself this year; in fact it lost a little bit of itself when Herbert Blau resigned as co-director on January 13, leaving Jules Irving to carry on alone. The Blau-Irving operation has functioned not so much as a true repertory company building a backlog of productions as it goes along, with its own company of actors learning a repertory of roles; rather, the Blau-Irving regime has offered what amounts to a series of one-shots with special players imported for the leads: O'Sullivan for *The Alchemist,* Gloria Foster for *Yerma,* Quayle for *Galileo.* The Lincoln Center management has renewed Irving's contract as sole director, so it must have full confidence in his future plans. It is certainly to be hoped that such plans will include the production of American scripts, both new and old. If American playwrights have not written and/or are not writing scripts worthy of production by an American company, then we had better give up the whole New York permanent repertory experiment right now and give the Vivian Beaumont Theater to the Cafe LaMama.

The Association of Producing Artists Repertory Company (APA-Phoenix) put one toe into Broadway last season with the revival of *You Can't Take It With You,* found conditions warm and hospitable, and so spent this entire season there. Both in the choice and performance of its plays, APA demonstrated the kind of taste, ensemble skill and occasional individual flair that should be at first expected and finally demanded of any repertory company seeking to make lasting friends. The APA company has stayed together and played together since its formation in 1960 by its director, Ellis Rabb.

There's no question of stars drifting in and out of this company for special performances. When Helen Hayes joined for the 1966-67 season she came to play, and play she did—as Mrs. Candour in *The School for Scandal* (the hit of this repertory), Signora Frola in *Right You Are* and Mother in *We Comrades Three* (the New York debut of an adaptation of Walt Whitman that didn't quite work on the stage). The company also offered *The Wild Duck,* their vest-pocket spectacular *War and Peace* and their American comedy hit *You Can't Take It With You.* They had the skill and assurance of a group that has been performing these works long enough so that now they could give lessons—*Right You Are* since 1960 and *The School for Scandal* since 1961. Miss Hayes has signed up for another season and, yes, Broadway is lucky, the APA-Phoenix will be back next season.

One of the three other repertory visitors was ANTA's touring troupe, the National Repertory Theater offering Molière, Noel Coward and Eugene O'Neill *(A Touch of the Poet)* for two weeks of a less-than-distinguished New York appearance. England's D'Oyly Carte made an American tour this year, stopping at Broadway with its productions of Gilbert & Sullivan operettas. The fifth of the season's repertory groups was also from England: the Bristol Old Vic with skillful revivals of *Measure for Measure, Hamlet* and *Romeo and Juliet.*

Side by side with the repertory there were 13 one-at-a-time revivals during the season. Peter Weiss's *Marat/Sade* appeared in a re-staging, a curious example of the revival of a play only one season after its first run. There was an all-star Broadway presentation of the George S. Kaufman-Edna Ferber comedy *Dinner at Eight* reflecting the new interest in Kaufman's work inspired by last season's APA production. This season we had Kaufman's *The Butter and Egg Man* off Broadway, the musical *Sherry!* (based on Kaufman and Hart's *The Man Who Came to Dinner*) as well as *Dinner at Eight*. The latter is about dinner guests preparing to gather for a party given by a hostess who will let nothing stop her from going through with it, not even the suicide of one of the prospective guests, nor her husband's imminent ruin and physical collapse. Performed by Walter Pidgeon, Ruth Ford, Arlene Francis, June Havoc, Darren McGavin and others of similar acting calibre, the Kaufman-Ferber work had a touch of old-fashioned Broadway glamor about it. It's curious to note, too, that these guests were dining at 8 p.m. and yet expected to be taken to a musical where they would arrive only a *little* late for the first-act curtain. Ah, 1932!

The success in recent seasons of *You Can't Take It With You* and *The Glass Menagerie* in Broadway revivals adds force to the argument that New York can supply an audience for the American straight-play library, but not a theater. This season the City Center moved to fill the need. In addition to its regular program of musical revivals, it offered three expertly produced plays: Clifford Odets' *The Country Girl*, with Jennifer Jones, Rip Torn and Joseph Anthony; Maxwell Anderson's *Elizabeth, the Queen*, with Anne Meacham; and Tennessee Williams' *The Rose Tattoo*, with Maureen Stapleton in the role she created in the original Broadway production. The latter was the biggest success of the three and moved to the Billy Rose Theater to continue its run following the City Center engagement.

In addition, of course, Miss Dalrymple and her City Center Light Opera Company kept reminding us of the American musical theater's glorious heritage with a season full of revivals: *Guys and Dolls, Carousel, Finian's Rainbow, The Sound of Music* and *Wonderful Town*. New York City Opera did Gian Carlo Menotti's *The Consul* again. And the New York State Theater of Lincoln Center, under Richard Rodgers' guidance, offered a handsome summer production of *Show Boat* and brought *Annie Get Your Gun*—with Ethel Merman—to Broadway in the fall after its spring debut at Lincoln Center and summer tour. This *Annie* was revived so effectively, with so much valuable new material, that it received one vote as the best musical of 1966-67 in the New York Drama Critics Circle voting (from Henry Hewes).

This was a disproportionately large revival year, to be sure, with 32 productions alongside only 19 new American plays and 8 new musicals on Broadway. But it served many purposes, some better than they have been served in recent seasons. The past paraded by in works by Shakespeare, Sheridan, Pirandello, Ibsen, Jonson, Lorca, Molière. And, for a change, in the American parade with Rodgers & Hammerstein, with Loesser and Kern there were some straight play writers, too: Kaufman, Odets and Maxwell Anderson, O'Neill and Tennessee Williams.

Off Broadway

The 1966-67 season off Broadway amounted to 69 productions of record, as compared with 66 last year and 73 two years ago. These broke down into 29 plays, 8 musicals, 8 foreign plays in English and 5 revues (a total of 50 new works as compared with 40 a season ago), plus 10 revivals, three for-eign-language productions and 6 specialty shows. By "off Broadway" we mean a production which employs a professional Equity cast, invites criticism at a designated opening and has a regular schedule of public performances.

The number that really counts off Broadway is the number of exciting shows, and in this respect 1966-67 tested very high. Three off-Broadway productions made the Best Plays list and others were close. In recent seasons, off Broadway seemed to be relying on revivals of its "standards"—Albee, Beckett, Pinter, Ionesco, Genet—or to be merely toying with sensation. 1966-67 was the season it went back to work.

Jean-Claude van Itallie's *America Hurrah* was a program of one-acters which made the Best Plays easily in this one-act year, and which was Kerr's and Nadel's first-choice play in the Critics Voting. Its author subtitled it "Three Views of the U.S.A.", but indeed it was only one view expressed three ways: the view that certain elements of American life in which some take great pride may cause others the most acute anguish; a view expressed with powerful irony and most inventive stage style. The first playlet, *Inter-view,* was a fugue of four job-seekers and four interviewers which expands out of the employment agency to include many of the painful brush-offs of city life (including city death). The second, *TV,* showed three viewers at a rating organization slowly swallowed by the TV programs they are paid to watch, like rabbits going down the throat of a boa constrictor.

The third, *Motel,* was a masque of three dolls: a motel-keeper house-proud of her establishment, and two guests who rent a room only to wreck it. The three "characters" were larger-than-life papier-mache figures worn by three actors. Their grotesque appearance with huge grinning, nodding heads was matched by grotesque behavior in which the guest dolls, a man and a woman, make love and scrawl obsenities—raw, subway-men's-room obscenities—in large, easy-to-read letters and drawings on the motel room walls before they pull these same walls down. They do this as a lark, grinning and nodding, while the motel-keeper doll continues to advertise her place in glowing terms, and lights flash and a siren shrieks warning. Thus the American motel *ideos*—the concept of mass-produced convenience—contains the seeds of its own de-struction. Creature comforts appeal not to the best within us, but to the bestial *creature,* van Itallie seemed to be saying as he lifted a corner of the veil for a glimpse of what the creature looks like. All three of these highly imaginative one-acters were to some extent contraptions, and their directors—Joseph Chaikin for *Interview* and Jacques Levy for *TV* and *Motel*—deserve extra credit for a smooth and potent production.

Clark Gesner's musical adaptation of the Charles M. Schulz comic strip "Peanuts" was a risky undertaking—"Peanuts" addicts might have lynched the perpetrator of a merely adequate rendition. But Gesner won his dare hand-somely with *You're a Good Man Charlie Brown,* a wonderful show which is easily a Best Play and received several citations in the Critics Circle voting for best musical.

You're a Good Man Charlie Brown was a series of episodes in which Charlie Brown (the born loser), Snoopy (a canine superstar), Lucy (the shrew), Schroeder (the Beethoven fancier), Linus (hugging his blanket) and Patty (blonde and bubbleheaded) cope with baseball, the Red Baron, Lucy's tantrums, kite flying, a book report on "Peter Rabbit," a glee club rehearsal

The 1966-67 Season off Broadway

PLAYS (29)

Undercover Man
Until the Monkey Comes
Command Performance
Match-Play and A Party for Divorce
A Whitman Portrait
Who's Got His Own
This Here Nice Place
AMERICA HURRAH
Three Hand Reel
Javelin
Viet Rock
The Infantry
The Ox Cart
Night of the Dunce
The Displaced Person
Kicking the Castle Down
The Deer Park
Sometime Jam Today
The Rimers of Eldritch
MacBird!
Fortune and Men's Eyes
Not a Way of Life
Chocolates
Gorilla Queen
Harold and Sondra
The Party on Greenwich Avenue
The Death of the Well-Loved Boy
To Bury a Cousin
A Time for the Gentle People

MUSICALS (8)

My Wife and I
Autumn's Here!
Man With a Load of Mischief
The Penny Friend
The Golden Screw
Shoemakers' Holiday
YOU'RE A GOOD MAN CHARLIE BROWN
Follies Burlesque '67

REVUES (5)

Below the Belt (cabaret)
Mixed Doubles (cabaret)
Skits-oh-Frantics!
An Evening with the Times Square Two
Absolutely Free

REVIVALS (10)

American Savoyards
The Mikado
Trial by Jury and H.M.S. Pinafore
Mardi Gras!
The Long Christmas Dinner, Queens of France and The Happy Journey
The Butter and Egg Man
Antigone
By Jupiter
Dynamite Tonite
To Clothe the Naked
The Coach with the Six Insides

FOREIGN PLAYS IN ENGLISH (8)

The Kitchen
Eh?
When Did You Last See My Mother?
The Wicked Cooks
HAMP
Carricknabauna
The Experiment
Drums in the Night

FOREIGN-LANGUAGE PRODUCTIONS (3)

Les Femmes Savantes
Die Brücke
Les Fourberies de Scapin

SPECIALTIES (6)

The Israeli Mime Theater
Blitzstein!
Baird Marionettes: *People Is the Thing That the World Is Fullest Of*
Davy Jones' Locker
The Harold Arlen Songbook
The Diary of a Madman

Plays listed in CAPITAL LETTERS have been designated Best Plays of 1966-67.
Plays listed in *italics* were still running on June 1, 1967.

and each other. These are matters familiar to readers of the comic strip, and in the show they varied in length just as printed episodes do. Some were fully developed scenes (like a Sunday page), others were one-panel blackout skits. All were in perfect key with our image of six-year-old Charlie Brown and his gang. Reva Rose made her face do exactly what Lucy's does on paper, with voice to match, in an uncanny performance. Bill Hinnant wore no special costume or makeup, but while he was on stage he became a dog—the very dog Snoopy who yearns to be a jungle animal but is chained emotionally to his supper dish. Joseph Hardy's direction should be credited for evoking these and the other excellent performances, and Alan Kimmel's set was simple and versatile: a white background to pick up changes of colored lights on a stage dressed with geometrical shapes, capable of being arranged to represent anything from a schoolroom to a doghouse. I don't see how *You're a Good Man Charlie Brown* could have been better; why, it was almost as good as "Peanuts."

John Wilson's *Hamp* is a third off-Broadway script in this year's list of Best Plays. *Hamp* completed the British sweep of the New York theater season; it was by far the best drama. It reached way back for its subject to the Battle of Passchendaele in 1917, in the story of a British soldier who is tried, convicted and shot for desertion. In the eye of this somewhat familiar moral storm Wilson has found the heart of the conflict between group and individual needs and responsibilities. It raised every question: should Hamp have been a soldier in the first place? Once a soldier, should he have deserted under any circumstance? Having deserted, should he receive mercy? Or should he be sacrificed to the needs of the group? *Hamp* dramatized both sides of these questions, and it also faced the physical horror of execution; the blood penalty that must be paid; the ritualism of this form of killing which helps to impersonalize it for everyone except the victim. The performances were painfully convincing, notably those of Michael Lipton as the defense attorney and Robert Salvio as poor left-footed Hamp. This lean, unremitting, rending and tearing drama was seen in New York previously in a movie version entitled *King and Country,* in the season of 1963. It has lost no force in the passage of time. Its symbols may be borrowed from World War I, but its moral dilemmas remain to trouble us this very hour.

There were many other 1966-67 achievements in the smaller playhouses. The first act of *Fortune and Men's Eyes* was high up among the season's best work, in an account of homosexuality in prison among four cellmates: a dyed-blond "queen" (played by Bill Moor with no quirks barred), his idealistic young victim, a tough gangster-type who likes to protest that he is no "pansy" and a farm boy (Terry Kiser) who becomes one of them through experience with each. John Herbert, the author, once spent six months in a Canadian prison, and his subject matter, appalling though it may have been, was expressed in such a way that it did not directly exploit sensationalism. It was a commendable effort, unfortunately vitiated in the second act in shouting and loss of clear purpose or resolution.

Another off-Broadway standout wasn't sensational *enough:* the much discussed *MacBird!* Its author, Barbara Garson, used Shakespearean parody as a magnifying glass to lampoon the political scene, with MacBird (an LBJ-like figure in the drawling person of actor Stacy Keach, a ragged eagle) instigating the murder of his chief "John Ken O'Dunc," a murder which is then avenged by John's brother "Robert Ken O'Dunc" (played by William Devane to resemble, uncannily, the junior Senator from New York). The savagery of *MacBird's* opening attack was exciting, so far outside any consideration of truth or taste that it could not possibly give offense. But the joke became tangled in its own tricks and parallelisms, both Shakespearean and Johnsonian, losing its momentum and even its spirit of total irreverence.

Also promising a good deal more than it was able to perform was Norman Mailer's *The Deer Park*. Its avowed intention (in the opening scene) was to reveal sin in high Hollywood places (or maybe, the script suggested, the setting was not really Hollywood but some sort of dream-world limbo). Most of its sinning (happily heterosexual) was pretty mild stuff compared with the off-Broadway average.

One of the year's most attractive off-Broadway productions was the musical *Man With a Load of Mischief,* an innocent, almost operetta-like concept. Set in an inn in 19th century England, this one sang a troubadour's tale of a nobleman in a secret romantic escapade with the Prince's mistress. But the lady, it turns out, prefers the nobleman's valet (played by Reid Shelton in excellent voice). John Clifton's music for *Man With a Load of Mischief,* like Ben Tarver's book, had great charm. Other musical highlights of the off-Broadway year were *Autumn's Here!* (a musicalization of the Ichabod Crane story) and *Dynamite Tonite,* a comic opera with emphasis on acting by Arnold Weinstein and William Bolcom, previously produced off Broadway by the Actors Studio in 1964, reworked in a staging at Yale Drama School, and, in this production, attracting one citation in the Critics Circle voting (from Martin Gottfried). Out of the past came a successful revival of the Richard Rodgers-Lorenz Hart musical *By Jupiter,* plus *Blitzstein!* (a program of his works) and *The Harold Arlen Songbook.* The outstanding revue attractions were both cabaret and both by Rod Warren: *Below the Belt* and *Mixed Doubles.*

Causes pleaded stridently off Broadway included the anti-war protest, most conspicuously expressed in *Viet Rock,* which made ironic comment and presented adverse examples in a persuader-device of theatrical production. Also polemic was the war-is-hell message of *The Infantry.* The little man's fight for identity against the establishment was celebrated in the British comedy *Eh?* about an employee who deliberately pushes all the wrong buttons in a dye works. One of the season's more sensational experiments was *Gorilla Queen,* a comedy which explored the subject (and some of the possibilities) of sex deviation in the story of a female ape-goddess and the men who worship her.

In a somewhat nobler spirit of experimentation, the Messrs. Edward Albee, Clinton Wilder and Richard Barr—under the banners of Theater 1967 and Albarwild Theater Arts Inc., and with the assistance of a Rockefeller grant— put on a series of five American play programs. Two were revivals: an evening of Thornton Wilder one-acters and a production of George S. Kaufman's ·*The Butter and Egg Man.* Three were new works: Frank Gagliano's *The Night of the Dunce,* Lanford Wilson's *The Rimers of Eldritch* and Grandin Conover's *The Party on Greenwich Avenue.* All were received with respect (particularly *Rimers,* about narrow-mindedness and injustice in a small town) but none achieved ranking among the season's leaders in popularity. The same was true of three major European importations: Arnold Wesker's *The Kitchen,* Günter Grass's *The Wicked Cooks* and Christopher Hampton's *When Did You Last See My Mother?*

Dorothy Raedler's perennially competent American Savoyards were present off Broadway in 1966-67, complementing Broadway's visiting D'Oyly Carte. Bil and Cora Baird's marionette theater was a standout entertainment. Off Broadway also had its Brecht (the American premiere of *Drums in the Night*), its revival success (Jean Erdman's return with her *The Coach With the Six Insides,* inspired by *Finnegans Wake*) and even its Joel Grey performance—in Guy Lombardo's Jones Beach musical *Mardi Gras!*

Such parallels might embarrass devotees of off Broadway who balk at any suggestion that it might become a "little Broadway," a scale model of the commercial theater. Nevertheless, in 1966-67 off Broadway has rivaled Broadway with the quality of its work, and, in some ways, beaten it. Off Broadway came up with two *new* authors on the Best Play list (Gesner and Wilson; van Itallie was previously produced in the program *6 from La Mama*), whereas Broadway found only one. Off Broadway came up with a musical, *You're a Good Man Charlie Brown,* to equal anything uptown, at least in imagination; it came up with a black, contemporaneous, inventive *America Hurrah;* it came up with the only "serious" play in serious contention for this year's bests. Broadway not only couldn't find a drama the equal of *Hamp;* it couldn't even assimilate *Hamp* itself, apparently, because this London script could have been acquired for production uptown just as well as downtown. So, in 1966-67, off Broadway has done what Broadway could or would not do, and has done it extremely well—and surely that is one of off-Broadway's highest aims, achieved.

Side-by-side with the elegant formalities of the Broadway theater; mixed in with the Equity casts and regular performance schedules off-Broadway; tucked away out of sight of most critics in converted churches, libraries, cafes—and sometimes even in theaters—is a form of tributary stage activity which for want of a better name has come to be known as "off off Broadway." The name is unsatisfactory, if only for the reason that it is a put-down; the use of the word "off" twice tends to assign it a level below other theater activity. The truth is, its fermentation rate is the highest in town, and sometimes it raises its head above Broadway itself: for example, two-thirds of *America Hurrah* surfaced from off off Broadway. And as a Best Play of 1966-67, *America Hurrah* can be said to have o'ercrowed no fewer than 67 Broadway and 66 off-Broadway productions.

Offstage

Behind the scenes, 1966-67 was a year in which the New York theater watched newspaper after newspaper go under; a year in which small steps were taken toward the solution of some of the theater's more pressing institutional problems; a year in which Richard Maney, theater press agent, historian, raconteur and all-purpose eminence—who inspired the character Owen O'Malley in the hit comedy *Twentieth Century* by Ben Hecht and Charles MacArthur—retired with the following characteristic comment to his many Broadway friends and associates:

> Of course I'm going to miss the theater.
> But at 75 plus, I thought it the better part of valor to go AWOL while I still had a few of my marbles. If I've learned anything in the theater

it is that everyone stays on too long: playwrights, musical saw players, acrobats and David Merrick.

I'm one of the theater's fortunates. Rarely have I been idle for more than a week or two in the last 40 years. Few stars can make such a boast.

I raise my glass to you, Sirs!

RICHARD MANEY

While Maney was calling it quits, some of his best friends on the papers were finding themselves quite unwillingly disfranchised. As the season of 1965-66 ended, an ominous silence had fallen upon many New York presses. The *Herald Tribune, Journal-American* and *World-Telegram & Sun* had ceased publication April 24, 1966 pending the working-out of union agreements re their proposed merger. Historically, as their names indicate, they were the accumulation of seven newspapers. To the theater, as of the end of the 1965-66 season, they represented three drama critics—Walter Kerr, John McClain and Norman Nadel—and three outlets for theater news, advertising and reporting.

The original plan to come back with three papers proved unworkable. On August 15, 1966, the *Herald Tribune* folded, not with a bang—not in the full agony of a final edition with all editorial flags flying—but silently, in suspended publication, with a whimper about the generic problems that face *all* newspapers: union intractability, rising costs, competition from other media. The *Trib's* value to the New York theater was inestimable and, as far as can be seen now, irreplaceable. It was the Other Voice. In past decades it offered Broadway producers a versatile instrument (as opposed to the *Times's* inflexible format) for bringing their shows to the attention of the public. Under the direction of the late Arthur H. Folwell and those who succeeded him, its New York theater coverage spoke through the typewriters of such as Percy Hammond, Richard Watts Jr., Howard Barnes, Lucius Beebe, Bert McCord, William K. Zinsser, Walter Kerr, Stuart West Little, Judith Crist and myself. The *Trib* was no easy publicity mark, but it was steadily *interested* in the theater, and, with its passing, Broadway lost a loyal friend.

No sooner had the *Trib* folded, when a reshuffling took place at the *Times.* Stanley Kauffmann departed and Walter Kerr, Supercritic, took over drama criticism's superjob on a *Times* which now did not even have the *Trib's* competing voice to reckon with. The shopping-service aspects of this position; its almost absolute life-and-death power over individual productions, could be only an enormous embarrassment to a critic determined to fulfill his highest artistic function. An attempt to mitigate this monstrous economic side-effect of *Times* criticism is planned for next season. The job is to be split in two. Instead of writing both daily and Sunday, Walter Kerr will write Sunday criticisms only, and Clive Barnes—the *Times's* present dance critic—will do the daily reviews. In the meantime, the policy instituted by Stanley Kauffmann of attending shows at their last preview performance, to give him more time to consider his review, was abandoned. As one *Times* insider expressed it, "We're through with all of *that."*

The newly-merged afternoon-and-Sunday paper finally began publishing in the fall, with Norman Nadel as its drama critic. The late John McClain, who had been highly and warmly regarded in drama criticism (at the *Journal-*

American) as a spokesman for the man-about-town, ceased writing play reviews. The new *World Journal Tribune* lasted almost as long as the drama season, then folded on May 5, 1967. With its demise the last traces of seven daily New York newspapers—the *World, Telegram, Sun, Journal, American, Herald* and *Tribune*—simply vanished. Broadway, which had begun the year with six daily newspaper critics (Kauffmann, Kerr, Nadel, McClain, John Chapman of the *Daily News* and Richard Watts Jr. of the *Post*) ended it with three (Kerr, Chapman and Watts).

The advantage to the theater of having as many critics as possible (if you are going to have any at all) seems obvious. The clamor is louder when you have a hit, and wide divergence of opinion sometimes acts as a net when you don't. The influence of the TV critics has been growing steadily, and it is possible that in coming seasons they will perform some of the function of differing opinion once performed by their newspaper colleagues. An infallible sign of the TV commentators' growing stature was the banning of one of them by David Merrick from his opening-night press list. The target of Merrick's opprobrium was the exceedingly perspicacious and entertaining Edward Newman of WNBC-TV. Otherwise, for the most part, Merrick took it easy on the critics this season—mellowed, no doubt, by the success of his shows including Carol Channing's *Hello, Dolly!* tour which lasted 1,272 performances from November 18, 1963 through June 11, 1967, grossing a total of $17,015,018 including $310,000 for one 10-performance week in Oklahoma City.

Actors' Equity doesn't negotiate a new contract with Broadway's League of New York Theaters until 1968, but there was some agitation this season over the employment of foreign actors in New York shows. Forty-eight actors picketed Lincoln Center in February, protesting the casting of Margaret Leighton in a revival of *The Little Foxes* and Anthony Quayle as *Galileo*. Equity members held a meeting on this foreign-actor issue and voted 491 to 2 to demand that permission to hire a foreign (except Canadian) actor on Broadway or at Lincoln Center be required from a majority of Equity's own 72-member council. Meanwhile, British actors offered the information that in the past seven years British Equity's record of employment of American actors in England has been "Yes" 524 times and "No" only 18 times.

Also in the matter of organizations, the Metropolitan Opera Company opened triumphantly in its new theater in the Lincoln Center complex. The acoustics were fine and the theater handsome and comfortable, so the move was a success—except for a few gremlins like unexpectedly large deficits and a couple of dressing rooms walled up by mistake during construction and discovered by accident. The installation is so large and complex that a Pentagon-like security system of passes controls the coming and goings of Metropolitan Opera personnel, and few have Q clearance for the entire building. Meanwhile, highly-publicized efforts to save the old Met failed—it was scavenged by souvenir hunters and then reduced to a heap of rubble.

The Ziegfeld Theater, too, disappeared from its familiar chunk in the Sixth Avenue skyline, razed because it was economically inefficient to operate. And at season's end it was disclosed that interests including the Rockefellers and Time Inc. had bought The Playhouse; ominously, tenants of offices in the theater's building were notified that the space would no longer be available.

On a more positive note, the New York Shakespeare Festival's new year-round headquarters on Lafayette Street were progressing toward completion; their new, 300-seat Anspacher Theater was expected to be ready for the autumn opening of a series of seven new American playscripts. The headquarters will include a second 300-seat theater and other facilities.

The 1966-67 season saw the publication, under the auspices of the Twentieth Century Fund, of another major study on the performing arts in America, prepared by William J. Baumol and William G. Bowen, both of Princeton, and entitled *Performing Arts—The Economic Dilemma*. Its particular hang-up was what it called the "income gap" between rising costs and relatively static earnings in live performances (there's no way, the report reasoned, significantly to reduce the cost-per-performance of a live string quartet by automation, which is the answer to rising costs in other areas of activity). The total performing-arts income gap has now reached $25,000,000 (the report estimates) and is growing—except on Broadway which, the study admitted, is holding its own economically. The study also offered a per-seat estimate of the Broadway situation. Musicals (average cost per performance, $6,509) cost $4.90 a seat to put on; straight plays (averaging $3,077) cost $2.83. The cost of the theater tickets, the report added, is only 53 per cent of the cost of a Broadway evening.

In any fall-off of production it is mostly flops that are missing. When a thaw sets in, *this* iceberg melts much faster on the bottom than it does on the top. To illustrate, four decades ago the prolific season of 1926-27 brought forth 188 new plays and 49 new musicals as compared with 66 and 16 (off Broadway included) in 1966-67. Here were the Best Plays of that 1926-27 season, as chosen by Burns Mantle: *Broadway, Saturday's Children, Chicago, The Constant Wife* (foreign), *The Play's the Thing* (foreign), *The Road to Rome, The Silver Cord, The Cradle Song* (foreign), *Daisy Mayme* and *In Abraham's Bosom*.

Well, was the Best Plays list of that 237-show season three times as interesting as the one in this volume's 82-show season? Certainly not. Forty years ago they had Robert E. Sherwood, Sidney Howard, Maxwell Anderson, George Kelly; Somerset Maugham and Ferenc Molnar. Today we have Edward Albee, Jerry Bock and Sheldon Harnick, *Robert* Anderson; Harold Pinter and Peter Shaffer. They had George Abbott on that 1926-27 Best Play list, true, but we may have him on ours *next* year. The top of our iceberg is solid and bright—so what if the bottom is much smaller?

In sum, 1966-67 may have been a defensive year in the New York theater—but the position was well defended. The theater functioned; it *was;* it introduced new work worthy of its past traditions, and it held the door wide open for a future that seems, now more than ever, illimitable.

John Wood, Noel Craig and Brian Murray in *Rosencrantz and Guildenstern Are Dead* by Tom Stoppard.

1967-68

THE NEW YORK theater season of 1967-68 was allergically sensitive to the temper—or, rather *dis*temper—of the times but held few mirrors up to contemporary events. This year of shocking assassinations, when the city, the state, the nation and the world were in an acute phase of sociological and political distress, dramatists were peering almost myopically at the intimate stresses of the human psyche. By far the most popular single subject was sexuality—dramatized or lampooned in all four or five sexes. Intrafamily stresses also came in for a large share of attention. With a few exceptions, shows which edged too close to the factual issues of the day wilted like the wings of Icarus in the sun's rays. The distemper of this era of disillusionment, this age of anxiety, was clearly evident in the blackness of the comedies, the absence of anything like *joy* from the theater's mood; or, to put it the other way, in the fact that "square" theater was out and even the most sorrowful subjects must be twisted into odd, wry shapes before presentation to an audience.

This was not an escapist season by any means. The Broadway musical stage, that traditional refuge of the tired business man, was becalmed and rolling in mediocrity, even in a season in which it might have attracted more audiences than usual, because *everybody* was tired. But if the season was not escapist, neither did it aim for semi-documentation of these times. In its close attention in rich playscripts to father-son relationships; to husband-wife stresses both comic and pathetic; to homosexuality in several phrases, the New York theater both on and off Broadway was going to the root rather than the branch of our discontent for its material.

American playwriting brightened in 1967-68, and its light shone out and around the towering scripts imported from England. The New York Drama Critics Circle and the Pulitzer Prize committee withheld awards for American playwriting; well, that's their hang-up. It's true that the season's very best play, in my opinion, was a British script—*A Day in the Death of Joe Egg* by Peter Nichols—and British work further stimulated the New York season in Tom Stoppard's *Rosencrantz and Guildenstern Are Dead,* Charles Dyer's *Staircase* and John Bowen's *After The Rain.* Right up among these on the 1967-68 Best Plays list, however, were three substantial scripts by veteran American playwrights: *The Price* by Arthur Miller, *I Never Sang for My Father* by Robert Anderson and *Plaza Suite* by Neil Simon. It's true that plays by Edward Albee, Frank D. Gilroy and Tennessee Williams fell short of their authors' best work, but on the British side so did plays by Harold Pinter and Bill Naughton. The theater is measured by its successes, not its average, and the dynamically creative state of American playwriting, its sheer vitality, was conspicuous in the three off-Broadway scripts on the Best Plays list—*Scuba Duba* by Bruce Jay Friedman, *Your Own Thing* (winner of the Critics Prize for Best Musical) by Donald Driver, Danny Apolinar and Hal Hester and *The Boys in the Band* by Mart Crowley—all professional playwriting debuts.

The 1967-68 Season on Broadway

PLAYS (25)

Dr. Cook's Garden
Johnny No-Trump
Daphne in Cottage D
What Did We Do Wrong?
More Stately Mansions
The Trial of Lee Harvey Oswald
The Ninety-Day Mistress
Something Different
Everything in the Garden
Spofford
How To Be a Jewish Mother
Before You Go
The Prime of Miss Jean Brodie
I NEVER SANG FOR MY FATHER
Avanti!
THE PRICE
PLAZA SUITE
Carry Me Back to Morningside Heights
The Guide
Weekend
The Seven Descents of Myrtle
Mike Downstairs
The Exercise
Happiness Is Just a Little Thing Called a Rolls Royce
The Only Game in Town

MUSICALS (10)

Henry, Sweet Henry
Now Now, Dow Jones
The Happy Time
Darling of the Day
Golden Rainbow
Here's Where I Belong
The Education of H*Y*M*A*N K*A*P*L*A*N
George M!
I'm Solomon
Hair

SPECIALITIES (6)

Judy Garland at Home at the Palace
Eddie Fisher-Buddy Hackett at the Palace
Marlene Dietrich
By George
Brief Lives
Portrait of a Queen

REVUE (1)

Leonard Sillman's New Faces of 1968

REVIVALS (16)

South Pacific
Life With Father
The Tenth Man
The Little Foxes
Lincoln Center Rep:
Saint Joan
Tiger at the Gates
Cyrano de Bergerac
APA-Phoenix:
The Show-Off
The Cherry Orchard
Brigadoon
City Center:
The Pirates of Penzance
H.M.S. Pinafore
The Mikado
The Yeomen of the Guard
Patience
The King and I

FOREIGN PLAYS IN ENGLISH (17)

Sing Israel Sing (reopening)
The Unknown Soldier and His Wife
Keep It in the Family
Song of the Grasshopper
The Birthday Party
A Minor Adjustment
AFTER THE RAIN
ROSENCRANTZ AND GUILDENSTERN ARE DEAD
There's a Girl in My Soup
Halfway up the Tree
The Promise
APA-Phoenix:
Pantagleize
Exit the King
STAIRCASE
A DAY IN THE DEATH OF JOE EGG
Loot
Soldiers

FOREIGN-LANGUAGE PRODUCTIONS (9)

Jewish Theater of Poland:
Mirele Efros
Mother Courage
The Grand Music Hall of Israel
Les Ballets Africains
Vienna Burghteater:
Professor Bernhardi
Das Konzert
Maria Stuart
Einen Jux Will Er Sich Machen
The Venetian Twins

HOLDOVER SHOWS WHICH BECAME HITS DURING 1967-68

BLACK COMEDY
CABARET
Don't Drink the Water
THE HOMECOMING
I Do! I Do!

Plays listed in CAPITAL LETTERS have been designated Best Plays of 1967-68.
Plays listed in **bold face type** were classified as hits in *Variety's* annual list of hits and flops published on June 5, 1968.
Plays listed in *italics* were still running on June 1, 1968.

Even in two shows that ranked so near to the top ten as makes almost no difference—*The Prime of Miss Jean Brodie* by Jay Allen and *Hair* by Gerome Ragni, James Rado and Galt MacDermot—American playwriting (in two more professional debuts) shone. Let's try it the other way around, to test it: 1967-68 was a dim year for our dramatists, who produced only *The Price, I Never Sang for My Father, Plaza Suite, Scuba Duba, Your Own Thing, The Boys in the Band, The Prime of Miss Jean Brodie* and *Hair*. Nonsense.

Statistically this season showed manifold improvements over last. There were 84 programs produced on Broadway in 1967-68 (see the one-page summary accompanying this article), as compared with 78 last season, 76 the year before and 81 the year before that. Last season's total was overloaded with revivals; this season the volume of new American work climbed back from its alarming 1966-67 low (19 plays and 8 musicals) to the level of previous seasons—25 new plays and 10 new musicals (compared to 25 and 11 in 1965-66 and 25 and 10 in 1964-65). The total of new foreign plays in English climbed from 10 last year to 17 this year. There were two more specialty shows and two more foreign-language productions. Only the number of revivals declined, from a massive 32 last season to 16 in 1967-68.

Financially, the 1967-68 results were cheering. For the fourth straight year (according to *Variety* estimate) Broadway set a new all-time record total gross well over the $50 million mark at $58,941,849. In addition, the gross from road companies brought the grand total from first-run legitimate theater at more than $104 million, topping the $100 million mark for the first time. (It isn't possible to estimate at close range with any degree of accuracy how much of this is net profit, except to assert that costs and losses did not amount to this much; certainly the year as a whole *was* profitable in at least seven figures.) The phenomenally high Broadway gross was earned by a large number of successful straight plays in combination with the holdover musical blockbusters, but without the usual infusion of new popular musical entertainment. There were no striking new Broadway musicals until *Hair* turned up near season's end.

The number of playing weeks (if 10 shows play 10 weeks, that's 100 playing weeks) in the 1967-68 season was 1,257—fourth highest in Broadway history behind 1,325 in 1947-48, 1,295 in 1965-66 and 1,269 in 1966-67. Notice that the playing-week total in the past three seasons has been exceptionally high (even if attenuating slightly). This indicates not that there are more shows but that the ones we have are running longer, which helps to account for the record grosses when coupled with high ticket prices, particularly on weekends, when the modern theater does most of its business. In 1967-68 the Broadway ticket topped out at $12; next year a $15 top has already been announced for a forthcoming musical.

Financially, when 1967-68 was good it was very, very good, but when it was bad it could be extremely expensive. Musical flops put a multi-million-dollar strain on the Broadway bankroll. David Merrick's *Mata Hari* folded out of town in December to the tune of $500,000 (according to *Variety* estimate), and this was only the beginning. *I'm Solomon* died for $700,000 and *Darling of the Day* fared almost as badly (this would make these two the costliest musical flops ever). *Here's Where I Belong,* which closed after its opening night performance, set a new record for a one-performance Broadway loss: $550,000. *The Education of Hyman Kaplan* lost about $550,000 and *Henry, Sweet Henry* piled up an estimated deficit of $400,000. The total losses on Broadway musical flops measured well over $3,000,000 by May 31.

For David Merrick, 1967-68 was a roller coaster ride. His *Mata Hari* folded out of town, and two other Merrick musicals—*How Now, Dow Jones* and *The Happy Time*—limped through the season. Despite these and other annoyances, Merrick finished the season with his richly-deserved reputation as an outstanding showman-impresario not only intact but enhanced. To his list of achievements, Merrick now adds the production of *R & G*, which won both the Critics and Tony awards for the best play of the season. He brought the new Tennessee Williams play to Broadway (with a big publicity boost in the much-publicized quarrel between himself and the author over the title, which was changed from *Kingdom of Earth* to *The Seven Descents of Myrtle*); and the production of a new Tennessee Williams play is the proper business of the art to which Williams has contributed so much. Merrick deserves as much praise for setting it up on Broadway as though it had been a prizewinner. And while he was at it, Merrick also produced the season's biggest hit—and he did it almost without moving from his office chair, in somewhat the same way that Zeus produced Athene full-grown from his own skull. Merrick re-cast his long-run musical *Hello, Dolly!* with Pearl Bailey as Dolly and Cab Calloway as Horace Vandergelder, backed up by an all-Negro cast, and the result was the hottest $9.90 ticket in town for a 5-year-old musical that has already grossed $45,000,000 in America and about $100,000,000 worldwide. That's showmanship, daddyo. So was the incident in Washington, D.C. on Nov. 4, at one of the tryout performances of Pearl Bailey's *Dolly*, when at the end of the show an enthusiastic couple in the audience was invited to join the cast onstage for a final chorus of the title number—the couple being President of the United States and Mrs. Lyndon Baines Johnson. So was the billing which Merrick arranged for himself in the Playbill for *How Now, Dow Jones*. The note read simply, "DAVID MERRICK (Producer) Mr. Merrick is known as the distinguished producer of *Breakfast at Tiffany's*." This year he can bill himself as the producer of *Mata Hari*, too. He can remind us of his flops and leave it to others to keep the record of his many distinguished credits.

Another of the season's characteristics was the repeated success of script material from other days. George Kelly's comedy *The Show-Off* (1924) was a Broadway hit in APA-Phoenix Repertory, with Helen Hayes a standout in the mother role. Michel de Ghelderode's *Pantagleize* (1927) was also well received in production by the same troupe. Lillian Hellman's *The Little Foxes* was revived successfully. Shakespeare received a kind of back-handed homage in *R & G*, in the off-Broadway musical *Your Own Thing* (whose book is based on *Twelfth Night*) and a camp *Hamlet* produced by Joseph Papp. The season's most glamorous performance was one that we have enjoyed before in other media: Marlene Dietrich doing her own thing in a one-woman show.

The sharpest disappointment of the 1967-68 season was its inability to come up with a musical blockbuster to match the holdovers from other years: *Hello, Dolly!* (1963-64), *Fiddler on the Roof* (1964-65), *Man of La Mancha* and *Mame* (1965-66) and *Cabaret* (1966-67). The musical *Hair* is a well-deserved hit, of course, but it was borrowed from previous off-Broadway production and came uptown much too late (April 29) to rescue the Broadway season.

While not escapist in temper, the 1967-68 theater season offered a dram of consolation in these perplexing times. The constant theatergoer, after his twentieth or thirtieth play about Man as Fortune's Fool, as the last to know or to understand the *force majeur* overwhelming him, could breath a sigh of partial relief: "Well, I'm not paranoid after all, something really *is* out to get me." If the season had any keynote play, it was *R & G*, with two fops being nudged towards death without ever getting the word about what is killing them or why, scarcely even aware that the passionate events of *Hamlet* are taking place around them. The two father plays—*The Price* and *I Never Sang*—sympathized with sons who had made gestures of affection, even major sacrifices, only to discover (the plays concluded) that paternal selfishness and hostility are inevitable. In three plays—*Scuba Duba, Joe Egg* and *Staircase*—the individuals being tortured dramatically or comically were victims of emotional forces beyond their control and sometimes even their perception: despair over a handicapped child (*Joe Egg*), sexual alienation (*Scuba Duba*) and homosexual antagonism (*Staircase*). Neil Simon sent up the whole matter of Man as Victim in a burst of farcical fireworks in the last of three *Plaza Suite* one-acters, in which the father of a bride is thrown into a frenzy when his daughter, on her wedding day, locks herself in the bathroom for no comprehendable reason. On and off Broadway the Fool was the plaything of his Fortune: the boys at the mercy of their neuroses in *The Boys in the Band*, the king kicking and screaming against death in Ionesco's *Exit the King*, the Indian so helpless as to make himself the inevitable target of toughs in Horovitz's *The Indian Wants the Bronx*, Pantagleize ignorant of his own revolution in de Ghelderode's *Pantagleize*—finally, the whole species suffering from the flaws of its violent and authoritarian nature in some all-too-near future century in *After The Rain*.

The theater season displayed two other characteristics which I would like to note before going into a play-by-play report. First and most obviously, in an effort to move closer to their audiences, to penetrate deeper into their minds and hearts, many playwrights have pushed their characters all the way to the apron of the stage to address the audience directly. In these chatty conveyances of confidence (as in *Spofford*), these elucidations of the events of the play (as in *I Never Sang*), these confessions and elaborations of agony (as in *Joe Egg*), it isn't the playwrights themselves who speak directly to the audience, but their characters *in character*. This isn't a case of Shakespeare setting the stage of his "wooden O" with language, it's more like a Greek chorus, the citizens telling you where it's at right now, in Thebes. Rosencrantz and Guildenstern did it from time to time (in *R & G*, not in *Hamlet*). *After The Rain* began with the no-nonsense entrance of a lecturer who stepped to a podium, told the audience to pay attention and delivered a history lesson in which was embedded the gradual discovery that the lecturer is, in reality, the villain and the audience itself the true victim of the play.

So this was a season in which, for one thing, we have had the Greek chorus as both hero and villain. Secondly—and so much less obviously that I offer it as an impression, a cloud no bigger than a playwright's fist which nevertheless shows no sign of going away—the plays of 1967-68, like the people of 1967-68, were preoccupied with causes and relatively indifferent to consequences. In the theater, this has the effect of eliminating most of the conventional third act; the part that goes into what happens as a *result* of all the stresses that have built up from the first act and burst at the end of the second. Just after the point of decision, of climax, is the point at which, it seems to me, we sometimes drop the whole subject, as though effects were either totally predictable or relatively much less important than causes. *I Never Sang for My Father,* for example (the strongest that comes to mind), is a play in which father and son build up to a big confrontation, whose consequences are described in less than a page of narration as the play ends. If this sample is indeed part of an esthetic development, it is further evidence of the theater's allergic sensitivity to its environment. This is an era in which we seek not so much to punish or reward as to understand; in which we are not often required to accept the full responsibility for our actions; in which we sometimes judge even violence not by its effect but by its causes. Small wonder, in these circumstances, that "Act III: The next morning" seems to be disappearing from the playwriting esthetic.

Broadway

Some shows are born hits in a blaze of box office popularity. Others are made by movie sales and other special factors. This year's success of the one-woman show whose title says it all—*Marlene Dietrich*—was no fluke of accounting. Miss Dietrich's Broadway debut was one of the year's memorable events, projecting songs and glamor in a style that won her both instant city-wide popularity and a special Tony Award to crown her achievement.

The resounding popular success of the new-play season was Neil Simon's *Plaza Suite,* a triptych of one-acters looking into the lives of three couples occupying in turn a suite at the Plaza Hotel in New York, couples perfectly played by George C. Scott in three different facets of masculine dominance and Maureen Stapleton in three different moods of feminine perseverance. The first couple is middle-aged, married but losing contact. The magic is gone, and they are in trouble—a tired kind of emotional trouble in which each laugh ends in a wrench of despair. The second couple acts out a satire on sex play, as a visiting Hollywood star invites his childhood sweetheart to come in from New Jersey for an afternoon of getting reacquainted. The third couple has a daughter who is getting married today, in about a minute and a half, and she has locked herself in the bathroom and refuses to come out. This last is a farce in which Scott soars to parental fury and plunges into dark wells of humiliation in a hilarious sequence. The program was directed by Mike Nichols, and what more is to be said of Nichols now, after his steady succession of hits on stage and screen? In this season of 1967-68 he has reached a height of celebrity and adulation at which he might be expected to cross a kind of timberline and lose intimate contact with contemporary reality. There's no sign of any such happening in Nichols' work. His insight is unfailing, his touch unerring in any combination of comedy and drama (in the direction of this season's hit revival of Lillian Hellman's *The Little Foxes* as well as in *Plaza Suite*). What more, indeed, is there to be said about Neil

Simon? His plays speak louder than any critical praise. He is the Molière of the high-rise era; he knows his contemporaries intimately and he treats them affectionately but never too gently, always living up to our greatest expectations of laughter.

Another hit comedy was British and, like many others this season, amused in its own oblique fashion about the generation gap. Terence Frisby's *There's a Girl in My Soup* made it on Broadway after a long and successful London run. It was comedy frappé, about a middle-aged bachelor gourmet (Gig Young) who prides himself on his prowess with women but meets more than his match in a teen-aged mod (Barbara Ferris) who moves in to keep house with him. She is reconciled, finally, with the boy friend her own age—not a moment too soon for her deflated middle-aged lover.

For once, however, it was the darker shades of theater that dominated the season. The presence on the hit list of Arthur Miller's *The Price* and Tom Stoppard's *Rosencrantz and Guildenstern Are Dead,* as well as Jay Allen's *The Prime of Miss Jean Brodie,* leads inevitably to the conclusion that so-called "serious" theater is not, after all, lying in conspicuous decay like an unburied corpse; in fact, it may not even be dead. True, these are neither classically-formed tragedies nor plays which attack their subjects with the uncompromising gravity of a script like last season's *Hamp.* In them, the comic spirit often makes a jack-in-the-box appearance. Often they borrow, if not the uniform of comedy, at least some of its insignia. But they are plays which can be called serious—on balance.

Miller's *The Price* is the first playscript since the two (*After the Fall* and *Incident at Vichy*) written for the Elia Kazan-Robert Whitehead operation of Lincoln Center Repertory downtown. The celebrated and controversial *After the Fall* contained a scene in which the hero, Quentin, determines to continue his education, even though this self-preoccupation implies a lack of feeling for his father and brother, who need his help at home, in the business, in hard times.

This theme has been expanded to become the whole matter in *The Price,* which dramatizes the results of such a situation, 20 years later. The scene in the new play is the attic of a New York house cluttered with all the furniture from its glory days (a middle-class materialistic fantasy of harp, chiffonier and rowing oar designed by Boris Aronson). Here the brother (Pat Hingle) who stayed to help, now a policeman whose only fortune is his personal honor, has a head-on collision and recrimination with the brother (Arthur Kennedy) who ran out on the whole family problem, continued his training and became a rich and successful doctor. They meet in the attic to sell the jointly-owned furniture to an 80-year-old dealer (a role created by David Burns on the road, then, after Burns' illness, taken over and consummately realized by Harold Gary). The furniture dealer is a grand old comedy character. He is as Tevye might be after coming to America and making money. But the dealer and the furniture are only pawns in the game of guilt played by the brothers as they reproach each other—the one for abandoning their father, the other for a self-pitying pose of moral superiority. In the middle is the policeman's wife (Kate Reid) who never misses a chance to remind her husband how poor they are and what advantages they might have had, were it not for his instinct for self-sacrifice. The interplay is effective, and it is good Miller, which is to say strong, clean-lined, direct and often going deep into emotional complexity. The play concludes that each of us does his own thing for selfish reasons and winds up with whatever life he has bought and paid for (one brother in proud penury, the other in neurotic affluence). Arthur Miller's generation is one which began with the sweet illusion that spirituality was all, materialism nothing. In *Death of a Salesman* Miller let us hear an ominous rumble of truth for our time: that material tensions in this materialistic age can serve as an instrument of tragedy. Miller's *The Price* reverberates with some of the same thunder: in these times no emotion or moral position is entirely free of material influences.

Tom Stoppard's *R & G* was more flippant in manner but equally sharp in its sting. This script won the New York Drama Critics Circle Award and the Tony Award for best play in the American debut of its young British author. The script treats the matter of Hamlet's long-named schoolmates like a photographic blow-up; it takes the scant material from the Shakespeare script and magnifies it a hundred times until Rosencrantz and Guildenstern are seen in all their grainy innocence, with the main part of *Hamlet* only dimly visible around the fringes. While the two are in the foreground wondering who's who and what's what and why they're here at Elsinore, the terrifying events of *Hamlet* take place in the corner of their eyes, uncomprehended, in the deeper shadows of Desmond Heeley's eerily suggestive setting. Thus the theme of Stoppard's play was prototypical of our era: Rosencrantz and Guildenstern in their doublet and hose are stand-ins for Everyman interrupted in a happy-go-lucky course by overwhelming events. Rosencrantz and Guildenstern (who in their ignorance betray Hamlet to Claudius as unfeelingly as Hamlet in his turn betrays them to death) are never going to get the word, but they are surely going to get the axe—that's the heart of the matter. Brian Murray and John Wood in the title roles, and Paul Hecht as the Player King who keeps issuing ironic warnings to the doomed pair, served the material so well that they all received Tony nominations, in an unprecedented citation of three performers in the same play. Noel Craig, too, made his shadowy Hamlet a figure of feral menace, and Derek Goldby's direction played a major part in the success of Tom Stoppard's brilliant Broadway debut.

A choice of the very best play produced professionally in New York during the 1967-68 season would narrow down to a decision between two imported British hits: *R & G* and *A Day in the Death of Joe Egg*, the playwriting debut of its author, Peter Nichols. The critics and the Tony voters gave their deep and flourishing bow to *R & G*. My own choice by a narrow margin of preference is *Joe Egg*, which was billed by its own author in the program as a "comedy" but is much the darker of these two gray playscripts. *Joe Egg* contains many more laughs and is much more harrowing with its examination of a husband and wife in their 30s coping with a child so handicapped that it cannot perform the simplest function for itself and is little better than a vegetable. Like *R & G*, *Joe Egg* is a play about human beings at the mercy of inexorable fate; but in the latter case the fate is grindingly realistic instead of poetic, so that the sufferers in the grinder react realistically: as their nerve is stretched to the breaking point, they start giving off jokes. The couple in *Joe Egg* is beyond tears, beyond even the metaphor of Rosencrantz and Guildenstern. Their world is so bleak that only jokes will help—and almost all the jokes, the horrid ones as well as the funny ones, have been used up by the time the play begins. Albert Finney played the husband clowning at the end of his rope, and Zena Walker the wife who is barely managing to cling to a straw of hope, in two fine performances. From time to time in the play, husband or wife would come downstage to tell the audience how it really was. The confidences in *Joe Egg* were no less harrowing than the jokes, in a shattering experience of theater.

The Prime of Miss Jean Brodie was another on-balance-serious hit, but here the comic spirit prevailed in scene after scene. This is an American script by Jay Allen, based on Muriel Spark's novel about a Scottish schoolteacher in the 1930s. It had its premiere in London in a widely praised production starring Vanessa Redgrave; then it moved homeward across the Atlantic to Broadway, where Zoe Caldwell played Jean Brodie and won the Tony award for the year's best female performance in a straight play. Miss Brodie is a "character" built out of will, passion and humor, a dedicated Edinburgh girls' school teacher in the "prime" of early middle age. She is a romantic who considers herself and her pupils the *"creme de la creme"* of human society. Miss Brodie encourages them to believe that they are a chosen few, born and destined to appreciate fine poetry, music, art and conversation and at the same time to be excused from ordinary educational discipline and even conventional morality. The male members of the teaching staff make love to Miss Brodie (who returns the favor when she has a mind to), while the female principal of the school is out to "assassinate" her from her beloved teaching job because she is jealous of Miss Brodie's influence on her class. Miss Brodie finally makes a fatal misjudgment: she believes that fascism as manifested in the Spanish Civil War is a romantic, even chivalric movement. And so she is indeed "assassinated" by a favorite pupil who feels that Miss Brodie underestimates her worth and so, impulsively, she bears the tale of Miss Brodie's fascist sympathies to her enemy the principal. Miss Brodie falls from the heaven of her teaching position as doubtless she deserves (in the London version of the play she is a suicide; in the Broadway version she is merely cast adrift). But in the meantime her defiance of the forces of gravity in the excitement of her teaching, the pride and humor of her personality, were a delight of the Broadway season, totally realized in Zoe Caldwell's memorable performance.

Three of our most distinguished American playwrights found something less than instant popular support of their 1967-68 work on Broadway, but made the hit list by virtue of the sale of movie rights to their scripts (which must prove something: either that screen audiences are still less demanding than stage audiences, or they are more celebrity-conscious about authors). In two of these three cases the scripts also represented the common difficulty of drawing definitive boundaries of comedy or drama (none was billed as comedy, none was without humor or poignancy). Frank D. Gilroy's *The Only Game in Town* was one of the season's peak moments of heterosexuality. Gilroy's tale of a couple of lonely young show business people (Tammy Grimes and Barry Nelson) finding each other in Las Vegas and engaging in an affair which, in spite of their flippancy, solidifies slowly into deep-felt love and inevitable marriage ("The only game in town") was written and presented with comic insight, with sincerity and expertise—a likable play but one which met difficulty in today's rough Broadway waters. *The Only Game in Town* probably has a future in the American theater repertory. Somehow, though, May 1968 on Broadway was the wrong time and the wrong place for its first appearance. The comedy-drama style to which we've become accustomed was better exemplified (though not as well realized) in Edward Albee's *Everything in the Garden,* an adaptation of a Giles Cooper play about suburbanites who find that they can have all the cars, swimming pools, imported vodka, greenhouses and other status symbols—everything in the garden, in fact—if only their wives will bring in the $$$ by working part time as high-priced prostitutes in the big city. That's the kind of black-comedy twist we expect when an earnest subject (in Albee's case, materialism) or emotion is raised in the modern theater: not Romeo and Juliet but Punch and Judy. Contemporary as it was in style, the Albee play finally lost control of its joke (as the suburbanites casually murder one of their number who begins to embarrass them) and became opaquely instead of glossily black in mood.

Of clearly serious intent was the third of the screen-rights hits, *The Seven Descents of Myrtle,* in which our great playwright Tennessee Williams once again put himself to the task of a drama of desire and frustration. In it, Williams ties a fading burlesque actress (Estelle Parsons) in wedlock to a golden-haired mamma's boy (Brian Bedford) who owns a farm worked by his swarthy half-brother (Harry Guardino), the sort of fellow who takes his eyes off a sexy calendar picture only to ogle his brother's neglected bride. *The Seven Descents of Myrtle* is Williams as before—not at his best, but in regular form—yet the whole play seems to teeter on the edge of camp, or we were *expecting* it to cross over into camp like so many other modern plays which raise the subject of desire and frustration, only to avoid coming to grips with them and copping out into black comedy. Maybe *Seven Descents* doesn't reach us at this time because, although Williams is aiming exactly where he aimed before, we are no longer sitting there. Here too is a script, though, that may have a future in stock and repertory.

Another dramatic work that made the hit list was Eugene O'Neill's *More Stately Mansions,* which brought Ingrid Bergman back to the American stage and confronted her with Colleen Dewhurst in two of the season's vivid performances. The O'Neill script was judged not yet ready for production by its author at the time of his death, but it was prepared for this staging by José Quintero (his eighth O'Neill play) from notes and other indications as to how the playwright intended to proceed. *More Stately Mansions* takes up O'Neill's chronicling of early America where *A Touch of the Poet* left off. Now Sara Melody (daughter of the village tavern-keeper Con Melody) has married Simon Harford of the important big-city Harfords. But all does not work out happily ever after; Sara (Colleen Dewhurst) has won Simon's (Arthur Hill) hand but must fight for his loyalty and even his love against Simon's unyielding mother (Ingrid Bergman). The struggle between the two women is larger than life, a struggle of goddesses. As a whole, this was a murky drama which nevertheless had its moments depicting these Junos in conflict.

Broadway waited until the 11th hour of the 1967-68 season to find anything like a musical blockbuster of the kind which has been its mainstay in this decade—and even then it borrowed from its kid brother. *Hair* originated off Broadway as the first production of Joseph Papp's New York Shakespeare

Festival Public Theater, and it didn't move uptown to Broadway until late April (after a stop-off as a special attraction at the night club known as Cheetah). *Hair* was an explosion of musical theater, a rock 'n' roll 'n' rebellious entertainment with a loud, irresistible score by Galt MacDermot; a now-generation book and lyrics by Gerome Ragni and James Rado (who also played leading roles), directed with acute sensibility by Gerald Freedman off Broadway and with wild excitement by Tom O'Horgan on Broadway. It touched and delighted audiences downtown and shocked and delighted audiences uptown. On Broadway it was a bigger, louder presentation which seems surely destined to become the only solid musical hit of the season.

There must come a moment in the life of an up-tight adolescent (I imagine from reading the *Village Voice* faithfully) at which he decides to freak out of the cliches and unreasonable hangups of the "real" adult world; a moment when he decides to join those of his generation, sometimes called "hippies", who are unreachable any longer by any persuasion or appeal except love and soul-brotherhood. This moment of determination to do one's own thing, this act of confirmation of the rebellious spirit, is the moment that *Hair* captures, prolongs and splinters into its dozens of jagged comments on sex, drugs, military service, money, religion, etc., etc. The libretto about a hippie's decision whether to accept or resist being drafted into the Vietnam war had pathetic and chilling overtones downtown; uptown it was camped out of any earnest meaning. For example, the young man's arguments with his parents in the original version were instances of blindfolded people groping for each other across the generation gap; in the Broadway version it was low comedy, with each parent played by three performers of mixed sexes. This loss of narrative focus isn't much of a problem in the all-out, high-volume, hyperthyroid Broadway *Hair,* whose whole impact is far less than that of its insolent parts—parts like Sally Eaton singing of carbon monoxide and sulphur dioxide in "Air", and of love in a ballad whose tenderest regret is that the boy she loves isn't the father of the unborn child she is carrying; parts like Shelley Plimpton's teeny-bopper love song, "Frank Mills"; parts like Ragni's positively acrobatic performance in every defiant, bushy-haired (the title *Hair* is a salute to the shaggy trademark of modern youth) moment of the show. And speaking of defiant moments, *Hair's* first-act curtain number was a be-in with a tangle of bodies choreographed to end in a heap under a gauzy blanket—except for a group of the performers, both boys and girls, who stand for a beat or two fully lit and facing the audience stark naked in a "shock of recognition" moment that rendered Robert Anderson's outlandish suggestion of an actor naked onstage in last season's *You Know I Can't Hear You When the Water's Running* totally and finally done, a *fait accompli*, obsolete. Oddly enough, this radical development was added to the Broadway version; it didn't take place off Broadway (and I am told that the number of actors and actresses in this tableau varied from one performance to another—each did it only when and if he felt like doing it). But off Broadway and on, with or without gimmicks, *Hair* was a detonation of a musical that shook up its audience and made them hear the hippie's cries of joy in living ("I got life, mother!") and of anger ("——you, Margaret Mead!") at any sign of generalization or conformity.

Those were the hits and probable hits of the 1967-68 Broadway season.

Their subject matter was on the dark side, immersing us deep in the agony of parents of a vegetable child; in the wanton murders of two uncomprehending young men; in the unnegotiable resentment of brothers; in the destruction of a glorious personality; in the clash between wife and mother. Our only hit musical harped on two of our most pressing social problems—alienated youth and the Vietnam war. Our funniest comedy began on a haunting note with a loss of communication between a husband and wife; another laughed through clenched teeth at suburban avarice, and only one splashed about happily in a foamy environment of sex and nonsense. To borrow a Jerry Herman punch line that must be almost two decades old by now but gains in meaning with each passing year, "Oh, what a lovely theatrical season we've had!"

Of course it was only a couple of years ago that we were all viewing with alarm the absence of so-called "serious" theater works, the scarcity even of temper in the comedies and musicals. This year the playwrights led the adventurous theatergoer into a terra incognita of strange new shapes like *Joe Egg, R & G* and *Hair*. It was a challenging and exciting season, as the theater once again began to cultivate its black tulip in rich, dark blooms.

After The Rain is a fantasy that edges oh, so craftily into its dark conclusions about human beings surviving a second Flood "two hundred years after The Rain of 1969." It begins as a "lecture" with the theater audience as the lecture audience. Its "actors" are prisoners who have committed some breach or other of the laws two centuries hence (they are kin to *Marat/Sade's* performing inmates). As part of their rehabilitation program, they have been hypnotized and trained to play the roles of survivors on a raft in the Flood, acting out the illustration of the Lecturer's "historical" account. A handful of men and women survived (the play-within-the-play demonstrates) under the ruthless leadership of an egotistical, authoritarian, lower-middle-class accountant who set himself up first as dictator, then as god. Alec McCowen is domineering and detestable as the god Arthur, nasal and small-minded in his authority, a contrast to Paul Sparer as the donnish Lecturer, who directs the "actors" as he unfolds the tale. We find, at last (after Arthur is killed in a revolt by his companions) that the principles laid down by Arthur—symbolic of man at his worst—are those which govern the new "free" society two centuries later. Like *Marat/Sade*, *After The Rain* exists on many levels. Its characters represent ourselves, today (on the raft); ourselves viewed with dimming acquaintanceship centuries later (the raft events as history); hypnotized prisoners of the future waiting to play ourselves; and finally (in the case of the Arthur character) a man of the future who manages to throw off the hypnotic veil and, awake, hates what he has become. Vivian Matalon's staging of this intertwined material was impeccable, at times ballet-like. *After The Rain* is a mind-expanding script which for some inscrutable reason didn't find a large audience on Broadway (though it was a hit in London and Paris). I confidently predict that it will find a niche in future production by those who dare greatly in order to achieve much.

The father-son relationship, touched on in Arthur Miller's *The Price*, was the whole matter of Robert Anderson's *I Never Sang for My Father*, about a 40-year-old son trying to establish an affectionate relationship with his aging father and—despite a deeply sincere effort—failing. Where Miller's father-figure was only a clinging memory, Anderson's is frustrating his son, not in memory, but right there on the stage. As played by Alan Webb in one of the season's best performances, he touches the heart at one moment as he tries to concentrate on choosing a coffin for his wife's funeral; at the next moment, he becomes a detestable, wiry little bundle of senile ego, unknowable, unreachable, unloveable. After many failures to build a bridge to his father, the son (Hal Holbrook) gives up, and that's that; that's the point of the play. The consequences, if any, are not explored. This is a generation-gap drama, not in a contemporary but in a universal sense: neither son nor parent, so widely separated by time and yet so closely bound by family kinship, is able to forget himself and suppress his own convictions and feelings long enough to project understanding toward the other—or, if this happens occasionally, it never happens to son and parent at the same moment, so that the instant of perfect understanding and love never happens. *I Never Sang for My Father* was first written as a movie. Scenes and locales flowed into each other under Alan Schneider's direction, with settings symbolized by light projections within Jo Mielziner's triple-arched set. For example, the coffin showroom was represented by rectangles of light projected onto the stage floor, in a scene which was visually as well as emotionally haunting. *I Never Sang for My Father* was not only a powerful experience of theater, it was also a triumph of American playwriting combined with Broadway stagecraft.

It would be appropriate at this point to move smoothly into a run-down of other serious matters raised on Broadway in 1967-68, except that in the modern theater is becoming harder and harder to draw meaningful lines between "comedy" and "drama." This season 17 shows were billed by their authors in the program as "comedies"—one of them was *Joe Egg*. And a leading newspaper, commenting on the renaissance of "serious" theater, made a list of 8 noteworthy "dramas"—one of them was *Joe Egg*. So what's in a name? New nerves are tingling in the theater of today; the old skin that established the boundary between flesh and air, between comedy and drama, is sloughing away. This is an era, in the theater as in the streets, of laughter born of tears; tears born of laughter.

This was especially true of the two Best Plays about homosexuality, a subject which our theater explored more thoroughly than ever before this season. One of them, *Staircase*, by the British actor-playwright Charles Dyer, was a haunting two-character study of a couple of middle-aged "hair stylists" joined in a love-hate alliance against loneliness and despair. They have nothing but each other, and that is not much (they keep observing in joke after cruel joke at the expense of their own ludicrous physical and personality characteristics). One of them, Harry, is physically awkward, the butt of several of nature's pranks, generally passive and easygoing except that he wishes he had been born an effective male. The other, Charles, is wiry, nervous, taunting, emotionally unstable—he has been capable both of marriage and of a recent public display of transvestitism while drunk that is going to land him in court. Both are lonely (but Harry is lonelier than Charles, a slow, pathetic figure as portrayed by Milo O'Shea in the year's top straight-play performance). Both are frightened (but Charles, volatile, an easy prey to remorse, is more frightened than Harry). Often they make fun of each other simply to reassure themselves that the other one is really *there*, that neither is alone in the hostile world. As in *Joe Egg*, however, there is a notable lack of joy in the laughter as these two misfits joke past the cemetery where lies buried all their masculine pride. Their neurosis has destroyed everything except their continuing ability to feel and suffer. Unbeautiful as the subject of *Staircase* may sound, it is beautiful in its insight and sympathy.

In Mart Crowley's *The Boys in the Band* off Broadway, six homosexuals are giving a birthday party for a seventh, attended by a male prostitute and one "straight" guest who arrives uninvited. In each character the neurosis takes a different form, varying from a pipe-smoking Ivy League schoolteacher (Laurence Luckinbill) to a barelegged, camping interior decorator (played in full color but without offense by Cliff Gorman) who tells the others "I've known what I was since I was four years old." The host at the party (Kenneth Nelson) is 30-ish, high-strung, warped by a doting mother but somewhat ashamed of his homosexuality, taking out his hang-ups in attacks on the others. The birthday boy is a pockmarked ex-figure skater (Leonard Frey) with no inhibitions whatever. The guests include a soft-spoken Negro, (Reuben Greene) two young men in blue jeans, one aggressive (Keith Prentice) and one a diffident observer, mother-spoiled (Frederick Combs). With Peter White as the shocked "square" (who just may not be quite as sharp-cornered as he believes himself to be) and Robert La Tourneaux as a cowboy-costumed male version of a dumb female prostitute, these are the manifestations of neurosis which the playwright and his director, Robert Moore, combined with great skill into a harrowing stage portrait of the neurosis itself. In doing so, *The Boys in the Band* gave no offense to taste or decency. Like last season's *Fortune and Men's Eyes* about homosexuality in prison, the first act tends toward comedy; but then in the second act when the script must reveal the tension underneath the warp, there is an onslaught of bitterness leading to hysteria. Yet there was no emotion, no sympathy evoked by the second-act tears that had not already been evoked in the first-act laughter; that has been a weakness of the theater's treatment of this theme so far in the 1960s. Nevertheless it was handled with admirable sensitivity and skill in *The Boys in the Band* by actors, director and playwright, as it was in *Staircase,* a couple of plays that turned the lights on in a dark corner of human experience.

Among new American plays on Broadway, it's safe to say that the short-lived *The Trial of Lee Harvey Oswald* was a work of serious dramatic intention (but minor accomplishment) which imagined that President Kennedy's assassin was alive and on trial for his crime. In the first act, "witnesses" present much of the real, available evidence against Oswald, and in the second Oswald himself takes the stand to plead that he was the tool of a conspiracy. The season offered one minor melodrama—Ira Levin's *Dr. Cook's Garden*—with Burl Ives as a Vermont small-town doctor improving the breed by killing out all the undesirable human beings in his practise. Mary Mercier's *Johnny No-Trump* was a drama of a young man contending with father images. It was withdrawn from production after only one performance and a mixed press with strong enthusiasm on the pro side. I am told by its producer Richard Barr that he will bring it back to Broadway in a planned schedule of Theater 1969 repertory next season. On the borderline of drama was Stephen Levi's *Daphne in Cottage D,* with Sandy Dennis and William Daniels in a two-character exploration of emotional distress starting out as a bright, bantering drinking party and ending up as a mutual confession of betrayal and guilt. R.K. Narayan's novel *The Guide* was dramatized by the late Harvey Breit and Patricia Reinhart, with its Indian setting and story of a con man who persuades a village he's a saint, then comes to believe in his own beatitude as he tries to relieve a drought. George Panetta was also writing about a kind of saint in *Mike Downstairs:* a resident of Manhattan's Little Italy doing his earnest best to assist his neighbors through the tensions of modern life and, finally, killed for his pains (but Panetta has labeled this play a comedy). Actors' hangups were the subject of Lewis John Carlino's *The Exercise,* a two-character situation in which an actor and actress practise their art by "improvising" impressions of their own emotional disturbances.

Surveying the list of new foreign plays on Broadway in 1967-68, one finds drama—historical drama—in Rolf Hochhuth's *Soldiers* translated from the original German by Robert D. MacDonald. Like Hochhuth's *The Deputy* (which presented Pope Pius XII as soft in his opposition to the Nazi policy of genocide), *Soldiers* was another creaking machine of a play designed to spread guilt as widely as possible. The time of the play is 1943; Stalin is England's most effective ally, holding most of the Nazi army at bay, so that Russian cooperation is Winston Churchill's first priority. Churchill is seen as condoning (if not actually arranging) the death of his friend General Sikorski because of Sikorski's embarrassing insistence on the recognition of Polish territorial rights at Stalin's expense. Churchill is also represented as adopting a policy of cruel and immoral mass bombing of German civilian population centers, in lieu of a second front on the Continent. An uncannily believable and sustained portrayal of Winston Churchill by John Colicos was hypnotically interesting; the actor created, not a replica, but a strong impression of the great man. As for the message of the play, it is suspect; Hochhuth is the sort of writer who has used the words "Hiroshima" and "Auschwitz" in the same sentence as though they have the same moral implications. The bombing of cities (Hochhuth insinuates in *Soldiers*) is a war crime committed by all in equal guilt, but unpunishable because not outlawed by the Geneva Convention. The script had been booked for production by Laurence Olivier and Kenneth Tynan at England's National Theater but was opposed by the Lord Chamberlain and then brought over here for production by Tynan, Herman Shumlin (who produced Hochhuth's *The Deputy*) and others. Looking upon it as a purported documentary, it seems only a little more foolish to ban than to sponsor its Teutonic sophistries.

Also on the dramatic side, Eugene Ionesco's *Exit the King* was produced on Broadway in an American premiere by APA-Phoenix. It is a paranoid and absurdist nightmare, a fantastic but relentless account of the death of a king who is not pushed but ticked slowly toward his end through an hour and a half of protest against time's inexorable movement toward decay and oblivion. A young second wife consoles Berenger; but his first wife, played with metallic precision by Eva Le Gallienne, is first among those who insist that Berenger's time has come and that he must get on with it and die without making a fuss. This weird experience of theater was enhanced by Rouben Ter-Arutunian's setting—a strange, brown, geometrical Nowhere which transformed itself at the moment of Berenger's death into a Nowhere wrapped in Saran. A new Russian play by Aleksei Arbuzov dealt with a universal theme —the love triangle—in a grave manner, setting up a "design for living" with two youths and a girl who meet as souls lost in the rubble of the siege of Leningrad in World War II. The three maintain their ties through the years, and the girl marries both of the men in turn. This Russian script was not without a sparkle of the comic spirit, and it was so irridescently well-acted by Eileen Atkins, Ian McKellen and Ian McShane that it deserved a larger share of the Broadway audience than it was able to attract.

There's no use pretending as I pass from a report on *The Promise* to a thought about Peter Ustinov's *The Unknown Soldier and His Wife* that I am crossing some well-marked border between drama and comedy. But if there is a border—a lightening of the mood, an alleviation in the terrain—it is here. The characters in *The Unknown Soldier* were hurting badly as they dragged themselves off to war time after time through the ages, killing the Unknown Soldier and widowing his wife again and again for the many causes of history. But always the woes consoled themselves in irony and sarcasm, in a show directed briskly by John Dexter as a black farce. Other foreign comedies of the year shared the general characteristic of being strong in the bass; there was no great abundance of joy. Michel de Ghelderode's *Pantagleize* made its New York debut in an APA-Phoenix production spread across the stage in symbolic revolutionary action by John Houseman and Ellis Rabb. Pantagleize (played by Rabb) is a nonentity whose only offense is that he feels happy one morning and comments that it is a nice day, thus unwittingly giving the signal for the start of a revolution that is destined to destroy him (what else?). De Ghelderode's 1930s play didn't seem all that relevant to the 1960s, but it was full of colorful incidents expertly performed. The late Joe Orton's black comedy prototype *Loot* exported a few laughs with its juggling of a corpse in order to hide stolen cash in the coffin, but the best part of this show was the performing by George Rose as an inept and crooked Scotland Yard man and Carole Shelley as a murderous nurse. Another British comedy, Bill Naughton's *Keep It in the Family,* can be added to the list of the season's father plays. With the locale changed to Boston for American audiences, it worked the theme of the domineering parent who finally goes too far, so that his family rises in revolt. Still another British comedy was Harold Pinter's *The Birthday Party,* about a slovenly young man visited in his boarding house by two strangers who at first throw him a party which ends on a note of horror, then, next morning, spruce him up and cart him away to some strange and probably gruesome destiny. *The Birthday Party* was written by Pinter before his magnificent *The Homecoming* which was last season's best on Broadway. Coming after it in production here, *The Birthday Party* seemed shallow and unfulfilled, merely an experimental step on the way to the masterpiece, though it was well served in the acting of James Patterson as the young boarder, Ruth White as the confused boarding-house keeper, Ed Flanders as the sinister visitor, and the rest of the cast. Other foreign comedic efforts, less than satisfactory, were *Song of the Grasshopper,* a Spanish comedy about a romantic loafer (played by Alfred Drake), and *A Minor Adjustment,* a Canadian sex comedy about a father's effort to tame his rebellious son by arranging for his seduction.

Peter Ustinov's *Halfway up the Tree* (his second script of the season, a British comedy which had its world premiere in New York shortly before its

London premiere) and Henry Denker's *What Did We Do Wrong?* both were cheerful plays about harried fathers who decide if they can't lick their hippie kids they're going to join them and out-hip them. The British version was colored with the wit and style of Ustinov's older-generation brand of verbal comedy, as a British general (Anthony Quayle), a ramrod of a man, returns home from duty in the Empire to find his unmarried daughter pregnant and his son a hippie dropout. Instead of losing his cool, the general takes guitar lessons, grows a beard and goes outside to live in a tree. Paul Ford is the harried American parent in Denker's version, a suburbanite saddled with a bossy wife and a dropout son—so of course he stages his own rebellion and becomes a hippie. The gags were broader in the Denker version, but the aim was the same in a trans-Atlantic playwriting coincidence.

With an exception or two like Ustinov's script, the season's foreign comedies were hedged with attitudes that were rueful, enigmatic or black; not so American comedies, which in several cases aimed for the "laff riot" kind of effect. The most effective of these was Carl Reiner's *Something Different,* a wildly improbable tale of a one-play playwright (Bob Dishy) trying to repeat his success by recreating within his suburban affluence the atmosphere of his mom's battered kitchen, in which he wrote his one hit. Reiner directed his own play (and the lead would have been right for him had he wished to play it), which was the season's most interesting loser. It had the best sight gag (twin boys, one white and one black) and some of the funniest gags, but it was a situation comedy that started somewhere and went nowhere. It left you wishing that Carl Reiner would write another play soon; it was a stylistic achievement that did credit to Reiner and to the Alan King group of producers who brought it to Broadway.

Herman Shumlin's *Spofford* was another light-hearted show, about a retired chicken farmer whose rustic domain is under invasion by expanding suburbia. Spofford makes it his business to observe closely and take mental notes on the strange new breed of beautiful people who are making a Westport of his Arcadia, while one of *them* is wooing his granddaughter. Portrayed in full Yankee acerbity by Melvin Douglas in one of the year's top performances, he confides his findings and conclusions directly and frequently to the audience in a play constructed as a long comedy monologue with occasional sketches. Pert Kelton was cool and sensible as a widow with a nature so warm that not even a locked sacroiliac can wipe the smile from her face. Miss Kelton and Douglas staged a middle-aged courtship which was not only the most ingratiating part of *Spofford* but also one of the major delights of the season.

The subject of sex was an American comedy favorite in the season of 1967-68. It appeared in both boy-meets-girl and boy-meets-boy form in Samuel Taylor's *Avanti!* about an American square and a British mod in a Rome hotel suite, egged on by an Italian fixer (played with great relish by Keith Baxter) who is waiting for either one of them to get lonely. Sex came around again in J.J. Coyle's *The Ninety-Day Mistress,* about a girl who shrinks from lasting attachments and so places a time limit on her affairs; and again in Lawrence Holofcener's *Before You Go,* in which a would-be actress comes into the Greenwich Village apartment of a would-be sculptor to get out of a thunderstorm and stays to make love. Among other comedy subjects was the matter of *How To Be a Jewish Mother,* a series of sketches sprinkled with songs with a two-character cast of Molly Picon in the title role and Godfrey Cambridge as a lot of other characters. American racial stress was treated comically by Robert Alan Aurthur in *Carry Me Back to Morningside Heights* (which opened and closed before the Columbia tumult and had no connection with it), staged by none other than Sidney Poitier in his first outing as a director, in which a starry-eyed Jewish youth indentures himself to a Negro law student (Louis Gossett) as a slave, to try to atone in small part for historical injustice; and by Gore Vidal in *Weekend,* mixed with politics, in a comedy about a Presidential candidate whose son brings home a Negro mistress (played with energy and charm by Carol Cole, Nat King Cole's daughter, in a promising Broadway debut), in order to embarrass his father—who promptly turns the whole situation into a political asset. Finally, in comedy, the war between a forcefully ambitious wife and a shy husband was treated farcically in *Happiness Is Just a Little Thing Called a Rolls Royce* which lasted for only one performance but may be remembered as one of the first plays in which a character sets out rather casually to get high on marijuana.

There were no hits as of May 31 among the Broadway season's haircut musicals. But winner or not, *How Now, Dow Jones* took a pleasantly high-spirited view of the stock market, enjoying the occasional bright blaze of a Carolyn Leigh lyric or a sudden George Abbott sight gag. Also profiting from an agile leading performance by Anthony Roberts as a young man on the way up in Wall Street, and from a standout supporting performance by Hiram Sherman as a tycoon who has already arrived and means to stay, *How Now, Dow Jones* had its enjoyable moments—and indeed, that's the most that could be said for the entire 1967-68 Broadway musical season until *Hair* came along. Among these momentary rewards was Alice Playten's schoolgirl villainess in *Henry, Sweet Henry,* about well-bred teen-agers adventuring in New York's streets (based on *The World of Henry Orient*). There was Robert Goulet's strong performance of a footloose French Canadian photographer coming home to visit his family (including David Wayne as his spry old dad) in *The Happy Time,* which also was distinguished by Gower Champion's choreography and by the use of color slides and movie footage as part of Peter Wexler's settings, a step forward in the scenic art. There was Patricia Routledge's star turn as a widow being courted by mail by a famous artist in *Darling of the Day* (based on Arnold Bennett's *Buried Alive*). There was the splashy Las Vegas opening number, plus excellent vocals by Steve Lawrence and Eydie Gorme and a promising supporting stint by young Scott Jacoby, in *Golden Rainbow,* the musical based on Arnold Schulman's play *A Hole in the Head.* There was Tom Bosley as an immigrant grabbing life with both hands in *The Education of H*Y*M*A*N K*A*P*L*A*N* based on the Leo Rosten stories. There was incomparable Joel Grey putting out a high-voltage portrayal of George M. Cohan, strutting and singing a wide repertory of Cohan numbers in *George M!* based on the musical star's life and works. There were Rouben Ter-Arutunian's exotic part-Eastern, part art nouveau settings for the lavish but ill-fated *I'm Solomon,* and in the season's single Broadway revue, *Leonard Sillman's New Faces of 1968,* there were moments of musical and satirical freshness. This was Sillman's 11th show under the title which he has made famous. These with *Here's Where I Belong* (the musical based on John Steinbeck's *East of Eden*), which lasted for only one performance, made up the musical scene on Broadway in 1967-68. It was a dark mass like the void of chaos itself, lit here and there by the starlight sparkle of individual contributions.

The season's 1967-68 specialties included, in addition to Marlene Dietrich, Judy Garland in her third solo-show appearance at the Palace, and Eddie Fisher and Buddy Hackett in a two-man show at the same theater. George Bernard Shaw was portrayed by Max Adrian in *By George,* devised by Michael Voysey from Shaw's writings. Roy Dotrice impersonated an aged and gossipy John Aubrey, the 17th century biographer, in *Brief Lives,* adapted by Patrick Garland from Aubrey's writings about the famous personages of his era, and displaying a setting designed as a jam and clutter of museum pieces of the period by Julia Trevelyan Oman. Finally on the list of specialties there was *Portrait of a Queen,* a biography of Queen Victoria assembled from her diaries and letters and from those of contemporaries who helped illuminate her reign. Dorothy Tutin played Victoria from girlhood to widowhood with a graceful and winning sincerity, and James Cossins contributed a remarkable vignette of Gladstone.

Among the foreign-language visitors to Broadway were The Jewish State Theater of Poland with stately Ida Kaminska as Brecht's Mother Courage; The Grand Music Hall of Israel, one of whose performers, Geula Gill, was nominated for a Tony Award; The Vienna Burgtheater impressing all comers with expert ensemble performances of a German repertory which included *Einen Jux Will Er Sich Machen* (He Wants To Have a Good Time), the comedy which formed a basis for Thornton Wilder's *The Matchmaker,* upon which *Hello, Dolly!* was based; and, visiting Broadway for the second straight season, the colorful and sometimes topless *Les Ballets Africains* from the Republic of Guinea. Finally, Broadway received a visit from The Theater of Genoa doing Goldoni's *The Venetian Twins.* Its hopelessly involved mistaken-identity plot was played with joyous caperings and harlequinades, with frequent asides to the audience in English and without insisting on making Goldoni's ironic point about the flexibility of ethics. Alberto Lionello in the dual role of the twins—one a bravo and one a craven—communicated as heartily as any silent-screen comic. His encounter with himself at the town privy as the twins "meet" for the first and only time is a memorable comedy routine.

Revivals

Last year's spate of 32 revivals eased off to a merely handsome total of 16 in 1967-68. The surprise success of the revival season was George Kelly's *The Show-Off* as produced in repertory by APA-Phoenix. The surprise was not so much that there proved to be a strong comedic kick left in this 1924 script about a well-meaning braggart—that has been proven before in stage and TV revivals. The surprise was in the shift of the play's emphasis in this production from show-off Aubrey Piper (the starring role played by Lee Tracy off Broadway and Jackie Gleason on TV) to his foil, Mrs. Fisher, his skeptical and outspoken mother-in-law played in this APA version by none other than Helen Hayes. Under Stephen Porter's direction the old script was re-focussed around Miss Hayes's detailed and engaging performance.

APA did for *The Show-Off* this season what it did for *You Can't Take It With You* two seasons ago; instead of kidding it or exploiting it they shed new light on it and stood it up straight in all its enduring comic glory. APA-Phoenix rounded out its 1967-68 Broadway visit at the Lyceum with an unremarkable staging of *The Cherry Orchard,* but the troupe had already won more than enough applause for the Kelly play and the two fascinating European plays—*Pantagleize* and *Exit the King*—dealt with in a previous section of this report. APA-Phoenix has grown into an American repertory unit of such stature that it no longer leans on its scripts but enhances them, informs them, lights them with ideas of acting, staging and design.

Another outstanding 1967-68 revival was the staging of Lillian Hellman's *The Little Foxes* as a guest production at the Vivian Beaumont Theater in Lincoln Center. The wounds inflicted by the greedy, materialistic Hubbard family as they scrape at the world and each other seem as painful as ever in Miss Hellman's powerful script, produced by Saint-Subber as an all-star presentation (most notably with George C. Scott as Ben Hubbard, Anne Bancroft as Regina, Margaret Leighton as Birdie and E.G. Marshall as Oscar), directed with perfect control and clarity by Mike Nichols and designed in deliberate ostentation by Patricia Zipprodt. Following its limited Lincoln Center engagement the production moved to Broadway with some of the stars switching roles, others moving out of and into the cast. The changes didn't matter; this *The Little Foxes* remained a treat as well as a rarity, a revival that became a hit in the full competition of a commercial theater season on Broadway.

The smooth, impressive mounting of the Hellman play at Lincoln Center helped to point up the general fruitlessness of the effort being expended by the Repertory Company of Lincoln Center, in residence at this same Vivian Beaumont Theater. It is learning, yes, but much of its lesson is obsolete. This year the group mounted adequate revivals of Shaw's *Saint Joan,* Anouilh's *Tiger at the Gates* and a new English version by James Forsyth of Rostand's *Cyrano de Bergerac.* Lincoln Center Rep can't be expected to produce on a Saint-Subber all-star scale (though I admired very much Edward Zang's performance as the Dauphin and Michael Annals' costumes for *Saint Joan*). It can't even hope to compare in ensemble virtuosity with such as APA—it isn't ready yet, and comparison would be unfair. Its most pressing problem, it seems to me, is the much more obvious one of a choice of plays. Lincoln Center Rep did not choose to do *The Little Foxes* or *The Show-Off* or any other American play. It relied on standard European scripts, not even new (to New York) like APA's de Ghelderode and Ionesco plays. I suppose it could be argued that the casting of Diana Sands in the title role of *Saint Joan* was an effort to give the play contemporaneous overtones, but they never materialized. Miss Sands realized Shaw's Maid as a symbol for all time and people, in a fine performance in which negritude nevertheless counted for nothing.

Suppose Lincoln Center Rep had mounted three perfect productions of *Saint Joan, Tiger at the Gates* and *Cyrano de Bergerac?* What then would have been accomplished as the 1967-68 result of all the energy that has gone into Lincoln Center's massive act of theatrical parturition, its effort to give birth to a New York repertory company; this agony of Elia Kazan and Robert Whitehead, of Herbert Blau and Jules Irving and all the Rockefellers wheeling in their appointed courses? The answer would have been: nothing that could not have been done better by Jean-Louis Barrault, Laurence Olivier and the Comédie Française. Until the American actors and directors at the Vivian Beaumont start working on American plays (at least part of the time), they will not proceed one single step along the path that Kazan and Whitehead started to take, and that APA-Phoenix has followed so painstakingly and with such distinction.

It should be noted right here that Lincoln Center Rep deserves applause for its smaller-scale experimental activities in its basement theater, the little Forum. Here were staged new programs by American playwrights, reflecting more credit on the company than anything it has done since Kazan put on two new Arthur Miller plays several seasons ago. Two of these programs were formally presented to the public as off-Broadway shows: Mayo Simon's double bill of one-acters, *Walking to Waldheim* and *Happiness,* and Ron Cowen's full-length *Summertree.* The latter provided the season's most probing reflection on the Vietnam war, in the fanciful context of a young man's thoughts and dreams as he is trying to grow up but is swallowed by the draft and killed in the war. David Birney as the young man, and Philip Sterling as his well-meaning father bogged down in materialistic cliches, were especially effective. The vignettes of *Summertree* cannot be the ultimate goal of a great American repertory company, but they are a more appropriate stop-off along the way than *Tiger at the Gates.*

The Music Theater of Lincoln Center provided a summer production of the Rodgers & Hammerstein masterpiece *South Pacific* under Richard Rodgers' personal supervision, with Giorgio Tozzi as Emile de Becque and Florence Henderson as Ensign Nellie Forbush. Our good New York City Center gave us not only the City Center Gilbert & Sullivan Company in five expert Savoyard programs; not only The City Center Light Opera Company in highly professional re-stagings of *Brigadoon* and *The King and I;* but also The City Center Drama Company in revivals of American straight plays: *Life With Father,* with Dorothy Stickney playing the Vinnie role she created on Broadway, and *The Tenth Man,* both in their first New York professional revivals. As in the cases of *The Show-Off* and *The Little Foxes,* it was a pleasure to note the enduring vigor of these fine American scripts. They are the mined and smelted treasure of the art form, growing in supply season after Broadway season, waiting to be borrowed by anyone with the wit to use them with skill and respect.

Off Broadway

Burdened with rising costs and a creeping hit psychology, the tributary theater known as off Broadway nevertheless was still resisting in 1967-68 the forces influencing it to become a sort of junior Broadway. Hit musicals and comedies were conspicuously present, to be sure, but the air was not yet dangerously polluted with commercialism. Off Broadway was still trying out new forms and subjects, tinkering with the musical theater, probing the nature of man through various avenues of his sexual nature, and in so doing treading paths seldom if ever before trod in the theater. Off Broadway was still a Mecca for the one-act play, the esoteric revival, the facing of existentialist "facts". 1967-68 reached a peak with the musical *Your Own Thing,* which is not only a Best Play and the recipient of the New York Drama Critics Circle award for the year's best musical (the first off-Broadway musical so honored); it also issued a challenge to the whole theater and beyond the theater to the audience with its theme of "Know thyself" (translated into modern language as "Do your own thing").

The off-Broadway season tested high on every important count in 1967-68. There were 72 productions of record, as compared with 69, 66 and 73 in recent seasons. These 72 productions broke down into 27 new American plays, 8 musicals, 10 new foreign plays in English and 4 revues (a total of 49 new works almost equaling last year's high total of 50), plus 15 revivals, 4 specialty shows and 4 foreign-language programs. In 1967-68, as last season, three off-Broadway shows made the Best Plays list in competition with the best that Broadway had to offer: *Scuba Duba, Your Own Thing* and *The Boys in the Band* (and *Hair* came very close). Off Broadway came up with the most trenchant comment on the Vietnam war in *Summertree,* described with Lincoln Center Rep's other productions in the previous section of this report. Off Broadway's high spirits were displayed in the provoking two-character play *The Beard;* in Joseph Papp's oddball *Hamlet;* in Ed Bullins' *The Electronic Nigger and Others*—and most impudently in the bouncing bare-breasted scene in *Scuba Duba.* All this and the Drama Critics prize too? It was a *very* good year.

The critics prizewinner *Your Own Thing* is based on Shakespeare's *Twelfth Night* in the sense that its leads, Viola and Sebastian, are sibling look-alikes (and in our modern age, dress-alikes and haircut-alikes) who are shipwrecked in Illyria, neither knowing that the other has survived the wreck. Here's where *Twelfth Night* ends (except for a few quotes from Shakespeare sprinkled into the script) and the 1960s begin. The duke of *this* Illyria is called Mayor John V. Lindsay, and the twins gravitate into the society of pop rock 'n' roll singers. The joke in the beginning is that no one knows which is the brother and which the sister, which is boy or girl; and the topper is that after a while no one cares (do your own thing!). The book by Donald Driver is salted with asides, some of encouragement and some of moral indignation, while images of John Wayne, Shirley Temple, Queen Elizabeth I, Humphrey Bogart, Everett Dirksen and the Sistine Chapel God Himself are projected onto the scenery. Still photos, movies and comic book balloons are set into the live action wherever they can enlarge a mood or throw a comic curve, in a sort of multi-media show. The lyrics by Hal Hester and Danny Apolinar (who also appears onstage as a member of the rock 'n' roll singing group) are monosyllabic but effective in the context of the heavy rock beat. Leland Palmer as Viola, in love with a boy who thinks *she's* a boy but loves her anyway, was far and away the year's most engaging musical actress. Making sport of Shakespeare's work was a popular gimmick last season. Off Broadway saw a camp revival of *A Midsummer Night's Dream,* Joseph Papp's fun-house *Hamlet* and *another* musical based on *Twelfth Night,* the relatively short-lived *Love and Let Love.*

The other off-Broadway Best Plays were comedies: *The Boys in the Band,* described earlier in this report, and *Scuba Duba,* which was billed in the program by its author, Bruce Jay Friedman as "a tense comedy." Its central character is an immature young American wandering around the salon of his rented French Riviera chateau dressed in a bathrobe, carrying a scythe and generally making an ass of himself because his wife has left him for a black scuba diver. All of it—even the scene in which an old broad bounces through the salon naked to the waist, looking for something to read—is written, directed and acted a few degrees too earnestly for farce. Nor is it black comedy —there is no leer, no exaggeration of evil just for the hell of it. It's the tense comedy of a clown act, with Jerry Orbach as the bewildered and bereft husband getting laughs at his clownish defenses against pain. His only comfort is the girl next door, played by Brenda Smiley, a model who soothes him with anecdotes from her past, all so weird that it's a wonder she could have survived them, let alone talk about them so blithely. *Scuba Duba* is a disquieting work, staged disquietingly by Jacques Levy in perfect style. The joke is on our tense hero three ways: he's a clown when he's trying to control himself, he's a clown when he lets himself go, and in either case he's the goat of a ruthlessly humiliating situation when it turns out that his wife's lover is not a black skin diver at all, but a black poet—the husband's intellectual as well as his romantic superior. Tense comedy indeed—and most skillful variation of the comic art.

Another of off Broadway's wildly tossing crests in 1967-68 was the "tribal love-rock" musical *Hair,* which was the opening production of Joseph Papp's New York Shakespeare Festival Public Theater season downtown in his new theater, the Florence Sutro Anspacher, a handsome, multi-level, arena-stage house converted from the Astor Library. When its limited engagement ended, *Hair* would not fold up and go away. It was taken uptown to the discoteque *Cheetah* and then to Broadway, where as we go to press it is firmly established as the only solid musical hit of the season, and as such was previously described in the section on hits.

The creation of a Broadway hit is remarkable in itself, but Papp's first season indoors yielded far more than that. Each of his three productions following *Hair* was provocative theater, though none could be classed as a total success. His *Hamlet* did not come off, but its spirit of adventure, its boldly demonstrated conviction that any play, even *Hamlet,* can be freshly revealed by imaginative innovation, is exactly the spirit required of any such experimental troupe as this one (and certainly Papp no longer needs to prove that he could put on an exciting Shakespeare revival if he chose to play one straight). The Public Theater's third offering, Jacov Lind's *Ergo,* directed by Gerald Freedman, was a grotesque dissection and magnification of the elements of the German character, in order to trace the roots of Nazism. The final production, Vaclav Havel's *Memorandum,* directed by Papp, was a farcical Czech expose of an inhumanly mechanized society, further dehumanized by an artificial language to be used for business communication, a language no one can master. These were challenging plays for both producer and audience. They were received with general, if not total, appreciation— but what really matters is that here, in a theater partly supported by public funds, the public arts interest was being well and truly served in experimental efforts to expand for the public benefit the theater art as a whole, rather than

The 1967-68 Season Off Broadway

PLAYS (27)

Jonah
The Niggerlovers
Fragments
Beyond Desire
SCUBA DUBA
The Beard
Where People Gather
American Place:
Father Uxbridge Wants To Marry
The Ceremony of Innocence
The Electronic Nigger and Others (Three Plays by Ed Bullins)
Endecott and the Red Cross
Lincoln Center Forum:
Walking to Waldheim and Happiness
Summertree
The Peddler and the Dodo Bird
A Certain Young Man
The Indian Wants the Bronx and It's Called The Sugar Plum
Oh, Say Can You See L.A. and The Other Man
Saturday Night

The Bench
Scarlet Lullaby
Two Camps by Koutoukas
Tom Paine
Rate of Exchange
THE BOYS IN THE BAND
The Hawk
Muzeeka and Red Cross
Collision Course

SPECIALTIES (4)

I Must Be Talking to My Friends
Take It from the Top
Winnie the Pooh
I Only Want an Answer

MUSICALS (8)

Now Is the Time for All Good Men
Hair
Curley McDimple
Love and Let Love
Have I Got One for You
YOUR OWN THING
Who's Who, Baby?
The Believers

REVUES (4)

In the Nick of Time
In Circles
Jacques Brel Is Alive and Well and Living in Paris
Fun City

REVIVALS (15)

Arms and the Man
A Midsummer Night's Dream
American Savoyards:
Patience
H.M.S. Pinafore
The Gondoliers
The Mikado
Iolanthe
Hamlet
No Exit and The Little Private World of Arthur Fenwick
Iphigenia in Aulis
Summer of the 17th Doll
House of Flowers
The Victims
Winter Journey (The Country Girl)
Private Lives

FOREIGN PLAYS IN ENGLISH (10)

The Poker Session
Stephen D
Public Theater:
Ergo
The Memorandum
The Trials of Brother Jero and The Strong Breed
Negro Ensemble:
Song of the Lusitanian Bogey
Kongi's Harvest
Goa
The Four Seasons
Carving a Statue

FOREIGN-LANGUAGE PRODUCTIONS (4)

University of Chile:
La Remolienda
ITUCH Anthology
Le Treteau de Paris:
Le Tartuffe
En Attendant Godot

Plays listed in CAPITAL LETTERS have been designated Best Plays of 1967-68.
Plays listed in *italics* were still running June 1, 1968.

to play it safe and enhance private reputations. My only quarrel with Papp, Freedman and their interesting troupe would be in the choice of two foreign scripts while our own authors are clamoring to be produced. Let's hope the Public Theater's record improves in this one respect. It could scarcely be bettered in others.

The American Place Theater, too, had a noteworthy season of experimental production with four *American* plays. Their first effort, Frank Gagliano's *Father Uxbridge Wants To Marry,* was a difficult and sometimes obscurely symbolic work describing man as the victim of his own life, in a play about an elevator operator who is to be supplanted by automation and who loses control of his machine at the same time that he is caught up in agonized reminiscence. American Place was more communicative with its second play, Ronald Ribman's *The Ceremony of Innocence,* an account of Ethelred the Unready's efforts to bring peace to his realm in 1013, offered by its author as a parable, or at least a silhouette, of our own time. The third production at American Place was Ed Bullins' *The Electronic Nigger and Others,* a program of one-acters whose third and strongest play, *Clara's Ole Man,* was a grim mood piece about the lower depths of South Philadelphia, peopled by twisted minds in twisted bodies (with a piercingly accurate portrayal of a spastic child by Helen Ellis, and of an overbearing lesbian by Carolyn Y. Cardwell). These plays were experiments leading toward what will surely be a major Bullins play to come. It seems necessary to add, only because of the title, that the author and characters of these plays are Negroes. The title was changed to *Three Plays by Ed Bullins* after the program was moved to the Martinique Theater to continue its run when its American Place booking ended.

Finally, American Place presented Robert Lowell's *Endecott and the Red Cross,* rich in language and symbolism as it dramatizes two Nathaniel Hawthorne stories about the Puritan leader Governor Endecott suppressing his compatriot British colony at Merry Mount in 1630—stamping it out with fire and musket because of its establishment and Church of England character, its hedonistic practises and its policy of selling guns and whisky to the Indians. This play was originally intended to form part of Lowell's historical trilogy *The Old Glory,* which included the one-acters *My Kinsman, Major Molineux* (Boston just before the Revolution) and *Benito Cereno* (events aboard a Spanish slave ship in 1800), produced by American Place on November 1, 1964. *Endecott and the Red Cross* was to have begun the trilogy with its assault of the grim Puritans upon Thomas Morton's cheerful colony of maypole dancers—an example, of course, of still another dichotomy in the American personality even as it was being formed. Kenneth Haigh, as Endecott, gave a strong-chinned portrayal of a flawed hero, in this version rewritten and expanded from the 1964 script. Lowell's characters are set firmly on their feet, but some of his symbolism remains obscure to me. For example, Endecott is presented as a man of some charity who tones down many of the harsher punishments suggested by his colleague, the minister Palfrey, and yet he coldly orders the shooting of an inoffensive dancing bear which acts out its astonished pain and dies, suffering. The act robs Endecott of any identity as a rational human being, and—though it probably has significance which escapes me—distorts all the other values of Lowell's script, which came out finally as an interesting but puzzling play.

The Negro Ensemble Company realized this season the dream of its artistic director, Douglas Turner Ward, its executive director, Robert Hooks, and other members of its staff and acting company to establish a Negro-oriented repertory and training group in New York City. It is true, and cannot quite be shrugged off, that this is a form of segregation, like the all-Negro company of *Hello, Dolly!* (and many liberals urged Merrick to integrate Pearl Bailey's cast as he was planning the production). But I admit that in the case of the Negro Ensemble Company (and *Dolly*) a reasonable man would have to conclude that the end (enlarged Negro employment and opportunity) justifies the means (a segregated company). The occasional casting of a Diana Sands in a leading role, or that token presence in a chorus of countesses in a Court of Versailles number, are too narrow an opportunity for Negro actors. In the summer of 1967, when Frederick O'Neal, president of Equity, claimed that Broadway was under-employing Negroes, Richard Barr, president of the League of New York Theaters, argued that the modern realistic theater reflects society, so that not until society integrates can there logically be more Negro characters, and thus wider employment, in the plays. In that case, it could be said that The Negro Ensemble Company is what's happening until society integrates. 1967-68 was its pilot season as it stretched its new muscles in *Song of the Lusitanian Bogey,* a Peter Weiss drama of protest against the exploitation of Africans in European colonies; in a revival of *Summer of the 17th Doll;* and in a new play by the Nigerian author Wole Soyinka, *Kongi's Harvest,* contrasting the old with the new Africa. Soyinka is 32, British-educated, with experience at the Royal Court Theater in London. His work was introduced to off-Broadway audiences earlier in the season in an independently-produced program of his one-acters *The Trials of Brother Jero* and *The Strong Breed,* both set in Africa, about a false prophet and the ritual sacrifice of a teacher. Soyinka was in jail in Nigeria as a political prisoner at the time his one-acters opened in November, 1967. *Kongi's Harvest* came along in April as his second representation here this season. It was a full-length work including singing and dancing, a challenge for the Negro Ensemble. This group will conclude its first year in June 1968 with a production of Richard Wright's adaptation of *Daddy Goodness.* The company showed steady development through the year, and its choice of plays was adventuresome. It has gone a long way toward a total justification of its means in its very first season.

In other organized off-Broadway activity, Dorothy Raedler's American Savoyards presented still another season of excellent Gilbert & Sullivan revivals. The Bil Baird marionetteers contributed a delightful *Winnie the Pooh.* And there were two distinguished foreign visitors: The Theater Institute of the University of Chile and Le Treteau de Paris.

The organized producing groups help to broaden the base of each off-Broadway season, but usually it's the way-out individual effort that gives the tributary theater its heightened color. Off Broadway as on, sexuality was a popular subject—all sizes and shapes of sexuality in *Scuba Duba, Hair, Your Own Thing, Clara's Ole Man* and *The Boys in the Band.* Michael McClure's *The Beard* was a heterosexual hang-up, a two-character play whose characters were not so much sex partners as sex symbols: Billy the Kid and Jean Harlow caught in a symbolic battle of the sexes in a symbolic eternity, finally resolving their struggle in a symbolic sex act on the stage. An imported script by Arnold Wesker, *The Four Seasons,* was another two-character affair taking place in an abandoned house and making the comment that loss of innocence is linked with loss of meaning in life. There was even a play—*Scarlet Lullaby* —about the reform of a prostitute through her association with an innocent child.

Turning from sex to violence, the latter was the subject of a most sensitively perceptive study in Israel Horovitz's one-acter *The Indian Wants the Bronx.* Here is Man as the prototype Victim, in the person of an East Indian waiting for a bus to the Bronx in the wee small hours of the lonely morning, long after the buses have stopped running. Two young toughs happen by, notice him (he sticks out like a sprained thumb), begin to tease him (he cannot speak English) and finally beat him and reduce him to a state of terror for much the same reason that Mallory climbed Mt. Everest. The Indian was so conspiciously *there,* so conspicuously lost and defenseless, so obvious a victim that he seemed an incomplete image until his torturers happened along to complete the circle. It takes two to make an act of violence, Horovitz seems to be saying, a victim as well as a bully (and in real life there are more torturers than potential victims; one has only to stand on a dark corner and wait, as for a bus).

John Allen considered the subject of revenge and its corrosive effect on the human spirit in *The Other Man,* a compelling one-acter about a Jew who has made his one-time Nazi torturer a prisoner and is now torturing him. This play appeared on an Allen program of one-acters which took its title from the second playlet, *Oh, Say Can You See L.A.,* a way-out satire on modern decadence, with song-and-dance characters. The Irish playwright Hugh Leonard was represented twice off Broadway early in the season, almost back-to-back, with *The Poker Session,* a study of a mental patient after his release from the hospital, and *Stephen D,* an adaptation of James Joyce's autobiographical works about his life from childhood through university years. Jerome Kass, author of *Monopoly* two seasons ago, was present again off Broadway with a full-length play, *Saturday Night* about a Bronx librarian with dreams of grandeur and intellectual eminence (it received Martin Gottfried's vote for best American play in the Critics Circle balloting). Paul Foster created a vivid portrait of a flawed hero in the biographical-historical *Tom Paine.* Some of off Broadway's most interesting work crowded into the end of the season with John Guare's *Muzeeka,* a satiric comment on middle-class values (symbolized by the vapid music dispensed by a taping firm) and the Vietnam war and its TV coverage; and with a program called *Collision Course,* a sampler of 11 playlets on now subjects by such writers as Jean-Claude van Itallie, Lanford Wilson, Terrence McNally, Jules Feiffer and Israel Horovitz.

Musically, off Broadway came up smiling not only with *Your Own Thing* and *Hair,* but also with *Curley McDimple,* a successful Mary Boylan-Robert Dahdah spoof of child stars in general and old Shirley Temple movies in particular. Then there was the musicalization of Gertrude Stein's fragment *In Circles,* a series of tentative beginnings of conversations among articulate young people on a chateau terrace, set to music by Al Carmines and choreographed movement under Lawrence Kornfeld's direction. It was one of those off-Broadway productions which may be described as "interesting". Here and there a Stein image or a Carmines music theme took flight, but for the most part it was a mind-blower, of an experience trying to dig Miss Stein's meaning in such disconnected lines as "Papa blows his noses," "Cut wood" and "A circle is a necessity, we each have our circle." Elsewhere off Broadway, the songs of the Paris-based Belgian composer Jacques Brel were cordially celebrated and presented in the Village Gate cabaret revue *Jacques Brel Is Alive and Well and Living in Paris.*

Among the season's off-Broadway revivals, Euripides's *Iphigenia in Aulis,* not seen here since 1921, was mounted most effectively by Circle in the Square under Michael Cacoyannis's direction, with Irene Papas as Clytemnestra. Its drama of the impending sacrifice of the innocent in order to attain a military goal was an ancient Greek drama with strong modern overtones. Some of the same contemporary echoes were heard in a noteworthy revival of Shaw's *Arms and the Man* under Philip Minor's direction.

Looking back on the off-Broadway season as a whole, I am struck by its energy and drive to express everything in terms of theater. The word "struck" is exactly what I mean—I can't think back over the off-Broadway year without being assaulted in heart and mind by a series of memory images: long-haired, clown-suited Danny Apolinar singing in *Your Own Thing* that nature had not formed him to resemble the prince in the fairy tale, so why should he torture himself pretending to be such a one? . . . . . Jerry Orbach clutching an irrelevant scythe in *Scuba Duba* and striving desperately to find a straw of sense in his sea of nightmarish troubles . . . . . bushy-haired Gerome Ragni trying to love everybody all at once in *Hair* . . . . . Cliff Gorman camping through *The Boys in the Band* . . . . . the sterotyped smile of John Cazale as the East Indian and the bored resignation to violence of Al Pacino and Matthew Cowles as the bullies in *The Indian Wants the Bronx* . . . . . the smirking dominance of Carolyn Y. Cardwell in Ed Bullins' *Clara's Ole Man* . . . . . the bland self-satisfaction of Philip Sterling driving his son into the Army in *Summertree* . . . . . all right, even "Papa blows his noses." Such moments of truth on the stage stop us short and make us take account. There was a time when off Broadway's 1967-68 images might have shocked a majority of us; but in the last decade our literary and performing arts have led most of us slowly through barriers of tabu, superstition, prejudice, modesty, preconception and other hang-ups, so that now we have been trained to observe what once would have merely blown our minds. It's next to impossible to shock today's off-Broadway audience—at least not with any revelation of human suffering or aspiration. I confess that I was shocked—mind-blown out of any delicate appreciation of the play's values—by the slaughter of the bear in Robert Lowell's play. But strike us the off-Broadway theater can and should—and did in 1967-68; often profoundly and, in the case of its dramatized encouragements to know and be thyself, perhaps even with a lasting effect on the general social attitude and philosophy.

Offstage

Behind the scenes of play production, an important 1967-68 development was the concerted effort by theater and New York City authorities to encourage the building of playhouses into new office structures in the Broadway area. Building code regulations in combination with other factors had made it generally unfeasable to combine theaters with office or apartment space under the same roof, so that in the present construction boom the theater might have found itself pressed for lebensraum by the new anthills in its own yard. Now, with the help of Mayor John V. Lindsay and others concerned with the welfare of New York's legitimate stage, in hearings and discussions with various City powers and agencies, the way has been eased and it was more than likely at press time that 1,600-1,800 seat legitimate playhouses would be included in each of the new office structures on the sites of the Astor Hotel and Capitol Theater. The technicalities of the arrangement are complicated, but what it amounts to is an interpretation of the building code —in the Broadway area only—compatible with theater interests, public interest and safety and of course the profit interest of the builders.

The theater count is one of the art form's vital signs. In recent years the Broadway count has remained fairly steady in the low 30s, with theaters shifting in and out of availability—the Palace in, the Ziegfeld out and so forth. This year the ANTA-Washington Square Theater was lost to Broadway production—but it had been only recently (in 1963) gained. Far more significantly, the Playhouse at press time was booked for the bulldozer to make way for a new office complex whose mentors include Rockefeller interests. The fact that they also have announced their intention to include a new theater in their plans for this site is not entirely reassuring. One veteran theater observer pointed out that new builders tend to think big and are likely to plan large theaters (like the ones designed for the Astor and Capitol buildings) rather than medium-sized ones, like those being demolished. This change in the physical environment could induce esthetic change. No longer will the American theater need actors with large voices and personalities projecting to fill a theater in immediate dramatic or comic contact with the audience. The actor will be projected mechanically through microphones in big productions tailored to fit the bigger houses; or he can reach audiences with a whisper in a tiny 300-seat off-Broadway environment. If the present trend continues, there will be no in-between.

The issue of whether American playwrights should permit their scripts to be produced in South Africa (in order to fight Apartheid with the box office proceeds), or whether they should withhold permission for performances before South Africa's racially segregated audiences, continued to heat up in 1967-68. Neil Simon had permitted *The Odd Couple* and *Barefoot in the Park* to be done there under the first rationale, but this season he switched to the starve-'em-out-culturally position and withheld permission to perform *Sweet Charity* after "second thoughts" about a country "that denies its *majority* of citizens their basic civil liberties." Paddy Chayefsky too declared his works unavailable for South African production.

And speaking of involvement, 1967-68 saw an unusual instance of bringing a social problem onto the stage itself, not merely as the subject of dramatization but in a sort of happening. The tortures of drug addiction were reenacted in a presentation called *The Concept,* not by actors, but by actual victims of this illness. Ex-addicts described and acted out the agony and some of its methods of cure at Daytop Village, Staten Island, communicating their own experiences directly to the audience with minimum intervention of playwriting. They had a basic program of material to be presented, but many of the details and words were improvised from performance to performance.

In subsidy, the regional and experimental theater continued to benefit from foundation support in five- and six-figure grants. Federal support of the arts administered by the National Foundation on the Arts suffered from a cut in appropriations by Congress, but not before a grant of $200,000 had been made by the National Endowment to the Theater Development Fund. This Fund is the professional stage's best hope for subsidy where it will do the most good, and it is now organized and ready to function during the 1968-69 season. With the abovementioned Federal money and other grants received from the Rockefeller Brothers and Twentieth Century Funds and the Mary Reynolds Babcock Foundation, this Fund will support the occasional, especially deserving but not instantly popular New York show by purchasing blocks of tickets during the earlier weeks of its run, and at the same time helping to develop theater audiences by giving these tickets to students and other selected groups. This would give a deserving show a broader hearing and perhaps even buy it the time to develop an audience and become self-sustaining.

New York theater enjoyed virtual freedom from censorship in 1967-68. City authorities took a long, hard look at *The Beard* and, commendably, decided to leave it alone. The New York *Times* rejected a *The Beard* quote ad full of sexual references (without which reviewers couldn't describe the play), and *The New Yorker* ignored the show in its off-Broadway listings after its critic decided it was "unworthy of review." But in our town there were nothing like the police problems which *The Beard* encountered in San Francisco and Los Angeles, or the Lord Chamberlain problems of *America Hurrah, Soldiers* and Edward Bond's *Early Morning* in London this season.

Union activity during the 1967-68 season included a new three-year contract for stagehands. During its term the top weekly minimum will rise to $204 for department heads, $156 for key men and others. Actors Equity reached a new agreement with the League of off-Broadway Theaters and Producers, by which actors' minimums will rise from $65-$130 a week to $75-$150 a week over a three-year period, with stage managers getting $20 more. Actual amounts in individual cases are based on box office receipts off Broadway, so the contract has a bonus clause written into it to benefit actors performing in playhouses so small that the grosses could never be large even if the play is a long-run hit. After a 44 weeks' run in such a situation, actors will receive $7.50 a week extra. In exchange, Equity agreed that its off-Broadway performers could be signed to run-of-the-play contracts of 9 months' duration.

As the season ended, Broadway was facing a renegotiation of its Equity contract, which expired June 2, 1968. As we were putting this volume to press, a League of New York Theaters proposal was rejected by the Equity membership. Principally at issue were the minimum salary, the employment of chorus members and a difference of opinion over when and how to control the casting of foreign actors in Broadway shows. The latter problem is complicated by fiscal as well as esthetic considerations: actors' salaries in speaking roles are almost invariably negotiated far above the minimum level, and there is always the possibility (some actors believe the inevitability) that British actors will settle for a good deal less pay than their American colleagues in the same roles. In any case, the casting last season of Anthony Quayle in *Galileo* and this season of Margaret Leighton in *The Little Foxes*,

and of Eileen Atkins, Ian McKellen and Ian McShane in *The Promise*—all
non-British roles—and finally almost in the middle of negotiations of Nicol
Williamson to replace George C. Scott in *Plaza Suite*—an American actor in
an American role—were red flags to the Equity bull. On Monday, June 17,
the actors struck (a relatively painless process for a union most of whose
members are out of work anyway at any one time). 19 Broadway shows went
dark. David Merrick decided to close *How Now, Dow Jones* and *I Do! I Do!*
permanently, and Joseph Cates and Henry Fownes closed *A Day in the Death
of Joe Egg* (the three shows had run their course at the box office anyway
but might have been kept running for a while, for the benefit of those employed in them). Settlement of the strike was reached in an all-night session
June 19 at Gracie Mansion under the watchful eye of Mayor Lindsay. The
parties agreed to a minimum wage increase from $130 to $155 over the
three-year contract period and an employment arrangement for choristers by
which they could not be dismissed after 20 weeks (as they could previously)
but need not be replaced if they left voluntarily. Alien performers are never
to be hired as replacements for American actors, and all disputes about the
employment of aliens are to be resolved by binding arbitration. On the evening of June 20 the lights went back on again at 16 Broadway shows. It was
estimated that the strike cost actors $80,000 in salaries and producers
$400,000 in gross receipts for the 4 canceled performances.

Among theater critics the year's major development was the slotting of
Clive Barnes into the job of daily theater reviewer at the New York *Times*.
Walter Kerr voluntarily handed over this daily stint so that he could concentrate on his series of critiques in the paper's Sunday drama section. Barnes
became the Lord High Everything Else of the *Times* drama desk as he continued to review dance while he took over the reviewing of Broadway productions and selected off-Broadway, out-of-town and other performing arts
events. Also at the *Times,* Arthur Gelb replaced Joseph G. Herzberg as the
overlord of the paper's cultural coverage. William H. Glover of the AP was
elected president of the New York Drama Critics Circle, succeeding Norman
Nadel. Richard Watts Jr. was the playwrights' choice as the "most perceptive" critic of the season by a small plurality in annual poll conducted by
The Dramatists Guild Quarterly. The prime example of critic-baiting was a
thrust and riposte of telegrams between David Merrick and Clive Barnes,
following unfavorable Barnes comments on Merrick productions (Merrick:
"The honeymoon is over." Barnes: "I didn't know you cared.").

A major promotional effort by the League was the glamorization of the
Tony Awards ceremony in which citations for the theater's 1967-68 "bests"
were bestowed at the Shubert Theater in an evening of network TV coverage
and a galaxy of stars (some of whom like Audrey Hepburn, Jack Benny,
Gregory Peck and Groucho Marx hadn't been on a Broadway stage in a long
time). The show was a good one, but the Tony Awards themselves were
subjected to several technical limitations which robbed them of a portion of
their meaning and were the subject of controversy long before the ceremony
took place. An arbitrary cut-off date for the nominations in March (in order
to schedule a TV show before the summer doldrums) prevented consideration of *George M!, Hair* and other spring shows until the next calendar year
—and required the inclusion of several productions from last season. Reper-

tory companies including the APA-Phoenix at the Lyceum on Broadway were excluded by the League's rules, as were *all* off-Broadway productions. Distinction between "leading" and "supporting" players was confused by technicalities of billing.

Such were the revels of 1967-68—the revels of the New York commercial theater. By any possible measurement, Broadway is still the scene. It's where it's at. Even the names of its major tributaries—off Broadway and off off Broadway—are love-hate relationships with the parent. Their names signify that they are *not* Broadway, they are *removed* from Broadway—but not very far; a measurable distance, not a million light years of heredity, style, technique or even intent.

Broadway is where it's at in deed as well as in name. Its best outgoing playscripts become staples of stock and other activity from coast to coast and pole to pole, even when these scripts didn't make it the first time out on Broadway (c.f. *Tiny Alice, Slow Dance on the Killing Ground, The Lion in Winter,* etc.). Broadway can provide an atmosphere of appreciation for the outstanding incoming works of the world theater, however far out, from *Marat/Sade* to *R & G,* including Ionesco and Pinter at their best. Broadway can assimilate all new forms of theater as they reach a state of operational efficiency (c.f. *The Homecoming, R & G, Hair,* etc.); and although Broadway economics work against experimentation in the early stages of new theater forms, where is a major scene of such experimentation? Around Broadway, near Broadway, of course, and this is no accident. All three of the off-Broadway scripts on this season's Best Plays list were mounted by producers who also have Broadway productions in the works or in being. Broadway is not a mere stagnant receptacle of is tributaries, its tides rise and flow back into the small playhouses in the form of ideas, talent and money, refreshing the experimental activity in its turn.

As for environment, Broadway's continuous insistence on freedom of expression has created in New York a theatrical environment in which almost anything goes that can stand up and walk. It was not in commercially polluted New York that such scripts as Michael McClure's *The Beard* ran into trouble, it was out in the pure Rockefeller and Ford-blessed ether of the hinterlands. Homosexuality came under close study with a new dramatic insight during 1967-68, and the subject was accepted almost as unselfconsciously by Broadway audiences in *Staircase* as it was by off-Broadway audiences in *The Boys in the Band.*

Yes, the New York theater is where it's at in name, in creativity, in freedom of expression and in audience appreciation, and Broadway is both the parent and the child of its time and place. Our musical theater is evolving rapidly, and yet *Hello, Dolly!, Fiddler on the Roof, Man of La Mancha, Cabaret* and *Hair* can play side by side, inviting comparison to the detriment of none, like the beauties in Paris's judgment. Some of these productions are years old, but which is tired, which is obsolete? The answer, of course, is not one of them. Time does not wither nor custom stale this wench of infinite variety, this best effort of the Broadway theater which in good and bad seasons, in old and new forms, is created not only to dazzle but also to light the way; not only to startle but inform, not only to delight but also to last.

Howard Da Silva, *center,* as Benjamin Franklin in a scene from the musical *1776,* book by Peter Stone, music and lyrics by Sherman Edwards.

PHOTO BY MARTHA SWOPE

1968-69

CALL IT A SEASON of transition, of strange new theater forms and strange new plays and playwrights from the hinterlands—but don't insist on burying Neil Simon and overpraising Julian Beck. In 1968-69, at last, you could see plainly that an old theater tradition was dying and a new one was being born; but the process was still in its early stages. The moribund retained most of his signs of vigor, while the new life was in the embryonic state. A swinging good old-fashioned comedy like *Forty Carats* still held the field against the way-out efforts of a *We Bombed in New Haven,* even though it was perfectly clear to the New York theatergoer which one represented the past and which the inevitable future, perceptible at last, after several seasons of groping and experimentation with new theater forms, like a seed trying to find out what kind of a tree it is going to be.

Actors were speaking to audiences directly, stepping right down into the auditorium and coaxing spectators to take their clothes off. It now seems certain that the theater of the future will be a theater of more direct contact between play and audience, with the audience not just a group of passive observers like movie or TV watchers, isolated by the convention of an invisible fourth wall, but instead taking on an active relationship with the play.

This was a season, moreover, of experimentation with nakedness onstage, not so much on Broadway as in the smaller playhouses. Males and females in various combinations peeled, groped and pressed against one another. Very little came of it all except publicity, and not much of that. There was hardly even a sense of shock. Theatrically speaking, the nudity and mimed fornication accomplished so little, at the cost of so much effort, that perhaps we have got *that* notion out of the way at last, once and for all.

There was much dramatizing of headlines in the year's best work—not today's headlines, yesterday's, in *The Great White Hope, 1776, The Man in the Glass Booth* and *In the Matter of J. Robert Oppenheimer.* Rising from last season's absolute nadir, the Broadway musical skyrocketed back into prominence with two boldly original shows—*1776* and *Celebration*—with *Zorbá* and *Promises, Promises* also helping to restore the reputation of this uniquely American theater form.

And speaking of sources, the year's best script was developed, not in the New York atmosphere, but in Washington, D.C. *The Great White Hope* had its premiere at the Arena Stage during the 1967-68 season, with James Earl Jones as the boxer Jack Jefferson and Jane Alexander as his mistress, directed by Edwin Sherin. Thus it was literally a play produced in regional theater and sent "on the road" to Broadway, where it topped everything around. *Oppenheimer,* too, had its American premiere in regional theater last year, in the Center Theater Group production in Los Angeles, and came to New York with the leading players and director. Broadway "created" only three of its top ten shows this year: *1776, Celebration* and *Forty Carats,* which Jay Allen adapted from a French script.

Statistically, the season was about average. There were 76 programs pro-

119

The 1968-69 Season on Broadway

PLAYS (24)

Lovers and Other Strangers
The Cuban Thing
Woman Is My Idea
Box-Mao-Box
THE GREAT WHITE HOPE
We Bombed in New Haven
A Cry of Players
Morning, Noon and Night
The Goodbye People
Jimmy Shine
The Sudden and Accidental Re-education of Horse Johnson
FORTY CARATS
Fire!
The Mother Lover
Play It Again, Sam
Does a Tiger Wear a Necktie?
But, Seriously . . .
The Wrong Way Light Bulb
Zelda
The Watering Place
The Dozens
Cop-Out
The Gingham Dog
My Daughter, Your Son

SPECIALTIES (5)

Marlene Dietrich
Gilbert Becaud Sings Love
The National Theater of the Deaf
Trumpets of the Lord
The World's a Stage

MUSICALS (12)

Her First Roman
Maggie Flynn
Zorbá
Promises, Promises
The Fig Leaves Are Falling
CELEBRATION
Red, White and Maddox
Canterbury Tales
Dear World
1776
Come Summer
Billy

REVUE (1)

Noel Coward's Sweet Potato

REVIVALS (23)

My Fair Lady
West Side Story
APA-Phoenix '68:
The Show-Off
Pantagleize
Theater 1969:
The Death of Bessie Smith and The American Dream
Krapp's Last Tape and The Zoo Story
Happy Days
APA-Phoenix '69:
The Cocktail Party
The Misanthrope
Cock-A-Doodle Dandy
Hamlet
D'Oyly Carte:
H.M.S. Pinafore
Patience
The Mikado
The Pirates of Penzance
Iolanthe
Lincoln Center Rep:
King Lear
The Miser
Carnival!

Minnesota Theater:
The House of Atreus
The Resistible Rise of Arturo Ui
Hamlet
The Front Page

FOREIGN PLAYS IN ENGLISH (6)

LOVERS
THE MAN IN THE GLASS BOOTH
The Flip Side
Rockefeller and the Red Indians
IN THE MATTER OF J. ROBERT OPPENHEIMER
HADRIAN VII

FOREIGN-LANGUAGE PRODUCTIONS (5)

Compagnie Villeurbanne:
The Three Musketeers
George Dandin
Tartuffe
The Megilla of Itzik Manger
Fiesta in Madrid

HOLDOVER SHOW WHICH BECAME HIT DURING 1968-69

Hair

Plays listed in CAPITAL LETTERS have been designated Best Plays of 1968-69.
Plays listed in bold face type were classified as hits in Variety's annual list of hits and flops published in midsummer 1969.
Plays listed in italics were still running on June 1, 1969.

duced on Broadway in 1968-69 (see the one-page summary accompanying this article), as compared with 84 last season, 78 the year before, 76 the year before that and 81 the year before that. The important figure—the volume of new American work—has remained reassuringly steady except for that alarming drop-off in 1966-67. This season there were 24 new American plays and 12 new musicals produced on Broadway, compared with 25-10 last year, 19-8 in the alarming year before that, 25-11 the year before that and 25-10 the year before that.

The slight decline from last year in overall volume of play production is accounted for by the sharp drop in the number of foreign plays in English—only 6 as compared with last year's 17. There was a corresponding rise in the number of revival programs from 16 last year to 23 this year, which helped keep production activity at a level normal for the 1960s.

There was also a small decline in the Broadway theater's combined gross and activity (as per *Variety's* annual estimate). For the fifth straight year Broadway's total gross topped the $50 million mark, but for the first time in five years it fell short of a record. Broadway took in a handsome $57,743,416 during the season of 1968-69, as compared with last year's record high of almost $59 million. Its additional gross of $42,601,016 for Broadway road companies in 1968-69 made the Broadway theater a better than $100 million dollar proposition overall for the second year in a row.

In the matter of playing weeks (if 10 shows play 10 weeks that's 100 playing weeks) there was also a dropoff. There were 1,209 Broadway playing weeks in 1968-69 (including 101 weeks of previews), continuing the slight but steady decline in previous seasons, from 1,295 in 1965-66, 1,269 in 1966-67 and 1,257 in 1967-68. On the bright side of this statistic, *any* playing week total in the 1,200s is exceptionally high (the record was 1,325 in 1947-48), so that in 1968-69 Broadway was still going strong with a $57 million gross that is the second-highest in its history.

To establish, briefly, a context for these production figures, let us note that 1968-69 was the season in which the box office price for the hottest weekend musical ticket leapt to $15 (for *Promises, Promises* and *Zorbá*), with tickets at the $12.50 level a commonplace. The straight-play top rose to $9.50 (for *White Hope*), and off-Broadway producers found that the traffic would bear $10 a seat at the leading small-house hits *(Dames at Sea, Adaptation/Next* and last season's *The Boys in the Band).*

Half a million bucks was the going rate for mounting a Broadway musical. The total tab for six conspicuous 1968-69 musical flops *(A Mother's Kisses, Her First Roman, Maggie Flynn, The Fig Leaves Are Falling, Billy* and *Come Summer)* amounted to $3,300,500. Straight Broadway plays were being capitalized around $100-150,000. At the same time, rising *net* profit totals had reached at least the following levels by last spring for this sampling of shows: *Hello, Dolly!* $5,886,150, *Man of La Mancha* $4,000,000, *Mame* $1,289,554, *You Know I Can't Hear You When the Water's Running* $564,763 (on an investment of $135,000), *The Price* $70,000 (on an investment of $100,000), *The Boys in the Band* $210,000 (on an off-Broadway investment of $20,000).

Of course, 1968-69 brought disappointment to some, often those of whom we have the highest expectations. Aeschylus for one, and Edward Albee for another, bombed at the Billy Rose. Esthetically, this was a season of so many plays about sex that one wished for a sexy play to come along—but none ever happened. It has been said that the realistic theater reached its full bloom when, in a restaurant scene, David Belasco caused to be placed onstage a fully operative steam table. In this season of 1968-69 the realistic theater of David Belasco seemed to be giving way to newer, more dynamic, more imaginative forms—but before the old theater vanished it was trying to get in all the nakedness and fornication omitted during the decorous Ibsen-Chekhov-Belasco decades. Like an aged roue trying everything once before the end comes, the theater in 1968-69 dallied in the copulatory antics of men and women, men and men, women and women, men and animals. Belasco can rest in peace— it was all done, all literally represented, and with real steam coming up. The only thing was, the truly sexy play never arrived.

A less conspicuous but probably more vital development in the theater esthetic was this business of direct playwright-to-audience and actor-to-audience communication in the theater. The living stage is trying to make the most of the unique characteristic that sets it apart from movies and TV: the audience and the play are physically present *together* in the theater, *living*. Instead of pretending that an invisible fourth wall separates the two, the theater of 1968-69 was pulling down not only the invisible wall but the other three walls of the setting as well, binding the play and the audience into a single intense unit of experience within the four walls of the playhouse.

Thus the script of *The Great White Hope* contains passage after passage, line after line of dialogue underlined by the playwright with the general direction that all such lines are to be spoken *directly* by the actor to the audience— no pretense that the play is to take place independently of its witnesses. Thus Joseph Heller's *We Bombed in New Haven* is constructed as a "rehearsal" of a "play" at which the "actors" frequently appeal directly to the audience; in fact, the irony of the audience reaction, or lack of it, to the events onstage is the whole point of the script. Thus, off Broadway, *The People vs. Ranchman* broke the auditorium into blocks of seats and stages, laid out irregularly like sections of a Mondrian painting. Thus, even farther off Broadway at the Brooklyn Academy of Music, The Living Theater issued its gentle summons to the *Paradise Now* audience to shed its inhibitions (and its clothes) and enter into a whole new, anarchic but meaningful relationship of actors and audience. During the show performers and observers were gradually homogenized into one group of people, indivisible.

The transition from the theater of the uniformed maid dusting the furniture behind the invisible fourth wall, to the new theater of naked actors sitting in the audience's lap, is of course far from complete. The shining new theatrical form of our Columbus-like dreams is still far over the horizon; but in 1968-69, at least there were signs of new life floating past us in the waters of play production. It is a major disadvantage in this season of passage that the division of styles onstage tended to divide the audience. In previous 20th century decades, with a stable theatrical form, everyone knew approximately what to anticipate in a musical, comedic or dramatic evening on Broadway, and therefore each show of quality had a satisfactorily broad-based audience potential. In the theater of 1968-69, almost any individual production worth naming *(Forty Carats; Adaptation/Next)* was calculated either to entrance or offend either Aunt Hattie from Scarsdale or her hippie niece, but seldom both the same at the same production. As tastes begin to fragment, so does the size of the potential audience for any one show, forward-looking or backward-reaching. In a transition season like this, playgoers were warier than ever of finding themselves in the wrong theater. The New York *Times* drama reviewer, with his virtual monopoly on directing audience traffic because of the paper's position in the New York area, had an ever weightier *negative* influence than ever on the success factor of each production. (His *positive* influence was less certain; for example, his enthusiasm could not drive the Broadway theatergoer to Theater 1969's repertory of Albee and Beckett revivals, nor to the sex-play one-acters *Lovers and Other Strangers.*)

As a result of taste fragmentation, of *Times*-watching and of other factors this season, several inventive and richly endowed shows failed to attract the attention that they might deserve in the healthiest of all possible theatrical environments. Herb Gardner's *The Goodbye People,* for example, though handicapped with a slow-starting first half, built into one of the most poignant experiences of the season, not only in its writing but also in Milton Berle's portrayal of an aged Coney Island concessionaire determined to do or die in making a comeback with the grand opening on the beach—in February—of a hot dog stand.

In many cases where the footprints of Prometheus clearly showed, as in *The Goodbye People,* the public failed to get excited. Don Petersen's excellent play *Does a Tiger Wear a Necktie?* deserved a much longer run than the 39 performances it received. So did Lanford Wilson's 5-performance *The Gingham Dog,* with George Grizzard's shattering portrayal of a Southerner in despair at the failure of his marriage to a Harlem Negro. Perhaps the greatest loss to the 1968-69 Broadway theatergoer was his failure to find out in time that the Tom Jones-Harvey Schmidt *Celebration* was one of the rare new experiences of the Broadway musical's rapidly developing art/entertainment form. The book of *Celebration* is a fable about a lad who wants permission to plant a garden in the yard of a demolished church, of which he has been able to rescue only the Eye of God (a symbol of the sun) from the heap of shattered stained glass. A rich roue competes with the boy for the attention of a venal young dancer who wants it all no matter what she has to do to get it. This triangle is compressed on all its sides by the schemes of a vagrant philosopher, played by Keith Charles. *Celebration's* lyrics are strongly poetic. It suffers its moments of cynicism and despair, even of ugliness, but its theme of regeneration always finds the upbeat ("beneath the snow/there's a tiny seed/ and it's gonna grow!"). Vernon Lusby's choreography illustrated each sardonic turn of the fable, and the design was a visual marvel of symbolic scenery, costumes and gargoyle masks by Ed Wittstein.

Like *Man of La Mancha* in its early weeks, which it somewhat resembles in mood, *Celebration* struggled forward in an effort to find its audience. It was urged on by the enthusiasm of a few major critics and it also basked in loud and joyful applause from the members of the public who half-filled its auditorium—but it could survive no more than 109 performances. Lack of public information and/or appreciation of a worthwhile show is the worst that can happen in any theater season. Underneath all the affluent statistics and eager esthetic hopes and dreams of 1968-69, there was a mushy layer of doubt, of unwarranted skepticism. Playgoers lacked the spirit of adventure in a rather adventurous season, and this cost the theater the full appreciation of some of its best work.

Broadway

Exactly half the Best Plays made the hit list. Irish playwright Brian Friel made it early with his second Best Play in three seasons: *Lovers* in the Dublin Gate Theater production, with Art Carney added to the cast, which had its American premiere at the Vivian Beaumont during the summer festivities and then moved downtown to the Music Box. *Lovers* was billed as "A Play in Two Parts," but it was more like a pair of one-acters with separate characters, joined by the same Commentator. In the first playlet, *Winners,* two young lovers appear on a sunny Irish hilltop the day before their wedding in an idyll of schoolboy and schoolgirl youth on the very threshold of maturity and eager to begin the future. Meanwhile the Commentator (Carney) is reading from his newspaper that in some way, no one knows exactly, the two lovers (played in exuberant high spirits by Dublin Gate's own Fionnuala Flanagan and Eamon Morrissey) were drowned on the lake that perfect afternoon. They are "Winners" drowned at their moment of greatest joy, in a skillful mood piece which participates in the newest stylistic trend in expressing the sorrowful events *directly to the audience* in the words of an observer.

In Friel's second playlet, *Losers,* the Commentator tells us of his own courtship, marriage and war of wills with his wife's invalid mother. It is a hilarious struggle for command of the household in which the devout old woman recruits the very saints to her cause. The husband can win a battle or two, but inevitably he cannot win the war against this subtle woman. In this playlet the Commentator is more than just a link between the audience and events. He is up to his neck in the play, but he keeps coming "outside" the house to report to the audience on how he thinks he is doing. The two halves of *Lovers* show Friel exercising his previously established (in *Philadelphia, Here I Come!*) ability to draw accurate sketches of vulnerable human beings, both comic and poignant.

The second hit from abroad was *Hadrian VII,* another outstanding British play with a like performance by Alec McCowen as a penniless misfit whose many efforts to enter the priesthood have been frustrated. He imagines himself the first British Pope in hundreds of years—and what a pontiff he makes of himself, a veritable John XXIII, in his efforts to pull the vainglorious princes of the church back to the first principles of their shepherd's duty. Peter Luke's play is based on the life and works of a debatable turn-of-the-century literary figure named Frederick Rolfe (alias Baron Corvo) who wrote the original version of this daydream as a novel, *Hadrian the Seventh,* and who appears as the leading character of the play. Rolfe was indeed rejected for the priesthood several times, and *Hadrian VII* represents a breakout of frustrated dedication, a dream in compensation for the reality of failure. The final irony of the play is that even in his imaginings Rolfe's enemies penetrate the Vatican and destroy him. *Hadrian* is a playwriting debut and a most successful one, an almost noble dramatic treatment of spirituality.

The most conspicuous success of the year, however, was not foreign but American: the Critics, Pulitzer and Tony Award-winning *The Great White Hope,* the Broadway debut of its author Howard Sackler and the vehicle for a magnificent performance—that of James Earl Jones as Jack Jefferson, a Negro heavyweight boxer who reaches the fistic heights of the world championship, only to be pulled inexorably down by the unanswerable gravity of American racial prejudice. Both play and performance were polished in a regional theater production last season at the Arena Stage in Washington, D.C., and they reached Broadway in gleaming condition. Sackler's script (which, as previously noted, addresses itself to the audience frequently in single lines of dialogue or elaborate setpieces) is written mostly in blank verse rhythm and has a narrative flow through nineteen scenes in the United States, Europe, Mexico and Cuba. Its events were suggested by the real-life career of the black heavyweight Jack Johnson in America's extrovert period before and during World War I. The role of Jack Jefferson is written in colorful dialect and is spoken boldly by the actor Jones as though language like ring challengers were something to be conquered by force. What the New York boxing crowd, chagrined at finding a black man wearing the champion's belt, does about the situation is the story told in this play: how they hound the champion out of the country with trumped-up charges—he has accompanied his white mistress across a state line. They plunge him into poverty, despair and spiritual depletion, to the point at which he quarrels with his love and drives her to suicide. With all love and pride gone, he agrees to throw a fight to the newest White Hope. The black champion bloodies his white challenger savagely in the Havana ring in one last gesture of animal defiance before taking the arranged dive and accepting his ignoble fate, made to seem all the more piercingly unfair in contrast to Jones's noble, larger-than-life portrayal. Jane Alexander's performance of the loving and faithful-unto-death companion was also one of the season's best. The play spoke to 1968-69 audiences directly, not only in the dialogue directed outward by the playwright, but also in its deepest dramatic voice: it is not somebody else's prejudice which is an object of terror here, making the fighter an object of pity, but *our* prejudice, deep rooted in the past and hard as ever to kill in the present. It wasn't only one of our heroes, but our own villainy too that came under dramatic examination in *The Great White Hope,* the year's outstanding play.

Another Best Play on the hit list was *Forty Carats,* a finely-honed comedy adapted by Jay Allen from a French script by Pierre Barillet and Jean-Pierre Gredy, whose *Cactus Flower* was a Broadway hit three seasons ago. In this new one, Julie Harris plays a divorcee of 40 who at first enjoys, then resists, then finally succumbs to the attentions of a handsome, knowledgeable and persistent young man in his 20s. Every possibility of this May-August wooing is developed with a smooth interworking of script, performance and direction, the latter by Abe Burrows who also wrote and directed *Cactus Flower* and whose name is a very synonym of comedic skill.

The two other comedies on the hit list, *Jimmy Shine* and *Play It Again, Sam* were one-man shows of performance and personality. The man in *Jimmy Shine* was The Graduate, Dustin Hoffman, playing a born loser who accepts his status as an unsuccessful abstract painter with good humor and only slightly tarnished hope. This Murray Schisgal script is a series of episodes in which the loser goes back over his life remembering its major emotional crises, and there are times when mere words are inadequate for Jimmy Shine—he must express himself in songs (written for the play by John Sebastian). Like The Graduate, Jimmy is a generally inexpert but eager lover, and of course Dustin Hoffman made the most of this characteristic on the stage, as he did on the screen in the Mike Nichols movie.

The man in *Play It Again, Sam* was Woody Allen, also playing a loser-lover, in a script of his own fabrication. The role Allen cut out for himself was that of a movie critic whose wife has left him and who imagines that he is coached by an embodiment of Humphrey Bogart into seducing his best friend's wife. Romantically speaking, he is a mouse that finally roars. The mild-mannered antihero personified by Hoffman and Allen, the Jimmy-Sam figure of a shuffle-footed, daydreaming lover may be a kind of comic backlash from the wham-bam-thank-you-mam lover in most fiction of this James Bond era. At any rate, in two versions he was instantly popular on Broadway this season.

Broadway's musical writers came out of the 1967-68 inertia with a glorious fanfare of musical successes in 1968-69, one of them a Best Play. This was *1776*, the year's happiest surprise, a successful musicalization of the debate in the Second Continental Congress that led to signing of the Declaration of Independence (I know this sounds theatrically implausible but it's a fact). This wonderful show, with book by Peter Stone and music and lyrics by Sherman Edwards, is like no other before it, demonstrating again that the musical form developed on Broadway in the past 50 years is only beginning to realize its full potential. *1776* is no song-and-dance show, it is a drama of ideas with the interplay of characters and events leading toward a climax in which John Adams, Benjamin Franklin and Thomas Jefferson sacrifice their deepest beliefs about equality in order to gain the necessary unanimous vote for independence. When the political maneuvering becomes too emotionally intense for mere words, *1776* breaks into song—as when a young soldier of Washington's army tries to explain what it was like at Lexington and Concord. William Daniels's portrayal of the waspish John Adams was the best musical performance of the year, and many other *1776* contributions were outstanding including Jo Mielziner's single thrust-stage set representing the Congress but adjustable for moving the action out into Philadelphia occasionally; Patricia Zipprodt's costumes; Peter Hunt's direction, and so many of the performances that it seems almost unfair to single out Howard Da Silva's Franklin as the best of a uniformly interesting group. The emotional heat generated by this musical about a political debate is amazing—all the more so because when you entered the theater you knew how it was going to come out. After half an hour of *1776*, however, you weren't so sure. And finally you were made to understand that it didn't come out quite as red, white and blue as you thought it did.

Finally on the list of hits and probable hits were the season's two blockbuster expense-account ($15 a ticket at the box office for weekend evenings) musicals, both with subject matter fresh in the minds of movie fans: *Promises, Promises* based on the script of the Jack Lemmon comedy *The Apartment*, and *Zorbá* based on the same novel as the movie *Zorba the Greek*. Both shows were superbly produced, the first by David Merrick and the second by Harold Prince; both were imaginatively directed, the first by Robert Moore and the second by its producer; and each package contained elements of theater artistry that ranked among the top achievements of the season: the Burt Bacharach-Hal David score of *Promises* and its leading performance by Jerry Orbach, the Boris Aronson setting for *Zorbá* and the supporting performances of Maria Karnilova and Lorraine Serabian. Neil Simon salted *Promises* with the cool humor of the 1960s and Joseph Stein colored *Zorbá* red with primitive passion and motivation. In Miss Serabian's function as a Greek chorus leader cynically warning lovers to love fiercely because death comes early, Zorbá reached its emotional peak on exactly the same mountain *Cabaret* climbed with a male counterpart, the skull-faced emcee played by Joel Grey. In *Promises,* the Orbach performance of a Neil Simon character can't be denied its full measure of humor and style, yet the comic despair of business executives lacking a place for a 4 p.m. assignation seems somewhat pale in a season which has freely offered us (in Terrence McNally's *Sweet Eros*) the vision of a man tying a woman to a chair and stripping her preparatory to rape. The trouble with *Promises* and *Zorbá* is that they are deja vu in subject matter, specifically and generically, and in concept of what a Broadway musical should be.

This is not to quarrel with their success. Consider how dismal the theater season often seemed last year, when there was no handsome *Promises, Promises* or *Zorbá* to glamorize Broadway. Our theater needs all of its ingredients for a season of full, rich flavor; it needs the expense-account musicals as well as the dynamically original Best Plays and the way-out off-Broadway hits. The producers of these big 1968-69 musicals, David Merrick and Harold Prince, have contributed enormously to the most subtle progress of their art form in past years, and they will both do so again; maybe next year. Meanwhile they also make important contributions to the New York theater and its audiences by providing such entertainments as *Promises, Promises* and *Zorbá.*

One of the Best Plays from regional theater was *In the Matter of J. Robert Oppenheimer,* which marks the return of the Repertory Theater of Lincoln Center to this particular winner's circle for the first time since the Kazan-Whitehead era. This documentary play about Oppenheimer's security-clearance hearing during the McCarthy era of accusation and mistrust was written by a German playwright, Heinar Kipphardt, translated by Ruth Speirs and mounted in an American premiere by Center Theater Group in Los Angeles under the direction of Gordon Davidson, with Joseph Wiseman in the title role. Davidson directed the play in New York, with Wiseman repeating his portrayal of the angular, enigmatic physicist "Father of the Atom Bomb," so that Lincoln Center was playing host to the West Coast production. It proved a most distinguished guest; a tangle of intellectual positions and at the same time a taut courtroom-like drama echoing to the distant thunder of Alamogordo and Eniwetok.

Kipphardt's countryman, Rolf Hochhuth, has attracted much attention in recent years with his "documentary" plays in which the facts of history are rearranged, or juxtaposed, so as to form a propagandistic cop-out for Nazi guilt. Kipphardt's play is nothing of *that* sort. His search for some kind of truth within the weedy testimony of the Oppenheimer hearing seems inspired by curiosity rather than preconviction. Kipphardt is not trying so much to point a moral as to dramatize a conflict of moral values, and he has succeeded in this play. Certainly it is limited in scope, even with newsreel and other footage projected on screens behind its confining hearing-room setting. But in this modern theater where plays are being aimed more directly at the audience, the direct-testimony method of courtroom drama does not seem as static as it might once have seemed—particularly when expressed in the carefully-reasoned form of *In the Matter of J. Robert Oppenheimer.*

One last backward glance over the list of Best Plays reminds us that the scarcity of so-called "serious" drama, deplored by so many observers of New

York theater in the earlier 1960s, seems to have ended. *Oppenheimer* may not be tragedy in the classical sense, but it is totally serious-minded as it addresses its audience. Half of *Lovers* is a tragic idyll (the sheer high spirits of the lovers on this day of days will make them careless with a rowboat and bring them to destruction). And different kinds of semi-tragic heroes are victimized in the losing struggles of *The Great White Hope, Hadrian VII, The Man in the Glass Booth* and *No Place To Be Somebody.* A serious Best Play from abroad was *The Man in the Glass Booth,* with which the well-known stage and screen actor Robert Shaw made his debut as a playwright with the drama of a rich and powerful German-born American Jewish millionaire who for reasons of his own decides to pose as an Eichmann-like ex-Nazi. Played with ferocity and a twist of irony by Donald Pleasence, this onetime concentration camp victim frames himself as a Nazi war criminal and permits himself to be kidnaped to Israel for trial, for the most noble of reasons: he wants to honor the memory of the Nazis' victims with the sacrifice of himself. Posing as a Nazi who is unregenerate, remorseless, even boastful of his viciousness, he is giving his fellow Jewish victims the ideal villain of their most horrible nightmares, the villain they need to exorcise their hatred, instead of the apologists and buck-passers that they have seen in the courtrooms. His disguise is penetrated before the sacrifice can be consummated, but not before many powerfully prodding reminders not only of Nazi villainy but also of the need for continuing vigilance against any kind of repetition.

Another important drama this season was *Does a Tiger Wear a Necktie?,* a series of episodes presenting the hang-ups of juvenile drug addicts in detention "on an island in a river bordering on a large industrial city"—and the painted skyline behind the setting had the Gothic-arched look of New York Hospital viewed from Welfare Island. The episodes were tied together in Don Petersen's play (his first full-length work) by the character of an English teacher, played by Hal Holbrook, trying to offer his teen-aged pupils adult help without increasing their tensions. He even manages to establish a form of communication with an unregenerate tough-guy addict named Bickham—a name worth remembering because it is the role that provided the Broadway acting debut of Al Pacino (just as Sage McRae is the name of the character Marlon Brando was portraying when he walked onto the Broadway stage in *Truckline Cafe* in 1946). We have seen Pacino before—last year for example as the bully in *The Indian Wants the Bronx*—but in *Tiger* we saw him clearly as an electrifying acting talent. He was authentic in the ultimate degree in the play's most demanding scene, a virtual monologue, in which Bickham describes his great expectations of a first meeting with his long-gone father and his emotionally devastating shock and disappointment when the meeting actually took place. The scene itself is worthy of Pacino's performance and vice versa. Petersen's *Tiger* can be faulted on grounds of continuity, but never in regard to insight or empathy. The great majority of the theater audience which failed to attend one of *Tiger's* scant 39 performances missed what may be one of the most memorable playwriting-acting Broadway debuts of this era.

Other noteworthy efforts at dramatizing "serious" matters were the aforementioned *The Goodbye People* and *The Gingham Dog;* Leonard Spigelgass's *The Wrong Way Light Bulb* which dramatized today's slum-area frictions in the example of an apartment dwelling, formerly in an upper middle class Jewish neighborhood, now being taken over by upward-striving blacks and

Puerto Ricans, another play that deserved wider attention than it received; and William Gibson's *A Cry of Players,* viewing a young Elizabethan named "Will" in growing revolt against his squire's authority and his wife's emotional possessiveness, until finally he breaks away and runs off with a group of strolling players, dropping out of life and into the theater. Jack Gelber's *The Cuban Thing* was an effort to come to terms on the stage with the Castro movement. It attracted more attention in the streets than in the theater, stirring up anti-Castro agitators but closing after only one performance. John Roc's *Fire!* was an allegorical drama which searched the human spirit and sometimes found itself gazing into hell. Jerome Weidman's *The Mother Lover* also explored the darker areas of the human spirit in a triangular arrangement of mother, son and call girl; so did Lyle Kessler's *The Watering Place* in presenting the impact of a returning Vietnam War veteran on a dead friend's neurotic family; both the latter plays for only one performance each. Laird Koenig's *The Dozens* attempted a comment on the black link between Africa and America in the incident of a night club singer, her ineffectual husband and a fugitive African leader spending a night together. Julius J. Epstein's *But Seriously . . .* concerned itself with the marital and character tensions of a Hollywood writer —on the edge of comedy, except that the writer wept often. And finally, a musical based on Herman Melville's dire Billy Budd story, *Billy,* was the fourth of this season's Broadway shows to last only a single performance.

Of the season's 30 new plays in English, only eight billed themselves in the program as comedy. As an identifying label, this word "comedy" is like the little girl with the curl in the middle of her forehead in the nursery rhyme. *Forty Carats* was very, very good, and toward the end of the season Phoebe and Henry Ephron's *My Daughter, Your Son* invented a pleasant fancy about the planning of a full-scale wedding for the daughter of a screen writer and the son of a mid-Western dentist (and of course the happy couple has been living together in New York for months), with Robert Alda, Vivian Vance, Dody Goodman and Bill McCutcheon having a TV situation-comedy field day with the roles of the quivering parents. But the other six 1968-69 comedies were something else: *Lovers and Other Strangers,* an assortment of one-acters about married or soon-to-be-married couples' emotional hang-ups; *Woman Is My Idea,* about love among the Salt Lake City Mormons of the Brigham Young era; *The Sudden and Accidental Re-Education of Horse Johnson,* in which an average guy tries to study up on how to change the world; *Zelda,* about a world-ending hurricane of the same name (that's what we call *comedy*); and two British imports, *The Flip Side* about wife-swapping and *Rockefeller and the Red Indians,* a spoof of Westerns.

Where the theater has exerted its most vital energy in recent seasons has been in that mysterious area between nominal drama and nominal comedy— the area of *Rosencrantz and Guildenstern Are Dead* and *A Day in the Death of Joe Egg* and *Marat/Sade* and *A Delicate Balance* and this season the area of Joseph Heller's *We Bombed in New Haven* and Edward Albee's *Box* and *Quotations from Chairman Mao Tse-Tung (Box-Mao-Box).* Neither of these two new works was nearly as effective as the best of this genre in recent seasons; 1968-69 was not a vintage year for greyish comedy. Albee's newest work was incomprehensible (to me); not only because it failed to communicate during the time it played in the theater, but also because I cannot sense its creative purpose; I touch the wire and am convinced that it is cold. *Box-Mao-*

Box's curtain went up on an empty stage, set with the open frame of a boxlike cube. A recorded voice (Ruth White's in this production) made a protracted philosophical statement while the stage remained empty. Then four characters came on: an actor in a fixed-smile Mao mask who walked the aisles reciting chosen sayings of the Chinese leader, an emotionally disturbed woman (Nancy Kelly) in a deck chair who told a silent clergyman the most intimate secrets of her unfortunate marriage, and behind them a gaunt, elderly woman who recited the poem "Over the Hill to the Poorhouse"—and meanwhile, segments of the recorded voice were repeated. There was a kind of orchestration to this, of voices that differed in timbre, and a literary orchestration in styles of language that were as different as the tonality of instruments. But as far as I can determine there is no theme and (let's remember where we are) no theatrical gratification of any kind.

Joseph Heller's *We Bombed in New Haven* communicated more clearly; in fact, it is one of those plays in the newly-developing form. It not only made its appeal directly to the audience but also cast the audience in a major role. The spectators are the fall guys of this piece. The jokes in this comedy are not on the characters, but on *you.* The characters aren't supposed to be real, anyway, they are actors rehearsing a play about an American bombing squadron that goes on absurd missions like the bombing of Minneapolis. The squadron commander (Jason Robards) keeps stepping out of character to reassure the audience that the actors aren't really being killed on these missions, just "written out" of the story. The events of the play are *only* a story (Robards keeps reassuring us). This should be obvious—because (the squadron commander points out) if these events were real, if young Americans were *really* being sent off on bombing missions to kill or be killed, you, the audience, would rise up out of your seats to stop it, *wouldn't you?* That's the irony of *We Bombed in New Haven,* so that the presence of the audience to be reassured and not to act is absolutely essential to the point and performance of the play. If that isn't playing an active part in an evening of theater, I don't know what is. Heller's play is one-joke irony, and its incidents are repetitive, but it was one of the season's noteworthy events simply because of its contemporary style and highly relevant subject matter.

A couple of programs of dark-comedy one-acters provided noteworthy high spots. Within *Morning, Noon and Night,* a trio of one-acters, Terrence McNally's *Noon* was a joke at the expense of sex deviates. In it, a group of weirdos with totally different hang-ups have been summoned to the same rendezvouz, under the false pretenses of a mysterious caller, just for the mischief of placing lions and tigers and bears in the same cage to see what happens. John Guare's *Cop-Out* presented a pair of saw-toothed sketches. The first was a post-World War I skit about the generations of a German family in various stages of "passing" as Americans in America. The second was a series of two-character sketches of the violence and neurosis of the day, ending up with the man shooting the woman "dead" in the aisle of the theater. There she remained, so that the audience had to step across the "dead" actress on the way home.

In the elephant graveyard of Broadway production where the massive no-hit musicals go to die, there is left behind the occasional lingering memory of a tune, a performance or a design to show that the great beasts existed. *Dear World,* for example, can be remembered for Angela Lansbury's performance of Giradoux's Madwoman of Chaillot in musical version, and also for the title number, a standout show tune by Jerry Herman. The British musical *Canterbury Tales* was handsomely designed in lively colors by Loudon Sainthill. Underneath the fine feathers, though, was a jade of bawdy affectation, often in doubtful taste. Only one of the also-ran musicals left Broadway wishing it had stayed longer. This was *Red, White and Maddox,* a political satire which had been mounted in Atlanta, but, when Theater Atlanta lost its playhouse, became homeless and wandered north to Broadway. The show took direct aim at Georgia's onetime Pickrick Restaurant celebrity, now governor of the state, in an engaging performance by Jay Garner as Lester Maddox. Among the other mammoths (as previously noted, they cost their producers $3,300,500 in their aggregate of failure), one, *A Mother's Kisses,* folded out of town. Four others—*Her First Roman* (17), *The Fig Leaves Are Falling* (4), *Come Summer* (7) and *Billy* (1)—played a total of 29 performances. A sixth, *Maggie Flynn,* struggled for 81 performances through a story about a New York City orphanage in the Draft Riot days of the Civil War. The songs of *Maggie Flynn* linger in memory, however: "The Thank You Song," "Mr. Clown" and the title number from an admirable score.

The season's single revue, *Noel Coward's Sweet Potato,* compiled songs, sketches and play scenes from the work of the master. It seemed thin-blooded. The year's specialty shows included, besides Miss Dietrich, two unusual musical opportunities: Gilbert Becaud from France in a solo appearance, and a staged revival meeting called *Trumpets of the Lord,* with soaring gospel hymns. Then there was a silent show, the sign-language theater of The National Theater of the Deaf, which visited Broadway. A hypnotist, Sam Vine, appeared in a Broadway house for 7 performances of an audience-participation show called *The World's a Stage.*

Among the season's foreign-language exhibits the standout was the Compagnie du Théâtre de la Cité de Villeurbanne's camp version of *The Three Musketeers,* with antic stagecraft and performances adding tart modern flavors to the smooth old tale of d'Artagnan and Anne of Austria's diamonds. René Allio's kinetic scenery, including a stormy English Channel devised out of blue gauze, was a delightful and integral part of the action. The Compagnie also revived *George Dandin* and *Tartuffe.* An Israeli musical, *The Megilla of Itzik Manger,* which transposed the Bible story of the Book of Esther to a modern Middle European village, came around twice—once for its premiere and again for a return engagement. Finally, there was the lively Spanish zarzuela production *Fiesta in Madrid* at City Center.

Revivals

It was an outstanding revival season in the large number of plays brought out of the library and in the expertise of their airing. Perversely, it was also a season which found many partly subsidized producing organizations in deep trouble from insufficient support.

Among 1968-69's 23 revival programs (as compared with 16 last year and 32 the year before) there crackled the electric presence of an all-star production of *The Front Page* and an angry-young-man *Hamlet.* This year it wasn't all Gilbert and Sullivan (though we enjoyed our biennial visit from the incomparable D'Oyly Carte), it wasn't all Molière (though we had outstanding productions of *The Miser* by Lincoln Center Repertory and *The Misanthrope* by APA-Phoenix). This season we had Beckett too, and Albee, and T.S. Eliot; we had *West Side Story* at Lincoln Center's New York State Theater and *My Fair Lady* and *Carnival* at City Center.

This year, as last, Hamlet was very much a presence on New York stages, no doubt because the hung-up young Prince of Denmark relates in some way to today's hung-up youth. The under-30s of 1969 may or may not be confused, threatened, overprivileged, underloved, etc., but there is no doubt that they dig Shakespeare. During the past two New York seasons, while Zeffirelli's movie *Romeo and Juliet* was packing in the youngsters, Prince Hamlet was under continuous stage scrutiny, exposed to camp in the Joseph Papp production and portrayed eerily as a member of a hostile Establishment in *Rosencrantz and Guildenstern Are Dead*. This year we had Ellis Rabb emphasizing the paralizing effect of the Prince's inner conflict in the APA-Phoenix production, and we had Nicol Williamson's much-discussed *Hamlet* played as though John Osborne had both written and directed the tragedy, with the Prince as a nasal whiner, a lip-curler, shouting in accents strange to American ears but clearly not acquired at Elsinore or even Wittenberg. Played as a used-car salesman with a real grievance against the loan company (and played thus with brilliant accuracy by Williamson, who is one of our most accomplished actors), Hamlet descends to a level at which his emotional equipment is too flimsy for grand passion. The most understandable element of this production was the confusion of Ophelia, Gertrude, Polonius and Claudius as to what could possibly ail this sulky stranger-in-their-midst. The angry-young-man *Hamlet* didn't work onstage, but the season was more interesting because it was tried by so gifted an artist as Nicol Williamson.

The revival hit of the season was Harold J. Kennedy's staging of the Ben Hecht-Charles MacArthur 1928 newspaper play *The Front Page* with an all-star cast that included Robert Ryan as the managing editor, Bert Convy as Hildy Johnson, Katharine Houghton as Hildy's fiancee, John McGiver as Chicago's mayor and the selfsame Mr. Kennedy as Bensinger, the Chicago *Tribune* reporter. Kennedy's performance as well as his direction left us wishing he would visit Broadway more often than each decade or so. Kennedy put on *The Front Page* as though every nuance of political chicanery, every sharp tilt of a reporter's sarcasm was right out of today's headlines and press room instead of the 1920s. Two seasons ago APA-Phoenix proved you don't have to have a depression to appreciate the quixotic essence of *You Can't Take It With You,* and the same held true for *The Front Page.* The Hecht-MacArthur kind of reporter who would trade his mother-in-law for a good story and his fiancee for a page one byline went out long ago with the advent of the suburban-living wage and the public relations handout. But *The Front Page* remains insistently alive, and played on its own terms it was a delight.

The Hecht-MacArthur play was produced by Theater 1969 (Richard Barr, Edward Albee and Charles Woodward) as a kind of fund-raiser for the group's program of developing new playwriting talent. Previously in the season, Theater 1969 tried to mount repertory on Broadway (at the Billy Rose) without success. Their schedule began with Albee's new work *Box-Mao-Box* and then went on to revivals of some of the most distinguished works of the new theater: Albee's *The Death of Bessie Smith, The Zoo Story* and *The American*

Dream and Samuel Beckett's *Happy Days* and *Krapp's Last Tape*. The presence of such scripts as these on Broadway might cause some future historian of the theater to guess that in 1968-69 we were enjoying a period of cultural sophistication. He would be wrong. Despite an encouraging press, Theater 1969 Playwrights Repertory found no audience and closed early, leaving the Broadway scene the richer for its presence on the record and the poorer for its departure from the stage.

It was an economically troublesome year. Both subsidies and audiences were coming tough. The clamor from the ghettos for the attention and support of Congress and the private foundations was drowning out the rational and continuing need of the performing arts for some kind of subsidy. In competition with other, more urgent human needs, the arts as a whole and the theater in particular suffered a cutting-off of funds—that's as it should be, probably, but it made for long faces in the Green Room. For example, APA-Phoenix lost an expected $250,000 from the National Endowment owing to Congressional cutbacks, and this automatically deprived the troupe of another $250,000 in matching grants from the Ford Foundation. At the same time, the expected massive response of supposedly culturally-oriented America to good retrospective theater never materialized—not in New York, anyway. In New York, the culturally-oriented theater audience wants the same thing the tired business man wants: hits.

Thus, for want of a 1968-69 hit the APA-Phoenix was lost to Broadway in April, possibly permanently. In the past two seasons the popularity of *You Can't Take It With You* and then of *The Show-Off* had helped keep them going. This year APA-Phoenix brought back *The Show-Off* with *Pantagleize* for a brief fall engagement in repertory, but later in the season it could not find a hit among its four new productions. Personally, I looked forward to seeing Eliot's *The Cocktail Party* again; but I can't say that the APA's production was equal to the high-tension inferences of the script. Equally, *Cock-A-Doodle Dandy, Hamlet* and a well-executed *The Misanthrope* failed to stir the interest of the town. With no outside help in sight after a losing season, the APA-Phoenix now plans to split at the hyphen. The APA (Association of Producing Artists under Rabb's direction) will return to the University of Michigan. The Phoenix will go its own way, possibly as an adjunct to a university theater and/or an off-Broadway operation.

The Repertory Theater of Lincoln Center was also reported to be in financial difficulty, in a season in which it took great strides esthetically. Members of its company worked in both the showcase Vivian Beaumont Theater and its experimental basement Forum Theater (classified in these pages as an off-Broadway house). Each theater opened its season with two productions alternating in repertory: the Beaumont with *King Lear* and William Gibson's new *A Cry of Players,* and the Forum with John White's *Bananas,* which used reminiscences of burlesque as a vehicle for satire, and Charles Dizenzo's one-act play program *An Evening for Merlin Finch.* The outstanding element of these shows was Lee J. Cobb's performance of Lear, but they certainly opened Lincoln's Center's season with a bang of progressive programming. The memorable evening came later, with *In the Matter of J. Robert Oppenheimer.* The fourth and final production in the big theater was a very well-received staging of *The Miser,* ending the year with a classical flourish.

At the Forum, too, the season progressed from strength to strength. Follow-

The 1968-69 Season off Broadway

PLAYS (55)

Daddy Goodness
Futz!
An Ordinary Man
Another City, Another Land
Before I Wake
American Place:
  The Cannibals
  Trainer, Dean, Liepolt & Co.
  Boy on Straight-Backed Chair
Papp
Don't Shoot Mable
People vs. Ranchman
The David Show
Triple Play
The Grab Bag
Public Theater:
  Huui, Huui
  Cities in Bezique
  Invitation to a Beheading
  NO PLACE TO BE SOMEBODY
Sweet Eros & Witness
Papers
Possibilities
Forum Theater:
  Bananas
  An Evening for Merlin Finch
  The Year Boston Won the Pennant

Big Time Buck White
Americana Pastorale
Lemonade & The Autograph Hound
Beclch
Negro Ensemble:
  "God Is a (Guess What?)"
  Ceremonies in Dark Old Men (2 productions)
  An Evening of One Acts
  Yes Yes No No
Geese
Shoot Anything with Hair
ADAPTATION/NEXT
Open 24 Hours
Corner of the Bed
Frank Gagliano's City Scene
Stop, You're Killing Me
The Perfect Party
World War 2½
Lime Green Khaki Blue
God Bless You, Harold Fineberg
Someone's Comin' Hungry
War Games
The Honest-to God Schnozzola

A Home Away From
The Triumph of Robert Emmet
In the Bar of a Tokyo Hotel
De Sade Illustrated
Pets
Exhibition
Spiro Who?
The Transgressor Rides Again
Arf & The Great Airplane Snatch

SPECIALTIES (7)

The Fourth Wall
Walk Together Children
Chad Mitchell
The Wizard of Oz
To Be Young, Gifted and Black
An Evening with Max Morath
Make Me Disappear

MUSICALS (11)

Frere Jacques
The Happy Hypocrite
Month of Sundays
How To Steal an Election
Just for Love
Up Eden
Ballad for a Firing Squad
Dames at Sea
Horseman, Pass By
Get Thee to Canterbury
Peace

REVUES (2)

Now
Walk Down Mah Street!

FOREIGN PLAYS IN ENGLISH (7)

The Empire Builders
Tea Party and The Basement
The Inner Journey
Tango
Spitting Image
Man With the Flower in His Mouth
Philosophy in the Boudoir

REVIVALS (11)

Song of the Lusitanian Bogey (return eng.)
N.Y. Shakespeare:
  Henry IV, Part 1
  Henry IV, Part 2
  Romeo and Juliet
A Moon for the Misbegotten
In Circles (return eng.)
The Firebugs
Winnie the Pooh

Little Murders
The Millionairess
Of Thee I Sing

FOREIGN-LANGUAGE PRODUCTIONS (10)

Atelje 212:
  The Progress of Bora
  Ubu Roi
  Who's Afraid of Virginia Woolf?
  Victor
Die Brücke:
  Minna von Barnhelm
  Das Schloss
Piraikon Theatron:
  Iphigenia in Aulis
  Hippolytus
Tréteau de Paris:
  Quoat-Quoat
  Pique-Nique and Guernica

Plays listed in CAPITAL LETTERS have been designated Best Plays of 1968-69.
Plays listed in italics were still running June 1, 1969.

ing its two-play repertory, the Forum offered the American premiere of James Hanley's *The Inner Journey,* a dark study of tensions within a family of vaudevillians whose son is a dwarf. Finally there was the powerful drama by John Ford Noonan, *The Year Boston Won the Pennant,* using the baseball world and a baseball hero to symbolize Everyman as a wounded hero, ringed round with hostility and crippled little by little in mind and body until he is ripe for the kill. It was one of the best offerings of the off-Broadway year, tightly directed by Tim Ward and grimly acted by Roy R. Scheider, who resembles George C. Scott in both appearance and ability, in the role of the pitcher who has lost an arm. While all of this was going on under the artistic guidance of Jules Irving and Robert Symonds, the business leadership of Lincoln Center Rep passed into the hands of Robert Montgomery, who was elected to the presidency of the company's board of directors. There are problems, but Lincoln Center's immediate future is almost certainly secure. This year, at least, the organization seemed to have struck a proper balance in programming: a new American play, a new European play, a Shakespeare and a Molière in the big theater and four new-play programs in the small one. Lincoln Center Rep is now much nearer to the goal which, in recent seasons, the APA-Phoenix approached so closely: the establishment of an exciting, versatile, permanent *American* repertory ensemble.

Broadway was also offered a glimpse of how the grass grows on the other side of the repertory fence. The Minneapolis Theater Company from the Tyrone Guthrie Theater paid a visit with *The House of Atreus,* an adaptation of Aeschylus' trilogy about Agamemnon's homecoming and its aftermath, and Bertolt Brecht's *The Resistible Rise of Arturo Ui.* They were competent revivals whose impact on Broadway was slight—but any kind of evaluation in Broadway context is meaningless. Clearly, the Guthrie troupe is a great success in its own environment, and it has no added responsibility to electrify New York audiences to whom the APA-Phoenix, Lincoln Center, City Center and all the off-Broadway organizations have been readily available.

And speaking of City Center, it too curtailed its play-producing activity this season, in which Richard Clurman was selected to fill the chairmanship of the board left vacant by the death of Morton Baum. The City Center Light Opera Company mounted two musicals with their usual flair under Jean Dalrymple's supervision, but there was no season of American play revivals and no spring season of musicals. The City Center is in a transitional period, with plans to vacate their present theater, the old Mecca Temple, and move into new, more elaborate quarters.

To sum up, revivals and repertory tend to be classified in the public mind as "culture," and culture does not sell especially well in today's New York commercial theater environment. But this year with the Albee plays, *The Front Page,* the musicals, the Molière revivals and even the oddball *Hamlet,* the enjoyment of "our cultural heritage" was often indistinguishable from the enjoyment of pure theater.

Off Broadway

If you haven't seen everything yet, you didn't get around off Broadway much this season, because they tried just about everything. Nudity was commonplace, heterosexuality was square. In Rochelle Owens's *Futz!* it was man and pig; in *Geese* it was man and man in the first one-acter, woman and woman in the second. In Terrence McNally's *Sweet Eros,* a man tied a woman to a chair and then raped her. He was only pretending, but in at least one off-off-Broadway show, *Che!,* the actors were determined to do the real thing if they found they could (at least that's what the show's publicity led us to believe). *Triple Play* and *The Grab Bag* were programs of one-acters with a variety of sex deviation, and in the full-length *Spitting Image,* imported from England, two "married" male homosexuals have a baby. In Miss Owens' *Beclch,* sadism rules as queen of the jungle, and in *Pets*—let's see, in the three one-acters of *Pets,* a female painter intimidates her model with a palette knife, an old man is tied up, robbed and teased by a couple of young women, and a woman in a cage is attacked by a man with a whip. And speaking of sadism, de Sade's own *Philosophy in the Boudoir* (a series of bedroom incidents in the education of a young girl by libertines into the purpler forms of passion) was the subject of *two* stage adaptations, one under its own name and one called *De Sade Illustrated*—illustrated with slides, that is.

In *Winnie the Pooh* as done by the Baird marionettes, the animals are all cute and the jokes all pure—but then of course this show was a *return* engagement, a throwback to the dim, distant, innocent, pre-*Hair* era of a year ago.

Once you have mentioned what these plays *do,* you have just about said it all. The naked deviates made little impression on the theater art or audiences, despite their large numbers and uninhibited nature. This year they tried almost everything, but little of it worked theatrically.

Together with the outburst of sex off Broadway in 1968-69 there was an outburst of production: 103 productions of record compared with 72 last year and 69, 66 and 73 in recent seasons (see the one-page summary accompanying this article). This total included 55 new American play programs, more than double the 24 produced on Broadway this year and the 27 produced off Broadway last year. Had it accomplished nothing else, the 1968-69 off-Broadway season distinguished itself in this large number of American playwrights given a hearing, both in individual productions and on the schedules of the various permanent groups—American Place, the Public Theater, the Negro Ensemble Company, the Forum.

But the off-Broadway season *did* boast many other accomplishments, including two Best Plays. One of these was *Adaptation/Next,* a program of two one-acters, one by Elaine May and one by Terrence McNally (surely the most-produced playwright as well as one of the best on, off and off off Broadway this season).

In Elaine May's *Adaptation,* life is a bewildering game. The contestant, being alive, must perforce compete and try to move forward on the game board's squares. But inevitably in the struggle to raise a family and find the "security square" there are penalty cards to set the player back. "This is a hard game!" gasps exhausted Gabriel Dell as the contestant, after he suffers a humiliating reverse (he's a Hilton hotel man in Chicago during the Democratic convention), his son grows up to be a long-haired hippie and his wife orders him to move to one side and not block her view of the TV screen. Don't we know that it is a hard game—but in Miss May's capsule version it ends swiftly enough for the player when he is ordered by the grinning master of ceremonies to have a heart attack right there in the appropriate square.

Terrence McNally's *Next* is played in exactly the same key, with James Coco in the role of a middle-aged movie theater manager who for some utterly unexplained and unexplainable reason has been ordered to take an Army physical exam. The broad-beamed lady technician who is to give him the exam (Elaine Shore) is not at all sensitive to his feelings of humiliation and anxiety —her job is to examine him, and she means to do it. Miss May staged McNally's playlet as well as her own to reach out as far as possible with the farcical situations, without losing a balance of sardonic comment on man as the victim of his own monstrous system, in which he must not ask "Why?" because the machine issuing the instructions isn't programmed to answer that question.

In the second of 1968-69's off-Broadway Best Plays, *No Place To Be Somebody,* as in *Adaptation/Next,* the time is Now. *No Place* came along late in the season as a sort of afterthought of Joseph Papp's New York Shakespeare Festival. After the group had tried it out during their experimental Other Stage activities, it was decided to add it to the regular indoor season as a full-scale off-Broadway presentation at the Public Theater.

This decision was on the order of Papp's decision last season to produce *Hair.* The first playwriting work of the actor-director Charles Gordone, *No Place To Be Somebody* is a stinging account of an ambitious, aggressive, ruthless—and black—owner of a bar in a West Village neighborhood controlled by white hoodlums. Characterized by its author as "a black black comedy," it is an outcry of a play, with its black characters including a poet, a thief, a ballet dancer and a whore, set in abrasive action against white characters including a busboy, an idealistic college girl, a judge, an assortment of killers and a whore. This is an uproar of a play, with explosions of violence knocking over furniture and people and explosions of language to match. The script is unique in that 90 per cent of the dialogue is punctuated with exclamation points; apparently Gordone wrote his play to be shouted. Yet this is not an angry play. The black poet addresses the audience directly, several times, on the subject of blackness and prejudice, but his mood like that of the play is more arrogant than angry; it lacks the ingredient of fear. *No Place* is acted by the most successful ensemble since last year's *The Boys in the Band,* headed by Nathan George as the bar owner, Ronnie Thompson as the seedy white busboy and Ron O'Neal as the poet, and blended so carefully that the performance of one actor who doesn't seem to know the first thing about his craft is turned into an asset of naivete. Of several good plays this year about the contemporary black condition, *No Place To Be Somebody* was clearly the most relevant and most powerful.

Another relevant, powerful drama on much this same subject was *Ceremonies in Dark Old Men,* the professional playwriting debut of Lonne Elder III with a script about an ex-vaudeville dancer, now an unsuccessful Harlem barber, whose family is inexorably pushed toward dishonest means of earning an adequate living. *Ceremonies in Dark Old Men* was produced by the Negro Ensemble Company under the artistic directorship of Douglas Turner Ward— who, under his acting name of Douglas Turner, played the barber in *Ceremonies* at the head of an ever more cohesive Negro Ensemble troupe. Other standouts in this production were David Downing as Bob; the barber's youngest, most cynical and most vulnerable son, and Samual Blue Jr. as Blue Haven, an emissary from the underworld. The barber is a man who makes mistakes but is unfailingly decent and often courageous, retaining some hope even as he moves closer and closer to tragedy. The script, written by Elder more than three years ago, is more compassionate, more direct than most of the angry-young-black-man writing of 1969. That the mood has darkened and the complexity of the problem increased in the past three years is no reflection on the play, which was staged by Edmund Cambridge to take advantage of its simplicity of construction and clarity of expression. *Ceremonies* was produced twice off Broadway this season: first in the Negro Ensemble Company's regularly-scheduled limited engagement, and again by Michael Ellis for an indefinite run in an off-Broadway house.

This season, off Broadway was developing a hit pattern of its own for those very few productions which attained the apex of the popularity pyramid. A show like last year's *The Boys in the Band* or this year's *Adaptation/Next* could raise its top price (applicable to most of the seats in the small houses) from an off-Broadway norm of $5-$7 to $10, which evidently the traffic will now bear. *Dames at Sea* entered the winner's circle with its hilarious take-off of Dick Powell-Ruby Keeler movie musicals. Like all good parodies, this George Haimsohn-Robin Miller-Jim Wise baby extravaganza paid homage to the lovable old format in the very observance of its cliches—and each and every cliche was minutely and delightfully observed in *Dames at Sea,* from the heroine's wrinkled-forehead emoting and machine-gun ferocity with the taps, to the show-biz slang and slant of the plot, with most of the action taking place "in rehearsal" and finally, lacking a theater, playing the opening performances on the deck of a convenient battleship in New York harbor. The performances were good parody, too, including those of Bernadette Peters as "Ruby" and Sally Stark standing hands on hips and tossing bleached-blonde curls and sarcasms as "Joan." The director of *Dames at Sea,* Neal Kenyon, got all his ducks in a row with their tails up, in this year's logical successor to such off-Broadway musical hits as *Your Own Thing* and *You're a Good Man Charlie Brown.*

Among the other off-Broadway musicals, a minstrel-show format based on Aristophanes' *Peace,* a campy version in which a nobleman rescues the goddess Peace from heaven and brings her home, has enjoyed a long run, owing in large part to the Al Carmines score (and the Carmines musicalization of Gertrude Stein's *In Circles* played a return engagement). *Horseman, Pass By,* a musical arrangement by Rocco Bufano and John Duffy of writings of W.B. Yeats, also attracted the attention of connoisseurs, albeit in a limited run. There was a *Canterbury Tales* musical off Broadway as well as one in 1968-69, *Get Thee to Canterbury,* but it fared not even as well as its Broadway cousin. The Mata Hari musical dropped by David Merrick out of town last year turned up this season off Broadway under the title *Ballad for a Firing Squad,* but it didn't make it in this league either.

One of the season's most effective plays in the new genre was Megan Terry's *The People vs. Ranchman,* loosely based on the Caryl Chessman case, a farcical treatment of the punishment impulse in society. Ranchman, an admitted and almost boastful rapist, looks down from the Olympian height of his jail cell upon the conflict raging below between those who agitate to free him because there isn't enough evidence against him (his victims may have been more willing than they can admit to themselves) and those who agitate to hang, electrocute and/or shoot him. The characters seethe from one part of the theater to another—the action was staged by Robert Greenwald in various parts of the auditorium, with the audience seated in blocks among the stages—everyone had at least one scene take place in his lap. In the pro-Ranchman contingent were two blacks and three hippies; anti-Ranchmanites were a soldier, a baseball player and the Girl Next Door. William Devane's performance of the grinning, unrepentant Ranchman was one of the season's standouts, as he was executed over and over again until society's urge to violence seemed far more evil than any trivial crime Ranchman might have committed.

Off Broadway also received Tennessee Williams's latest work, *In the Bar of a Tokyo Hotel,* about a painter (Donald Madden) in the final stages of failing artistic powers, and the selfish wife (Anne Meacham) who refuses to sympathize with his bewilderment. A fair amount of the Williams fire burned hotly under the surface of this play, which might have blazed into a real conflagration if the painter's suffering had been more clearly exposed to the audience's view. Instead, the wife monopolized the attention with her hang-ups, in a play that seemed wrongly balanced.

Other highlights included an outstanding revival of Jules Feiffer's *Little Murders,* a 7-performance Broadway flop two seasons back, a limited-run hit in repertory in London, and now a palpable off-Broadway hit and the standout of the year's list of 11 revivals. Somewhat rewritten for this new production, *Little Murders* found the means of communicating its farcical, bitterly ironic attitudes toward violence to New York audiences. Also present in the limelight were a pair of Harold Pinter one-acters, *Tea Party* and *The Basement,* sketches of a tired business man, and of a pair of friends conniving for the attentions of a woman; based on TV plays and providing a kind of between-meals snack of Pinter until his next swinging new play comes along. There was a program of semi-biographical writing collected from the late Lorraine Hansberry's work and presented under the title *To Be Young, Gifted and Black.* There was a popular one-man show by Max Morath accompanying himself on the piano in turn-of-the-century song numbers. There was Slawomir Mrozek's *Tango* in translation, the noted Polish playwright's comment on the nature of totalitarianism, in the form of a play about a conservative son who disapproves of his parents' extravagant behavior and tries to impose his will on them. There was a successful and popular group called *The Fourth Wall* which offered improvisations at each performance.

Of the major producers of a schedule of off-Broadway plays on a subscription basis, Joseph Papp's New York Shakespeare Festival was the most active, with a summer season of revivals outdoors in Central Park (the two *Henry IVs* and *Romeo and Juliet*) and a busy winter season indoors at the Public Theater. Papp's schedule of four new American plays included, besides *No Place To Be Somebody,* Russell McGrath's adaptation of Vladimir Nabokov's *Invitation to a Beheading,* the black comedy of a man awaiting execution by he knows not whom for he knows not what, providing yet another in the long list of Kafkaesque plays on and off Broadway this season. In his first two seasons of theater indoors, Papp has certainly distinguished himself, last year with *Hair* and a pair of interesting European scripts, this year with four new American scripts including a Best Play. Papp has steadfastly insisted on reaching out with every indoor production, instead of once in a while playing it safe. He ended his season in financial difficulty like every other enterpreneur, facing curtailment of the 1969 summer program. Nevertheless his is a highly creative performing-arts group which must be sustained somehow, even in hard and distracting times, if we are to maintain any pretense at all to culture as a spinoff of affluence.

Another of our cherished off-Broadway subscription organizations, Th American Place Theater, presented a 1968-69 schedule of four new-play programs, of which Ronald Tavel's *Boy on the Straight-Back Chair* attracted the most attention with a study of the character and motives of a young man who has committed mass murder. American Place's final production, Kenneth Cameron's *Papp* (no connection with Shakespeare Joe), was an imaginative play about religion changed into a primitive, barely recognizable form in the post-holocaust future. Still another group, Lincoln Center Repertory, as previously noted, ran a four-play schedule in its small Forum Theater, with good results.

The Negro Ensemble Company was going from strength to strength in its second year of operation. It ran through most of the summer with the late Richard Wright's adaptation of a French play about a religious charlatan, *Daddy Goodness,* presented in repertory with a return engagement of last season's *Song of the Lusitanian Bogey,* about Portuguese policies in Africa. For the new season, Negro Ensemble mounted a three-play schedule which included *Ceremonies in Dark Old Men,* plus a program of one-acters, and Ray McIver's *"God Is a (Guess What?)"*—you guessed it, in this manifestation He is black. All these works had themes of and attitudes toward blackness, as the Negro Ensemble continued to work toward the creation of a permanent black ensemble for the performance of black-oriented plays.

Elsewhere in the off-Broadway pot-pourri there was, among the new American plays, an effort to express the new generation's goals and discontents in the mouths of three college-student characters in *Spiro Who?* Among specialties, there was a cheerful and imaginative new Baird marionette show. *The Wizard of Oz.* Among revivals, there was a creditable re-staging of Eugene O'Neill's *A Moon for the Misbegotten* which ran for 199 performances; and an effort was made to bring back *Of Thee I Sing,* the 1931 Gershwin musical which won the Pulitzer Prize and was the first musical to be named a Best Play, but the production was short-lived. Among new foreign plays presented in English were two American premieres of Luigi Pirandello one-acters in translation on the program *The Man with the Flower in His Mouth.* Distinguished foreign visitors were the Yugoslav troupe Atelje 212 with a program that included Edward Albee's *Who's Afraid of Virginia Woolf?* in Serbo-Croat, plus the German Die Brücke, the Greek Piraikon Theatron and France's Le Tréteau de Paris.

To sum up, 1968-69 was a big year off Broadway in volume of activity, in the impetus of the top hits and in the quality of individual achievement (and, it goes without saying, in the cost of production). In looking back on an off-Broadway year, however, we should ask ourselves whether it functioned merely as a junior Broadway or whether it continued to serve its own unique purpose. The latter was clearly the case in 1968-69. The best of its new work —*Adaptation/Next, No Place To Be Somebody, Dames at Sea, Ceremonies in Dark Old Men, The People vs. Ranchman*—resembled the style, shape and content of Broadway hardly at all. The program of one-act plays is a frequently-recurring form off Broadway, where it serves more than an entertainment function; it is a sampler for playwrights and plays. There were 20 programs of one-acters presented off Broadway this season, 17 of them one-man shows displaying for better or for better-luck-next-time the work of Israel Horovitz, Harold Pinter, Adrienne Kennedy, Terrence McNally, Charles Dizenzo, James Prideaux, Frank Gagliano, James Leo Herlihy, Ben Piazza and others.

Finally, off Broadway found the handle for *Little Murders,* thus adding still another to the list of Broadway scripts *(Summer and Smoke, The Crucible, The Iceman Cometh,* etc.) which proved their full capacity when reaching off-Broadway revival. Certainly the tributary theater has continued to serve its unique theatrical purposes in 1968-69, affording many the opportunity to try —even to try nakedness as a form of frankness, perversion as a form of passion—and some the opportunity to find fulfillment not attainable elsewhere.

Offstage

Outside the theaters, the Broadway sound of 1968-69 was the sound of the jackhammer, as the office-building boom crept over westward and penetrated the theater district like the prongs of an exercise in military strategy. The Playhouse went the way of the Astor, Capitol, Paramount and Roxy, with office towers mushrooming on the sites. True, the city authorities have bargained with the developers for new theaters: zoning laws limiting the size and shape of new office buildings are to be relaxed slightly in exchange for the inclusion of new theaters within the construction. Many "official spokesmen" for various branches of the theater think this is an adequate safeguard for the legit stage's physical future. Others do not, citing two reasons why new theaters-within-offices are not true replacements for the old: 1) any change in the size and shape of the playhouses will influence the form of the plays, with the intimate type of production finding less and less lebensraum and 2) dispersal of theaters into office buildings, some of them placed above street level, will cost the Broadway area its compact, show-biz-flavored theater district. While the arguments continue a theater vanishes—and at least a half dozen of the old legit playhouses, maybe as many as a dozen, face the imminent and deadly threat of progress.

This was the season that the Theater Development Fund began to function in aid of selected productions on and off Broadway by means of subsidized ticket purchases. The Fund operated in 1968-69 with an endowment of about $400,000, some of it Federal and some private foundation money. The Fund comes into the picture *after* a play is in production (so that it has no influence on which plays are to be produced). Before the chosen play opens, the Fund may buy a block of tickets to increase the advance sale and tide the show over the first few weeks, as it did this season, $10,000 worth, in the case of *The Great White Hope.* Or the Fund may circularize a special segment of the public, offering cut-rate theater tickets and paying the difference on the box office price, to broaden the base of the theater's audience generally and an individual play's in particular as it did, $25,000 worth, for *We Bombed in New Haven.*

At the Dramatists Guild, the playwrights' organization, Sidney Kingsley declined to run for a fifth term as president, and Frank D. Gilroy was elected to take his place. In May it was decided by the Guild Council and active membership to alter the organization's constitution so as to offer off-Broadway playwrights the same full membership rights (and duties) as their Broadway colleagues. Until this action was taken, off-Broadway authors had been "associate members" of the Dramatists Guild and could not vote or serve on its Council. Now they can, in a step which may ultimately have a very important effect on the status and even the art of playwriting.

The drama critics had an active year in the rough-and-tumble of industrial relations with David Merrick, Alexander H. Cohen and others. Clive Barnes of the New York *Times* was a frequent target because of his paper's make-or-break influence on the Broadway box office. After the Equity strike last June, Merrick stated facetiously that he would desist from hiring foreign actors if the *Times* would do the same with its English-born drama critic. During the Tony Awards warm-up before the ceremony went on TV, Cohen, the master of ceremonies, introduced "Clive Barnes," and onto the stage came a man dressed in a gorilla suit. The producers of *The Flip Side* requested that Barnes *not* cover the opening of their show, so Dan Sullivan did and reported unfavorably on it as did a majority of critics (Sullivan has since transferred to the Los Angeles *Times* as its drama critic). The New York *Times* Sunday critic, Walter Kerr, drew fire from Julian Beck, who blamed Kerr's denigration of his show *Paradise Now* on Kerr's "loneliness," his non-participation in the performance, his refusal to accept the actors' invitation to all members of the audience to come up on the stage and take their clothes off.

The question of whether and when foreign actors are to be employed in Broadway shows has been one of the running controversies within the theater. Certainly it had much to do with the Equity strike in June. As part of the strike settlement, it was decided to set up an arbitration procedure to mediate cases in which a producer insists on hiring a foreign actor over Equity's objection. Norman Nadel served as the abitrator in at least one case this season (he decided against the producer), but a major confrontation between Equity and Merrick on this issue, over the all-British cast of *Rockefeller and the Red Indians,* was avoided at the 11th hour after Equity O.K.'d the employment of the English personnel. Like most controversies in the theater, therefore, this one has not entirely cooled off and continues to simmer on the back burner.

Ditto the running dispute with the Union of South Africa over production rights to American playscripts. Most American playwrights object to the production of their works for segregated audiences, but the copyright tribunal in that country ruled that it can overrule authors in this matter and grant compulsory licenses for production. This was done in the cases of *West Side Story, Man of La Mancha* and *Fiddler on the Roof.* Appropriate protests were filed through available channels, but the dispute still seethes.

One that seems to have been settled was the flare-up between the authors and producers of *Hair.* Gerome Ragni and James Rado, stars as well as authors of the Broadway musical, were experimenting onstage with new material. Rado and Ragni were replaced in their roles and barred from the theater by the producer, Michael Butler. After a few days and several meetings, all parties finally reached an understanding about a procedure for introducing new material, the boys returned to their roles and everything returned to smash-hit normal at the popular rock musical.

In a season in which almost every imagineable sex act was mimed onstage, with actors appearing in various degrees of the nude from suggestive to total, there was surprisingly little censorship activity. The New York theater cannot be said to be suffering the pangs of censorship in the way, say, the London theater did before the historic office of play censor (Lord Chamberlain) was abolished by act of Parliament, taking effect on Sept. 26, 1968 (the opening date of *Hair* in London was deliberately scheduled after that date); or the Paris theater did last September when Andre Malraux, France's minister of culture, dismissed Jean-Louis Barrault from the Odeon following a dispute arising from events during the student rebellion. Nevertheless there seems to be a limit to what even the New York authorities will tolerate, and this limit seems to have been reached finally with the off-off-Broadway production of *Che!*, a symbolic drama of modern ideologies in which nudity, explicit sex acts (both straight and kinky) and the characters of Che Guevara, the President of the United States and a nymphomaniac nun are all stirred together in a kind of sociological-political metaphor. After *Che's* opening performance the police arrested the cast, the producers and other personnel on charges which included obscenity and consentual sodomy. All were later released on bail and subsequent performances of *Che!* were held in the East Village. Still, it was not the facts of the case but its implications that must be given some attention in any review of the 1968-69 season.

This is the problem: the pre-opening publicity had included the boast that actors playing Che and the nun would not only mime the sex act called for in the play, they would *do* it in reality, if they were able to at any given performance. Whether this is to be taken with a grain or mountain of salt is beside the controversial point. It raises a question even for those who take the extreme, purist anti-censorship position. Even those who make it an article of faith that the theater should be able to mime *anything* must pause to ask themselves whether it is also permissible to *do* anything—or is there a borderline between art and reality, and, if so, where does this border lie? Obviously, only Nero himself would consider it a curtailment of artistic freedom to insist that murders on the stage must be mimed, not performed. The fact that an overt sex act might offend some people is no reason for banning it from the stage (those people who might be offended can stay home). But is it a curtailment of artistic freedom to insist that this act be mimed, not actually performed? As this 1968-69 season of transition ended, no truly satisfactory answer had been found to this question raised by the *Che!* case.

In November 1968, in France's Chamber of Deputies, a legislator attacked Andre Malraux's proposal to establish cultural centers throughout France, on the ground that the contemporary theater had little to offer but "unrelieved metaphysical anguish." Malraux replied: "Don't you know the two greatest French poets aside from Victor Hugo—Baudelaire and Rimbaud? Are they not bitterness incarnate? And is our civilization not dominated by gloom?"

In May 1969, Angus Duncan, executive secretary of Actors' Equity Association, issued a policy statement: "It is not the policy of Actors' Equity to be guided by considerations of morality, literary merit or artistic value. . . . . (But) when a performer is required to disrobe as the sole prerequisite for a job, then both his dignity and his artistic integrity are under attack."

The theater season of 1968-69 was not entirely dominated by gloom and/or nudity, though there were times when it might have seemed that way. But this was a season in which environment took on a special importance; in which the theater was as continuously aware of its environment as a violin teacher with a parade going by. The plays and musicals of 1968-69 existed not in a mere social, political or artistic "climate," but in a savage weather of events. The theater year had just begun last June when the second of two horrible assassinations rocked the world. This was followed by the shameful happening at the Democratic convention in Chicago. Then there was the Presidential election (in which theater folk took a less conspicuous part than usual) and a change of government. During the Christmas Season, as *Forty Carats* opened on Broadway, man at last reached and orbited the moon; and along with the Christmas carols on the radio there was the booming poetry of Genesis coming down through the quarter-million miles of space between Apollo 9 and the earth, and suddenly after all these earthbound millenia there was an incredible new perspective on our planet in the photos of an earthrise as seen from the moon's surface.

And as if this weren't enough environment for one year, there was the continuing tragedy of the Vietnam War and the painful efforts toward peace. There were the campus rebellions; the have vs. have-not tensions; the increasing computerization of society; the polarizing race troubles.

The theater responded to this heavy 1968-69 environmental presence with renewed effort at finding new forms and ideas. After the environmental shocks of 1968-69, it is unlikely that human beings will settle for the same world they lived in before—or the same theater they enjoyed before. The world, we know, is going to the moon and stars. The theater's destination isn't that clear yet, but at least the art form was aroused and on the move in a season that, taken as a whole in retrospect, must be judged a pretty good one. Like the world, the theater is going *somewhere,* and for the time being we must settle for enjoyment of the adventure for its own sake, maintain our faith in survival and even in progress, and await results.

1987 PERSPECTIVE: And so the 1960s closed with men on the moon, the U.S. still embattled in Vietnam and the theater entering the final phase of its 20th century metamorphosis from a popular entertainment to a special cultural occasion. In the year-by-year reports here in "Curtain Times" there was no historian's mission to identify and follow major trends through the New York stage's tumultuous past. Still, the seeds of what our theater has become in the 1980s could be seen dropping all over the place and taking root in the events of the 1960s: for example, that the newly-formed National Endowment was helping local subsidy to raise the public consciousness and new theater complexes across the country; that Cafe LaMama and Caffe Cino, undertaking the Herculean labor of producing a play a week, started something in 1965 whose effect "may become measurable in the future." It certainly has. This beginning of the off-off-Broadway germination has grown into a boon to new playwrights, with nearly 100 groups now putting on something like 200 shows each season.

Yes, 20 years ago the price of a Broadway ticket seemed very high at $9.90. But "Cabaret" then broke the sawbuck barrier in 1967 with a $12 top, and we might have known where this inflationary spiral would lead— though even today we can't tell where it will end.

It was about 1968, we notice, that we stopped using the word "Negro" in favor of "black." At this same time, Alexander H. Cohen came up with a scheme to glamorize the obscure Tony Awards with TV presentations, to light up the darkening Broadway skies. Onstage, scripts came out of the closet with important statements about homosexuality, out of clothes in all kinds of experiments, sexual and asexual, with naked performers, and into fashion with first casual use of marijuana in a play.

We couldn't help thinking wishfully in making predictions during those years; and so, like all hopes, there were those that were fulfilled and those that weren't. Not all the new playwrights for whom we predicted a great future lived up to expectations, but most did, and we were right in asserting in passing that plays like "The Lion in Winter" and "A Delicate Balance" would go on to far greater glories than indicated by the Broadway audience's indifferent reception. We didn't recognize immediately that the "wild excitement" imparted to the Broadway "Hair" by director Tom O'Horgan, as compared with the "acute sensibility" of the prior off-Broadway version directed by Gerald Freedman, would turn this moody musical into a huge international blockbuster, the most popular musical of all time as of its day. We overestimated the esthetic potential in eliminating the fourth wall and making direct contact with the audience (though it worked very well in some shows), and of incorporating new theaters in office and hotel skyscrapers, but not the stifling effect on theater of the dwindling of critical voices, as most of New York City's major newspapers went out of business.

As this account of New York theater in the late 1960s began, the Tom Jones-Harvey Schmidt off-Broadway musical "The Fantasticks" was already 2,120 performances old. It had opened May 3, 1960 and kept on attracting audiences, though no one imagined the true extent of its staying power. It remained where it opened, at the Sullivan Street Playhouse, not only for the rest of the 1960s but all of the years covered in this volume, enduring as an outstanding achievement and unique symbol of this whole generation of theater. As I write these lines from the perspective of 1987, "The Fantasticks" finally announced that it would close on June 8 of 1986 after an unprecedented run of 10,864 performances — and then, when it began to sell out as a result of the closing notice, decided to continue its longest run ever, by far, on the professional New York stage. It is a glorious symbol of all the activity described in this volume, as well as proof emphatically positive of the power of good theater in any age.

O.L.G. Jr.

PART II:
THE EARLY SEVENTIES

ZERO MOSTEL AS LEOPOLD BLOOM IN "ULYSSES IN NIGHTTOWN"

Stacy Keach, *foreground,* as Buffalo Bill and Manu Tupou, *top,* as
Sitting Bull in *Indians* by Arthur Kopit.
PHOTO BY MARTHA SWOPE

1969-70

IT WAS like this in 1969-70: there was no cluster of exciting shows until deep in April; off-Broadway hopefuls folded literally by the dozen (33 productions lasted less than two weeks, 10 of these less than one week, 7 for only one performance); our most reliable playwrights seemed baffled, even paralyzed by the demands of the developing theater form and kept their new works, if any, to themselves; instead of one great homogenious appetite for theater, there was a decided schism between the lacquered audiences at *Applause* and the soft, rapt, furry faces at *Stomp;* production costs continued toward the roof (I do not say ceiling because apparently there is no ceiling, not even at the $1 million level), at the same time that the audience buck was coming tough; and, last straw, the sound of the air compressor and jackhammer intruded into the venerable theater district, as office-builders continued to threaten the very physical existence of the Broadway theater as we've known it for decades.

And yet . . . and yet there was a season, and a pretty good one too, esthetically and even financially. As an added irony, it was conventional plays and not audience-confrontation or subliminal ones that dominated the year's best work. In the big theaters, *Butterflies Are Free, Child's Play, Last of the Red Hot Lovers* and *Applause* came on as comfortable as old slippers with a love story, a thriller, a comedy and a glamor musical—no surprises here. In the smaller playhouses the cream of the crop included the straightforward *The Effect of Gamma Rays on Man-in-the-Moon Marigolds* together with the stylistically bizarre but safely constructed *The White House Murder Case* and *What the Butler Saw.* Among the ten Best Plays, the farthest out in form were *Indians, Company* and *The Serpent: A Ceremony* in that order.

The number of shows produced on Broadway declined to 68 productions of record in 1969-70 (see the one-page summary accompanying this report) from 76 last year, 84 the year before and 78 the year before that. But the most important element of this total—new American scripts—has remained reassuringly steady. This season there were 21 new American plays and 14 new musicals on Broadway, compared with 24-12 last year, 25-10 the year before that, 19-8 in alarming 1966-67, and 25-11 and 25-10 in the two years before that. Off Broadway this season the total productions of record jumped to a whopping 119 as compared with 103 last season, including 69 new American musicals and playscripts (see the one-page summary accompanying the off-Broadway section of this report).

Not surprisingly, *Variety's* annual estimate showed a dropoff in Broadway's total gross for the second year in a row. The decline amounted to more than 7 per cent, as the Broadway take for the 52 weeks of 1969-70 came to $53,324,199 as compared with last year's $57.7 million and the year before's record high of $59 million. In the matter of playing weeks (if 10 shows play 10 weeks, that's 100 playing weeks), there was a continuing decline. There were only 1,047 playing weeks on Broadway (including 74 weeks of previews) in 1969-70, as compared with 1,209 last year, 1,257 the year before, 1,269 the year before that and 1,295 the year before that.

The 1969-70 Season on Broadway

PLAYS (21)

A Teaspoon Every Four Hours
INDIANS
The Penny Wars
BUTTERFLIES ARE FREE
Operation Sidewinder
Angela
Love Is a Time of Day
LAST OF THE RED HOT LOVERS
Watercolor & Criss-Crossing
Brightower
Sheep on the Runway
Paris Is Out!
Gloria and Esperanza
CHILD'S PLAY
Norman, Is That You?
The Chinese and Dr. Fish
Grin and Bare It! & Postcards
A Place for Polly

Inquest
The Engagement Baby
Wilson in the Promise Land

SPECIALTIES (4)

Nat. Theater of Deaf
Sganarelle
Songs From Milk Wood
Charles Aznavour
Marcel Marceau

MUSICALS (14)

Jimmy
Buck White
La Strada
Coco
Gantry
Georgy
Purlie
Blood Red Roses
Minnie's Boys
Look to the Lilies
APPLAUSE
Cry for Us All
Park
COMPANY

REVIVALS (18)

Oklahoma!
In The Matter of J. Robert Oppenheimer
Amer. Conservatory
Tiny Alice
A Flea in Her Ear
Three Sisters
Three Men on a Horse
The Front Page
Lincoln Center Rep
The Time of Your Life
Camino Real
Beggar on Horseback
Henry V
Our Town
Private Lives
No Place To Be Somebody

Harvey
Candida
The Boy Friend
The Cherry Orchard

FOREIGN PLAYS IN ENGLISH (3)

A Patriot for Me
The Mundy Scheme
Borstal Boy

FOREIGN-LANGUAGE PRODUCTIONS (8)

Grand Kabuki
Chushingura & Kagami-Jishi
Kumagai Jinya & Momiji-Gari
The New Music Hall of Israel
Comédie Française
La Troupe du Roi & Amphitryon
Dom Juan
Les Femmes Savantes
Le Malade Imaginaire
Rabelais

HOLDOVER SHOW WHICH BECAME HIT DURING 1969-70

1776

Plays listed in CAPITAL LETTERS have been designated Best Plays of 1969-70.
Plays listed in **bold face type** were classified as hits in *Variety's* annual list of hits and flops published June 3, 1970.
Plays listed in *italics* were still running June 1, 1970.

Looking for a silver lining, *Variety* noted that road productions of Broadway plays were doing better than ever, grossing $48,024,325 (and thus giving Broadway its third $100-million season in a row) for 1,024 playing weeks. The figures speak for themselves—Broadway activity was going down, not up —but we would like to add our own qualification. The season was very late in starting (for example, seven of the ten Best Plays opened in the last half of the season). *Applause* didn't arrive until March, *Company* until April. During the final weeks of 1969-70, when all its new shows were finally on, Broadway was out-grossing the comparable weeks of 1968-69, rolling along at the rate of $1.2 million a week.

To sketch a context for these figures, the ticket ceilings held pretty much at last year's levels. Broadway's hottest weekend musical tickets were highest priced at $15 (and *Coco* asked this price for week nights as well), with the straight-play top pegged generally at $8.50. *Coco, Applause* and *Company* pushed the matinee top up a notch from $8 to $9. Off Broadway, the producers of a solid hit could continue to get $10 a ticket as they had been ever since *The Boys in the Band* established this pattern in the 1967-68 season. A very special case *Oh! Calcutta!* was able to charge a $15 top for most seats and $25 for the first two rows. Curiously, Broadway was more hospitable than off Broadway to the tight-budgeted theatergoer, who could see *Hair* for $4 or *Fiddler on the Roof* for $2.80 and *Company* for $2 in the least expensive seats but would have to pay $5 for the minimum-priced seats at most off-Broadway hits.

Production costs for musicals, according to *Variety* estimates, were just about anything you wanted to pay: *Coco* $850-900,000, *Cry for Us All* (it lasted 9 performances) $750,000, *La Strada* (it lasted 1 performance) $650,000. The operating expenses of trying out and opening could bring the total capital loss much higher, estimated by *Variety* to be in the neighborhood of $850,000 for *La Strada,* $720,000 for *Georgy* (it lasted 4 performances) and close to $1 million for *Jimmy's* 84-performance career. Straight plays were a bargain in comparison: *Indians,* whose production cost was relatively high, came in for $240,531 (*Variety* reported), but *Butterflies Are Free* was mounted for only $71,000, a real bargain, only a few dollars more than the cost of a lavish off-Broadway flop. A *very* lavish off-Broadway flop like *Mahagonny* cost $350,000, the highest of off-Broadway record, and lost more than that. *Salvation,* an off-Broadway musical hit, came in for $37,682. Another figure for the context: Seymour Vall was doing a musical called *Blood Red Roses* off Broadway, when a funny thing happened on the way to production—he decided to bring it to Broadway instead. The production budget for this show (it lasted 1 performance) was $65,000 for the original off-Broadway venture, $175,000 for the same show on Broadway. We shouldn't leave this subject without adding that if the stakes were high, the pots were sometimes fat. Among *net* profit estimates published during the season were these: *Hello, Dolly!,* $7,775,526 on a $350,000 investment; *Fiddler on the Roof,* $5,907,552 on $400,000; *The Boys in the Band,* $600,000 on $20,000; *Man of La Mancha,* $4,600,000 on $200,000.

For the second straight season there was a good deal of talk about the emergence of a directors' theater in which improvisational techniques would bypass the playwright or use his work as a scaffolding on which to hang the garlands of interpretive artistry. But for the second straight season it was anything but a directors' year. Producers? No one goes around saying "As David Merrick goes, so goes Broadway," but maybe they should give it some thought. Like Broadway itself, Merrick had moderate success with a combination of new material *(Child's Play)*, a popular revival *(Private Lives)* and the hardy old survivors *Forty Carats, Promises, Promises* and *Hello, Dolly!*, which took yet another new lease on life with the arrival in town of Ethel Merman to play its title role. At season's end, *Dolly* was well on the way to overtaking *My Fair Lady* and becoming the longest running Broadway musical of all time.

Harold Prince, almost alone among a group of "experts" in an early-season New York *Times* symposium, insisted that Broadway is still where it's at if you have what it takes, and he proved his point with the musical *Company*. Arthur Whitelaw (together with Max J. Brown and Myron Goldman) drew a high pair back to back with *Butterflies Are Free* and *Minnie's Boys;* so did David Black with *Paris Is Out!* on Broadway and *Salvation* off.

For some, the season brought disappointment. Cassius Clay failed to make a show business career out of his role as an activist lecturing about black pride and liberation to the members of a social club in the musical *Buck White.* The ex-heavyweight champion's performance was devoutly sincere but not quite at ease, like a high school debate over the Constitution. John Osborne, too, fell short of expectations for his treatment of the subject of homosexuality in *A Patriot for Me,* based on turn-of-the-century characters in the Austrian military aristocracy. The theatrical high point was a drag ball presided over by Dennis King costumed and mannered as a grande dame. Also from abroad, Brian Friel's *The Mundy Scheme* (a plan to bring prosperity to Ireland by converting it into a cemetery for the world's overcrowded cities) was not the biting satire of our hopes from this distinguished Irish playwright. John Patrick dealt unsuccessfully with love among college students in *Love Is a Time of Day,* and Dore Schary was practically assaulted by the critics for his effort to examine in *Brightower* the problem of right of privacy, in the drama of a Hemingway-like writer who suffers a nervous breakdown—it lasted only one performance but apparently was strong enough to support a Tony nomination for Geraldine Brooks for best performance by an actress, in the role of the writer's wife. Murray Schisgal's program of one-acters failed to take a strong comic hold on the subjects of marriage counseling (in *Dr. Fish*) and race snobbery (in *The Chinese*), though in the latter playlet there were outstanding performances by Joseph Bova and Alice Drummond as the proud Chinese parents of a young man who is somewhat ashamed of them and is passing for Jewish in the neighborhood.

Successful or unsuccessful, show people were joining their audiences in the season of 1969-70 in a kind of space exploration. While astronauts walked on the moon and children dreamed of visits to the planets and stars, the New York theater was blasting off from its old fourth-wall-set, realistic-theater concepts and exploring its own inner space, trying to discover whether there can be found in new forms of theatrical expression a cluster of new meanings or merely a vast and vacuous emptiness. As the earth was beginning to seem stuffy and confining to a hugely expanding mankind, the old theater was too limited a form now for the art's wildest dreams. So 1969-70 tended to be an adventurous year in which anything including the worst was possible; anything, from a naked cast in *Grin and Bare It!* to audience participation in pulling a huge sheet of plastic over the entire auditorium as an image of our sealed-in environment in *Stomp* to the brilliant break-through of *The Serpent.*

Anything could happen—even an old fashioned but still satisfying evening of conventional theater.

Theater style was fragmenting in 1969-70, partly because of this growing dissatisfaction with the old forms, and partly to satisfy the fragmenting taste of the New York audiences. Time was when we all knew what we wanted and what we meant when we spoke of "a good comedy" (*Harvey* or *Private Lives*), "a good musical" (*Oklahoma* or *The Boy Friend*) or even "a good drama" (Arthur Miller/Tennessee Williams). We still enjoy such shows— many of them, in fact, appeared as popular revivals this season. But now there's a growing audience that wants something else/something more/something different, an audience that grew up in this age when television has been repeating, and exhausting, all the possible linear comic and dramatic situations. Thus, Neil Simon's *Last of the Red Hot Lovers* with its situation-comedy premise and Jules Feiffer's *The White House Murder Case* with its sick-joke fantasy are two fine theater comedies, funny and meaningful, but in such completely different ways that there's no reason to insist that a devotee of one must necessarily enjoy the other (it is possible, but not inevitable).

In 1969-70 the audience fragments overlapped in some areas, and when they did not they were often large enough to support the theater of their special taste. The trick was to get the right person to the right show. At one performance of the rock musical *Salvation,* two graceful white-haired ladies were helped to their third-row seats by uniformed chauffeur who opened their programs for them to the first credits page and disencumbered them of their furs. It's perfectly possible that these ladies enjoyed the outspoken put-on of moral poses, including the number "Stockhausen Pot Pourri" in which the cast first whispers, then speaks, shouts and finally orchestrates, as it were, all the major four-letter obscenities (certainly they hadn't heard *that* on television). But for the most part it is mis-matching of audience to show in these days of way-out experimentation that provokes all those cries of alarm over what is becoming of our beloved theater. It is indeed *becoming,* growing, and that's the important point.

What is sometimes called "new theater" to distinguish it from our old Henrik Ibsen-to-Tennessee Williams friend is setting off in as many directions as Stephen Leacock's impetuous horseman; and two of them may be leading somewhere. For the past couple of seasons we've had plays which make overt and direct contact—sometimes even physically—with the audience, instead of keeping their third-person distance as in the conventional fourth-wall theater. These new plays sometimes go so far as to insist that the audience assume a role in the events being dramatized, if only to accept a portion of the guilt for the play's motivation, which in the old theater was pretty much the exclusive possession of the villains. An example of direct-contact theater in 1969-70 was LeRoi Jones's *Slave Ship,* a dramatic exercise with a single purpose: to polarize the audience into two *hostile* camps of black and white, right there in the theater, now. In a series of sketches it traced the history of white America's inhumanity to blacks in incidents of the slave trade, Southern slavery, growing rebellion and modern militancy. A blue police light revolving at the slave ship's masthead was one of its dramatic points of reference; another was a pleading, half-naked black teenager dropped at the foot of the audience during a slave auction scene to bring them into the picture, so to speak. But the purpose of *Slave Ship* was involvement, not the arousing of sympathy;

anger, not love. After its adverse examples have been dramatized, an actor costumed as a Masai warrior exhorts the blacks in the audience to stand up (in order to separate them physically and visually from the whites) and join him in a song of black solidarity. Standing and separate in their Negritude, they are then told that their race mission is to destroy the white beast and all his works—not necessarily their seated white neighbor in the audience, but not necessarily *not*. That was the purpose of the play, and it left a cold wind blowing through the exit doors as the audience filed out, silent, hostile, polarized. For better or for worse, *Slave Ship* was an example of direct-contact, role-for-the-audience theater that really worked.

A second important direction of change was toward what might be termed peripheral-vision, or subliminal, playwriting. It's what you see out of the corner of your eye, what you don't *quite* hear, or what you hear *after* the words have been spoken that counts. What is literally being done or said on the stage may be intended to distract the conscious mind, with its increasing resistance to the simple linear premise, so that the playwright's real intentions can slip into the eye's corner, slide into the ear between the literal meanings. Thus, the program of new Harold Pinter one-acters offered off Broadway at Lincoln Center Repertory's small Forum Theater—*Silence* and *Landscape*—mesmerized the audience with characters who were themselves in a sort of trance of introspection. They speak their long, image-filled thoughts not so much to communicate with one another (there is no cross-pollination of dialogue in these plays) as to hear themselves think. I found *Landscape* particularly effective, with its middle aged man and woman (Robert Symonds and Mildred Natwick) daydreaming in a kitchen setting that is a monotone gray, drear as their burned-out marriage. Their spoken thoughts made no interconnection (indeed, all connection between them is broken never to be repaired) except that each is imagining what could be, sexually. She is dreaming of a warm sand dune and a tender wooing; he of catching his wife at the dinner gong and getting her attention long enough to make love right there in front hall. Pinter's stream of images was like an electric current carrying powerful feelings of isolation and loss that would be very difficult indeed to communicate in any conventional theater form.

In the same way, at Lincoln Center Rep's Broadway-sized Vivian Beaumont Theater, Sam Shepard's new play *Operation Sidewinder* was one of the most imaginative scripts of the season and one of the best in this "subliminal" style. A computer built to resemble a giant rattlesnake which escapes from the Air Force compound into the desert . . . a hippie protagonist who guns down an innocent garage mechanic taking too long to fix his car . . . two black militants cruising in a black Cadillac convertible with painted flame licking from the front wheel bays . . . kookie generals and a Dr. Strangelove scientist . . . Hopi Indian rituals and designs . . . this was a sauce with too many strong ingredients for any literal taste. It was the aftertaste of *Operation Sidewinder* that counted, though, not any narrative logic in this mad, mad, mad view of a world on a trip of violence, crazed with force and power. One example of the very great and still-rising importance of rock music in our culture was the use by Shepard in *Operation Sidewinder* (which is certainly not a musical) of a rock group, The Holy Modal Rounders, to comment on each hallucinatory episode in song, as a sort of narrator.

Another outstanding example of "new" theater was The Open Theater's

The Serpent: A Ceremony which combined the abovementioned developments —audience contact and corner-of-the-eye communication—with its own development in the creation of material for the stage. The Open Theater is an off-off-Broadway group which specializes in the ensemble improvisation of scenes and characters. The way it works is this: someone, maybe a playwright but maybe an actor or director, gets an idea for a scene; perhaps a playwright supplies a few lines of dialogue or narration to go on with, perhaps not; at any rate, the writer, actors and director improvise around the idea in a collaborative process of creating a scene. This is a technique which has received a great deal of critical attention recently in evaluations of the work of Jerzy Grotowski, the Polish director (the subject of some consideration later in this report). Thus *The Serpent's* creative credits read: "Created by The Open Theater Ensemble, words and structure by Jean-Claude van Itallie, under the direction of Joseph Chaikin, associate director Roberta Sklar."

Van Itallie's words are few, but they are very effective. He seems to have found a way of writing short takes of narration that keep on reverberating in the mind while the actors go about their mimed business of interpretation. When the serpent himself, played with extraordinary ensemble skill by five writhing actors, touches Eve with an apple and then challenges her belief in God's threats with "Have you died?", an apocalyptic moment has taken place not only in the serpentine contortion or Eve's puzzlement but in the frighteningly simple three *words* themselves. Likewise Eve's question to the serpent about free will—can she "listen to God and not to you?" if she wants to; likewise the narrative introduction to Cain's murder of Abel: "And it occurred to Cain/To kill his brother/But it did not occur to Cain/That killing his brother/Would cause his brother's death/For Cain did not know how to kill" which echoes in imagination over an entire memorable scene in which Cain at first tries to kill his brother by pulling his hand off his arm. Messily but finally Cain succeeds in his murderous purpose and then tries to bring Abel back to life and movement. "And it occurred to Cain/To kill his brother" —if van Itallie has found a way to write a scene like this in a few short lines, it is not an abandonment of artistic prerogative but a refinement of it; a challenge, not a surrender, to the interpretive artist.

The Open Theater troupe of actors worked its own wonders with van Itallie's ideas (and it is pertinent to note here that in the company's other excellent new work, *Terminal,* there are the same vivid one-by-one acting effects in a series of comments about death and dying but not the same strong and cohesive underpinning—call it playwriting—that gives *The Serpent* its special power). The performing was exceptional, with fascinating detail and profound depth of understanding and communication of human nature to match the Biblical size of the concept (and, in two cases, a profound understanding of animal nature, in Peter Maloney's exact portrayal of dull ovine egocentricity, in a sheep eating grass out of Abel's dead hand, and in Paul Zimet's heron walking unmolested through the violent events of Eden, fluttering his wings and raising his crown in a perpetual state of astonishment). "I no longer live in the beginning/I've lost the beginning/I'm in the middle," cry the women of *The Serpent,* which has indeed brought the theater from where it was yesterday onto a new path—with, as usual, a playwright, the gifted Jean-Claude van Itallie, pointing the new and exciting way to go.

This breeding of new styles and tastes doesn't necessarily make for a firm, esthetically predictable, financially stable theater. It certainly didn't work that way in New York in the season of 1969-70. But neither does it make for a picturesque downslide dominated by moribund preconceptions. The good old tree is hollow here and there, certainly; the theater as we know it was in deep trouble artistically and financially, as we have suggested. But those who conclude that the theater is in decline didn't go to many shows this season. Those who did couldn't help noticing a characteristic that stood out from all the others: new growth all around, on the stage and in the audience, everywhere.

Broadway

The best script of the 1969-70 bests, in our opinion, was Arthur Kopit's *Indians,* about the opening of the American West. It would be absurd to define this play, in terms of its Broadway appearance, as a 96-performance "flop." *Indians* came to New York following a world premiere production by the Royal Shakespeare Company in London and an American premiere production at the Arena Stage in Washington, D.C. It is destined, certainly, for an illustrious career on the world's stages, where it will enhance the reputation of American playwriting.

Indians takes the form of a dramatic memoir. The Buffalo Bill era is preserved in glass museum cases on the curtainless stage as the audience files in. Then the glass cases disappear and the artifacts come to life as Buffalo Bill Cody himself (Stacy Keach) "gallops" to the jutting apron to open another glorious Wild West show. But he finds he can't proceed without trying to justify certain events in the opening of the West to you, the audience; he'd rather confide in you than lie to you. The glories of the past were flawed if you look at them in a strong light: the buffalo as a species was nearly wiped out and the Indians nearly annihilated in the name of progress and adventure. No one cared, not the President of the United States, not the Congress, not even the Western heroes like Bill Cody and Wild Bill Hickok, because young America needed expansion and heroic legends at this crucial period in its growth. Buffalo Bill didn't realize (he pleads), *couldn't* have realized how his name and fame were to be used as a larger-than-life disguise for exploitation and savagery. In a moral sense he is innocent, and Sitting Bull doesn't blame him even after Bill is unable to prevent the U.S. Cavalry from slaughtering the chief's whole tribe. Sitting Bull doesn't accuse, he merely wonders: "We had land . . . You wanted it; you took it. That . . . I understand, perfectly. What I cannot understand . . . is why you did all this, *and at the same time* . . . professed your love."

No, it isn't Buffalo Bill who takes the tragedy on his conscience, or the politicians onstage. It is the *audience,* heirs of the conquerors, whose conscience is put to the torch, who are forced into the role of villain. With excellent direction by Gene Frankel, *Indians* reached its climax and fulfillment not in the events on the stage (no change took place in the characters there) but out in the auditorium where we were forced to re-examine some of our value judgments through a crack in our beloved national epic of the Old Wild West.

Another Broadway drama on the Best Plays list was the thriller *Child's Play,* a first play by Robert Marasco about mysterious evil pervading a boys' school and inciting the students to acts of apparently meaningless violence which satisfy some unknown craving. All elements of this play combined for eerie effect: Joseph Hardy's exceedingly careful direction, Jo Mielziner's dark staircase and gloomy faculty-room setting, and especially Fritz Weaver's telling portrait of a teacher too preoccupied with his job to bother about defending himself from envy and slander until it is too late. Rather like Henry James's *The Turn of the Screw, Child's Play* projected but never really named its terror in a mystery that refused to spell out all of its secrets even at the final curtain. In part, this script is an example of the trend toward subliminal communication in playwriting. Marasco addressed his work not entirely to conscious logic, but in part to instinct. Deep down below the level of conscious thought (the playwright assumes), the audience understands *by instinct* that the events in *Child's Play* are a microcosm of our time, a time which expresses itself in acts of seemingly irrational violence (read any issue of any newspaper) as a surfacing, particularly in the younger generation, of a deeply-imbedded evil that is very difficult to identify and root out. Thus this work, which seemed at first glance to be traditional in form and subject, was one of the season's most topical as well as most effective scripts.

From abroad, the season was enhanced by *Borstal Boy* adapted by Frank MacMahon from the late Brendan Behan's autobiographical account of his arrest at 17 years of age as an IRA sympathizer carrying a suitcase full of dynamite to England, and his subsequent arrest and incarceration, first in a prison and then in a boys' reformatory called a "borstal." This production won the New York Drama Critics Circle and Tony Awards as the best play of the year, yet it was less a dramatic structure than an evening of colorful anecdotes and bad-boy expressions spoken with ingratiating Irish charm by Niall Toibin uncannily impersonating Behan as an adult commenting in epithet and song on the actions of Frank Grimes as Behan as the idealistic young revolutionary. The youth, of course, is a victim of his own violent politics—in his shy, warmhearted way he might have blown off people's arms and legs as messily as any blood-lusting veteran revolutionary if he hadn't been caught in time to prevent it. *Borstal Boy* was an entertaining and sometimes moving concert of verbal images and attitudes; a good show with many attractive theatrical and literary elements, but certainly not the best "play" of 1969-70, or anywhere near it, in our understanding of the word.

There were three other noteworthy "serious" dramas this season, all home grown. Elliott Baker's *The Penny Wars,* a David Merrick production which Barbara Harris staged in her first time out as a Broadway director, was a stark view of a family coping with the Depression after the father dies of a heart attack; and of the eventual failure of the stepfather, a warm-hearted immigrant dentist played by George Voskovec, to bear up under the economic and emotional pressures of those difficult times. Donald Freed's *Inquest* reopened the Ethel and Julius Rosenberg atom-spy case in the theater-of-fact genre with this message emblazoned on the backdrop: "Every word you will see or hear on this stage is a documentary quotation or reconstruction from events." Perhaps so, but the words were carefully selected to honor the memory of the Rosenbergs (most sensitively played by George Grizzard and Anne Jackson) as innocent victims of McCarthyism, and their lawyer (James Whitmore) as the single clear, true voice of advocacy within a judicial system gone bloody mad with paranoia. It was a frankly biased effort to arouse sympathy, rather than to seek new understanding with new light as in the case of last season's *In the Matter of J. Robert Oppenheimer*.

Finally, in ANTA's 1969-70 schedule of showcase bookings in New York of regional theater productions (of which more later in the section on revivals), there was the Trinity Square Repertory Company's production of Roland Van Zandt's dramatic pageant *Wilson in the Promise Land*, brought in from Providence, R.I. for the last week of the New York season. Under Adrian Hall's direction, with William Cain playing the president crippled in body and spirit by war and its aftermath, this script is a judgment rendered against the American purpose in selected quotations orated by costumed symbols of historical viewpoints: Abraham Lincoln, George Washington, Franklin D. and Teddy Roosevelt, John F. Kennedy (quoted by Wilson), hippies, etc. Again, this was more of a persuader than a play, a political cartoon.

One of the two Broadway comedies on the Best Plays list was Leonard Gershe's *Butterflies Are Free*, a boy-meets-girl story in the realistic fourth-wall theater genre which nevertheless seemed one of the freshest as well as pleasantest of the year's entertainments. The boy (Keir Dullea) is a clean-cut refugee from Scarsdale living in an East Village apartment; the girl (Blythe Danner) is the warm, outspoken blonde in the apartment next door. Not long after they meet they open the connecting door; but what costs them the time and difficulty of the play is the collateral fact that the boy's Scarsdale mother feels sorry for him because he is totally blind. Her instinct is to protect him from the life that he wishes to embrace; but the boy hardly ever feels sorry for himself, and the girl never, which brings them through the crisis safely. *Butterflies Are Free* was its author's first straight Broadway play (he did the book for the musical *Destry Rides Again*). His final scene between the two young people was one of the most attractive love scenes in a long, long time of theatergoing.

The other Broadway comedy on the Best list is Neil Simon's *Last of the Red Hot Lovers*, with James Coco as a middle-aged restaurateur trying to live it up sexually but failing with three different women in a three-ring circus of satire on (and insight into) contemporary emotional attitudes and behavior. As we have come to expect in a long succession of Simon shows, *Red Hot Lovers* was a skillful and enjoyable work; and as we have no right to expect, it was part of the astonishing but continuing expansion of a playwriting career which defies even the superlatives of description. It sounds like legend but it is true that Simon once had *four* hits running simultaneously on Broadway (*Barefoot in the Park, The Odd Couple, Sweet Charity* and *The Star-Spangled Girl*) for a combined total of 3,367 performances. Almost unbelievably, as of the 1969-70 season Simon had a whole *new* batch of three hits running simultaneously: *Plaza Suite, Promises, Promises* and *Last of the Red Hot Lovers*. *Variety* called him "Legit's all-time top playwright.

Two more comedies helped brighten the Broadway scene this season. Richard Seff's *Paris Is Out!* cast Sam Levene as a crotchety Jewish grandpa being cajoled by his wife (Molly Picon) into his first reluctant trip to Europe. The family-friction humor was well paced in Paul Aaron's direction, and Levene's performance was another memorable episode in what is surely the longest and funniest case of heartburn in stage history. Humorist Art Buchwald r'ared back and delivered a Broadway play this season, *Sheep on the Runway*, a foreign-policy joke about an American newspaper columnist who stirs up a hot war in an otherwise peaceful and obscure Asian mountain country. It benefited greatly from the presence in the role of the harried American ambassador of David Burns who, like Sam Levene, knows where all the best laughs are buried in the character of a victim of outrageous circumstance.

The remaining handful of comedies on the Broadway season's list came and went like turnpike traffic. *A Teaspoon Every Four Hours* (a Jewish family comedy co-written by and starring Jackie Mason) held 97 preview performances—a new record high—but closed after its formal opening night for a one-performance official run. Faring not much better were *Angela* by Sumner Arthur Long (a romantic involvement between a middle aged woman and a TV repairman); the Philip Magdalany one-acters *Watercolor* and *Criss-Crossing* satirizing modern patterns of sex and violence; Julie Bovasso's series of episodes in an artist's development in *Gloria and Esperanza;* Lonnie Coleman's *A Place for Polly* about the problems of a young woman married to an ambitious and rather unscrupulous book publisher; the anguish of an Ohio father (played by Lou Jacobi) who visits his son in New York only to discover that the young man is part of the gay set, in *Norman, Is That You?;* or *The Engagement Baby,* a hapless effort to levitate a situation in which a prosperous Jewish ad man finds that his college sweetheart, who is black, bore him a son.

Even the naked comic stresses of *Grin and Bare It!*, about a girl taking her fiance home to meet the family who, it seems, are nudists, could survive only 12 performances on a Broadway whose audiences are no longer attracted by nudity per se. It is worth noting also that the *Grin and Bare It!* actors who played the script stark naked modestly put on their dressing gowns for the curtain calls in order to demonstrate that these were not naked *actors* up there on the stage; they were actors playing naked *characters.* As soon as they stepped out of character they clothed themselves.

Among the 14 musicals presented on Broadway in 1969-70, the most satisfying was *Applause,* the Tony Award-winning show based on the same Mary Orr story as the movie *All About Eve,* with book by Betty Comden and Adolph Green, music by Charles Strouse and lyrics by Lee Adams. While we deplore the modern system of warming over successful movie or play material to make a musical (often it's a serving of leftovers buried in catsup), we must admit that *Applause* was a happy combination of creative efforts. The story about the ambitious young actress Eve flattering her way into the middle-aged star's favor in order to promote a Broadway career of her own provided a good backstage context for production numbers: the opening-night party, the night out on the town, the high spirits of the chorus "gypsies" at Allen's restaurant, the chic supper party in the star's apartment. The green-room maneuverings made a sturdy vehicle for a leading character with the glamor which most of the Broadway musical stage lacks these days. She is Margo Channing, the no-longer-young but still vibrant star, played by Lauren Bacall in her free-swinging, man-eating style. Miss Bacall is a lioness who never was a pussy cat; her Margo is younger and suppler than Bette Davis's was on the screen, but no less ferocious in defense of her career and her man. She was backed up by a good score, a fine production directed and choreographed by Ron Field in Robert Randolph's settings, and strong support by Penny Fuller as the scheming Eve, Len Cariou as the director Margo loves, Bonnie Franklin as a bouncing chorus gypsy and Lee Roy Reams as Margo's loyal hairdresser. It all blended together and worked very, very well as a show.

Another Best Play musical and the Critics Award winner was *Company,* most imaginative of the Broadway musicals, produced and directed by Harold Prince, with lyrics *and* music by the noted word artist Stephen Sondheim and book by the actor George Furth in his playwriting debut. *Company* wasn't based on yesterday's hit material; it is an original contemplation of the shiny, swinging and shallow (unfortunately) young marrieds who are "making it" in New York, and their friend Robert, "Bobby Baby," who is persistently single, though heterosexual. *Company* didn't look like any other show—it looked more like a vaudeville set for a trapeze act with a geometrical framework designed by Boris Aronson to stand in for the spiritless rectangularity of the new high-rise environment, a setting in which actors were permitted to travel vertically on a built-in elevator as well as horizontally from one to another part of their New York forest. *Company* didn't *feel* like any other show; from the beginning when Elaine Stritch abrasively rubs her fellow-guests at a birthday party the wrong way by characterizing them as "Lois and Larry Loser," and then the cast goes into an ingratiating musical "Bobby Baby" greeting of the 35-year-old birthday boy, you could almost taste the shine on the plastic society whose surface *Company* was going to scratch. The show repeated what was virtually the same episode over and over, as Robert (Dean Jones) goes from one couple to another, finding that each marriage is to some extent merely an accommodation against loneliness. If for no other reason— and there isn't much else in the world these characters inhabit—they are together for the sake of each other's company. Thus, *Company* ran hard in place, and eventually ran down, despite the efforts of Prince, Aronson and Sondheim (whose lyrics work many wonders, including a rhyme for "personable"—"coercin' a bull"). But *Company's* shortcomings as well as its advantages were clear evidence that they dared admirably to try.

Another of the season's big four musicals, *Purlie,* came along late in the season with *Applause* and *Company. Purlie* was a musicalization by Ossie Davis, Philip Rose and Peter Udell of Davis's play *Purlie Victorious,* about a resourceful black preacher who returns to his home town down upon the Swanee River and rallies the Uncle Toms to throw off the burdensome domination by their white "Cap'n" once and for all. *Purlie* converted racial antagonism into an edge of humor and an outburst of song, and it also profited from its performances including Cleavon Little as Purlie and Melba Moore as his beautiful young "protegee."

Then there was *Coco* and Katharine Hepburn playing Gabrielle Chanel in her heads-up, wiry way, as though the lady were a tennis champion instead of a dress designer. Alan Jay Lerner's book and lyrics worked noticeably better than the score or even the elaborate production. Nevertheless, Broadway owes a backward glance of gratitude to this show, which opened in December and carried on for weeks and weeks as the lone new musical excitement. And one of its better ingredients was Rene Auberjonois' performance as Coco's young, envious, effeminately-mannered colleague who is gleeful that Coco's new dresses seem at first to be a disaster. *Coco* had its faults, but it was there, with Katharine Hepburn and all, when it was most needed.

Another musical, which boasted an attractive score by Larry Grossman and Hal Hackady but was generally underrated, was *Minnie's Boys* about the struggles of the Marx Brothers to make it in show biz urged on by their mom (Shelley Winters as Minnie Marx, nee Shean, sister of Gallagher's vaudeville partner). Wisely confining themselves to suggestion rather than impersonation, Lewis J. Stadlen (Groucho), Daniel Fortus (Harpo) and Irwin Pearl

(Chico) adroitly portrayed the brothers in the hard times before their famous comic characterizations were set into the shapes we knew and loved. Also lightly nostalgic was *Jimmy,* with Frank Gorshin playing New York's 1920s Mayor James J. Walker in a musical reminiscence. *La Strada* based on the Fellini movie, *Gantry* based on the Sinclair Lewis novel and *Blood Red Roses* (an original anti-war musical set in the Crimean War era and once intended for off Broadway) failed expensively and instantly after only one performance each, like elephants shot in the eye. *Georgy* based on the British movie *Georgy Girl,* with Dilys Watling in the lead, lasted only 4 performances; *Park,* a production of Baltimore Center Stage, a four-character original about parents and their children deliberately meeting as strangers in a park to get a fresh view of each other, survived only 5 performances in a Broadway visit; *Look to the Lilies* based on *Lilies of the Field* with a Jule Styne-Sammy Cahn score and Shirley Booth in the Mother Superior role, lasted only 25; *Cry for Us All,* based on *Hogan's Goat,* stayed around for only 9.

Foreign visitors to Broadway in 1969-70 included the Grand Kabuki from Japan; a new edition of the Israeli revue *The New Music Hall of Israel;* the Comédie Française with four Molière programs. Individual visitors from abroad were Jean-Louis Barrault in his own devising of a singing, dancing, dramatized avant-garde presentation entitled *Rabelais,* based on the works and life of that free-swinging author; Charles Aznavour with his songs; and Marcel Marceau with his programs of BIP and other pantomimes. Domestic visitors included The National Theater of the Deaf offering *Sganarelle* and a Dylan Thomas program *Songs From Milk Wood,* plus a series of showcase bookings of regional theater programs, mostly revivals, reported in the next section.

Revivals

For the past few seasons the APA-Phoenix, a coalition of University of Michigan based regional theater and a New York production organization, dominated the Broadway revival scene with a series of notable productions at the Longacre. This year APA-Phoenix split at the hyphen and the two entities went separate ways. Ironically, what they could not accomplish in combination last season they each accomplished separately in 1969-70: a booming revival hit on Broadway. Ellis Rabb's Association of Producing Artists (APA) mounted the Tammy Grimes-Brian Bedford reenactment of Noel Coward's *Private Lives* which David Merrick presented to a New York that applauded its verbal and emotional acrobatics as though they were Neil Simon's latest. T. Edward Hambleton's Phoenix Theater in its turn sponsored the James Stewart-Helen Hayes *Harvey,* which became one of the town's hottest tickets at the ANTA theater, as well as John Lewin's *The Persians* adapted from Aeschylus' *Persae* with modern connotations about the personality of Xerxes-like aggressors. Both the Phoenix and APA are continuing as entities, the latter's new project being its customary annual autumn schedule of plays at Ann Arbor in Michigan's Professional Theater Program.

This revival season was one in which gain balanced loss. Like APA-Phoenix, the City Center found it no longer economically feasible to produce the revivals which have provided such nourishing supplement to the Broadway diet in seasons past. Losses were piling up above any possibility of subsidy, and so there were no City Center musicals this year. The summer *Oklahoma!* at the New York State Theater of Lincoln Center and à new Broadway production of *The Boy Friend* were the year's only surfacing of our musical heritage.

But lose one, win one: the City Center's Jean Dalyrymple went over on part time loanout to The American National Theater and Academy (ANTA) where, in collaboration with ANTA's executive producer Alfred de Liagre Jr., she helped direct the use of the ANTA Theater as a Broadway showcase for visiting troupes from regional theater and elsewhere. The programs included the Trinity Square Repertory Company production of Roland Van Zandt's *Wilson in the Promise Land,* the Playwrights Unit's *Watercolor* and *Criss-Crossing* and the Cafe La Mama's *Gloria and Esperanza.* Mostly, though, these guest programs tended to be revivals. Thanks to ANTA, Broadway audiences could see Edward Albee's chilling *Tiny Alice* again, as well as Georges Feydeau's *A Flea in Her Ear* and Chekhov's *Three Sisters,* all in William Ball's American Conservatory Theater (of San Francisco) productions. Likewise, ANTA presented Len Cariou (later the male lead in *Applause* opposite Lauren Bacall) in the American Shakespeare Festival of Stratford, Conn. version of Shakespeare's *Henry V;* Henry Fonda, Elizabeth Hartman, the late Ed Begley and Mildred Natwick in the Plumstead, L.I. Playhouse production of *Our Town;* the John Fernald Company from Rochester, Mich., in *The Cherry Orchard;* and, co-sponsor with the Phoenix, the smash hit *Harvey.* ANTA also chose to provide a limited-engagement showcase for last year's original off-Broadway production of Charles Gordone's *No Place To Be Somebody* which played 16 Broadway performances following the termination of its run downtown at the Public Theater (it was subsequently re-mounted in an off-Broadway revival which was still running when Gordone won the Pulitzer Prize in drama, a most commendable bestowal of that often debatable award, the second Pulitzer for a work that originated off Broadway—the first was *In Abraham's Bosom* in 1927—and incidentally, the first to a black playwright).

Win one, lose one . . . the American straight-play revivals at the City Center were now out of the question, of course, but this season Lincoln Center Repertory turned its attention to the American playshelf with an all-American season of one new play (Sam Shepard's provocative *Operation Sidewinder*) and three revivals: William Saroyan's limpid *The Time of Your Life,* Tennessee Williams' strangest and in some ways most contemporary script, *Camino Real,* with Al Pacino as Kilroy, and finally the art vs. materialism fantasy of the 1920s *Beggar on Horseback* by Marc Connelly and George S. Kaufman, with added music by Stanley Silverman and lyrics by John Lahr, and a spectacularly elaborate production designed by Michael Annals to stretch even the Vivian Beaumont Theater's well-developed production muscles.

It's neither our admiration for these individual scripts nor mere chauvinism that causes us to applaud Lincoln Center's decision to put on American plays for its 1969-70 season. It is a matter of esthetic priorities. In this country we are developing our own kind of theater, both dramatically and musically, out of the traditional forms we inherited from other cultures. The first business of a New York-based and New York-supported permanent repertory company, surely, should be to acquire proficiency in the production of American plays, just as the comparable British and French companies are first of all adept at interpreting their home-grown works, with foreign material sometimes staged as a special event. The Lincoln Center company is certainly not proficient yet, and it is heavily dependent on guest stars, but with an American season they are at least headed and moving in the right direction.

In addition to its regular season, Lincoln Center offered an instant revival of last year's successful *In the Matter of J. Robert Oppenheimer*. Also back in town trailing last season's glory was the Harold J. Kennedy revival of *The Front Page,* which not only retained its well-deserved popularity through a second season but also became a kind of a club for outstanding performers, as star (Molly Picon, Robert Alda, Maureen O'Sullivan, Jan Sterling, Jules Munshin, Paul Ford, Butterfly McQueen) replaced star (Helen Hayes, Peggy Cass, John McGiver, Dody Goodman) even in minor roles. In other star appearances in revivals, Celeste Holm did *Candida* and audiences were given the opportunity to re-acquaint themselves with Sam Levene's memorable performance of Patsy the gambler in *Three Men on a Horse.* This show wasn't able to develop the staying power of *The Front Page* or in recent seasons *You Can't Take It With You* and *The Show-Off*—the power to make it as an individual commercial Broadway hit. It was nevertheless a real asset to the season and emphasizes the need for some kind of permanent establishment to provide this kind of show with at least a partial shelter from the hard economic necessities of the commercial New York stage.

Off Broadway, revival activity was relatively light, with only 13 as compared with Broadway's total of 18. Ibsen was prominently represented by the New York Shakespeare Festival production of *Peer Gynt* in Central Park and the Opposites staging of *Hedda Gabler.* A revival of *The Madwoman of Chaillot* presented best-selling novelist Jacqueline Susann in the role of one of the madwomen, Mme. Josephine, but it was short-lived nonetheless. *Room Service,* with Ron Leibman in the lead, received a fresh viewing, as did Clifford Odets' *Awake and Sing.*

William Hanley's *Slow Dance on the Killing Ground,* a Best Play which lasted only a short time on Broadway, reappeared off Broadway this season, and so did *Dark of the Moon,* the witch-boy fantasy revived somewhat in the nude. Popular reappearances of off-Broadway scripts which had recently ended their regular runs but were brought back for another look included the abovementioned *No Place To Be Somebody* as well as John Herbert's prison play *Fortune and Men's Eyes* (in a new production directed by Sal Mineo and laced with explicit staging of homosexual practises), Ron Cowen's antiwar *Summertree* and Beckett's *Endgame* in a new interpretation by the gifted Open Theater troupe. With these off-Broadway efforts added to the presentations of Lincoln Center Repertory, ANTA, APA, Phoenix and the others in the larger theaters, the 1969-70 revival season in New York was perhaps a little short of outstanding classical presentations, but it was a valuable element of the whole culture and entertainment scene.

Off Broadway

Off Broadway in 1969-70 carried on from the previous season with its spate of new-play production. The tributary playhouses once attracted experimenters because of their relatively low production costs; and now they have also become attractive to the Broadway producers (many of whom tried their

The 1969-70 Season off Broadway

PLAYS (53)

The World of Mrs. Solomon
Tonight in Living Color
Fireworks
Time for Bed—Take Me to Bed
Pequod
The Glorious Ruler
A Black Quartet
Sourball
The Reckoning
Silhouettes
The End of All Things Natural
The Ofay Watcher
Calling in Crazy
American Place
Five on the Black Hand Side
Two Times One
The Pig Pen
And Puppy Dog Tails
A Scent of Flowers
The Haunted Host
Rose
Who's Happy Now?
The Disintegration of James Cherry
Passing Through From Exotic Places
The Moon Dreamers
Seven Days of Mourning
The Brownstone Urge
Love Your Crooked Neighbor
Negro Ensemble
The Harangues
Brotherhood & Day of Absence
The Memory Bank
Slave Ship
Transfers
The Jumping Fool
THE WHITE HOUSE MURDER CASE
Contributions
Nobody Hears a Broken Drum
Nature of the Crime
The Unseen Hand & Forensic and the Navigators
THE EFFECT OF GAMMA RAYS ON MAN-IN-THE-MOON MARIGOLDS
The Nest
And I Met a Man
The Persians
How Much, How Much?
The Republic
Colette
The Moths
The Shepherd of Ave. B & Steal the Old Man's Bundle
Lemon Sky
Chicago 70
Open Theater
THE SERPENT
Terminal
Candaules, Commissioner

MUSICALS (16)

Man Better Man
Promenade
Salvation
Rondelay
Public Theater
Stomp
Sambo
Mod Donna
The Last Sweet Days of Isaac
I Dreamt I Dwelt in Bloomingdale's
Billy Noname
Show Me Where the Good Times Are
The House of Leather
Lyle
Mahagonny
The Drunkard
The Me Nobody Knows

FOREIGN PLAYS IN ENGLISH (11)

Hello and Goodbye
A Whistle in the Dark
Crimes of Passion
The Local Stigmatic
Little Boxes
Lincoln Center
The Increased Difficulty of Concentration
Landscape & Silence
Amphitryon
The Criminals
Dear Janet Rosenberg, Dear Mr. Kooning
WHAT THE BUTLER SAW

Unfair to Goliath
Joy
Exchange
This Was Burlesque

REVUES (10)

Oh! Calcutta!
The Hoofers
The American Hamburger League
From the Second City
Gertrude Stein's First Reader
Love & Maple Syrup

FOREIGN-LANGUAGE PRODUCTIONS (11)

Arena Conta Zumbi
Polish Lab Theater
The Constant Prince
Acropolis
Apocalypsis Cum Figuris
Die Schauspiel
The Marriage of Mr. Mississippi
Philipp Hotz & The Firebugs
Iphigenie in Tauris
Le Tréteau de Paris
Le Grand Vizir & Le Cosmonaute Agricole
Lettre Morte & Architruc
La Lacune, La Jeune Fille a Marier & Les Chaises
Oh! Les Beaux Jours

REVIVALS (13)

N.Y. Shakespeare
Peer Gynt
Twelfth Night
Fortune & Men's Eyes
Summertree
Hedda Gabler
No Place To Be Somebody
The Madwoman of Chaillot
Lulu
Dark of the Moon
Room Service
Slow Dance on the Killing Ground
Awake and Sing!
Endgame

SPECIALTIES (5)

Whores, Wars & Tin Pan Alley
Go Fly a Kite
Baird Marionettes
Whistling Wizard & Sultan of Tuffet
Winnie the Pooh
Akokawe

Plays listed in CAPITAL LETTERS have been designated Best Plays of 1969-70.
Plays listed in *italics* were still running June 1, 1970.

luck in the little theaters this season) because of the handsome commercial possibilities which accrue to an off-Broadway hit. The traffic will now bear $10 a ticket for the whole house at off-Broadway successes (as compared with $8.50 top for a straight play on Broadway), with much smaller overhead for salaries, percentages, etc. Then, once a show is established, there is a market for additional productions across the country and around the world, where there is no concern whatever as to whether a good American script originated on Broadway or off. Even limited to 300 seats (as compared with 800 in the smaller Broadway houses) it never seemed desirable to Richard Barr to move *The Boys in the Band* or to Jordan Hott and Jack Millstein to move *Dames at Sea* uptown.

Thus, the season brought a whopping 64 new-play programs off Broadway, 53 of them American (see the one-page summary accompanying this report. Add to this number 16 new book musicals and 10 new revues, and you have a landslide of theatrical offerings. The volume of new work in English was about the same in 1969-70 as last season. There were 119 productions of record off Broadway in 1969-70 as compared with 103 the year before, but the increase was largely in revival and foreign-language production, plus a big numerical jump from 2 to 10 in the revue category.

One trait that did *not* carry over from the previous season, we are happy to report, was the monotony of sex—interest, yes, but preoccupation, no. If there was any single characteristic the 1968-69 sex plays had in common, it was that they were largely unsuccessful. They failed to attract audiences as the movies seem to do with this kind of material. Consequently, 1969-70 brought only a handful of such attractions. One of them was the exception that proves the rule, the out-and-out orgy *Oh! Calcutta!,* a smash hit by all standards except critical, where it suffered almost universal condemnation not as a shocker but as a bore. It was indeed not quite a shocker and almost a bore, but with a few points of interest along the way. Item: the opening number, in which each member of the cast one by one, individually, removes all his/her clothes was very cleverly conceived with backdrops of blown-up photos of the performer in various informal poses, in order to hold up the (clothed) personality of this human being before your eyes so that the body being revealed on the stage is never just a naked body, but the receptacle of a person.

And note: *Oh! Calcutta!* was the first production to demonstrate clearly and beyond any question of a doubt that a naked actor or actress onstage takes the mood right back to the Garden of Eden—not to original sin but back before that, to original innocence. Innocence, sheer *innocence* is the quality produced onstage by total nudity, no matter how suggestive the material being offered. Thus, in *Oh! Calcutta!* the bare, vulnerable skin and revealed glandular structure of the performers was at war with the subject matter. In those scenes which combined dressed and undressed actors—as in the skit where a young couple (naked) volunteer for a sex experiment to be witnessed by a group of burlesque-show medical types (clothed)—it was the clothed people whose smirks and obscene gestures seemed outrageous in the presence of naked innocence. In the Broadway *Hair* a couple of seasons ago, the shock of innocence provided by the suddenly naked cast at the end of Act I was entirely appropriate to the musical's story of babes in the hippie woods; in the salacious *Oh! Calcutta!* innocent nakedness is entirely *in*appropriate and tended to defeat the show's purpose.

Nudity itself as a instrument of showmanship was only sporadically employed. On Broadway there was the nudist play *Grin and Bare It!* and off Broadway in *The Nest,* for example, an actor licked cake icing from an actress's bare breasts and audiences coudn't have cared less—the play lasted for only one performance. *And Puppy Dog Tails* played a homosexual love triangle partly in the nude. An unclothed revue entitled *The Way It Is* tried a long string of 60 "previews" but no great interest was aroused and it folded in mid-January without ever holding a formal opening, dropping all of its $65,000 investment.

Homosexual affections were under some scrutiny in *The Haunted Host* and, from England, in John Bowen's *Little Boxes,* a program of one-acters whose second playlet, *Trevor,* was an amusing complication of two young women, lovers living in adjacent apartments, who are visited on the same day by their respective families and arrange for the same man to pose as their fiance. On the heterosexual side, the season included the musical *Rondelay* based on Schnitzler's good old *La Ronde,* and *Love and Maple Syrup,* about love in Canada, both naive in comparison to last season's whippings, rapings and adaptations of the works of the Marquis de Sade.

The socio-political mess attracted the skillful attention of several of our most gifted off-Broadway writers this year. LeRoi Jones's *Slave Ship* was a vivid piece of activist theater, described previously in this report. Racism and the black condition were the subject of Frank Cucci's *The Ofay Watcher,* about a white scientist's discovery of a pill to turn blacks into whites, with Cleavon Little as a black hobo hired as a guinea pig for an experiment which turns into a Grand Guignol of horror. Another strong variation on this theme was the musical *Billy Noname,* by Johnny Brandon and William Wellington Mackey, with Donny Burks in a standout performance as a young American black struggling not only against handicaps but also with success, trying to make a choice between personal ambition and soul-brother militancy. At American Place, Ed Bullins's new play *The Pig Pen* was a somewhat mystifying (and eventually stupefying) description of black-white relations in terms of a pot-sex-rock-alcohol orgy the night that Malcolm X was killed. Presumably, the party represents a kind of easy, *de facto* racial accommodation that existed before this tragic event. At the end of the play, the party is over; news of the murder arrives by radio, and everybody splits (and presumably this is the moment at which society itself splits into black and white elements). And twice during the party, a porcine Keystone Cop rushes in blowing his whistle like mad, dancing around and striking furniture with his truncheon (does Bullins mean that before Malcolm X's death police violence was rather comic, a bad-guy stereotype?). Bullins's symbols were vivid, but confusing: if the boorish, swinish pot party is to be taken as a sample of society when things were possible, then surely there were no Edens lost in the final shuffle of *The Pig Pen.*

Also examining various aspects of the black condition were *A Black Quartet* of angry one-acters by Ben Caldwell, Ronald Milner, Ed Bullins and LeRoi Jones; *Sambo,* a New York Shakespeare Festival Public Theater musical harping on black alienation; Joseph A. Walker's *The Harangues,* staged by the Negro Ensemble Company and drawing parallels between the black man's African tribal and American sociological problems; Douglas Turner Ward's *The Reckoning,* confronting a white Southern governor and a black pimp; the same author's new *Brotherhood,* a one-acter about latent racism among pretended liberals, and his *Day of Absence,* revived by Negro Ensemble which kept its franchise at the St. Marks Playhouse this season but fell short of its distinction of earlier play schedules; and the Ted Shine program of one-acters, *Contributions,* sketches of crackers and black militants.

On another socio-political subject, Jules Feiffer's *The White House Murder Case* alternated scenes on the battlefront in an imagined future war with Brazil (the "Chicos") with scenes in the White House. The self-deluding hypocrisy of a "future" president and his associates is so rampant in Feiffer's stage caricature that murder either on a mass or personal scale is ludicrously inevitable. In Feiffer's fun-house-mirror view, soldiers on the battlefield are slowly coming apart from the effects of their own nerve gas, and much the same sort of thing is happening at commander-in-chief level, where the nerve gasses of power and militarism are destroying their creators—in a setting that was dominated by an apparition that looked like a half-starved chicken worked over to look like an eagle by a third-rate taxidermist. Feiffer's skill with both drawing and writing pens in newspaper cartoons is one of the treasures of modern literature, and the actors and director of *The White House Murder Case* were on their mettle to reproduce the ironic visions of Feiffer's play-script. It must have been easier for the scene designer to realize his eagle than for the actors to realize his President, Secretary of Defense, Postmaster General and others in this Dr. Strangelove government. There may come a day when *The White House Murder Case's* sick joke will be almost unintelligible to theater audiences—let's hope so, anyway. In the meantime, more than any other script on or off Broadway this year it reflected the distemper of the times.

Many other plays in the off-Broadway stream came to grips with the dilemmas of the day, but none quite so effectively. Sam Shepard's program of one-acters, *The Unseen Hand* and *Forensic and the Navigators* provided images of the false values and destructive impulses of contemporary life. The one-acters of Jon Swan's *Fireworks* took off on the press, war and cocktail parties; idealism vs. practical politics was the issue in Robert Shure's *Sourball;* Ronald Ribman's *The Burial of Esposito* from his one-act program *Passing Through From Exotic Places* was a study of a father who has lost his son in the Vietnam war; Julie Bovasso's *The Moon Dreamers* dwelt on the irony of man's reach for the moon while his platform Earth suffers from so many imperfections; Larry Cohen's *Nature of the Crime* raised the question of whether and to what extent a scientist can be said to own his thoughts; *Chicago 70* hit upon the idea of combining material from Lewis Carroll's *Alice's Adventures in Wonderland* with Judge Hoffman's Chicago courtroom at the recent conspiracy trial, with gratifying results; and so on and on, again and again, on stage after stage, repetitious as a picketer's chant.

Curiously enough, it was in the 1969-70 musicals that off-Broadway authors made some of their most telling socio-political statements. *Salvation* by Peter Link and C.C. Courtney lambasted religious and moral poses with a bright young cast and a loud young rock combo, Nobody Else. In 1970 the rock lyric has taken on a life of its own as a literary form, a vehicle for emotional expression, philosophical debate, political activism—you name it, the rock lyric can and does express it daily from audio sources and from the stage itself in the likes of *Hair* and *Salvation. Salvation's* lyrics deal with such matters as the Vietnam war ("Let the Moment Slip By"), the literal interpretation of the Bible ("Deuteronomy XVII, Verse 2") and tenderness ("If You Let Me

Make Love to You Then Why Can't I Touch You?" with wit and insight.

Another rock musical, *Stomp,* also tackled issues of our time like sexual inhibition, air pollution, the generation gap. This show was devised by a group who call themselves The Combine at the University of Texas and brought to New York at Joseph Papp's New York Shakespeare Festival Public Theater (they also visited Paris this season as part of the Theater of the Nations program). It was a wild and woolly multimedia presentation which used all four sides of the auditorium as though it had been designed to be played in a basketball court, with the audience involved directly in the action. *Stomp* had no individual writing or acting credits and no script, so that it was played slightly differently, but always with an irresistible flair, at each performance.

The Public Theater's 1969-70 season was wholly devoted to protest musicals with *Stomp, Sambo* and *Mod Donna,* the latter one of two off-Broadway presentations that echoed with the shrill cries of Women's Liberation (the other was Ed Wode's *The Republic,* an adaptation of an Aristophanes comedy about women taking over the government of Athens). Early in the season the Maria Irene Fornes-Al Carmines musical *Promenade* satirized our world as seen through the eyes of a pair of convicts, and it remained for 259 performances as one of the year's major delights. *The Last Sweet Days of Isaac* was a small but wide-reaching musical by Gretchen Cryer and Nancy Ford which took on both sex and violence (and the nature of reality) in its tiny format. Austin Pendleton and Fredricka Weber filled the stage with two characters, first as a boy and girl trapped in an elevator and second as a pair of protesters lodged in jail and, though in separate cells, brought even closer together in spirit than they were in the elevator, as the boy watches on TV his own accidental death at a protest demonstration. Revues like the Chicago troupe's *From the Second City* and *Exchange* also made socio-polical scenes of varying intensity. Likewise in the form of a musical, *The Me Nobody Knows* brought onto the stage a collection of writings by ghetto children of many races expressing their frustration, their alienation, their imprisonment in the lowest dungeon under the mountain of American affluence. The sincerity of their expressions of distress, the general absence of anger in their longings, radiated warmly from the stage in this show performed by a talented young cast led by Northern J. Calloway through a soft rock score by Gary William Friedman.

In addition to the sex games and socio-political object lessons, there were plays that dealt with the abiding subject of the human being and his emotions. The most probing inner-space exploration of the year was Paul Zindel's *The Effect of Gamma Rays on Man-in-the-Moon Marigolds,* the New York Drama Critics Circle award-winner (for Best American Play) and a powerfully conceived, directed (by Melvin Bernhardt) and acted drama. This script was originally produced in 1964 at the Alley Theater in Houston, and it has taken a long, laborious time to reach the New York stage (partly because a New York TV version was panned by TV critics). Zindel's script is about a widow and her household of women without men: an epileptic daughter of hostile and unbalanced temperament; a dreaming younger daughter whose imagination has been captured by the atom and all its works; and an aged crone whose board money is essential in their grimly penurious circumstances. There's no silver lining in this dark cloud of family life, not even a marigold lining as the mother, played on an edge of despair by Sada Thompson in one of the year's best performances, misses her chance to bask in the reflected glory of her daughter's success with a science class experiment with radioactivity and flowers. Pamela Payton-Wright as Tillie the dreamer, Amy Levitt as the mind-blown adolescent with too much lipstick, even Judith Lowry as the sere and wrinkled Nanny, made their contributions to a play which showed human nature frayed back to expose the ugliness of fear and despair.

Another family closeup was Oliver Hailey's *Who's Happy Now?*, a script organized as a son's exhortation to his mother, years later, about the relationships of his youth back in a hard and bitter area of the Southwest where his father kept company with a saloon woman and his mother accepted this as a fact of life and managed to hold onto some shreds of pride and home life. This excellent script was excellently served in its New York production by Ken Kercheval, Teresa Wright and Robert Darnell as son and parents. *Who's Happy Now?* has been acclaimed in previous stagings at the O'Neill Foundation, the Mark Taper Forum in Los Angeles and the Washington Theater Club, so that its place in theater repertory is assured. It was New York's loss that it wasn't able to pick up off-Broadway audience support for more than a 32-performance run. Ditto for Lanford Wilson's *Lemon Sky,* also a study of family relationships which combined a straight-from-the-shoulder narration with dramatized flashbacks in an account of a 17-year-old boy's heartfelt and to some extent heartbreaking attempt to make close contact with his selfishly preoccupied father.

A Scent of Flowers by James Saunders was a luminescent vehicle for Katharine Houghton as a young girl who has committed suicide and re-lives and re-evaluates the stresses leading to her demise. Circle in the Square presented *Seven Days of Mourning* by Seymour Simkes, a dark drama of reaction to a daughter's suicide by a Jewish family who refuse to mourn her in traditional fashion. From England, Thomas Murphy's *A Whistle in the Dark* was another exceptional dramatic script, an outcry against brutishness and its inevitable self-defeat, in the story of an Irish father and brothers visiting the youngest married son in England and smashing into his life with their anti-British prejudices and ham-handed ways.

The season's best foreign script on or off Broadway, however, was the late Joe Orton's farcical *What the Butler Saw,* a compendium of theatrical comment on sexual behavior and mores in the form of a Feydeau-like treatment of a hectic day in the life of the director of an exclusive psychiatric clinic. This is the play that was greeted by jeers and catcalls at its West End debut last season and was lambasted by nearly every one of the London critics—but, clearly, Orton's cleverly orchestrated and enormously witty play will survive this lapse of expertise. Joseph Hardy, who also directed *Child's Play* this season, tuned it to farcical concert pitch, with characters running in and out in various stages of undress and transvestitism, ogling each other with joyless passion. *What the Butler Saw* wasn't just camp or black jokes, it had a high gloss on its cynicism, and a method in its madness. It makes one regret even more the plays which Orton, dead by violence long before his time and obviously at the height of his powers, now will never write.

A couple of Orton's darker pieces—*The Ruffian on the Stair,* about a warped, murderous middle-aged couple, and *The Erpingham Camp,* in which vacationists go berserk and destroy their environment—also appeared off Broadway briefly under the portmanteau title *Crimes of Passion.* Such one-acter programs were staples of the 1969-70 off-Broadway season, with 27 playwrights represented on 18 bills. Among the best of the year was *Dear Janet Rosenberg, Dear Mr. Kooning* by Stanley Eveling, a British playwright who provided Catherine Burns with a role to shape into one of the year's top performances as a sweet young thing hero-worshiping a mediocre middle-aged novelist and gradually eating him alive. The second playlet on Eveling's program, *Jakey Fat Boy,* was a lampoon of modern sex mystiques; both were evidence of a playwriting talent that performed much and promises more. Another notable twin bill was John Bowen's *Little Boxes* which combined the aforementioned *Trevor* with *The Coffee Lace,* about a group of vaudeville actors broke, unwanted and reduced to selling their very last object of value so as not to skip their traditional anniversary party. Still another English bill, *A Local Stigmatic,* presented several short Harold Pinter sketches on the same program with the title play, a one-acter by Heathcote Williams (and as previously reported, Pinter was further represented by the double bill of new plays at Lincoln Center).

A major event of the 1969-70 theater season was the visit to New York in an off-Broadway context of Jerzy Grotowski's pioneering Laboratory Theater of Wroclaw, Poland, with three programs: *The Constant Prince* (a mad society's torment of its gentle prince, based on a Calderon play), *Acropolis* (combining Biblical, Homeric and concentration-camp images suggested by a Polish work) and *Apocalypsis Cum Figuris* (a pot pourri of excerpts from various sources on the subject of the Second Coming). Grotowski's is a very special and certainly pretentious form of theater which has been criticized, analized, canonized and whipsawed, jeered and cheered on an international scale. Before audiences carefully limited in size (40 to 90, depending on the work) and prepared in mood by a reverential attitude that had nothing to do with the fact that the troupe was appearing in a converted church, the Polish company specializes in very high-intensity ensemble performances which demand more intense concentration from the watchers than conventional theater usually does. *Acropolis,* for example, enacts the grunting agonies of concentration camp inmates building their own doom machine out of gas pipes and dumping their dying into wheelbarrows like so many cement sacks. But the performance is based on a script which in its turn was preoccupied with Biblical and Homeric themes, so that simultaneously these gifted actors, including the outstanding Ryszard Cieslak as "Esau-Hector," represent parallel Homeric and Biblical images. An *Acropolis* program note explains: "Grotowski changed the setting of the drama from the Royal Castle (in Wyspianski's original script) to the Extermination Camp. In this production the characters . . . . . seem to come out of the crematorium smoke in vapors of mass extermination. The Biblical and Homeric scenes are performed by prisoners of the concentration camp. In a kind of daydream they act out their sorrow and consolation, their despair and hope, their cynicism and faith. The reality of the myth and the reality of the camp interpenetrate. . . . . A prisoner asks a fellow prisoner about his identity, then knocks him down and crushes him to death with a wooden shoe. This is the Bible episode of the first encounter of Laban and Jacob, who is wandering in search of a wife."

Baffling as these multiple meanings sound in this "clarification," they are even more obscure in performance—particularly if the observer has no knowledge of Polish. The general impression of a Polish Lab performance is of a vivid flash of intensely humanistic material—but what? It doesn't matter, however, whether the audience enjoys or understands the performance—it isn't for them, anyway, it is for the actors in the way that a religious ceremony is primarily for the celebrants. The audience is the suffered presence of a congregation. You are a witness to the act of the Grotowski troupe, and then you go away quietly without applauding, or discussing what you have seen; you are permitted, however, to reflect on it at your leisure. It is true that a strong subconscious rapport is established between the ensemble and its small audiences, and it is also true that many of the individual images stay with you long after the performance is over, if not the continuity or general impact of the work. In the short acquaintanceship of the group's New York visit, it looks as though Grotowski has devised a theater for the interpretive artist as opposed to the creative artist, a theater in which the actor-director can tailor a play-script as he would an overcoat to fit the form and style of his own imagination at the expense of the playwright's vision; he can take a Calderon script, say, and dye it purple, cut out huge patches, attach ornamentation, etc., until the result no longer resembles the model. It becomes, rather, the "creation" of the actor and director, not of the author, whose original idea the play might no longer fit or suit. Grotowski's provocative experiments are said to be a continuity from the work of Artaud, influencing other directors like Peter Brook (with his *Marat/Sade*) and modern performance groups including The Open Theater, whose *The Serpent: A Ceremony* is a Best Play of 1969-70. But let Grotowski have the last word on his own work, quoted from an explanatory program note:

"In our productions next to nothing is dictated by the director. His role in the preparatory stages is to stimulate the creative associations for which the impulse comes from the actors and to organize the final structure in which they assume a specific shape. It is one of the basic principles of our method of creation to have this kind of interplay in which director and actors give as much as they take, ceaselessly exchanging, sometimes passively, sometimes actively, the creative germs of the coming performance. This exchange does not take place at the level of discussion either; it is in essence an exchange of our life experience, a reciprocal offering of the signs of our biographies, of what I would call our '*arrière-être.*' If someone choses to call this melting-pot of creation 'Grotowski,' fair enough. But it must be clearly understood that this is only a symbol and that the reality is a division of responsibilities among the members of a group to which I am happy to belong."

Among the many, many 1969-70 off-Broadway programs there were some that took no part in setting trends of artistic revolution or social comment, but which brightened various corners of the city. *Joy,* for example, was exactly what its name promised, with a cabaret-style collection of Brazilian-style songs performed by Oscar Brown Jr. (who also wrote them), Jean Pace and the Brazilian instrumentalist Sivuca. A group of showcase productions brought into prominence good old-style vaudeville dancing *(The Hoofers),* assorted works by Gertrude Stein *(Gertrude Stein's First Reader),* the views of a Tel Aviv newspaper columnist presented in revue form *(Unfair to Goliath),* African music, dancing and poetry (Negro Ensemble Company's *Akokawe* with the Mbari-Mbayo Players), burlesque as Ann Corio remembers it *(This Was Burlesque)* and even Benjamin Franklin *(Go Fly a Kite,* with Fredd Wayne impersonating the great man). Zoe Caldwell, Broadway's beloved Miss Jean

Brodie, scored another acting triumph in *Colette* impersonating the noted French authoress and life-stylist, in a script adapted from autobiographical material by Elinor Jones. Among the year's specialties was a new Baird Marionette production, *The Whistling Wizard and the Sultan of Tuffet*. Distinguished visitors were the Arena Theater of Sao Paulo, Brazil, performing an historical play in Portuguese; Die Schauspiel Truppe of Zurich doing Goethe, Max Frisch and Friedrich Duerrenmatt in German; and Le Tréteau de Paris with a four-program sampler of contemporary French theater: Samuel Beckett's *Happy Days* (the French-language version) and three programs of one-acters by Rene de Obaldia, Robert Pinguet and Eugene Ionesco.

A selection of Kurt Weill's German and American theater music was available off Broadway under the title *Whores, Wars and Tin Pan Alley*. One of the season's major disappointments was the first professional New York production of the Weill-Bertolt Brecht *The Rise and Fall of the City of Mahagonny* under the abbreviated title *Mahagonny*. The work was adapted by Arnold Weinstein and staged by Carmen Capalbo in a production which took its time in many weeks of previews to get ready for opening night. The biting anti-materialism of Brecht's 1930 script (about a wholly materialist society established in an American town named Mahagonny by criminals) has survived the decades together with Weill's music. But the work itself, usually presented by opera companies, was uncomfortable within the context of the commercial musical theater. *Mahagonny* was a misfit this time around, an 8-performance disappointment but truly a case of book and score waiting for some kind of Godot of future New York production.

American Place Theater, under Wynn Handman's continuing guidance, kept up the good work of providing a showcase for new plays at its St. Clements Church base. Its season included a drama of dark psychological and emotional pressures (*Mercy Street* by Anne Sexton), a Harlem family comedy with echoes from the battle between the sexes (*Five on the Black Hand Side* by Charles L. Russell), a double bill of one-acters *(Two Times One)* by Charles Dizenzo and David Scott Milton, and Ed Bullins' newest script, the aforementioned *The Pig Pen*.

In its little Forum Theater, regarded as an off-Broadway house in tandem with its Broadway-sized showcase the Vivian Beaumont, Lincoln Center Repertory placed most of its 1969-70 emphasis on scripts from abroad (it was doing American plays in the large theater). In addition to the program of Pinter one-acters, the Forum offered a whimsical Czechoslovakian comedy of a scientist caught in the entanglements of modern existence (Vaclav Havel's *The Increased Difficulty of Concentration*) and a sparkling new *Amphitryon* by the German playwright Peter Hacks, translated by Ralph Manheim. The single American script of the Forum's season was *The Disintegration of James Cherry* by Jeff Wanshel, an inner-space exploration of a young man's nightmarish fancies, symptoms of terror in contemporary living translated into poetic images.

Yes, and there were other programs—quite a few in fact—which may have added little to the development, lore or enjoyment of the off-Broadway scene in 1969-70; but they were *there*, which in itself is a matter of importance. Off-Broadway production is an area in which numbers count, because large numbers of shows mean large numbers of playwrights heard, directors energized, actors seen, ideas exposed.

Offstage

Offstage as well as on, change was blowing in the wind during 1969-70; the same wind that was breezing fresh ideas of dramaturgy through the new scripts; the same that was blowing through the office skyscraper construction jobs on former theater sites.

One of the major offstage developments matured late in the season and was concerned with the physical sizes of the professional New York theater. Both Broadway and off Broadway operate according to standards set by contract and mutual agreement between managers, artists and craftsmen, and each has its separate organization of producers and theater owners: the League of New York Theaters (Broadway) and the League of off-Broadway Theaters. The off-Broadway League's jurisdiction encompasses playhouses with audiences of 299 or less; the Broadway League customarily deals with playhouses of 800 or more.

What about the middle ground between these two figures? Studies were made this season of the possibility of setting up a "Middle Theater" situation for in-between-sized activity in the area of a potential weekly gross not to exceed $25,000. Theaters which might come under this classification are the 499-seat Eden (where *Oh! Calcutta!* has been housed) and the new Twin Arts (West 48th St.), Hudson West (West 57th St.) and Edison (West 47th St.) theaters. Broadway houses could also be used for Middle Theater shows if portions of the auditorium were roped off to limit the size of audience and potential gross.

The office-builders continued their relentless incursion into the Broadway theater district, encouraged by a rationale that goes something like this: our legit playhouses are occupying valuable midtown real estate for only a limited number of hours a day and weeks a year, therefore this space should be put to more serviceable use as the site of an office skyscraper which would be operating around the clock all year long. This is exactly the kind of people-per-dollar-per-square-foot-per-second reasoning which has led us to the comfortable, easy, reassuring, humanistic environment which all of us, New Yorkers in particular, enjoy so thoroughly in this seventh decade of the 20th century.

Thanks to Mayor John V. Lindsay and other city planners, the theater district won't be wiped out, but it may change in character. Special regulations on the use of building sites in the Broadway area make it more profitable for the office-builders to include replacement theaters in their skyscraper designs, and this is being done. So the Playhouse is gone; the Morosco and the Helen Hayes are doomed; and the Cort, Broadway, George Abbott and Belasco Theaters are earmarked for oblivion. Replacement theaters are being drawn into the plans of the monoliths destined to occupy their sites, but whether these will satisfy all the demands of the continuing dramatic art form—the demands of intimate dramas as well as large musicals—is still moot.

On the plus side of the construction situation, the handsome new Juilliard Theater went into operation at Lincoln Center, and the boom in off-Broadway production was matched by an off-Broadway theater-building boom. This year there were 26 playhouses ranging in size from tiny to medium, some brand new and some remodeled, ready for occupancy, that weren't in existence last season.

The critics, as usual, were stirring around and being stirred in 1969-70. Concern over the New York *Times* daily reviewer's power (whoever might hold the job) to make or break a show with his single opinion was growing in every corner of the theater. Many suggestions for relieving the situation—which must be almost as embarrassing to the job's incumbent, Clive Barnes, as it is for the theater—were being discussed, some with *Times* personnel. Measures actually taken proved ineffective, however.

Also, the whole matter of the *Times* daily critic making a swing to London to report on new shows for his New York paper has been under discussion. In a page one story, *Variety* reported in September that "allegedly" the chances of a pair of London successes—*40 Years On,* with John Gielgud, and *The Secretary Bird*—to be optioned for and produced on Broadway were diminished if not altogether ruined by unfavorable opinions expressed in Barnes columns sent back to his paper during his London visit. Writing in the *Dramatists Guild Quarterly,* British playwright Frank Marcus complained that his play *Mrs. Mouse, Are You Within?* "had been mentioned most favorably in the pages of the New York *Times* by three London critics; nevertheless, Mr. Barnes's adverse report killed its chances as far as America was concerned." The point to be inferred from Marcus's complaint—that the *Times* has plenty of other sources of information about London plays without putting them to the commercial hazard of the New York reviewer's comment in advance of New York production—seems to be a good one.

Back home, at long last Barnes managed to soften David Merrick's hardnosed hostility towards critics. Merrick *praised* the *Times* critic in his presence while both were appearing on a New York TV show: "I highly approve of Barnes. I feel that my plays will be fairly and properly appraised in the New York *Times.* I think he loves the theater and hopes each time he's going to see something wonderful." Barnes's astonished reply: "I fear for my career."

The New York drama critics as a group came under criticism for not making the best use of tickets allotted to them; not bothering to return them when they didn't plan to use them, or coming alone and thus leaving the seat beside them empty (there's some justification for this latter practise; I have become convinced that many legit playhouses have been "refurbished" to allow for cramming in more and smaller seats in narrower rows to increase the auditorium's capacity; the empty seat gives some leg room and avoids severe constriction of the muscles and consequent lapses of concentration).

And finally on the offstage subject of critics, Louis Harris and Associates prepared a survey on *Critics and Criticism in the Mass Media* which established the following profile of the composite critic: a man (81 per cent), working for a male editor (98 per cent), average age 45, on the job 6 years, Protestant (47 per cent), liberal (57 per cent), with a college degree (75 per cent) in English or literature (51 per cent) or journalism (23 per cent), who went into journalism and became a critic by chance (50 per cent), who has worked for his medium in some capacity other than criticism (60 per cent), with admitedly too great an emphasis on the manner of expression at the expense of content (66 per cent), under some pressure from advertisers (21 per cent), employers (19 per cent), supervisors and editors (17 per cent), publicists and promoters (13 per cent) and personal threats (10 per cent).

A couple of censorship problems arose and/or continued on 1969-70. The *Che!* case was decided in Manhattan Criminal Court with the ruling that the play, containing the representation of 23 sex acts, was obscene without redeeming social value. Its author, producer and other personnel received fines. The decision is being appealed; meanwhile the result tends to encourage prosecutors everywhere. If the decision had gone against them, the censorship forces might have thrown up their hands and abandoned the field for a time, at least.

A tricky situation developed with the U.S. Department of State over a proposed Middle and Far-East tour of avant-garde playlets produced under the supervision of Gordon Davidson in the Mark Taper Forum's "New Theater for Now" series. Short works by Jules Feiffer, Lanford Wilson, Jean-Claude van Itallie, Israel Horovitz, Terrence McNally and others—among the finest talents the American theater has to offer—were placed in production for the tour; then, abruptly, in October, less than two weeks before the tour was to begin, the whole project was cancelled by the State Department with a vague explanation of "unstable and changing political conditions in the host countries." Authors of the playlets cried "censorship;" but an insider suggested that it might be "not so much a matter of censorship as of fear" lest the plays offend the antediluvian tastes of congressmen who hold the purse strings for State's cultural programs.

In the area of subsidy, NBC earmarked $1 million to back selected shows. The administration in Washington decided on $40 million as the sum to be asked for the National Endowment on the Arts and Humanities, about double the previous year's Federal subsidy, but still very small in comparison to, say, $477 million to the National Science Foundation for "pure science," or New York City's $75 million budget for arts and humanities programs. Of the previous year's Federal allotments, only $2 million went to the performing arts.

Among individuals who figured in offstage events was Dore Schary, in the thick of it as usual, appointed to the newly-created post of Commissioner of Cultural Affairs of the City of New York by Mayor John V. Lindsay and sworn in April 27. Queen Elizabeth II made it *Sir* Noel Coward, and the honors lists also elevated the world's leading English-speaking actor, Laurence Olivier, to a life peerage. There was a reshuffling of personnel at Lincoln Center, where John D. Rockefeller III retired as chairman of the board and was replaced by Amyas Ames—and Robert Montgomery resigned as president of The Repertory Theater of Lincoln Center, reasons undisclosed. And speaking of Rockefellers, a close associate of Rockefeller cultural interests, Nancy Hanks, was named to replaced Roger L. Stevens as chairman of the National Council on the Arts.

In politics, show people stood up to be counted on various contentious occasions, in what was certainly a stormy season. In the autumn there was the Moratorium, a mass demonstration for peace climaxed in New York City by a Bryant Park rally with many stage stars on the dais. A post-curtain observance in May—a moment of silence in memory of the students killed at Kent State University, followed by the reading of a text protesting the incursion of American troops into Cambodia—was organized by a theater committee of five persons under Kermit Bloomgarden's direction.

At season's end, in a decision which might eventually have exerted a profound effect on the theater if it had gone the other way, the U.S. Supreme Court struck down a Federal statute making it a crime for an actor to wear a U.S. military costume if his character reflects discredit on the service. The case involved an incident in which the law was invoked against a protester who staged an anti-war guerrilla theater skit outside the draft induction center in Houston, Tex. The Court's decision was unanimous. Justice Hugo L. Black stated in the opinion that such incidents might be "crude, amateurish and perhaps unappealing," but that "an actor, like everyone else in our country, enjoys a Constitutional right to freedom of speech, including the right openly to criticize the Government during a dramatic performance."

Following Vice President Spiro T. Agnew's now-celebrated attack on those he envisioned as "effete snobs" in the communications media, the annual membership meeting of Dramatists Guild playwrights, composers and lyricists framed and adopted this resolution: *"Resolved: It is the sense of the Dramatists Guild at its annual meeting to assert and affirm our belief in the freedom of the press and the freedom of the various media; and to deplore specifically the succession of threats by the administration to attempt to intimidate the media, the press and for that matter everybody else in the country."*

It was ironic to reflect that only a few months previously, when the 1969-70 season began in June, there existed off Broadway a topical revue with the year's most un-prophetic title: *Spiro Who?*

The days of the 1969-70 New York theater season were days of change, not only in the notoriety of Spiro somebody but in all things visible and invisible including the art of the theater; days of *becoming,* of metamorphosis taking place and continuing to take place, with no end to the process in sight. The important question for the theater in the season just past is not, Was it a good one? (yes, in spots) or Was it a bad one? (no, not really) but Was it one of change or stagnation?

We hasten to proclaim it one of change, not all for the better of course, but with vigorous economic and artistic forces continuously churning within. Those who jest at the theater's scars by calling it the Fabulous Invalid do not understand the nature of its wounds. The theater is a fabulous convalescent, constantly recovering from some staggering blow of imagination which disrupts the system, knocks the props out from under the steadiest old artistic concepts and makes the whole art form see stars.

How went the theater in 1969-70? Painfully, thank you, painfully but not lamely; determined to strike every note from sexual outrage to political contempt, to try every dramatic trick from attacking the audience to Pinteresque non-communication, and to defend its freedom of choice against all intrusions of power and censorship; slowly, boldly, hopefully making progress as the seasons change.

Alexis Smith, *left,* in a scene from the musical *Follies,* book by James Goldman, music and lyrics by Stephen Sondheim.

PHOTO BY MARTHA SWOPE

1970-71

MOST of our leading playwrights took this year off, and most of the best new scripts represent new growth, a greening rather than a yellowing. *Sleuth* is a first play by Anthony Shaffer. Yes, *Conduct Unbecoming* is ostensibly a nostalgic collection of scarlet-uniformed pukka sahib characters, but its real subject is highly contemporaneous—the cruelty deep-rooted in man's nature—and it was its author's, Barry England's, first major professional stage production. *The Philanthropist* was Christopher Hampton's Broadway debut with a new play (his Ibsen adaptations preceded it by a few weeks). *The Gingerbread Lady* is the first Neil Simon play with a cutting edge as well as a sharp point. *The House of Blue Leaves* is John Guare's first full-length play. *Home* was David Storey's American theater debut. *Follies* may have a nostalgic title, but it is not so by any means; written by James Goldman and Stephen Sondheim, it is brilliant and innovative. *Steambath* may be Bruce Jay Friedman's second Best Play, but it's the first anywhere in which God has been personified as a Puerto Rican steam room attendant.

But lest anyone suppose that in a time of social and political unrest new New York theater was an ostrich burying its head in detective stories, marital/alcoholic tensions and beach ball production numbers, we point to the fact that one of our Best Play co-authors—Father Daniel Berrigan—is in jail this summer of 1971 for anti-war protest "crimes" including the actions described in the Berrigan-Saul Levitt dramatization *The Trial of the Catonsville Nine*. Still another Best Play author, Athol Fugard—whose *Boesman and Lena* is a piercing example of the human condition on the receiving end of racial prejudice—is considered a troublemaker in his native South Africa, which denied him a passport to come to New York for rehearsals of his play in June.

Yes, the number of shows produced on Broadway declined to 56 productions of record during 1970-71 (see the one-page summary accompanying this report) from 68 last year, 76 the year before and 84 the year before that. This figure is all the more distressing because the new-American-play category suffered the greatest decline. There were only 14 new American straight play programs produced on Broadway this season along with the 11 musicals, compared with 21-14 last year, 24-12 the year before and 25-10 the year before that. What's more, or rather less, of these 14 new plays six were Limited Broadway productions under the new "middle theater" agreement (of which more anon), so that there were only eight—count 'em on your fingers—eight American plays produced in 1970-71 in the old Broadway sense of the word production.

Is "distressing" a strong enough word for this development? Wouldn't "alarming" be more accurate? I make bold to say no at this time. There is no great attentuation of playwriting—the 39 new American straight-play programs produced off Broadway this season tell us clearly where our replacement playwrights are, and the New York audience continues to make hits out of the best material that comes to Broadway, even at today's prices. As long as there is a sizeable playwriting and audience potential, there is the condition for a

The 1970-71 Season on Broadway

REVIVALS (15)

Charley's Aunt
Othello
Lincoln Center Rep
The Good Woman of Setzuan
The Playboy of the Western World
An Enemy of the People
Antigone
Hay Fever
Ibsen Rep
A Doll's House
Hedda Gabler
Hamlet
No, No, Nanette
A Midsummer Night's Dream
The School for Wives
Johnny Johnson
Dance of Death

PLAYS (14)

Opium
Gandhi
Les Blancs
The Castro Complex
The Candyapple
Foreplay
THE GINGERBREAD LADY
Happy Birthday, Wanda June
Four on a Garden
And Miss Reardon Drinks a Little
Father's Day
All Over
Scratch
Lenny

MUSICALS (11)

The Rothschilds
Two by Two
The Me Nobody Knows
Lovely Ladies, Kind Gentlemen
Soon
Ari
Oh! Calcutta!
FOLLIES
70, Girls, 70
Frank Merriwell
Earl of Ruston

SPECIALTIES (4)

Bob and Ray—the Two and Only
Paul Sills
Story Theater
Metamorphoses
Emlyn Williams as Charles Dickens

HOLDOVER SHOWS WHICH BECAME HITS DURING 1970-71

Applause
Company

FOREIGN PLAYS IN ENGLISH (8)

CONDUCT UNBECOMING
Not Now, Darling
SLEUTH
HOME
A Place Without Doors
Abelard & Heloise
THE PHILANTHROPIST
How the Other Half Loves

FOREIGN-LANGUAGE PRODUCTIONS (4)

Light, Lively and Yiddish
The President's Daughter
Orlando Furioso
National Theaters of Japan

Plays listed in CAPITAL LETTERS have been designated Best Plays of 1970-71.
Plays listed in **bold face type** were classified as hits in *Variety's* annual list of hits and flops published June 9, 1971.
Plays listed in *italics* were still running June 1, 1971.

healthy theater. Production statistics don't tell the whole story. Those who yearn for the good old 200-play seasons of the 1920s should go back to the old Burns Mantle *Best Plays* volumes and read some of the descriptions of the plots with third-act resolutions brought about by remorse, suicide, fortuitous heart attacks, etc. Why don't we have all these plays today? Maybe we do, on daytime TV.

Meanwhile, the problem of high production costs, consequently an ever-more-limiting ticket price increase, linked with the high-risk factor inherent in the power of the New York *Times* daily reviews, poisons the environment. Luckily, the art form itself is vigorously healthy, and it is surviving. And the theater as an institution is not just sitting there; it is working hard to solve its problems, which is another good sign. The new 7:30 p.m. curtain for the convenience of commuters and the "middle theater" arrangement for encouraging producers are evidence of the effort the theater is making to change with the times and lifestyles of its patrons. In the meantime—as the figures distressingly show—many Broadway playwrights and producers are holding off, waiting for conditions to improve.

In 1970-71, the going rate for the best seat at a Broadway musical (fifth row center at *Follies,* say, on a Friday night) was $15, with musical matinees pegged anywhere from $7 to $9 a seat and the cheapest seat at midweek going for $5 or $6. For a straight play on Broadway $8.50 was the usual price for a top ticket; prices above $9 were in existence, but rare. Off Broadway, prices varied somewhat according to degree of popular appeal and even of subsidy, but a young man taking his Friday night date to an off-Broadway show would have been well advised to expect to pay $7.50 each for front row seats and $4 in the last row.

It's almost embarrassing to report, here in the midst of all the modern theater's difficulties, that the *Variety*-estimated total Broadway theater gross for 1970-71 was a healthy $54,941,023, an increase over last year's $53 million, possibly creeping back toward that record high of $59 million in 1967-68. Road productions of Broadway shows continued to do better than ever, grossing $50,079,434 compared to last year's $48 million (and thus giving Broadway its fourth $100-million-plus season in a row: $105 million plus, the highest on record). In the matter of playing weeks (if ten shows play ten weeks that's 100 playing weeks) Broadway registered 1,099 this season compared with 1,047 last year and 1,200-odd in the four previous years. The high 1970-71 gross is explained not by great activity, therefore, but by higher ticket prices and longer runs for the high-priced holdovers. The two longest-running musicals in Broadway history were both playing in 1970-71: *Hello, Dolly!* which set a new record of 2,844 performances before it closed, and *Fiddler on the Roof* which in turn would break *Dolly's* record in July, 1971.

Within the overall figures there were conspicuous individual triumphs and tragedies. The Alan Jay Lerner musical *Lolita, My Love* folded in Boston to the tune of a $900,000 loss, while *Dolly* was reporting a $9,000,000 net profit on its $350,000 investment and still counting. Some of the year's ongoing successes, according to *Variety* reports, were *Hair* ($2,098,000 on $150,000), *Coco* with Katharine Hepburn (which grossed $206,131 in a single week on the road, in Chicago), *Sleuth* ($160,314 net on $150,000 at season's end and still going strong), *Fiddler on the Roof* (about $7 million net on $350,000), *Man of La Mancha* ($5 million on $200,000) and *The Boys in the Band*

($580,000 net on $20,000 in New York, $120,000 on $70,000 in national companies). According to an estimate published by the theatrical financing division of the New York State attorney general's office, "average capitalization" for shows was $300,000 for Broadway and $47,000 off Broadway. But an "average" figure is meaningless in a situation in which a small-scale straight play can squeak onto Broadway for $110,000 whereas an unsuccessful *Lovely Ladies, Kind Gentlemen* could cost $600,000 to produce and lose more than that in an unprofitable tryout.

As a matter of fact, if our season did not run a complete metaphysical gamut it at least touched both ends at A and Z with effective personifications onstage of both God and Satan. As we have noted, God appeared in *Steambath* in the form of an authoritative, awesome Puerto Rican, guardian of the anteroom to eternity, played by Hector Elizondo. Satan appeared in the form of a small-town Yankee lawyer as portrayed by Will Geer in Archibald MacLeish's short-lived *Scratch*. Both were highly successful, formidable portrayals—put them onto the same stage, and *there* would be a play.

The directors could point with pride to Peter Brook, who found a whole new way of doing *A Midsummer Night's Dream;* directors and producers to Harold Prince, who followed last season's pacesetting *Company* with 1970-71's pacesetting *Follies*. Among other producers who both dared and succeeded in this perilous interval were Morton Gottlieb and Helen Bonfils, David Merrick (of course), Hillard Elkins (who brought *Oh! Calcutta!* uptown into the respectable neighborhood of his *A Doll's House* and *Hedda Gabler*), Saint Subber, Alexander H. Cohen (who produced a dandy Tony Awards TV show in collaboration with his wife, Hildy Parks, and then went on to win the Critics Award with *Home*), Zev Bufman, T. Edward Hambleton (still astride his Phoenix as it rose from the ashes) and the remarkable Joseph Papp who now has five auditoriums in working order at the Public Theater on Lafayette Street, put on ten shows (not counting experimental stagings) this season and, when he fell as usual into financial difficulties, summoned the City of New York to his rescue.

Among those who fared less felicitously in 1970-71 were Joseph Kipness and Lawrence Kasha who produced and then immediately closed Oliver Hailey's *Father's Day* after only one performance, following an unfavorable *Times* review—though high praise soon began pouring in from other sources including major weeklies, and the continuing profits from *Applause* might well have influenced the producers to take a longer chance on *Father's Day* (to be fair, Mr. Kipness has since commented that maybe he could have used a little hindsight at the right moment). The Hailey play, about three divorced women meeting their ex-husbands for cocktails, has already been produced again, by the Washington, D.C. Theater Club, and will undoubtedly survive its New York experience.

Another of the year's major playwriting disappointments was Edward Albee's *All Over,* an effort to dramatize the importance and significance of life in the contrasting situation of a death watch, with friends and family hovering around a dying man and indulging their own impulses and emotions. It seemed formless, almost purposeless, with the John Gielgud staging hurling the spoken observations out into empty, echoing space without any compression. It should be reported, however, that *All Over* attracted adherents who praised it highly; it was the first choice of Clive Barnes, Harold Clurman, William Glover and Edward S. Hipp for best play and of George Oppenheimer for best American play in the Drama Critics Circle voting.

The considerable Gallic fascination of Danielle Darrieux proved unable to carry the heavy weight of *Coco* after Katharine Hepburn left it to go on tour, and the gross dropped by $70,000 the first week the one star replaced the other in the Broadway cast. Shelley Winters made an unsuccessful foray into playwriting with three one-acters on a program entitled *One Night Stands of a Noisy Passenger,* romantic shipboard episodes. Judith Anderson tried playing Hamlet for a couple of special performances at Carnegie Hall, neither the first time the Prince of Denmark has been portrayed by an actress, nor the most effective. The Roundabout tried an off-Broadway *Hamlet* with an all-male cast including the actor playing Gertrude. Still another *Hamlet,* an amateur one mounted by the combined efforts of the Oxford and Cambridge drama societies under Jonathan Miller's direction, was brought over here for a brief tour.

Probably the year's most conspicuous individual waste of time and talent was Norman Wisdom's in a tasteless sex farce called *Not Now, Darling* dragged all the way from England even though we have a continuing domestic surplus of this commodity. Shirley Booth wrestled with Noel Coward stylization in a revival of *Hay Fever* and didn't quite manage a draw. After the success of *No, No, Nanette* it must have seemed a good idea to bring back a collection of Gershwin numbers as an off-Broadway musical, but *Do It Again!* failed to attract much attention.

Titles like *Foreplay* (one actor refused a role in this show because he would not play a nude homosexual love scene), *The Immaculate Misconception, Score* and *Stag Movie* found the theater still trying to sell sex in one form or another, more often than not in some fun-house-mirror distortion. It didn't succeed without an additionally supportive quality like the satirical viewpoint of *The Dirtiest Show in Town,* the innocence of the commune characters in *Touch* or the consuming emotions of a historical love affair in *Abelard & Heloise,* which included a nude love scene played by Keith Michell and Diana Rigg in the title roles.

There were two adroit manipulations of spacetime onstage, one of them in *Follies* (of which more later in this report) and another in the British comedy *How the Other Half Loves,* thoroughly Americanized on Broadway under the direction of Gene Saks, with Phil Silvers and Sandy Dennis as neighbors whose spouses are making it, not quite clandestinely enough. The spacetime trick is that a single living-room set serves for both households. The couples aren't aware of each other, of course; they are supposed to be in separate houses, but the audience sees them as two couples inhabiting the same room at the same time. The chef d'oeuvre of this play by Alan Ayckbourn, which happened to be the season's best light comedy fare, is a dinner party, or rather *two* dinner parties taking place at the same table with the same guests on two succeeding nights—one party a success and the other a disaster.

In the deep water where the currents run slow they were setting in the same directions as in recent seasons. 1970-71 continued to be a time of change, we hope of development, within the theater art. Audience tastes continued fragmenting into a group of audiences instead of a great monolith. There was one audience for *No, No, Nanette,* another for *Home,* another for the manic-depressive *Alice,* and so forth. More and more obviously, it seemed, the New York theater was dividing into two theaters like some unicellular creature overcome with an impulse to grow; not the Broadway/off Broadway separation, not straight/musical, not even square/far out, but a comfortable/uncomfortable theater division which crossed all other dividing lines; the comfortable theater as we have always known it existing side-by-side with the uncomfortable theater as it is bound to become, stretching our minds until it strains our imagination, stimulating our senses to the threshold of pain.

The "uncomfortable" new theater has abandoned the old rubber-tired ride in favor of roller-coaster speed and excitement. It continued to experiment with forms of theater that tear down that reassuring fourth wall and reach out for direct contact with the audience. As Walter Kerr put it in a Sunday *Times* article, "The audience has got to have more rehearsal time. It is being asked to do so many things these days." It was asked to touch elbow-tips as a symbolic taking-part in the affectionate activities of the off-Broadway musical *Kiss Now*. At *Commune,* it was asked to share the experience of collectivism by removing shoes upon entering the theater and creating a huge pile of footwear symbolizing community and togetherness, along with the inconvenience of trying to find your own shoes after the show. In John Guare's fine *The House of Blue Leaves* the characters kept telling the audience more about themselves than they would tell each other, but this was more in the nature of extended stage asides than a radical form of stagecraft.

New styles of playwriting were flashing like colored lights all over the city. *Follies* was breaking new ground, and so was Paul Sills's *Story Theater* and *Metamorphoses,* adapting myths and fairy tales to the stage with an unusual mix of narration, mime, a few words of dialogue and a musical background. This was a form of collaborative rather than literary theater with all the tricks of stagecraft used to punch up the ironies of fairyland: the sky really *is* falling as near as makes no difference, and the gods *will* use mortals as their playthings, and it is the lot of human kind to put up with its tortured destiny.

There were many variations on the subliminal style practised so expertly by Harold Pinter and Samuel Beckett and so assiduously by others, a style like a negative impression of a photo image, in which the actual words spoken are a counterpoint to the unspoken meaning, in which the words that count are the words between the lines bringing images to mind after the image expressed. David Storey's New York Drama Critics Circle best-play-award-winning *Home* was an example of this stylistic development, and also of the fact that it runs great risks of noncommunication between playwright and audience. Suppose the audience does *not* hear the words between the spoken lines, what then is left on the stage? The two Pinter one-acters *Landscape* and *Silence* revived this year by Lincoln Center Repertory at the Forum Theater are problematical in this respect, even though their author is a master of the medium. *Home*, too, is stylistically curious but perilously inarticulate with its insistent groping, and almost always missing hold, through the murky memories and cliche-ridden habits of speech of two old fogies who, granted, are brain-damaged by senility or some other tragedy of the psyche (Storey is never clear on this or any other point) but who, judging from the scraps of conversation left to them, would have bored the bejesus out of everybody on the best day they ever had. I am one of those to whom *Home* communicates very little except a modicum of compassion for the human condition; about as much, say, as an average segment of *Marcus Welby, M.D.* True, with Ralph Richardson and John Gielgud playing the two staring old men there is for a while the illusion that, yes, something important *is* being said between the lines and happening in the pauses, because of the brilliant inventiveness of character detail which these two perfectly polished, highly reflective artists bring to their roles. Obviously, there are some to whom *Home* communicates—New York's distinguished drama critics, for example, ranked it the best play of the year, bar none. Well, my choice for the best is *Follies,* or for one without music *Sleuth.*

In substance as well as in form and style the currents of the "uncomfortable" new theater were running the patterns of recent seasons. A sense of outrage is pushing most other subjective concepts off the stage; not invented outrage, but feedback of outrage plucked from life like an ugly *objet trouvé* and shaped by the playwright into recognizable dramatic form. Look at the subjects of some of season's most effective work. *Boesman and Lena* pictures human beings reduced to the status of swamp animals. *The House of Blue Leaves* is an oil-and-water mixture of intimate human agony and a black-comedy effort to murder the Pope. *Alice in Wonderland* becomes a horror tale in which the Dormouse at the Mad Hatter's tea party crams his mouth and smears his face with food in a stomach-turning image of degraded appetite. *Follies* gambols in the wreckage of exposed and shattered pretenses. *The Trial of the Catonsville Nine* is a polite protest in courtroom-scene form, but its outrage is—and there is no greater outrage anywhere among the louder theatrical noises of 1970-71—that the facts and events it represents onstage really happened. Even the Broadway theater's numero uno, Neil Simon, was writing in *The Gingerbread Lady* about an alcoholic nymphomaniac and her friends the homosexual and the narcissist.

Within all this artistic turmoil the "comfortable" theater continued to exist, however, and even to flourish. There is no shadow of a doubt that a large segment of the audience continued to demand and enjoy the likes of *Sleuth, No, No, Nanette* and the Ibsen repertory. Artistic changes and changing audience tastes are mirror images of each other, though there may be some chicken-and-egg debate about which comes first. The theater as we have known it and the theater as it is becoming are drifting farther and farther apart, because the old theater is anchored fast, and so are the tastes and styles of some audiences. The increasing gap is one of the factors that is creating the illusion of an era of nostalgia—the new theater is making old-style theater *seem* nostalgic.

Taking a wide-angle view of the season of 1970-71, we see that our versatile theater is capable of assimilating both *Sleuth* and *Home,* both *Follies* and *Nanette,* and of recruiting an audience for each; but while our new theater is developing and gaining strength, our old theater as of this date is still in the ascendancy, economically at least, and its partisans still in the majority. Coming out of *Follies,* I overheard an elderly dissatisfied customer, a square audience peg in the roundest hole of the season (and with a title like *Follies* they must get a lot of those), complain to his companion: "They haven't had *my* kind of musical since *Suzie Wong.*" Very well, sir, you're entitled to your opinion, your taste and your enjoyment, and you are still in the majority—but you are *not* entitled to pretend that the New York stage belongs in the grip of some sort of retrogressive impulse like nostalgia, rather than in the main stream of the steady, sometimes uncomfortable but inexorable progress toward the more exciting theater of the future.

Broadway

The best of the 1970-71 straight plays *Sleuth* , is a confrontation be--

tween a snobbish intellectual (the detective story writer played by Anthony Quayle) and his wife's proletarian and persistent lover (a charmless but quick-witted young man played by Keith Baxter). The dangerous games they play with each other in jealous rivalry, trying with frightening masquerades to unman each other, are most cleverly conceived in Anthony Shaffer's script and executed by the cast. The author is the twin brother of the much-cited playwright Peter Shaffer.

Sleuth was the most conspicuous of many works by British authors which dominated the straight-play scene on Broadway this season. *Home* has been covered earlier in this report, as have *Abelard & Heloise* and *How the Other Half Loves*, which enhanced the Broadway scene. A third British play on the Best Plays list is *Conduct Unbecoming*, the London-New York playwriting debut of a new author, Barry England. His was a colorful tale of warped values among the British officer caste of an Indian regiment in Her Majesty Queen Victoria's Imperial army in the late 1800s. One of these proud, scarlet-uniformed, pig-sticking pukka sahibs commits a clandestine act of most ungentlemanly violence, and the play's problem is to discover who is the guilty party, in a formal midnight inquiry in the officers' mess. The performances of Donald Pickering as the spit-and-polish adjutant who conducts the trial, and of Jeremy Clyde as a tipsy, new-fledged subaltern who would like nothing better than to be kicked out of all this and sent home, were noteworthy vignettes within an ensemble of notable performances by the British cast. Again, there are the fibers of reality running through what is ostensibly a simple, theatrical tale of suspense in a highly colorful setting. Barry England's play is also a dramatic demonstration that callous and unspeakable violence against dumb animals can lead to callous and unspeakable violence against human beings and is in fact an extension of the same reprehensible impulse to shed blood—a truth that can't be overstressed, either in Imperial India or here and now in the land of the free and the home of the brave.

A fourth British play on the Best Plays list is Christopher Hampton's *The Philanthropist,* a provoking piece of work which opens by spattering blood all over the wall in the incident of a suicide, leaving the audience in shock and in quaking anticipation of what may happen next. Nothing similar ever does; what follows is the polite and deferential self-destruction of an intellectual who sells his manhood for a mess of good manners and an uncontrollable impulse to accommodate everybody. The script is a character study of a philology professor who has succumbed to early training and is now buried alive in attentive mannerisms and the literal meanings of words. Hungry women, egotistical authors, concerned friends revolve around him; he always pays attention but cannot understand. He is bound to destroy his romance, his friendships and himself, not with a bang but with impeccable courtesy, without raising his voice or using a word wrongly. Alec McCowen gave one of his perfectly detailed performances, sustaining every quirk and whimsy of this professor, and he was nobly assisted by Ed Zimmermann as a friend on the faculty, Penelope Wilton as a sexual virago, Jane Asher as a bewildered fiancee and Victor Spinetti as a novelist whose ego is sometimes battered but never broken. Hampton's adaptations of Ibsen's *A Doll's House* and *Hedda Gabler* were hot tickets even before *The Philanthropist* arrived; again, a happy combination of playwriting and acting skill, with Claire Bloom in vibrant and career-expanding interpretations of Nora and Hedda. Hampton's *When Did You Last See*

My Mother? off Broadway in 1967 was one of the first of the new-era dramas of sexual involvement.

Turning to the American list, our choice for the best would have to be *Follies,* the musical that not only had widely varied effects on the fragmenting audience, but even fragmented its own enthusiasts. There are those who hated *Follies* and those who loved it; and even among those who loved it, there were some who shrugged off its book. I am not one of them. To me *Follies* was uniformly imaginative, varying never in quality but only in intensity from scene to scene. Remember that its title is *Follies,* not *The Follies;* it wasn't a girlie show, but a haunting and emotionally moving treatment of the foolishness and heartache of human pretenses. The theater itself being a kind of pretense, the appropriate setting for *Follies* was a bare, ruined stage where once the sweet showgirls sang, now littered with the rubble of plaster ornamentation, its half-demolished roof open to the sky. In this dead pretense of a theater there takes place a reunion of middle-aged former show people who are themselves the living results of the pretenses, the "follies," projected by their 20-year-old selves when they were young and playing on Broadway. These memory-images of youth were present onstage as actual people, in black and white to contrast with the grown-up characters, haunting the mature characters with their past selves. Seldom did the memory-figures make direct contact with their future selves; they were true to the strange principles of spacetime governing the relationship between memory and reality.

Each of the leading characters has been indulging his or her folly, brought to a critical state by this boozy reunion and finally and achingly exposed in an ironic "Loveland" sequence staged in Valentine lace, with beribboned showgirls and chorus boys in powdered periwigs. At the heart of the matter was the pervasively sad and increasing *felt* story of two promising marriages gone to seed: the stately Alexis Smith with a coldly successful politician-diplomat, John McMartin, and the wistful Dorothy Collins with a traveling man, Gene Nelson, who loves her but cheats on her. They and their problems are symbols, certainly, but the symbols are appropriate to our times and circumstances, and extremely empathetic. When all their follies have been mercilessly exposed in the ironies of "Loveland;" when the youth-figures have disappeared in the wings; when the party is over and the married couples are left alone to face one another in the dawn coming through the holes in the roof of Boris Aronson's magnificently haunted setting, a form of emotional catharsis has taken place, seldom if ever before experienced in the musical theater—less than tragic, perhaps, but strangely akin to the emotional mood of the burial scene in *Death of a Salesman.*

The very concept of *Follies* was partly responsible for its distinction as this season's best-of-bests, but it also inspired each of its contributors to a best effort, and therefore it took fire from many torches. The powerful book was written by James Goldman, author of *The Lion in Winter;* the lyrics and music had the stinging precision of the Stephen Sondheim we already admired in *Company* (*Follies* is *Company* once more, with feeling). Alexis Smith has matured into a star of the first magnitude who was equally capable of carrying the show with unbending poise, or of stopping it with a barelegged "Loveland" number called "The Saga of Lucy and Jessie." Yvonne De Carlo, Ethel Shutta and Mary McCarty also supplied show-stopping interludes. All of the foregoing adds up to a tribute to the producing-directing expertise of Harold

Prince and Michael Bennett. Whoever did what at what moment, it was all done brilliantly for *Follies,* a pacesetting musical for our new theater.

The best American straight play of the Broadway season was Neil Simon's *The Gingerbread Lady,* a head taller (it seemed to me) in a group of interesting if imperfect works that included *Les Blancs, Happy Birthday, Wanda June, And Miss Reardon Drinks a Little, Scratch* and *All Over.* Simon, easily the most successful playwright of his generation—and deservedly so, on the basis of his comic insights—has moved slowly from the bright optimism of *Barefoot in the Park* toward the shadows of *Visitor from Mamaroneck* (in *Plaza Suite*) and *Last of the Red Hot Lovers,* finally to arrive at the dark corner of *The Gingerbread Lady.* The lady of Simon's title is an alcoholic nymphomaniac whose two well-meaning best friends—a homosexual actor and a narcissistic ex-beauty queen—keep stumbling against her, driving her ever closer to the brink of self-destruction. What saves her, and indeed the play itself, is the character's (and Simon's) sense of humor, her tendency to veer in the direction of irony rather than self-pity. Simon's wit rescued his indifferently-made play (which is somewhat distorted in construction, owing to extensive rewrites). Maureen Stapleton played the lady as the most perceptive spectator as well as the most involved participant in her own fight to survive, in the season's outstanding performance by an actress in a straight play. This fight was lost in the first tryout version of *The Gingerbread Lady,* which must have been as suspenseful as a stone's fall to the ground; in the final rewritten version it was beginning to be won, maybe, with the help of a daughter (played by Ayn Ruymen) who simply refuses to give up on her alcoholic mother. This script was a logical progression in Neil Simon's developing mood as a playwright, and, with a few flaws, a worthy addition to the Simon canon.

Paul Zindel too was contemplating lost ladies in his *And Miss Reardon Drinks a Little,* a study of three sisters, all school teachers, one married, one (not the drinker) more than a little neurotic, all somewhat alienated from reality, which finally invades their privacy in the form of the married couple downstairs. Zindel won the 1971 Pulitzer Prize for last season's off-Broadway *The Effect of Gamma Rays on Man-in-the-Moon Marigolds;* in his second produced play the passion is all there but the play not quite, though it enjoyed an extraordinarily capable ensemble of performances including those of Estelle Parsons (as the drinking Miss Reardon), Julie Harris as the neurotic and Nancy Marchand as the married one, the take-charge type.

The late Lorraine Hansberry's work-in-progress *Les Blancs,* with text prepared for production by her husband Robert Nemiroff, was a dramatized textbook of the black dilemma. It centered on James Earl Jones as a completely Western-civilized, citified African who visits his native village to attend his father's funeral and resists letting himself be caught up in the local web of revolt and violence. He wants nothing so much as to get back to his white wife in respectable London—possibly with some reason, because the people in his native village, white and black, tend to be attitude symbols. Another of the season's noteworthy serious efforts was Archibald MacLeish's *Scratch,* a play suggested by Stephen Vincent Benet's story *The Devil and Daniel Webster,* in which Webster (Patrick Magee) confronts Old Scratch (Will Geer) in a mock-trial contest for the forsworn soul of a Yankee farmer. In the first act, MacLeish the poet faces us with the fact of an America in which even a good man like Daniel Webster might yield to the devilish temptation to preserve the Union at the price of Liberty—individual liberty, for example, by supporting the Fugitive Slave Act to appease the Southern voters. This was an image of potentially tremendous impact and might have been worth exploring more deeply than the final act, a colorful but conventionally theatrical trial scene, was capable of doing.

Another slice of Americana on Broadway was *Lenny,* a dramatic celebration of the life and works of the controversial night club comedian Lenny Bruce, who was willing to use any means up to and beyond obscenity, blasphemy, etc., to expose the hypocrisies of the late 1950s and early 1960s, when he made himself equally conspicuous on stages and in the courts. This show was not so much of a documentary as a poetic idealization, with Lenny presented as a champion of freedom of speech (or, rather, the victim of our sometimes fear and hatred of really free speech), much sinned against and scarcely sinning at all. I'm in no position to judge its veracity; I can only say that Julian Barry's script, which seemed to be made in large part out of Bruce's night club monologues, aroused my interest in the character without letting me believe in him as a personification of ruthless honesty. What I did believe in thoroughly, thanks to a memorable performance by Cliff Gorman as Lenny, was a vital personality, a racing engine impossible to control and guaranteed to self-destruct. Gorman played the camping Emory in *The Boys in the Band* to perfection on stage and screen; as Lenny he pulled out all the stops, including even a little camp, of a highly sophisticated and powerful acting talent, and the music came out loud and clear from one end of the scale to the other. The 1970-71 drama season made a star out of Cliff Gorman, and that may prove to be one of its outstanding contributions to theater history.

On the lighter side, Kurt Vonnegut Jr.'s playwriting debut with *Happy Birthday, Wanda June* was an auspicious one. With Kevin McCarthy as a modern Hemingway-like Ulysses who returns home to find his Penelope married to a doctor, the play is a put-down of adventurous hero types. Many of its scenes and character vignettes were very funny in broad farcical style, notably the performance of William Hickey as the mighty hunter's side-kick, the somewhat simple minded "Looseleaf Harper." Another long reach for farce was made in *Four on a Garden,* four man-and-woman comedy skits credited to Abe Burrows, with Carol Channing and Sid Caesar in good form as the lady and the house painter, the old couple trying a last fling, etc.

Happy Birthday, Wanda June was one of several shows transferred to or produced on Broadway under the new agreement covering smaller playhouses in the Times Square area. It used to be referred to as a "Middle Theater" arrangement. Now it's "Limited Gross Broadway Theater Agreement"—we call it "Limited Broadway" in this volume—enabling shows in playhouses near Broadway to come in with union concessions and generally lowered production costs, in order to minimize the risk of and thereby encourage experimentation. *A Place Without Doors,* the Barbara Bray translation of Marguerite Duras's study of a murderess, was brought from its American premiere at the Long Wharf in New Haven to a Limited Broadway house. With Mildred Dunnock as an interrogated prisoner explaining but never elucidating the reasons that drove her to kill, this was exactly the kind of theater novelty that the Limited Broadway arrangement was designed to encourage. (The French version of this play, *L'Amante Anglaise,* was produced off Broadway this year by the visiting Tréteau de Paris, with Madeleine Renaud as the murderess and Claude

Dauphin as the interrogator.)

Except for this French play and *Wanda June,* however, the new arrangement produced nothing but disappointments: the short-lived *Opium* based on Jean Cocteau's diaries, *Gandhi* with Jack MacGowran in episodes of the great Indian leader's life and career, *The Castro Complex* about sex fetishism, *The Candyapple* with a comedy of Roman Catholic attitudes and *Soon,* a rock musical romance. The Limited Broadway deal was designed to apply not only to the middle-sized theaters between 299 (off Broadway) and 600 (Broadway) capacity; it aimed also to encourage Limited Broadway production in large houses with auditoriums roped off to limit the seating and consequently the potential weekly gross. No show took advantage of this part of the opportunity in 1970-71, but it is expected that Limited Broadway production in regular Broadway houses will get under way next year. The one-performance musical *Frank Merriwell, or Honor Challenged,* based on the Burt L. Standish stories, was widely reported as a Limited Broadway show, but it was not—it opened under a regular Broadway contract.

For most of the season the list of new Broadway musicals was dominated, not by *Follies* which came along late, but by two hefty early-season shows, *Two by Two* and *The Rothschilds.* Top individual efforts in *Two by Two* (the story of Noah adapted by Peter Stone from Clifford Odets's play *The Flowering Peach*) included Richard Rodgers's score, with Martin Charnin's lyrics suiting the Rodgers musical style; and Danny Kaye's Noah who at the beginning of the play is too old to do God's will but shakes off his years to become spry enough to command his unwilling family to their fateful voyage. This was an outstanding performance by a skilled and experienced musical comedy star (I am speaking of the Kaye performance at the beginning of the show's run, before he suffered a muscle injury and decided to adapt his role and indeed the whole show to his infirmity, abandoning much of Noah and filling in with more and more straight Danny Kaye in his new performance). David Hays's setting of weathered boards and light projections provided a rugged Old Testament atmosphere for the story of a famous Jewish family in a historically tough spot.

The same might be said for *The Rothschilds,* which traced the fortunes of the banking family from the ghettos to the courts of Europe. Rothschilds are treated with good humor and affection in Sherman Yellen's light-hearted book, to which Keene Curtis gave strong support in performing all the smiling anti-Rothschild villains from the local nobleman to Prince Metternich. Another musical with a strong book was *70, Girls, 70* about a group of enterprising senior citizens—led by Mildred Natwick, Hans Conried and Lillian Roth—who steal for profit and fun, suggested by the story of the film *Make Mine Mink,* in a stage version prepared by Fred Ebb, Norman L. Martin and Joseph Masteroff.

Two off-Broadway musical hits moved uptown and became part of the Broadway scene: *The Me Nobody Knows,* the charming show based on the writings of underprivileged city children, and the fabulous *Oh! Calcutta!* (and *You're a Good Man Charlie Brown* reappeared on Broadway in June as a new season began). Leon Uris's *Ari,* an effort to make a musical out of episodes in his novel *Exodus* about Jewish refugees struggling to reach the promised land of Israel, was short-lived. So was *Earl of Ruston,* a rock musical by C.C. Courtney and Peter Link (author of last season's excellent *Salvation*) and

C.C.'s brother Ragan Courtney. This show was an arrogantly daring effort to push out the frontiers of the musical stage with the re-enactment of the life of a small-town misfit, the Courtneys' cousin Earl Woods, who died young after a hapless life spent partly in mental institutions. Earl's mother, Leecy R. Woods Moore, was actually present onstage to comment about her son. Earl himself was played by the Courtney brothers, two actors playing one character who communicates with himself a lot. It was an imaginative, stimulating musical which, finally and unhappily, wasn't able to put over its leading character as a tragic figure or even as a compelling *raison d'être* for all this talented commotion.

Specialty shows supplied more than their ordinary share of flavor to the Broadway season. *Bob and Ray—the Two and Only* brought Bob Elliott and Ray Goulding (TV and radio comedians and satirists whose work has included the popular cartoon ad characters Bert and Harry Piel) in a collection of their tongue-in-cheek interviews and characterizations. There was *Story Theater,* discussed earlier in this report. Emlyn Williams stopped off briefly at Lincoln Center's Alice Tully Hall with his famous impersonation of Charles Dickens, in an evening of excerpts from that author's works. Among foreign-language productions, the Italian romantic adventure extravaganza *Orlando Furioso* was an early-autumn arrival on the entertainment scene (classify it Broadway, off Broadway or what you will—it was produced in a huge air-bubble auditorium raised for the occasion in Bryant Park). The production list also included two Yiddish-language musicals, Ben Bonus's *Light, Lively and Yiddish* (a romantic contrast between the folk of the old and new worlds) and the sentimental romance *The President's Daughter.* And the National Theaters of Japan gave three performances each of Noh and Kyogen plays, demonstrating these forms of traditional Japanese theater to New York audiences at Carnegie Hall.

Revivals

This season was a vintage year for revivals. The number was somewhere near average—15 on Broadway and 20 off—but here and there among them the excitement ran exceptionally high. We mentioned earlier in this report that the Christopher Hampton-adapted Ibsen repertory starring Claire Bloom ran with no moss on the old scripts but plenty of ice on the Friday night tickets. An even bigger hit—the hit of the Broadway season, in fact—was the revival of the Otto Harbach-Frank Mandel-Vincent Youmans *No, No, Nanette* with its hit tunes "Tea for Two" and "I Want to Be Happy" and its airy book about a Bible manufacturer who can't resist offering aid and comfort to lonely young girls—platonic comfort, that is. There's nothing about *Nanette* to suggest that it might make a special appeal to audiences of the 1970s, or strike a particular spark of fond recollection. The nostalgia in this show was superimposed on the material rather than evoked from it. Charming Ruby Keeler was recruited to smile engagingly in scene after scene as Nanette's mother, and to stop the show in Act I with a selection of tap routines that summoned up innocent Saturday afternoon visions of *Forty-second Street.* Patsy Kelly was cast as a maid locked in battle with her hated enemies the vacuum cleaner and the doorbell. Raoul Pene du Bois's costumes and scenery were exactly as we could hope the 1920s looked, as affectionate a caricature as were Donald

Saddler's dances and Busby Berkeley's production numbers. Burt Shevelove adapted and directed *Nanette* for flair rather than condescending camp, so that the sharper performances like those of Bobby Van and Helen Gallagher blended well with the smoother, more nostalgic ones of Miss Keeler and Jack Gilford as the benevolent Bible man. *Nanette* was a supremely skillful coup of theater which inspired the loose talk about a "nostalgic" trend which others will undoubtedly try to imitate before long.

One of the season's most contemporary works of stage art was based on one of the theater's most glowingly patinaed treasures—William Shakespeare's *A Midsummer Night's Dream* as produced by the Royal Shakespeare Company and directed by Peter Brook, brought to Broadway for a limited engagement (thank you, David Merrick Arts Foundation). The contemporary theater, many believe, is moving away from a playwrights' and toward a directors' medium, and certainly this revival is one of the shows that could support that belief. As presented with unfailing directorial imagination, the play seemed almost brand new; the fairy tale was no longer etherial, no more sprites with gauzy wings, but an intensely *physical* magic. Against Sally Jacobs's glaring white three-walled setting, the actors in their orange and purple robes were psychedelically present, as though dressed in day-glo. They moved three-dimensionally, climbing ladders and swinging from trapezes. They clung and twined in acts of love at ground level; here, love is a physical enchantment, and Titania's infatuation for Bottom is based entirely on her imagination of his sexual prowess, so that their relationship takes on the flavor of a joke about the traveling salesman and the farmer's daughter. Brook's version of *A Midsummer Night's Dream* had the quality of a chemical trip rather than a poetic one. Done in this way it was still great theater—and you needed the comedy of Bottom and his joiners and bricklayers doing their silly play about Pyramus and Thisbe in the court scene at the end, to bring you back to earth, to the proportions of reality. Brook and the company chose to interrelate the court and forest scenes of this *Dream* by means of dual casting, i.e.: the actor and actress playing Theseus and Hippolyta also played Oberon and Titania. This helped integrate the play and corresponded neatly with the ensemble style of the British acting company, who made many contributions to the show but never tried to preempt it. This was a director's triumph and one of the Broadway season's major entertainments.

Another example of the high level of excellence attained by many of the season's revivals was the Tony Award for best actor to Brian Bedford as Arnolphe in the Phoenix's production of Molière's *The School for Wives*. This is the role played in New York by Louis Jouvet in a previous Broadway production, in French, in 1951. The *Best Plays* record lists no previous New York production in English, but Lewis Harmon remembers an English-language production of *The School for Wives* off Broadway more than 20 years ago, before the complete off-Broadway production schedule became a matter of record in these volumes.

Shakespeare was well represented with *A Midsummer Night's Dream;* three *Hamlets;* the American Shakespeare Festival *Othello* with Moses Gunn, which visited Broadway briefly; a popular off-Broadway *Macbeth* rearranged by the director, Dino DeFilippi, so that the action took place as though in Macbeth's imagination—he didn't take direct part in the action; and, of course, the perennially wonderful Shakespeare-in-Central-Park mounted under Joseph Papp's eagle eye. This year he gave us a three-play "Wars of the

Roses" consisting of *Henry VI* in two full-length parts followed by *Richard III* on the third evening, tracing the violent quarrels of the York and Lancaster factions through the bloody murders to the "glorious summer" of the first Tudor, Henry VII. As an act of special dedication, Papp put on the three plays together, continuously, for one all-night performance beginning at dusk on Saturday, June 27 and running till dawn Sunday, June 28. Three thousand enthralled New Yorkers packed the Delacorte Theater and heard, to their added delight, Richmond's question at Bosworth Field "How far into the morning is it, lords?" answered "Upon the stroke of four" at exactly 4:03 a.m. When the three-play marathon ended in the dawn's early light, the audience gave the players a ten-minute standing ovation. Later on in the season, Papp's indoor New York Shakespeare Festival organization at the Public Theater scored with a very well-received revival of Pirandello's *Trelawny of the "Wells"*.

Lincoln Center Repertory enjoyed a season of distinguished revivals in the large Vivian Beaumont Theater. Productions were skilled, and the plays chosen were tough-fibered: Brecht's *The Good Woman of Setzuan*, Synge's *The Playboy of the Western World* (marking the centennial of the author's birth), Sophocles's *Antigone* and Arthur Miller's adaptation of Ibsen's *An Enemy of the People*—the only American work, alas. On its smaller Forum Theater stage, Lincoln Center Rep revived Harold Pinter's *The Birthday Party, Landscape* and *Silence* and Paul Shyre's version of Sean O'Casey's autobiographical *Pictures in the Hallway* on a schedule which also brought two new playscripts, of which more later.

Off-Broadway revivals of unusual interest included the Roundabout Theater's *Uncle Vanya* and *She Stoops to Conquer* as well as its previously mentioned all-male *Hamlet*. Beckett's *Waiting for Godot* was expertly revived under Alan Schneider's direction. Eugene O'Neill's *Long Day's Journey Into Night* was one of the hits of the off-Broadway season as staged by Arvin Brown and acted by Robert Ryan, Geraldine Fitzgerald, Stacy Keach and James Naughton and Paddy Croft. Dale Wasserman's *One Flew Over the Cuckoo's Nest*, about a patient resisting but finally overwhelmed by the terrors and cruelties of a mental institution—played on Broadway by Kirk Douglas in 1963 and now off Broadway by William Devane—was successfully revived in a partially rewritten version. And both *Dames at Sea* and *Colette* played return engagements off Broadway this season, the former in cabaret at Plaza 9. *Woyzeck* appeared, too, but only briefly and without much distinction.

On Broadway, the revival season began with a limp *Charley's Aunt* and ended with short-lived efforts to bring back *Johnny Johnson* and *The Dance of Death*. In between, however, was a banner season for the old scripts. It was easy to fall into the habit of forgetting all about Elizabethans and remembering Peter Brook's *A Midsummer Night's Dream* as one of the most exciting new plays of the season. And I was asked several times, "Are you going to pick *No, No, Nanette* as one of the ten best?" (Being a revival, it isn't eligible.) These productions were more than just museum-piece curiosities. Like the living theater that created them originally, they retain that spark of eternal fire ready to flame for the artist who learns their secret.

Off Broadway

Where have all the new American plays gone? They have gone off Broad-

The 1970-71 Season off Broadway

PLAYS (39)

The Cage
The Dirtiest Show in Town
STEAMBATH
The Emerald Slippers
Three by Ferlinghetti
Children in the Rain
Public Theater
The Happiness Cage
Subject to Fits
Underground
Candide
The Basic Training of Pavlo Hummel
Happy Birthday, Wanda June
Alice in Wonderland
My House Is Your House
American Place
Sunday Dinner
The Carpenters
Pinkville
Roundabout
Tug of War
Chas. Abbott & Son
The Immaculate Misconception
Score
A Dream Out of Time
Negro Ensemble
Perry's Mission & Rosalee Pritchett
Ride a Black Horse
Commune
One Night Stands of a Noisy Passenger
The Shrinking Bride
In New England Winter
Istanbul
Scenes From American Life
THE TRIAL OF THE CATONSVILLE NINE
THE HOUSE OF BLUE LEAVES
Acrobats & Line
Things That Almost Happen
Behold! Cometh the Vanderkellans
The Olathe Response
King Heroin
And Whose Little Boy Are You?
Any Resemblance to Persons Living or Dead . . .

SPECIALTIES (7)

MacGowran in the Works of Beckett
Here Are Ladies
Baird Marionettes
Whistling Wizard & Sultan of Tuffet
Ali Baba
Winnie the Pooh
Theater of the Balustrade
Tarot

MUSICALS (13)

Whispers on the Wind
Blood
Sensations
Touch
Ododo
Stag Movie
The Survival of St. Joan
Look Where I'm At
A Day in the Life of Just About Everyone
The Red White and Black
Kiss Now
The Ballad of Johnny Pot
Godspell

REVIVALS (20)

N.Y. Shakespeare
The Chronicles of King Henry VI, Part 1
The Chronicles of King Henry VI, Part 2
Richard III
Sambo (mobile)
Dames at Sea
Trelawny of the "Wells"
Colette
Roundabout
Hamlet
Uncle Vanya
She Stoops to Conquer
Hamlet (Ox-Camb)
Macbeth
Waiting for Godot
Forum Theater
The Birthday Party
Landscape & Silence
Pictures in the Hallway
One Flew Over the Cuckoo's Nest
Long Day's Journey Into Night
The Homecoming
Woyzeck

FOREIGN PLAYS IN ENGLISH (6)

The Nuns
BOESMAN AND LENA
Slag
Saved
The Dream on Monkey Mountain
Ac/Dc

REVUES (6)

To Be or Not to Be—What Kind of a Question Is That?
Earthlight
Cooler Near the Lake
Do It Again!
The Proposition
Six

FOREIGN-LANGUAGE PRODUCTIONS (4)

Golden Bat
Die Brücke
Amphitryon
Kurve & Kleinbürger-hochzeit
L'Amante Anglaise

Plays listed in CAPITAL letters have been designated Best Plays of 1970-71.
Plays listed in *italics* were still running June 1, 1971.

way, where the action is, where Charles Gordone's *No Place To Be Somebody* and Paul Zindel's *The Effect of Gamma Rays on Man-in-the-Moon Marigolds* have carried away the Pulitzer Prize two years in a row. If American playwrights were content to spend their efforts on works for the "comfortable" theater, they'd be on Broadway with the British playwrights—but they're not, they're writing new-theater scripts which get a hearing more readily in the smaller playhouses. There are 39 new American play programs in the "Plays Produced off Broadway" list for 1970-71 (see the one-page summary accompanying this article). This is a lot of action; somewhat less than last year's flood of 53 (costs are going up and risks are slightly higher these days off Broadway, too) but still an impressive volume of creative effort.

The quality results are also comparable to last year: four Best Plays off Broadway in both seasons, three American and one foreign. The foreign script on the 1970-71 best list was Athol Fugard's haunting *Boesman and Lena,* about a "hotnot" couple (in Apartheid parlance this identifies their degree of blackness) of shack dwellers chivvied from place to place at the whim of the white *baas,* living not only *on* the white man's cast-off trash but *as* the white man's cast-off trash, in a lean-to in the mud of a river estuary. Lena is weary and resentful, Boesman weary and frightened, brought to almost unbearable reality in the performance of Ruby Dee as Lena and first James Earl Jones, then Zakes Mokae, as Boesman. Fugard, a white South African playwright, director and actor, who established an international reputation a few seasons ago with *The Blood Knot,* and who has been active in black theater enterprises in his own country, was denied a passport by South Africa to come to New York to attend rehearsals of his play because, in Fugard's words, "The government thinks I'm a potential source of trouble"—an exquisite form of trouble, if *Boesman and Lena* is a sample.

The first of the season's American off-Broadway Best Plays to open was *Steambath,* a dark comedy by Bruce Jay Friedman, author of the previous Best Play *Scuba Duba.* In his new script Friedman is joking about life from the point of view of death. His protagonist is a young man (played by Anthony Perkins, who also directed) who finds himself dead and waiting for eternity in a sort of anteroom which in Friedman's imagination takes the form of a steam room attended by a nervously energetic Puerto Rican who is God. Now, God is a busy man who has his floors to mop, his towels to wash and his auto crashes on the freeways to supervise; but he takes time to listen to his customers' strange tales before he hustles them out of the door that leads to forever. The play is about the young man's protests that he must go back, his life is unfinished (in reality, there was nothing in his life worth going back to, and he will realize this in the next second or two after the curtain comes down). Hector Elizondo's personification of God was one of the season's notable acting achievements, and Friedman's saw-toothed edge of humor was as sharp as ever, in a painfully funny show.

John Guare's *The House of Blue Leaves* was another outstanding new script, also a black comedy, also toying with religious imagery, but somewhat more bitter than Friedman's. Guare, like Friedman, senses life as a comedy even in its most painful or exalted moments. His play is about a middle-aged sufferer, a zookeeper whose mentally disturbed wife seems like part of his menagerie, who dreams of escape from his piteous niche in Queens by means of writing and selling songs to a friend who makes movies in Hollywood. The play takes place on the day of Pope Paul's visit to New York in 1965, which through Guare's eyes becomes an analogy of muddled values, with nun and starlet equally the object of respect and scorn, and with suffering humanity—exemplified by the poor mind-wandering wife—the least of anybody's worries. The zookeeper becomes a figure of compelling sympathy as played by Harold Gould, a brave swimmer drowning in one of the Gowanus Canals of life. His girl friend in the apartment below, whose idea of hell is Sandra Dee losing her hair curlers the night before her first movie, is a vivid caricature of *Reader's Digest* values. The characters in *The House of Blue Leaves* often feel the need to speak to the audience directly; and in many other ways, too, this guaranteed sugar-free script is one for our new theater. It burns as it goes down like a good shot of rye whisky, and it richly deserved its New York Drama Critics Circle citation as the year's best American play.

The fourth of the off-Broadway Best Plays, the third by American authors, was *The Trial of the Catonsville Nine,* written by one of the nine who lived it, Father Daniel Berrigan, and adapted for New York production by Saul Levitt. It was constructed as a poetic condensation of the trial of the Berrigan brothers, both of them Roman Catholic priests, and seven others for seizing handfuls of draft board files and burning them in the public square at Catonsville, Md., on May 17, 1968, as an act of protest against the Vietnam war (the defendants were found guilty and sentenced to two to three and one-half years' imprisonment). As the judge and lawyers go about their business and the defendants state their motives and justifications and protest an oppressive United States presence not only in Vietnam but in such other parts of the world as Guatemala, the play grew on you like a fine painting of an historical event. Father Daniel Berrigan is an often-published poet, and the script quotes many passages from his works. The play had scant physical action but increasing sympathy for everyone caught in this moral and legal cobweb. The Berrigans (impersonated by Ed Flanders and Michael Kane) and their friends don't want to go to jail, but they want us all to understand fully that dropping napalm on children is a horribly and unmitigatedly evil act. The Federal judge (William Schallert) doesn't want these Christian soldiers punished in a real prison for their symbolic "crime"; but under the law he has no option to exercise his personal sympathies. Neither does the prosecuting attorney (Davis Roberts), a black man in this re-enactment as at the real trial; he bears the defendants no malice, but he never compromises with the facts of his open-and-shut case. The jury too is charged to make its decision on the basis of law, not sympathy. Staged with scrupulous attention to clear communication by Gordon Davidson of the Mark Taper Forum in Los Angeles, where the play was first performed, *The Trial of the Catonsville Nine* was a combination documentary play and practical demonstration of our present political and moral dilemma. The Berrigans did what they had to do; the Court did what it had to do, and we the jury are witness to events over which we have no direct control but for which we too are called to account (and after the end of the play we watched a stark black and white newsreel of the events at Catonsville, leaving the audience with an image of the pitiful reality of the protest). Staged in a church which huddles near the travertine ostentation of the Lincoln Center complex (and transferred from there to Broadway just after season's end), here was a piece of highly effective theater for our time, as relevant as a body count.

Turning from the sublime to the frequently ridiculous, off Broadway is where they began taking it all off a few seasons ago; where *Oh! Calcutta!* first flourished; where yeasty four-syllable obscenities became household words; where the Marquis de Sade became the most-trammeled source for theatrical material since Holinshed. Off Broadway was beginning to emerge from this blue period in 1970-71, but some vestiges remained. Tom Eyen's facetiously-titled *The Dirtiest Show in Town* facetiously represented itself to be about pollution. It was a satire on various conspicuous aberrations of our society including both pollution and sex deviation, a collection of pungent caricatures flawed by witless efforts to represent naked sex acts explicitly on the stage. Naked sex acts invariably shatter whatever illusion a show has been able to create; there are no longer any character or play up there on the stage, merely bare actors in an exhibition for voyeurs. Stripped (if you will excuse the expression) of its extraneous orgies, *The Dirtiest Show in Town* would have been and indeed was one of the season's most flavorful evenings of episodic theater. What critics were beginning to call "the obligatory naked scene" was still in evidence this season, on Broadway and off (for example, there was a shower bath scene with a pretty blonde in *Steambath* which had no roots in the play and had no effect on it one way or the other), but no show since *Oh! Calcutta!* has succeeded on this one quality alone.

Each of the organized off-Broadway producing groups made its special mark, with Joseph Papp's New York Shakespeare Festival Public theater the standout in both quantity and quality. Papp was living precariously and energetically in 1970-71, perhaps a little more so that usual in both categories. The season had scarcely begun when he let it be known that he needed extra financial help to complete his season of summer Shakespeare in Central Park. No sooner did he get past this crisis than an even greater one loomed: construction costs of creating several theaters in the former Astor Library building on Lafayette Street had mounted over the $2 million mark, and the whole project was in severe financial jeopardy. Meanwhile, in his five auditoriums (the Estelle R. Parsons, the Florence S. Anspacher, the Other Stage, Martinson and South Halls) Papp mounted one show after another of challenging, not always successful but always provocative theater—ten programs including musicals, specialties, revivals and new work that demonstrated eloquently the energy, the taste, the dedication of this gifted impresario, and above all the real usefulness of *all* these auditoriums to him and to the theatergoing public. Clearly, Papp and his Shakespeare Festival operation are among the richest of the city's (and the state's, and for that matter the nation's) cultural treasures, comparable to England's Royal Shakespeare, Royal Court and National Theaters in demonstrating the possibilities of subsidized or semi-supported theater. Papp appealed to the city to help him out, supporting his argument (it was reliably rumored) with an English translation of the word used so effectively by Cambronne at Waterloo. In any case, Mayor John V. Lindsay's impoverished municipality somehow found the money to buy the Public Theater building (paying off the remodeling costs) and leasing it back to Joseph Papp. This was a decision which will do credit to those involved in making it, roughly in the same proportion as that which has accrued to Secretary Seward for insisting on the purchase of Alaska.

Papp didn't come up with a *Hair* or a *No Place To Be Somebody* in his city-owned building this season, but his ten-show program pulsated with imagination, from Dennis J. Reardon's new script *The Happiness Cage,* which began Papp's 1970-71 season with a fantasy about medical experiments in inducing human happiness, to David Rabe's strong new script *The Basic Training of Pavlo Hummel,* which ended it on a contemporary note about an unhappy young man doomed to serve in the army in the Vietnam war and to die in a Saigon fragging. In between were the hit revival of *Trelawny of the "Wells"* and a *Candide* constructed from improvisations by the Organic Theater Company of Chicago; two fascinating solo shows, Siobhan McKenna's *Here Are Ladies* portraying heroines of Irish literature, and homage to an illustrious talent with *Jack MacGowran in the Works of Samuel Beckett;* a musical *Blood* loosely based on the *Oresteia* and done by the same young people who did last year's *Stomp* but not quite a match for their previous inspiration; a pair of new one-acters about the black condition, by Walter Jones and Edgar White, under the portmanteau title *Underground;* and *Slag* by David Hare, a British script presented in London by the Royal Court, about the last three teachers remaining at a moribund girls' school, a metaphor of British society.

Finally, and by no means least challengingly, the Public Theater came up with *Subject to Fits,* described by its young author Robert Montgomery (no relation) in a program note as follows: "*Subject to Fits* is neither adaptation, dramatization nor translation of Dostoevsky's inimitable novel *The Idiot.* The greatness of Dostoevsky's masterpiece is inseparable from its novelistic form, and any attempt to literally transpose it into another art form could not help but undermine its wholeness and alienate its power. *Subject to Fits* is a response to *The Idiot;* it is absolutely unfaithful to the novel; it uses the novel for its own selfish purposes; it does not hold the novel responsible. As such, it is entirely original—smacking of *The Idiot,* dreaming of *The Idiot,* but mostly taking off from where *The Idiot* drove it."

Whatever the roots of *Subject to Fits* may be, what appeared on the stage was a kind of realized nightmare of demented effusion and forlorn hopes, with Andy Robinson in a juicy performance of Prince Myshkin and with a rock score throbbing painfully behind the fantasies which emerged from the Dostoevsky work. The play is a kind of object-lesson critique of Dostoevsky, an acrobatic and juggling act of words, ideas and poses. It either grabbed you or it didn't; it grabbed enough critics to take sixth place in the best-play voting (and it was the first choice of two critics, Martin Gottfried and Jack Kroll). Love it or leave it, *Subject to Fits* was a progressive work of new theater, typical of Joseph Papp's imaginative production policy and the standout of his 1970-71 season.

Wynn Handman's American Place Theater was as always a showcase for playwrights. Its most interesting 1970-71 work was *The Carpenters,* a first professionally-produced play by a new author, Steven Tesich, who was born in Yugoslavia and emigrated to America at age 14. His play was a strong, if pessimistic, image of the generation gap. A hard-working husband and father (Vincent Gardenia) decides to take a day off from work, and in staying home finds that he is unwanted by his wife and hapless children, one of whom is going to kill him if he can. His family is coming apart like the home that shelters them, and there is no carpenter capable of making repairs. The father's contribution to the home (in the light of Tesich's play), which is security and authority, is no longer of any importance to grim, self-centered, directionless new America. Tesich's judgment was harsh but his perception keen, and we eagerly await more scripts from this promising new source.

Family guilt and recrimination also was the subject of another American Place production, Joyce Carol Oates's symbolic *Sunday Dinner,* about a ritual feast at the graveside of a family's departed mother. George Tabori considered the brutalizing effect of military training and the Vietnam war in *Pinkville.* American Place's season ended with a work-in-progress, Sam Shepard's *Back Bog Beast Bait,* which was not submitted for review at the playwright's request—a privilege available to all American Place authors and sometimes exercised, in circumstances designed to give the playwright the greatest possible encouragement and opportunity while subjecting him to the least possible pressure.

The development of black theater is the aim of the Negro Ensemble Company, and presumably its season can be accounted a success because its series of programs was offered under the portmanteau title "Themes of Black Struggle," and one of them offended a lot of people. This was *Ododo* (the Yoruba word for "truth"), a musical review of the black man's history in North America viewed as repeated episodes of hate and injustice leading to a present status as an inevitable revolutionary—a kind of release of pent-up fury on the stage. Perhaps it satisfied some inner longing in black members of the audience; but Clive Barnes of the New York *Times* may have been speaking for a large segment of theatergoers when he wrote in his review: "The black nationalism of shows like *Ododo* makes me realize that I am white . . . . . it is a purely racist show, and I am not prepared to feel deliciously masochistic guilt for crimes I did not commit."

In the course of its season under the direction of Douglas Turner Ward and Robert Hooks, the Negro Ensemble Company also brought in *Perry's Mission* and *Rosalee Pritchett,* a pair of one-acters about the contemporary black condition; *The Dream on Monkey Mountain,* a play by a Trinidadian, Derek Walcott, a poetic image in the form of a black convict's dreams; and, finally, *Ride a Black Horse,* the dramatization by an Ohio professor, John Scott, of the emerging conflict between the black liberal-intellectual community (personified in the play by a college teacher) and the radical impulses of the ghetto leaders.

The Chelsea Theater Center staged a schedule of interesting productions in its loft over at the Brooklyn Academy of Music, and two of them were eventually brought across the river for brief runs in Manhattan. One of the latter was Edward Bond's *Saved,* one of the darkest and most controversial of the dark British plays, containing the now-famous scene in which a baby is stoned to death. It was directed by Alan Schneider in its American premiere. The other production transported from Brooklyn to Manhattan was *Tarot,* a rock musical pantomime with tarot card deck characters playing out the adventures of The Fool. In the course of its season the Chelsea Theater Center imported Heathcote Williams's *AC/DC,* about pinball machines, TV sets and other electronic contraptions as hallucinations of our time, to Brooklyn but not to Manhattan.

On its small Forum Theater stage, Lincoln Center Repertory presented A.R. Gurney Jr.'s close scrutiny of America, *Scenes From American Life,* a time machine that traveled from the Depression years through our present travails into what the playwright conceives to be an inevitably Orwellian future. Lincoln Center Rep was also preparing another new play—new to America, that is—for production in the Forum. It was Friedrich Duerrenmatt's adaptation of Strindberg's *The Dance of Death,* entitled *Play Strindberg,* which was in previews as the season ended.

Elsewhere in off Broadway's new-play production list, a highlight was Israel Horovitz's *Line,* about five ill-assorted people jockeying for position in a line waiting for we know not what, insulting and loving each other to pass the time. A young musician (Richard Dreyfuss) manages to outwit the others much of the time, monopolizing first place, in a metaphor of the artist's drive to succeed. The play is witty and perceptive in the writing and was capably acted by a good cast throughout its one-hour running time. Horovitz also supplied an amusing curtain-raising sketch entitled *Acrobats,* about a husband-and-wife team having a family quarrel during their balancing act.

Irv Bauer's *A Dream Out of Time* was another standout, one which suffered an interference of its run by the strike of off-Broadway actors in mid-season. It contrasted two generations of a Jewish family in New York, with Sam Levene representing a generation which worked its way out of the Lower East Side, and James J. Sloyan as the brightly promising modern young man radicalized by the failures of the American dream. There was a drama of prison life, *The Cage,* written by an ex-lifer Rick Cluchey and performed by a cast of ex-inmates. In another part of the forest, Ed Bullins is working on a 20-play cycle about the black experience in the industrial areas of America's North and West. The second of them, *In New England Winter,* surfaced briefly at the Henry Street Playhouse (the first was *In the Wine Time* depicting a world of winos, petty holdups and general hopelessness). Bullins's plays are getting harder and harder to see, as he arranges to have them produced farther and farther out on the edges of the New York professional theater. This is too bad for most theatergoers, because he is a major playwrighting talent who ought to have a wide hearing. Another of the year's achievements in the tributaries was *King Heroin,* a drama of drug abuse written, directed and produced by Al Fann at St. Philip's Community Theater in Harlem.

The potpourri of 1970-71 off-Broadway entertainment included the satisfying ingredient of the Bil Baird Marionettes in three programs from the repertory. Of the six revues, only the improvisational *The Proposition* caught on for any length of time; the new edition of Second City, *Cooler Near the Lake,* did not. A glorious Japanese rock musical enlivened the earlier part of the season: *Golden Bat,* brought over here by the Tokyo Kid Brothers who describe themselves as "La Mama, Tokyo" and the Golden Bat itself as "a popular Japanese comic strip character who, like a phoenix, died and was reborn . . . . . a symbol of *matsuri*—the hopes, dreams and will of the young generation."

Of the 13 home-grown musicals produced off Broadway this season, only *Godspell* and *Touch* were hits. *Godspell* was a rock musical takeout of the Gospel according to St. Matthew, with Jesus in clown makeup as a folk hero, and with an irresistible mood of innocent wonder in the stylized re-enactment of his life and sacrifice as adapted and musicalized by Stephen Schwartz and John-Michael Tebelak (with one additional number by Jay Hamburger and Peggy Gordon). *Touch* was something else, a joyous musical celebration of the communal way of life of contemporary young people, written by Kenn Long, Amy Saltz and Jim Crozier. Another of the off-Broadway musicals, *The Ballad of Johnny Pot,* about a Johnny Appleseed character who scatters cannabis instead of pippins, took extraordinary measures following lukewarm reviews: it staged an admission-free performance. The theater was jammed even on a rainy night, with turn-aways accommodated on later evenings (so much for the myth that you can't give away tickets to a show that isn't a hit). The experiment was curious but ultimately ineffective. When the show returned to charging admission, action at the box office was scant and it closed after a two-week run.

Such was the off-Broadway theatergoing experience in 1970-71: a modest abundance of average skill and considerable variety, hitting its share of the high spots which rise out of the seething effort in any New York theater season. It was often relevant to contemporary life, and vice versa; off Broadway may have had some small effect on our times with telling programs like *The Trial of the Catonsville Nine,* and in return our troubled times were having some effect on off Broadway. Certainly some portion of the potential audience was kept away from the tributary theater, or at least rendered very cautious, by the increasing upset in the city streets. The bright-light, theater-cluster areas like Lower Second Avenue, Sheridan Square or the East Seventies weren't much affected, but off-Broadway theatergoers thought twice about seeking entertainment at some lone theater up a dark and taxiless side street. A recent off-Broadway theater-building boom came to an abrupt halt, as the planners reassessed their plans in a troubled city. The off-Broadway theater is calculated to survive any number of artistic revolutions. But it is highly susceptible to the side effects of civil unrest and urban blight, and it is ardently to be hoped that this threat will disappear in better days to come.

Offstage

Whatever may be the problems of the New York legitimate theater as compared with its golden age a few decades ago, 1971 was a year in which theater people were taking action to meet and solve them.

This was the season in which the 7:30 curtain became a reality. The League of New York Theaters under Richard Barr's leadership had approved changing the Broadway curtain time from 8:30 to 7:30 p.m., and so had David Merrick (who brought a 1960 experiment in a one-day-a-week early showing to an abrupt end by switching his shows back to 8:30). The reason for moving the curtain time up was, in Barr's words, "to reduce the time span between the end of the business day and the start of performances, to allow our audiences to get home an hour earlier."

It had been argued that even an 8:30 curtain didn't allow Manhattanites time for a truly leisurely dinner before the theater. With the earlier curtain time, they could have supper afterwards as many Londoners do, and the suburbanites wouldn't have that long 5:30-to-8:30 wait for the shows to begin, and they might be able to get the baby sitter home before midnight. Besides (it was whispered), there was street crime in the Broadway area as elsewhere in the city, and it might be well to get the public home an hour earlier.

Another much-discussed dream implemented into contractual reality in 1971 was the Limited Gross Broadway Theater Agreement (previously called "middle theater" and referred to generally in this *Best Plays* volume as "Limited Broadway"). Technically speaking, the term "Broadway" with its scales of salaries and percentages to artists, technicians, rentals, etc., applies to theaters seating more than 600. "Off Broadway" with its different scales applies to those seating 299 or fewer. Thus there is an area between which is now defined as "middle theater" or "Limited Broadway"—and there are houses right in the Broadway area like the Edison Theater which come under these new rules. But even more importantly for the future, it is hoped, the "Limited Broadway" rules are also designed to permit a producer to rope off some of the seats in a regular-sized Broadway house so that his maximum weekly gross would not exceed $25,000 at a top reduced to $5. Under these conditions, he could mount a show with Limited Broadway cost concessions. If he finds he has a smash hit on his hands, the producer may elect to remove the ropes and move up to full Broadway status (and cost levels) after four weeks (but a show scaled originally to Broadway cannot move *down* to Limited Broadway).

Other efforts to improve the general condition of the theater included the movement by the League of New York Theaters and others formally to establish the Times Square area as a "special district," with a high saturation of police and other municipal attentions including taxi lines, in order to create an environment favorable to theatergoing. Mayor John V. Lindsay gave his approval to this effort, particularly as it might apply to extending the zoning area in which office-tower builders would be encouraged to include theaters in their structures.

One of the season's most trying events was an Actors Equity strike of off-Broadway actors and stage managers which began on Monday, Nov. 16, involved 200 people in 17 struck shows and lasted for 31 days through Wednesday, Dec. 16 (but most of the 13 shows that resumed didn't get going again until the following week; two never reopened and two had transferred out of the strike jurisdiction to Broadway and Limited Broadway). The strike ended when Equity and the League of Off-Broadway Theaters and Producers, whose spokesman was Paul Libin, agreed to send major issues including salary, welfare and pensions to arbitration. Salary minimums for actors before the strike were $75-$150 depending on the weekly gross of each off-Broadway production. The League offered $90-$165 and Equity was demanding $125-$265. The arbitrator fixed the sum at $100-$175 this year rising to $125-$200 in 1974, and Libin commented on the arbitrated package: "It will mean the slow death of off Broadway as we know it" because of increased production costs. The shows that closed during the strike were *What the Butler Saw* after a long run and *Score* after a short one; and in addition the play *A Dream Out of Time,* which had only just opened to favorable notices, never regained its momentum.

There were hassles over the critics with Clive Barnes, the daily drama reviewer of the New York *Times* in the center of the turbulence because of the economic power of the paper's reviews, a matter of life or death to most productions. The Dramatists Guild—the organization of playwrights, librettists, composers and lyricists on and off Broadway—made an effort under the leadership of its then president Frank D. Gilroy to persuade the *Times* to do something, *anything,* about this situation which the paper's own critics have often characterized as repugnant even to them. In a meeting and an exchange of correspondence with A.M. Rosenthal, the paper's managing editor, the dramatists suggested such possible mitigations as a box score of other critics run along with the *Times's* daily review, or a panel of guest critics who might offer additional opinions. The *Times* found all the suggestions unworkable, though expressing sympathy for the problem of playwrights whose work lives or dies with the views of only one man (it was never suggested that Clive Barnes was the wrong man, or that his reviews be inhibited in any way, only that some means be found to take some of the economic curse off them).

The *Times* critic went the extra mile with the dramatists; he sat down unarmed and unescorted with 70 of them at Guild headquarters one afternoon in an open discussion and fielded all questions up to and including "What are your qualifications, Mr. Barnes?" (His reply was, "What are your qualifications as a playwright? Chiefly you do the job.") At one point in this exchange he explained that power is almost as disconcerting to a dedicated critic as it is to those he is reviewing—it is *influence* the critic strives to exercise, not power, Barnes told the gathering. Meanwhile the intolerable situation remains.

The instinct to reach out toward subsidy grew in reverse proportion to the weakening performing-arts economy. The National Endowment continued to function under the direction of Nancy Hanks, President Nixon's appointee, granting $731,750 to 26 resident professional theaters in 24 cities, and $207,500 to 22 experimental groups like Cafe LaMama, Chelsea Theater Center, etc., in eight cities. This was only a drop in the bucket of need. The Theater Development Fund continued to sustain the professional New York theater in its especially effective and double-barreled way of coming to the aid of shows *after* they are produced.

Our public and private efforts to support the theater are commendable, but they shouldn't obscure the fact that in the United States we have no such subsidized organizations as England's National Theater, Royal Shakespeare Company and Royal Court, from whence come a considerable number of those excellent plays which steal the limelight of our Broadway seasons, some of them risky concepts which might never have reached full-scale production in an unsubsidized, private commercial theater. But even London's fine publicly-financed theaters are a mere detail. Here's one figure that says it all. West Germany spends $2.42 per person annually in government support for the arts; Sweden and Austria $2 per person; Canada $1.40; Israel $1.34; England with its great subsidized theaters a measly $1.23. Here in the United States, where we spent $1,125 per person on highways in 1970, the annual per capita support of the arts is 7½ cents.

Finally, the season's most poignant offstage event took place only just offstage, in a Philadelphia theater. On Friday night, March 12, David Burns collapsed on the stage of the Forrest just after his big Act II number in the musical *70, Girls, 70*. He died a few moments later in the wings, of a heart ailment that had been troubling him for some time. He had lived the life of an actor, and he made such a mark on the entertainment scene that he already enjoyed, if that is the word, the sincerest type of adulation in the many bald imitations of his technique and personality to be found all over the media. The sad occurrence of his final exit was so remarkable in its sheer theatricality that we must note it here. Without stepping out of character, David Burns died the death of an actor, on the stage in a starring role, at the height of a distinguished career, on a Friday night with a good house, his big number finished, nothing in his ears but the sound of applause.

As though taking its cue from the popularity of *No, No, Nanette,* the 1971 TV show celebrating the 25th anniversary of the Antoinette Perry (Tony) Awards presented a cavalcade of numbers from the Tony Award-winning musicals over the years. This was a much more entertaining show than the Academy, Emmy or other 1971 awards programs on television, as the Broadway musical stars of the past and present sang and danced 25 years of show-stopping numbers from Rodgers & Hammerstein to Strouse & Adams by way of Lerner & Loewe, Bock & Harnick, Frank Loesser, Meredith Willson, Leonard Bernstein, Jerry Herman, Stephen Sondheim and all the others.

Like the 1970-71 drama season itself, this musical cavalcade was not merely a nostalgic savoring of the past, it was also a progress right up, into and through the present toward the future. Certainly the Rodgers & Hammerstein songs sounded wonderful—they always will, and by the way this very season's Broadway musical stage was brightened by still another lilting Rodgers love song, "I Do Not Know a Day I Did Not Love You" from *Two by Two.* But the significant point is that Broadway enjoyed wearing the laurels of *Carousel,* *My Fair Lady* and *Guys and Dolls* without standing on them. "Oh What a Beautiful Morning" or "This Was a Real Nice Clambake" may not be titles immediately relevant to our time, but for our time Broadway has come up with "Another Hundred People Just Got off the Train" from *Company* or "I'm Still Here" from *Follies.*

As the Tony Awards cavalcade of musicals demonstrated, the theater's past has been glorious—but in 1970-71 it is ringing out as many echoes of the future as echoes of the past. The New York theater is beset with economic, sociological, journalistic and even real estate difficulties, as we have outlined. It is caught in a tide rip of violent artistic change at a moment when the quiet backwaters of the comfortable past offer not even the illusion of safety from the turbulent present. Our theater is in all kinds of difficulty except the worst kind of all: stagnation. It is puzzled and perverse and at times discouraged, but—to borrow a line from the 1971 Tony Award winner *Applause*—"But alive, that's the thing! But alive!"

William Hickey, Gene Fanning, Cherry Davis and Brad Sullivan in *Small Craft Warnings* by Tennessee Williams.

PHOTO BY MARTHA SWOPE

1971-72

LOOKING back on the New York Theater season of 1971-72, we can see splashes of bright color all over the place; but we have to admit that the predominant hue was gray. This was a season of gray subject matter and gray, half-realized achievement. Its best work, the imported full-length Harold Pinter play *Old Times*, was a misted memory of Paradise lost performed in a bleak white-on-white setting so that if you missed the point intellectually you'd be sure to grasp it visually—if you were one of the relatively few Broadway theatergoers who went to see it. The season's best musical, *Ain't Supposed to Die a Natural Death*, was a grim reminder of conditions in the black ghetto done as a series of chants, with a poetic but songless score. The season's most lavish showcase musical, *Sugar*, was based on an old movie. Its biggest musical hit, *Jesus Christ Superstar*, was a nightmare version of the passion and crucifixion.

In April the New York *Times* was able to announce "All Broadway Stages Occupied or Booked" wonder of 1972 wonders, all 30-odd Broadway theaters were full of shows in the waning weeks of the season. Unfortunately, grayly, they weren't also full of audiences. Only one show was selling out, Neil Simon's *The Prisoner of Second Avenue* (a comedy about the frustrations of high-rise living, admittedly funny, but focused on a man having a nervous breakdown within four gray walls of a drab modern apartment).

The number of shows produced on Broadway—most in first-class, a few in "limited" or "middle" productions—held steady at 56 in 1971-72 (see the one-page summary accompanying this report). This was the same number as last year, after a dropoff from 68 the year before, 76 the year before that and 84 in 1967-68. Some encouragement can be drawn from the rise in the number of American straight play programs produced on Broadway this season to 19 from last season's all-time low of 14; and in the slight rise in the number of American musicals from 11 to 13 in 1971-72. This overall production statistic in 1969-70 was 21 plays and 14 musicals, 24-12 the year before that and 25-10 in 1967-68. Off Broadway the American straight play number was higher, too, with 43 programs as compared to 39 last year. With musical production steady and straight plays reversing their previous downward curve, there is certainly some cause, if not for rejoicing, or even for guarded optimism, at least for renewed determination.

It was the other numbers that took on overtones of gray this season—the relatively few people on the streets of the Broadway area at show time (and the far from festive mood of those who were showing up), the prohibitively high cost of a top ticket, the soaring price tag on every aspect of production. On Broadway, the going rate for fifth row center on Friday night at *Jesus Christ Superstar* was $15, and the same every night at *Sugar*. It cost $9 for the best seat at the new Neil Simon on weekends, $8.50 week nights; $8 and $6 at *Sticks and Bones* on Broadway. Weekend matinee top for plays was running around $8, for musicals $8-$10. Off Broadway, Joseph Papp was

The 1971-72 Season on Broadway

PLAYS (19)

The Trial of the Catonsville Nine (transfer)
Solitaire/Double Solitaire
The Incomparable Max
Unlikely Heroes
THE PRISONER OF SECOND AVENUE
Twigs
Fun City
The Love Suicide at Schofield Barracks
MOONCHILDREN
Night Watch
STICKS AND BONES (transfer)
Children! Children!
Voices
Elizabeth I
Promenade, All!
All the Girls Came Out to Play
Ring Round the Bathtub
An Evening With Richard Nixon And . . .
Tough to Get Help

MUSICALS (13)

Jesus Christ Superstar
AIN'T SUPPOSED TO DIE A NATURAL DEATH
The Grass Harp
Two Gentlemen of Verona (transfer)
Wild and Wonderful
Inner City
Grease
The Selling of the President
Sugar
Different Times
Hard Job Being God
Don't Play Us Cheap!
Heathen!

REVIVALS (12)

You're a Good Man, Charlie Brown
No Place To Be Somebody
On the Town
Lincoln Center Rep
Mary Stuart
Twelfth Night
The Crucible
There's One in Every Marriage
The Sign in Sidney Brustein's Window
The Country Girl
A Funny Thing Happened on the Way to the Forum
Captain Brassbound's Conversion
Lost in the Stars

REVUES (2)

That's Entertainment
Don't Bother Me, I Can't Cope

SPECIALTIES (1)

Black Light Theater of Prague

HOLDOVER SHOWS WHICH BECAME HITS DURING 1971-72

Bob and Ray, the Two and Only
Coco
Lenny
The Me Nobody Knows
No, No, Nanette
Two by Two

FOREIGN PLAYS IN ENGLISH (9)

To Live Another Summer, To Pass Another Winter
Narrow Road to the Deep North
OLD TIMES
Only Fools Are Sad
Murderous Angels
Anne of Green Gables
VIVAT! VIVAT REGINA!
Wise Child
The Little Black Book

Plays listed in CAPITAL LETTERS have been designated Best Plays of 1971-72.
Plays listed in **bold face type** were classified as hits in *Variety's* annual list of hits and flops published June 7, 1972, or judged imminently likely to become hits.
Plays listed in *italics* were still running June 1, 1972.

playing his hits for $5 weekdays, $6 weekends, but an expensive $7.50 was more like what you would be asked to pay for a good seat at an off-Broadway success on a preferred night.

According to *Variety* estimate, the average production cost of a Broadway musical had risen to $534,000 (and this is an *average,* the big ones couldn't open for anything like that sum). For straight plays the average had reached $141,000. Off Broadway, costs for a musical ran from $100,000 up and for a play $40,000 up. At these prices, New York producers began to look enviously in the direction of London (where this season the West End actors were negotiating a raise in the weekly minimum from $43 to $72, while Equity's weekly Broadway minimum is now $185). In October, the American musical *Ambassador* was produced in London for $240,000 as a sort of tryout for Broadway. It wasn't a success, but it would have cost three times as much to find this out on Broadway. In April London saw a $450,000 musical version of *Gone With the Wind,* reputedly London's most expensive musical ever, but a half-price bargain compared to the estimated Broadway cost.

In this context, *Variety's* summary of the season gives no great cause for rejoicing—nor any significant jolt of alarm. The total Broadway gross for 1971-72 was $52.3 million, off from last year's $54.9 million and way under 1967-68's record $59 million but still a sizeable sum. Touring Broadway productions grossed $49.7 million in 1971-72, so that the season's total take was well over $100 million. In the matter of playing weeks (if ten shows play ten weeks that's 100 playing weeks) Broadway registered 1,092 (plus 65 previewing weeks) this season as compared with 1,099 last year, 1,047 the year before that and 1,200-odd in the four previous years.

There were a few patches of blue in the gray overcast. According to *Variety* estimates, *Fiddler on the Roof's* net profit on its $375,000 investment reached $7,215,000 as it climbed toward the top of the heap to become the longest-running show in Broadway history at its 3,225th performance on June 17, 1972. As *No, No, Nanette* reached the break-even point on its $650,000 investment, it had an additional near-$1 million advance sale already in hand. *Sleuth* has netted more than $1 million on its $150,000 investment; *Promises, Promises* and *1776* about $1.5 million each on $500,000; *Oh, Calcutta!* $310,000 on $100,000.

Unhappily, there were also the patches of blacker significance drifting through the weeks of production. *Old Times,* the season's best play, was mounted for $100,000 and lost $120,000 in a Broadway run of 119 performances. *The Rothschilds* was still in the red for $650,000 of its $850,000 production cost when it closed after a run of no less than 507 performances. *Follies,* last season's best musical and indeed one of the outstanding theater works of the decade, eked back about $160,000 of its nearly $800,000 production cost until, in midwinter, the sands began to flow the other way and the gap to widen again.

The one-performance run of the melodrama *Children! Children!* reminded us that there were five of these single-performance flops this season on Broadway. The others were *Wild and Wonderful,* a musical about the big city youth movement; *Ring Round the Bathtub* about an Irish-American family in Chicago during the Depression; *Tough to Get Help,* a suburban situation involving a rich liberal and the black couple who work for him; and *Heathen,* the Robert Helpmann-Eaton Magoon Jr. musical about Hawaii in 1819 and

1972. Off Broadway there were ten: *Drat!, Memphis Store-Bought Teeth, Two if by Sea* (musicals), *In the Time of Harry Harass, Brothers, Whitsuntide, Cold Feet, Masquerade* (the latter a part of the 1972 Elizabeth I canon, dramatizing her relationship with the Earl of Oxford), the Roundabout Repertory's American premiere production of the late John Whiting's 1947 play *Conditions of Agreement,* and *The Soft Core Pornographer,* for which the New York *Times's* Clive Barnes produced the following tag line for his unfavorable review: "What less can I say?"

Few of our so-called "established" playwrights ventured out into the threatening overcast of 1972. Of those who did, only a handful distinguished themselves. Among those who missed a hold on Broadway were Robert Anderson with *Solitaire/Double Solitaire* and the Messrs. Lawrence & Lee with *The Incomparable Max.* Off Broadway, Ed Bullins's *The Duplex,* a slice-of-life play about an all-night party in a black California community (stylistically akin to the same author's *The Pig Pen*), fell far below the very high standard of acute observation and intensity of expression which this distinguished playwright has set in his better works. In the Broadway instances of Anderson and Lawrence & Lee it was more the form than the performance which raised difficulties. Both *Solitaire* and *Max* were one-act play programs, Anderson's a back-to-back pair of wry comments on the final victory of machines over man in the first play and the tensions of married life in the second; Lawrence & Lee's a pair of dramatized Max Beerbohm short stories about clairvoyance, sandwiched in between character vignettes of Beerbohm himself (played by Clive Revill) as a sort of commentator. Both programs were written and acted with a wit and flair worthy of the Broadway spotlight, but by their very nature as one-acters they couldn't add up to the big play, the big evening which now more than ever the Broadway theater craves from its precious Andersons, Lawrences & Lees. George Furth's one-act play program *Twigs* made it on Broadway this season on its strength as a vehicle for a big Sada Thompson virtuoso appearance as much as on its own inner values. *Unlikely Heroes* did not, even though it was sterner stuff than either *Solitaire, Max* or *Twigs* in its three one-act episodes of the Jewish experience, adapted by Larry Arrick from Philip Roth stories: a Jewish army sergeant's efforts to be fair to a malingering Jewish recruit, a Jewish poppa's ill-fated romantic adventure with an amorous widow, and, last but warmest, a young Jewish lawyer's inner torment and outward metamorphosis as he resists the enforcement of suburban zoning laws on a Hebrew school. The episodic or stream-of-vignettes means of expression seemed to be cropping up all over the place this season in both song and story, as though life were too pungent a matter to taste in any but little bites; notable shows which partook of this style included *Ain't Supposed to Die a Natural Death, Older People, Don't Bother Me, I Can't Cope, And They Put Handcuffs on the Flowers* and to some extent even *Where Has Tommy Flowers Gone?* and *Small Craft Warnings.* Even so, the one-act play program doesn't adapt easily to Broadway's high-cost, big-deal environment (*Twigs* and *Plaza Suite* to the contrary, perhaps for special reasons), or even in ever-higher-costing, bigger-dealing off Broadway these days except as an almost self-consciously non-commercial showcase for playwriting talent. The customary spate of off-Broadway one-act play programs dwindled this year to a mere trickle of five: Martin Craft's *Out of Control;* Eugene Yanni's *Friends* and *Relations; Black Visions* (a Public Theater showcase for the work of Sonia Sanchez, Neil Harris and Richard Wesley in one-acters dealing with contemporary black problems and emotions); a notable staging at American Place of Ronald Ribman's *Fingernails Blue as Flowers* and Steve Tesich's *Lake of the Woods;* and, from London, Tom Stoppard's *After Magritte* and *The Real Inspector Hound.*

The producer of the year both on and off Broadway was Joseph Papp. He brought two of his New York Shakespeare Festival Shows to Broadway—the musical *Two Gentlemen of Verona* from Central Park and the drama *Sticks and Bones* from the indoor season at the Public Theater—and carried off both major Tony awards, the first working of this hat trick since David Merrick did it with *Hello, Dolly!* and *Luther* in 1964. Papp's off-Broadway production of *That Championship Season* won the Critics Award in a hot contest with *Sticks and Bones* (and both of these were named Best Plays), while *Verona* easily ambled off with the Critics Award for best musical. Underneath this glittering tip of the Papp iceberg lay a large mass of exceptionally imaginative theater indoors and out, including *The Black Terror, Iphigenia, Older People* and a rare opportunity to see Shakespeare's *Timon of Athens* on its feet.

As for the redoubtable David Merrick, he deserves a cheer from the New York theater for staying with it, for producing show after show in a variety of genres. He was a sign of life in an entertainment form showing too many patches of barren ground, from which too many of the Harold Princes were temporarily absenting themselves, and in which Richard Barr's Theater 1972 was having bad luck with short-lived shows. Merrick produced two Best Plays, *Moonchildren* and (with Arthur Cantor) *Vivat! Vivat Regina!;* a big musical, *Sugar;* and the Canadian adaptation of Feydeau's farce *There's One in Every Marriage,* which was a *succes d'estime.*

In spite of all the talk in recent seasons about a new era of directors' theater, there was little sign of directorial exaltation over playwriting in 1971-72. The year's best direction of a straight play was Peter Hall's of Pinter's *Old Times,* yet not for a moment would anyone consider him the *auteur* of the evening. In the case of top musical direction, Burt Shevelove's of the *A Funny Thing Happened on the Way to the Forum* revival, the director was indeed the *auteur* both literally and figuratively, since he both directed and rewrote his own book for the occasion. The scripts were outstandingly well served in directorial stints like Alan Schneider's of *Moonchildren,* Gilbert Moses's of *Ain't Supposed to Die a Natural Death,* Jacques Levy's of *Where Has Tommy Flowers Gone?,* Nathan George's of *The Black Terror,* Fernando Arrabal's of his own *And They Put Handcuffs on the Flowers,* Joseph Hardy's of the Stoppard one-acters, A.J. Antoon's of *That Championship Season,* Gower Champion's of *Sugar* and Mike Nichols's of *The Prisoner of Second Avenue* (the Tony Award winner, and in his acceptance speech Nichols took pains to acknowledge Neil Simon as the *auteur* of this popular comedy).

The conspicuous exception to this deferent directorial attitude was Tom O'Horgan, whose garishly imaginative wonder-boy approach to theater is bound to elbow the playwright to one side. Certainly O'Horgan was the *auteur* of last season's *Lenny* and to a great extent of this season's *Jesus Christ Superstar;* and to a lesser but some extent in his staging of the Eve Merriam musical *Inner City.*

With such talents and excitement going for it, how could the New York theater find itself trapped in a gray season? One reason may be that very few of the most skilled of both younger and older generations of American playwrights saw fit to offer any script at all in New York this year. There was no

Miller, no Albee, no van Itallie, no Feiffer play this season; we must thank
our lucky stars that we had a Simon, a Guare, a McNally, a Williams. In the
1971-72 environment of economic strain, social upset and esthetic dichotomy,
the playwrights, it seems, are hanging back.

Audiences are hanging back, too, and perhaps for much the same reasons.
The strange behavior of audiences and playwrights may be two sides of the
same coin. Consider first the economic strain: the price of a ticket, high as it
is, is only a small part of the onerous cost of theatergoing, which is now
scaled at the level of the special occasion rather than of casual drop-in entertainment. It piles up all the extras that a special occasion demands: cocktails,
dinner, taxis, dress, etc. Nowadays even the off-Broadway theater has priced
itself out of range of casual pleasure. Even in this era of inflation, $7.50 (the
usual off-Broadway top) is a lot of money for admission to anything and too
much for careless mild rapture, even when that is available at an off-Broadway
show. No wonder a large part of the audience, particularly the less affluent
young section, is hanging back—and it is obvious that this economic strain
also has an inhibiting effect on the playwright. The box office won't give you
your money back if you don't like the show, so the advance shopping information services—that is to say, the daily drama reviewers in general and the
daily reviewers of the New York *Times* in particular—have more and more
power over the life or death of plays on and off Broadway, in proportion as
costs rise. Many playwrights are reluctant to submit their scripts to the judgment of one man, however dedicated and qualified this one man may be. They
hold their scripts back waiting for the situation to improve, which it shows no
signs of doing. Thus economic strain is a blade which slashes at the theater
both ways, at both audience and dramatist.

So does the spiky bludgeon of social unrest. The legitimate stage has done
much to enhance the quality of New York life over eight or nine decades, and
vice versa, but it is now getting a bad name by association with the city to
which it has contributed so much. Sensational bad news travels fast, and New
York's crime-in-the-streets publicity is offered up daily not only to theater
audiences in the city and its suburbs but also to those many ardent fans of
New York theater across the country who customarily make an annual pil-
grimage to Broadway. The extent and frequency of crime in New York's
streets are exaggerated in these reports, of course, and small mention is ever
made of countermeasures such as increased police visibility and scrutiny in
key theater areas, especially Times Square, and other admirable programs
organized by the city and the theater committees to meet the problems of civil
disorder without turning the world's most interesting city into a police state.

It is almost never emphasized that the centers of legitimate stage activity
are the objects of special supervision. The theatergoer's attention may be captured by some weird-looking specimens of humanity on his way to and from
the theater (*everybody* comes to New York) in a free street show often more
colorful than the one he is on his way to see at $9.90 per, but the activity
of theatergoing is an almost entirely safe recreation even in permissive New
York. The peace is being kept, and perhaps the next step will be to improve
the atmosphere. The threat of culture shock in a visit to the Times Square,
Lower Second Avenue or Sheridan Square areas, let alone violence, is enough
to scarce off many members of the audience. Certainly there is today a
freaked-out atmosphere over what should be the Gay White Way of imagina-

tion and excitement, inhibiting the playwright's drive to make the scene as well as the audience's, tempering his satisfaction in a success by making him wonder if anybody really cares about his painstakingly hand-made work of art in this swirl of stamped-out divertissements and stamped-down humanity.

There was a day when the New York theater audience was one big, admiring unit of homogenized taste, and the theater art grandly homogenized in form and style to suit the massive majority. Over the last decade, however, American theater artists have been struggling to emerge from this cocoon. They have been experimenting—often successfully—with new forms, new means of expression, a new theatrical language. In doing so, they have divided the audience, carrying some along with them on the adventure of change but repelling others. Today there are two separate theaters existing side by side in New York, with—to some extent—separate audiences for each. Here is another two-edged sword; with this esthetic dichotomy, any given play has only a portion of the potential audience it had before, not because the theater audience is smaller (it isn't) but because it has been split into partisan sections.

There is no doubt in my mind and heart that *Follies*—book, lyrics, the whole thing—is one of the great musicals of the decade if not of the century; that *Sticks and Bones* is a highly sophisticated work of new theater expressed on at least three levels; that *Old Times* is a masterpiece of the new subliminal form of theater expression; that *The Prisoner of Second Avenue* (which doesn't belong in this group but, more properly, to the old form) is only "mindless" if one considers Molière's comic fancies mindless. What I doubt is that the first three of these shows will ever find it possible to reach, or are even designed to reach, a large majority of the theater audience.

One Wednesday afternoon last season I dropped in at two Broadway matinees to check replacement performances. I went to the first act of *Vivat! Vivat Regina!,* and the ladies who made up most of the audience were clearly loving the spectacle. They were spellbound, and as I left the theater at intermission I heard them discussing the play itself rather than irrelevancies, a sure sign of involvement. They could hardly wait for the second act to begin.

Around the corner at the matinee of *Sticks and Bones* it was another story. The house was nearly full and you could feel the tension, all right—but it was the wrong kind. This audience was not gripped by the play, as the off-Broadway audience had been, it was in a state of esthetic alarm. It was afraid of what was going to happen next, not in empathy for the characters, but in self-defense. When the Vietnam veteran in this play decides to cut his wrists (it is one of his delusions, I think, but is presented on the stage as though it were actually happening, with a straight razor and a lot of red fluid), the audience was horrified. If there had been an easy way out they would have poured into the street seeking the womb-like reassurance of their special buses. When the curtain went down, about a third of the audience pressed for the exits without waiting for the actors to take their bow (and yet I must also report that I was astonished at the volume and enthusiasm of the applause of those who remained in their seats).

This is what can happen when an audience is mismatched to a play in our era of esthetic dichotomy. It's the job of the theater's institutions to solve the problems of economic strain, whether through organized subsidy or restructuring the economy of production or both. It's ultimately New York City's job to keep the problems of social unrest from polluting the experience of theater-going or enjoying any other art, because there is everything to lose—without the stabilizing environmental influence of its powerful arts contingent, New York would become just another city, just another desert on the edge of a jungle. But the theater's third major problem, that of esthetic division, is a highly personal matter between the playwrights and their audiences.

Here is where the theatergoer must play his major part in the development of the art form. First and foremost, he must understand that there are at least two and probably several kinds of theater nowadays, not just one, and that one kind is not easily judged by the standards of the other. Of course he has every right to ensure his enjoyment, which is what the theater is all about, by taking extra pains to find a show to match his personal taste (that's what keeps the critics powerful). But occasionally he should take a chance just for the hell of it, or maybe for the love of the theater. You *Sticks and Bones* people—stop turning up your nose at *Vivat,* it's a colorful and entertaining *coup de théâtre.* You *Vivat* people—come on over to see a challenging play like *Sticks and Bones* once in a while. Do it in the spirit of adventure, and don't be afraid to hate it if you do, or give in to it if you can; but don't give up on the theater because some evening you find yourself attending a show that's not for you. Your kind of show is almost certainly playing just around the corner.

Broadway

A "hit" in the true Broadway meaning of the word isn't merely a show that is hard to get into on a Friday night in December, but a show which pays off its production cost (it may be easy to get into but become a "hit" by virtue of a movie sale or a profitable road tour). In recent seasons, however, the word "hit" has been losing a lot of its magic. With higher costs hopefully compensated by longer runs, few productions, however popular, reach the break-even point in the season in which they opened. And very often Broadway doesn't have either the first or the last word on a playscript as it once did. Plays now come to Broadway from previous regional or foreign production which has already established their position in world theater. A good script ignored on Broadway for some special reason may take on an illustrious life of its own elsewhere on world stages or in other media. So we make no special point in this resume about which 1971-72 offerings were "hits" and which were "flops" except that this information is recorded in the one-page summary of the Broadway season accompanying this article.

The bests of 1971-72 straight plays were, in the opinion of the *Best Plays* editor, two which by a coincidence carried the imprimatur, if not the byline, of Master Will Shakespeare. These trans-Atlantic rivals were Harold Pinter's *Old Times,* first produced by London's Royal Shakespeare Company, and David Rabe's *Sticks and Bones,* first produced on the indoor program of the New York Shakespeare Festival and later brought uptown to Broadway. Pinter's third full-length play (the other two were *The Caretaker* and *The Homecoming,* both Best Plays of their seasons) was like his others a comment on the human condition in general, rather than a headline-relevant work like Rabe's. As far as external reality is concerned, *Old Times* had a deceptively simple subject: a movie director and his wife receive the wife's former London roommate (herself married and living in Sicily) for a weekend visit to their farmhouse home in England, near the coast. This pale concept was further washed out by John Bury's white-on-white setting, often with white furniture blending into the white walls, in a design statement subtly harmonized to the play. The weekend visit is a white-on-white excuse for a situation, in a play which was not concerned with present reality but—as its title *Old Times* implies—with the half-seen, half-heard, almost subliminal events of the past, existing only in memory and nearly drowned in it. In contrast to *Rashomon* in which a single episode is remembered differently in sequence, *Old Times's* stream of past incidents is remembered simultaneously by its three characters, but differently, like a musical composition performed by an instrumental trio who do not play long in unison but break into scintillating harmonies and discords. Hard facts are as fleetingly experienced as single musical notes: is this really the first time the husband (Robert Shaw) and the roommate (Rosemary Harris) have met, or did they in fact once spend an evening together in a London bar, while he "gazed" (Pinter lays special stress on the word) up her skirts at underwear borrowed from her roommate, his future wife? Did this wife (Mary Ure) share a very strong emotional attachment with the other woman while they were roommates in London? Did the husband try to make love to both women on a single evening, and does he now regret he married the one instead of the other? Acted with uniform sensitivity and directed likewise by Peter Hall, *Old Times* never supplied direct answers but was entirely fascinating as it asked the questions. At the end, when the husband suddenly weeps for a few moments and then as suddenly ceases, you perhaps did not know exactly why, but you couldn't help feeling sad along with him, in an intuition of Paradise somehow lost. *Old Times,* our choice for best of bests, never quite caught on with New York audiences, though it was a close runner-up in the Critics Circle voting for best foreign play and was awarded a special citation; nor was it originally produced in the commercially-exposed side of the London theater, but in the shelter of the Royal Shakespeare Company's organization and subsidy, as was *The Homecoming* and other Pinter works. Their existence ahead of their time in the spotlight of public attention is a powerful argument for subsidy and strong evidence of its potential rewards.

The best American play of the season was David Rabe's *Sticks and Bones.* Rabe is a Vietnam war veteran who made his professional playwriting debut last season at Joseph Papp's Public Theater with *The Basic Training of Pavlo Hummel* (the New York Shakespeare Festival's longest-running show to date, 363 performances before it closed this season). In that first play Rabe's protagonist is a soldier finally killed in Saigon; in his second, *Sticks and Bones,* his Vietnam war veteran comes home, wounded and blind, to a Henry Aldrich-type American family that remains as stubbornly blind to his spiritual despair as he is to the physical world around him.

There are at least three separate levels of action in this play. First, there is the veneered middle-class American home life with the family resisting any emotional intrusion by their veteran or his memories of war; a teen-aged son's excruciatingly cheery "Hi mom, hi dad" loses not a shade of its day-glo brightness because his blinded brother is home from a cruel war, agonizing in the room upstairs. The soldier is alone on his own private level of experience, haunted by dreams of killing and of love. The living memory figure of the

Vietnamese girl he left behind him follows him around the house, and he is often unable to distinguish between the real and the hallucinatory. He's ready to believe that his family would quite casually recommend that the best solution for him would be to cut his wrists, when in reality—or apparent reality—they are only talking about some TV show they saw the night before.

The third level of *Sticks and Bones* is a sort of mezzanine between the two, where they sometimes meet and set off explosions like a contact of matter and anti-matter. Caught on this split-level, neither completely comfortable either with the family or with the veteran, is the father, played by Tom Aldredge in the season's best performance by an actor. His wife (played by Elizabeth Wilson in the year's best supporting performance by an actress) is comfortably secure in her conviction that a little snack of fudge and milk cures any but the most major upset, in which case you call in the priest. But the husband is at the center of the storm, trying to cope, but buffeted by self-contradicting winds, in a play we have all been waiting for; a play which explores some of the deeper cracks in the American spirit caused by the Vietnam war. *Sticks and Bones* was the close runner-up for the Critics Award (and like *Old Times* won a special citation) as well as the Tony winner, a credit to the theater and to David Rabe who newly but surely joins the ranks of our leading young playwrights.

The man who produced *Sticks and Bones* off Broadway and then brought it into the more intense limelight of the West Forties, Joseph Papp, was widely quoted in the press this season as having declared that Broadway can no longer muster an audience for serious drama. I've always been uneasy about that phrase "serious drama" as a possible redundancy, but it has a certain usefulness. Drama may imply serious, if not tragic, themes, but in our contemporary theater it often uses the moods and devices of the human comedy to frame its tragic implications. Plays like *Old Times* and *Sticks and Bones* probably ought to be called dramas (if a classification is demanded) because they are only comedic when their winds are blowing nor'-nor'-west; the pathos, even the agony at times, is stronger than the irony. They are black comedy-dramas, or something like that; dramas if you will, but not "serious drama" in the straightforward, pike-thrusting sense of that phrase.

Neither is Robert Bolt's *Vivat! Vivat Regina!*, another Best Play imported from the London stage. Any story in which one of the two leading characters has her head cut off in the last scene is probably going to be called a drama; but there is a romantic light touch in the handling of this series of queenly vignettes, with only a whiff of pentameter. Bolt presents his queens as young women who must make a choice between reigning and loving, of growing to maturity either as monarch or as woman but not both. Elizabeth opts for England, Mary for romance, and such is the story of their lives in this play. Elizabeth becomes vividly a queen, Mary vividly a woman; and, at last, each envies the other's lot. The spectacle was enhanced by the excellent designs of Carl Toms both in costumes (rich and elegant) and in scenery (simple, spare, versatile), and the drama was powered by a dominating Eileen Atkins performance as Elizabeth, memorable even in a year of many Elizabeths on stages and screens. The Virgin Queen and her reign received much dramatic attention in every medium this season, even twice more on Broadway, once in the revival of Schiller's *Mary Stuart* at Lincoln Center and again in Paul Foster's *Elizabeth I,* an historical cartoon with the events of the reign and the ideas and ambitions underlying it presented through a company of 16th century street actors.

Two wholly serious Broadway dramas added interest and dimension to the season. Romulus Linney's *The Love Suicide at Schofield Barracks* took the shape of an Army inquiry into the suicide of a commanding general and his wife in full public view at a barracks Halloween party. Gradually the investigation discloses that the suicide was an act of protest against the Vietnam war, with Mercedes McCambridge and William Redfield in standout performances on the witness stand. *Murderous Angels,* a play by Conor Cruise O'Brien staged at the Mark Taper Forum in Los Angeles before coming to New York under Phoenix Theater auspices, was another script that brought some thunder to the atmosphere in a dramatization of the Dag Hammarskjold-Patrice Lumumba confrontation in the Congo in the 1950s, which ended fatally for both. The Irish author of the play was the Secretary-General's representative in Katanga at the time of these events, but in his effort to write a play instead of an historical tract he juggled the facts and characters to suit his purpose. This brought a flood of criticism down upon his work in New York by those who resented what they considered a demeaning characterization of Lumumba, and equally by friends of Hammarskjold who didn't approve of the way he was presented. But viewed as an invention for the stage, *Murderous Angels* had a strong premise: since it was Lumumba's responsibility to arouse his compatriots to effective rebellion against their oppressors, and Hammarskjold's responsibility to keep them cool in order to avoid a confrontation of great powers over the issue, there arose an almost tragic conflict of interests which forced two "angels" to murder each other in their holy causes, inevitably, as a tragic mutual duty. It is a pity that O'Brien had to use real names in his drama, which might well have stood on its own feet without historical buttressing, avoiding odious historical comparisons. *Murderous Angels* didn't find an audience on Broadway, nor did *The Love Suicide at Schofield Barracks,* nor even the off-Broadway hit *The Trial of the Catonsville Nine* when it transferred to Broadway for a brief visit in June. These experiences and Mr. Papp's observation to the contrary notwithstanding, this doesn't prove that the audience isn't there.

That popular form of not-wholly-"serious" drama, the thriller, was variously represented this season. Besides the short-lived *Children! Children!,* there was *Night Watch* by Lucille Fletcher, author of the famous radio play *Sorry, Wrong Number.* In the new play she presented yet another menacing husband and agonizing wife (played by Len Cariou and Joan Hackett under Fred Coe's concise direction) in a cat-and-mouse game which held quite a few chills and a fair share of surprises. Richard Lortz's ghost story *Voices* had the makings of a memorable one-act play about a couple seeking refuge in a gloomy, empty house in a snowstorm, only to find the place haunted. As a full-length play it spread itself too thin, despite consistently strong performances by Richard Kiley and Julie Harris as the couple and the other-worldly atmosphere enhanced by Peggy Stuart Coolidge's ghost-music score.

Returning to the Best Plays list, the best comedy of the year was Neil Simon's ninth straight Broadway success (most of which were also hits in the *Variety* sense of the word) and sixth Best Play, *The Prisoner of Second Avenue.* As the Molière of our era, Simon takes the position of a fellow-sufferer mindful of our woes—with a streak of anger that has broadened almost consistently since the happy times of *Barefoot in the Park*. Simon's prisoner in the new play is a high-salaried adman who has all the modern inconveniences money can buy in his 82d Street high-rise: failing plumbing, hostile neighbors, garbage smells, burglar risk as high as the rent and a couple of German airline hostesses living it up on the other side of the thin wall. When he loses the job that pays for all of this luxury, the adman goes over the edge into a nervous breakdown. Life has insulted him one too many times, and he insults it back by blowing his mind. His wife takes over the breadwinning chore and his brother and three sisters, who haven't paid him a visit in nine years, gather self-righteously to help their baby brother who has lost touch with reality. This family scene, with Vincent Gardenia as the brother trying to herd his sisters into some kind of line of practical support, is worthy of Molière in its cartoons of avarice, role-playing, hypocrisy, sibling rivalry, etc. Mike Nichols's Tony Award-winning direction drew every bit of sense and nonsense into the open and helped evoke excellent performances from Peter Falk and Lee Grant as the beseiged husband and wife. That's how Neil Simon views the way we live, as a state of seige under regular assault, with no help in sight from the fortress walls. The fact that a miraculously gifted playwright is still able to treat this as a subject for comedy made *Prisoner* one of the more cheering thoughts of the season.

Another outstanding comedy (self-styled a "comic play") and Best Play on Broadway this season was *Moonchildren,* the professional New York debut of its author, Michael Weller. It is about college students in the 1960s, huddling together in their dormitory and living fantasy lives by mutual agreement, shrinking from a reality which they are sure is growing increasingly materialistic, crass, hostile. In their own imaginative way they are whistling past the graveyard which they fear their planet may become. Weller's *Moonchildren* are Terrence McNally's *Tommy Flowers* ten years earlier. As college seniors in the 1960s they are lovingly and innocently reinventing themselves and their lives (one pair of youths decide they are brothers whose father is a trapper; no invention is too unlikely to be accepted without skepticism by the others). Later in the 1970s, turning 30, most of them will have sharpened a *Tommy Flowers* edge by losing their innocence without solving their problems. Not in this comedy, though; here their instinctive response to life is still affectionate. With James Woods, Kevin Conway, Edward Herrmann and Cara Duff-MacCormick heading an attractive ensemble under Alan Schneider's exceptionally skillful direction, the script's faults (repetitiousness, a confusion of destination) were minimized and its virtues (texture, imagination, insight into the motivations of contemporary youth) maximized.

Five other Broadway attractions billed themselves outright as comedies. David V. Robison's *Promenade, All!* was a sketchbook of an American family in transition from the late 19th century to the present, pausing at four stops along the way—1895, 1920, 1945 and now—to acquaint us with six generations of individuals facing their personal and business crises. The nine members of the Huntziger, later Hunt, family whom we meet on this trip are an appealing assortment of pleasure-loving or fortune-hunting products of their eras, played to the absolute limit by Richard Backus (all the young men), Anne Jackson (all the women), Eli Wallach (the driving or neurotic types) and Hume Cronyn (most notably as a 93-year-old who volunteers for a sex experiment). This was a fresh and comfortable patch of blue drifting across the stormy season. Another comedy, *Fun City,* by Lester Colodny, Joan Rivers and Edgar Rosenberg, projected Neil Simon's New York into a future when all services will be breaking down but we will all be used to it. Gabriel Dell, Miss Rivers and Rose Marie worked hard for the laughs in this play, which also featured the season's most distinguished bit-part casting: Paul Ford in the minuscule role of an aged mailman. A third self-styled "comedy" was the short-lived Richard T. Johnson-Daniel Hollywood script *All the Girls Came Out to Play* about a writer and his agent who seclude themselves in the suburbs to work on a show, are mistaken for homosexuals by the community and exploit this error by demonstrating to the suburban wives that they are not. The fourth was a French comedy adapted by Jerome Kilty and produced here under the title *The Little Black Book,* with Richard Benjamin as a gullible bachelor and Delphine Seyrig as a stranger who forces her way into his life and slowly begins to fascinate him, for some unknown reason; she (the character, not Miss Seyrig) was the most repellent nuisance to appear on a stage this season. Finally there was *Tough to Get Help,* a comedy about a rich advertising man's suburban household and the black couple who maintain it, unshriven even by the direction of Carl Reiner.

Gore Vidal's *An Evening With Richard Nixon And . . .* was a ponderous political satire on the President's opportunistic career and all-American style, overloaded with double and triple framing and a portentous historical perspective. Beginning as a Pro and Con argument, it soon enlists the shades of Kennedy and Eisenhower as chief advocates of either side, with George Washington as judge and everyone else in the modern history books brought into the act. It fared slightly better than the season's other political foray, *The Selling of the President,* but not much better. It made a sitting duck-type victim out of Nixon (played bravely and even admirably by George S. Irving), his entourage and even his family, so that its partisan zeal was weakened by embarrassing personal comment, blunting its point about the Nixon regime being merely the inevitable product of decades, even centuries, of instinctive American imperialism.

Among other scripts which must on balance be classified as comedies even though they didn't make a point of it in the billing was George Furth's *Twigs,* one of the season's most conspicuous successes, with Sada Thompson carrying off the year's female starring honors in a quadruple performance. *Twigs* was four playlets centering on the woman in each of them. The first is a newly-divorced, young middle-aged, middle-class housewife who succumbs gracefully to the first attractive man she meets, the mover who helps her set up the furniture in her new apartment. The second is a drudge who once had a chance in the movies but is now married to an insensitive boor. The third is happily married in a suburban sort of way and enjoys a playful relationship with her husband. The fourth—and this is the punch line of the collection of playlets—is a bent, aged but verbally active old crone who is the mother of all the previous three and detests any hint of sentiment in her relationship with her offspring. She is a handful (I don't want to usurp the playwright's prerogative by saying more about her specific goals) and she is also a sort of summing-up of her three daughters, as Miss Thompson made abundantly clear in her virtuoso performance.

A pair of English black comedies turned out not to travel very well, but at least they added an extra taste to the season. Simon Gray's short-lived *Wise Child,* about a criminal on the lam disguised in women's clothes, was an attenuated joke about sexual identity. Its acting was more sustaining than its subject, however, with Donald Pleasence snarling in his female get-up, Bud Cort as his youthful accomplice and especially George Rose as a smirking pervert who runs the hotel in which the other two are hiding out. Lincoln Center Repertory tried Edward Bond's *Narrow Road to the Deep North*, a batch of sprawling, episodic comments about fascism, colonialism, idealism and other conceits of human beings in the mass. Bond's play is set in the 17th, 18th and 19th centuries in Japan, where and when, presumably, submission was a habit and violence a way of life. It was one of the meatier offerings of 1971-72, and Dan Sullivan staged its tumultuous, if somewhat obviously symbolical, episodes with clarity and fluidity on the Vivian Beaumont's thrust stage.

On the musical scene, Melvin Van Peebles arrived in town and started putting out Broadway musicals as though he planned to do Neil Simon's thing, except that he produced them, wrote the music as well as the words and directed one of them himself. 1971-72 was a year in which several Broadway musicals had something but none everything, and Van Peebles's *Ain't Supposed to Die a Natural Death* emerged onto the list of Best Plays by virtue of its originality and its power. The author has practically invented his own form to present ironic, impassioned snapshots of the black ghetto. His subject is the agonies and the very scarce joys of life on the bottom of the scale where poverty, crime and neglect are facts of life along with love, beauty and charity. Van Peebles's music was an unobtrusive accompaniment to lyrics which were not sung, but spoken in a rhythmic continuity something like a poem, something like a recitative, something like narration. *Ain't Supposed to Die a Natural Death* is a strange mutation of musical theater, using the idiom and imagery of the musical stage to great effect under the direction of Gilbert Moses, with an acting ensemble so uniformly gifted that it seemed almost unnecessary to single out one of them, Beatrice Winde, for a Tony nomination. For its finale, the musical confronts the audience and declares "Put a curse on you!" for even passive complicity in events depicted on the stage. I could have done without the Van Peebles curses, but nevertheless I admired his most inventive use of the musical theater.

Having gathered his Broadway momentum, Van Peebles coasted in with *another* interesting musical this same season, *Don't Play Us Cheap!*, an antithesis of his previous work, without a mean bone in its body; without a curse or even a sneering "the man" in its dialogue. This one was a warm, friendly fantasy about a couple of would-be evil spirits disguising themselves as humans and trying to break up a family party in Harlem on a swinging Saturday night. These are just folks enjoying themselves and each other, expressing themselves in song when the spirit or spiritual moves them (the music for this show is happier, more folk-songey, and the lyrics are almost conventionally styled). The party goers include an enchanting young girl (Rhetta Hughes), her wise and unfailingly benign aunt (Joshie Jo Armstead), a needle-shaped neighbor (Avon Long) and a handsome young evil spirit (Joe Keyes Jr.) who discovers to his shame that he isn't really so evil after all. With his two musicals, Van Peebles poisoned Broadway with hate and then brought forth the antidote love, all in the same season, in a remarkable display of musical energy and virtuousity.

The year's most popular musical was the Tom O'Horgan staging of *Jesus Christ Superstar*. Like *Ain't Supposed to Die a Natural Death*, this was a visualization of material previously published on records, a rock concert version of the Gospel story with music by Andrew Lloyd Webber and lyrics by Tim Rice which had already gained international renown in a best-selling LP record album. In O'Horgan's hands, this material became *Lenny* with Biblical overtones; *Hair* in Galilean dress. The character of Jesus in the last seven days of his life was almost submerged under the fantastic (and undeniably color-ful) scenery by Robin Wagner and costumes by Randy Barcelo, with the crowd scenes as full of monstrous and unexplained images as the corners of a Hieronymus Bosch painting. Herod camping across the stage on his wedgies . . . Caiaphas and his priests suspended in air on a framework of dinosaur bones . . . Jesus having a tantrum as he drives the money-changers from the temple . . . the soul of Judas (played by Ben Vereen, a black actor) in space on a trapeze decorated with pretty girls and peacock feathers . . . this was an evening of raw, often indigestible, stage imagery, sometimes in questionable taste but as unstoppable as a circus. The lyrics are rock-opera streamlined, and yet respectful of the subject (for example, in the Last Supper scene, Jesus reproaches his friends with indifference: "For all you care, this bread could be my body/For all you care, this wine could be my blood"). But unlike last season's *Godspell, Superstar* had no reverential tone. The American Jewish Committee and the Anti-Defamation League of B'nai B'rith protested the show because it represents Caiaphas and his henchmen as prime movers of the crucifixion, "unambiguously lays the primary responsibility for Jesus's suf-fering and crucifixion to the Jewish priesthood. The priests are portrayed as hideously inhuman and Satanically evil; contemptuous, callous and blood-thirsty. There is no warrant in the New Testament either for the attribution of primary guilt or for the caricatured characterization." The protest implied for *Superstar* a significance which otherwise seemed hard to find in its comic-strip versions of villainy. The show's producer, Robert Stigwood, stated in rebuttal that these incidents were "confrontations of a reformer and the Es-tablishment which continually recur in the history of man." *Superstar* had very little religious meaning, nor would it win prizes for artistic taste, but it was a prime example of the Tom O'Horgan beaux-arts-ball type of musical extrava-ganza.

O'Horgan's second musical of the season, *Inner City,* was sterner stuff but unable to find an audience on Broadway, possibly because it existed in the shadow of the Van Peebles material. This was a series of fairy tale-parodying musical takeoffs on the outrages of the black ghetto, based on Eve Merriam's book *The Inner City Mother Goose,* with song titles like "You'll Find Mice" and "Twelve Rooftops Leaping." Linda Hopkins won a Tony for her efforts in this show, conceived and directed by O'Horgan, which suffered, perhaps unfairly, from being the second of two Broadway musicals and one of many 1971-72 stage works about the black condition.

It was David Merrick's prerogative to supply Broadway with a big showcase musical, the kind that attracts expense account customers and stimulates the pulsebeat of show business all over town. *Sugar* filled this bill admirably. Peter Stone's book recreated 101 per cent of the fun of the Marilyn Monroe movie on which it was based, *Some Like It Hot,* about two musicians hiding out from menacing Prohibition-era gangsters by disguising themselves as women and joining an all-girl orchestra. Jule Styne and Bob Merrill provided a happy jazz-era score and Merrick found an absolutely gorgeous and talented comedienne, Elaine Joyce, to play the Monroe part (Miss Joyce has none of the voluptuousness of a sex goddess, but she is so well proportioned that her beauty is a joke at other women's expense). Robert Morse clearly had a wonderful time with the Jack Lemmon role, playing all the double and even triple entendres of a masquerade in which the costume gradually gains dominance over its wearer until he becomes confused about his identity. Gower Champion put it all together very adroitly indeed as director and as choreographer. Even the designs by Robin Wagner and Alvin Colt were fun. *Sugar* was an entertainment in the most cheerful sense of the word, welcome as the flowers in early April when it finally appeared on the New York scene.

Two other musicals helped lift the spirits of the season, both originating far from the Times Square area but both finally making it there. Joseph Papp's production of *Two Gentlemen of Verona* (dropping Shakespeare's *The* from the title on Broadway) originated in Central Park as a New York Shakespeare Festival summer giveaway but proved so popular that it moved to Broadway in the fall at a $15 top. This was Galt MacDermot's first Broadway score since *Hair*—masterful stage music, if less than a masterpiece—and the John Guare-Mel Shapiro adaptation kept Shakespeare's lovers revolving like hurrying planets around the wisp of a tale. The attractive cast was headed by Raul Julia and Diana Davila as one of the couples and Clifton Davis and Jonelle Allen as the other, the latter pair stopping the show with a lively duet called "Night Letter." *Two Gentlemen of Verona* was warmly received by the critics, but coolly by the public at first; evidently the audience was reluctant to shell out hard cash for a show that had been given away free only a few weeks before. This block soon dissolved, however, and *Verona* went on to become a success and win the Critics Award for best musical as well as the Tony.

Another high-spirited session was *Grease*, which managed to whip up some quite genuinely appealing nostalgia for the Elvis Presley-James Dean, rock musical tempest-in-a-teapot era of the 1950s. This show written by Jim Jacobs and Warren Casey opened downtown at the Eden Theater on Second Avenue, but it was operating on first-class Broadway contracts and thus was classified as a Broadway production. It was easily worthy of the name, with a very bright book and score and Barry Bostwick (lapsing into a James Dean saunter whenever threatened or embarrassed, as protective coloration), Adrienne Barbeau and Timothy Meyers heading a cast which bore down hard on the humor of high school characters with grease slicking down their hair and mischief in their hearts. Facetiously billed as the *No, No, Nanette* of the 30-year-olds, *Grease* was fun for all ages and moved uptown to the Times Square area at season's end.

Among the shorter-lived Broadway musical efforts were an adaptation of Truman Capote's *The Grass Harp*, highly praised in some quarters for its Claibe Richardson-Kenward Elmslie score, and the effort to make a musical out of Joe McGinnis's book *The Selling of the President*, about the merchandizing, Madison Avenue-style, of Richard Nixon's 1968 campaign (in the show the date was put forward and the candidate was a fictional senator, played by Pat Hingle). Micki Grant's bright and lively *Don't Bother Me, I Can't Cope* came to Broadway in a middle theater production of topical musical diversion, some of its score based on calypso, Gospel and other folk sources, with even the ghetto themes traced out with wit and style under Vinnette Carroll's driving direction. This was an Urban Arts Corps production which had originally appeared in New York and elsewhere in a slightly different form.

A Howard Dietz-Arthur Schwartz musical revue *That's Entertainment* was a collection of song numbers from their distinguished past shows, but it lacked any point of view or other *raison d'être* over and above the music itself. A new musical written and directed by Michael Brown, *Different Times,* was only tenuously premised on an episodic story line about several generations of an American family, and the score wasn't one of Brown's best. The Supreme Being Himself found his way onto the stage in Old Testament episodes musicalized in *Hard Job Being God* which, like the Creation, ran for only 6 performances.

Three foreign musicals visited Broadway in 1971-72. The Israeli production *To Live Another Summer, To Pass Another Winter* was a topical musical revue mostly about Israel's emergence as a nation; an image of a forthright, self-possessed, determined—and when driven to it, arrogant—new society expressed in songs, sketches, a sense of humor and the appealing performances, in English, of a young Israeli cast. A second import from Israel, *Only Fools Are Sad,* was a paean to the simple, pious life expressed in an anthology of Hassidic songs and stories translated into English. A third import was *Anne of Green Gables,* a Canadian musical version of the novel about an orphan girl's childhood. Also touching at these shores was the Black Light Theater of Prague, a vaudeville of trick staging with fluorescent shapes animated by black-clad actors in a black setting.

Revivals

It was a small but healthy year for revivals, with only a dozen each on Broadway and off, (11 fewer than last year's total), but with several notable accomplishments in the list. Burt Shevelove updated his and Larry Gelbart's book for *A Funny Thing Happened on the Way to the Forum,* staged it in Los Angeles and finally brought it to Broadway with Phil Silvers as Pseudolus and Larry Blyden as Hysterium, a new comedy team honored by both Tony Awards for actors in the musical category. Blyden is too good an actor to settle for a career as a straight man; but on the basis of his performance here he is much too good a straight man not to make the most of this exceptional opportunity, playing the house slave with a myopically persistent belief that his world is the best of all possibles, even though angels might fear to tread in it. Under Shevelove's direction the jokes seemed fresh and very, very funny, and the Stephen Sondheim score included two numbers that weren't in the original production: "Farewell" in the first act and "Echo Song" in the second. Last year Shevelove came up with the season's biggest hit, the revival of *No, No, Nanette,* while Sondheim was creating the brilliant *Follies.* This year, together, they have again lit up the Broadway sky, and I suspect that if Plautus had it this good in the 1961-62 production, he certainly couldn't have had it any better.

The Maxwell Anderson-Kurt Weill musical *Lost in the Stars* also received a first-rate revival production mounted at Kennedy Center in Washington and brought to New York after a couple of stopoffs. Based on Alan Paton's *Cry the Beloved Country,* and originally billed as a "musical tragedy," this is a book show with musical interpolations, about two South African families, one black and one white, brought together in an ultimate agony of social malaise, an almost senseless murder. The performance of Brock Peters as the black country minister whose son turns to crime was a standout in this context, a late 1940s poetic design in which brotherly love seems to shine somewhere behind the dark clouds of racism in a more heartbreaking but less cynical view than we are used to in these darker days. A similar effort to mount a revival of the ebullient Betty Comden-Adolph Green-Leonard Bernstein musical *On the Town* in a full-scale Broadway production fizzled out expensively, leaving little more than the memory of another Bernadette Peters acting coup in the role of Hildy the lady taxi driver. Likewise, the durably popular *You're a Good Man Charlie Brown* failed to attract an audience with a Broadway revival production early in the season.

Neither did there seem to be much of an audience for the uptown restaging of the recent Pulitzer Prize drama *No Place To Be Somebody* by Charles Gordone, but two more venerable scripts attracted attention with the alluring twinkle of their starring performances. Clifford Odets's *The Country Girl* and George Bernard Shaw's *Captain Brassbound's Conversion* both jumped from the Kennedy Center to Broadway, the former for a run, the latter for an engagement limited to two weeks. With Jason Robards, Maureen Stapleton and George Grizzard as the backstage characters in the Odets play about an aging but talented star and his apparently man-eating wife, *The Country Girl* proved to be a still-valid comment on the nature of emotional commitment. Ingrid Bergman was the big attraction in *Brassbound* (which she had just previously done in London), adding her personal grace to the indomitable character of Lady Cicely in the Shaw comedy.

Off Broadway, Sean O'Casey's *The Shadow of a Gunman* alone among the revived straight plays was able to make a run for it, probably because it played upon already-tingling emotions with its drama of violence in the Dublin "troubles" of the 1920s, now echoing tragically through streets of Ulster. Mid-20th century scripts which tried unsuccessfully to stage comebacks this season were Saul Bellow's *The Last Analysis,* Sidney Michaels's *Dylan* and, uptown, Lorraine Hansberry's *The Sign in Sidney Brustein's Window.* David Merrick deserves applause for bringing in the Stratford, Canada version of the Georges Feydeau farce *There's One in Every Marriage* in an adaptation by Suzanne Grossman and Paxton Whitehead, in a production whose acting and direction left little to be desired and therefore indicated that in the present, problematical Broadway commercial context there's not much of an audience for the ephemeral frivolities of Feydeau, even when well executed. Still another echo of the theater's glorious past, the drama *Rain,* made a short-lived appearance downtown. Last season's *Alice in Wonderland,* on the other hand, came right back this season and once again was warmly embraced by both critics and audiences.

In organizational production of revivals, the New York Shakespeare Festival's summer program outdoors at the Delacorte gave New Yorkers the opportunity to see two very seldom-produced Shakespeare plays: *Timon of Athens* (with Shepperd Strudwick in the title role) and *Cymbeline* (offered under the title *The Tale of Cymbeline*). According to the *Directory of the American Theater, 1894-1971,* which lists all plays, authors and sources of Broadway, off-Broadway and off-off-Broadway shows named in all the 56 *Best Plays* yearly and retrospective volumes, this was the first *Timon* produced professionally in New York (it's about a rich man who tries to buy friendship and suffers a King Lear-like rejection when his money runs out). The third offering of Joseph Papp's outdoor season was the musical *Verona* which went on to become a Broadway success.

Another major revival-producing group, Gene Feist's Roundabout, mounted creditable productions of Ibsen's *The Master Builder,* Shakespeare's *The Taming of the Shrew* and Shaw's *Misalliance.* Over in Brooklyn, the Chelsea Theater Center took a breather in the midst of a season of challenging new plays and put on a revival of John Gay's *The Beggar's Opera,* with "musical realization" by Ryan Edwards. The show not only delighted audiences in Brooklyn but later moved into the McAlpin Rooftop Theater, hopefully settling in for a run.

This brings us finally to the subject which we must inevitably confront in these yearly summaries of revival activity in New York: The Lincoln Center Repertory Company in its glittering facility, the Vivian Beaumont Theater. Its finest hour this season was the revival of Arthur Miller's *The Crucible* with Robert Foxworth in the pivotal role of the drama about Salem witch-hunting, written at the time of the Sen. Joseph McCarthy Communist-hunts of the 1950s but acquiring a broader relevance with the passage of time. A criticism by Arthur Miller of the Lincoln Center board of directors was first printed in the spring of 1972 in the playwrights' own publication the *Dramatists Guild Quarterly* and later received a wider circulation in the *Times* and *Variety.* Miller's point—made in connection with an effort to prevent the demolition of the Forum Theater and the Beaumont's repertory storage space to make room for some kind of movie program—was that it's futile for critics and other commentators to confine their remarks to the material presented on the Beaumont's stage or even the efficacy of Jules Irving's artistic directorship, when the problem begins with the Lincoln Center board of directors' apparent ignorance of and indifference to what is required in dedication and currency to start and maintain a repertory theater. The decision to revive *The Crucible* had no connection with Miller's comments; the necessary permission for a revival production was acquired through channels before Miller's criticism appeared. But the decision was a good one; revivals of American plays like *The Crucible* are what Lincoln Center should be all about. And if the organization had maintained Elia Kazan's and Robert Whitehead's original momentum toward creating an American repertory company, they might possess two other Miller plays, *After the Fall* and *Incident at Vichy,* in their permanent repertory today, because the Lincoln Center company was the first to produce them.

Wishing won't make it so, however, and the fact is that the Lincoln Center board, or somebody up there, did arrest the Kazan-Whitehead development; and if there has been purpose or progress in the work of Lincoln Center since then, it cannot be seen by the naked eye (occasional excellence, yes, now and then an imaginative or challenging single production—a company in being, perhaps, but without any sense of *becoming*). On Lincoln Center's 1971-72 Beaumont schedule, Edward Bond's *Narrow Road to the Deep North* was stimulating theater and Schiller's *Mary Stuart* was right in step with this season's parade of Elizabeth I-Mary Queen of Scots plays. But neither the production of British scripts nor the pursuit of trends would be found among the mandates extended to Lincoln Center Repertory by that part of the theatergoing public which hoped—and maybe somewhere, faintly, still hopes—that it would some day become an American company along the lines of the Old

The 1971-72 Season off Broadway

PLAYS (43)

The Justice Box
Charlie Was Here and Now He's Gone
Public Theater 1971
Dance Wi' Me
Black Girl
Georgie Porgie
Out of Control
WHERE HAS TOMMY FLOWERS GONE?
Friends & Relations
A Song for the First of May
A Gun Play
In the Time of Harry Harass
Public Theater 1972
STICKS AND BONES
The Black Terror
Iphigenia
Black Visions
THAT CHAMPION- SHIP SEASON
Older People
The Hunter
Lincoln Cent. Forum
The Duplex
Suggs
Negro Ensemble
The Sty of the Blind Pig
Frederick Douglass
Masquerade
El Hajj Malik
Kaddish
American Place
Fingernails Blue as Flowers &
Lake of the Woods
Sleep
The Chickencoop Chinaman
Nightride
22 Years
Rosebloom
Brothers
The Web and the Rock
Whitsuntide
In Case of Accident
SMALL CRAFT WARNINGS
The Soft Core Pornographer
God Says There Is No Peter Ott
Cold Feet
The Divorce of Judy and Jane
Anna K
The Silent Partner
Jamimma

MUSICALS (10)

The Two Gentlemen of Verona
Leaves of Grass
Drat!
F. Jasmine Addams
Richard Farina
Memphis Store-Bought Teeth
Wanted
Two If by Sea
God Bless Coney
Sweet Feet

REVUES (3)

Look Me Up
Uhuruh
Harkl

REVIVALS (12)

The Last Analysis
N.Y. Shakespeare
Timon of Athens
The Tale of Cymbeline
Roundabout
The Master Builder
The Taming of the Shrew
Misalliance
Dylan
The Shadow of a Gunman
Alice in Wonderland
The Beggar's Opera
Rain
One for the Money

SPECIALTIES (6)

The James Joyce Memorial Liquid Theater
Baird Marionettes
The Wizard of Oz
Peter and the Wolf
Kumquats
JFK
Walk Together Children

FOREIGN-LANGUAGE PRODUCTIONS (2)

Szene 71
Kabale Und Liebe
Der Prozess

FOREIGN PLAYS IN ENGLISH (11)

Lincoln Cent. Forum
Play Strindberg
People Are Living There
The Ride Across Lake Constance
Love Me, Love My Children
Chelsea Theater
THE SCREENS
The Water Hen
A Ballet Behind the Bridge
Theater: Fair of Opinion
And They Put Handcuffs on the Flowers
The Real Inspector Hound & After Magritte
Conditions of Agreement

Plays listed in CAPITAL letters have been designated Best Plays of 1971-72.
Plays listed in italics were still running June 1, 1972.

Vic or the Comédie Française. The fourth program on this year's Beaumont schedule, a revival of Shakespeare's *Twelfth Night*, was a wholly competent exercise in station-keeping, in schedule-filling. It's not Lincoln Center's lack of performance that is mainly in question, it is its lack of policy. Arthur Miller said it all when he wrote: "The first order of business now is to get clear in our own minds what (a repertory) theater is, what it can do and what is financially needed to do it. Then if we are convinced of its value, a considered, serious attempt must be made to transform Lincoln Center into such a theater."

Off Broadway

When in mid-year *Variety* characterized the 1971-72 off-Broadway season as "possibly the worst in a decade," the newspaper was speaking of the drab performance of even the more prominent shows at the box office. Once a blissfully carefree, artistically because financially liberated, often experimental Elysian Field of New York play production, the off-Broadway theater is now being made heir to all the cost and other commercial and social problems that have beset its big brother to the north, including ever-expanding demands from the theatrical unions and guilds.

The rising cost of off-Broadway production ($100,000 average for musicals, $40,000 for straight plays according to *Variety* estimate) seems to have inhibited musical production more than play production in 1971-72. This may be partly because many of off Broadway's plays are produced by organizations like Joseph Papp's New York Shakespeare Festival which are partly subsidized and partly supported by subscription lists. There were only ten musicals produced off Broadway this season, as compared to 13 last year and 16 in 1969-70. In contrast, there were 52 new straight play programs in English as compared to 45 last year, reversing direction toward the total of 64 in 1969-70.

Of these 1971-72 straight play programs, 43 were new American scripts, again reversing direction from last year's 39 toward the spate of 53 in 1969-70 and 55 in 1968-69. But *Variety's* "worst season in a decade" comment was applicable to audience response if not to production volume. 1971-72 was a season in which off Broadway's top attractions suffered neglect at the box office. A contributing factor might be that the going top for most off-Broadway offerings was $7.50 with some exceptional draws priced as usual up to $10—much too expensive for the casual but stimulating evening out which has been off-Broadway's thing, particularly when compared to the price of admission to other casual entertainment like the movies; and only a couple of dollars cheaper than the price of the exceptional evening on Broadway, with its sense of special occasion. If there ever has existed an off-Broadway theatergoing "habit," particularly among the adventurous young people in the audience, surely it was threatened by these high admission prices, and exacerbated by the geographical diffusion of off-Broadway theaters in all corners, some of them dark, of a city whose state of social unrest inhibits many entertainment-hungry citizens from leaving their homes for any reason.

Certainly the *Variety* comment isn't applicable to the esthetics of off Broadway in 1971-72. Unprecedentedly, it won half the Best Play citations with *Sticks and Bones, That Championship Season, Where Has Tommy Flowers*

Gone?, *Small Craft Warnings* and *The Screens*. It carried off all three Critics Awards for best play, best foreign play and best musical and, in raids uptown, both major Tony Awards. Its deepest gloom was the failure to command strong support for *Tommy Flowers* or the Al Carmines musical *Wanted;* its brightest hours were its hospitable reception of a new play by Tennessee Williams, and the emergence of what is certainly a major new playwriting talent in David Rabe, who not only won major prizes with *Sticks and Bones* but also set the present long-run record at Joseph Papp's Public Theater with *The Education of Pavlo Hummel's* 363 performances.

The Williams play *Small Craft Warnings* was a fine theater piece, unstructured but communicative. An inner flame of poetry is what warms it up, not its outward energies. It takes place in a third-rate but tolerantly hospitable bar and grill on the California coast, and as in Saroyan's *The Time of Your Life* it is what the characters are, not what they do, that tells the tale. Its patrons are small souls, not great ones, come to grief; character rejects, if you will, from the great Williams works of the past. The stud is a degraded Stanley Kowalski trying to work the men's room; the nymphomaniac is a Blanche Dubois without the slightest pretense of refinement. A talkative frump romanticizing her long-dead younger brother could be Laurette Taylor's beautician, while the bartender is an Eddie Dowling-like observer of the passing scene which he neither approves nor disapproves, but tolerates. A homosexual played by Alan Mixon is the only commanding presence; all the others, including a drunken doctor, have long since admitted defeat and learned to live with it. The director of an obviously dedicated cast, Richard Altman, kept the Williams brilliance shining through the melancholy haze of the subject matter, in a very good play by a great playwright.

Another highlight of the off-Broadway season was Terrence McNally's *Where Has Tommy Flowers Gone?* with Robert Drivas as a 30-year-old child of the 1950s adrift in the stormy sea of New York in the 1970s, living by his larcenous ingenuity, looking for warm patches in a cold, cold world. McNally's first full-length play, presented on Broadway in the 1964-65 season, was a very black comedy about such symptoms of end-of-the-world malaise as homosexuality and sadism, with no sentimentality, entitled *And Things That Go Bump in the Night*. It was maybe the first really cool play, years ahead of its time; a Broadway flop which has since been produced successfully all over the world, reviewed in New York with myopic distaste by such heavy-lidded critics as Otis L. Guernsey Jr. poking at it with a stick in his comments published in *The Best Plays of 1964-65*. Well, the times and maybe even the critics—some of them breathing a little hard—have finally caught up with McNally. His *Tommy Flowers* is a cool portrait of disillusioned youth viewed without a trace of sentimentality or extra affection, without any special pleading for his cause, no quarter asked and none given, in a string of episodes in which the Jacques Levy direction helped unify the style and point of view. What does Tommy Flowers—30, rootless, jobless, unfulfilled—want? He has grown up in a world in which the movies, TV, comic strips and especially Holden Caulfield have exposed him to everything, so of course he wants *everything*. He has no means or will to pay for it, and his response to frustration becomes a game of ripping off Bloomingdale's and Howard Johnson's. His grin is a Robin Hood grin; his merry men are an old man, a young girl and a dog named Arnold who luckily does not expect too much out of life. As his world grows colder and colder, Tommy Flowers still grins, but now it's a *risus sardonicus* and he has a home-made bomb in his knapsack. Tommy (played by Robert Drivas with perfect clarity through all his sudden changes of mood and key) isn't a hero, an anti-hero or a villain. You don't have to make a standard emotional response to him, but you'd better take him into consideration as McNally does with consummate playwriting skill, and stand out of the way when the bomb goes off.

Another of off-Broadway's distinguished Best Plays was *That Championship Season,* a reflective drama cast in the conventional realistic theater mold by its author Jason Miller and directed by A.J. Antoon to squeeze every drop of gall from its gradually contracting circumstances. In it, members of a 1952 state basketball championship team, now in their 30s, gather for an annual reunion at the house of their former coach, now retired. They are here to remind each other and themselves of their triumph, relive it with jokes, back-slapping and beer busting among hale fellows well met. The trouble is that their lives have gone sour. Somehow the qualities that won them the championship are losing them the game of life, even though they still have the outward insignia of lettermen. One of them is mayor—but he will almost certainly lose the next election to someone he considers a nonentity. Another is a captain of industry—but a polluter who in his own view is respected for his money alone. Another is a school official—but he feels the others have held him back from further advancement. The fourth is a self-taught alcoholic, and proud of it. Only the Coach still believes that they won something of value back there in 1952, and if they will all stick together and remain true to the old values of aggressive elitism it will all somehow come out right (even though one of his "boys" vomits into the precious silver trophy).

The ensemble portraying these desperate loser-winners was truly a championship team whose members were Walter McGinn (the drunk), Charles Durning (the mayor), Michael McGuire (the teacher), Paul Sorvino (the tycoon) and last but certainly not least, Richard A. Dysart as the Coach. Since a basketball team consists of five members, it is obvious that someone is absent from this play. They talk about him a lot—his name is Martin and he shuns these reunions because he feels they won the championship by foul and ruthless means urged on them by the Coach, and should have given the trophy back. Martin doesn't show up at this reunion, either, so we will never know whether he messed up his life like the others, or was saved by his recognition of the hollowness of their competitive values. In any case, *That Championship Season* was a most effective work of conventionally-oriented theater, the winner of the Critics Award, scheduled as of this volume's press time to follow in the footsteps of *Sticks and Bones* and move from the Public Theater uptown to the Broadway area early in the fall of 1972.

Still another off-Broadway Best Play was *The Screens,* Jean Genet's script using colonialism in Arab countries as a stark symbol of human behavior at its worst, written in 1959 but never produced in its entirety in Paris until 1966 because of the sensitivity of the Algerian question, presented here this season in its American premiere in an English translation by Minos Volanakis at the Chelsea Theater Center. The Chelsea is a production and performance group whose activities are centered across the river from Manhattan in the Brooklyn Academy of Music, a long way off Broadway. It has nevertheless acquired over the past few seasons a courtesy off-Broadway classification in all lists because of its presentation of consistently challenging theater season after season in premieres of plays like LeRoi Jones's *Slave Ship* and Heathcote Williams's *AC/DC*. Now the Chelsea has topped its previous achievement with Genet's long (over 5 hours), crowded (more than 40 players), episodic but virulent play about society's drive toward self-destruction, exposed in suicidal colonial policies in Africa and in a masochistic native anti-hero named Said who marries the ugliest girl he can find and steers their lives into crime toward an apocalypse of deliberate and total disaster. *The Screens* is written in the absurdist style, unleashing Genet's imagination in sudden, almost unbearable purple bursts of brutality and degradation (but seldom suffering; looked at through Genet's tinted glasses, evil and pain are not suffered, they are merely lived and sometimes even enjoyed). *The Screens* gained no strength from its structure, which is non-existent, but from its tragic mood expressed in poetic symbols of nihilism in its happiest moments, horror in its unhappiest. The designs by Robert Mitchell and Willa Kim, the direction by the translator, Volanakis, and the performances of a large company on its mettle combined with the 5-hour Genet script to produce a massive experience of theater which won the Critics Award for best foreign play over the formidable competition of the new Harold Pinter script.

The Chelsea Theater Center continued its most distinguished season to date with the unusual *Kaddish,* a visualization and dramatization of the Allen Ginsberg poem about his mother, a glowing and poignant memoir which transferred to Circle in the Square for an extended run in Manhattan. A bouncing revival of John Gay's *The Beggar's Opera* was also moved to Manhattan after its regularly-scheduled run in Brooklyn. For its season's finale, Chelsea turned once again to the American premiere of a European work, in English: *The Water Hen,* a play by Stanislaw Ignacy Witkiewicz, a Polish playwright who committed suicide in 1939 and whose plays have only recently been produced and appreciated. Written in 1921, *The Water Hen* is a comedy which seems to anticipate the theater of the absurd by decades in a wild, symbolic fantasy about a timeless seductress (a "water hen") who enchants several generations of a family.

A recurrent theme this season off Broadway as well as on was the black condition. While Broadway mounted its images musically in *Ain't Supposed to Die a Natural Death, Inner City, Lost in the Stars, Don't Play Us Cheap!* and the revue *Don't Bother Me, I Can't Cope,* off Broadway posed its questions dramatically. The best of these plays was the Negro Theater Ensemble's production of Phillip Hayes Dean's *The Sty of the Blind Pig* taking place, not in the kaleidoscopic 1970s, but in the 1950s just before the civil rights movement. It painted a picture of black family life in Chicago in primary colors. Mother (Clarice Taylor, her elbows as sharp as her principles) and her gambler brother (jaunty Adolph Caesar) are proud members of an older generation which would scorn to suffer identity problems. Somehow, however, the daughter senses that she is not what she will become, and her association with a blind street singer looking for his lost love sharpens her perceptions even more. She is like Tony in *West Side Story,* vibrating with an inner knowledge that "something's coming." She and her family seemed to be real rather than symbolical black personalities caught accurately in their small and special segment of time.

Another matter of special relevance raised this season on the Negro Ensemble Company's program was the career and writings of Frederick Douglass, a onetime slave who became a noted abolitionist, recapitulated in *Frederick Douglass . . . Through His Own Words.* The company also presented Lennox Robinson's *A Ballet Behind the Bridge,* as well as a full schedule of less formal work-in-progress stagings.

Still another effective off-Broadway dramatization of the black condition was J.E. Franklin's *Black Girl,* produced by the New Federal Theater at the Theater de Lys, about an upward-mobile family in a small Texas town. Some of its members drag it down with unhappy gravitational forces of cynicism and selfishness, but there is vision here, and an energy which impels others into an escape velocity toward a more fulfilling life. Also prominent on the off-Broadway list was *El Hajj Malik,* an intense reenactment of the life of Malcolm X, with different actors playing Malcolm in succeeding episodes, a technique which proved both a strength and a weakness to the play. It emphasized the universality of the black leader's appeal, but it tended to blur the human focus in a script which already was determined to sacrifice intimacy of personal detail in favor of volume of protest.

Vinie Burrows returned to town in her distinguished one-woman show *Walk Together Children,* with its cavalcade of black imagery in folk songs and other writings from slave days to the present. The abovementioned New Federal Theater moved from Henry Street to the Ellen Stewart Theater (renamed the New Federal) in May, bringing with them *Jamimma,* the Martie Evans-Charles play which had received a workshop viewing earlier in the season. This was a sensitive study of a black girl prepared to bear the illegitimate child of a lover who isn't worthy of her, facing life in today's Harlem.

The black condition was also brought into concern within Joseph Papp's indoor schedule of productions at the Public Theater. Richard Wesley's *The Black Terror* was an explicit play about an executioner for a group of black activists. Though this human paradox functions most efficiently as a killer, still he doubts the final worth of violent methods as a means of changing society. This was a strong play, tautly directed by Nathan George, explosive, brutal, melodramatic. Its author Wesley was produced a second time this season by the Papp organization, as his one-acter *Gettin' It Together* was part of the four-play program *Black Visions.* Other programs which filled the Public Theater's stages during a busy and conspicuous year were *Dance Wi' Me,* a former Cafe LaMama experimental comedy-with-music about an attractive loser, and *Iphigenia,* a free rock-musical adaptation by Doug Dyer, Peter Link and Gretchen Cryer of the Euripides dramas in Aulis and Tauris. Then there was *Older People,* a rueful but sympathetic study of old age in various poses, many humorous, of regret, arrogance and failing powers, especially sexual, by John Ford Noonan, a member of the new generation of playwrights. This was a pungent, if uneven, piece which had its place in Papp's well-rounded season (with a list of seven productions, they can't all be prize winners). Finally among Papp's full-length programs came Murray Mednick's *The Hunter,* a murkily symbolical drama of two soldiers in Civil War uniform who capture a passing hunter, crucify and then kill him, in an enigmatic puzzle of hostilities.

Over at Lincoln Center, no sooner had the furore over the possible demolition of the Forum Theater (about which more hereinunder, in the "Offstage" chapter of this report) died down than the Forum was right back in the news again with a controversial production of the distinguished black playwright Ed Bullins's *The Duplex;* controversial because Bullins objected strenuously and publicly to the Forum's production concept of his play (a rambling and indifferent slice-of-black-life string of episodes, very minor Bullins). Elsewhere on the Forum schedule this season the Lincoln Center company chose to present a series of scripts by foreign authors: Friedrich Duerrenmatt's *Play Strindberg,* a somewhat camped black-comedy rewrite of *The Dance of Death;* Athol Fugard's *People Are Living There,* a conversational review of social conditions in South Africa; and a translation of *The Ride Across Lake Constance,* an unstructured collage of words and characters by the Austrian playwright Peter Handke. For those who conceive the Forum's purpose, as Lincoln Center Rep's experimental arm, to be the stretching of the company's muscles and the audience's mind in avant garde works of *American* theater, the final program was more relevant: *Suggs,* a play about a romantic youth from the sticks who plunges eagerly into city life and is gradually disillusioned by its crushing imperatives, written by a noteworthy new American playwright, David Wiltse. The Forum has known its finest hours in the introduction to its public of such as Wiltse, Ron Cowen (*Summertree*) and John Ford Noonan (*The Year Boston Won the Pennant*), representative as they are of healthy new growth and evolution within the domestic genus of playwrights.

1971-72 proved to be a disappointing year for devotees of the American Place Theater, the organization which has encouraged so many talented new writers and offered such fascinating theater under the groined ceiling of St. Clement's Church on a side street over west of Ninth Avenue. This year American Place moved to a fine new installation at the bottom of a skyscraper near Sixth Avenue, and it was as though their familiar energy had been absorbed in the move, with too little remaining for the stage. Their first program in the new facility was a portmanteau of the one-acters *Fingernails Blue as Flowers* and *Lake of the Woods,* telling comments on our maladjusted society but certainly lesser Ronald Ribman and Steve Tesich than American Place has presented before. Jack Gelber's *Sleep* was a mildly entertaining comedy about the fantasies of a guinea-pig volunteer in a pompously scientific experiment on the nature of sleep. American Place's final production had a somewhat wider grasp: *The Chickencoop Chinaman* by Frank Chin, a cry from the heart of the yellow minority victimized in 20th century America as faceless, identityless exotic cultural stereotypes, but individualized in the play's Chinese-American hero, a talented and suffering loner who once had a childhood daydream that perhaps the Lone Ranger was an Oriental good guy wearing a mask to conceal the shape of his eyes. The play shares a general tendency this season to ingest emotions and conflicts in little bites instead of big ones.

Among the rest of off Broadway's 1971-72 straight plays the subject matter was far-ranging and variegated in style. *Nightride* by Lee Barton (a pseudonym) contrasted old and new homosexual attitudes, in a confrontation between a distinguished but now over-the-hill playwright who has never openly acknowledged his homosexuality either in plays or in private life, and a young rock star who boasts of it proudly. This was darkish comedy which benefited greatly from the performance of Lester Rawlins as the playwright whose flaming intelligence and sense of the ridiculous carries him through the most awkward, even violent, situations. Another script which addressed audiences on the subject of homosexuality was George Birimisa's *Georgie Porgie,* a study of a homosexual's relationship with his wife, mother and lovers which opened in midsummer to mixed notices but ran well into the fall. *The Divorce of Judy and Jane* peered at the subject from yet another angle in a short-lived and short-focused study of a group of Lesbian types.

The convicted killer Charles Manson was viewed as an innocent victim of society in *22 Years,* and Yale M. Udoff's *A Gun Play* also contemplated the violence of our times, in the setting of a once-chic restaurant. Harvey Perr's *Rosebloom* considered the uses and nature of violence in a dark study of intensifying passions among a cripple and his wife and mother awaiting the return from prison of his father. Originally produced at the Mark Taper Forum, it deserved a longer run than its scant 23 performances.

Tolstoy's *Anna Karenina* provided Eugenie Leontovich with a theatrical springboard: take a group of actors rehearsing a stage version of *Anna Karenina* and switch back and forth between old Russia and modern New York, commenting on the tragic love story—and other pertinent matters—even as the love story unfolds. As written, acted and directed by Miss Leontovich *Anna K* was salty theater, episodic like so much of the season's works but certainly one of its off-Broadway highlights.

A foreign play that added a new flavor to the 1971-72 brew was Fernando Arrabal's *And They Put Handcuffs on the Flowers,* which had previously made its American premiere in an off-off-Broadway experimental staging. It is a script of great power about political prisoners degraded to the lowest levels of physical and mental suffering by the very fact of their incarceration as well as the cruelty of their captors. It was written in French by the Spanish playwright Fernando Arrabal (who was once jailed by Franco), translated by Charles Marowitz and presented here under Arrabal's own direction. This included arranging for the audience to grope its way into a darkened theater with irregularly-arranged seats to give an impression of confinement before the play even began. The gruesome episodes (this work is episodic *too*), often charged with shock, culminate in an execution by garroting simulating all the horrible physical details including the emptying of the naked victim's bladder after "death," a noteworthy feat of performance, if not of esthetics. Powerful as it is, this Arrabal protest play is nevertheless like Lewis Carroll's grin without the cat: a violent play without developed characters, physical horror disoriented from humanity, disgust almost without pity, monstrously imaginative but insubstantially human.

No less flavorful at the other end of scale was another foreign program, Tom Stoppard's entertaining exercises in the absurd in his one-acters *The Real Inspector Hound* and *After Magritte.* In the latter, he sends up a Scotland Yard inspector, satirizing all investigative gravity with a farcical construction of preposterous circumstantial evidence, all pointing toward a totally wrong conclusion. The longer piece, *Inspector Hound,* manages to draw its cartoons in depth, and in double projection, taking off a typical murder play at the same time as it exposes the vanities, petty jealousies and propensities of critics covering the play's opening. These works were slight as well as short, but the balancing skill of the author of *Rosencrantz and Guildenstern Are Dead* was fully evident in them. Also from abroad, John Whiting's 1947 play *Conditions of Agreement* was given an American premiere production at the Roundabout. It was a play of sinister implication stopping short of action, with politely British characters abrading each other with memories of an accidental death, menacing each other with threats of unnameable evil but never quite bringing themselves to touch each other.

Other than *Two Gentlemen of Verona, Wanted* was the only moderately successful American book show of the off-Broadway season. David Epstein's libretto viewed the bad guys of American history in a new light, as honored rebels against the oppressive law-and-order forces of their day. This amiable cur-bites-Rin Tin Tin reversal of identities took an added lyric bounce from the Al Carmines score. Here again was a show which merited a wider audience than it could gather in its 79 performances, but this was that kind of a season. The American past turned up more than once more as the subject for off-Broadway musical treatment; even Walt Whitman got into the act in a musical adaptation entitled *Leaves of Grass.* A Canadian import, *Love Me, Love My Children,* exploring the big city youth counter-culture, was an attractive visitor which freshened the off-Broadway musical scene for most of the season.

A spirit of youthful energy invigorated *Hark!* with an ensemble of attractive performers singing songs about almost everything relevant to today's living. It came along in late spring and also freshened the scene with its music by Dan Goggin and Marvin Solley and lyrics by Robert Lorick. A topical cabaret revue, *Look Me Up,* settled in at Plaza 9 for a long run, while a visiting revue from San Francisco, *Uhuruh,* stayed only a week. A foreign-language visitor was the Szene 71 group from Schweinfurt with a Schiller play and a new dramatization of Kafka's *The Trial,* presented in German. Standout specialty programs were the perennially favorite Bil Baird Marionettes and an experience entitled *The James Joyce Memorial Liquid Theater,* an evening of audience participation in fun, games and physical sensations up to and including a couple of respectful kisses. Jeremiah Collins appeared in *JFK,* adapted from the records of the late President's administration. Finally, there was *Kumquats,* a trifle whose subtitle says it all: "The World's First Erotic Puppet Show."

In sum, it was a difficult year off Broadway—but the difficulty was less often artistic than financial; the art form itself was less often guilty than victimized. That preoccupation with nakedness and perversion so conspicuous in recent seasons seems to have pretty much disappeared (or maybe we're noticing it less). Light shone in the gloom, reflecting from the coppery newness of David Rabe and from the deeply glowing patina of Tennessee Williams.

Offstage

Offstage as on, theater activity tended to come in shades of gray, with very few flashes of lightning. There wasn't even a really rancorous controversy over a critic (the best ones were *between* critics), not even involving David Merrick. Merrick let everybody know he was still a law unto himself by switching his shows to an 8 p.m. curtain when everybody else on Broadway was opening at 7:30, but this was little more than a muscle-stretching exercise. There was one brief flurry over the use of quotations from critics' reviews in promotional material. The city's watchdogs made a move to regulate the use of "false and misleading" quotations used out of their context. The city soon mitigated its attitude, however, when various organizations including the Authors League pointed out that quote-ad surveillance would constitute a violation of freedom of the press and "the rights of authors, publishers and producers under the First and Fourteenth Amendments," placing such ads at the mercy of "the varying subjective judgments of many officials."

A citizens' committee of 19 persons under the chairmanship of Eugene R. Black Jr., sponsored by the New York State Council on the Arts and the New York City Cultural Council, financed with the help of New York State and the Rockefeller Brothers Fund, with a research staff headed by the same William J. Baumol who put out a report on the performing arts five years ago, made a close study of the theater and came to the surprisingly rose-colored conclusion that "The extent of decline of activity on Broadway has sometimes been exaggerated in the press . . . . . Broadway has been the base and bulwark of the American stage, in spite of the profit incentive. Most of what is good and enduring in our theatrical heritage has emerged from the hard trial-and-error of Broadway-type presentations and our best new works will probably continue to come from this source."

The word "subsidy" was on the tip of every theater tongue, with economic pressures mounting, with the object lesson of Harold Pinter's *Old Times*— originally produced in the subsidized shelter of the Royal Shakespeare Company—staring Broadway in the face, and with Joseph Papp demonstrating with play after play in the Public Theater how much subsidy can accomplish when it links arms with imagination. For the live performing arts, subsidy is no longer a matter of whether but of when and how much, to whom and under what circumstances. In 1971-72 as in previous seasons, the Theater Development Fund was doing its helpful thing, supporting the commercial-theater shows its committee deemed worthwhile by purchasing blocks of tickets to strengthen a show's economic position after it has been produced but before it has caught on, and distributing those tickets to audiences who might otherwise not be motivated or able to attend a live theater performance.

Congress voted $29,750,000 to the National Endowment for the Arts for 1971-72. Major grants to theater organizations across the country amounted to somewhere near 10 per cent of this total Federal money for the arts. Among New York theater organizations, Joseph Papp's received $125,000, the Phoenix Theater $50,000, American Place $25,000 (for administrative staff development), Chelsea Theater Center $50,000, LaMama Experimental Theater Club $75,000, Negro Ensemble Company, $75,000, Repertory Theater of Lincoln Center $25,000 (for Forum productions).

New York State appropriated $14,000,000 this season to its Council on the Arts, and some of this was expected to filter through to the legitimate stage. New York City, which spends $23,000,000 a year on museums, zoos, gardens, etc., limits its performing-arts aid to a paltry $1,200,000 of which Joseph Papp gets a well-deserved $350,000 share.

Only one 1971-72 production—*Solitaire/Double Solitaire*—availed itself of the Limited Gross arrangement, in which the Broadway producer agrees to limit his potential weekly gross to $25,000 by cutting ticket prices and/or roping off part of the theater, in exchange for certain salary and royalty concessions by the theatrical unions and guilds. This experiment wasn't a success. The theatergoing public actually tended to become suspicious of the lowered prices, for one thing; and for another, those connected with the show reported a prevailing feeling of "lacklustre" because of their second-class financial status.

A former distinguished editor of the *Best Plays* volumes, John Chapman, celebrated his 50th anniversary with the New York *Daily News* in the spring of 1971. Then about a month later, on July 1, 1971, he announced his retirement from the post of drama critic which he had held for so long, and he was succeeded by Douglas Watt. Illness, not disaffection, was the cause of his retirement, and his death in mid-winter deepened the gloom of this gray season. John Chapman loved all kinds of theater (he always thought it strange that his colleagues would never join him in classifying grand opera as "theater" in its truest sense) and he was beloved by its practitioners. He leaves bright memories of warm friendships and a distinguished career as the drama critic who succeeded Burns Mantle on the *News* and in the editorship of five of the *Best Plays* volumes, 1947-48 through 1951-52.

Among the producing organizations, off-off-Broadway groups were joining together for unified action, and so were eight of the city's black-theater troupes. The Black Theater Alliance, which will try to attract more aid from Federal and other sources, is made up of The Bed-Stuy Theater Inc., the Afro-American Studio for Acting and Speech, the Afro-American Total Theater, the New Heritage Repertory Theater, the Brownsville Laboratory Theater, the Afro-American Singing Theater, the New World Workshop and Theater Black. Delano Stewart of Bed-Stuy was named Black Theater Alliance's first president. American Place Theater moved from St. Clement's Church to gleaming new quarters in a new theater and allied facilities built into the bottom of an office skyscraper on 46th Street east of Broadway. The 300-seat house is the first new Broadway-area theater built expressly for the legitimate stage in 38 years.

A good deal of energy was expended behind the scenes this season on ways to make theatergoers happier and theatergoing more convenient and satisfying. An experiment in the use of the American Express credit card to buy Broadway theater tickets was put into effect in March. Once again the Tony Award ceremonies focused the TV spotlight on Broadway theater in a coast-to-coast network program, and again this was the best of the annual award shows on TV, thanks to the expertise of Alexander H. Cohen who produced it. Locally, first steps were taken toward establishing a Theater Hall of Fame in the Broadway area, in the Grand Gallery of the new Uris Theater built into an office tower at Broadway and 50th Street.

Stepping back from the 1971-72 New York theater season to take a long view before it disappears over the horizon, you can see both the stigmata of invalidism and the insignia of fabulousness. The farther away we get, the more the gray predominance blends into the grayness of everything else, while the slashes of bright color are visible for a long time in the rays of memory. The theater's best work is well worth saving and remembering, and there seems to be no internal stunting of its growth as an art form. Why then is its very existence called to judgment in each passing season? Why is it so extremely sensitive to every disturbance of the economic and social environment? Why are we so relieved every June when the first report of that new musical going into production or this famous playwright's new work to be produced in the coming fall promise us that once more, at least, there will be a new theater season in New York?

Looking at 1971-72 from afar, one might conclude that the theater is in an all-out struggle to maintain its position as a popular art instead of permitting itself to fade into a closet art. No one (or at least no one I know) talks of a crisis in chamber music, nor is its vigorous existence as a closet art form much affected by the increase of crime in the streets. If in the late 20th century the theater became a closet art as it has in some periods of its history, you would be hearing only about its fabulousness and nothing about invalidism. It would become a cultural imperative to attend a play or two a year at a university, or museum, or theater club, or as a subscriber to a touring attraction. A few students would still study playwriting, and there might still be a group of ardent diehards—comparable, say, to the fans of Irish football—who would amuse themselves by putting on plays in some dark corner of New York City, managed, no doubt, by Joseph Papp.

In this decade, though, the theater is anchored much too firmly to the popular scene—if only by means of its musical stage—to be led off into the closet. The hardy hit musicals account for a large portion of those $100 million dollar grosses, and they keep reminding the public in the West Forties how satisfying and thrilling a good live entertainment can be. The situation, then, seems to clarify in the long view: a fadeout is not really available to the theater as we know it, not while it continues to show vigorous signs of life and growth. The theater must remain a popular art, and those precious portions of it which have economic difficulty must be sustained by popular subsidy. The American culture must ask itself not what the theater costs or what it might bring in, but what it is *worth*. The answer to this comes in huge superlatives; from every point of view, the theater is hugely worth America's support. We must respond accordingly, and soon, if we are to have dramatic art in the 1970s and 1980s as well as anodyne, a culture as well as media, a life as well as an economy, human beings as well as a society.

Jack Albertson, Lewis J. Stadlen and Sam Levene in *The Sunshine Boys* by Neil Simon.

PHOTO BY MARTHA SWOPE

1972-73

ANTICIPATION . . . disappointment . . . surprise . . . anticipation . . . disappointment . . . surprise . . . that's the roller-coaster rhythm of every New York theater season. Yearly, great expectations are aroused by the announced shows. For example, in September 1972 we knew we were going to get new scripts by Tennessee Williams, Arthur Miller, Neil Simon, Stephen Sondheim, Jean Kerr, Paul Zindel and Gerome Ragni. In accordance with the laws of human nature, we anticipated not merely new delights from these richly gifted dramatists, but masterpieces on the order of *A Streetcar Named Desire, Death of a Salesman, The Odd Couple, A Funny Thing Happened on the Way to the Forum, Mary, Mary, The Effects of Gamma Rays on Man-in-the-Moon Marigolds* and *Hair*—and all in the same season, naturally.

Disappointment must always follow as inevitably as September becomes October and November and December. Early in the year even the successes seem less than fulfilling, not yet having taken on that larger-than-life magnification which comes partly from the repetition of the title day after day in capital letters in the newspapers' alphabetized listings. Disappointment is January's other name. The lamentations of the drama critics fall upon the pages like snow, celebrities badmouth the theater on all the talk shows, and parodists compose a new verse for Jerry Herman's "Oh, What a Lovely Theatrical Season We've Had."

And then, surprise . . . a couple of scripts jostle the imagination in a new way, and/or a spring musical suddenly gives Broadway the polish and excitement it needs to make all its other shows look attractive. Surprise . . . all at once, the shows that have managed to live through the winter suddenly seem better than anyone has a right to expect from the creative artists of one performing-arts form in a single season.

Last year it was *That Championship Season, Sticks and Bones* and the vibrating musicals based on the black experience that finally produced the surprise of a good showing. In 1972-73 it was Joseph A. Walker's off-Broadway-to-Broadway-commuting *The River Niger* and Lanford Wilson's off-off-Broadway-to-off-Broadway-commuting *The Hot l Baltimore*, together with the Stephen Sondheim-Hugh Wheeler musical *A Little Night Music*, that finally brought the shining rabbit out of the battered hat. And, true to form, Neil Simon's *The Sunshine Boys*, Arthur Miller's *The Creation of the World and Other Business* and Jean Kerr's *Finishing Touches* grow increasingly worthy of a major place in the canons of their illustrious authors as we reflect upon them, "blossoming even as we gaze."

In 1972-73 as in other recent seasons we enjoyed the added distinction of fine British scripts, most notably David Storey's *The Changing Room*, Simon Gray's *Butley* and, off Broadway, Paul Ableman's *Green Julia*. Add in a successful playwriting debut—Bob Randall's with *6 Rms Riv Vu*—and you certainly have an admirable 1972-73 Best Plays list.

The number of shows produced on Broadway in 1972-73 dropped only very slightly to 54 from an overall total of 56 (including "limited" and "middle" productions) last year and 56 in 1970-71—thus maintaining some sort

The 1972-73 Season on Broadway

PLAYS (16)

That Championship Season (transfer)
6 RMS RIV VU
The Lincoln Mask
The Secret Affairs of Mildred Wild
THE CREATION OF THE WORLD AND OTHER BUSINESS
The Last of Mrs. Lincoln
THE SUNSHINE BOYS
Look Away
The Enemy Is Dead
Let Me Hear You Smile
FINISHING TOUCHES
Status Quo Vadis
Out Cry
42 Seconds From Broadway
THE RIVER NIGER (transfer)
No Hard Feelings

MUSICALS (13)

Dude
Hurry, Harry
Pippin
Lysistrata
Dear Oscar
Ambassador
Via Galactica
Tricks
Shelter
A LITTLE NIGHT MUSIC
Seesaw
Cyrano
Smith

REVUES (2)

Jacques Brel Is Alive and Well and Living in Paris (transfer)
Nash at Nine

HOLDOVER SHOWS WHICH BECAME HITS DURING 1972-73

Don't Bother Me, I Can't Cope
Grease
Jesus Christ Superstar
The Prisoner of Second Avenue

FOREIGN PLAYS IN ENGLISH (4)

BUTLEY
The Jockey Club Stakes
No Sex Please, We're British
THE CHANGING ROOM

FOREIGN-LANGUAGE PRODUCTIONS (2)

From Israel With Love
Pacific Paradise

SPECIALTIES (3)

Here Are Ladies
Bunraku
Marcel Marceau

REVIVALS (16)

Man of La Mancha
Lincoln Center Rep
Enemies
The Plough and the Stars
The Merchant of Venice
A Streetcar Named Desire
Much Ado About Nothing (transfer)
Circle in the Square
Mourning Becomes Electra
Medea
New Phoenix
The Great God Brown
Don Juan
Purlie
Don Juan in Hell
Irene
Emperor Henry IV
The Women
The Play's the Thing (transfer)

Plays listed in CAPITAL LETTERS have been designated Best Plays of 1972-73.
Plays listed in **bold face type** were classified as hits in *Variety's* annual list of hits and flops published June 6, 1973 or judged likely to become hits.
Plays listed in *italics* were still running June 1, 1973.

of plateau after a dropoff from 68 in 1969-70, 76 in 1968-69 and 84 in 1967-68 (at the end of the season David Merrick voiced his opinion that Broadway production will probably maintain its present level in the foreseeable future). Of this 1972-73 Broadway total, 16 were new American plays and 13 were new musicals as compared with totals of 19-13, 14-11, 21-14, 24-12 and 25-10 in previous seasons (so that the number of musicals is slightly up, even with production costs astronomically increased). There was a sharp decline in the off-Broadway production of new American playscripts from 43 last year to 28 in 1972-73, probably a result of the changing character of the off-Broadway environment from informal and experimental to a more formal and ever more expensive "little Broadway."

Ticket prices stayed about the same as they have in recent seasons since reaching but not exceeding that $15 Broadway musical top, $9 for a Broadway play and around $7.50 for a hot off-Broadway ticket if there was such a thing this year. Production costs were continuing to rise like the price of everything else, and it was whispered that one of the Broadway musicals actually cost as much as $1 million. In this context, *Variety*'s annual summary of the Broadway season contained both good and bad news. First, the good news: for the ninth straight year the combined 52-week New York and road-company gross for all legitimate stage attractions was more than $100 million ($100,431,571 according to *Variety*'s figures), with the road's share of this total a whopping, record-breaking $55,532,992, going over the $50 million mark for the first time. Now, the bad news: the total 52-week Broadway gross had shrunk to $44,898,579, the lowest in 10 years, down from $52.3 million last year, $54.9 million in 1970-71 and way under 1967-68's record $59 million.

In the all-important matter of playing weeks, which measure the activity of the Broadway stage (if 10 shows play 10 weeks, that's 100 playing weeks), the total dropped to 878, the lowest since *Variety* began keeping these figures in the late 1930s, down from last year's 1,092 and way below the plateau of 1,200 in the late 1960s. Paradoxically—*Variety* noted—there were more box office successes this year than last. Furthermore, by mid-May 1973 there seemed to be arising in the theater a feeling of optimism, an instinct that some nadir had been passed, some corner turned, as *Irene* and *A Streetcar Named Desire* set new weekly gross records and brave new productions were being announced for 1974.

There is another footnote that should be added to the 1972-73 summary. Those massive $50-million-plus Broadway grosses and 1,000-plus playing week totals of recent years were accomplished with the very considerable help of a group of smash-hit holdovers playing year after year in some of the longest runs in history, comfortably padding the annual statistics. These included *Hello, Dolly!*, *Fiddler on the Roof*, *Man of La Mancha*, *Hair*, *Promises, Promises*, *1776* and *Oh, Calcutta*—all of which added greatly to the activity and grosses of other seasons but none of which played for any appreciable segment of 1972-73. We can at least hope that beneath the low tide of numbers Broadway is taking a leaf out of Neil Simon's book. When a bunch of his hits closes, Simon gets busy on a stack of new ones, and there's not much wrong with Broadway that it couldn't cure in a big hurry by doing likewise.

With the shadow of these generally downbeat statistics, there were shining highlights as well as black holes. This was the year that *Fiddler on the Roof* topped *Life With Father*'s record June 17 with its 3,225th performance and went on to establish an all-time Broadway long-run record of 3,242 performances before finally closing on July 2 (and meanwhile, off Broadway, *The Fantasticks* played through another year of the longest continuous run of record in the American theater, reaching its 5,443d performance at season's end). According to *Variety* estimates, *Fiddler* has returned $8,347,500 *net* profit on its original $375,000 investment and has sold more than 2,000,000 cast albums, an impressive showing albeit only a fraction of *Hair*'s 4,000,000 or *My Fair Lady*'s 8,000,000.

But then there was *Dude,* which spent more than $100,000 to remodel the Broadway Theater to suit its unique form and personality, and then folded to the tune of $900,000; and *Via Galactica,* nicknamed "daughter of *Dude"* because it had the same composer, Galt MacDermot, and suffered a similar fate, a $900,000 loss after a minuscule run. These two musicals plus *Ambassador, Lysistrata, Tricks* and *Shelter* lost their backers a total of over $3 million. Under the perverse economic conditions of the contemporary stage it would be a mistake to assume that all these shows fell as far short artistically as they did financially; in this game, quality and success don't always play on the same team. One of our landmark musicals, *Follies,* lost $674,443 of its $792,596 cost in its Broadway run and increased its deficit to $700,000 before ending an unsuccessful road tour prematurely in Los Angeles.

Last season's best play, David Rabe's *Sticks and Bones,* not only failed to find an audience in its transfer to Broadway but was cancelled in a scheduled TV version on CBS March 9, presumably because it might have offended viewers oversensitized to its Vietnam War theme at a time when the prisoners were coming home (and also probably because it offended some of the network affiliate programmers, who previewed it on closed-circuit TV and were put off by its highly imaginative, split-level dramatic form). The tribulations of *Sticks and Bones* are doubly ironic because of the great success of its Public Theater stablemate, Jason Miller's *That Championship Season,* which was a big box-office hit in *its* move to Broadway and added to its 1972 Drama Critics Award the 1973 Tony and Pulitzer Prize.

Arthur Miller's fine, if not widely popular, *The Creation of the World and Other Business* was a $250,000 straight-play loser on Broadway. So was *Status Quo Vadis,* Donald Driver's satire on the stratification of American society, with each character wearing the number of his station in the tale of a brash Number 5 who dares to love a haughty Number 1. A big success in its original Chicago production, *Status Quo Vadis* was unenthusiastically received on Broadway and closed after only one performance $235,000 in the red. Other 1973 Broadway productions which gave up after only one viewing were Don Petersen's *The Enemy Is Dead, Let Me Hear You Smile* by Leonora Thuna and Harry Cauley and starring Sandy Dennis, Jerome Kilty's *Look Away* (one of the season's three plays about Mary Todd Lincoln), Louis Del Grande's *42 Seconds From Broadway* and the Sam Bobrick-Ron Clark comedy *No Hard Feelings* starring Eddie Albert and Nanette Fabray. The year's hapless one-night stands off Broadway were three musicals (*Crazy Now, A Quarter for the Ladies Room* and *Buy Bonds, Buster*), three plays (*Blue Boys* by Allan Knee, *Echoes* by N. Richard Nash and *A Phantasmagoria Historia of D. Johann Faust,* etc. by Vasek Simek) and the revival of *We Bombed in New Haven*—thus making a total of 13 unlucky shows in the 1973 New York professional theater which lasted only a single performance. Another off-

Broadway musical called *Smile, Smile, Smile*, about the inept ruler of a desert island paradise, lasted a whole 7 performances but drew the shortest review of the year from Clive Barnes of the New York *Times*, only three sentences long. The first identified the who, what, when, where of the production. The last two were: "It was called *Smile, Smile, Smile*. I didn't, I didn't, I didn't."

The directors came on strong in 1973, which in musicals was a vintage year for the directing choreographer (Bob Fosse of *Pippin*, Michael Kidd of *Cyrano*, Gower Champion of *Irene*, Michael Bennett of *Seesaw*, Donald Saddler of *Berlin to Broadway With Kurt Weill*). Among other notable stints of staging were A.J. Antoon's of *Much Ado About Nothing*, Alan Arkin's of *The Sunshine Boys*, Michael Rudman's of *The Changing Room*, Harold Prince's of-*A Little Night Music*, Joseph Anthony's of *Finishing Touches*, Roderick Cook's of *Oh, Coward!*, Richard Foreman's of *Doctor Selavy's Magic Theater*, Douglas Turner Ward's of *The River Niger*. The producer of the year was Joseph Papp—who else?—with his two transfers *That Championship Season* and *Much Ado About Nothing* and his takeover of Lincoln Center. As far as his regular indoor season at the Public Theater was concerned, however, it wasn't quite as interesting overall as that of American Place.

After a writing-directing triumph in the movies, Frank D. Gilroy returned to the theater with *Present Tense*, a short-lived off-Broadway program of four experimental playlets, contemporary skirmishes in the never-ending war between men and women. Other former Pulitzer Prize winners who had difficulty finding their feet in the theater this season were Tennessee Williams, Paul Zindel and Abe Burrows. Their problems were not the season's most conspicuous, however. That distinction is the sole property of the *Hair* team of authors, Gerome Ragni, James Rado and Galt MacDermot, who separately and in pairs came up with three new musicals which managed only 51 performances combined. Besides *Dude* and *Via Galactica*, there was *Rainbow* off Broadway with James Rado-authored book (in collaboration with his brother Ted), music and lyrics. *Rainbow* was a musical fantasy of a Vietnam casualty's life after death, almost a sequel to *Hair*. A king-sized collection of rock compositions and pastiches, it poured out 42 numbers in youthful indignation at a universe that isn't as loving as it should be. It was as ardent as *Hair*, and very imaginative, but it lacked *Hair's* coherence both in style and substance.

Much the same could be said about *Dude*. With book and lyrics by Gerome Ragni and music by Galt MacDermot, it didn't so much probe the meaning of existence as strike at it with a sledgehammer in the hope that it might reveal itself in shattering. It, too, was an ardent show, vibrating with rock rhythms, spilling all over a specially-rebuilt theater so that its symbolic characters could descend on wires from symbolic heaven or roam all over the symbolic earth in search of truth, climbing a "mountain" in the balcony aisles or wandering the deep "forest" of the orchestra pit area (the stage itself was placed about where fifth row center should have been). For all its effort and aggressive imagination, *Dude* like *Rainbow* was more of an experience for the performers than for the audience.

Finally from a *Hair* contributor there was *Via Galactica*, opening the new, cavernous and uncomfortable (for the show) Uris Theater with a musical fantasy of the world 1,000 years from now. It was an almost operatic musical, all sung to the music of Galt MacDermot (who, by the way, was additionally represented this year by the musical interludes in Rochelle Owens's *The Karl*

Marx Play), with words by Christopher Gore and Judith Ross. As one of only four, or 40, or perhaps 400 theatergoers who enjoyed this show, I find myself slowly forgetting its faults and remembering its glowing MacDermot score (including a notable rock ballad, "Children of the Sun") and its entertaining comic-book concept (the comic-book form doesn't seem to do well on the New York stage—c.f. *Superman, Status Quo Vadis, Warp I*, etc.—but there are those of us who enjoy its bright primary dramatic colors). Its "book" was both fantastic and relevant: if you felt threatened in 1972 you would hate 2972 when all human beings have become happy but will-less robots controlled by a headpiece attached at birth, except for a handful of rebellious individualists who plan to escape to another solar system where they can be free. The brains of the outfit is a disembodied head riding around on a mobile heart-lung machine (played by Keene Curtis with great relish) and the brawn is a space adventurer, played by Raul Julia. Peter Hall staged the action with space ships hovering over the audience and with a trampoline-covered stage on which the actors' bounces suggested a low-gravity environment, thus making the most of the show's adventure-comic ambiance. The climax was an ironic reversal of the United States Cavalry charge we all grew up on, with a spidery, villainous space cruiser with aluminum belly marked "U.S.A." threatening to doom the rebels at the last second. *Via Galactica* lasted only 7 woe-begone performances, and, come to think of it, I do remember one of its flaws: the orchestra was playing so loudly at the performance I attended that it was hard to hear what was being sung. People in the balcony began shouting to the orchestra to tone down so they could hear the words. They were obviously caught up in the show or they wouldn't have cared what the characters were saying—or, rather, singing. Maybe some of them would agree that *Via Galactica* was one of the most satisfyingly *theatrical* concepts of the season, and that MacDermot's excellent score balanced out some of this year's shortcomings of the *Hair* collaborators.

We anticipated . . . in some cases, particularly at the beginning of the season, we were disappointed . . . but finally the surprises came along and the season ended on a rising pitch of accomplishment and optimism. Viewed in perspective, the 1973 New York professional theater season was a sculptural, stationary attraction of line and form, rather than of kinetic energy. It lacked thrust, drive, purpose, boldness. Last year the effort to experiment with new kinds of theater side-by-side with well-made structures of the old form was vividly exemplified in 1972's two outstanding American plays—the challenging, difficult, triple-tiered *Sticks and Bones* and the conventional *That Championship Season,* both dramas. They symbolized the growing split in the form and among audiences of the modern theater art; a split which was weakening the theater commercially, perhaps, but which was producing a dynamic tension among creative artists which frequently proved inspiring.

This season it was as though someone had pulled out the plug connecting this dynamo of invention to its energy source. 1972-73 never ventured beyond *Pippin* or *Shelter*—absurdist Broadway rock musicals—in experimental concept. Except for an occasional *succes d'estime* and the institutional productions, there was hardly anything doing off Broadway, let alone any thrust of experimentation, while on Broadway—symbolically—the creators of the bittersweet musical milestone *Follies* were toying, skillfully but conservatively, with operetta. It was that kind of a year; a year of musicals and comedies; entertaining and restful, an intermission in the artistic abrasion of the recent past.

Broadway

The 1973 best of bests, in the opinion of the *Curtain Times* author, was the play imported from London by the Long Wharf Theater in New Haven, David Storey's *The Changing Room*. In this new script, as in *Home*, Storey's purpose is to fashion an exact copy of a time, place and circumstance, without much decorative overlay of "plot" or underlay of "theme." In *Home* Storey zeroed, or maybe Xeroxed, in on two less-than-distinguished old men struggling feebly in a web of senility; in *The Changing Room* the object of the playwright's scrutiny is a less-than-distinguished North Country professional rugby team in its locker room before, during and after a game. This is not the rugby of the green playing fields of Eton, but a merciless, brutish form of the game having a special appeal to fans who are only a generation or two removed from the merciless, brutish life of a Victorian-era coal miner. Storey, who himself was once a rugby player of professional ability, has keenly observed the team and its hangers-on, as one by one the men drift into the locker room to peel off their street clothes together with whatever gentling values their outside world may possess. They put on clean uniforms and a special set of values for the duration of the game: the obligatory extra effort, the need to work together as a team, the endurance of pain in bone-crushing action to take place on a frozen field, the urge to demonstrate some kind of commitment to one another in locker room byplay and jokes. There is no conflict except the game in *The Changing Room,* no resolution except the passage of time. The players get themselves "up" for the opening whistle; they collapse between the halves; for a few moments they are rambunctiously elated by victory, then slowly they deflate as they put on their street clothes and street manners and depart individually.

In its effort to produce an exact copy without any retouching, *The Changing Room* was performed with physical reality, without any encumbrance of modesty. That is to say, the players changed into and out of their uniforms as casually as they would in a real locker room as men among men. They let it all hang out, and it is to the great credit of Michael Rudman's staging that the cast performed this aspect of the play without either hesitation or exploitation. This rare example of total mass male nudity on a Broadway stage was so far from being shocking, so fluent a part of the stage action, that most members of the audience didn't become conscious of it until after it was well under way. The Long Wharf production of Storey's British play was cast with American actors (whose North Country accents sounded fine to these inexperienced ears), and to single out any one of this coordinated group of artists would seem to slight the others (though John Lithgow won a Tony and a Drama Desk Award for his portrayal of a battered, sobersided veteran). They were an admirable ensemble in an admirable play which received seven of the 20 first-choice votes in the New York Drama Critics Circle balloting and won their consensus and their 1973 award for the best play of the season regardless of category. It was the eighth foreign script to win the Critics' best-of-bests in the decade, with only *The Subject Was Roses* and *The Great White Hope* taking top honors for American playwriting in their respective seasons in the ten years beginning with John Osborne's *Luther* in 1963-64.

The best American play of the year, other opinions to the contrary notwithstanding, was Neil Simon's *The Sunshine Boys,* a study of human beings on the threshold of senility so amazingly sensistive, with a touch so light and yet so accurate, you hardly realized how good a play it was until you'd had time to reflect on it. Where *The Changing Room* was a kind of stunt, *The Sunshine Boys* was a finely disciplined work (and in every important respect the other play's peer) about two crotchety old show-biz pros, once-famous comedians, trying to solve the problem of getting along with each other long enough to do one of their old skits on a TV special. It was spare but wholly sufficient, with just enough humor, just enough pathos, just enough caricature but not an ounce more than enough for a comment on the aging process that was both deeply felt and highly entertaining. I wouldn't presume to try to identify Alan Arkin's direction apart from the other contributions; the play seemed to be driven forward by its own inner logic, which in itself is evidence of Arkin's skill. If there were performances this year that seemed better than Jack Albertson's and Sam Levene's as the septuagenarian vaudevillians and Lewis J. Stadlen's as the nephew who hero-worships them, it must have been because there were juicier roles. Simon has labeled *The Sunshine Boys* a "comedy." Whatever you call it, it is a superbly crafted piece of theater. Simon may have written funnier plays, but never one that demonstrated such total mastery of his art.

The 1973 season was a year of comedies, to be sure, but not all of them called themselves by this name. On Broadway, for example, only five scripts were self-styled comedies (and, perversely, a Broadway-bound musical which called itself *Comedy* folded out of town). A Best Play selection whose author did *not* identify his work as a comedy was *6 Rms Riv Vu* (the title being an abbreviation in the style of an apartment-to-let classified ad) by Bob Randall, who made his professional playwriting debut with this tale of a youngish middle-class New York couple, very much married to two other people, meeting by chance while inspecting an empty apartment and inevitably gravitating into a brief encounter. This was a very small concept very well realized in Randall's characterization of two people who can have this unique fling but never a real affair. The sexual revolution is not for them, they fall between the stools of the generations; they were brought up on Wonder Woman comics and the last scraps of 19th-century morality, and if they go on from this empty apartment to a real hotel-room rendezvous the first thing she would do, instinctively, would be to wash his socks. The playwright's inventiveness, together with that of the director, Edwin Sherin, and Jerry Orbach and Jane Alexander as the couple, sustained a play physically limited most of the time to two characters in a cavernously empty set, but expansively comic in its observation of two people who can make love but never be lovers, who can change their luck but never their stripes.

Arthur Miller's *The Creation of the World and Other Business* was far from a bundle of laughs, but certainly its approach was comedic rather than dramatic, even though it was not specifically labeled a comedy in its Broadway billing. The author of *After the Fall* here peruses the relationship between man (and woman), God and the Devil at the time of the Fall. Miller's Garden of Eden is a place where paradox commands more attention than principle. The puzzle of the coexistence of good and evil is the concern of this work, setting forth its theme in a subtitle for the play's first act: "Since God made everything and God is good—why did He make Lucifer?" Miller looks and often writes like an Old Testament prophet, but in *The Creation* he is in a Shavian humor, not pointing morals or sounding alarms but fashioning ironies which are very closely reasoned behind their highly-polished facets, like the electric moment at which God places His accusatory and at the same time protecting mark on the murderer Cain. As he so often does in these tales, Lucifer (George Grizzard) stole most of the scenes from God. The production was uneven, with the characters sometimes failing to come to grips with one another, following changes of directors in the midstream of preparation. But Miller's *The Creation* is a muscular comedy which will undoubtedly live on in future productions around the globe and even in New York.

Another Best Play and Robert Whitehead production was Jean Kerr's *Finishing Touches,* a comedy in fact and name. In this one, Mrs. Kerr's laugh-laden subject is the onslaught of middle age. Her idiom continues to be the American suburban (but intellectually oriented) family, viewed through that unremitting sense of humor which makes it so much fun to go to any of Mrs. Kerr's plays. In this one, father (Robert Lansing) is a professor perplexingly infatuated with a pretty girl in his class, and very much in need of a hoped-for promotion as an incentive for going on with his life. Mother is still handsome, still full of the take-charge instinct, still witty, still Barbara Bel Geddes. Three sons scaled from 22 to 11 make all those amusing comments which Mrs. Kerr hears around her house all the time but which, oddly, no one else's children ever seem to come up with. It's all in fun, of course; there is, finally, no place for Lucifer at Mrs. Kerr's table, not even for the harmless consummation of a *6 Rms Riv Vu.* In Mrs. Kerr's family stories the world is a constantly troubled place where, thanks to a modicum of common sense and the persistent influence of the eternal verities, things nevertheless work out. There is no danger that the New York stage will be tainted in some way by her optimism, because no one else writing for the theater today can draw her kind of conclusion so adroitly, so warmly, so convincingly, let alone so entertainingly.

Other scripts billed as comedies on Broadway in 1973 included Paul Zindel's *The Secret Affairs of Mildred Wild,* about an overblown housewife living drably above a candy store in a clutter of movie magazines, escaping from her various crises by fantasizing herself into scenes from 1930s movies, imagining that she is Shirley Temple or, in a particularly aggravating moment of family strife, Fay Wray in the clutches of King Kong. The fantasy scenes created by Zindel and directed by Jeff Bleckner were more valid comically than the straight husband-and-wife involvement from which they sprang, even with Maureen Stapleton's firm grasp on the title role.

A more satisfying comic fancy was the imported *The Jockey Club Stakes* by William Douglas Home, a London comedy of good and bad manners of that vanishing mannered breed, the British aristocrat. In it, three lordly cronies who run the Jockey Club are investigating a charge of race-fixing, at first in stern and righteous judgment; and then, when it develops that one of their own class is the culprit, conniving at a smooth, plausible cover-up. The three rascally old patricians were played by Wilfrid Hyde-White, Robert Coote and Geoffrey Sumner as though W.S. Gilbert were prompting from the wings. He would have been as gratified by their comic skill as was the black-tie theater audience which apparently still hides away somewhere and was brought out by this play. The amusing antics onstage were almost outdone by the absurd performances of a few critics who tried to pin a tail of social significance on this play, attacking it as decadent, but succeeded only in pinning asses' ears on themselves. *The Jockey Club Stakes* is no more significant socially than the bubbles in a glass of champagne, and its existence is totally justified for identical reasons: it tastes good, it's fun. Such was not the case, alas, with a second imported British comedy, *No Sex Please, We're British,* with Maureen O'Sullivan as a respectable matron whose home is flooded with unwanted porn literature because of a mistake in communications. Now, *that's* socially significant.

Turning from comedy to drama on 1973 Broadway, one turns and turns again, scanning and re-scanning a space which, if not quite a void, is a thinly-settled line of country. Not until very late in the season did Broadway get an American drama of Best Play quality, and like last year's *Sticks and Bones* and *That Championship Season* it was a transfer from off-Broadway institutional production. The closest rival of *The Sunshine Boys* as the best American play of 1973, Joseph A. Walker's *The River Niger* was a standout in its articulate sensitivity to the special circumstances of a black family living in today's Harlem. Originated off Broadway by the Negro Ensemble Company and then moved to Broadway for a continuing run, this was certainly the best all-around production in the six-year history of the Douglas Turner Ward-Robert Hooks group, a cut above its two previous standouts *Ceremonies in Dark Old Men* and *The Sty of the Blind Pig.* Some scripts about the contemporary black condition dissipate their energy hammering away at the enemy like Punch with the alligator, but not this one, which hardly ever mentions "whitey" or "the man" and never "Mr. Charlie." It seeks to define battlefields, not enemies, in its closeup of a Harlem father, a poet forced to paint houses for a living. He is a good provider, a loving husband and a devoted parent, somewhat alcoholic but above all a man of great courage and wisdom who is not going to start his war of rebellion until he is sure the terrain suits him. His son is a U.S. Air Force trainee, and his father is proud of him; but the son rejects the white man's uniform just as he rejects the black man's street militancy, and he chooses the law and law school as his battlefield. An excellent ensemble of NEC actors portrays this family and their friends. Douglas Turner Ward played the father as he directed the play, with strong feeling, and the same is true of the performances of Roxie Roker as his wife, Les Roberts as their son, Graham Brown as a West Indian doctor friend of the family, and all others on their periphery. *The River Niger* is the title of a Walker poem about the life force of the black people, its imagery linking the Niger to the Mississippi and the Hudson, as well as of the play itself, which is at its best in dealing with the poetry of the black experience and at its worst in flashes of red melodrama which provide a convenient ending but are not in key with the delicacy of Walker's writing at its best. Walker is the author of two previous NEC-produced plays—*Ododo* and *Harangues*—and this early promise has flowered in *The River Niger,* which received five first-choice votes, as many as any of the other contenders, on the Critics Circle first ballot for Best American Play.

Two other distinguished scripts with fairly serious thrust were the British imports *The Changing Room* and *Butley*—though if either of their authors insisted on calling his work a comedy, we would raise no serious objection. In contrast to the ensemble-performed slice-of-life Storey play, Simon Gray's *Butley* was a star turn by the brilliant Alan Bates in the season's best performance by an actor. His role was that of a college professor whose character has been eaten away by termites of sexual dissatisfaction and academic disillusionment long before the play begins. What we see on the stage is the day the whole structure of his life collapses. The younger man who has been sharing his office, his apartment and his life goes off with another, more solid companion; his ex-wife has decided to marry a rival professor whom he considers a clown and a clod; he cannot seem to relate to his students or perform his academic duties; he cannot pick up a simple object from his desk without dropping it; he has even cut himself shaving. Finally he has nothing left except the intellectual prop of quoting nursery rhymes as though they contained the wisdom and poetry of the ages. He has not a shred of confidence or self-respect, and Bates's performance shows every leaking seam, every chipped surface, every frayed nerve connection. Hayward Morse, too, was particularly good as the smooth, ambitious, unflappable young professor who keeps his cool under assault from Butley's eccentricities but also coolly leaves him for a better man. The original London direction was by Harold Pinter, and one must assume that James Hammerstein followed it as closely as he could in staging the play here. Anyhow, there is distinction enough to go all the way around among the contributors to this richly rewarding show.

Elsewhere in drama on Broadway in 1973 there were the three scripts about Mary Todd Lincoln and a kind of theatrical experiment by Tennessee Williams. James Prideaux's *The Last of Mrs. Lincoln* studied the tortured widowhood of this ill-fated woman who, after the murder of the President, watched one son die and the other seemingly betray her with cruelty disguised as kindness, suffered agonies of penury, and choked on the poisoned air of the asylum before finding a kind of peace on her deathbed. Julie Harris gave us an impassioned portrait of Mary Todd, in the year's best performance by an actress, in a strong play in the mournful atmosphere of William Ritman's settings. V.J. Longhi's *The Lincoln Mask* was a more philosophical work, set at Ford's Theater on the night of the assassination and flashing back over the career of Lincoln (Fred Gwynne) as a man so fanatically devoted to a cause—the concept of equality and abolition of slavery—that he will ultimately decide to stake and sacrifice millions of lives in an effort to achieve his grand and noble purpose; a paradox with obvious modern overtones. In this one, Eva Marie Saint's Mary Todd was a Southern belle devoted to Lincoln's cause but grief-stricken at its impact on her world. The last of the three Mary Todd Lincolns was played by Geraldine Page in Jerome Kilty's *Look Away,* on the eve of the President's widow's departure from the asylum, discussing the past with a loyal black confidante.

The Tennessee Williams experiment, *Out Cry,* was a re-working of a Williams script entitled *The Two-Character Play,* previously produced several times on this continent and abroad. It was an exorcism of emotion rather than an evocation of it, in which a brother and sister, performers stranded by their troupe, put on a two-character play which is in reality some kind of parable of their real emotional stresses and guilt feelings. It was philosophically curious but dramatically unsound, a real disappointment in comparison to Williams's triumphant *Small Craft Warnings* last year.

Leading the season's parade of 13 Broadway musicals was—as usual—a Harold Prince show, *A Little Night Music,* with Stephen Sondheim at the top of his virtuosity, and with a beguiling book by Hugh Wheeler based on Ingmar Bergman's film *Smiles of a Summer Night* (as you probably don't remember, it was about the ways of love on a Swedish country estate on Midsummer's Eve, when the sun never sets and the characters from both drawing room and scullery wander in pairs among the birch trees throughout the long, warm twilight). This show took an operetta form, not as a pastiche but in a very high style. These northern midnight follies concern themselves with a middle-aged husband (Len Cariou) who is enduring an unconsummated marriage with a teenaged wife (Victoria Mallory), meanwhile amusing himself with his onetime mistress (Glynis Johns), all guests at the country estate of an elderly chatelaine (Hermione Gingold) who couldn't care less who does what to whom as long as the dinner table conversation sparkles. All colors of burlesque were screened out by the Sondheim-Wheeler-Prince treatment, which filtered through a sophistication as delicate and provocative as the lighting of the midnight sun (an off-white mauve, or perhaps ivory). Sondheim's waltz score insists gently, with a consistent lilt but never a blare. His lyrics scale the show's every peak, most notably in Miss Johns's show-stopping blues number "Send in the Clowns." They are also marvellously acrobatic when they feel like it ("raisins" rhymed with "liaisons," "virgin" with "submerge in," "women" with "indiscrimin-ate"). Every major element of this show including Prince's direction, Boris Aronson's grove of phallic birch trees, Florence Klotz's elegant costumes, Tharon Musser's lighting, the starring and supporting performances including the maid (D. Jamin-Bartlett), the butler (George Lee Andrews) and a wooden soldier (Laurence Guittard) ranks among the best that the Broadway theater has to offer.

Broadway also owed much to *Pippin,* which came along early in the year and played a lone hand for many weeks as the only new musical interest of 1973. With book by Roger O. Hirson and a Stephen (*Godspell*) Schwartz score, this was a theater-of-the-absurd concept about a young man trying to "find" himself in the heat of battle, romance, revolution and other turbulences, but in the long run discovering nothing worth finding out about himself or the world around him, and finally settling rather cheaply for domestic ease. The young hero happened to be called Pippin or Pepin, son of Charlemagne, and the show had a period atmosphere in the extremely attractive and imaginative sets by Tony Walton and costumes by Patricia Zipprodt, but history was not to be studied here. This was a free-swinging, free-dancing show under Bob Fosse's energetic direction, not a period piece, as Pippin's career was acted out like a series of vaudeville sketches by a group of clowns (shades, at least, of commedia dell'arte) led by Ben Vereen's notable presence as the Leading Player and commentator who maintains contact with the audience. The cast also included Irene Ryan, the nationally beloved Grandma of TV's *The Beverly Hillbillies,* in the role of an elderly cut-up (it was her last; she died during the run of the show). In a year of little experiment and less musical appeal until *Night Music* came along at the end of February, *Pippin* was a standout entertainment and a stand-in for the dormant avant garde.

A couple of plays were set to music with quite considerable success, though you would scarcely think of them as "musicals" in the rich, full-bodied sense of that term. Edmund Rostand's *Cyrano de Bergerac,* in a new Anthony Burgess adaptation, turned up as a *soi-disant* musical entitled *Cyrano,* but in spite of the ruffles and flourishes the play remained very much the thing here. Christopher Plummer played Cyrano expertly as a poet, a bit of a roisterer and a cosmically persuasive lover, with panache as long as his nose. In this version of the play, Plummer pauses once in a while to express himself in song—this is a "musical," after all—as in "No Thank You," about Cyrano's insistence on being independent of all forms of patronage and control, and "I Never Loved You" to Roxana as he is dying, trying to maintain his masquerade to the very end. Plummer reached the heart with the thrust of his performance, side-by-side with the music, whose peak moment occurred when Leigh Beery (Roxana) stopped the show with a lyric "You Have Made Me Love"—but Michael Kidd's direction didn't stress musical moments. He enhanced Cyrano's presence with manner and movement as though the whole world were an adjunct to the waving white plume on the Gascon's hat, in a thoroughly handsome show with sets by John Jensen and costumes by Desmond Heeley.

William Gibson's play *Two for the Seesaw* also was musicalized. The score by Cy Coleman and Dorothy Fields heightened the New York flavor with Broadway and barrio numbers, but here again the play predominated under the direction of Michael Bennett, who also took over the writing of the book in the late stages of *Seesaw's* production. Michele Lee was every inch the Second Avenue gamine Gittel Mosca, the warm-hearted dancer who comes to rue the day she permitted herself to fall in love with that lonesome lawyer from Nebraska.

The revival of *Irene* starring Debbie Reynolds got a mixed notice from President Nixon when it played Washington. The President called it "A great show . . . . . a good family show . . . . . a lot of fun" but predicted that it might not be popular with New Yorkers. It was well received when it finally reached Broadway, however, with Miss Reynolds, George S. Irving, Patsy Kelly and Peter Gennaro's dances receiving Tony nominations. *Irene* opened the new Minskoff Theater in the skyscraper which has replaced the Astor Hotel on Broadway, and though the show was technically a revival it must be viewed as a contemporary effort in any consideration of the 1973 musical scene. Its book about a male coutourier and a beautiful piano tuner in the carefree days of 1919 was re-worked by Hugh Wheeler (his second hit libretto of the season) and Joseph Stein from an adaptation by Harry Rigby (*Irene's* producer, who had previously helped revive *No, No, Nanette*) and more songs were added (some of them by Charles Gaynor and Otis Clements) than were retained from the original Harry Tierney-Joseph McCarthy score. Certainly *Irene* was offered by its collaborators and accepted by its audience as a show for now, not an antique.

Elsewhere on the musical stage the rewards were only partial. *Shelter*, with book and lyrics by Gretchen Cryer and music by Nancy Ford, was an ambitiously inventive, modern-idiom fairy tale about a TV writer who lives in a Tony Walton vision of a TV studio set, with background projections of anywhere on earth he wants to be, in company with a computer named Arthur and occasional visits from beautiful women. As done by Marcia Rodd and Terry Kiser in the leads under Austin Pendleton's direction, *Shelter* seemed to have been shaped by warm hands but a cold heart. In another part of the musical forest, Rene Auberjonois's rendering of Scapin in *Tricks,* a musical version of the Molière comedy brought up from regional production by the Actors Theater of Louisville, Ky. where it originated, was a commedia dell'-arte design of great virtuosit , disembodied in a nervously ineffectual show. Melina Mercouri blazed briefly in a Michael Cacoyannis-Peter Link adaptation-with-music of Aristophanes's anti-war comedy *Lysistrata.* Howard Keel escorted Danielle Darrieux onto the New York stage for a brief hour in *Ambassador,* based on a Henry James novel and defying the fates by coming to New York against the strong current of an unsuccessful tryout on the London stage last year. *Smith* put forward Don Murray in a pleasant but short-lived fable about a square who becomes trapped in a dream that he is the hero of a stage musical. Two other ill-fated Broadway musical efforts were *Hurry, Harry,* like *Pippin* about an overprivileged young man trying to find a life worth living, and *Dear Oscar,* an attempt to musicalize the life and conflicts of Oscar Wilde. Additionally, there was one new musical revue, *Nash at Nine,* paying homage to Ogden Nash and his writings, some of them set to music by Milton Rosenstock, with E.G. Marshall in the center spotlight.

The first of many distinguished visitors to 1973 Broadway was also a revue, the long-run off-Broadway cabaret production *Jacques Brel Is Alive and Well and Living in Paris,* which moved uptown for a limited engagement before going on tour. Israel sent over the revue *From Israel With Love,* a production of their Army entertainment groups. Maori folklore played the Palace in *Pacific Paradise,* a New Zealand compendium of songs, dances and games. New York audiences were also treated to Siobhan McKenna in her portraits of women in Irish literature (*Here Are Ladies*), Marcel Marceau's miming and the Bunraku Puppets of the National Puppet Theater of Japan, all three in return engagements, all incomparable special talents.

Revivals

Writing in the New York *Times Magazine* about the then-doubtful situation at the Lincoln Center theater facility, Walter Kerr observed that the versatile New York stage is a whole repertory theater already in being, and maybe that's why it's so hard to establish another separate one in the same city. This season the New York theater did indeed put on a huge repertory of 35 revival productions, 16 on and 19 off Broadway. From Maxim Gorky to Cole Porter, the season wore a coat of many familiar colors, some of them antique and some of them as modern as a re-staging of Joseph Heller's *We Bombed in New Haven,* Richard Kiley in *Man of La Mancha,* or *Purlie* stopping in for a brief revisit.

This was the season in which Jules Irving finally gave up trying to establish a sort of repertory operation in New York. Like a prime minister faced with the fact that he cannot form a viable government, Irving resigned as director of the Repertory Theater of Lincoln Center before the season had begun. Irving had led the organization to many an achievement but no discernable long-range purpose. Ironically, his post-resignation season was one of his most successful, beginning with Maxim Gorky's 1906 play *Enemies* about fragmenting Russian society, never before mounted in a full-scale New York production like this one with Joseph Wiseman, Nancy Marchand and the Lincoln Center company under Ellis Rabb's direction, in a Maharam Award-winning setting by Douglas W. Schmidt. This was followed by a production of Sean O'Casey's *The Plough and the Stars* whose drama of the Easter Rebellion in Dublin is a kind of parable of modern Irish troubles, and by an Ellis Rabb-modernized version of *The Merchant of Venice,* setting it in the now era of *la dolce vita,* dresed in Pucci, with Portia (Rosemary Harris) living on a yacht and Shylock (Sydney Walker) as a dark-suited counting-house square—but nevertheless raising the usual controversy over Shakespearean anti-Semitism.

Jules Irving's last program at the Vivian Beaumont Theater was certainly one of his finest hours, a revival of Tennessee Williams's powerful drama *A Streetcar Named Desire* with James Farentino as Stanley Kowalski and Rosemary Harris as Blanche Du Bois, again under Rabb's direction. It was so well received by Lincoln Center subscribers and others in the theatergoing public that its engagement had to be extended, and in May it broke the house record for a non-musical at the Beaumont with a week's gross of $60,797.

Meanwhile, at Lincoln Center Repertory's smaller theater, the Forum, a season of new experimental works by several well known playwrights, contemplated if not actually scheduled, was canceled after the opening program. This Forum finale too was one of the more rewarding efforts of Irving's tenure, a series of four Samuel Beckett one-acters, three seen previously (*Happy Days, Krapp's Last Tape* and *Act Without Words 1*) and one world premiere (*Not I*, a monologue of a woman talking desperately and effusively in an effort to stave off death), performed by Hume Cronyn, Jessica Tandy and Henderson Forsythe under Alan Schneider's direction.

The Forum's season was curtailed for the same reason Jules Irving resigned: the Lincoln Center Board couldn't raise enough money to finance either the Beaumont or the Forum adequately. Irving's regime always operated in a state of near-beggary and at the same time under continuous fire from critics, present company included, demanding that Lincoln Center Rep serve this or that high purpose. If Walter Kerr's observation about repertory theater in New York is correct, and I believe that it is, then to attempt to create a separate one here is to attempt the near-impossible. New York is one of the world's great financial capitals, however, so presumably it *is* possible to raise large sums of money here for noble arts enterprises—witness the Beaumont's next-door neighbor, the Metropolitan Opera. If Irving's departure from Lincoln Center marks the end of the dream of a large-scale permanent repertory company in New York, probably for a decade or a generation, then our loss is to be blamed more upon the board's shortcomings in pursuit of the possible than on those of Irving and his collaborators in the producing and acting company in pursuit of the impossible.

Joseph Papp, who will take over both Lincoln Center theaters next year, repeated the New York Shakespeare Festival's 1972 *Two Gentlemen of Verona* success with yet another streamlined Shakespearean production which moved on from summer in Central Park to Broadway in winter. Papp's *Much Ado About Nothing* was staged as though it had been written by Booth Tarkington, set in the America of the early 1900s and clothed by Theoni V. Aldredge in ice cream suits and Gibson Girl dresses. The wooing of Beatrice (Kathleen Widdoes) and Benedick (Sam Waterston) was as disarming as the brass-band rags and oom-pah-pah music written by Peter Link and Scott Joplin. The show floated pleasantly along despite the weight of one of Shakespeare's least workable comic subplots. The New York Shakespeare summer season at the Delacorte also presented a potent *Hamlet* by Stacy Keach under Gerald Freedman's direction and a new musical folk fable, *Ti-Jean and His Brothers*, a symbolic affirmation of life by the West Indian poet Derek Walcott. During the winter season downtown at the Public Theater, New York Shakespeare staged *The Cherry Orchard* with James Earl Jones and Gloria Foster heading a cast which was all black, for whatever reason and to no special effect.

Speaking of Shakespeare, the entry of Papp's musical version of *Two Gentlemen of Verona* on the longest-runs list at 627 performances marks the first time that a Shakespeare title has appeared on this honor roll of shows that have played more than 500 performances of record in a single production in the New York professional theater. The Bard has never made it on his own, and unless we've overlooked something, his works have appeared there only four additional times in musical versions more or less loosely based on his plays, as follows: *Kiss Me Kate* (1,070 perfs.), *West Side Story* (732 perfs.), *Your Own Thing* (933 perfs.) and the off-Broadway revival of *The Boys From Syracuse* (500 perfs.)

Two other institutions mounted revivals in Broadway theaters: T. Edward Hambleton's New Phoenix Repertory Company which, like its mythical namesake, rises triumphant from the flames of each new burning circumstance; and Circle in the Square in its uptown phase at the brand new, massively-named Circle in the Square Joseph E. Levine Theater. John McMartin and Paul Hecht headed the Phoenix company in two outstanding productions in repertory: Eugene O'Neill's *The Great God Brown,* with its examination of an artist's spiritual dichotomy set in a new time frame of 1916-1936 and directed by Harold Prince successfully disguised as a straight-play director; and Molière's *Don Juan* (sometimes known as *Dom Juan*) as adapted and directed by Stephen Porter. The Circle in the Square came to grips with O'Neill, too, in the *Mourning Becomes Electra* trilogy cut to three and a half hours, with Colleen Dewhurst under Theodore Mann's direction; followed by Irene Papas playing Euripides's *Medea* in a version adapted and staged by Minos Volanakis. All these revivals offered the New York playgoer valuable new acquaintance and sometimes new insight into important segments of the theatrical past.

The 1973 "New York Repertory Theater" also included three large-scale Broadway revivals individually produced as star vehicles. *Emperor Henry IV* was the Pirandellian context of a Rex Harrison portrait of a dreamer dazed in an accident and suffering for many years the delusion that he is an 11th-century monarch, a delusion supported by his faithful retainers who dress up in costume and play the game with him. Even after he regains his senses, the object of all this attention continues to pretend even to himself that he is Henry IV because he prefers a life of vivid illusion to one of boring reality—one of Pirandello's famous variations on this theme. Harrison was both whimsical and commanding in this highly intellectual diversion, a Hurok concert of a stage production.

A clutch of stars turned out in a period revival of Clare Boothe Luce's once daring, now rather ingenuously disarming, study of the feminine gender in its 1936 manifestation, *The Women,* starring (in alphabetical order) Rhonda Fleming, Kim Hunter, Dorothy Loudon, Myrna Loy and Alexis Smith, with Leora Dana and Doris Dowling also in the cast. The men had their innings in a revival of George Bernard Shaw's *Don Juan in Hell,* performed as a staged reading in the style designed by Charles Laughton in 1952, also an exercise of intellectual brilliance ably served by Paul Henreid (the Commander), Ricardo Montalban (Don Juan) and Edward Mulhare (the Devil), with Agnes Moorehead playing Dona Ana as she did in the original production.

The final Broadway revival program of the season was *The Play's the Thing,* a transfer from off Broadway produced and performed by the Roundabout Theater Company, a group which continues to defy the law of repertory gravity in New York City. Its curve is ever upward as it annually presents a series of programs with a top-notch repertory cast, usually under Gene Feist's elucidating direction. This year the Roundabout presented *Right You Are* (still another Pirandello illusion-and-reality puzzle), Beatrice Straight as the guest star in a starkly effective staging of Ibsen's *Ghosts* and an ebullient, accent-on-comedy staging of the Molnar work which eventually wound up on Broadway. The Roundabout's 1973 season also included a program of Chekhov readings and, as in 1972, one program of new material, *American Gothics,* a compendium of four moody one-acters by Donald Kvares. This organization seems to have changed its name this season from the Roundabout *Repertory* Company to The Roundabout *Theater* Company, but there has been no change in the continuing high level of its aspiration and performance. We *have* a professional resident company in New York, the Roundabout, in 1973 stretching its well-disciplined muscles and extending its influence north toward Broadway.

Still another off-Broadway repertory company was fledged this year: City Center Acting Company, a group of players who made up the Julliard Acting Ensemble a year ago and now, having graduated from school, sticking together in an effort to find a lasting place in the New York theater scene. With John Houseman as artistic director, they presented a large, versatile and uniformly creditable program which included Sheridan's *The School for Scandal,* Paul Shyre's adaptation of John Dos Passos's *U.S.A.,* the Jacobean tragedy *Women Beware Women* by Thomas Middleton and Maxim Gorky's *The Lower Depths,* as well as Brendan Behan's *The Hostage* and James Saunders's *Next Time I'll Sing to You.* The troupe will further justify its name next April in a scheduled two-week engagement at City Center's 55th Street Theater.

Also in revival off Broadway was the Gertrude Stein-Virgil Thomson work *The Mother of Us All,* a 25-year-old operatic composition presented at the Guggenheim Museum but far from a museum piece in its celebration of the life and times of Susan B. Anthony, the noted 19th-century suffragette whose struggle was a deep root of Women's Lib. Cole Porter's *You Never Know* surfaced for a brief moment in a shaky production. Ayn Rand's famous gimmick play, *Night of January 16th,* a courtroom drama in which the jury is selected from the audience and there are two endings depending on its verdict, was resurrected for a short time under the title *Penthouse Legend.* And *Spoon River Anthology,* the Edgar Lee Masters works of Americana adapted for staged reading by Charles Aidman, was seen in a return engagement.

Add to this imposing list of revivals the specialty programs like The Bil Baird Marionettes' popular perennials *Winnie the Pooh* and *Davy Jones' Locker,* the one-man program of readings and songs *Shay Duffin as Brendan Behan,* or The Everyman Players version of *The Pilgram's Progress,* and you have an ever-widening circle of renewed acquaintance with the distinguished past. In 1973 alone the New York repertory theater in the Walter Kerr sense brought us productions of Gorky, O'Casey, Shakespeare, Tennessee Williams, O'Neill, Euripides, Shaw, Molière, Ibsen, Joseph Heller, Sheridan, Behan, Thomas Middleton, James Saunders, Beckett, Chekhov and others. What could another so-called permanent repertory company do for an encore?

The 1972-73 Season off Broadway

PLAYS (28)

Public Theater 1972
The Corner
Present Tense
Coney Island Cycle
Public Theater 1973
Wedding Band
The Children
Siamese Connections
The Orphan
American Place
The Kid
Freeman
The Karl Marx Play
Baba Goya
American Gothics
F.O.B.
Blue Boys
Negro Ensemble
THE RIVER NIGER
Please Don't Cry and Say No
Mystery Play
The White Whore and the Bit Player
Welcome to Andromeda & Variety Obit
The Tooth of Crime
Brother Gorski
An Evening With the Poet-Senator
THE HOT L BALTIMORE (transfer)
Echoes

MUSICALS (16)

Buy Bonds, Buster
Joan
Ti-Jean and His Brothers
Safari 300
Aesop's Fables
Speed Gets the Poppies
Crazy Now
Lady Audley's Secret
Lady Day: A Musical Tragedy
Doctor Selavy's Magic Theater
The Contrast
The Bar That Never Closes
Say When
Rainbow
Thoughts
Smile, Smile, Smile

REVUES (7)

They Don't Make 'Em Like That Anymore
Berlin to Broadway With Kurt Weill
Oh Coward!
A Quarter for the Ladies Room
National Lampoon's Lemmings
Hot and Cold Heros
What's a Nice Country Like You Doing in a State Like This?

SPECIALTIES (8)

The Sunshine Train
Baird Marionettes
Winnie-the-Pooh
Davy Jones' Locker
Band-Wagon
Anton Chekhov's Garden Party
Shay Duffin as Brendan Behan
Fly Chelsea to Brooklyn
The Pilgrim's Progress

REVIVALS (19)

N.Y. Shakespeare
Hamlet
Much Ado About Nothing
Roundabout
Right You Are
The Play's the Thing
Ghosts
We Bombed in New Haven
City Center Company
The School for Scandal
U.S.A.
The Hostage
Women Beware Women
Next Time I'll Sing to You
The Lower Depths
Lincoln Center Forum
Happy Days & Act Without Words 1
Krapp's Last Tape
The Mother of Us All

Penthouse Legend
Public Theater 1973
The Cherry Orchard
You Never Know
Spoon River Anthology

FOREIGN-LANGUAGE PRODUCTIONS (8)

Jewish of Bucharest
The Dybbuk
The Pearl Necklace
Yerma
Die Brücke
Der Frieden
Woyzeck
The Grand Music Hall of Israel
El Grande de Coca-Cola
Le Médecin Malgre Lui

FOREIGN PLAYS IN ENGLISH (9)

Chelsea Theater
Sunset
Kaspar
GREEN JULIA
Not I
The Trials of Oz
L'Été
Crystal and Fox
Alpha Beta
Owners

Plays listed in CAPITAL LETTERS have been designated Best Plays of 1972-73.
Plays listed in *italics* were still running June 1, 1973.

Off Broadway

The numbers tell quite a lot of the off-Broadway story: there was a sharp drop in the number of straight-play programs in English to 37 from 52 last year, down even from the 45 produced in 1970-71 and only a little more than half of 1969-70's 64.

Of these, only 28 were new American plays, as compared with 43 last year, 39 the year before and more than 50 in each of the two previous years.

The production of musicals, on the other hand, jumped to 16 (18 if you count a couple of revues heavily oriented to their scores; see the one-page summary accompanying this report), up from 10 last year and 13 the year before, back to the 16 musicals produced in 1969-70. And when we say that the numbers tell quite a lot of the story, we mean also that in a distressingly large proportion of these cases the shows were just statistics, here today and gone into the column of figures tomorrow. Of all the musicals—excepting the revues—there was only one solid success (*Doctor Selavy's Magic Theater*). Among straight plays, the off-Broadway output, which last season shared the Best Plays list evenly with Broadway, produced only three Best Plays in 1972-73, and two of these were brought in from outside. One—Paul Ableman's *Green Julia*—came from the London stage and another—Lanford Wilson's *The Hot l Baltimore*—from off off Broadway.

There was seldom any mood of experimentation, any thrust of innovation in the smaller playhouses this season. The creative style of even the best work tended to be conservative. Shrinking straight-play and expanding musical volume . . . reluctance to experiment, with a consequently lower level of invention . . . rising production costs and substantial ticket prices . . . if all of this seems *deja vu*, it is, we saw it all happen before on Broadway. Off Broadway appears to be changing from a free-swinging adventure into some sort of mini-commercial theater, inheriting all the problems which have for so long burdened Broadway. New York City's crime-in-the-streets publicity affects off Broadway even more adversely than it does the Times Square area because its little theaters are scattered in many dark corners of a Manhattan many of whose residents are reluctant even to venture forth on broad avenues in broad daylight. The truth is that the theater areas both on and off Broadway are as close to 100 per cent secure at show time as anywhere in any city in the world, but ballyhoo counts more than truth in matters like this. The fact remains that in 1972-73 off Broadway was suffering all of Broadway's ills on top of those uniquely its own, with only the organizations like the Public Theater, Negro Ensemble, American Place and Chelsea seeming to have any sort of viable answer to the double dilemma.

The only bona fide unsubsidized, independent off-Broadway production to make the Best Plays list this year was *Green Julia*, a British comedy by Paul Ableman first produced in 1965 at the Edinburgh Festival by the Traverse Theater. It was its author's first full-length play, and when it was brought in to London in the season of 1965-66 it was selected by Ossia Trilling as one of the year's outstanding new British works. *Green Julia* had its American premiere at the Washington, D.C. Theater Club under Davey Marlin-Jones's direction May 9, 1968 and was still a long time coming to New York. It was well worth waiting for, like a good tune that finally catches on. Ableman's script is a song of youth, a "Gaudeamus Igitur" for an era when sentiment is out of fashion and emotional manifestation of student brotherhood is frowned upon. The play's flood of mocking, parodistic words and poses exchanged between two college roommates breaking up housekeeping after graduation is camouflage for their real (but not clearly perceived even by themselves) feelings of sadness and loneliness at their imminent parting. Their studies completed, they are poised on the threshold of great adventure, one as a botanist and one as an economist, and they are making a pretense of celebrating the event with champagne and a lady friend (Julia, who dawdles in a bar downstairs and never shows up). Underneath this surface is a premonition that they have grown too close together for comfort as individuals in the outside world. These two roommates are *Moonchildren* at the end of their graduate studies, three or four years older but still insecure, playing a private game of charades and assuming the characters of priests, doctors, soldiers, etc. and improvising dialogue as a ritual to ward off reality for an hour . . . a minute . . . a second more. But reality will finally intrude, and when it does there is a moment of mutual hatred at their interdependence. As the more vulnerable of the two—the botanist—Fred Grandy gave a performance which was surely the beginning of an important acting career. The other, more dominant role was originally played by Moonchild James Woods, a fine actor whose performance nevertheless couldn't have been any better than that of his replacement, John Pleshette, who took over the part shortly after the opening. In every department including the direction by William E. Hunt, *Green Julia* was one of the engrossing evenings of theater in 1972-73.

The best of bests off Broadway this season, we feel, was Joseph A. Walker's compelling *The River Niger*, about a Harlem family. The only full-scale program produced by the Negro Ensemble Company in 1972-73, it was an instant success and was later brought to Broadway and has already been described in the Broadway section of this report. The third off-Broadway Best Play, Lanford Wilson's *The Hot l Baltimore* (the missing "e" in the title is meant to be a letter missing in the dilapidated sign of a run-down hotel), was a transfer upward from its original production off off Broadway by the Circle Theater Company. It won the New York Drama Critics Circle Award as the best American play of 1972-73 and an Obie best-play citation, and it is worthy of these distinguished honors. Describing a day's activity in the lobby of a soon-to-be-razed, once-quality-but-now-shabby hotel, *Baltimore* weaves together the lives and fading dreams of its seedy tenants. But unlike Wilson's *Balm in Gilead,* a similarly structured look at low life in an inner-city greasy-spoon diner, *Baltimore's* tone is not dispassionate and clinical but intensely romantic, a poignant salute to the illusions we build to act as buffers against the intrusion of reality. The characters are easily-identifiable prototypes—a grumpy old geezer, sentimental hookers, a belligerent young man on the run from the law and a batty old lady who claims contact with ghosts—but under Wilson's pen they become fresh and vital once more.

American Place had an outstanding season in its new Sixth Avenue home in a skyscraper's basement, with its *Freeman* and *Baba Goya* ranking close to the top ten, and with Robert Coover's *The Kid* and Rochelle Owens's *The Karl Marx Play* (which included a musical score by the ubiquitous Galt MacDermot) making their tart comments on idolatry of heroes and philosophers. Phillip Hayes Dean's *Freeman,* like his *The Sty of the Blind Pig* last year, was a commentary but not a diatribe on the black condition, presenting a conformist black family making it in the middle class but unable to persuade their aggressively independent misfit son to go along. The son tries first to use, then to subvert "the system," and he follows that different drummer stubbornly to his doom.

In a lighter treatment of the argument for doing your own thing no matter what, Steve Tesich's *Baba Goya* brightened up the final weeks of American Place's season with another disharmoniously funny view of a way-out American home like his previous full-length play *The Carpenters* (also produced by American Place). In *Baba Goya* we have a mother (Olympia Dukakis) who has been through three or four husbands and several children and is hungry for more—more children, preferably adopted orphans, to replace those who have grown up, and another husband to replace the current one when he dies, which he and she believe will be soon. During most of the play a malefactor of Japanese extraction is chained to a radiator, and an old guy runs around insisting on *not* being called "grandpa"—this is the kind of thing that goes on in Tesich plays and is incapable of brief explanation. This playwright has a knack of welding bits of the absurd into fairly naturalistic situations.

The season at Joseph Papp's Public Theater produced no blockbusters on the scale of 1972's *Sticks and Bones* and *That Championship Season*, but there was never an idle moment down on Lafayette Street. The Public led off with Alice Childress's *Wedding Band*, a reflection on the black American South in the recent past. The time is the summer of 1918, the place is a seaside community in South Carolina, and the matter to be dramatized is a love affair which crosses a color line sharply drawn and primly observed by both factions. Ruby Dee and James Broderick played the ill-fated lovers who know they can't win but will insist harder and hold out longer than most, in a Ming Cho Lee representation of the cozy and homogenized black world of adjoining back yards—the real world (Miss Childress seems to be saying in her play) where real values are established and observed, regardless of what parades may be going by in the street out front. Co-directed by its author and Joseph Papp, *Wedding Band* was the leading attraction of a Public Theater season which included Michael McGuire's *The Children*, a nightmare fantasy of family relationships; Dennis J. Reardon's *Siamese Connections*, about a bad apple in the basket of a family which has lost another son in Vietnam; and, finally, a new David Rabe script, *The Orphan*, about an individual doomed in advance by the established circumstances and preconditions of the world around him, like Rabe's Pavlo Hummel and his blinded Vietnam veteran in last year's prizewinning drama. His new protagonist was an Orestes re-enacting his story as a parable of our own era. It was creditable but not memorable, like the Public Theater's season as a whole, marking time and getting in trim for next year's great leap forward when Joseph Papp will take over the Lincoln Center facilities.

Fly Chelsea to Brooklyn was the title of one of Chelsea Theater Center's programs this year; and, indeed, Chelsea has been both a vehicle and a destination for cultural adventure across the river at the Academy of Music. Whether reviewing the life and times of Billie Holiday as portrayed by Cecelia Norfleet in the musical *Lady Day: A Musical Tragedy*, or looking back on the special world of Jewish Russia early in the century in Isaac Babel's *Sunset*, the Chelsea's programs are always reaching, always challenging. This year's peak was *Kaspar*, by the avant garde German playwright Peter Handke, about a 16-year-old boy in an animal condition, unable to speak or walk, suffering the spiritual agonies of slowly being trained and transformed into a human being, with particular attention to the function of language as a humanizing force. The role of Kaspar (which means "clown"), played by Christopher Lloyd, was the perpetual center of the play's concentration through 15 closed-circuit TV screens as well as in the flesh onstage. The final Chelsea program, the first named, was a portmanteau invitation to a mini-festival of guest attractions put on by theater groups which flew into Brooklyn from the mid-West and West.

Elsewhere on the list of straight plays, Terrence McNally's *Whiskey,* about a booze-ridden touring troupe of Western performers, was an amusing collection of black comedy skits. Jean-Claude van Itallie appeared with an even blacker but not quite so comic script, *Mystery Play,* an absurdist murder yarn in which all the characters are killed off (the trouble was, they were all easily expendable and the play seemed to improve as the stage emptied). Van Itallie's return to the mainstream theater after his long sojourn off off Broadway, during which his only work of record was the brilliant *The Serpent,* was an important event regardless of any one script, and we earnestly hope he has come out to stay out. Tom Eyen's *The White Whore and the Bit Player,* a famous off-off-Broadway piece based somewhat on the life of Marilyn Monroe, surfaced in a production at St. Clement's (whose status as a production center for this, McNally's *Whiskey* and other plays is now a borderline case between off and off-off). *The Children's Mass,* about transvestism and the New York City sex and drug scene, was a promising playwriting debut for the actor Frederick Combs.

Green Julia was much the best of the English-speaking imports off Broadway this season, but not the only one of at least passing interest. Brian Friel's *Crystal and Fox* was a dark but rather effective play about a brooding showman, the leader of a third-rate touring Irish entertainment troupe, bent on the destruction of himself and of those around him. E.A. Whitehead's *Alpha Beta* was a relentlessly abrasive two-character study of a marriage going from bad to worse over a period of almost a decade, with Laurence Luckinbill in a flashy performance as the husband and Kathryn Walker slowly but finally and firmly stealing the show with her portrait of an indomitable woman caught in a domestic trap and determined both to do her duty and to see that others perform theirs toward her. *The Trials of Oz,* a semi-documentary play about the British trial of the editors of the magazine *Oz* for obscenity aimed deliberately at school children, should also be classed as an import because it was previously presented in London in a Royal Shakespeare Company reading, though never fully produced there.

The off-Broadway season also brought a number of foreign-language visitors: The Jewish State Theater of Bucharest with *The Dybbuk* and *The Pearl Necklace,* Spain's Nuria Espert Company in a production of *Yerma,* Germany's Die Brücke with *Der Frieden* and *Woyzeck,* The Grand Music Hall of Israel and France's Le Jeune Théâtre National. Finally, delightfully (and probably not quite accurately classified as a foreign-language production), there was *El Grande de Coca-Cola,* a multi-national endeavor written for the British stage by members of its cast, with an American (Ron House) in top authorship billing. This zany show was set in Honduras, where the owner of a run-down night club is trying to con customers with a fake "Parade of Stars," and it was performed in a sort of Spanish, fractured with most other leading languages of the Western world, but understandable and appealing to all in its short but sweet one-hour context.

The miniature pleasures of the one-act-play form seemed less and less comfortable in the New York stage environment this season. The old days of the Albee, Pinter and Beckett programs were days of bold experimentation off Broadway, which once was especially hospitable to the imaginative one-act statement. Now that off Broadway is being tainted with cost problems and their attendant hit-psychology syndrome, however, the one-act play programs have attenuated in both number and stature. Lincoln Center Repertory's Forum Theater schedule of Samuel Beckett one-acters was a distinguished exception, including as it did the world premiere of *Not I*. The year's best new short play (albeit performed with an intermission) was Ron Whyte's *Welcome to Andromeda* about a bedridden young cripple (David Clennon) overprotected by his mother and trying to induce his nurse to put him out of his misery while his mother is out of the house—presented on the same program with Whyte's one-acter *Variety Obit*, a frivolous musical bit about a show-business family. The season brought only five other one-act programs, all off Broadway: *The Corner*, a Public Theater production of plays by Ed Bullins, Oyamo and Clay Goss; and four one-playwright programs, Frank Gilroy's *Present Tense*, Peter Schuman's *Coney Island Cycle* done by the Bread and Puppet Theater, a Donald Kvares program of four plays produced by the Roundabout under the portmanteau title *American Gothics*, and Townsend Brewster's *Please Don't Cry and Say No*. This is quite a change from only five seasons ago, when there were 20 off-Broadway programs of one-acters including the Best Play *Adaptation/Next*.

On the musical side off Broadway in 1973, revues took a major share of the bows. The hit of the year was *Oh, Coward!*, Roderick Cook's compendium of Noel Coward songs interspersed with word passages from his plays and prose writings. The filaments of Coward's wit still carried their powerful charge in a show which could have been viewed as a sort of swan song and eulogy for its author, a posthumous tribute to one of the century's most sparkling literary lights who died last winter at his home in Jamaica. In fact, the show was intended as nothing of the sort. It was produced with only pleasure in mind long before Coward died, and Coward came to see it during a New York visit. Like everybody else, he enjoyed it. His fragile tunes making their highly sophisticated observations, meant for a time when amusing one's self was a serious part of the business of living, have retained their power to entertain and even move the audiences of this battered era.

The late Kurt Weill was also roundly celebrated in a popular off-Broadway revue, *Berlin to Broadway With Kurt Weill*, billed as "a musical voyage" through shows like *The Threepenny Opera, Knickerbocker Holiday, Lady in the Dark* and *Lost in the Stars*, stopping to revisit about 40 song numbers. It was a melodic bonanza. On the subject of revues, a comic bonanza arrived at the Village Gate late in the season, *National Lampoon's Lemmings*, co-written and assembled by its producer-director Tony Hendra (like David Frost a graduate of England's TV hit *That Was the Week That Was*) as a sort of theatrical spin-off from the humor magazine named in the title. With music by Paul Jacobs and Christopher Guest, it fired away at all the usual topical revue targets like sex and politics and especially the world of pop music, peaking in its version of "The Woodchuck Festival of Peace, Love and Death" as a young people's mass-suicide ritual.

Of the 16 book musicals off Broadway in 1973, only one attracted a sizeable audience: *Doctor Selavy's Magic Theater,* conjured up by Richard Foreman as a parody of a case history in a madhouse (proving once again that you can make a musical out of almost *anything*), with a versatile score by Stanley Silverman and Tom Hendry. It was a clever raising of the eternal question about who is sane and who crazy, which the reality and which the delusion. Another book show of more than routine interest was *Joan,* a musicalization of the Joan of Arc story by Al Carmines, that prolific off-off-Broadway composer whose work often adorns and/or challenges the professional theater. Still another musical of note was Derek Walcott's *Ti-Jean and His Brothers,* a folk fable by the Trinidadian poet about three brothers symbolic of affirmative human attributes like strength and intellect, pitted against the Devil, with music by Andre Tanker, the first new, modern work presented by the New York Shakespeare Festival in its Central Park seasons. Other lesser efforts in this busy but not very productive musical season off Broadway, which began with the single-performance *Buy Bonds, Buster* and ended similarly with *Smile, Smile, Smile,* included a William Russo rock musical rendition of *Aesop's Fables* and others of *Lady Audley's Secret* and Royall Tyler's *The Contrast* (produced in New York in 1787, the first comedy of record by an American playwright). A gospel program entitled *The Sunshine Train,* assembled and staged by William E. Hunt and featuring The Gospel Starlets, Clara Walker and the Carl Murray Singers, proved to be one of the season's more popular off-Broadway attractions.

Offstage

The behind-the-scenes story of the year began the last week in October when Jules Irving confirmed reports of his resignation as director of the Repertory Theater of Lincoln Center. The story ended—or, rather began again—with the announcement tentatively put forward March 7 and finally confirmed in May that Joseph Papp's New York Shakespeare Festival would take over at the Vivian Beaumont and Forum Theaters, using the former to house mostly new plays and the latter as a year-round showcase for the plays of William Shakespeare.

These events had roots in the Elia Kazan-Robert Whitehead era when the Lincoln Center Repertory board, apparently refusing to understand the function of a permanent repertory company, dismissed Kazan and Whitehead and replaced them with Jules Irving and Herbert Blau from the West Coast. Having failed one set of gifted impresarios, the board then failed the second. In all the years of the Irving regime, this board never provided the financing necessary, let alone appropriate, to a first-class repertory operation. They nearly permitted the Forum to slide into the oblivion of motion picture re-runs; they nearly permitted an intrusion into Lincoln Center Repertory's affairs by interests alien and maybe even antipathetic to the legitimate theater; they nearly permitted the irrevocable dismantling of the facility's specially-designed storage space for repertory productions. They did permit the financing to fall into disarray, so that there were no funds to continue the Forum's season beyond the Beckett repertory and barely enough to carry out the Beaumont's 1973 schedule.

This and other major policy problems left Irving with no alternative but to resign. The board appointed a committee to study the situation, and at first it was thought that the Beaumont could be booked for a series of outside attractions in 1973-74 (the touring *Man of La Mancha* had enjoyed a very profitable run there during the summer of 1972). At one point David Merrick wanted to lease the Forum for a three-year period of experimental production of about a half-dozen plays a season but was unable to reach a satisfactory agreement which did not also include the Beaumont, in which he had no interest. Then, on March 7, came the announcement that many had hoped for but few really expected: Joseph Papp would take over at Lincoln Center, not instead of but in addition to operations at the Public and Delacorte Theaters, if adequate financing was available. Just as there is New York Shakespeare Festival Public Theater, there is now also to be New York Shakespeare Festival at Lincoln Center, and *Joseph Papp's board will replace the Lincoln Center board.*

The arrangement was contingent on raising money for operations, and Papp immediately and boldly doubled the anticipated, budgeted, annual Beaumont-Forum deficit from the previous $750,000 to $1.5 million. Of this, $500,000 was to be raised by the Shakespeare Festival board and the rest from other sources. Papp made it clear that he expected a firm commitment to a five-year deficit of $7.5 million, but he declared himself officially go for the full mission after Mrs. Samuel I. Newhouse presented him with a $1 million donation, following a $350,000 grant from the Rockefeller Foundation. Mrs. Newhouse's magnificent gift was of momentous importance, not only because of its size but also because of its unusual character. It was earmarked for operations, for putting on plays, not putting up a building with the donor's name on a brass plaque. Mrs. Newhouse has donated life itself to the theater art form, and the urge to put up a plaque anyway in honor of this rarely discerning patron is irresistable.

Papp's policy at Lincoln Center will be exactly the same as at the Public Theater and exactly the opposite of Lincoln Center Rep's: he will present new plays, not classics. "We are coming in as a contemporary force in what is basically a classic constituency," Papp told the *Times,* and he is also coming in with complete artistic, managerial and financial autonomy. If the present 25,000 Beaumont subscribers don't like the kind of plays he produces (Papp said), he'll try to find an audience that does. Off the top of his first thoughts he rather views the Public Theater as a continuing showcase for the more experimental kind of plays and the Beaumont Theater for more finished ones, though the distinction will not be sharply drawn.

A major growing sociological threat to the theater in 1973 was the porno industry in both its fleshly and its vicarious forms. Prostitutes and their pimps were crowding the edges of the theater district, some of whose legitimate playhouses were reportedly on the verge of takeover by porno flick operators, while massage parlors and peep shows were outbidding legitimate enterprises for rentable space. Early in the season the Shubert organization rattled the saber, hinting it might start selling off theaters if the cheapening of the Times Square area was allowed to continue unchecked. The city moved in to eliminate the porno nuisance wherever it impinged on theatergoing. Efforts to acquire the Bijou, Ritz and Little Theaters for the porno circuit were thwarted. A concerned theater industry is working with a concerned city government to maintain a glamorous environment for enjoying the theater. They have gone a long way toward pushing out crime and porno, and they will keep on working until theatergoing is as it should be in image as well as in fact.

The Shubert organization itself was troubled in 1973. In a power shift, three executive directors—Gerald Schoenfeld, Bernard B. Jacobs and Irving Goldman—took over the active management of the company from Lawrence Shubert Lawrence, the late Lee Shubert's grand-nephew, who was named chairman of the board. Differences between the troika and Lawrence soon came to the surface in the form of court proceedings, in which Lawrence attempted to oust the executive directors and regain control of the organization and the Shubert Foundation. The suit was unsuccessful and has been appealed.

Trouble with the musicians' union caused *Pippin* to cancel its tryout booking at the Kennedy Center Opera House in Washington, D.C., until the musicians agreed to compromise as to the number of men employed and their salaries, and *Pippin* rescheduled the booking. As always in the course of a long, hotly creative theater season, some shows had director trouble including *The Creation of the World and Other Business* which started with Harold Clurman and ended with Gerald Freedman; *Irene* which started with John Gielgud and ended with Gower Champion (and there is a lesson in *that* somewhere); and *Cyrano* which started with Michael Langham and ended with Michael Kidd. The directors as a group raised a specter when their organization, the Society of Stage Directors and Choreographers (SSD & C) negotiated a contract with the producers (represented as always by the League of New York Theaters) which, in SSD & C's own words in a notice to its members, "established the principle that directors and choreographers have property rights. The League has agreed that they will not authorize publication in any form of the 'work' of the director or choreographer. In immediate practical terms this means that the final prompt script of a Broadway production may not be published without the consent of the director or choreographer who has staged the production."

In reality it meant nothing of the sort; it meant only that the SSD & C was waving its plume above the parapet, with the producers whistling and looking up at the sky, playing innocent bystanders. The Dramatists Guild, the organization of playwrights, composers, librettists and lyricists, who do in fact own the written material, was never a party to any such agreement and promptly advised its members to be on guard against and resist any encroachment upon their property. The SSD & C members are paid for what they do, the Dramatists Guild pointed out, and their work belongs to the production whose script, in turn, belongs to the playwright (who is compensated, not by any salary, but by a share of the box office receipts when and if—a very big if—they begin coming in). A lot of words were exchanged but no material issue joined in this matter in the 1972-73 season, and it looked as though the whole controversy might vanish in a slow dissolve.

Some critics complained openly that producers were catering to Clive Barnes of the *Times*, sometimes shifting opening dates to suit his convenience (he has a particularly tight reviewing schedule since he covers dance as well as theater), regardless of the inconvenience to other critics. And inside the Critics Circle there were indigestive rumbles about *Variety's* publishing the intimate and sometimes controversy-ridden details of the group's private meetings. But with David Merrick mostly absent from the theater scene in 1972-73, there was no one to goad the critical fraternity into excesses of righteous indignation individually or in combination, so that the pundits maintained a fairly low profile.

There was a positive sign of growth in 1973 in the completion and putting-into-operation of new theaters built into high-rise office structures, a fruition of the city's program to give developers in the Broadway area valuable concessions in the building regulations if they will include theaters within their skyscraper designs. The first of these was American Place's new home below ground level at 46th Street and Sixth Avenue, opened last season, an intimate, efficient and pleasant environment for experimental activity (but one hypersensitive and dissenting playwright commented, "I don't like it, I can feel that whole building weighing down on top of me"). In contrast, the word for the three new Broadway houses which opened this season is cavernous. The Uris, the Minskoff and the Circle in the Square Joseph E. Levine Theaters seem to have been designed as though bigness had the same value in stage housing as it does in office buildings. *Via Galactica* managed to fill the Uris, but they needed a space ship and an amplified rock band to do it; *Seesaw* seemed to shrink in its vastness. The Minskoff opened with the expansive *Irene,* but even so there were complaints about a feeling of remoteness in the balcony. The Circle in the Square's new uptown arena-stage facility is great for the massive emotional content of O'Neill and Euripides, but a Yankee Stadium for an intimate presentation like Siobhan McKenna's *Here Are Ladies.*

On the plus side, these theaters are more comfortable, with much more width and breadth of individual seating room than in the Shubert-era Broadway houses (and the slight inconvenience of the so-called "continental" aisleless seating arrangement, with access to the seats laterally through the wider-spaced rows, is small in comparison to the pleasure of the increased *lebensraum*). Also, these new theaters *are,* they exist, and they are a great deal better than nothing—which is what we might have been left with, were it not for the Mayor Lindsay administration's concern for the future of the legitimate theater and its district.

On a personal note, Stephen Sondheim was elected to succeed Robert Anderson as president of the Dramatists Guild, the fourth time a dramatist from the musical side has been named to lead this authors' organization (the other three were Richard Rodgers, Alan Jay Lerner and the late Oscar Hammerstein II).

Alexander H. Cohen produced another good Tony TV show and made a good point in a letter to *Variety* about "the custom of allowing the marquees of shows which have closed to remain standing on Broadway theaters until an incoming production displaces them." He pointed out that leaving the name of an unsuccessful show on the marquee of an empty theater turns Broadway into a "Street of Flops" which have strutted and fretted their brief hour upon the stage and then, instead of being heard of no more, continue having their titles blazoned on Broadway's prime promotional space, like names on elaborate tombstones. Cohen asked in his letter, "Would any other industry trumpet its mistakes in this fashion? It is of course regrettable that most of the shows in question didn't find acceptance and that the theaters they played in are dark. But must we continue to remind the public of their fate?" He urged that marquee signs be taken down as soon as a show closes and, while the theater remains vacant, the space be used to promote living hits.

The theater's efforts to set up some kind of center for the last-minute sale of unsold tickets at reduced prices were suspended at the beginning of the season, then picked up again and brought to fruition under the auspices of the New York City Cultural Council and the Office of Midtown Planning and Development, together with the Theater Development Fund. A Ticket Center was set up in a booth in Duffy Square offering unsold tickets to Broadway and off-Broadway shows at cut-rate prices, on the day of the performance only. And also locally, a Theater Hall of Fame has been established in the spacious lobby of the Uris Theater and the first group of 90 names of theater greats from the period 1860-1930 are now permanently affixed. Five more names are to be added each year.

Those who look back over the 1972-73 drama season seeking signs and portents are apt to find more than they can conveniently interpret. Something is happening to the theater in this decade, all right—but what? Off Broadway seems to be middling and Broadway, unable to middle with any degree of commercial viability, is concentrating on the big, conventional theater concepts—does that augur good or bad?

One of the prime movers of the 1970s, Joseph Papp, is certainly bullish on the New York theater and the American playwright's ability to keep its stages full of excitement. Papp voices his confidence in the continuing strength of the *Broadway* theater when he says that shows which prove popular at the Public or the Beaumont are to be "summarily moved to higher ground," that is, transferred to Broadway, which obviously he expects will retain its firm, large-scale commercial eminence. David Merrick, the leading Broadway producer of the era, interviewed in the New York *Times* at the end of a 1973 season in which he scarcely participated at all, voiced his conviction that Broadway production will stabilize at about the present level. "I think things are improving now," he said, and he intends to come on strong next year with a play and two musicals.

Most would agree with Papp and Merrick that even with all its perplexing 1972-73 symptoms, the theater still looks like an art form for the millenia, adaptable, enduring, endlessly inventive. Even if we can't read all the signs clearly, at least we know that the New York theater is still in action, in motion, and we have a pretty clear idea of where it is bound. If it can live down its particular problems of urban blight, rising costs, artistic dichotomy, developmental encroachment and critical tyranny; if it can shake off all the minor afflictions of the age like traffic jams and power blackouts, then all that remains for it to do is merely to devise entertainments to fascinate and astonish not only its regulars—who have already seen everything the theater has been able to offer since the 1920s—but also attract audiences of a new generation which is bored with walking on the moon.

Ed Flanders, Jason Robards, *foreground,* and Colleen Dewhurst in the Broadway revival of *A Moon for the Misbegotten* by Eugene O'Neill.

PHOTO BY MARTHA SWOPE

1973-74

THE most indelicate theatrical season since Sodom and Gomorrah has left us wondering what the New York stage plans to do for an encore. In 1973–74 we saw a naked man mount a naked woman in a Broadway show, hardly a believable illusion, more like watching a third-rate magician attempt the Indian Rope Trick —success was clearly impossible. Off Broadway we saw a naked man pretend he was going to mount another naked man for an entire act (actors playing the French poets Verlaine and Rimbaud) in what was certainly the superlatively cathartic sequence of the year, though perhaps not for the first reason that comes to mind. It aroused real pity for the actors, not as characters but as human beings, for their defenseless and prolongued exposure in this impossible context.

In another Broadway session we saw a virile young man murder a handsome young woman and bear away her naked corpse to have his necrophiliac way with it offstage, in a rare instance of modesty if not of the highest behavioral standards. The human form was in conspicuous display all over town, even if it necessitated the intrusion of a spurious gesture like the violent baring of a lady's breasts in *When You Comin' Back, Red Ryder?* This sculptured asset was attractively showcased in *Ulysses in Nighttown,* but the image that the Joycean nightmare insisted on leaving with us wasn't the gentle curve of naked, reflective Fionnuala Flanagan as Molly Bloom. Oh no, it was, rather, this same lady's intimate contact with a chamber pot on the stage—and, finally, the androgynous side show of Swen Swenson costumed in black lace panties and black leather jock strap, heavily eye-shadowed and cracking a whip.

The 1973–74 season was blatant verbally as well as epidermically. The descriptions of male homosexual practises in *Find Your Way Home* and of child molestation in *Short Eyes* spared few sensibilities. The vital forces of these two Best Plays absorbed and transcended any shock in their subject matter, however. *Find Your Way Home* is a drama of love and loneliness, not sex, and *Short Eyes* is a drama of man's inhumanity to man, not perversion. The revival of *Ulysses* or David Rabe's new *Boom Boom Room* were earthbound to the sensationalism of their subject matter, but the Hopkins and Piñero plays easily lifted the weight of their physical imagery. So did *Creeps,* a sensitive script about prejudice against people who are "different" (in this case spastics), though it was anything but attractive in a filthy men's room setting, with all the concomitant action the place implies.

Add to all this the year's other immoderate conceits, such as the ballad about venereal disease in *Over Here!* and exploration of other dark corners of the human experience in the neuroses in *Bad Habits,* the cruel disillusionment in *Red Ryder* and the shame lurking under the urbanities of Noel Coward's *Song at Twilight,* and you have maybe the century's best prototype for the famous sarcastic Jerry Herman lyric "Oh, what a lovely theatrical season we've had!"

The reach and the grasp of Broadway seemed to diminish somewhat in 1973–74, but the volume of production repeated that of last season: 54 shows, including as "Broadway" offerings those offered under special contracts at the smaller Times Square theaters like the Bijou and the Little. Thus the dropoff from 84 productions in 1967–68, 76 in 1968–69, 68 in 1969–70, 56 in 1970–71, 56 in 1971–72 and 54 in 1972–73 seems to have bottomed out. It took a lot of revivals

The 1973–74 Season on Broadway

PLAYS (10)

Children of the Wind
Veronica's Room
Vivian Beaumont:
Boom Boom Room
What the Wine-Sellers Buy
SHORT EYES (transfer)
THE GOOD DOCTOR
Thieves
An American Millionaire
My Sister, My Sister
BAD HABITS (transfer)

MUSICALS (9)

Raisin
Molly
Gigi
Lorelei
Rainbow Jones
Sextet
Over Here!
Ride the Winds
The Magic Show

REVUES (1)

Good Evening

FOREIGN PLAYS IN ENGLISH (8)

Crown Matrimonial
Full Circle
The Au Pair Man
FIND YOUR WAY HOME
The Freedom of the City
NOEL COWARD IN TWO KEYS
My Fat Friend
JUMPERS

SPECIALTIES (7)

An Evening With Josephine Baker
Liza
Clarence Darrow
Music! Music!
Words and Music
Sammy
Will Rogers U.S.A.

REVIVALS (19)

Circle in the Square:
Uncle Vanya
The Waltz of the Toreadors
The Iceman Cometh
Scapino
The Desert Song
A Streetcar Named Desire
New Phoenix:
The Visit
Chemin de Fer
Holiday
The Pajama Game
City Center Company:
Three Sisters
The Beggar's Opera
Measure for Measure
Scapin
Next Time I'll Sing to You
A Moon for the Misbegotten
Candide (transfer
Ulysses in Nighttown
The Dance of Death

HOLDOVER SHOWS WHICH BECAME HITS DURING 1973–74

A Little Night Music
Sugar
The River Niger

Plays listed in CAPITAL LETTERS have been designated Best Plays of 1973–74.
Plays listed in *italics* were still running June 3, 1974.
Plays listed in **bold face type** were classified as hits in *Variety's* annual list of hits and flops published June 5, 1974 or judged likely to become hits

(19) to bring that 1973–74 total up to 54, however, as there was a marked drop in new American play production: from 16 last year to 10 this, from 13 musicals to nine. New foreign plays in English doubled from four last year to eight this, materially helping Broadway to make a season of it.

The worst attenuation continued to take place in the all-important matter of playing weeks (if ten shows play ten weeks, that's 100 playing weeks). According to *Variety's* figures, Broadway hit another new low in playing weeks in 1973–74 of 852, as compared with 878 or 889 (as variously reported) in 1972–73 and 1,092 in 1971–72, way off the 1960s plateau of 1,200 playing weeks. The total 52-week gross was up slightly according to *Variety's* figures, however, to $46,250,772 from less that $44 million last season, but way off the $52.3 million the previous year and the record $59 million in 1967–68. This increased Broadway gross may have occurred because of a slight increase in the proportion of more expensive shows to less expensive ones, or even maybe a small rise in attendance, but it wasn't because of a rise in the top ticket price, which hung in there for still another year at $15.

It was on the road, not on Broadway, that the most noticeable drop took place of more than $10 million, to a total 52-week 1973–74 gross of $45.3 million as compared with almost $56 million last year. *Variety* attributes this 18 per cent drop to "the dearth of multiple-company touring musicals such as *Hair* and *Godspell,* which bolstered the totals substantially in recent seasons." For that matter, almost the same could be said of Broadway itself, where the presence of three or four blockbusting musical holdovers brought crowds into the theater district and padded the totals for season after season in the 1960s.

The returns won't be in on this season's successes for a while yet (it takes longer than ever for a show to recoup its production cost), though *Lorelei* came to town trailing a golden $5 million gross from its long road stint, and the hit British revue *Good Evening,* with Peter Cook and Dudley Moore repeating some of the song and satire gems from *Beyond the Fringe* together with new sparklers, recouped before the snows melted and had reached the $40,000 profit mark on its $120,000 investment. Off Broadway, the success story of *El Grande de Coca-Cola* was writ large, but in relatively small numbers: 112 per cent profit on an initial investment of $30,000. Meanwhile, *Sleuth* finally closed after 1,222 cat-and-mousey performances and a profit of $1,700,000 on its $150,000 investment; *Pippin* was passing the $1,188,000 profit level; and Broadway's all-time longest-run show, *Fiddler on the Roof,* touring, reached $4,515,000 profit on its $375,000 investment, and still counting. In this connection, *Variety* published a summary of Harold Prince's record as the producer of 20 shows including *Fiddler* and *A Little Night Music* in 21 seasons. Prince has scored 11 hits in his 20 tries (and two of the others still have a chance to get into the black), for an 84.87 per cent return, or a net profit of $5,868,000 on a total investment of $6,915,000.

Bad news happens faster and is more quickly reported in *Variety's* estimates. Sixteen unsuccessful 1972–73 musicals had lost their backers a total of $6,150,000 when all was said and done and the last one, *Seesaw,* had finally gone on the road. This *succes d'estime* was figured as the most expensive of the 16, a $1,250,000 loss (a show can loose much more than its original investment by staying open and fighting a losing cause in the Broadway theater, where a near-hit can be something like a second-best hand in poker). *Variety* estimated that *Seesaw* lost $750,000 in addition to its production cost of $500,000. Losses on the unsuccessful 1973–74 musicals as reported by *Variety* amounted to $2,040,000 as of our press time, as follows: *The Desert Song* $200,000; *Rachael Lily Rosenbloom and Don't You Ever Forget It* (which closed in previews at the Broadhurst) $500,000; *Molly* $600,000 (on a $400,000 investment); *The Pajama Game* $300,000; *Gigi* $440,000. Still another failed musical, *Rainbow Jones*, closed after only one Broadway performance, with no estimate of its loss available.

Among the straight Broadway plays, what there was of them, *Children of the Wind* was the shortest-lived with only 6 performances. The most expensive failures according to *Variety* estimate, however, were *Boom Boom Room*, the David Rabe play that cost Joseph Papp's group an estimated $250,000 at Lincoln Center, *Full Circle* and *Crown Matrimonial* at deficits of $150,000, *Veronica's Room*, the Ira Levin thriller which ran a respectable 75 performances but dropped $125,000 of its $225,000 cost, and *Freedom of the City* at the $100,000 level. Off Broadway there were two plays and two musicals which came and went for only one performance each: *The Boy Who Came to Leave, The Indian Experience* and the musicals *Kaboum!* and *Pop* which went the way of their titles.

In this season which saw more revivals produced at the Broadway level than the combined Broadway total of American plays and musicals, there was heavy reliance on the strength of our acting establishment to carry the season along. It was fully justified in the performance. The vivid personal images were topped by Michael Moriarty as the hustler in *Find Your Way Home*, Jason Robards and Colleen Dewhurst as O'Neill's star-crossed lovers in *A Moon for the Misbegotten*, Lewis J. Stadlen's Dr. Pangloss in *Candide* and Julie Harris's threadbare queen in *The Au Pair Man*.

A director who scored twice this season was Harold Prince, who provided the year's top musical staging in *Candide* and also put on a notable revival of *The Visit* in New Phoenix repertory. Robert Moore was also doubly effective in musical and straight categories with *Lorelei* and *My Fat Friend*. Edwin Sherin added *Find Your Way Home* to his summer *King Lear*, and A.J. Antoon directed Simon and Strindberg.

Joseph Papp limited himself to two directing stints *(Boom Boom Room* and *As You Like It)*, but he was the busiest of producers as he took over the legit theaters at Lincoln Center in addition to his nest of theaters in the Public downtown and the action at the Delacorte in Central Park. Not counting workshop or experimental productions, Papp produced 15 shows during the 1973–74 season: three in Central Park, six at the Public Theater, four (not counting a transfer) at the Beaumont and two in the Newhouse (formerly the Forum). They weren't all good, but they all had a vitality, a thrust; and certainly Papp enjoyed his share of success this season with one Best Play, the Critics Award-winning *Short Eyes*, and several that came close, including *The Au Pair Man, What the Wine-Dealers Buy* and *The Killdeer*. No one who likes theater could fail to applaud Papp's energetic determination to lift the American theater out of its doldrums into the heavens, single-handed if necessary.

A little off-off-Broadway troupe under the artistic direction of Marshall W. Mason, The Circle Repertory Theater Company, was even more successful, or luckier, or whatever, in finding new scripts. They stole a big piece of the show last year with *The Hot l Baltimore* and an even bigger piece this year with *Red Ryder* and *Sea Horse*, first produced at the Circle Theater and subsequently elevated to commercial status. In the opinion of the *Best Plays* editor, they were certainly 1973–74's two best American scripts. Orin Lehman had a hand in the off-Broadway presentation of *The Sea Horse* (together with Kermit Bloomgarden and Max Allentuck), and he also produced *Creeps* off Broadway, so that together with Circle Repertory he has the distinction of producing two Best Plays this season.

What were the playwrights doing? Researching back alleys of the Casbah for ever more bizarre experiences to color their future work? Just sitting around waiting for better times? Well, a handful of them—Ira Levin, David Rabe, Neil Simon, Herb Gardner, Murray Schisgal—were hanging in there on Broadway, in each case with a script that was of more than passing interest, and the same was true of Terrence McNally, Mart Crowley, Arthur Laurents, Ed Bullins and a few others off Broadway. They helped keep the franchise for the American playwriting establishment at this dismal time when every empty theater presents a temptation for someone to tear it down for real estate development.

Where where the others? Well, Arthur Miller was teaching at Michigan, experimenting there with a new work in progress and adapting his *The Creation of the World and Other Business* into a musical called *Up From Creation,* apparently just for the hell of it. Tennessee Williams was experimenting off off Broadway and working on a new play for possible production by David Merrick (who was off somewhere making a movie). Edward Albee was teaching, experimenting with off-off-Broadway production and getting a new play ready. Sidney Kingsley and Jules Feiffer were trying to cast new scripts. Jerome Lawrence and Robert E. Lee were teaching, directing and writing books. Lanford Wilson was acting in an off-off-Broadway revival. Frank D. Gilroy and Robert Anderson were writing movies. Israel Horovitz was having the first of a nine-play series produced on regional stages.

On the Broadway musical stages it was much the same story. The shows that counted were more nostalgic than inventive. All leaned heavily on a well-remembered score, playscript or performance, and the major one that could be classified "original"—*Over Here!*—was the most nostalgic of all. The likes of *Raisin* and *Lorelei* helped keep audiences coming to Broadway, but the most inventive element of our proud Broadway musical theater in 1973–74 was the new staging of *Candide.* Off Broadway was the showcase for the most imaginative new musical material this year, with Al Carmines's *The Faggot.*

Where were our Broadway musical authors? Well, Stephen Sondheim and Burt Shevelove were staging their own idea of Aristophanes's *The Frogs* in the Yale swimming pool (and Sondheim wrote some new lyrics for *Candide*). Jerry Herman was working on *Mack and Mabel* for future production. Mary Rodgers and Sheldon Harnick did the score for a new Bil Baird marionette show, *Pinocchio.* Richard Rodgers, Jerry Bock, Tom Jones, Harvey Schmidt, Lee Adams, John Kander and all the others who could be mentioned were between shows, we must suppose. The stalwarts who put in an appearance with Broadway material included Jule Styne, Betty Comden, Adolph Green, Hugh Wheeler, Alan Jay Lerner, Frederick Loewe, Stephen Schwartz (and Sammy Cahn in person), and they deserve our applause both for the substance and value of their work and for helping to keep some of the streets lighted.

One of the reasons why so few ventured forth this season was that the dramatist's so-called "chance to fail" is shrinking fast in the modern commercial theater. It can be said that off off Broadway offers the American playwright his chance to succeed, as witness the progress of a *Red Ryder,* a *Sea Horse* or a *Short Eyes* as they evolve from the seething OOB embryo. The chance to fail is quite another matter, however. It is or should be a function of the commercial, not the experimental, theater, as important to its vitality and development as to the business of drilling oil wells: the established producer and dramatist's chance to fail in the center ring, in a full-scale commercial production with no effort spared, without causing irreparable damage to the financial or ego structures. Under modern pressures, this chance to fail has all but disappeared from Broadway and is fading fast off Broadway. What is left of it can be preserved only by means of at least partial subsidy (as in the case of David Rabe and *Boom Boom Room*)—subsidy either by an enlightened, arts-conscious public, or by setting aside a portion of the profits from commercial-theater hits, or both.

Broadway

The best of bests in this problematical year, all things considered, was a Broadway offering (albeit a foreign script), *Noel Coward in Two Keys,* an eight-year-old British program. Being the work of a master dramatist, it shrugged off its age as a matter of no consequence in a sparkling Richard Barr-Charles Woodward production which enjoyed the services of the original London director, Vivian Matalon. In the 1966 London production there were three plays divided into two evening's programs: *Shadows of the Evening* (about a terminally ill man determined to reconcile his wife and his mistress to the fact of his impending death, so that they could all get some fun out whatever time he had left); *Come Into the Garden Maud* (about the liberation of a henpecked American millionaire); and *A Song at Twilight* (about the previously hidden but now surfacing homosexuality of an internationally famous writer). On Broadway, the first was dropped and the third abridged slightly to make a single, also memorable, evening of Noel Coward in top form in the twilight of his own years, dwindling down to a precious few that ended with his death in Jamaica in March 1973. Coward played the male parts in London as Hume Cronyn did in New York. The characters have differing conflicts and personalities, but they are all men of distinction coping grandly with a climax in their lives, in an elegant Swiss hotel suite which was the same set for all three plays. In the two plays done in New York, Coward makes the direct statement that vanity and greed are eventually self-defeating (in *Maud*); and that in all forms of love, honesty is the best policy (in *Twilight*). The larger implication of the total program was even more striking. Coward's characters insist on maintaining standards of excellence even though all about them may be crumbling, and so did Coward as a playwright—standards of characterization, manner, wit, *mise-en-scene* and everything else that goes into an evening of theater. This is finished work with a high polish, of a kind all too seldom encountered on the stages of today. Hume Cronyn playing wide open as two husbands, Jessica Tandy as two wives—one selfish, the other managerial—and Anne Baxter as two intruders—one loving, one designing—served the play very well on the three points of Coward's triangles. *Noel Coward in Two Keys* (London title: *Suite in Three Keys*) was the last but certainly not the least of the now-treasured works in the canon of this great 20th-century playwright.

Easily the next-best of the year's Broadway productions was another script by an English author, John Hopkins, this one bearing down very firmly on the matter of homosexuality. This subject pained the characters in Coward's play; not so in Hopkins's *Find Your Way Home.* Here homosexuality is a matter of devouring involvement, with Michael Moriarty in a brilliant portrayal (the best male performance in a season of exceptionally good performances) of a young man who,

when suddenly suddenly deserted by his lover without explanation, was so agonizingly bereaved that he could ease the pain only by immolating himself in the
extreme degradations of a hustler. When his lover—a husband who finally decides
to leave his wife—returns as unexpectedly as he once left, the homosexual hustler
begins a long climb back from the pit into which he has sunk, toward some kind
of daylight. The dialogue of Hopkins's play is vividly (and to some, shockingly)
explicit about physical homosexual practises. His play is not so much about
homosexuality, however, as it is about love and the consequences of its depriva-
tion. It's obviously difficult for a playwright to deal objectively with such matters
—discussing, recriminating, threatening, surrendering—without resorting at
times to the literary tactics of soap opera (and commentators have been quick to
point out that Hopkins is an experienced TV writer). For the most part, however,
the English author of *Find Your Way Home* kept his play from being spoiled by
this taint, in a forthright script which had its world premiere in this New York
production.

Still another British play imported to Broadway made its way onto the Best
Plays list: Tom Stoppard's *Jumpers* which may turn out some day to be the play
of the decade if someone finds a way to communicate to an audience the full depth
and breadth of its witticisms and conundrums on the subject of God, the universe
and the true meaning and value of human life on earth. When in the last scene
the heroine, a neurotic but appealing musical comedy star, sings the deceptively
simplistic lyric line "Two and two make roughly four," this is a staggeringly
comprehensive philosophical observation which can be appreciated only if the
listener has noted and understood clearly the meaning of all the verbal stunts
which have gone before in Stoppard's scintillating but difficult play.

The problem is that in this production *Jumpers* never seemed clear about
anything, in particular 1) whether it really wanted to be a play at all and 2) if
so, what kind of a play it wanted to be. On the surface it showed itself an
extremely loose-jointed absurdist farce collected in setpieces unrelated in style, or,
apparently, any sort of useful "plot". There was a nugget hidden in each and every
segment, however, in a play that dares greatly and is great or nothing. The
"jumpers" of the title are acrobats, college professors who are also gymnasts, to
make a kind of running pun of mental and physical agility. A murder takes place
in the first scene and the corpse keeps bobbing up. Sportive sex also breaks out
here and there, but the heart of the matter lies in the philosophical dissertations
of a logician (Brian Bedford) preparing to debate the existence of God, and in the
distressed cries of his wife, the singing star, protesting that astronauts have robbed
the moon of its Juneyness. The sheer joyous acrobatics of Stoppard's language
invite comparison with a Coward or a Wilde. Bedford's interpretation was perfect, combining as it did a meticulous articulation with an absent-minded-profes-
sor appearance and manner. The Stoppard-Bedford combination worked well
enough in this New York (via Washington) production to whet the appetite for
a fuller realization of the entire play some day, if indeed that is possible.

If there was any large mass of solid worth in this Broadway season, it was the
group of attractive foreign plays lined up behind the three foregoing. First there
was Royce Ryton's *Crown Matrimonial,* the abdication of Edward VIII (played
by George Grizzard) as witnessed from the point of view of Queen Mary and
others in her drawing room. This British script was somewhat bloodless, not
being able to introduce the key character of Wallis Warfield into the exclusively
royal circle, but it came to life in a scene depicting the distress of the Duke and
Duchess of York (Patrick Horgan and Ruth Hunt) upon learning that duty would

call them away from their private family life to sit on the uncomfortable throne. Another British script, Charles Laurence's *My Fat Friend,* was a platform on which to display the entertaining performances of Lynn Redgrave as a compulsive eater nevertheless determined to lose weight for love's sake, George Rose as her middle-aged and devoutly homosexual boarder who urges her toward her heterosexual goal with fast friendship and an even faster wit, and John Lithgow as a young Scottish square, also a boarder, who does all the cooking and all the straight lines. Under Robert Moore's light directorial touch, these three provided a textbook example of soap-bubble entertainment.

Another foreign script adept at managing the flash and flow of language was Hugh Leonard's *The Au Pair Man,* with Julie Harris and Charles Durning as character symbols of British royalty declining in everything but pride, still served by loyal, subservient, but perhaps a bit restless Irish vigor. This two-character play took place in a set designed by John Conklin to symbolize British imperialism crumbling around the regal lady and her au pair man as they move through their intricate charade (for example, she is always seeking to borrow his pen, his literary tradition, to use as her own). It was a clever piece, acted as carefully as it was directed by Gerald Freedman, much the best of the 1973–74 plays originated at the Vivian Beaumont.

Two other imports were of a darker hue. Brian Friel's *The Freedom of the City,* set amidst the present Irish troubles, might have enjoyed a longer run in easier times. It searched deep inside the lives of three innocent victims of overzealous police action—two men and a woman who take refuge in the town hall during a Londonderry demonstration and are shot dead as they emerge, bewildered and unarmed. Friel uses a flashback technique he has used before (in *Lovers*) to shine the special lighting of hindsight on the ambitions and emotions of the living from the ironical vantage point of death. A special technique, equally ironic, was also useful to Peter Stone's adaptation of Erich Maria Remarque's play *Full Circle,* about the fall of Berlin in 1945. The play points to the similarity between totalitarian systems, Nazi and Communist, by emphasizing the identical nature of the last-gasp Gestapo actions in the early scenes and the first-blush-of-victory actions of the conquering Russians in the final scenes, with the identical actors playing the two sets of violent characters, wearing two sets of uniforms but a single set of values.

The best American play of the Broadway season was undoubtedly but not surprisingly Neil Simon's *The Good Doctor,* a collection of 11 sketches suggested by the life, career and stories of Anton Chekhov. Chekhov's point of view as a story-teller is what gives this program whatever unity it possesses, at it deals with one after another of the social and emotional characteristics of his highly class-conscious Russian society. It is Chekhov's sense of humor which Simon obviously admires most, and obviously there is no one better qualified to make the translation from printed page to an entertaining evening of theater, enhanced by Christopher Plummer's vigorous portrayal of the Russian writer, plus strong acting support in various roles by the entire ensemble: Rene Auberjonois, Barnard Hughes, Marsha Mason and Frances Sternhagen. Other embellishments were a concert of atmosphere-establishing music and songs written for the play by Peter Link (with lyrics by Neil Simon) and a colorful and versatile Tony Walton set. In *The Good Doctor,* Simon wasn't exactly writing a play in the fullest sense of the word, but he kept a curtain up on 1973–74 Broadway to excellent advantage and lengthened his incredible chain of successes.

Herb Gardner's *Thieves* was also a series of episodes, comments on life today in harried New York City, strung together on a thread of a plot about a young wife (Marlo Thomas) who is considering getting both an abortion and a divorce. Even in 1970s New York it is fairly obvious how that little difficulty is likely to be resolved; meanwhile Gardner does his thing in arresting monologues like that of the brother in his *A Thousand Clowns* and of the hot dog stand operator in his *The Goodbye People.* Here in *Thieves* it is the young wife's father, a cab driver played to the hilt by Irwin Corey, who pours out a parent's ultimate position statement on married daughters who contemplate abortions; and there's also a fumbling tramp (William Hickey) who talks to himself a lot about the difficulty of working up some kind of specialty which will bring him success in his chosen occupation: panhandling. *Thieves* was constructed like a string of beads; it was the baubles that counted for something, not the connections.

Ira Levin's *Veronica's Room* was the year's best-made American play to reach Broadway. This was a melodrama about a heroine's visit to a strange, gloomy mansion whose occupants (Arthur Kennedy and Eileen Heckart) aren't the friendly fatherly and motherly couple they at first seem to be. It was a melodrama with a difference, however, in that our foolhardy heroine (Regina Baff) does *not* escape the clutches of the villains, and it turns out that their deeds are motivated by a variety of dark perversions—which may have confused some but surprised nobody in this season of 1973–74. The old couple, it turns out, are an incestuous brother and sister who have produced a necrophiliac offspring upon whom they dote, in an atmosphere so noxious that murder seems almost a cleansing act. With Ellis Rabb directing a fine cast (whose fourth member was Kipp Osborne as the son), *Veronica's Room* was a raw, red helping of evil served up for the pure flavor of it.

Still another well-made American play, Ron Milner's *What the Wine-Sellers Buy* produced on Joseph Papp's Lincoln Center schedule, dramatized the dilemma of a black youth at the crossroads: shall he choose the strait, narrow and seemingly hopelessly, permanently deprived path of righteousness his good mother has taught him to take, or shall he listen to the blandishments of the flashy, high-heeled and well-heeled pusher next door and go for the bread, even if he must pimp his own fiancee to get it? Dick A. Williams made the most of the dope peddler—in a key of never-failing amusement at the ease with which evil seems always to get the upper hand—under Michael Schultz's careful direction. With this effective slice-of-life drama; with *The Au Pair Man;* with A.J. Antoon's firmly-staged revival of *The Dance of Death;* with the transfer uptown of the Best Play *Short Eyes* following its acclaimed debut downtown at the Public Theater; and, yes, even with David Rabe's controversial new play *Boom Boom Room,* Joseph Papp's first season at the Vivian Beaumont was one of adventure for the Lincoln Center subscription audiences (and audiences who aren't adventurous don't belong at Papp productions). They said it couldn't be done, but Papp has done it; he brought the Beaumont into the mid-1970s, without any major sacrificing of standards downtown. The only feat Papp was unable to accomplish in 1973–74 was dominate his rivals with a single, towering piece of theater as he has done in the past (though at least he won a Critics Award with *Short Eyes*). Rabe's *Boom Boom Room* was supposed to be that piece of theater, and there is disappointment only, not dishonor, in its failure to live up to great expectations. A random account of how a go-go dancer became entrapped in life and in her unrewarding profession, with sharp flavorings of promiscuity, incest, homosexuality, etc., etc., this play set out to explore some rugged terrain of human experience, apparently without the proper equipment, the emotional experience and/or insight, to accomplish its mission. Any idea of Rabe's is obviously worth trying onstage, however, and the only unworthy element of the whole experiment was the public outcry raised by Papp over Clive Barnes's put-down review in the New York *Times*. What should be borne in mind through such trying episodes is that Rabe will write another play; Papp and Barnes, each an adept in his own field, will continue to live eyeball-to-eyeball; and maybe the next time out everyone will cover himself with exceptional distinction.

Other American playwrights who ventured Broadway this season with less than happy results were Jerry Devine with *Children of the Wind,* a dark show-biz drama about an actor attempting a comeback, and Murray Schisgal with *An American Millionaire,* a black farce about violence, affluence and assorted hapless maladies of our time. On the fringe of Broadway at the Little Theater appeared Ray Aranha's *My Sister, My Sister,* a play about a black woman growing up in the white-dominated South of the 1950s, in a series of sensitized episodes flashing backward and forward over her life. This play was first produced in regional theater by the Hartford, Conn., Stage Company and made its way to 44th Street via an off-off-Broadway tryout at U.R.G.E.N.T., in the feeder mechanism which is becoming so important to today's theater.

The dropoff in new Broadway musical production from 13 in 1973 to nine this year was matched by a drop in voltage. Revivals have loomed over the musical stage in recent seasons, but in each year there was at least one new work with greater stature than the old: *No, No, Nanette* had its *Follies* and *Irene* its *A Little Night Music.* This season, however, there was nothing new on Broadway that could stand up to the revival of *Candide. Over Here!* came the closest, though its concept was so nostalgic that it certainly *seemed* like a revival. It provided a vehicle for a Broadway appearance of the two surviving Andrews Sisters, Maxene and Patty, with a Will Holt book about World War II G.I.s to be trained and entertained, and a Richard M.-Robert B. Sherman score to entertain them. Patricia Birch's dances were an amusing evocation of the jitterbug era, with Samuel E. Wright, John Mineo and Ann Reinking most notably putting the choreography into action. The show also had a "big band" in full view of the stage, and it had Janie Sell acting out its musical comedy version of a Nazi spy and finally providing a third note of harmony in the Andrews Sisters' song numbers. These two great performers sang up a storm on Broadway, including what they called a "third act," with the Andrews Sisters stepping out of character and doing a medley of their old hits after the last line of the book was finally out of the way, nostalgically evocative of that rhythmic and harmonic perfection once attained by adding the now-stilled voice of LaVerne. *Over Here!* was warm, it was fun in an undemanding sort of way, but hardly a flagship show for an entire Broadway season.

Raisin, the Tony Award winner, also had its moments in a Robert Nemiroff-Charlotte Zalzberg-Judd Woldin-Robert Brittan musical rendition of Lorraine Hansberry's prizewinning play *A Raisin in the Sun,* about a black family upwardly mobile in the Chicago of the 1950s. Virginia Capers as a loving and understanding mother and grandmother and Ralph Carter as the child of the family came on with particularly engaging performances. Performance was the thing in *Lorelei,* too, as Carol Channing returned to town in the justly famous person of Lorelei Lee. Subtitled "Gentlemen Still Prefer Blondes," this show goes back to Lorelei as a widow "remembering" some of her 1920s *Gentlemen Prefer*

Blondes adventures, almost a revival but not quite with its four new numbers by Jule Styne, new lyrics by Betty Comden and Adolph Green and new book material by Kenny Solms and Gail Parent. Another old-fashioned concept cloaked with some novelty on the musical stage this season was *The Magic Show*, an effort to set the amazing feats of an accomplished illusionist (Doug Henning) within the context of a Broadway musical. It was a good try, with lively, contemporaneous Stephen Schwartz musical numbers and fantastically adept acts of "magic" by its star, but it suffered from that old infirmity, book trouble.

Two other old friends, *Gigi* and *Molly* found Broadway less hospitable. *Gigi* was an adequate stage adaptation by Alan Jay Lerner and Frederick Loewe of their hit movie musical, with Alfred Drake impeccable in the Maurice Chevalier role, but stage audiences responded less than enthusiastically to its live presence in their midst. Likewise the effort to transpose Molly Goldberg to the musical stage, with Kay Ballard in the role created and made famous in every entertainment medium by Gertrude Berg, met with little success. The same was true, alas, in the case of *Ride the Winds,* with John Driver music, lyrics and book about an 11th century Samurai, on view for only 3 performances. And finally on the 1974 musical scene, intricate sexual pairings did not help *Sextet* nor animal fantasies rescue *Rainbow Jones* down on the bottom of this all too meager heap.

The 1973–74 Broadway specialty list included *Music! Music!,* a tuneful cavalcade of American music from late 19th century New Orleans jazz to rock 'n' roll, number upon number of old favorites staged by Martin Charnin with footnotes by Alan Jay Lerner. Also prominent in this category were the previously-mentioned semi-concert appearances of Josephine Baker, Liza Minnelli, Sammy Davis Jr. and Sammy Cahn (and it's getting harder and harder to draw the fine line of definition between a Broadway solo "show" and a concert which happens to take place in a Broadway theater. The Tony Awards committee reached across that line to hand a special award to Bette Midler for playing the Palace in what was styled, reviewed and has to be categorized as a concert rather than a Broadway show.)

There were no such reservations about still another solo, Henry Fonda's appearance as Clarence Darrow in a one-man show billed as "a play by David W. Rintels." Fonda evoked the personality of this dynamic lawyer who dared mightily and could laugh at his own shortcomings. The performance seemed so smoothly accomplished, so effortlessly and at the same time perfectly done, that the star's physical collapse which ended the show's Broadway run came as a surprise as well as a sorrow. Star and playwright were capable of calling up in the audience's imagination many of the characters to whom or about whom Darrow was speaking when he wasn't addressing the audience directly: defendants, plaintiffs, judges, juries, even wives. *Clarence Darrow* was well conceived, well acted and crisply directed by John Houseman, one of the year's most satisfying entertainments. In another specialized performance, James Whitmore portrayed Will Rogers in a one-man show adapted and staged by Paul Shyre, dropping in on Broadway following a long cross-country tour.

Revivals

An enormous proportion of the 1973–74 New York theater's effectiveness was achieved under the heading of revivals. Broadway's biggest straight-play hit was a revival: the superb Jose Quintero staging of Eugene O'Neill's *A Moon for the*

Misbegotten showering credit on all participants including Colleen Dewhurst in an earth-mother portrayal of Josie Hogan—easily the best starring female performance of the year—and Jason Robards as James Tyrone Jr. in an equally telling performance which was as near to the year's best as makes very little difference, with Ed Flanders in powerful support as Phil Hogan. Not since *That Championship Season* (which closed this year after 844 performances) has a drama established itself as a sellout hit on Broadway, and very seldom has a revival achieved such status without the presence of an overwhelmingly popular star; still less a revival of a play whose emotional tensions can be summed up under the pejorative contemporary meaning of the word "heavy" and which wound up its original 68-performance run with only an indifferent reputation as a second-rate item in O'Neill's first-rate canon. Then along came Quintero to change this duckling into a swan of swans.

But this was that kind of a season for revivals. The most popular Broadway musical, too, was a revival: *Candide,* the 1956 Leonard Bernstein-Lillian Hellman-Richard Wilbur musical which has built up more renown over the intervening years with its original cast recording than it ever did in its 73-performance first run on Broadway. This year it reappeared with a new book by Hugh Wheeler adapted from the Voltaire work and added lyrics by Stephen Sondheim and John Latouche, all restaged with the golden touch of Harold Prince. This revamped *Candide* was first tried out off Broadway at Chelsea Theater Center in Brooklyn, then moved to Broadway as the musical of the year. It still is as it was in 1956 (when it was named a Best Play of its season) a musically and verbally sophisticated satire on concepts of good and evil in human affairs—the "newness" of the 1974 *Candide* is more conceptual than spiritual. The book covers about the same ground, taking Candide through his episodes of adventure, from gullible pupil of Dr. Pangloss ("All for the best in the best of all possible worlds") to disillusioned but still hopeful man of the world ready to shed pretension and concentrate on making his own little garden grow.

Lewis J. Stadlen, the Groucho Marx of *Minnie's* and the nephew of *The Sunshine Boys,* was perfect as Dr. Pangloss and other dryasdust pontificaters, in the year's top musical performance. Mark Baker as Candide was somewhat more effective and Maureen Brennan as Cunegonde less so than the players in the original production, winning one and losing one in the comparison. Physically, this *Candide* concept was volatile, with the action taking place all over the auditorium (including sometimes its ceiling) and with the spectators seated in clumps all over the place, some of them in direct contact with the action. The show adapted itself to last year's radical physical alterations of the Broadway Theater for and by *Dude,* so that some good can be said to have finally come out of that debacle. If they don't tear down the Broadway, it is now a handy tool for shaping a new kind of theater, a sort of architectural blendor capable of stirring the performers and the audience together in one great intermingled unit of experience, as in this resounding *Candide.*

Another conspicuous Broadway revival was *Ulysses in Nighttown,* a segment of James Joyce's masterpiece dramatized by the late Marjorie Barkentin for off-Broadway presentation in the 1958–59 season and now remounted on Broadway with Zero Mostel playing Leopold Bloom as he did in the first production. As I indicated in the opening paragraphs of this report, I found it more vulgar than effective (except in the quality of performance and design, most notably the costumes by Pearl Somner). This play needed to soar to high reaches of imagination if its excursion into one man's overblown vision of a red light district was going to work on the stage. It was cruelly pulled back down to earth time after time, however, by grossly insensitive stress on the body's orifices and protuberances. If *Ulysses* is ever revived successfully, Zero Mostel may be the one to play it, but there has to be a better way to stage it.

The Circle in the Square began the 1973-74 season (which by tradition is dated from June 1) with a masterful revival of *Uncle Vanya* staged and co-adapted by Mike Nichols, with standout performances by Nicol Williamson as Voinitsky and George C. Scott as Astrov, designed by Tony Walton at the top of his form— the first and surely one of the best shows of the year. Circle in the Square followed with two more top-drawer revivals on its 1974 schedule: *The Waltz of the Toreadors* as interpreted by Anne Jackson and Eli Wallach under Brian Murray's direction, and *The Iceman Cometh* staged by the Circle's own Theodore Mann, with James Earl Jones a resonant Hickey. With programs such as these, it's almost incredible that Circle in the Square was brought to the edge of oblivion this season because of financial difficulties, which seem to be the common lot in this decade of our discontent and disorientation. As we went to press, the group was still the subject of much concern among theater folk but was equipped for the beginning, at least, of another season in 1975. They were enjoying an extra boost in both box office and prestige from their guest production from overseas, the Young Vic's popular *Scapino* with Jim Dale captivating Broadway audiences in the title role of this version of Molière's hardy farce, which had already made a hit off Broadway earlier in the season as a guest production at the Chelsea Theater Center.

Solidly mounted revivals of *A Streetcar Named Desire* (last year's Lincoln Center production restaged for downtown by Jules Irving) and *The Pajama Game* (staged and enhanced with some new material by George Abbott) ventured into the commercial fray of Broadway and emerged with honor but not much glory. An earlier effort to breathe life into *The Desert Song* seemed too little and too late, and its sister revival production of *The Student Prince* closed on the road.

The luck of the Broadway draw was much better in the organizational revival productions like those of New Phoenix with three treasures of the stage offered in repertory: Friedrich Duerrenmatt's *The Visit* directed by Harold Prince (a New Phoenix artistic director), Philip Barry's still-charming *Holiday* and Feydeau's *Chemin de Fer,* a fugue of flirtation expertly played by Rachel Roberts and the other members of the repertory ensemble under Stephen Porter's direction. Likewise, John Houseman's City Center Acting Company enjoyed a good season at the Billy Rose Theater with a versatile program of *Three Sisters, The Beggar's Opera, Measure for Measure, Scapin* (in a special performance for children) and *Next Time I'll Sing to You.* The difficult Shakespeare play was directed successfully by Houseman himself.

In case you weren't counting, that makes 19 Broadway revival productions in 1973-74, three more than last season even in this year of attenuated action in the large theaters. In the smaller ones, the story was the same. Off Broadway came up with 22 revivals, three more than last year. Shakespeare predominated in this area, with the productions last summer of *As You Like It,* the James Earl Jones *King Lear* and a return engagement of *Two Gentlemen of Verona* in Central Park at the Delacorte, and with innovative New York Shakespeare productions of *Troilus and Cressida* (staged as camp) and *The Tempest* in Lincoln Center's small theater, formerly the Forum, now renamed the Mitzi E. Newhouse Theater in recognition of its new namesake's thoughtful and bounteous patronage. (This group also put on *Macbeth,* but only as a workshop production.)

Shakespeare was also prominently on display in the offerings of four visiting English troupes imported by the Brooklyn Academy of Music in association with Brooklyn College, creating a series of cultural events that would have parted the waters of the East River to make way for theatergoers migrating to Brooklyn, were there not already a sufficiency of bridges and tunnels for this purpose. The first group of English visitors to the Academy's Opera House was the Royal Shakespeare Company with its production of *Richard II* under John Barton's direction, with Ian Richardson and Richard Pasco alternating as Richard and Bolingbroke who deposes him, as though to place double emphasis on the mutability of human affairs. In the Academy's smaller Leperq Space, three members of the British company performed a "new" work, *Sylvia Plath,* a stage arrangement and presentation of selections from that poet's writings.

The next group to fly the Union Jack over Brooklyn's cultural center was the two-year-old cooperative ensemble called the Actors Company playing the second *King Lear* of the season in repertory with a little-known Chekhov play *The Wood Demon, The Way of the World* and a novel and challenging program of verbal acrobatics called *Knots,* created by the Scottish philosopher R.D. Laing.

The third group to arrive in Brooklyn was the Young Vic with *The Taming of the Shrew* in repertory with their *Scapino* (which was later brought to Broadway by Circle in the Square) and Terence Rattigan's amusing bit of 1930s fluff *French Without Tears.* Finally there came to Brooklyn another Royal Shakespeare troupe headed by Michael Redgrave and Sara Kestelman in two remarkable anthology programs: *The Hollow Crown,* a compendium of writings and statements by kings and queens of England and about them by Shakespeare and other observers, which played once before in New York in 1963; and a brand new anthology, *Pleasure and Repentance,* a collection of writings about the ways of love from Sir Walter Raleigh up to and including the Beatles.

Our own leading off-Broadway troupe, the Roundabout Theater Company under the persistent and consistently able direction of Gene Feist and Michael Fried, presented New York with yet another busy, distinguished season. This was the group's longest year, beginning in early summer with Pinter's *The Caretaker* starring William Prince and continuing into April with W. Somerset Maugham's *The Circle* with Natalie Schafer, Christopher Hewett and David Atkinson. The three Roundabout programs in between were *Miss Julie* on a bill with the American premiere of a short French madame-and-butler farce called *The Death of Lord Chatterly,* by the French author Christopher Frank; another Strindberg, *The Father,* with Robert Lansing as the Captain; and a Chekhov, *The Seagull,* both the latter adapted by Feist, who directed all the programs except the double bill, which was directed by Henry Pillsbury. This worthy troupe, which has taken the word "Repertory" out of its name probably because it now schedules its programs seriatim, is to off Broadway what the New Phoenix and City Center are to Broadway itself, a going and active concern which does not always touch the heights with each production but does sometimes, and which maintains those standards of taste and performance which give New York theater its good name.

The straight-play revival hit of this off-Broadway season was *Moonchildren* by Michael Weller, a darkish comedy about 1960s undergraduates clinging to the last few weeks of the fantasy life they've created for themselves in their dormitory, with its special language and code of behavior, before being thrust out into what is clearly going to be a painfully cold world. This play was first produced on Broadway in 1972, the New York playwriting debut of its gifted author, but it survived only 16 performances—mostly because at that time audiences were fed up with hearing about the exploits of rebellious youth on every hand and were loath to expose themselves to it further, voluntarily, as entertainment. *Moonchildren* was named a Best Play of its season, though, and now it has become a solid commercial hit off Broadway, as directed by John Pasquin. Parenthetically, its author fared less well this season with a new effort to castigate Vietnam policies and events in the form of the musical *More Than You Deserve,* produced for a short run at the Public Theater.

Finally among this year's off-Broadway revivals, there were two productions at opposite ends of the stylistic scale: the Greek Art Theater's *Medea* and a return engagement of the revue *Jacques Brel Is Alive and Well and Living in Paris,* which already made off-Broadway history in its first run of 1,847 performances. The ever-increasing energy devoted to breathing new life into the theater's past is a flower in the thistle of the modern theater's environment.

Off Broadway

The nitty gritty of the contemporary New York theater's economic and artistic problems is exposed off Broadway, where costs have risen in multiples, not just percentages (it cost seven times as much to produce Mart Crowley's three-character *A Breeze From the Gulf* off Broadway in 1973–74 as it did to produce his nine-character *The Boys in the Band* in 1968, $70,000 vs. $10,000). The volume of off-Broadway production was bound to fall off this season, and it did: straight-play programs in English from 37 last season (and 52 the season before) to 35 this year; new American plays from 28 last year (and 43 the season before) to 27 this year; new musicals from 19 down to six. Revivals were up slightly, as previously noted, from 19 last season to 22 this year. The overall total of off-Broadway programming has been recorded in recent *Best Plays* volumes as follows: 119 in 1969–70, 95 in 1970–71, 87 in 1971–72, 87 in 1972–73 and 76 in 1973–74 (a steady decline, though the inference to be drawn isn't quite as simple and straight-lined at it looks at first glance, perhaps.)

Certainly there doesn't seem to be any parallel waning of artistic standards off Broadway. On the contrary, six of the 1973–74 Best Plays had their initial commercial-theater productions off Broadway, the largest number in the history of this 55-year old series: *The Contractor, When You Comin' Back, Red Ryder?, Creeps, Bad Habits, Short Eyes* and *The Sea Horse.* It is significant of the new era that two of these were pre-tested foreign scripts, two were transfers pre-tested off off Broadway in Circle Theater productions and a fifth was produced organizationally—that is, as part of the schedule of a semi-subsidized organization, rather than as an individual production standing on its own commercial feet. Of this year's half dozen Best Plays off Broadway, only one, *Bad Habits,* made it solo. There could hardly be a more persuasive illustration of the great value of experimental facilities to develop new works, either in the form of the off-off-Broadway work-in-progress production or under the umbrella of a subsidy.

Off Broadway's 1973 best-of-bests was *The Sea Horse,* the best American play of the whole New York year, a remarkably sensitive portrayal of a persistent wooing. She (Conchata Ferrell) is the owner-manager of a waterfront bar; built like a beer barrel and sleeps in the barroom loft, often alone. He (Edward J.

The 1973–74 Season off Broadway

PLAYS (27)

The Boy Who Came to Leave
Nellie Toole & Co.
Nourish the Beast (return engagement)
A Breeze From the Gulf
American Place:
  House Party
  Bread
A Festival of Short Plays
The Year of the Dragon
Public Theater:
  Lotta
  Barbary Shore
  Les Femmes Noires
  SHORT EYES
  The Killdeer
  The Enclave
  WHEN YOU COMIN' BACK, *RED RYDER?*
Felix
BAD HABITS
Ridiculous Theater:
  Hot Ice
  Camille
Negro Ensemble:
  The Great Macdaddy
  A Season-Within-a-Season:
    Black Sunlight
    Nowhere to Run, Nowhere to Hide
    Terraces
Heaven and Hell's Agreement
Once I Saw a Boy Laughing
THE SEA HORSE
A Look Back at Each Other

MUSICALS (6)

The Faggot
Antiques
More Than You Deserve
Fashion
Kaboom!
Pop

REVUES (3)

Sisters of Mercy
The Indian Experience
Let My People Come

FOREIGN PLAYS IN ENGLISH (8)

The Death of Lord Chatterly
Chelsea:
  THE CONTRACTOR
  Total Eclipse
  The Foursome
  CREEPS
Royal Shakespeare:
  Sylvia Plath
  Pleasure and Repentance
  Knots

FOREIGN-LANGUAGE PRODUCTIONS (2)

The Man From the East
Le Roi Se Meurt

REVIVALS (22)

Delacorte:
  As You Like It
  King Lear
  Two Gentlemen of Verona
Roundabout:
  The Caretaker
  Miss Julie
  The Father
  The Seagull
  The Circle
Candide
Medea
Moonchildren
Newhouse:
  Troilus and Cressida
  The Tempest
Royal Shakespeare:
  Richard II
  The Hollow Crown
Actors Company:
  The Wood Demon
  King Lear
  The Way of the World
Young Vic:
  The Taming of the Shrew
  Scapino
  French Without Tears
  Jacques Brel Is Alive and Well, etc.

SPECIALTIES (8)

Nicol Williamson's Late Show
I Love Thee Freely
Baird Marionettes:
  The Whistling Wizard, etc.
Pinocchio
Dear Nobody
I Am a Woman
The Wild Stunt Show
Ionescopade

Plays listed in CAPITAL LETTERS have been designated Best Plays of 1973–74.
Plays listed in *italics* were still running June 1, 1974.

Moore), a seaman with a flair for engines, and a stubborn wooer with an almost limitless supply of compassion, enjoys the lady's favors—such as they are—but is finally determined to persuade her to marry him and hack at least a thin portion of happiness out of their lives, if it takes him all night from closing time to opening time the next day (as it does). She has seen her beloved father killed by a drunken customer and has learned everything about how to survive and sometimes even enjoy herself, except how to love. He knows that their best hope lies in making a commitment to each other for better or worse, and he means to get "yes" for an answer even though it is like trying to milk a water buffalo; her skin is thick enough to resist all but the most pointed emotional penetration. His isn't, and this situation, plus the skill of the two actors and the Marshall W. Mason direction, provided a very full two acts of theater, even with only two people onstage. Mason is the artistic director of off off Broadway's Circle Repertory Theater Company, which launched last year's *The Hot l Baltimore* and this year's *Red Ryder* and *Sea Horse,* all transferred to commercial productions after their worth was proven at the Circle. *The Sea Horse* opened off Broadway as the work of one "James Irwin," which turned out to be a *nom de plume* for its co-star, Edward J. Moore, who had written the play as a vehicle for his own performance but didn't see fit to run double jeopardy as both actor and author. He succeeded admirably in both persons, reminding us that perhaps the good old practise of writing for specific actors, a la Shakespeare, Molière, etc., should be put to use more often in the modern theater.

The first of the Circle's two plays to graduate into the commercial theater this season and reach Best Play status was *When You Comin' Back, Red Ryder?,* another debut of a new American playwright, Mark Medoff (that new growth *will* continue to appear, no matter what), and another strong piece of conventionally styled playmaking. Red Ryder—the hero of a once-popular Western comic strip—ain't never comin' back to the pages of your local newspaper or anywhere else, the author is saying, nor is any other symbol of America's lost innocence in this era of disillusionment. Medoff's characters are collected in a third-rate diner in the Southwest, across the street from a motel just off the highway. Among them are a couple of dreamers (Bradford Dourif as the night man, still clinging to pieces of the Red Ryder ideal, and Elizabeth Sturges as a day waitress making the best of her sorry lot), a couple of doers (Robyn Goodman as a concert violinist and James Kiernan as her attendant husband) and a catalyst (Kevin Conway as a drug-smuggling bully who terrorizes all the others in the manner of *The Petrified Forest* and takes pleasure in smashing each and every one of their Red Ryder hopes and pretensions because he has long since lost the last vestige of his own). Bill Stabile's flyblown cafe set, Kenneth Frankel's direction and the performance of a closely-knit cast all contributed to the very great effectiveness of Medoff's play. Set in the late 1960s, *Red Ryder* might be summed up as the embitterment and self-destruction of one of the mid-1960s *Moonchildren,* a resolution which offers itself all the more readily because Conway was an unforgettable image in the Broadway production of the Michael Weller play.

A third off-Broadway Best Play by a new author was *Short Eyes,* which climbed the ladder all the way up in a single season. It began with an off-off-Broadway production by the Theater of the Riverside Church, then moved to off Broadway in its New York Shakespeare Festival production downtown at the Public Theater where it won considerable acclaim including the Drama Critics Award for the best American play of the year, and finally moved up to Broadway status when the Papp organization transferred it uptown to the Vivian Beaumont for an extended run. *Short Eyes* is a drama of life in prison, with inmates divided into three ethnic cliques—white, black and hispanic—living in close quarters in an uneasy truce. Their single point of agreement, of temporary solidarity, is their hatred of any child-molester, or "short eyes," who is an untouchable pariah in their tripartite society. This play was written by a former convict, Miguel Piñero, who was still on parole at the time of his play's opening. He cast his drama with members of a prison theater workshop called The Family, many of whose members continued to work together on the outside under the guidance of Marvin Felix Camillo, who brought them to Riverside as a resident company and directed *Short Eyes* on all its stages.

The bulk of the off-Broadway schedule downtown at the Public was exploratory, reaching, purposeful, never scaling as high a peak as *Short Eyes*, which could and should not be expected of a large production schedule of not-necessarily-finished work. There were new plays by Robert Montgomery (*Lotta*) and Jay Broad (*The Killdeer*, drawing a bead on a suburban Willie Loman); the Michael Weller-Jim Steinman musical *More Than You Deserve;* a Jack Gelber adaptation of Norman Mailer's *Barbary Shore*, a study of Marxism veneered with mystery drama; and *Les Femmes Noires*, details of the contemporary black experience in a script by Edgar White. The Joseph Papp organization did more than its share for the New York theater in 1973–74 and had its share of success, while establishing a powerful momentum of production all around the town.

A fourth American off-Broadway Best Play was the work of the distinguished professional Terrence McNally, who in his new comedy *Bad Habits* turned his laser beam onto the opposing forces of self-indulgence and self-denial. The medium for his message is the nursing home, in this case an unmatched pair of them, and the types of patients—alcoholics, eternal misfits, deviates, etc.—who might avail themselves of their services. Like two other of the year's Best Plays (*Noel Coward in Two Keys* and *The Good Doctor*), McNally's is a program of short plays, two one-acters set in sanatoria with opposite theories of treatment: in *Ravenswood* anything goes, patients are put on soothing high-cholesterol diets and encouraged to do and/or have their thing, whatever it may be; in *Dunelawn* nothing goes except a shot of tranquillizing drug which turns the most eccentric and difficult patients into identical vegetables. The two plays are a unit, however, in making their author's observation that in the long run it may perhaps be more bearable to suffer the consequences of, say, smoking than to suffer the dehumanizing frustration of not smoking (figuratively, not literally—as in other McNally comedies there is little to be learned about the taste of *Bad Habits* by studying the list of its ingredients). An ensemble juggled the eight extravagant characterizations in each play under the direction of Robert Drivas, who has starred in McNally plays in his time and is comfortable with the basically black-comic McNally style. At season's end *Bad Habits* moved to Broadway, but I am happy to have made its acquaintance in a smaller theater, with actors brushing by me up and down the aisle, in close contact with its pleasantly weird sense of values.

Chelsea Theater Center weighted its schedule with imports this season, most notably *The Contractor*, a 1970 play by David Storey, written the year before his Critics Award-winning *Home* but only now reaching New York in the Chelsea production which won the Critics Award for the best of bests in 1973–74. In this play as in his others, Storey distills the most acidulous implications from what appears to be the most watery of situations, as assorted workmen put up a marquee for the wedding party of their boss's daughter and then take it down again the day after the ceremony (the wedding party itself doesn't take place on stage, only the preparation and aftermath). Into this tiny frame Storey gets a huge chunk of the contemporary scene with its haves and have-nots, workers and drones, rough diamonds and smooth-polished obsidians. The contractor himself is the tent-pole character—it is his workmen, his tent, his daughter, an allegory of his life that is passing before his eyes as the marquee goes up and down. A major challenge of this play is to personify every member of a variegated company, and the acting ensemble under Barry Davis's direction, led by John Wardwell as the contractor, met the challenge admirably.

Candide, also a Critics Award-winner, was Chelsea's only American work on its 1973–74 schedule. One of its other imports was Christopher Hampton's *Total Eclipse,* a play about the strong attachment between the French poets Verlaine and Rimbaud in which the Messrs. Christopher Lloyd and Michael Finn played just about the whole second act naked in a succession of bedrooms (like *Candide, Total Eclipse* experimented with a multiplicity of acting areas interspersed with the audience seating, so that the action moved from place to place freely, in the style of a novel). Chelsea wound up its season going from the ridiculous to the ridiculous with *The Wild Stunt Show,* a zany topical revue which originated as a popular touring entertainment for London pubs and streets.

Another foreign script which made the Best Plays list in an off-Broadway production was *Creeps,* a study of nerve-damaged spastics written by a Canadian, David E. Freeman. *Creeps* was a hit and an award-winner in Toronto, after which it was produced in Washington, D.C. at the Folger Theater before its arrival in New York for an unfortunately short run of 15 performances. Its author is himself a cerebral palsy victim, but *Creeps* isn't about handicaps — its characters have pretty much learned to live with theirs. It's about prejudice, as a group of men with various muscle and speech infirmities gathers in the filthy washroom of a "sheltered workshop" for the handicapped to discuss their principal grievance: the so-called "normal" members of society, even the members of their own families, look on them as pariahs to be hidden away in the attic or in institutions. Once in a while they are permitted to become the objects of organized charity, but they are never to be treated as human beings or allowed to develop their own capacities in their own way. *Creeps* is a strong play by a gifted author who at this writing already has another hit in Canada. Once again we can report that it was very capably interpreted by another of those solid ensemble casts we've enjoyed this season, this one under the direction of Louis W. Scheeder.

Neither American Place nor the Negro Ensemble Company produced one of the Best Plays this season (though a 1973 NEC graduate, *The River Niger,* won the 1974 Tony), but they brought on some of the better off-Broadway offerings. The NEC's *The Great Macdaddy* was an imaginative musical parable of the black experience, with Macdaddy (David Downing) wandering across the U.S.A. looking for an old friend named Wine (Graham Brown) but generally finding nothing but trouble caused by villainous Scag (Al Freeman Jr.). It was a rare instance of a black Morality play in which Whitey is not the only evil. NEC simultaneously put on what it called *A Season-Within-a-Season,* a series of four new plays presented in limited rather than full-scale engagements.

American Place put on the new Ed Bullins, *House Party,* like so much of his recent work a series of vignettes or statements about the black experience as he witnesses it. In this case it was framed in the theater as a kind of night club show. The American Place schedule also included David Scott Milton's *Bread* and a one-act play program of scripts by William Hauptman, Lonnie Carter and Maria

Irene Fornes. The last and most effective of the organization's new-play programs was *The Year of the Dragon* by Frank Chin (author of *The Chickencoop China-man*), a study of two generations of a San Francisco Chinatown family, with a predictably bitter indictment of the restricted quality of life imposed on such a family by a combination of its own traditions and those of American society. In addition, American Place's production of last year's Steve Tesich family comedy *Baba Goya* returned for an off-Broadway run as an individual presentation at the Cherry Lane under the new title *Nourish the Beast*.

Charles Ludlam's well-established off-off-Broadway troupe, the Ridiculous Theater Company, surfaced in the commercial theater with the wild and woolly *Hot Ice*, a spoof of corpse-freezing, detective fiction and just about everything else in a putative theft-and-murder mystery written and direct by Ludlam and catering expertly to the special taste for theatrical camp. Ludlam ended his season by playing Camille in his own vision of the Alexandre Dumas play done by his company in their usual outlandish style.

After the phenomenal success a few seasons ago of his *The Boys in the Band,* Mart Crowley's second New York-produced play, *A Breeze From the Gulf,* aroused great expectations. They weren't entirely fulfilled by this too-introspective study of a boy's growing up with the burden of a boozy father and neurotic mother, even though the acting of the three characters by Robert Drivas, Ruth Ford and Scott McKay was first-rate. The greatest expectation of all was satisfied, however: *A Breeze From the Gulf* was a more than routinely interesting play by an author who turns out to be a new playwright in the full meaning of the word, not just a fluke of one-time success. Another more than routinely interesting off-Broadway script was *The Enclave* by the distinguished dramatist Arthur Laurents. The enclave of his title is a mews which a close-knit group of friends plans to renovate and settle as their own private little island in the sea of the city —until the group is suddenly fragmented under the blow of learning that one of them plans to come out of the closet as a homosexual and live openly in their midst with his lover. The New York production of *The Enclave* (following one last season at the Washington, D.C. Theater Club) included a Robert Randolph set ingeniously adaptable to all the various homes. An effort at ensemble performing didn't quite come off, however; the supposedly very strong rapport among these characters at the beginning of the play was never convincing.

Also on the list of off-Broadway's one-at-a-time productions in 1973–74 was E.A. Whitehead's play *The Foursome* about the battle of the sexes, imported for a short run. A Peter Keveson psychological thriller which had premiered in West Germany, *Nellie Toole & Co.,* was remarkable more for the offstage incident it provoked than for anything it developed onstage. The actress Sylvia Miles so resented John Simon's review that upon meeting him at a party a few days after the opening she anointed him with a plate of food.

Musical production was more satisfying off Broadway than on, even with the season's attenuated volume. The year's best musical, *The Faggot,* sprang to life out of the mind of Al Carmines, the regisseur of the Judson Poets' Theater, who wrote, directed and performed in the show both in its original off-off-Broadway phase and later as it graduated to a commercial production for a run of 182 performances. It was a series of comments on homosexuality aimed as humor, as pathos, as historical reference to such as Oscar Wilde and Catherine the Great, and, in its best sequence, as the emotional undercurrent in various modern situations. *The Faggot* was a show of strength for the musical theater, as Carmines brought poetry, melody and sympathy to his complex subject.

Off Broadway's other standout new musical was *Fashion,* based on the 19th Century comedy by Anna Cora Mowatt in an adaptation by Anthony Stimac (who also directed), with Don Pippin music and Steve Brown lyrics. This show was subtitled "A New Style Musical Comedy," and it was indeed a triumph of tongue-in-cheek style perfectly comprehended and performed by every member of the company in every corner of the production. The antique comedy is about a would-be lady of fashion whose financier husband has cooked his books in order to keep her in clothes and parties; she in her turn is easy prey for a bogus count and other designing persons. The heart of the joke in this version, though, is that the whole show is presented as a run-through by a modern Long Island ladies' dramatic society doing an early American script, with all the roles played by women except for the one male hired by the society to "direct" the show. *Fashion* had only one dimension of music played on a piano at the side of the stage, but it had an extra dimension of satire realized in such performances as Rhoda Butler's Snobson, the financier's scheming clerk, or Henrietta Valor's Trueman, a wealthy friend from the West who is a square shooter and figures heavily in the denouement (and it *was* a rich, ripe, 19th century-type denouement, not just an ending).

Off Broadway was dotted with outstanding specialty shows, too, throughout the season. No sooner had the *Uncle Vanya* revival established itself as a Broadway hit than one of its stars, Nicol Williamson, hired a small hall across town and performed nightly an after-theater mix of narrative poetry, songs and sketches under the title *Nicol Williamson's Late Show.* It was a popular success, as was Jane Marla Robbins's "one-woman play" about the noted 18th century wit, Fanny Burney, and those who moved through her world. Love letters of the Brownings were dramatized in *I Love Thee Freely,* and Viveca Lindfors brought in her one-woman program of sketches by and about women, *I Am a Woman,* for a limited engagement. The Bil Baird Marionette Theater opened a new hit for its repertory, a puppet musical version of *Pinocchio* created by an illustrious team of musical theater dramatists: Jerome Coopersmith (book), Mary Rodgers (music) and Sheldon Harnick (lyrics).

The foreign-language visitors this year were *The Man From the East,* a Japanese musical production of the Red Buddha Theater with a rock score by Stomu Yamash'ta, and the Tréteau production in French of Ionesco's *Exit the King.* There wasn't much to shout about in the category of off-Broadway revues, the one notable occurrence being the production of Earl Wilson Jr.'s *Let My People Come,* self-described as "A sexual musical," which opened in January at the Village Gate but steadfastly refused to formalize its existence and invite the critics to an opening night; instead, it merely allowed its "previews" to fade imperceptibly into a run.

If any single rung in a ladder can be said to be the most important, then surely off Broadway was the major rung in the ladder of legitimate stage production in 1973–74. It came up with six of the Best Plays and the best new musical. As an arena of experimental activity it was shrinking, but it was still able to provide a few of the theater's most distinguished artists with the opportunity to try out a *Candide* or a *Bad Habits* before committing them to the siege perilous of the Broadway showplace. It proved hospitable to imported, pre-tested scripts as well as to the work of new, scarcely-fledged American playwrights emerging from off off Broadway as from a hatching egg. Off Broadway's most conspicuous flaw, the rising cost of production, is shared by every other segment of the live performing arts, including, probably, the blind street minstrel who has to pay more these days for his dog's food. But off Broadway's 1973–74 honors were handsomely won, and deserve our enthusiastic applause.

Offstage

Along Broadway the principal subjects of conversation and concern were about the same as everywhere else: Watergate and finances. There wasn't anything much the theater could do about the former except discuss it, but a lot was done about financing in efforts to energize both the box office and the subsidy sources.

The season's major achievement in this area was TKTS, the ticket booth in Duffy Square which distributes unsold seats for same-day Broadway and off-Broadway offerings at half price plus a small service charge which goes to maintain the booth. This Times Square Theater Center was opened June 25, 1973 under the sponsorship of state and city agencies and the Theater Development Fund, which manages it. The booth was an instant success and soon was credited with handling a significant proportion of the New York commercial theater's weekly gross. By the end of 1974, *Variety* estimated, TKTS had distributed 409,886 tickets for gross receipts of $1,860,568—or about 4 per cent of the total gross during the time period covered by the estimate. A TDF survey conducted by William J. Baumol came to the conclusion that this TKTS business represented a net increase in the size of the theater's audience, drawing patrons who probably would not otherwise have bought theater tickets.

One prominent Broadway production, *The River Niger*, the eventual 1974 Tony winner, refused to participate in TKTS, twofers or any other plan to fill empty seats at cut-rate prices. The show closed in November and went on tour rather than trying to stay open in New York by means of the sales plans. Its management, the Negro Ensemble Company, is making a special effort to attract to the theater new audiences from the black community; and, as an NEC spokesman stated in *Variety*, the organization's artistic director, Douglas Turner Ward, made the decision not to offer cut-rate tickets because he felt that "selling individual tickets on a cut-rate basis to some, while haphazardly excluding others, constitutes a breach of faith with those who buy at regular prices." Mr. Ward had insisted that regular box office prices at *The River Niger* be as low as possible from the very beginning of its Broadway run. The NEC to the contrary notwithstanding, TKTS is proving to be a real boon to the theater at a very difficult time.

The National Endowment and the New York State Arts Council came through with proportionate shares of subsidy for the New York theater, the sums increasing in 1973–74 as they have in past years, but nowhere near as fast as the needs of those putting on live entertainment. A survey conducted in 1973 by a Louis Harris affiliate, the National Research Center of the Arts, estimates that about 64 per cent of American taxpayers would be willing to pay $5 extra annually to support the arts (the per capita Federal support is now averages out to less than 25 cents a year). If that 64 per cent handed out $5 apiece next year, it would amount—the survey estimated—to about $495.5 million, as compared with $60.7 million actually allotted to the National Endowment for fiscal 1974. New York State's allotment to arts subsidy is to be $34.1 million in 1974–75, more than double the $15 million distributed the previous year.

Among gimmicks dreamed up to stimulate theatergoing was the free taxi service offered by the long-run Micki Grant musical *Don't Bother Me, I Can't Cope*. Ticket purchasers from all New York City boroughs except Staten Island were offered a free taxi ride one way, either to the theater or home after the show. Staggering curtain times was another means of catering to the customers (some like them early, some like them late). A new agreement with the stagehands permits the curtain to be raised at any hour, so long as it comes down before 11:30. As a general rule in 1973–74 the Broadway straight plays moved their curtains back to 8 p.m., while the musicals held to 7:30.

The legitimate playhouses themselves were a focus of rising concern in 1973–74. One of them—the versatile and useful Mercer Arts Center—suffered physical collapse in August when its Siamese twin, the Broadway Central Hotel, fell down. The theater complex had to be abandoned by the four off-Broadway shows then playing therein (*One Flew Over the Cuckoo's Nest, El Grande de Coca-Cola, The Proposition* and *Tubstrip,* which previewed for a while but never formally opened). The knowledge that theaters were crumbling downtown was not much eased by the thought that new ones were a-building uptown. The new Uris, Circle in the Square and Minskoff Theaters have proved usable but never quite comfortable for their inhabitants. The Uris is cavernously hard to fill even with a musical and may commit itself mostly to dance and concert productions next season. The Circle in the Square, too, is overlarge for the theater-in-the-round concept of its design. The approach to the Minskoff's auditorium is dominated through hugh glass windows by Broadway advertising displays, which have never been noted for their good taste; and its stage floor proved too rigid for dancers (alterations were made to correct this during a week's layoff of its incumbent *Irene*).

The deepest concern, though, was reserved for the encroachment of real estate interests into the Times Square area, threatening its glamor, prestige and very survival as an oasis of entertainment, of human architectural scale, of contemplative design in the midst of a broadening desert of uninteresting, intrusive, steel and glass monster office buildings. The announcement in the summer of 1973 that a planned 54-story, block-long hotel-office-store complex will further intrude on the theater district turned threat into dismal reality. This monster tower is to displace the Morosco on 45th Street and the Helen Hayes on 46th Street (and not incidentally the Bijou and Victoria Theaters and the Piccadilly Hotel). The Morosco (in bad repair) and the Hayes (with an obsolete balcony structure) are hard to defend except on the urgent general principle that the American theater needs an inviolate district in New York.

Among theater organizations busy doing their thing in 1973–74 was Actors Equity, which added new impetus to the commercialization of the off-Broadway theater—with all the attendant cost/price problems which that entails—by pressing the League of off-Broadway Theaters and Producers for a jump in actors' wages during early winter negotiations for a new three-year contract. Equity, cognizant of the profits which can accrue to a big off-Broadway hit, was asking for a $12.50 weekly raise in each of the three years of the contract (the previous off-Broadway actor's minimum was $125 to $200 weekly, depending on box office receipts). The managers, cognizant of the tremendous odds against achieving hit status today off Broadway and the rising cost of production sapping off Broadway's strength of experimentation, stood firm enough so that a strike almost took place. It was avoided when both sides agreed to submit the matter to binding arbitration, which decided on a minimum sliding from $127.50 to $175 over the three years, graduated upward to $210 to $245 when the box office receipts of an off-Broadway show reach $13,000 weekly—at which point the off Broadway and Broadway actors' minimum become equal. In another part of its thickening forest, Equity established dinner-theater weekly acting minimums of $136 to

$176. As for off off Broadway and Equity, Edward Albee delivered the word to a Drama Desk discussion meeting also attended by Donald Grody, Equity's executive secretary: "Leave us alone . . . ignore us . . . make out we don't exist. Just leave us alone." And, just after the end of the season, Equity came to a new agreement with the League for Broadway minimums rising to $285 in three years (and scaled from $347.50 to $395 on tour).

Richard Watts Jr., distinguished drama critic of the New York *Post*, announced his retirement following the end of the 1973–74 season. Watts pioneered movie criticism beginning in 1924 on the *Tribune*. He succeeded Percy Hammond as drama critic of the *Herald Tribune* in 1936. After serving in missions to Dublin and China in World War II, he joined the *Post* as drama critic in 1946, continuously sustaining his well-deserved reputation as one of the leading critics of his generation. He will continue to write a column for the *Post* but will pass along the daily reviewing chore.

Notable celebrations this season included the dedication of a room in the New York Public Library's theater collection at Lincoln Center to the distinguished actress Katharine Cornell and her husband Guthrie McClintic. Miss Cornell, whose last stage appearance was in *Dear Liar* in 1961, was too ill to attend the April 24 event (she died soon afterward at her home at Martha's Vineyard). Many other notables were present, however, at the dedication of this large reading room featuring displays of Cornell-McClintic memorabilia. George Gershwin, too, was celebrated in all kinds of observances of the 75th anniversary of his birth—Sept. 26, 1973—including concerts, sing-alongs, exhibitions, a Gershwin stamp, special record albums and five books.

That's how it went in the New York theater of 1973–74. We are almost half a century removed from the peak years of the mid-1920s when there were more than 200 Broadway shows annually; a quarter of a century removed from the booking jams, ticket-icing, etc. of the 100-plus show years at the turn of the mid-century. Here in the 1970s Broadway production has attenuated to barely 50, including only eight new American plays, like the tip of a south-drifting iceberg melting in the hotter and hotter sun.

What we should bear in mind is that half a century ago there was no bottom to the iceberg worth mentioning; no great mass of theater activity hidden under the glitter of Broadway. If the stage's tip has shrunk by one-half or three quarters, its hidden mass has grown hugely, until now there is in New York City within any 12 months a volume of legitimate stage activity that includes hundreds and hundreds and hundreds of "productions" off off Broadway in numbers that would have been unimagineable by any theatergoer of the 1920s. Granted, our commercial managers are bearing greater and greater financial burdens, and for some reason our better-known dramatists seem to have taken the year off in 1973–74. But if ever an iceberg was ready with hidden substance to rise and replace its melting tip, our theater is. If ever it held promise, it is now.

1987 PERSPECTIVE: Why did the season of 1971-72 seem so especially "gray" when it came up with "That Championship Season," "Sticks and Bones," "Vivat! Vivat Regina!", a new Neil Simon, a new Tennessee Williams, a new Terrence McNally, a new Harold Pinter, as well as "Jesus Christ Superstar" and "Grease"?

You had to be there. Politically (the Vietnam War), economically (stag-

flation, with rising costs impacting even off Broadway), esthetically (style and audience fragmentation that wasn't going away), sociologically (culture shock and danger in the streets) and physically (a sparsely lit and thinly attended Broadway area), the atmosphere was dreary. It really seemed that the theater was sliding uncherished into a dark age, with the exceptional show a mere flash of heat lightning. Even the good old word "hit" had lost its glamor as well as its effectiveness as a measure of success, now attained not by immediate Broadway popularity but by longer-range attributes like cross-country production and TV or movie action.

As far as I could tell, it was new, determined leadership like Gerald Schoenfeld's at The Shubert Organization, plus Alexander H. Cohen's persistence in glorifying a faltering Broadway with the Tony Awards show on national TV, that turned things around. Certainly it wasn't that producers became more adventurous, or playwrights more inspired, or tickets and costs any cheaper, or the audience more uniformly responsive, or theatergoing any more comfortable, with theater owners jamming in ever smaller and more uncomfortable seats and to-and-fro transportation becoming ever more problematical. But Mr. Schoenfeld and Mr. Cohen behaved as though they had inherited a seamless mantle of showmanship, insisted that others in their vicinity behave likewise, spruced up the place, encouraged shows like "Grease," "Pippin" and "The Wiz" to attract the young and other new audiences and managed to set an example that reversed Broadway's downslide and even started the whole city feeling a little better about itself.

Wishful thinking, we see clearly in perspective, didn't make anything so; it didn't bring about a major subsidy program for the New York theater (which may be the only live performing art in the world that's still expected to pay its own way). It didn't follow through on Joseph Papp's suggestion for a national theater, or on Broadway's "middle theater" program. It didn't solve the problems of Lincoln Center or make an international hit out of the space musical "Via Galactica" which I STILL believe has great possibilities.

Anyhow, it wasn't wishful thinking that turned Hyde into Jekyll or revivified the theater. It was a mysterious potion of two parts effort and one part faith, garnished with courage and set to bubbling with a dash of inspiration — and in the 1970s on Broadway, it worked.

O.L.G. Jr.

PART III:
THE LATE SEVENTIES

Jack Lemmon in *Tribute*

Ellen Burstyn and Charles Grodin in *Same Time, Next Year* by
Bernard Slade.

1974-75

THE fabulous invalid sat up and roared this season. The mood on Broadway changed 180 degrees from apathy to excitement. Perhaps there were a few too many more shows than hits, and perhaps audiences turned out in greater abundance than shows good enough to satisfy them. But when all was said and done and the 1974–75 New York theater season an accomplished fact, there was a consensus—more of a *feeling*, really—that a current of energy had suddenly been turned on.

Only a year ago, the show business newspaper *Variety* was dismissing the 1973–74 theater year with words like "dismaying," "a national invalid," "slump" (off 9.15 per cent), "discouraging" and "grim." By mid-season of 1974–75, *Variety's* tune had changed right around from dirge to triumphal march, now resorting to such phrases as "prairie fire," "the box office went wild" (up 25 per cent) and finally just plain "wow!" to sum up Broadway activity.

Asked to comment on the season's quality for better or for worse, leading New York theater spokesmen repeatedly cited the brightening mood ("The sense of excitement"—Anna E. Crouse, president of the Theater Development Fund; "The resurgence of interest on the part of the audience; the general awareness that the theater is still an active and powerful force"—Dore Schary, former New York City cultural commissioner). Their only reservations were the same old headaches that have plagued the so-called invalid for years: the scarcity of new works by American dramatists ("While we all appreciate the high-subsidized imports from England, many of them superb, I would prefer that kind of subsidized effort to come from the various theaters and organizations around our own country"— Richard Barr, president of the League of New York Theaters) and the commercial theater's special, insidious economic strictures ("Some of the most worthy shows don't do business"—Stephen Sondheim, president of the Dramatists Guild; "We still seem to be in a hit-or-flop economy"—Richard Lewine, vice president of the Dramatists Guild).

When the dust cleared we looked back on a Broadway year dominated by British scripts at the box office but not in numbers on the Best Plays list; on an off-Broadway year that staggered toward a dismal foregone conclusion like the dinosaurs in *Fantasia* and then came suddenly to life and began doing handsprings in the final couple of months.

The foreign works ran one-two-three in the New York Drama Critics Circle voting for best of bests: *Equus* by Peter Shaffer the winner, *The Island* by Athol Fugard, John Kani and Winston Ntshona the runner-up, with the other of the year's foreign Best Plays, Peter Nichols's *The National Health,* coming in third. The four American Broadway plays on our Best list were Edward Albee's *Seascape* (the 1975 Pulitzer Prize winner), the American playwriting debut of Canadian-born Bernard Slade with the smash hit comedy *Same Time, Next Year,* plus new works by a pair of the American theater's leading authors: Murray Schisgal with *All Over Town* and Terrence McNally with *The Ritz.*

Most of Broadway's 1974–75 musicals were a bit overripe, and off Broadway stole the musical show in the last two weeks of the season with *A Chorus Line*

The 1974–75 Season on Broadway

PLAYS (18)

Medea and Jason
Dreyfus in Rehearsal
Vivian Beaumont:
 Mert & Phil
 Black Picture Show
 Little Black Sheep
Tubstrip
Mourning Pictures
Fame
Who's Who in Hell
God's Favorite
ALL OVER TOWN
The Hashish Club
THE RITZ
SEASCAPE
SAME TIME, NEXT YEAR
Don't Call Back
We Interrupt This
 Program . . .
P.S. Your Cat Is Dead

MUSICALS (9)

Mack & Mabel
Sgt. Pepper's Lonely
 Hearts Club Band on
 the Road
The Wiz
Shenandoah
Man on the Moon
Goodtime Charley
The Lieutenant
The Rocky Horror Show
Doctor Jazz

REVUES (3)

The Night That Made
 America Famous
Clams on the Half
 Shell
Rodgers & Hart

FOREIGN PLAYS IN ENGLISH (8)

Absurd Person Singular
THE NATIONAL HEALTH
Hosanna
EQUUS
Royal Court:
 Sizwe Banzi Is Dead
 THE ISLAND
Saturday Sunday Monday
In Praise of Love

SPECIALTIES (3)

Flowers
A Letter for Queen
 Victoria
Marcel Marceau

REVIVALS (18)

Gypsy
Cat on a Hot Tin Roof
Circle in the Square:
 Where's Charley?
 All God's Chillun Got
  Wings
New Phoenix:
 Love for Love
 The Rules of the Game
The Member of the
 Wedding
Sherlock Holmes
As You Like It
London Assurance
Of Mice and Men
Good News
Dance With Me
Private Lives
Hughie & Duet
A Doll's House
The Misanthrope
The Constant Wife

RETURN ENGAGEMENTS (3)

Scapino
Brief Lives
Clarence Darrow

HOLDOVER SHOW WHICH BECAME HIT DURING 1974-75

The Magic Show

Plays listed in CAPITAL LETTERS have been designated Best plays of 1974–75.
Plays listed in italics were still running June 2, 1975.
Plays listed in bold face type were classified as hits in Variety's annual list of hits and flops published
 June 4, 1975

by Michael Bennett, James Kirkwood, Nicholas Dante, Marvin Hamlisch and Edward Kleban down at Joseph Papp's Public Theater (it moved to Broadway as soon as it could run out its subscriptions and get its bags packed). The other two off-Broadway productions on the Best Plays list were Mark Medoff's *The Wager* and Ed Bullins's *The Taking of Miss Janie,* both graduates of off-off-Broadway tryouts. The Bullins play was one of four excellent late arrivals off Broadway, the other three being Leslie Lee's *The First Breeze of Summer* at The Negro Ensemble Company (later moved to Broadway), Jonathan Reynolds's program of one-acters, *Rubbers* and *Yanks 3 Tigers 0 Top of the Seventh* and Gene Feist's *James Joyce's Dubliners.*

Broadway's production decline seemed to have bottomed out. The long dropoff from 84 shows in 1967–68 down to 56 in 1970–71 and 1971–72 and 54 in 1972–73 and 1973–74 was reversed with a total of 62 productions in 1974–75. Of course, it took 18 revivals to reach that figure (and there were 19 last year), but new American play production jumped from ten last year to 18 this, with musicals holding steady with a total of nine.

In the all-important matter of playing weeks (if ten shows play ten weeks, that's 100 playing weeks) Broadway jumped back to a total of 1,101 this year from its historical low of 852 last, perhaps a first step upward toward the 1,200 playing-week plateau of the 1960s. Broadway's total gross from the 52 weeks by *Variety* estimate was $57,423,297, the third-highest in its history, about $1.5 million under the record of 1967–68. Tickets were priced somewhat lower in those days, of course, but the 1974–75 increase of more than $11 million over last year and $13 million over the year before took place without any appreciable rise in ticket prices, which have held the line at the $15 top in recent years, until the musical *Chicago* broke through that ceiling in June, 1975 with a $17.50 top.

The road-show activity of Broadway productions also steadied and started to climb back from its sharp 18 per cent dropoff last season. Broadway shows grossed $50,924,844 on the road in 1974–75 as compared to $45.3 million last year, and this season's combined New York-plus-road gross of Broadway shows of $108.4 million was an all-time high, according to *Variety.*

Whatever story the numbers may tell, in the theater there's no such thing as a satisfactory season; who'd be satisfied with only 27 new American shows on Broadway—or 37 or 47 or 57? Something more and/or better is always just out of reach, but at least the reach lengthened considerably this season, statistically if not esthetically. Satisfactory? No, but at least encouraging, with the upturn in production and audience response, and with the excitement that arose on both sides of the New York footlights in 1974–75.

In this year of progress for the theater as a whole, individual achievements were sometimes spectacular. After winning the movie Oscar as the year's best actress, Ellen Burstyn went on to win the Tony for her performance in *Same Time, Next Year.* This remarkable, probably unprecedented double accolade raises the possibility that some day there may be a show-biz hat trick, or triple crown winner, or whatever it may be called, for someone who duplicates Miss Burstyn's feat and wins the TV Emmy too. Her stage vehicle was a hard-ticket hit, one of only three shows—the other two being *Equus* and *The Wiz*—which managed to generate that old-time box-office magnetism in a year of many survivors (accounting for those high overall gross figures) but strangely few solid individual successes.

For once or maybe twice, the Broadway producer of the year wasn't David Merrick. It was Adela Holzer, who presented two new comedies *All Over Town* and *The Ritz* and co-sponsored *Sherlock Holmes.* Merrick's season was a distinguished one, with three respectable, if not wholly successful, Broadway productions: *Mack & Mabel, Dreyfus in Rehearsal* and (with Kennedy Center) *The Misanthrope.* Kennedy Center and Roger L. Stevens also helped bring in *Absurd Person Singular* and *London Assurance;* but the year's extraterritorial producing honors went to Arvin Brown's Long Wharf Theater which pioneered *The National Health, The Island* and *Sizwe Banzi Is Dead* before their transfer to New York. Joseph Papp opened his customarily busy season with Anne Burr's *Mert & Phil,* which turned out to be his best work until the last-minute blaze of glory of his two Best Plays and Critics Award winners *(A Chorus Line* and *The Taking of Miss Janie).*

Impressive as the total 1974–75 box office activity may have been, in the list of individual shows the losses seemed more impressive than the gains. In the present economics of the theater, the bad news happens fast and good news is a long time coming after a production is far enough into its run to have paid off its cost. In these circumstances, according to *Variety* estimate. the long-run *Pippin* was the star performer with a $2,500,000 net profit on its $500,000 investment and still counting. A handful of other holdovers were reported in the black including *A Little Night Music* ($100,000 profit on $650,000), *A Moon for the Misbegotten* ($300,000 on $150,000), *Good Evening* ($100,000 on $120,000), *Scapino* ($15,000 on $50,000) and *The Magic Show,* with the off-Broadway revue *Let My People Come* reported having grossed over $1,500,000 and returned $350,000 on its $10,000 investment. Of this season's new shows, *Same Time, Next Year* (banking a steady $22,500 each sellout week) and *The Wiz* were estimated to be running in the black by season's end, with *Gypsy, Absurd Person Singular, In Praise of Love, Sherlock Holmes, Private Lives* and *The Constant Wife* also thought to be over on the profit side.

On the reverse side of this coin, *Goodtime Charley,* like *Good News,* was a debacle on a scale of an estimated $1 million plus (on an $800,000 investment). Other losses reported by *Variety* this season included *Mack & Mabel* ($750,000), *Dreyfus in Rehearsal* (another Merrick show, another $200,000), *Flowers* ($150,000), *Mourning Pictures* ($150,000), *Saturday Sunday Monday* ($275,000), *Fame* ($170,000 of $185,000), *Don't Call Back* ($160,000 of $165,000), *The Night That Made America Famous* ($400,000). *We Interrupt This Program . . .* ($285,000 on $300,000), *P.S. Your Cat Is Dead* ($132,500) and *The Misanthrope* ($70,000 on $175,000).

Even more discouraging was the fact that several of last year's most effective shows ended their runs in the red, as follows: *Noel Coward in Two Keys* (the 1973–74 season's best play, $100,000 loss on its $175,000 investment), *Bad Habits* (a Best Play, $150,000), *Lorelei* ($250,000 on $500,000), *My Fat Friend* ($100,000 on $175,000), the Andrews Sisters' *Over Here!* ($500,000 on $750,000, expected to recoup on the road but cancelled after contractual differences between stars and producers) and *Thieves* ($250,000 on $300,000). And on the roster of 1974–75 dismay, four Broadway and two off-Broadway productions opened and closed at the same performance:the abovementioned *Don't Call Back* and *Fame* plus *Medea and Jason* and *Mourning Pictures* on Broadway and *Four Friends* and *A Matter of Time* off. The perversity of famine amid this season's plenty was even more clearly illustrated in the irony of *Dr. Jazz* and *The Lieutenant* receiving multiple Tony nominations in the musical categories while their Broadway runs lasted only 5 performances for the former and 9 for the latter, with losses estimated at $900,000 and $250,000 respectively.

Standing off from the individual achievements of 1974–75 and taking a long look at the loops and whorls of the season as a whole, we conclude that the new sense of excitement isn't merely another show-biz illusion. There's a clearly perceptible resolve, a re-commitment if you will, on both sides of the proscenium. The theater's audience has been rather neglectful in this decade, but now, it seems, they've decided to take another, closer look. The New York theater in its turn —like an old trouper who unexpectedly finds himself with an eager crowd on his hands—has risen to the occasion, throwing together a revival here, pulling in a ready-made show from abroad there, rummaging everywhere for inspiration. The old pro lit the lights, pulled the curtains and somehow created a season that transcended the reality of its statistics. If you look too closely you can see that the props are a bit tacky: too small a number of new plays, too few American authors, a trace of mold here and there around the edges of some of the most popular musicals. If you look behind the scenes you'll find the same problems becoming more rather than less acute in these difficult times: a hit-or-flop economy, discouraged backers, attenuating foundation support, a sleazy theater district, high costs of production, etc. (one problem alleviated in the present circumstances is the high cost of theater tickets; they haven't come down, but inflation has made them seem less costly in comparison to everything else).

Tacky, moldy, problematical or whatever, the good old New York theater came on in 1974–75, put on a show for all those folks out front and left them wanting more. And more is what the theater will certainly strive for next season, when those crowds are certain to come back: more new plays, more inventive musicals, more hits.

Broadway

The conspicuous presence of British plays on Broadway this season was topped by the towering *Equus,* the fifth British script in a row to capture our admiration as the season's best-of-bests (the others being *Sleuth, Old Times, The Changing Room* and *Noel Coward in Two Keys). Equus* is a drama of almost classic power, and yet its design is simple and functional as small-town gossip. A psychiatrist (played by Anthony Hopkins), hearing that a stable boy (Peter Firth) has gone berserk and blinded his beloved animals with a steel spike, asks himself how and why such a thing could happen, much as we all do on reading in the newspaper about some seemingly senseless act of brutality. The psychiatrist's calling is not just to shake his head in dismay, but to try to find the answers—and this seeking and at last finding is Peter Shaffer's play, which goes deeper and deeper into the boy's psyche, past ordinary quirks of family strain and religious conviction, until it uncovers dark mysteries of love and worship that have the power to taint other characters.

The physical production was an arena of wooden benches occupied both by the actors (who stepped back and forth into the arena, in and out of their roles) and by a segment of the audience, in order to place no barrier of fourth-wall convention between active and passive witnesses to this ritual. The horses were graceful, bestial and uncannily real as symbolized by actors wearing cage-like suggestions of horses' heads and hooves and moving across the stage in the slow, jointed rhythms of the large animals. John Dexter's direction and John Napier's design (with the mime credited to Claude Chagrin) created a compelling stage illusion of horses and man-horse relationships that was much larger than life, much more illustrative than the presence of a real horse onstage ever could have been, reminding us once again of the great power of the theater at its best. In contrast, the "real" nude love scene seemed to pull *Equus* down to earth. It was just a blurred copy of reality, unworthy of the transcendent images in the rest of this fine play, whose worth was admirably realized by everyone who touched it.

No other drama achieved much stature on the 1974–75 Broadway scene; all other outstanding scripts from home or abroad were more or less streaked with comedy. Even the Athol Fugard-John Kani-Winston Ntshona South African plays—solemn as their overtones certainly were—were devised in the context of the human comedy, not as direct confrontations of drama. *Sizwe Banzi Is Dead* and *The Island* were coupled as a best-play "entry" in the Tony nominations, but we don't do so here because we view them as two full evenings, distinctly separate works. In a sense, they are a canon of work on a single theme—South African racism—developed over a period of time but presented in a single season, under special circumstances. They both ranked high among the year's best, but we don't think it would be appropriate to put them both on the Best Plays list. We've named *The Island* a Best Play rather than *Sizwe Banzi* because it is the stronger literary entity, the other being more mimetic.

A collaborative effort of Fugard, the author-director, and Kani and Ntshona, the performers, the plays were precise in their linkage of word and action and finely tuned in every detail, perfected in the long practise of performance in South Africa, in England, and finally here at the Long Wharf Theater in New Haven and then New York. In *The Island,* Kani and Ntshona impersonated cellmates in a political prison whose last resort of protest lies in the allegory of a two-character version of *Antigone* they're preparing for the annual prison show. Their partnership is placed under great stress when one of them learns he is soon to be set free, while the other will probably rot in confinement. *The Island* was a triple *entendre* of protest against the South African state's racist policies: first in the Creon-vs.-Antigone dialogue about the individual's duty to the state; second in the convicts' selection, planning and presentation of this material in their prison context; and thirdly, in the modern actuality of devising and presenting *The Island* in its authors' native land, where the rules of *apartheid* are so restrictive that Kani and Ntshona must be registered as Fugard's house servants in order to work with his theater group, because "artist" or "actor" isn't accepted as an employment category for South African blacks.

The comedic twists of *The Island*—the curious relations between the two men as they endure their hard time, and their rehearsing and dressing up for the play—put a curve on the script that probably helped get it past official objections. The same was true of *Sizwe Banzi* which begins with a Kani monologue describing the preparations for an inspection of an American-owned factory in South Africa, with the blacks' oppressive working conditions temporarily disguised for the benefit of the American visitors. The heart of the *Sizwe Banzi* matter, though, was the second part: a tipsy laborer considers changing identity papers with a man he finds lying dead in the street, in order to better his condition—but hesitates to do so because this would a sort of suicide, forever destroying the real identity in which he takes pride and comfort. The hard emotional and psychological consequences of tyranny were eloquently expressed in these fine South African stage works which dared to confront problems which wouldn't vanish when the curtain came down.

Another foreign Best Play processed in an American premiere at the Long

Wharf before coming to Broadway was Peter Nichols's *The National Health,* which found the means to satirize the assembly-line impersonality of socialized medicine as it becomes ever more mechanized, institutionalized, in order to broaden its democratic base. *The National Health* spread itself across its hospital-ward setting in episodes of fear, hope, cynicism, racism and death, in a sprawling script which sprayed little pellets of satire in all directions instead of seeking to drill a single hole like *Equus.* It cried out for an ensemble performance and received it from Leonard Frey (a sardonically efficient orderly), Richard Venture (a trembling ulcer patient), Rita Moreno (a West Indian nurse) and a large cast portraying all kinds of doctors, nurses and patients caught together on many levels between life and death; all presented under the inspired and inspiring direction of Arvin Brown, artistic director of the Long Wharf.

If this seemed a foreign-play-dominated season, it was because of the high quality of the imports, not their quantity. They numbered eight, the same as last year, all but one of them standout attractions. Terence Rattigan's newest script, *In Praise of Love,* was a bright, mannered comedy (though not billed as one) of deception and counter-deception with very dark shadows of mortality in the background. The husband and wife played by Rex Harrison and Julie Harris have come to terms with each other's eccentricities—his intellectual, hers emotional. There are many layers to be peeled off, however, and the truth was slowly revealed under Fred Coe's meticulous direction as something quite different and quite touching: she has a terminal illness; he knows it and is redoubling his selfish importunities, lest he betray the truth with a hint of sympathy; but she also knows he knows it and goes along with his game so that he won't be troubled. A friend (played by Martin Gabel) was a mirror in which the audience could see reflected its own reaction to the various discoveries in this very smoothly-crafted play.

There were a protracted suicide attempt and other sinister implications including a vicious dog in Alan Ayckbourn's *Absurd Person Singular,* but it was the only one of the foreign entries which forthrightly billed itself as a "comedy" and set its sights firmly upon humor. The play showed three British couples with vastly different backgrounds meeting at each other's houses for Christmas Eve parties over a period of years. The working-class couple (the late Larry Blyden and Carole Shelley) is on the rise, the aristocrats (Richard Kiley and Geraldine Page) are on the descendent, and the other two (Sandy Dennis and Tony Roberts) are muddling through the middle, in these times which are homogenizing mankind along with the milk. All these American actors played their roles with convincing British accents (and ideal ensemble proportion) under Eric Thompson's direction. Blyden in particular achieved a perfect caricature of the not-so-meek who are now inheriting the earth, or at least a few of its luxuries and ostentations.

Another foreign play, *Hosanna,* was an English translation of a French Canadian script by Michel Tremblay about a transvestite and his seedy, leather-jacketed friend. The play is said to be a parable of Canadian politics, but it was theatrically effective on its own, without the political key, in a second-act monologue by the transvestite, powerfully acted by Richard Monette. The eighth imported new script, an Italian family play by Eduardo de Filippo directed and designed by Franco Zeffirelli in an English production by the National Theater, proved somewhat topheavy and lasted only 12 performances.

American authors made a creditable showing side-by-side with their transatlantic competitors. They provided Broadway with 18 new plays this season, four of which were Best Plays, one by a new author. No American work had the shattering impact of *Equus* or the resounding social echoes of the South African plays. Their approach was almost uniformly comedic or melodramatic, and their attitude one of helpless laughter in unfathomable circumstances—certainly a valid concept for the mid-1970s.

Edward Albee's Pulitzer Prize-winning *Seascape* was his best work since *A Delicate Balance,* the lightest in his canon and his first full-scale Broadway directorial credit. His play seemed filled with light and air, as he studied a middle-aged couple trying to work off their post-picnic depression in a lonely oceanside sand dune by trying to figure out what if anything to do with the rest of their lives. They're mismatched in their desires for the future, and the playwright further mismatches them with a pair of humanoid sea-lizards trying to find out whether it would be worth the effort to evolve into land creatures. Each "couple" hopes for more than their past, ordinary lives have afforded. They're willing to try for the brass ring—if it exists. Their confrontation is brittle rather than harsh, with Deborah Kerr as the spokesman for the land and Frank Langella for the sea, and their discourse is prevented from taking on too much weight by Albee's direction. The seascape by James Tilton and the lizard costume designs by Fred Voelpel were as helpful to the play as its staging—even the large, saurian tails seemed to be easily-manageable parts of a living body.

These couples conclude, not unpredictably, that evolution is a game probably worth the candle, even in middle age and considering the loss of peace of mind which is the cost of knowledge. *Seascape* was a pleasant conceit expertly contrived, easily the best American play of the Broadway season and a notch above its nearest off-Broadway rival.

The vein of absurdist comedy yielded riches in two other American Best Plays: Murray Schisgal's *All Over Town* and Terrence McNally's *The Ritz.* They were both comedies of tenacity, with individuals holding to their own concerns in the face of profound disorder, like an earthquake victim saving an ash tray from a falling house. In *All Over Town* an eminent psychiatrist (Barnard Hughes) is sure that California will fall into the Pacific Ocean any day now, but what he's immediately concerned about is the strange case of a young man who has nine children by five different women, all on welfare. There's also a matter of mistaken identity when the eminent doctor assumes that the good breeder is a black man (Cleavon Little) who happens by, when in reality he is a shy young white man (Zane Lasky) who seems harmless and is by some happy magic irresistable to women. Schisgal's play finds fun in everything it can lay its hands on, which under Dustin Hoffman's direction (his professional debut) is plenty and includes sex, sociology, success and everything else brought within range of this energetic and perceptive farce.

McNally's *The Ritz* was a script very similar to Schisgal's in genre, though it was billed as a "comedy" while Schisgal's was billed as a "play"; in tone, not surprisingly, because the producer of both plays was Adela Holzer; and in directorial energy and skill—for Dustin Hoffman read Robert Drivas, though *The Ritz* was certainly not his debut. In it, a helpless fugitive from a gangster family quarrel (Jack Weston) finds himself hiding out, or rather in, at a Turkish bath during a sort of homosexual Homecoming Weekend. It's not long before he finds the kinks of some of his fellow guests more troublesome than his enemy's threats. His guides in this jungle of fetishists include Tony Award-winning Rita Moreno as a Latin Bette Midler trying to get a foot on the first rung of the ladder by performing in this most unpromising place, and F. Murray Abraham as a seasoned veteran of these purple occasions. The point of this as of other McNally plays was that anyone who can keep his sanity in the circumstances we all find ourselves in today ought to have his head examined. As in the three past McNally Best Plays, *The Ritz* made it both absurdly and delightfully.

Another comedy and the biggest straight-play hit of the season was the Broadway stage debut of its Canadian-born author, Bernard Slade: *Same Time, Next Year,* a heterosexual response to the strictures of our times in the assignations of a couple, more or less happily married (to other people), who take an intense pleasure in meeting secretly for a fling once a year in a convenient motel cottage. The audience is privileged to look in on a half dozen such trysts over a 25-year span, each making a comment on its unique time frame of hippies, hipsters, affluence, even of war. As the world knows, Ellen Burstyn played the warm, generous, sometimes affected woman, while Charles Grodin was overlooked by most award givers and nominaters in his equally sure portrayal of a middle-class husband and father torn between his desire to be with it and his deepest instinct against it, whatever "it" happened to be at the time. Gene Saks's direction insured renewed life and a fresh style in each repeat of the situation and made the most of the many verbal and visual jokes—short-range assets which did more for this play than any long-range overview.

This comic spirit dominated American playwriting this season and carried through from the best to the near-best, though sometimes showing its darker side. One of the half dozen new 1974–75 scripts which billed themselves as "comedy" rather than "play" was Neil Simon's *God's Favorite,* a telling of the Biblical Job tale as though it had taken place in a modern, affluent Long Island suburb. In the first part, Vincent Gardenia as Job is harried by a divine messenger in the fussily, elaborately eccentric person of Charles Nelson Reilly, a wingless but persistent angel who mined the same vein of dark humor that sometimes gives the stripping of King Lear by his daughters a comedic streak. The second part, with Job clinging to his love of the God who pulls his house and his life down around his ears, didn't work comedically and, unlike *King Lear,* couldn't go forward and make it as drama. The brighter moments of *God's Favorite* rank with Simon's best work; and if the play as a whole doesn't, it's because it was too adventurous in trying to find a new way of telling the old tale. The playwright's search for a new way of expressing himself was a fault of commission, at least, not of omission.

Another of the season's comedies, Peter Ustinov's *Who's Who in Hell,* seemed a thoroughly American play regardless of the author's nationality. It had its premiere in New York and pursued a satire of American attitudes in situation-comedy style, with George S. Irving (who has played Richard M. Nixon on Broadway and resembles him in this role) as an American President assassinated together with the U.S.S.R. Chairman (played by Ustinov in portly Slavic grandeur) by a young hothead (Beau Bridges) who in his turn is killed by police and thus joins his victims in an anteroom of eternity. It was a quick-witted script, but it settled too comfortably into its premise and went nowhere. This time the anteroom was an empty office entered through a one-way door (as in *No Exit*) and left by means of elevators. The last anteroom of eternity of any consequence onstage was a steambath in the play of the same name. This year there were steambaths all over the place, but they had no supernatural significance; they were earthbound in their function, as in *The Ritz* and the far less successful *Tubstrip,* which wandered nakedly onto Broadway for a few performances following a national tour.

Across the line and into the realm of drama, Garson Kanin stressed the irony and pathos of believing, in the times just before Hitler, that anti-Semitism was finally dead and buried in civilized Europe, in an adaptation of a French play-within-a-play, *Dreyfus in Rehearsal,* about a Polish troupe rehearsing a drama of the Dreyfus case. The scripts which Joseph Papp's New York Shakespeare Festival brought into the big theater at Lincoln Center were shaded for drama even more than comedy, the first and best being Anne Burr's *Mert & Phil* dramatizing the emotional impact of a mastectomy on a 20-year marriage, constructed in widening concentric circles. Then there was Bill Gunn's *Black Picture Show* depicting the intellectual decay and death of a black poet seduced by ambition and movie money; a shambles of innuendo and grief which wasn't helped by the author's direction of his own play. Finally, in Anthony Scully's *Little Black Sheep,* powerful neuroses worked on the priests in the Jesuit House of Study in New Haven, but none emerged to make a play of it—not even with the added fillip of a visiting nun with a compulsion to take all her clothes off. It was a script with a good deal of muscle but little coordination.

Conventional crime and violence occupied some of theater's attention inside the auditorium as well as outside in the streets this season. *P.S. Your Cat Is Dead* offered up Keir Dullea as a victim first of a burglary and then as the target of an attempted burglary of his emotions, as the thief, having failed to rob him, tries to seduce him. Norman Krasna's *We Interrupt This Program...* reached for total audience participation, as a gang of criminals takes over the theater soon after the "play" begins and holds the audience hostage for the freedom of a gang member who is in prison. The action had to be continuous. The sound, by Jack Shearing, created the illusion that the mayor, the police commissioner and a whole street full of police cars were milling around, jabbering on walkie-talkies just outside the theater. Broadway proved inhospitable to this pleasantly prickly conceit, but it might do well in production elsewhere. Lance Larsen's *The Hashish Club,* about a bad drug trip, arrived from Los Angeles and departed shortly. *Don't Call Back,* with Arlene Francis as a star who comes home to her New York apartment to find it taken over by a gang of criminal youths including her own son, gave up after only one performance.

In the domain of Broadway musical production, *The Wiz* stood head and shoulders above all its contemporaries, but it didn't have to stand very tall to do so. A hip version of L. Frank Baum's Wizard of Oz story, with a soft-rock score by Charlie Smalls and marvellously inventive design and staging by Geoffrey Holder and Tom H. John, this was distinctly a 1970s show, albeit with a 1930s book which had to be picked up and dusted off from time to time. *The Wiz* began by representing a tornado as a dancer whirling and twirling across a huge empty stage with a strip of black gauze attached to her head, revolving up into the flies —one of the best of its trip-like design fantasies. The season's other rock efforts on Broadway were *Sgt. Pepper's Lonely Hearts Club Band on the Road,* a Tom O'Horgan fancy taking off from the famous Beatles album but never becoming really airborne; and *The Rocky Horror Show,* a lampoon of the movies presented cabaret-style at the Belasco, which was remodeled for that purpose. Andy Warhol ventured into musical production this year with a fantasy of the space age entitled *Man on the Moon,* lasting a little longer than your average moonwalk, but not much; and Harry Chapin also ventured onto Broadway with a revue *The Night That Made America Famous,* a loud, multimedia compendium of those depressing country rock "somebody done somebody wrong songs" about how everything without exception is going to hell in a haycart.

Another standout of the Broadway musical year was another oldie: *Shenandoah,* based on the 1965 James Stewart movie by James Lee Barrett, also the co-author of this Broadway book with Peter Udell (its lyricist) and Philip Rose (its director). This one tells a tale of the Civil War about a widowed farmer, a rugged individualist who refuses to take sides and is determined to keep on raising his large family and let the war go by. It doesn't, of course—it reaches out to take him and his family by the throat. If emotions were always showing on the surface of this show, at least they were *there*, with an attractive score by Gary Geld to give them emphasis.

The historical past supplied all the other Broadway musicals with their fitful inspiration. *Mack & Mabel* looked back at the movies' silent era in a big, impressive show by the *Hello, Dolly!* authors—Jerry Herman and Michael Stewart—with Robert Preston and Bernadette Peters striving mightily in the leading roles of Mack Sennett, the comedy director, and his star Mabel Normand. *Goodtime Charley* took a leaf out of *Pippin's* book and went Gothic with a musical version of Joan of Arc's travails, with Ann Reinking as Joan and Joel Grey as the Dauphin Charles (the Charley of the title), and with a most effective design by Rouben Ter-Arutunian. *The Lieutenant* made a bold attempt to express itself in musical theater terms on the subject of the agonies of My Lai. Finally, *Dr. Jazz* turned inward for a cavalcade of music, tracing the development of jazz in a score mixing old and new numbers, with a slight show-business story for a book. None of these shows was without some spark, but none lit a fire anywhere big enough to warm Broadway.

A much warmer musical pleasure was *Rodgers & Hart*, which also looked backward in a collection of 98 songs by the great composer-lyricist team of the 1920s and 1930s. Subtitled "A Musical Celebration," it was based on a concept of Richard Lewine and John Fearnley which for purposes of statistical classification we can call a revue. The songs poured out—love songs in Part I, satirical numbers in Part II—with Donald Saddler dances but without any inconvenience of a book, performed by an enthusiastic young group under the enthusiastic and canny direction of Burt Shevelove. It was in every way a happy event whose only shortcoming was the lateness of its arrival in a season which could have used its brightly entertaining presence all winter long.

In addition on the 1974–75 musical scene, there were concert appearances by singing stars (among them Frank Sinatra) and rock groups not only in the sports arenas and concert halls but also in some of the larger Broadway theaters, whose owners discovered a season or two ago that a Sammy Davis Jr. or a Liza Minnelli in what amounted to a concert could attract audiences as well or better than such Broadway fare as was available to them. These are "fan" audiences, and one of their objects of adoration this year was Bette Midler, whose appearance at the Minskoff, entitled *Clams on the Half Shell*, was offered as a revue of sight gags, inside jokes and Midler vocals, backed by Tony Walton designs; a little more elaborate than others of its concert-like ilk, enough so, perhaps, to earn the name of "show." Others making concert appearances on New York stages this season included Charles Aznavour, Tony Bennett and Lena Horne at the Minskoff and Henry Mancini, Anthony Newley, Johnny Mathis and the Fifth Dimension at the Uris, a pair of new skyscraper "theaters" which have proved more useful for making noise than for uttering words.

This season's specialty shows were impressive. Lindsay Kemp's *Flowers,* a tragi-comic program of pantomime imported from London, was a sensitive exploration of transvestism in several phases, said to have been suggested by Genet's *Notre Dame des Fleurs.* Kemp devised, designed, directed and played the leading role in *Flowers.* Another arresting specialty production was Robert Wilson's *A Letter for Queen Victoria,* a mood-establishing but otherwise mysteriously jumbled collection of theater effects of monologue, music, mime, etc., in Wilson's unique style. The list of specialties was further distinguished by the presence of Marcel Marceau for a limited engagement of his Bip sketches and other pantomimes. Return engagements of Henry Fonda in *Clarence Darrow,* Roy Dotrice in *Brief Lives* and Jim Dale in his hit Young Vic production of *Scapino* also added to the season's store of theatergoing riches.

Revivals

This season as last, New York was a repertory extravaganza, with 37 professional revivals (18 on Broadway, 17 off Broadway and two return engagements of revivals), and who knows how many off off Broadway—perhaps more than 100.

Revivals serve five obvious purposes in the entertainment/esthetic context of the modern New York stage: 1) They provide a known quantity for star performers who might not dare risk failure in a personal appearance in new, untried work; 2) They provide entertainment for audiences as well as occupation for artists during periods when good new scripts are relatively scarce; 3) They test the imagination and muscle of all the theater's interpretive talent; 4) They give audiences an historical perspective on living theater the way a library does on the theater as literature; and 5) They sometimes discover, or uncover, dormant vitality in a vintage comedy or drama to the extent that it outgrows the original concept of the work revived.

The first four purposes were admirably served by the 1974–75 revival activity, the fifth less so than last year, when new productions of *Candide* and *A Moon for the Misbegotten* redefined these works for our theater. The popular success of this season's Royal Shakespeare production of William Gillette's antique *Sherlock Holmes* came nearest to serving such a purpose. It was a redefinition with elaborate scenic, melodramatic, costuming and performing devices adding a new dimension of sentiment, or perhaps camp, to the good old detective play, like the fifth or sixth re-reading of a horror cartoon. The elegantly tilted nostrils of John Wood as the great detective, the fuzzy hair of wild-eyed Professor Moriarty (Philip Locke), the lighted cigar in the gas-filled boiler room were all intended to invoke chuckles of recognition, not gasps of astonishment

John Steinbeck's *Of Mice and Men* was also reprocessed by casting a black actor (James Earl Jones) in the part of simple-minded, hulking Lennie, with Kevin Conway as his mentor George. The acting, direction (by Edwin Sherin) and design (by William and Jean Eckart) were top-notch, but the added interracial tensions gave little to the drama and actually blurred it in some scenes. Eugene O'Neill's drama of a mixed marriage, *All God's Chillun Got Wings,* was staged by George C. Scott at Circle in the Square with his wife, Trish Van Devere, as the white city girl who marries her devoted black childhood sweetheart and then disintegrates under the pressures of their relationship. It was a sound production, but its most conspicuous revelation was that the playwright didn't have a very strong grip on this weighty subject, by modern standards. The massive musical effort to put *Good News* on a modern pedestal was the conspicuous demise of the year, even with memorable tunes added to the score, the Abe Burrows touch in adaptation and staging, and Alice Faye leading the cast. S.J. Perelman's comedy *The Beauty Part,* long supposed to have been an innocent victim of a newspaper strike in its initial Broadway production, proved to be less than durable in an American Place production off Broadway. Lindsay Kemp's effort to re-examine Oscar Wilde's *Salome* with the addition of mime and other innovative concepts proved not very productive.

The 1974–75 revival season served purpose number 1 by making an international firmament of the New York theater scene, attracting star performers from all over the world to shine with their special colors in specially chosen circumstances: the high-tensile strength and sensuality of Elizabeth Ashley in Tennessee Williams's *Cat on a Hot Tin Roof* . . . a replay of Jim Dale's *Scapino* . . . Maggie Smith, embodying frivolity as Noel Coward's Amanda in *Private Lives* . . . Ben Gazzara throwing verbal punches as Erie Smith in O'Neill's monologue *Hughie* . . . the outward style and inward vibrations of Liv Ullmann in *A Doll's House* . . . charm and abrasion perfectly paired and contrasted in Diana Rigg and Alec McCowen in *The Misanthrope* . . . the glow of Ingrid Bergman in *The Constant Wife* . . . the subtleties of character brought by Michael Moriarty to the title role of *Richard III*.

Revivals also fulfilled the second-named purpose in providing live entertainment where there might otherwise have been a shortage. The great Broadway musical *Gypsy* was given a new look in the successful revival directed by its multi-gifted author, Arthur Laurents, and starring Angela Lansbury, who won a Tony Award for her reinterpretation of the Ethel Merman role. An excellent cast headed by Raul Julia disported itself under Theodore Mann's direction in the Circle in the Square revival of *Where's Charley?* The La Mama Plexus Company settled in for a Broadway run with *Dance With Me*, a comedy with music expanded as well as revived from its earlier 1971 productions at La Mama and the Public Theater.

The Public Theater played its part by inviting other companies to use such of its stages as happened to be empty. The visitors who helped expand Joseph Papp's 1974–75 schedule included the Shaliko Company in distinguished presentations of Bertolt Brecht's *The Measures Taken* (its first professional New York revival) and Ibsen's *Ghosts*. Also visiting downtown was The Manhattan Project in a return engagement of its revival of Samuel Beckett's *Endgame* and a new interpretation of *The Seagull* in the Andre Gregory's troupe's imaginative style. Brooklyn too was the scene of notable revival activity with its Academy of Music hosting the Royal Shakespeare Company, whose Ian Richardson headed a travelling troupe presenting Gorky's *Summerfolk* (its first professional New York production), *Love's Labour's Lost* and an abbreviated *King Lear*. This company also put on a new selection of Shakespearean excerpts on the subject of royalty and monarchy, entitled *He That Plays the King*, in its U.S. premiere. Finally in Brooklyn there was Chelsea Theater Center's amusing *Polly*, a handsome and lively refurbishing of John Gay's musical sequel to *The Beggar's Opera*.

The third major purpose of exercising and stretching artistic muscles was amply served all over town. The visiting Royal Shakespeare production of Dion Boucicault's 19th-century comedy *London Assurance* (about a lordly widower competing with his son for the attentions of a young heiress) was a gem of ensemble stylization, directed by Euan Smith and with Donald Sinden giving one of the season's outstanding performances as the aging suitor. Another British visitor to Broadway, the National Theater's *As You Like It*, stretched its muscles in the concept of this Shakespearean comedy performed by an all-male cast, little

The 1974–75 Season off Broadway

PLAYS (30)

Negro Ensemble 1974:
In the Deepest Part
of Sleep
Why Hanna's Skirt Won't
Stay Down
Naomi Court
Public Theater:
Where Do We Go From
Here?
The Last Days of
British Honduras
In the Boom Boom Room
(revised)
Our Late Night
Kid Champion
Fishing
Chelsea Theater Center:
Hothouse
Yentl the Yeshiva Boy
Santa Anita '42
THE WAGER
Ridiculous Company:
Stage Blood
Bluebeard
Hotel for Criminals
Four Friends
James Joyce's Dubliners
Negro Ensemble 1975:
The First Breeze of
Summer
Liberty Call
Sugar Mouth Sam Don't
Dance No More & Orrin
The Moonlight Arms &
The Dark Tower
Welcome to Black River
Waiting for Mongo

American Place:
Killer's Head & Action
Rubbers & Yanks 3
*Detroit O Top of the
Seventh*
Augusta
Parlo
Women Behind Bars
THE TAKING OF MISS
JANIE

FOREIGN PLAYS
IN ENGLISH (3)

The Burnt Flowerbed
The Advertisement
Bullshot Crummond

MUSICALS (12)

I'll Die if I Can't Live
Forever
How to Get Rid of It
The Prodigal Sister
Diamond Studs
Lovers
Be Kind to People Week
Philemon
A Matter of Time
The $ Value of Man
The Glorious Age
A CHORUS LINE

REVUES (5)

Some People, Some Other
People and What They
Finally Do
Pretzels
Broadway Dandies
The National Lampoon Show
In Gay Company

REVIVALS (17)

Delacorte:
Pericles, Prince of
Tyre
The Merry Wives of
Windsor
Roundabout Company:
All My Sons
The Rivals
Rosmersholm
*What Every Woman
Knows*
Public Theater:
The Measures Taken
The Seagull
Ghosts
Newhouse Theater:
Richard III
A Midsummer Night's
Dream
The Beauty Part
Salome
Royal Shakespeare:
Summerfolk
Love's Labour's Lost
King Lear
Polly

RETURN
ENGAGEMENTS (3)

Public Theater:
Alice in Wonderland
Endgame
The Wild Stunt Show

SPECIALTIES (11)

The World of Lenny Bruce
Chelsea Westside:
La Carpa de los
Rasquachis
The Mother
The Great Air Robbery
Baird Marionettes:
Peter and the Wolf
Alice in Wonderland
Blasts and Bravos
He That Plays the King
The Ramayana
The Dybbuk & Priscilla,
Princess of Power
The Magic of Jolson

Plays listed in CAPITAL LETTERS have been designated Best Plays of 1974–75.
Plays listed in *italics* were still running June 1, 1975.

more than a stunt in the context of the modern theater. This season's New Phoenix repertory was a triptych of sharp-edged comedies of similar mood but widely differing eras: Congreve's *Love for Love* (directed by Harold Prince in a season which he spent between musicals), Pirandello's *The Rules of the Game* and Carson McCullers's *The Member of the Wedding.*

Off Broadway, Gene Feist's steadily active Roundabout Theater Company expanded into a second theater in its midtown neighborhood by acquiring and remodeling the RKO 23d Street movie house and renaming it Stage Two, the Roundabout's Stage One being its former and retained headquarters at 307 West 26th Street. This organization's busy season of high-quality offerings included four revivals on its busy schedule: Arthur Miller's *All My Sons,* Ibsen's *Rosmersholm,* Sheridan's *The Rivals* and Barrie's *What Every Woman Knows.* Only Joseph Papp's Shakespeare operation comes anywhere near the Roundabout in establishing a New York repertory *presence.* This year in the Delacorte, Papp essayed the seldom-seen *Pericles, Prince of Tyre* with Randall Duk Kim in the title role and *The Merry Wives of Windsor* with Barnard Hughes as Falstaff. In the Newhouse Theater at Lincoln Center Papp followed the distinguished Moriarty *Richard III* with a production of *A Midsummer Night's Dream,* then turned the smaller theater over to the presentation of a new script, thus falling short of his announced ambition to have Shakespeare revivals continuously available to New York audiences in that modest facility.

Finally, purpose number 4—historical perspective on the living theater—is perhaps the most precious byproduct of all this revival activity in New York. No single repertory company could possibly serve so grand a purpose; it is possible only in the large context of a great world theater capital and only in a time when the audience appetite for live entertainment exceeds the supply of satisfying new work. New York City is such a place, and recent seasons have provided such a time. This one was no exception.

Off Broadway

Nobody told the off-Broadway theater that 1974–75 was going to be a great year—not until April, that is. Off Broadway just dawdled along until the last three months of the season, when all at once it seemed to get the word and caught up fast.

Once so vital to the experimental side of the New York theater, off Broadway is now priced so high in both production costs and tickets that experiment has become too expensive for both producer and show-shopper. In independent production, this tends to create a mini-Broadway with a repressive hit psychology. And the alternative, the semi-sheltered (by subsidy) institutional production with its semi built-in (by subscription) audiences, was also facing up to hard times of reduced funding from both government and private sources. It was still dominant in 1974–75, however, with 22 of the 30 new American playscripts produced in organizational schedules. On the independent side, there was one Best Play *(The Wager)* and one that came close *(Naomi Court)*—and of course the off-Broadway flagship continued to sail on proudly in the longest run of record in the American theater, as *The Fantasticks* gave its 6,281st performance on May 31 and still counting. There have been 3,788 productions of this extraordinary Tom Jones-Harvey Schmidt musical in all the 50 states and 248 productions in 54 foreign countries.

When the final numbers were in for 1974–75, off-Broadway production volume was up from last year, including a small rise in new American plays (from 27 to 30) and a doubling of new musicals (from 6 to 12), plus a spate of specialties and revues and the previously-reported high level of revival activity. The total off-Broadway programming has been recorded in recent *Best Plays* volumes as follows: 119 in 1969–70, 95 in 1970–71, 87 in 1971–72, 87 in 1972–73, 76 in 1973–74 and finally 81 in 1974–75.

One of the reasons why the off-Broadway season at times seemed less successful than it later turned out to be was that it went somewhat sour for Joseph Papp in 1974–75. Papp's New York Shakespeare Festival is the leading producer off Broadway (and by volume in all New York as well) with five auditoria in the Public Theater downtown, his open-air season in Central Park and his small "off-Broadway" Newhouse Theater in Lincoln Center. At season's end, Papp threw the towel in and his hands up with the announcement that he would abandon off-Broadway production and take over the Booth Theater on Broadway for the production of new scripts. The Public Theater is to be given over to off-off-Broadway-level, work-in-progress, limited-engagement-type productions and the Newhouse to children's theater. Also, in disgust at the lame audience response to his Broadway-scale new-play schedule at the Beaumont, Papp declared further that he plans to turn the big Lincoln Center theater over to revivals.

The heart of this matter seems to be that the off-Broadway production environment has now failed to support even so entrenched and subsidized a group as Papp's, so that he must move up the scale to Broadway or perish. But it's hard to draw any such definite or sweeping conclusion from Papp's 1974–75 season, in which the quality of the plays gave little reason for audience enthusiasm in any corner of the Papp empire for 11 of the 12 months. And Papp has never sustained himself by keeping his hits going off Broadway, he has always moved his successes into the bigger theaters, beginning with *Hair* in his first season at the Public. If he no longer considers himself an off-Broadway impresario, perhaps he is merely one of the last to discover that he never was.

In any case, Papp managed to end his season with a bang as well as a whimper. At almost the year's last second he brought one of the year's best plays into the limelight. Like last season's *Short Eyes,* Ed Bullins's *The Taking of Miss Janie* was developed off off Broadway and later acquired by Papp for commercial showing. *Miss Janie,* like some other Bullins plays, was first produced by Woodie King Jr.'s New Federal Theater at the Henry Street Playhouse. As a result of an agreement announced in April, Papp will now provide input into the New Federal schedule of productions and, in the case of the more successful ones, bring them before a larger public in his uptown or downtown facilities.

The New Federal Theater production of *Miss Janie* was brought to the Newhouse Theater under this agreement. It proved to be Bullins's best program-length script to date (it is a long one-acter, playing without intermission), a parable of race relations in the 1960s in the encounter between a black would-be poet (Adeyemi Lythcott) and his blonde classmate and devoted friend (Hilary Jean Beane) whom he suddenly rapes after years of friendship. Bullins has often used the party as a microcosm of life, a means of mixing attitudes to produce reactions of social conflict and comment. He does so again here, in a play dominated by characters symbolic of both black and white stupidities and by the bad vibes of outside 1960s events such as the shocking assassinations. *The Taking of Miss Janie* has a sharper focus under Gilbert Moses's direction than similar

Bullins works—*The Pig Pen* (to which this play is a kind of sequel) and *The Duplex,* to name two; its dialogue has the incisiveness of Bullins's best one-acters. *Miss Janie* won the New York Drama Critics Circle award as the best American play of the year in a close contest with *Seascape,* and it now brings Bullins his first Best Play citation.

Miss Janie was merely a guest in Papp's house, but *A Chorus Line,* also a Critics Award winner and by far the best musical of the season, was a member of the New York Shakespeare production family from its outset. It was a beautifully simple show: on a bare stage sometimes backed with mirrors in which audience and dancers can see themselves doubled (as in last season's *Jumpers*), a Broadway musical director lines up 17 chorus aspirants from which he is going to pick eight for the chorus of his show. Because some of them may have a side or two of dialogue, and to get some insight into their skills and personalities, he asks each of the dancers to tell him something about themselves. The "director" is more often than not a disembodied voice on the public address system, like a god or at least a Delphic sibyl to whom these young people open themselves in awe. They speak in the various idioms of the musical stage, sometimes singing, sometimes joking, sometimes drawing out painfully their secret sexual and other hangups, but more often dancing, for this is a dancers' show as conceived, directed and choreographed by Michael Bennett. It is about dancers, by dancers; incredibly lithe and disciplined bodies driven, it seems, by damaged and overcompensating psyches. They long and strive mightily for the safe and yet exciting, fulfilling anonymity of the chorus line. This theme is expressed in Edward Kleban's sensitive lyrics for a song called "At the Ballet" in which one of these insecure young people notes that in the ballet when you reach out your arms there's always someone there.

Marvin Hamlisch's *A Chorus Line* music is sophisticated, singable, danceable, never missing the mood any more than it would miss the beat. A great charm of this show was its seamlessness, nothing bulging out of proportion, a true ensemble of authorship, staging and performance, running without intermission. Donna McKechnie as a onetime leading dancer now trying to start all over again in the chorus and Robert LuPone as the poker-faced "director" of the show come on a shade stronger than the others, in a production that is as much a blend of performers as of colors in Theoni V. Aldredge's rehearsal costumes or the blend of score and emotion, as near perfect as the unison of a Rockettes finale.

One distinguished guest production and one late-blooming, smash-hit musical —and two Critics awards—not Papp's finest New York season, perhaps, but certainly not his worst. What then of the long list of 1974–75 New York Shakespeare Festival productions that caused him to consider abandoning off Broadway at the Public and new-play production at Lincoln Center? On the Public's schedule, Michael Weller's *Fishing* and Thomas Babe's *Kid Champion* showed some signs of theatrical vigor. The former, by the author of *Moonchildren,* looked in on a group of now-grown-up moonchildren, functionless and apparently aimless, groping for a meaningful existence and meanwhile taking drugs to pass the time. It at least established an atmosphere, a presence, onstage, as did the Babe play in a series of highly-flavored episodes in the life and times of a popular rock star (and Lindsay Crouse in the former play and Christopher Walken in the title role of the latter gave Public Theater audiences a little more than they found in their vehicles). Also at the Public Theater there was John Ford Noonan's portrait of a transvestite and his friends in *Where Do We Go From Here?,* one of many scripts on this subject this season, and not the best—the best was *Hosanna* on Broadway.

There was Ronald Tavel's *The Last Days of British Honduras,* a science-fiction-mystery treatment of the disappearance of Mayan civilization in the 12th century.

Last year, Papp introduced his new-play policy at the Beaumont with David Rabe's *Boom Boom Room,* a blurred, black character sketch of a go-go dancer. It didn't do well uptown, and it didn't do any better downtown this season in a revised version called *In the Boom Boom Room.* Such was Papp's off-Broadway new-play season in 1974–75 (the remainder of the Public's schedule consisted of guest productions, including revivals, by The Manhattan Project and Shaliko). No firm diagnosis of off-Broadway's condition can be made from shows like these —and the same is true of the those uptown at the Beaumont, described earlier in this report. If Joseph Papp meant what he said and has really drawn irrevocable conclusions about the future of off-Broadway and new-play production at the Beaumont from the fate of the shows he presented this season, he is wearing dark glasses to judge a thunderstorm.

The vital signs of independent off-Broadway production are a more reliable indication of its general health than any institutional play schedule—and unfortunately these continued to decline in 1974–75. The truth is as simple as a thermometer reading: production costs have risen in multiples, so experimentation is ruled out at the source; and ticket prices have risen so high ($8.50 for *The Hot l Baltimore,* $8.95 for *Diamond Studs,* for example, and not extraordinary ones) that audiences can't afford adventure, either, and support only the smash hits. This might be called the Broadway syndrome, and there's no doubt it is far advanced off Broadway too, where in 1974–75 there was only one Best Play in independent production as compared with three last season. This was *The Wager* by Mark Medoff, a script as sophisticated as Medoff's 1974 Best Play *When You Comin' Back, Red Ryder?* was elemental. *The Wager's* leading character is a graduate student (most forcefully realized in Kristoffer Tabori's performance), an intellectual gymnast who has deliberately dominated and suppressed every emotion within himself and is now capable of total dispassion—almost. He treats his fellow-students like flies placed there expressly for him to pull their wings off. He bets that his athlete-roommate can't seduce the married student next door without inciting her husband to murder and then does his best to induce both actions, the seduction being a kind of flagellation because he's rather drawn to the woman himself. She is openly and confessedly interested him him, but of course he won't respond to either her hints or, finally, her open pleas. *The Wager* was tried out off off Broadway last year and directed off Broadway this year by Anthony Perkins in a production which was only one interpretation—albeit a good one— of a subtle script that will have a different color in each production in theaters around the world. The fact that it couldn't survive off Broadway for more than 104 performances tells more about economic conditions in the smaller New York theaters today than all the shows in Papp's theaters put together.

Elsewhere in independent off-Broadway production, Michael Sawyer's *Naomi Court* provided two of the season's most keenly-felt, if abhorrent, experiences in a program of two one-acters tied together by their setting, a soon-to-be-razed apartment building. The first play showed a lonely woman creating an ideal middle-aged lover in her imagination to relieve her intense longing; the second was an episode of sheer menace with a little burglary and a lot of sex perversion thrown in.

Then there were two Tom Eyen amusements which opened off Broadway under individual auspices after having been tried by groups off off Broadway: *Why Hanna's Skirt Won't Stay Down,* a program of linked comedies about a pair of sisters, and *Women Behind Bars,* a takeoff of women's prison movies. The three 1974–75 foreign scripts did less for the off-Broadway season than their counterparts did on Broadway. They were *The Advertisement* (Italian, an emotional tangle in modern Rome); *Bullshot Crummond* (a British lampoon of detective thrillers); plus the one produced institutionally, *The Burnt Flowerbed* (the New York professional premiere at the Roundabout of Ugo Betti's 1952 play about an aging political leader).

Other independent off-Broadway production was more striving than succeeding (and if costs weren't so high, that's the way it ought to be off Broadway; an experimental theater's reach should often exceed its grasp). This was nowhere more apparent than on the musical stages. The year's musicals included *I'll Die if I Can't Live Forever* (a youthful expression of show-biz ambitions), *How to Get Rid of It* (an Eric Blau-Mort Shuman effort to musicalize Ionesco's *Amedée*), *Lovers* (a hymn to homosexuality), *Wings* (an effort to musicalize Aristophanes's *The Birds*), *Be Kind to People Week* (a harmonious chord in these discordant times, in a fable about a girl who wants to unite all the militant groups) and *The Glorious Age* (a Cy Young fantasy of medieval times).

Among the season's best off-Broadway musicals, *Philemon* was produced independently as a work in progress by Tom Jones and Harvey Schmidt in their Portfolio Studio and finally made available for public viewing for a few weeks in the spring. Based on a third-century Christian legend, it is a bloody, tortured tale of a clown who masquerades as a Christian leader in order to spy for the Roman tyrant until he's trapped by his role into real martyrdom. Both musically and dramatically, it was a powerful and memorable show, even if sometimes a little too heavy for its own strength. In contrasting mood, Chelsea Theater Center's *Diamond Studs* provided one of the season's pleasantest diversions with a stylized, folklorish musical about the life and times of Jesse James. *The Prodigal Sister,* a promising musical of the black big-city experience by J.E. Franklin and Micki Grant, was brought uptown by the New Federal Theater but couldn't find a commercial-theater audience. *The $ Value of Man* was yet another of those Byrd Hoffman Foundation (Robert Wilson) "operas" that seem to be offered almost exclusively for the amusement of the performers.

In the area of new playscripts, the institutional producers carried the day off Broadway. After a very slow start, with off Broadway looking about the way Joseph Papp says it does for months and months, the superior scripts came tumbling in on each other's heels. The Negro Ensemble Company can always be depended on to produce at least one very strong play every year; this year's was *The First Breeze of Summer* by Leslie Lee, a reflection on three generations of a black, now middle-class family, as the quarrels of the younger members set their much-admired grandmother to remembering some of the sacrifices and heartaches she had to suffer in order to bring them all this far. With Frances Foster in another of her portrayals of a lovable, indomitable matriarch under Douglas Turner Ward's direction, this was a highlight of the off-Broadway year which, following the present pattern, was set to move to Broadway in July. The NEC 1975 schedule included another "Season-Within-a-Season," a schedule of four programs of new plays by Burial Clay, Don Evans, Rudy Wallace and Samm Williams showcased for one-week runs each. Finally, NEC presented Silas Jones's *Waiting for Mongo,* a reality-fantasy kaleidoscope of the thoughts of a rapist in hiding.

American Place, too, took time to hit its stride this year. An effort to bring back S.J. Perelman's *The Beauty Part* got their season off on the wrong foot, and it didn't recover until April with the arrival of a new Sam Shepard program: *Killer's Head* (a murderer's thoughts in the electric chair just before the current is turned on) and the longer *Action,* produced last year in London by the Royal Court (a symbolic representation of the human condition by four bedraggled souls unable to take hold of themselves or their lives). Challenging as this program was, American place finished its season with an even bigger bang in a May program of two one-acters by an outstanding new playwright, Jonathan Reynolds. The first, *Rubbers,* was a broad satire on the machinations of the New York State Assembly (or any other such body), with an eager-beaver representative from Brooklyn (Laura Esterman) introducing a bill calling for open display of contraceptives in drug stores, over the loud objections of the entrenched, fossilized majority of her colleagues. It was like an erratic fast-ball pitcher, wild but with some great stuff—and that brings us to the second of Reynolds's plays whose title expressed its situation: *Yanks 3 Detroit 0 Top of the Seventh.* It was observed from the point of view of the pitcher's mound, where an over-the-hill Yankee pitcher has a perfect game so far but is slowly losing the confidence to complete it, and consequently his stuff except for a slider which his opponents are beginning to hit. Perfectly played by Tony Lo Bianco, the pitcher treats the audience to a batter-by-batter account of his fears of the moment—which is only a game, after all—and for his future, which is not. He tries to hide his fears from his thin-skinned catcher "Beanie" Maligma (Lou Criscuolo) and his manager, a rubber stamp of sports cliches. Both *Rubbers* and *Yanks 3 Detroit 0* were uneven in style, a problem which the director, Alan Arkin, wasn't able to solve, but they reached peaks of satire (and, in the latter case, of pathos as well) seldom attained in this season's shows. The success of this program caused American Place to suspend its subscriptions-only policy for the first time and open its box office for the sale of tickets to the public on a regular basis.

The name of Gene Feist's Roundabout Theater Company conjures images of bright revivals in its midtown setting, but like the other off-Broadway organizations it too presented a strong new script in its 1974–75 schedule. *James Joyce's Dubliners* was a study of the *Ulysses* author's youth and family life, dominated by his father (played by Stan Watt)—a stubborn, opinionated, courageous but debt- and booze-ridden parent who was surely destined to find a brilliant son among his nine children and bound to clash with him and finally drive him from the Joyces' poor excuse for a home in search of a more fulfilling life. Philip Campanella's original music and lyrics provided a punctuation of Irish ballads expressing the ineffable sweetness within the hard shell of despair, surviving under any and all pressures. *James Joyce's Dubliners* was as episodic as most biographical dramas, but at the same time a colorful and moving show with the sprawling succession of times, places and characters neatly compressed and plainly expressed under Gene Feist's direction. According to the credits, the script was based on James's younger brother Stanislaus's *My Brother's Keeper* and written by one J.W. Riordan whom we might hail as a promising new playwright if we weren't pretty sure that Riordan is none other than that same Gene Feist disguised in an Irish brogue and pseudonym. For whatever reason he may have chosen to adopt this bushel, decidedly there was a light under it.

Diamond Studs was the hit of Chelsea Theater Center's 1974–75 show, but it was only a small segment of Chelsea's energetic and eclectic schedule spread out across the river into both boroughs. In the home base in Brooklyn there were three new scripts and a revival, all of more than routine value: Megan Terry's *Hothouse,* trying for a comic blend by dissolving three generations of man-hungry women in alcohol; *Yentl the Yeshiva Boy*, adapted by Leah Napolin and Isaac Bashevis Singer from Singer's own story, with Tovah Feldshuh playing a 19th-century Polish girl so hungry for learning that she disguises herself as a boy in order to seize the opportunities denied to her sex; *Santa Anita '42*, Allan Knee's drama of Japanese Americans interned at a California racetrack during World War II; and *Polly,* the John Gay sequel to his *The Beggar's Opera,* a beautifully-mounted collector's item if there ever was one. *Yentl* proved to be the hardiest and most appealing element of Chelsea's home program and is to join the parade of off-Broadway hits bound for Broadway next season. In its Manhattan playhouse in the West Forties, Chelsea put on a "World Series" of guest appearances, including San Francisco Mime Troupe and a return engagement of London's *Wild Stunt Show.*

Over at Charles Ludlam's Ridiculous Theatrical Company they mixed and stirred their ingredients as before, with the usual result that Ludlam's fanciful productions came out a bright shade of purple. His *Stage Blood* was a *Hamlet* played by clowns (a group of touring players) using an amateur Ophelia and contriving a happy ending and anything else that might be good for a laugh, onstage or backstage. *Bluebeard* was more of the same special madness. Still another far-out ensemble, the Music-Theater Performing Group under the direction of Richard Foreman (the *Doctor Selavy's Magic Theater* man) tried a musical satire of film melodramas, *Hotel for Criminals,* with mixed results.

Many off-Broadway revues and specialties made bright little corners of entertainment here and there in the huge grey city. *Pretzels* was an assortment of tuneful and witty comments on urban foibles. *The National Lampoon Show* took off where *National Lampoon's Lemmings* left off, in its form of comic commentary. The revue *In Gay Company* provided an outlet for special interest in one direction; the one-man show *The World of Lenny Bruce* with Frank Speiser provided another (and a rare if not unique instance of a replacement in a one-man show when Ted Schwartz substituted for Speiser the last two weeks of the run).

The year's programs also included the Indian epic *The Ramayana* dramatized as a one-woman reading (by Jalabala Vaidya) in English; Paul Shyre's one-man presentation of H.L. Mencken and his works, *Blasts and Bravos;* and the National Theater of the Deaf in *The Dybbuk* and *Priscilla, Princess of Power,* the latter a comic-book-style entertainment based on a James Stevenson script about the prevalence of sugar in the American diet. And for the ninth season the Baird Marionettes offered a diet of delight with their version of *Peter and the Wolf* and a new marionette musical adaptation of *Alice in Wonderland* with book by A.J. Russell, music by Joe Raposo and lyrics by Sheldon Harnick, with Alice portrayed both by a marionette and a live actress.

If off Broadway is indeed d-e-a-d (Joseph Papp spelled it out to make sure the *Times* reporter got it right), then where did these 80-odd shows come from? Some were vanity productions, true. Others were plastic or worse. Still others were sheltered under special umbrellas from the direct, cruel blasts of this year's economic conditions. But there was also a group of a least ten good, solid, entertaining, challenging shows that might never have appeared under today's limited Broadway circumstances, or would almost certainly have passed unnoticed in the seething experimental crucible of off off Broadway's work in progress. True, it's much harder these days—which is to say much, much more expensive —to rare back and defy hubris with a single, independent off-Broadway production; and it must be agonizingly difficult, too, to mount a schedule of productions in a semi-subsidized organization, with the present shrinkage of public and private support for the performing arts. But it's not impossible—not yet, anyway, judging from our perspective on 1974–75 off Broadway. And until it is, if it ever is, never say die.

Offstage

In the strange economic and artistic climate of the 1974–75 season, stage production began to proliferate, even populating a new area: dinner theater so-called, a twofer proposition holding out the promise of dinner (not just a snack or a short-order meal) followed by a program-length live show to be enjoyed without moving from the table, where after-dinner refreshment often continues to be available, especially in the calculatedly long intermissions. The type of show, if not the food, tends to be light. This new development has scarcely touched New York City (possibly because of the many cabaret-style entertainments already available there), though the Belasco on Broadway was adapted for tables instead of aisles for the brief run of the imported musical *The Rocky Horror Show*. Indeed, dinner theater isn't aimed at the regular theatergoer at all, but at a new audience coaxed by the promise of being fed and cosseted into putting its toe into live-theater entertainment. An all-inclusive tab of, say, $13 per person would have about $5 apportioned as the show-biz share and the rest for food.

While dinner theater was creating new audiences across the country, the TKTS cut-rate ticket booths were doing the same right in Manhattan, in the heart of Times Square and down on Wall Street. These booths are a non-profit venture sponsored by the Theater Development Fund and others. Now in its second season, TKTS offers unsold same-day tickets to Broadway and off-Broadway shows at half price plus a $.50 surcharge for the tickets listed at less than $10 and $1 for the more expensive ones. During the 12 months of the season, according to *Variety* estimate, TKTS moved 652,864 tickets (more than half a million Broadway, the rest off Broadway and Lincoln Center) for receipts of $3,239,417. This amounts to somewhere between 4 and 5 per cent of the year's total gross. In the report on its first fiscal year in December, TKTS calculated that of the $2,339,618 taken in at its windows, $2,051,898 went to the theaters and only $287,720 for maintenance. The Wall Street TKTS base was new this season, and business there was disappointing, according to Hugh Sothern, executive director of the Theater Development Fund, but helpful in bringing new audiences into the theaters.

Some of theater subsidy's 1974–75 problems arose inevitably from troublesome economic conditions, and some did not. It was obvious early in the season that with money in increasingly short supply from both private and public sources, the various stage enterprises which rely heavily on subsidy were entering upon hard times, made still harder by pressures on the foundations to direct more and more of their shrinking resources to relieve sociological instead of artistic want. The National Endowment's $6.1 million in theater grants was up $2 million from the previous season but barely covered sharply-rising costs when spread thinly over the whole surface of the American stage. The Endowment roused some resentment with a $250,000 matching grant to the Royal Shakespeare Company for special educational performances and programs at American universities. Stage groups complained that American companies were more deserving of this American subsidy (it should be noted, however, that this was an education, not an arts, grant from the Endowment; at least the funds didn't come out of the arts pocket). The Federal arts allotment for 1974–75 was $74,750,000 out of $81 million requested by the Endowment. For next season, the White House has asked Congress for $82 million for the arts. New York State's subsidy was pegged at about $34 million to spread around its non-profit performing arts organizations ($21.5 million for basic support, $7.6 million for program funding, $5 million for community arts services), and the same amount has been requested for next year.

Among offstage activities of individuals this season was Neil Simon's decision to give himself a working Sabbatical on the West Coast. The most successful dramatist of the modern era moved from New York to California with his wife, the actress Marsha Mason, for a couple of years or so while his younger daughter goes to school there and while both the elder Simons fulfill movie commitments. Simon isn't turning his back on Broadway, which was alleged in some reports. He still owns the Eugene O'Neill Theater, where his 14th Broadway production, *God's Favorite,* was housed this season, and he hopes to have a new script ready year after next. In his own words, "I need a year off from the theater. Coming up with a play a year for so long a time has been rigorous, and I need a rest. But I certainly plan to be back."

Another distinguished legitimate stage artist, George Abbott, was getting ready to celebrate his 88th birthday and the 117th show with which he's been associated as actor, author, director or producer and sometimes a little of each. (The new Abbott show is *Music Is,* which he'll stage next season after writing the book.) Abbott's 116th show, according to *Variety's* count, was a hit revival of *Life With Father* which he directed this season in Seattle.

What is often referred to as the "critical fraternity" of those who cover American theater has been anything but fraternal. Unlike their European counterparts, American critics have never banded together in any organization (except for local groups formed solely to give prizes, like the New York Drama Critics Circle). They've never had a spokesman who could represent them officially at international convocations, etc. Now all that is changed. In August 1974, 23 working critics in various media in cities from New York to Los Angeles met under the auspices and roof of the Eugene O'Neill Memorial Theater Center in Waterford, Conn. and formed an American Theater Critics Association with this agreed-upon statement of purposes:

Since the American theater is beginning once again to become a truly national institution, we have formed an American Theater Critics Association in order to pursue the following goals:

1. To make possible greater communication among American theater critics.

2. To encourage absolute freedom of expression in the theater and in theater criticism.

3. To advance the standards of the theater by advancing the standards of theater criticism.

4. To increase public awareness of the theater as an important national resource.

5. To reaffirm the individual critic's right to disagree with his colleagues on all matters, including the above.

The bylaws of this new critics' organization call for an executive committee with staggered terms. Those elected were Henry Hewes (New York, executive secretary), Ernest Scheier (Philadelphia), Elliot Norton (Boston), Dan Sullivan (Los Angeles) and Clara Hieronymus (Nashville).

Lawsuits may be an unhappy means of settling arts controversies, but they often exert a profound influence on the economics and even the esthetics of the theater. A United States Supreme Court ruling in March, overturning lower-court rulings in support of a Chattanooga ban on the musical *Hair,* extended the freedom-of-speech protection of the First Amendment to the theater for the first time. The Authors League filed an *amicus curiae* brief in support of *Hair's* appeal in this case, prepared by Irwin Karp, the League's counsel, who commented as follows on the decision: "The results are not as satisfactory as those the Authors League and Dramatists Guild would have liked and have been seeking since 1957 —complete First Amendment protection against any restraint on the rights of adults to see any play or read any book they choose to read or view, regardless of its contents. But the. . . . opinion is a first step toward true First Amendment protection for the living stage."

Numerous copyright problems arose and were adjudicated during the year. Many of them arose—and many more will arise—from the new recording devices in both sight and sound, and from lack of clear definitions as to what is "fair use" of copyrighted material by these new duplicating devices. The revised Copyright Act itself, so long in committee, was finally passed by the U.S. Senate, but time ran out before it could get through the House in the 93d Congress. It has been re-introduced in the 94th by Sen. John J. McClellan, chairman of the Senate Judiciary Committee on Patents, Trademarks and Copyrights, and in the House by Rep. Robert W. Kastenmeier. It is expected that this first revision of the national copyright laws since 1909 will have a speedy and uneventful passage through the new Congress.

Such were the circumstances of the 1974–75 New York theater season, for better or worse (definitely better), for richer or poorer (definitely richer), in sickness and in health (paradoxically, in some ways more fabulous, in others more of an invalid). The year 1975 will go down in history not only as the one in which the United States of America began to close out its second century, but also— we ardently hope—as the one in which the theater's pendulum began a long upswing.

As we look forward to the Bicentennial, we can't help noting that no major Bicentennial observation is yet planned on or off Broadway. In line with today's decentralizing trend, the major observances will take place in regional and college theaters which have commissioned and/or held contests for Bicentennial plays. The biggest blast of all will take place, appropriately, at the John F. Kennedy Center for the Performing Arts in Washington, D.C., with a special American Bicentennial Theater season of old and new American plays produced by Roger L. Stevens, the Center's chairman, and Richmond Crinkley. With funding co-sponsorship from Xerox, the Washington theater complex will attempt to mount "a representative selection of American classics and new plays, drawn from the full range and repertory of the American theater."

The city of Washington didn't even exist in 1776, but it certainly will be the center of Bicentennial attention in 1975–76, theatrically as well as politically. Still, this American Bicentennial Theater celebration is also a Broadway theater celebration, if only by proxy. New York is where the theater was for those 200 years, and it's still where it's at as far as the majority of new work is concerned. Fly the flags and strike up the band, Washington, but remember your Revolution came from Boston, your Constitution from Philadelphia and your plays from New York and its good old Broadway.

Peter Evans, Paul Rudd, Terry Alexander, Dolph Sweet and
Kenneth McMillan in *Streamers* by David Rabe.

1975-76

LIKE any fine performance, the New York theater year of 1975–76 was largely a triumph of illusion. The impression of a crowded, brilliant season was as convincing as a great stage setting—and as fabricated. Grand new musicals and plays paraded through the theaters, flaunting their tip of the stage's massive creative effort—except that this season was a prop iceberg in a cardboard sea, all tip and no mass. There were enough leading attractions to break box office records, but there was no solid base of new shows underneath them on which the exception of a *Pacific Overtures* or *Streamers* or *Knock Knock* could stand tall.

Fortunately for everyone on both sides of the footlights, the illusion worked like magic, as it was supposed to. The smash hit, multi-prizewinning *A Chorus Line* stirred up so much excitement that for the first time in years there were rumors of ticket scalping (and never mind that this wonderful musical was last year's show, and a transfer from off Broadway). Star performances ranged from admirable (George C. Scott in *Death of a Salesman*) to heart-stopping (Irene Worth's in *Sweet Bird of Youth*)—and if you didn't look too closely you might not notice that, say, two-thirds of the Tony acting nominations were for roles in revivals, imports or transfers, not in new Broadway shows.

The illusion of a busy Broadway year was sustained by opening wide the doors of the theater libraries. Of 1975–76's total of 65 productions, 28—close to half the total effort—were revivals. New musical production seemed to be holding its own with 12 new entries, one transfer and three sizeable revues; but the production of new American plays was attenuated to next to nothing: three transfers from off Broadway and seven new scripts—seven which together played a total of only about 200 performances the whole season. The total Broadway playing weeks (if ten shows play ten weeks, that's 100 playing weeks) rose slightly to 1,136 as compared with 1,101 last year, well above the historic low of 852 the year before. The total was padded, however, with shows mounted elsewhere and brought in, like the five distinguished productions generated in Washington, D.C. as part of the Kennedy Center American Bicentennial Theater schedule produced by Roger L. Stevens and Richmond Crinkley with the help of a special grant from Xerox; or the year's outstanding Broadway drama, *The Runner Stumbles*.

Nowhere was the illusion more disarming than in the Broadway box office summaries. 1975–76 shattered the record for a season's total Broadway gross, amassing $70,841,738 as compared with the previous historical high of $58.9 million in 1967–68. This was a whopping increase of 20 per cent in the record and 23 per cent over last season's $57.4 million—and this highest gross ever was attained in spite of the fact that it was a short year for the musicals: only 48½ weeks long, as a musicians' strike shut them down for three and a half weeks in October, reducing the year's total income by an estimated $3.5 million. The season included the first $2 million week in Broadway history, the week of Jan. 4. With the road enjoying its second-best year ever with a $52.6 million gross, the total take for Broadway shows in 1975–76 rose to an un-

The 1975–76 Season on Broadway

PLAYS (10)

The First Breeze of Summer (transfer)
Lamppost Reunion
The Leaf People
Yentl (transfer)
Kennedy's Children
Murder Among Friends
The Poison Tree
KNOCK KNOCK (transfer)
Legend
THE RUNNER STUMBLES

SPECIALTIES (3)

Monty Python Live!
Shirley MacLaine
The Belle of Amherst

MUSICALS (13)

CHICAGO
A Chorus Line (transfer)
The Robber Bridegroom
The 5th Season
Treemonisha
Boccaccio
Home Sweet Homer
PACIFIC OVERTURES
Rockabye Hamlet
Rex
So Long, 174th Street
1600 Pennsylvania Avenue
Something's Afoot

REVUES (3)

Me and Bessie
A Musical Jubilee
Bubbling Brown Sugar

FOREIGN PLAYS IN ENGLISH (7)

TRAVESTIES
Habeas Corpus
THE NORMAN CONQUESTS
  Table Manners
  Living Together
  Round and Round the Garden
A Matter of Gravity
Zalmen or the Madness of God

FOREIGN PLAY (1)

Des Journées Entières Dans les Arbres

REVIVALS (28)

Angel Street
Phoenix Theater:
27 Wagons Full of Cotton & A Memory of Two Mondays
They Knew What They Wanted
Secret Service
Boy Meets Girl
My Fair Lady
Who's Afraid of Virginia Woolf?
D'Oyly Carte:
The Mikado
The Pirates of Penzance
H.M.S. Pinafore
Circle in Square 1975:
Death of a Salesman
Bicentennial Theater:
The Skin of Our Teeth
Summer Brave
Sweet Bird of Youth
The Royal Family
The Heiress
Circle in Square 1976:
Ah, Wilderness!
The Glass Menagerie
The Lady From the Sea
Acting Company:
Edward II
The Time of Your Life
Three Sisters
Vivian Beaumont:
Trelawny of the "Wells"
Hamlet
Mrs. Warren's Profession
THREEPENNY OPERA
Hello, Dolly!
Very Good Eddie

unprecedented $123 million-plus.

Audiences thronged Broadway's side streets in 1975–76, with many who couldn't quite afford the price of a ticket lining up at the TKTS booth on Duffy Square looking for a bargain (TKTS distributed more than half a million Broadway and almost a hundred thousand off-Broadway cut-rate tickets during the twelve months). The box office bonanza was achieved by a large increase in attendance, not by any significant increase in prices. According to an estimate prepared by Hobe Morrison in *Variety,* Broadway's attendance for the year was around 6,000,000—the importance of which to New York City may be judged in comparison to, say, the 4,000,000 drawn by all the New York baseball and football teams combined.

The top price for a Saturday night ticket to a hit Broadway musical moved upward last season from the previous $15 to $17.50, but only at *Chicago* in June and *Rex* in April, with the *My Fair Lady* revival priced at $16. Even with some upward ticket-pricing movement at other levels, inflation has made the once-shocking price of a Broadway show seem less forbidding. With attendance stimulated by a host of popular revivals like *The Royal Family,* a record gross resulted.

No one dares to suggest that the record was set because the shows were more attractive. Until someone can, even financial success must be viewed as somewhat illusory. For example, in this year of record theater prosperity there were, paradoxically, very few individually profitable shows. The handful of productions showing a profit, according to *Variety* estimate (see the one-page summary of the season accompanying this report), included last season's phenomenal *Same Time, Next Year* which by this season's end had grossed $5.3 million and was showing a $1.2 million profit on its relatively modest $230,000 investment.

The "star system," presumed burned out in the theater, flickered and then blazed back to temporary glory this season. In an engagement limited to ten weeks, Katharine Hepburn drew audiences to the admittedly second-rate *A Matter of Gravity* to the tune of a $350,000 profit on its $160,000 investment. Richard Burton took over the role of the doctor in the admittedly first-rate *Equus* which thereupon raised the price of its top ticket to $15 and packed them in with standees, doing 102 per cent of seating capacity for the 12 weeks.

Music concert stars visited Broadway theaters and could do no wrong. One event billed as "The Concert," with Count Basie, Ella Fitzgerald and Frank Sinatra in a two-week, 16-performance engagement at the Uris Theater priced at a $40 top, took in a higher two-week gross than ever dreamed of by a single "Broadway" attraction: $1,080,000. Shirley MacLaine with her "gypsies" made a two-week visit to the Palace in a song-and-dance revue which had scored a big hit in London and broke the Palace's record, taking in $329,000 for the 14 performances.

At the same time, failures were ever more conspicuous. Last season's shows which were drawing their bottom lines in 1975–76 included *All Over Town,* a 1975 Best Play which nevertheless lost $300,000 on its $275,000 investment. David Merrick folded Tennessee Williams's *The Red Devil Battery Sign* out of town to the tune of an estimated $360,000. The short-lived Broadway transfer of *Knock Knock* set its producers back an estimated $250,000. Even pre-packaged revivals could be costly if they didn't happen to catch on; American Bicentennial Theater's *The Skin of Our Teeth* and *Summer Brave* did fine in Washington but dropped $144,000 and $175,000 respectively on Broadway, according to *Variety* estimate. A pre-tested foreign script was no talisman against failure, either. A *Habeas Corpus* full of stars and seemingly doing business dropped $225,000 on $200,000; *Zalmen or the Madness of God* went for $300,000. Even *The Norman Conquests,* a hit in every respect except at the box office, ended up in the red, dropping $235,000 of its investment of $275,000.

The New York *Times* quoted Stephen Sondheim in an interview: "It takes . . . . . guts to do a show on Broadway these days. A man like Joseph Papp, who is funded by the government, puts on a show in a theater workshop, and when he deems that show worthy of transferring to Broadway, he brings it uptown. Well, where's the courage in that? The courageous guys are the ones who lay themselves on the line for a million dollars." Translated into the facts of 1975–76, this means some courageous guys named Roger L. Stevens and Kennedy Center productions dropped an estimated $1.2 million on the Yul Brynner musical *Home Sweet Homer* which lasted only one performance on Broadway after a long cross-country tour.

In such an economic context, the survival of Broadway as an arena for the exploration and development of the theater art is as illusory as a paper moon. It is impossible—or at the very least, foolhardy—to mount an untried script on Broadway these days. Simply, it costs too much and the chances of success are too small. Joseph Papp himself couldn't hack it with new plays at the Vivian Beaumont and lapsed this season into a revival schedule there. His plan to invade the West Forties with a series of new plays at the Booth Theater began and ended with the first one, Dennis J. Reardon's *The Leaf People* about a strange jungle culture, which ran only 8 performances, cost an estimated $400,000 (which Papp could probably afford, with his *A Chorus Line* a smash hit at the Shubert) and sent New York Shakespeare's experimental new-play-production program back downtown to the auditoria of the Public Theater where it belongs.

In such a context, Broadway has become no longer an arena but a showcase, a glamorous shop window for the display of all the items that caught on back in the recesses of the store. The pure theater artists of the cross-country and back-alley stages may turn up their noses at Broadway's exorbitant economy and crass commercialism, but Broadway is nevertheless the goal of their developmental efforts and the eventual destination of all their major successes. Off-Broadway hits move to uptown theaters faster than a speeding bullet; with regional theater hits and West End attractions it sometimes takes a little longer, but they all know where the big time is.

Broadway

Broadway in 1975–76 was a feast of revivals and a famine of new American plays. The pitiful list of ten new American plays was padded with transfers, two from last year's off-Broadway season: Negro Ensemble Company's *The First Breeze of Summer* by Leslie Lee, dramatizing a black matriarch's memories of three generations of her family's upwardly mobile struggle, a strong play which came close to last year's Best Plays list; and Chelsea Theater Center's *Yentl the Yeshiva Boy* by Leah Napolin from an Isaac Bashevis Singer story, with Tony nominee Tovah Feldshuh as a Jewish girl who disguises herself as a boy to qualify for male prerogatives.

Milan Stitt's *The Runner Stumbles* came to Broadway late in the season, pre-packaged in a production mounted at the new Hartman Theater in Stamford, Conn. under Austin Pendleton's direction. The play itself (previously seen in stagings at Yale, the Berkshire Festival and OOB) is a darkly-lit drama whose tortured characters grope among religious tenets and human longings for some solid truth to steady themselves. Its study of a nonconformist priest and a life-loving nun drawn together irresistibly—and tragically —was based on a 1911 episode in Michigan that ended in the priest's trial for the nun's murder. The play flashes back from the priest (Stephen Joyce) in his jail cell to the arrival of the cheerful young nun (Nancy Donohue) in his small parish, under the watchful eye of his dogmatically religious housekeeper (Sloane Shelton). These three collide with each other in powerful variations on the theme of loneliness.

On Broadway as well as off, the 1975–76 theater seems to be shedding its heavy clown makeup of recent years and giving more attention to dramatic themes and subjects, even stark ones like *The Runner Stumbles*. Louis LaRusso II's *Lamppost Reunion* was a late-night encounter in a Hoboken bar where a singing superstar, played by Gabriel Dell, pays a post-concert visit to cronies in the neighborhood where he grew up. The reunion is not a happy one, since the singer had once found it necessary to step on friends in reaching for the first rungs of the success ladder. There was flavor added: Frank Sinatra is also a singing superstar who grew up on the Jersey side of the Hudson, and the play was talked of as a drama *à clef* (Sinatra has a sidekick named "Jilly" whereas the star in the play has one named "Jobby").

Among other Broadway dramas was Ronald Ribman's *The Poison Tree*, originally produced in Philadelphia and pointing the finger at prisons as incubators, not of rehabilitation but of inhumanity. It was a strong play, forcefully acted by Moses Gunn in the role of a stoolie in spite of himself, tragic in spirit but not in size and therefore a little too heavy even for this year's Broadway. The reverse was true of Robert Patrick's *Kennedy's Children,* a non-play made up of alternating monologues by 1960s types crying out in pain at the evaporation of their fondest dreams in the heat of the 1970s. The characters—a kill-crazy Vietnam veteran, a suicidal sex goddess, a JFK-idolizer, etc.—might have attained tragic stature except that their vehicle, a concert of soliloquys, didn't have the shape of a real play, even though it survived a long journey through OOB and London in order to reach the West Forties.

In a somewhat lighter vein there was *Murder Among Friends* by Bob Barry, with Jack Cassidy playing and having fun with the role of a stage star whose coterie of friends all seem to be both villains and victims of their murderous intentions toward each other. In still another American entry, Samuel Taylor's effort to use the Western motif in a novel way in *Legend* didn't come off, even with Elizabeth Ashley doing the honors in the leading role.

However enthusiastically and widely a certain rebellion is being celebrated this year, the British are slowly repossessing their lost American colony, or at least that part of it running between 45th and 54th Streets on the West Side of Manhattan. For still another year British plays stole the Broadway scene. For example, there was Alan Ayckbourn's *The Norman Conquests,* three full-length comedies with the same set of characters and the same situation but not exactly the same events, presented like rotating repertory in successive performances. These plays interlock in time but not in space during a single family weekend at a British country house. That is to say, each play takes place in a different "part of the forest," showing what was going on in the dining room (*Table Manners*), the living room (*Living Together*) and the terrace (*Round and Round the Garden*) as the characters drifted from one room to another, in the same weekend's time frame.

What was going on mostly was that the others were accusing Norman (Richard Benjamin) of romantic dalliance, or trying to lure him into it, while he was managing to make "conquests" of his two sisters-in-law and his own wife. An all-star cast of Paula Prentiss, Ken Howard, Estelle Parsons, Barry Nelson and Carole Shelley occupied the other places at this family party, which could be joined at any point in the trilogy. These performances were even more clearly unified efforts, with the same actors playing the same characters in the same vein throughout the three plays. In our opinion, Carole Shelley deserves top 1976 acting honors in a secondary role, particularly for the scene in which she is trying to impart to a left-footed young veterinarian (Ken Howard) some information about the ways of love at levels higher than that of the birds and the bees. We also designate *The Norman Conquests* as the best of bests for 1976—not only because it's an unusual if not unique triple-play concept, but also because each of its three parts is an example of playmaking the equal of any other script on this season's Best Plays list.

And then there was *Travesties,* Tom Stoppard's Critics and Tony Award-winning comic travesty of an old man fumbling among dim memories of his service at the British Consulate in Zurich during World War II. Mostly for his own ego-gratification, he acts out a boastful and almost totally false acquaintanceship with great personages living in Zurich at that time: Lenin planning revolution, James Joyce writing *Ulysses,* and the Dadaists. *Travesties* is constructed like the *Alice in Wonderland* "Eat Me" episode, flashing forward and backward between muddled old age and immaculate youth, in Alice's rhythm of growing taller and shorter by turns. To borrow still another image from Alice, Stoppard's play is the grin without the cat: a preposterous concept worked out in dialogue that is in itself clever to the threshold of brilliance, with puns, limericks, literary and political allusions, double entendres—a shameless revel of language conducted by a master. Still, there's not quite as much of the cat visible as there was even in Stoppard's verbally acrobatic *Jumpers;* the outline of any sort of working play has all but disappeared. As theater, *Travesties* leaned very heavily on John Wood's memorable, kaleidoscopic acting of the scatterbrained fogey and featherbrained youth. But it also holds out a promise of a great play or plays to come if and when Stoppard can produce both grin and cat in a single context.

Lest we begin to think of British playwrights as infallible, we should pause briefly to consider two more of their contributions to the 1976 New York theater season. Alan Bennett's *Habeas Corpus* was an object lesson in vulgarity with jokes about falsies, drooling middle-aged desire, etc. etc. The presence in the cast of such notable performers as Jean Marsh (the Rose of *Upstairs, Downstairs*), June Havoc, Celeste Holm, Rachel Roberts, Kristoffer Tabori and Paxton Whitehead was no help; the only thing that helped was Donald Sinden's decision to give up on the play from time to time and chat informally with the audience.

The other British entry was Enid Bagnold's unsatisfactory *A Matter of Gravity,* an attempt to characterize the decline of our society and devise an appropriate response to it—commit yourself to an asylum to take refuge from the crazy people outside—which not even charming, witty, supremely poised and skillful Katharine Hepburn could levitate off the stage floor. Still another foreign entry, a translation from the French of Elie Wiesel's *Zalmen or the Madness of God,* also took on more weight than strength in its clash between a modern Russian community of Jews and the Soviet authorities. The year's only foreign-language production on Broadway was a Bicentennial gift to the New York theatergoer from the French government: an 11-performance limited engagement of the Renaud-Barrault company's production of Marguerite Duras's *Des Journées Entières Dans les Arbres* (Days in the Trees), directed by Jean-Louis Barrault, with Madeleine Renaud and Jean-Pierre Aumont as mother and son trying to perceive outlines of meaning in the strange twilight of their lives and perhaps of their form of civilization.

It was an active year for musicals, with the successes not quite balancing out the heavy disappointments. The year's outstanding show followed in the footsteps of *Company, Follies* and *A Little Night Music* as an innovative brainchild of composer-lyricist Stephen Sondheim, and producer-director Harold Prince: *Pacific Overtures,* an adventure among Japanese sights, sounds and styles. The imaginative book about Commodore Perry's arrival in the mid-1800s and impact on a Japan which had been isolated for 250 years was written by John Weidman (Jerome's son)in his professional stage debut, with additional material by Hugh Wheeler. The script, score and production viewed their subject through the "wrong," or Japanese, end of the telescope as compared with the "right," or American-musical end. All characters, including Americans, were played by Oriental actors, with men playing the women and Commodore Perry, for example, portrayed as a lion-devil, Kabuki-style. Exotic instruments and strange harmonies and cadences permeated the score, which avoided conventional Broadway show tunes. The lyrics soared into rich poetic fancies and then sparkled with pidgin-English humor. The styling in Prince's direction was flawless, of Boris Aronson's scenery fantastic, and of the cast seamless (with a standout performance by Mako in various roles including that of narrator).

The most popular new musical of the season was *Chicago,* a show in the *Carousel* tradition of transposing the characters and atmosphere of a strong play into the larger context of a full-scale Broadway musical. The play by Maurine Watkins had the same title, was described as a "satirical comedy," played 172 performances and was named a Best Play of 1926–27. Its tale of a 1920s love nest murderess in the midst of all the gangsters, molls and shysters of her era was as jazzier-than-life as the score, book and lyrics by John Kander, Fred Ebb and Bob Fosse could make it, enhanced by Patricia Zipprodt's costumes and Tony Walton's sets. Since its heroine was after all a killer—albeit an appealing one in the person of Gwen Verdon—*Chicago* stretched our sympathies perilously close to the breaking-point. It was a black musical whose production concept (not overlooking standout performances by Jerry Orbach, Gwen Verdon and Chita Rivera) was so stylishly colorful that the show merits a 1976 Best Plays designation for its new musical self, even with the borrowed finery of its original script.

Smaller in scale but immensely likeable was *The Robber Bridegroom,* a new musical wedged into the revival repertory of John Houseman's Acting Company. "Legendary Mississippi" was its setting for a pleasantly folksy folk tale about a gentleman highwayman and the women in his life, with book and lyrics by Alfred Uhry based on a Eudora Welty story, and with a sprightly and equally folksy score by Robert Waldman. Patti LuPone and Kevin Kline cut handsome figures as the romantic leads, but Mary Lou Rosato stole the show with her portrayal of a jealous, grasping witch.

And then there were three latecomers—*Rex, 1600 Pennsylvania Avenue* and *So Long, 174th Street*—of which much was expected and much too little realized. The first was a maximum effort by Richard Rodgers with a new lyricist, Sheldon Harnick, and a new librettist, Sherman Yellen, to bring Henry VIII into focus as a father-figure, both as ruler and parent. The book just barely managed to touch on the paradoxical love-hate relationship between daughter Elizabeth and her royal father, but it never got a firm grip on this promising subject, even though Nicol Williamson was a formidable Henry. Viewed in perspective, it's an achievement for *Rex* to have brought Rodgers and Harnick together in a new collaboration and evoked another memorable Rodgers number, "No Song More Pleasing." As a show, it accomplished little else.

1600 Pennsylvania Avenue produced still another promising new collaboration, with Alan Jay Lerner and Leonard Bernstein teaming up to portray American heads of state from George Washington to Theodore Roosevelt as householders—White House-holders, that is—thanks to the black people performing the menial chores downstairs, with Ken Howard playing all the presidents and Gilbert Price all the butlers. *1600 Pennsylvania Avenue* came into town so close upon the heels of *Rex* that it invited comparison. The team of Lerner & Bernstein made considerably less headway than the team of Rodgers & Harnick; in fact, this was one confrontation that Washington lost and a British king won.

A much nearer miss than either of these two majestic musicals was *So Long, 174th Street*, directed by Burt Shevelove and therefore, happily, a *funny* musical for once. Also for once, Joseph Stein's book based on his comedy *Enter Laughing*, about a high school boy headed for pharmacy school but full of ego and longing to become an actor, held its own with the musical elements provided by Stan Daniels, delivered by an enthusiastic and willing cast. The Shevelove "a funny thing happened" kind of humor broke out all over the place in the clowning of Robert Morse assisted by George S. Irving, many of the scenes having a life of their own like revue skits.

Even among the other 1976 Broadway musicals, nobody was cutting to a pattern. *The 5th Season* was a bilingual (Yiddish and English) musicalization by Luba Kadison and Dick Manning of Sylvia Regan's hit 1953 comedy about the New York City dress business. *Treemonisha* was a distinguished folk opera by the late, great Scott Joplin about an orphan girl's magical impact on her black community. Written in 1907, it had never been able to find a home on Broadway and wasn't comfortable there this season, its unique musical qualities notwithstanding. In *Boccaccio*, Kenneth Cavander and Richard Peaslee musicalized a set of stories from *The Decameron*, with the winsome D'Jamin Bartlett helping to interpret the romantic ironies. And then there was *Rockabye Hamlet*, in which the events of the celebrated tragedy were exposed to the heat and noise of a full-volume rock treatment. It was the rock style that broke under the weight of the play rather than the reverse, with only Alan Weeks managing to carry both successfully in his portrayal of an arrogant, dictatorial Claudius.

Punctuating the end of the Broadway musical season like an italicized exclamation point was *Something's Afoot,* a jolly take-off of a mystery-story situation in which ten guests and servants marooned on an island estate at a British house party are killed off one by one, much as in Agatha Christie's *Ten Little Indians* (the characters were different but the concept identical). The show was a broad spoof, with Tessie O'Shea kicking up her still almost agile heels as an Agatha Christie type of nosy and indomitable white-haired lady sleuth. Gary Beach, Liz Sheridan and others under Tony Tanner's direction prowled comically among pieces of gloomy Victorian furniture rigged to murder them in a number of heavy-handed ways. It was a proper treat, once you got with it. The collaborators—James McDonald, David Vos and Robert Gerlach—credited their source in a show-stopping number entitled "I Owe It All to Agatha Christie." To a large extent, allowing for an extra degree of suspension of disbelief and an extra step of pleasant outrage, they did.

The 1975–76 revues were outstanding, with clear-cut themes and or stylistic traits and inexhaustible energy in the performances. *Me and Bessie* was an outline of the life and career of the celebrated blues singer Bessie Smith. She wasn't directly impersonated, but her memory was clearly evoked by Linda Hopkins as the "Me" of the title. Miss Hopkins rendered Miss Smith's best-known songs with power and emotion, and at the same time narrated her life with a light touch, affectionate and appealing, in the year's best musical performance by an actress. *A Musical Jubilee* contained an abundance of noteworthy performances, with an all-star cast (Lillian Gish, Tammy Grimes, Larry Kert, Patrice Munsel, John Raitt, Cyril Ritchard and Dick Shawn) in a nostalgic history of the American musical with a continuity by Max Wilk and a collection of memorable numbers from shows. *Bubbling Brown Sugar* was also nostalgic and affectionate in its view of the glory days of Harlem in a lively reminiscence written by Loften Mitchell, strung with glorious song numbers of the 1920s and 1930s and performed effervescently by Vivian Reed, Avon Long, Joseph Attles and many others in a superbly accomplished musical ensemble under Robert M. Cooper's direction.

A charming addition to the 1975–76 Broadway scene was Julie Harris's impersonation of Emily Dickinson in the one-woman drama *The Belle of Amherst* by William Luce. Another appealing specialty was *Monty Python Live!,* a zany multimedia romp by the visiting British troupe whose antics are familiar to millions in the TV series *Monty Python's Flying Circus* shown here on Public Broadcasting.

Off Broadway

Where did all the new plays go this year? Most of those that surfaced in the New York professional theater in 1975–76 did so in the area we call "off Broadway"—which was preserving a marvellous illusion of life all through the season, despite the fact that Joseph Papp pronounced it finally and thoroughly dead more than a year ago. In this year of illusions, off-Broadway mounted what seemed to be a real season of 26 new American plays, five of

The 1975–76 Season off Broadway

PLAYS (26)

Finn MacKool
Public Theater:
  JESSE AND THE BANDIT QUEEN
  Rich & Famous
  So Nice, They Named It Twice
  For Colored Girls Who Have Considered Suicide, etc.
  REBEL WOMEN
American Place:
  Gorky
  Every Night When the Sun Goes Down
Circle Repertory:
  The Elephant in the House
  Dancing for the Kaiser
  KNOCK KNOCK
  Who Killed Richard Cory?
  SERENADING LOUIE
Dear Mr. G
Jinxs Bridge
Newhouse Theater:
  The Shortchanged Review
  STREAMERS
Cracks
The Primary English Class
Negro Ensemble:
  Eden
  A Season-Within-a-Season

The Hound of the Baskervilles
Vanities
Medal of Honor Rag
Caprice
Titanic

MUSICALS (6)

Boy Meets Boy
Christy
By Bernstein
Gift of the Magi
Apple Pie
Fire of Flowers

SPECIALTIES (7)

Conversations With an Irish Rascal
Baird Marionettes:
  Alice in Wonderland
  Winnie the Pooh
From Sholom Aleichem With Love
The Polish Mime Theater
Szajna's Studio Theater:
  Dante
  Replika

RETURN ENGAGEMENT (1)

Women Behind Bars

FOREIGN PLAYS IN ENGLISH (3)

The Collected Works of Billy the Kid
The Family (Parts 1 & 2)
Ice Age

FOREIGN PLAY (1)

Phèdre

REVIVALS (29)

Delacorte:
  Hamlet
  The Comedy of Errors
Roundabout:
  Summer and Smoke
  Clarence
  The Cherry Orchard
Classic Stage:
  Measure for Measure
  Hedda Gabler
  A Country Scandal
  Antigone
  And So to Bed
Light Opera:
  Iolanthe
  Naughty Marietta
  The Mikado
  The Vagabond King
  The Pirates of Penzance
  H.M.S. Pinafore
  The Gondoliers
  Patience
  The Student Prince
The Homecoming

Brooklyn Academy:
  Sweet Bird of Youth
  The Royal Family
  Long Day's Journey Into Night
  Henry V
  The Hollow Crown
  The Boss
  Woyzeck
American Place:
  Endecott and the Red Cross & My Kinsman, Major Molineux
  Benito Cereno

REVUES (3)

Tuscaloosa's Calling Me ...but I'm Not Going
Dear Piaf
Tickles by Tucholsky

Plays listed in **CAPITAL LETTERS** have been designated Best Plays of 1975–76.
Plays listed in *italics* were still running June 1, 1976.

which achieved Best Play status. This total of new American plays produced in a single season is down from off-Broadway's peak, but it holds its own fairly well with the totals of other years in the 1970s: 30 in 1975, 27 in 1974, 28 in 1973, 43 in 1972, 39 in 1971, 21 in 1970.

Certainly this continued vitality is illusory to the extent that the very great majority of these new plays, and all the five Bests, were produced in the shelter of subsidized organizational schedules. As Broadway built its illusion of a 1975–76 season out of revivals, off Broadway built one out of an Establishment with outside support (outside the box office, that is) of such production groups as New York Shakespeare, American Place, Circle Repertory, Chelsea and Negro Ensemble. When Joseph Papp says that off Broadway is dead, what he probably means is that it's a marionette without an economic life of its own, creating an illusion of life by means of strings pulled by benefactors.

If so, public money was never better spent, private support never affected an art form so directly and purposefully since the days of the Medicis. Off Broadway isn't necessarily or even usually the source of its own best work, which is often drawn in from experimental programs elsewhere. But it seems to be the major showcase open to American straight-play dramatists at the center of the American stage, which is still New York. Five of the six American Best Plays were produced off Broadway this season. In the theater's "two planks and a passion," the planks are essential to the passion, and off Broadway is sustaining a platform where otherwise none at all would exist.

No one puts private and public subsidy to better use than the abovementioned, esteemed Joseph Papp and his New York Shakespeare Festival. Activity in his many nooks and crannies uptown and downtown, indoors and outdoors, ranges from workshop-experimental to the most striking finished productions include three of the Best Plays, among them the Critics best-American-play award winning *Streamers* by David Rabe. Papp has produced all of Rabe's plays in New York: *The Basic Training of Pavlo Hummel*, *Sticks and Bones* (a Best Play plus a special Critics citation) and *Boom Boom Room*, both the original and the rewrite. He produced *Streamers*, too, in Lincoln Center's little Newhouse Theater uptown, but not before it had been tried out in front of New Haven audiences at the Long Wharf. We note this as symptomatic of the soft and changing state of the New York stage, in that a Papp playwright—perhaps *the* Papp playwright—would find it necessary to try out his script in regional theater prior to even an off-Broadway production by a group whose very specialty is generating new material.

Rabe's newest, the best American script of the year, attempted to delineate the American way of violence. Its characters are soldiers, but *Streamers* isn't a play about war. Most of its 1965 Virginia army Barracks inhabitants haven't seen combat yet. Their stresses are personal: the idealist (Paul Rudd) secure in his identity with middle America, the black (Terry Alexander) who has made a separate peace with society, the barracks gadfly (Peter Evans) alternately mocking and inviting homosexual behavior. Into this tense but not yet explosive situation is thrust an angry, deprived black (Dorian Harewood) who has *not* made peace with anyone including himself. He is a selfish, self-pitying misfit wracked by contempt for his peers and fear of loneliness. This barracks, a social microcosm, must purge him at once or suffer the inevitable consequences of his hostile presence. They don't purge him so they do suffer when his arrogance is detonated by rejection and explodes at knife-point into mindless acts of brutal, very bloody violence.

The characters were well developed and the action explicit to the point of shock under Mike Nichols's carefully thought-out direction. This was a strong play, albeit somewhat impulsive, with a confusion of imagery. When a middle-aged sergeant tells the young privates how, in Vietnam, he threw a grenade into the foxhole of an enemy sniper and held a lid down over him until the grenade exploded, the anecdote is obviously an analogy of the intrusion of the black killer into this closed barracks society. But the title image of a "streamer" —a parachute which fails to open—was never quite connected up with the play, just as the final violence seemed in a way disconnected because it was hugely out of proportion to its immediate cause, like an insane paroxysm. Perhaps, though, this was Rabe's point: a "streamer" and a senseless knifing are accidents indigenous to American life and could happen to anyone at any time. Anyhow, Rabe did again what he did with *Sticks and Bones,* reinforce a whole season with an arresting drama.

Another of Papp's Best Plays was a Western of sorts, *Jesse and the Bandit Queen,* whose two characters, Jesse James and Belle Starr, wrap their legends and emotions around and around each other until they look exactly alike: part criminal and part hero, part man and part woman, part fiction and part fact. This was not a true history, but a series of metaphors in which only the deaths of Belle and Jesse were acted out literally. The two outlaws in the play are being used as symbols (a fact which they resent heartily). America invented them, stuffed them with the straw of romantic cliches and dangles them as a charm to ward off historical doubt and guilt. This Jesse and this Belle are both themselves and characters in a *Police Gazette* adventure, both vulnerable and violent, incestuous, cruel, selfish and never adequately loved, dangerous to the very admirers who place them on a pedestal, dangerous especially to themselves. As played by Kevin O'Connor and Pamela Payton-Wright (and her accomplished replacement Dixie Carter after she left the cast early in the run), they were as unforgettable in David Freeman's play as they seem to be elsewhere in American story and song.

New York Shakespeare Festival's third Best Play, *Rebel Women,* was the work of another of Papp's "own" playwrights: Thomas Babe, who made his professional debut last year at the Public Theater with the well-received *Kid Champion,* about the downfall of a rock music star. His second play turned backward to the past for a warts-and-all snapshot-in-transit of another sort of hero, Gen. William Tecumseh Sherman, larger than life and as sure-footed as death on his march to the sea over the helpless body of the defeated South. The sickness of war is well advanced upon Sherman and his men as they camp for the night in a Georgia mansion occupied by four Southern women. These soldiers and their leader welcome the brief escape of love or its semblance, any way they can and in any form available, to sweeten the bitterness of their duty. The script was overweight here and there, but Sherman himself was solid muscle, viewed as a military pragmatist whose convictions are like laser beams melting all illusions and—strangely —one "enemy" heart, at least for a night. The role vibrated with the power of David Dukes's performance, and Kathryn Walker, Leora Dana and Deborah Offner reflected some of it back at him as Southern belles of greatly differing character and standards. The direction by Jack Hofsiss held the focus on the conqueror, while Babe's script succeeded admirably in cutting down one of the heroic statues of American history to the size and proportions of a human being.

Papp's season of new plays up and downtown included a batch of other interesting works. Preceding *Streamers* at the Newhouse was *The Short-changed Review* by Michael Dorn Moody, reflecting the troubles of our times in the bloodshot eyes of a middle-aged, liberal pop-music radio station owner, whose friends and relations let him down and weigh him down in numbers of ways. Following *Jesse and the Bandit Queen* into the Public Theater was John Guare's collection of inside show biz jokes in *Rich & Famous,* with the season's most effective comedy teaming of William Atherton, Ron Leibman and Anita Gillette acting out a fledgling playwright's fantasies on the occasion of his first opening night under the expert direction of Mel Shapiro. Then there was the Myrna Lamb-Nicholas Meyers opera-style musical *Apple Pie,* about a woman who escapes from Nazi Germany only to be persecuted in America by anti-feminists, this show directed by Papp himself. In addition to this distinguished collection of new work there were the outstanding revivals in Central Park and at the Vivian Beaumont, about which more in the next section of this report. Debatable as some of Papp's most authoritative pronouncements may be ("Off Broadway is dead" indeed!), there's never been anything to compare with the consistent interest and versatility of his 1975–76 production schedules all around the town.

Violence, whether overt as in a *Streamers* or implicit as in a *Jesse and the Bandit Queen,* is now a preoccupation of our stage as it has been of our screen. Violence as we know it was invented by Jules Feiffer in a play called *Little Murders,* and it provided a sort of counterpoint to the hilarious absurdities of Feiffer's new *Knock Knock,* produced by Circle Repertory Company and then moved uptown to Broadway. This comedic Best Play was about two middle-aged recluses (played in the off-Broadway cast by Daniel Seltzer and Neil Flanagan) living in a cottage in the deep woods, passing the time by quarreling, until suddenly their lives are touched and transformed by magic. They rub a lamp, and lo! not a genie but Joan of Arc in person (the blonde and comely person of Nancy Snyder) knocks on their door, is greeted by a shotgun blast but stays anyway and manages to loosen the bonds tying the two men to their preconceived attitudes toward reality and fantasy. This mixture of old and new jokes, acrobatic language, an exploding kitchen, constantly lurking violence, etc., was stirred and seasoned to amuse by its director, Marshall W. Mason, and amuse it certainly did, with a touch of Feiffer bemusement for extra flavor. After the move to Broadway, *Knock Knock* was refurbished with a new cast (Charles Durning, John Heffernan and Lynn Redgrave) and new direction by José Quintero, but there was no way to make it more hilarious—in its perplexing Jules Feiffer fashion—than it was downtown.

Like Joseph Papp, Mason and his Circle Repertory Company didn't rest on the laurels of a single Best Play this season. Their second was Lanford Wilson's *Serenading Louie,* still another brown study of developing violence, this time with marriage as its breeding ground. The play was about two youngish couples ten years out of college and nine years married, the ex-quarterback (Edward J. Moore) to the ex-homecoming queen (Tanya

Berezin) and his best friend (Michael Storm) to a self-possessed creature (Trish Hawkins) who demands such order in her marriage that she can hardly believe it when she discovers that her husband is spending a lot of time and emotion on a teen-ager. The other marriage is on the rocks, too, and here's where the greatest danger lurks. The quarterback can't stop adoring his college sweetheart even though he knows she's lavishing her favors on another man. *Serenading Louie* was a controlled, orchestrated series of revelations and reactions, with the characters sometimes cutting through the underbrush of suggestion, turning away from the play and speaking directly to the audience. Both homes were represented by the same stage setting, with the two families inhabiting it simultaneously, helping to make the play's statement that though these people may be individuals, neither their situation nor their problems are unique. The play moved smoothly through this unusual space-time arrangement under Mason's direction, which was as appropriately fluid for *Serenading Louie* as it was punchy for *Knock Knock*.

Circle Repertory's season also took in *The Elephant in the House* by Berrilla Kerr, a rewrite of a former Circle workshop production of a play about a bedridden New York woman who opens her house to peculiar strangers; *Dancing for the Kaiser* by Andrew Colmar, a London 1918 period piece; and A. R. Gurney Jr.'s *Who Killed Richard Corey?*, a further exploration of the subject of the poem by Edward Arlington Robinson. Circle Repertory is one of those emergent groups hard to classify as to its technical status—off Broadway or off off? Technically, Circle Repertory falls somewhere between the two categories, sometimes showing perfect off-Broadway conformation, but sometimes with the character of an OOB "showcase" in which Equity actors have special permission to appear under certain prescribed conditions. Having noted this, we hasten to add that Marshall W. Mason and his Circle are every inch professional. They've defined their own status with the quality of their shows, and whatever their dimensions may be, the rest of our theater, Broadway included, could do worse than measure up to them.

In its theaters in Brooklyn and Manhattan, Chelsea Theater Center put on an eclectic schedule of new, foreign, musical and revived shows. Chelsea's best this season was *Vanities* by Jack Heifner in his professional playwriting debut with a sweet-and-sour study of three women friends at crucial stages of their interwoven lives: as high school cheerleaders, as college seniors important in their campus roles and finally a half dozen years later with their potentialities frozen into adult characteristics, most of them unattractive. Their youthful absorption with self was clearly portrayed by the three-actress ensemble—Jane Galloway, Susan Merson and Kathy Bates—and not allowed to let up under Garland Wright's direction, even during intermissions when the performers remained visible at their vanity tables upstage, making up for the next scene.

Other 1975-76 productions at Chelsea Manhattan were a translation of the first half of Lodewijk de Boer's *The Family,* a Dutch play about life's tribulations on the outskirts of Amsterdam; and the cabaret musical *By Bernstein,* an assemblage of Leonard Bernstein show tunes which for one reason or another had been cast overboard in the course of production. In Brooklyn there was *Ice Age*, a translation of Tankred Dorst's lumpy indictment of a Norwegian author (played by Roberts Blossom) who supported the Nazis and now, as an old man, is reviewing his actions; and, finally, a Chelsea bow to the Bicentennial with Edward Sheldon's *The Boss,* a 1911 drama about industrial corruption which hasn't been revived professionally in New York before. With shows like these, Chelsea held firmly to its artistic franchise in both boroughs, though it was less than a banner year.

The Negro Ensemble Company has made a habit of starting late but coming on strong season after season down at St. Marks Place. *Ceremonies in Dark Old Men, The River Niger* and *The First Breeze of Summer* were some of its past accomplishments. This year it was *Eden* by Steve Carter, a careful, intimate examination of intra-racial prejudice in the friction between a vain and disdainful West Indian immigrant patriarch and the second-generation American black family living next door in the Harlem of the late 1920s. Samm-Art (he is Samm when he writes plays, Samm-Art when he acts) Williams and Shirley Brown acted the appealing young lovers star-crossed by Montague-Capulet strife, and Graham Brown played the austere and ferociously prejudiced West Indian parent who worships Marcus Garvey as the messiah to lead them all back in glory to Africa, where he believes they belong. This was a long but rewarding script, precisely directed by Edmund Cambridge. The NEC also staged their customary "Season-Within-a-Season" schedule of one-week showcase productions including *A Love Play* by the abovementioned Samm Williams.

American Place came up with a pair of strong new scripts in 1976. Steve Tesich's *Gorky* introduced the aging Russian dramatist and revolutionary on the eve of a surgical "operation" ordered by Stalin and guaranteed to be fatal. It then flashed back in Gorky's memory to his boyhood, his youth and his loves in episodes of both character development and historical interest. The other was Phillip Hayes Dean's *Every Night When the Sun Goes Down,* whose group of barroom escapists a la *The Time of Your Life* realize that even for them the time has come for social and environmental renewal. In a rare example of homage to the Bicentennial on the part of a New York theater, American Place brought back its famous Robert Lowell trilogy *The Old Glory* in a distinguished two-program revival, with *Benito Cereno* (about black slaves rebelling and capturing the Spanish ship on which they're being transported) playing by itself and *Endecott and the Red Cross* (the massacre of a white settlement by the white governor at Merry Mount, Mass.) and *My Kinsman, Major Molineux* (the first days of the Revolution in Boston) playing together.

All off-Broadway productions cited so far in this report took place in the shelter of organizations. Independent production was scarce this season, increasingly inhibited by ever higher costs, with returns limited by the size of the auditoria. Even so, two remarkable scripts were independently mounted: Israel Horovitz's *The Primary English Class* and Tom Cole's drama *Medal of Honor Rag,* both of them plays of increasing pressure performed in one seamless piece, without intermission. The Horovitz comedy created the world's most frustrating English language class of pupils, each of whom speaks a different native tongue and not one word of any other, and their night-school teacher (Diane Keaton), a neurotic who patronizes and scorns her class. This adventure in non-communication was cleverly conceived and firmly pushed to a hectic conclusion.

The pressure of *Medal of Honor Rag* builds dramatically and inexorably toward disaster, in a session with an Army psychiatrist (David Clennon) and his patient (Howard E. Rollins Jr.), a black Vietnam veteran who went berserk when he saw his buddies killed. He attacked and decimated the enemy single-handed and cannot now always control the memory of his rage. The Cole and Horovitz scripts were small packages of exceptional theater, in a modern context that seems to have room for large packages only.

Most of the year's off-Broadway musicals were produced independently and to the sorrow of those backing them. The single exception was *Boy Meets Boy,* with a special appeal accurately represented by its title. One of the revues won a place deep in the hearts of New York theatergoers: *Tuscaloosa's Calling Me . . . but I'm Not Going,* a winning collection of songs and sketches making the case for living in New York City, written by a talented trio of young aficionados: Bill Heyer, Hank Beebe and Sam Dawn.

Among the year's specialty attractions were two visiting troupes from Poland, the Polish Mime Theater and Josef Szajna's stark, pantomimic images of World War II horrors. In a lighter, sweeter vein, the Bil Baird marionettes were a standout as usual, with their two fanciful 1975–76 offerings, *Alice in Wonderland* and *Winnie the Pooh.*

With 26 new American plays (including five Best Plays), the off-Broadway season wasn't as illusory as Broadway's. It was enhanced by the continued very long-run presence of *The Fantasticks,* Tom Jones's and Harvey Schmidt's fantastic musical, the longest-running professional New York production of all time, now in its 17th year having started the new 1977 season June 1 with its 6,700th performance. Combine Broadway's two all-time longest runs—*Fiddler on the Roof* and *Life With Father*—and their total still falls short of *The Fantasticks* by more than 100 performances. Before this indigenous off-Broadway phenomenon calls it quits, it may very well add the runs of *Tobacco Road* and *Hello, Dolly!* too. The supremely distinguished Joseph Papp to the contrary notwithstanding, and whatever else happens or fails to happen, off Broadway can never be pronounced dead while *The Fantasticks* lives on.

Revivals

This was the season of the New York theater's center of gravity shifting markedly toward revival production, particularly on Broadway. Over the last two or three seasons, revivals have been on the increase, until in 1975–76 they were preponderant. On Broadway, 28 of the year's programs were revivals (there were "only" 18 last year), as compared with a total of 23 new American plays and musicals, including transfers.

Revivals were not only numerous in 1975–76, they were exceptionally successful. They provided the biggest new straight-play hit—*The Royal Family*—and three of the year's sizable musical hits—*Very Good Eddie, My Fair Lady* and *Threepenny Opera.* Revival casts, directors and designers received 19 Tony nominations, four of them winners: Irene Worth (best actress for *Sweet Bird of Youth*), George Rose (best musical actor for *My Fair Lady*), Edward Herrmann (best featured actor for *Mrs. Warren's Profession*) and Ellis Rabb (best director for *The Royal Family*).

Why this shift toward the theatrical past? The explanation must lie with the dismal science of economics, not with the glorious art of the stage. An already-proven script doesn't guarantee success, but it reduces the element of risk at a time when risks are becoming ever more expensive in failure and not all that much more lucrative in success. Audiences are increasing, and so production is stimulated. But new work is more dangerous, and so all the extra thrust is placed behind revival production.

The Bicentennial accounts for a small percentage of the increased revival activity. Six plays of the American Bicentennial Theater at Kennedy Center in Washington, sponsored in part by Xerox, were brought to New York by various producers: *Long Day's Journey Into Night* with Jason Robards starring and directing at the Brooklyn Academy of Music; *The Skin of Our Teeth* with Alfred Drake, *Summer Brave* with Alexis Smith and *The Heiress* with Richard Kiley and Jane Alexander (a memorable acting team, at least as effective as their original counterparts, Basil Rathbone and Wendy Hiller) to Broadway; and *Sweet Bird of Youth* and *The Royal Family* to both Brooklyn and Broadway. Miss Worth as a faded movie queen in the Williams play was a towering figure, but she did not eclipse Christopher Walken as her doomed lover, under Edward Sherin's direction. And not enough gratitude can be expressed for the presence in New York this season of Ellis Rabb's re-launching of the 1927 George S. Kaufman-Edna Ferber comedy about a theatrical "royal family" reminiscent of the Barrymores, living in the grand manner of their performances. The acting ensemble of Eva Le Gallienne as the matriarch, Rosemary Harris as the Broadway star, George Grizzard as her movie-hating movie star brother, Sam Levene as the Broadway producer and others of equal importance in lesser roles outshone even *The Norman Conquests* company as a coordinated group.

Among musical revivals were a charming new *My Fair Lady* and an inventive re-staging of *Very Good Eddie,* an ice-cream-suit Jerome Kern musical with boys and girls, led by Charles Repole, romancing on the Albany night boat in an updated book by Guy Bolton, perfectly stylized by Bill Gile's direction. In the face of these superb productions, our choice for the best musical revival of 1975–76 is the Joseph Papp *Threepenny Opera,* the last in a four-program season of revivals at the Vivian Beaumont in Lincoln Center that was as admirable as Papp's new-play program was distinguished. These Beaumont shows may have been designed at least in part as audience-pleasers for the subscription set, but each of them had a little something extra, a little something challenging to flavor the experience for any more adventurous theatergoer who might happen along. The sentimental journey of Pinero's *Trelawny of the "Wells"* became a lively abrasion of high society and low-living theater folk under A. J. Antoon's direction, with a carefully color-blended ensemble of character actors: John Lithgow, Marybeth Hurt, Walter Abel and Aline MacMahon among them. Even *Hamlet* seemed almost newly-minted, with an imaginatively flexible design by Santo Loquasto and a pixillated Hamlet (Sam Waterston) who was no match for his stern Uncle Claudius (Charles Cioffi). *Mrs. Warren's Profession* became a collection of cameo performances by Lynn Redgrave, Ruth Gordon, Milo O'Shea, Edward Herrmann (the featured-player Tony Award winner) and others trying to capture the emerging feminism of the young century by characterizing various attitudes toward it.

Even more ambitiously, Papp decided to restore the Bertolt Brecht-Kurt Weill *Threepenny Opera* to something approaching its original design by producing, not the smoothed-over Marc Blitzstein translation so popular off Broadway in the 1950s and 1960s, but a new translation by Ralph Manheim and John Willett more faithful to its abrasive source. Papp's own program note described his aspirations in part as follows:

> In comparing the lyrics and text of Blitzstein to the original, we discovered to our surprise that the Blitzstein adaptation excised much of the political and sexual thrust which is contained in our present translation and which gives the original German work its relentless power.
>
> It is clear that the intention of Brecht in this now-classic work was to assault the audience with his irony and views of life. By neatly fitting his abrasive words into conventional musical pattern, the 1954 adaptation had the effect of neutralizing much of the bite of Bertolt Brecht. While the lyrics of Blitzstein may be more "singable" than Brecht's rugged, gutter lyrics, they quite clearly are at odds with the dramatist's purpose and dramatic sensibilities.
>
> An example to demonstrate how Brecht's intent was softened by the 1954 adaptation:

Blitzstein:	*Brecht:*
Instead of, instead of	No they can't, no, they cant.
Goin' about their business and behavin'	See what's good for them And set their minds on it.
They make love, they make love;	It's fun they want, it's fun they want
Til the man is through	
And then she's sorry that she gave in.	So they end up on their arses in the shit.

> It is our hope that this remarkable new translation of *Threepenny Opera,* in its original and uncensored form, will give our audiences knowledge of the true power of one of the great works of our 20th century.

Raul Julia's bold-faced portrayal of Mack the Knife was a finishing master-stroke in a masterly revival further informed by Richard Foreman's direction, with echoes of Peter Brook's *Marat/Sade*. When, a year ago, the Beaumont's audiences failed to support Papp's kind of new plays produced there, the producer was forced to try to give them what they apparently want: distinguished occasions of conventional theater. His 1975–76 set of revivals has served them better than anyone could have presumed to hope, punctuated by this provocative and brilliant *Threepenny Opera*. It was more than a revival, it was a thrilling restoration.

Another challenger at the musical peak was *My Fair Lady,* a captivatingly faithful copy of the original, tracing every line of the Moss Hart direction and Cecil Beaton design, produced by the show's original producer, Herman Levin, and with Robert Coote again treating Broadway to his interpretation of Henry Higgins's friend Colonel Pickering. Ian Richardson played Higgins differently than Rex Harrison but as validly: a little more force, a little less charm. Christine Andreas was in good voice as his fair flower girl, George Rose clowned all over the place as her father Alfred P. Doolittle, and Jerry Lanning was so good as Eliza's vapid young man Freddy that he stopped the show with his rendition of "On the Street Where You Live." Having *My Fair Lady* back in all its enduring glory of music, comedy and romance was indeed a joyful reunion, one of the year's most satisfying events.

Circle in the Square also produced a vintage season, beginning in June with *Death of a Salesman,* in which George C. Scott directed himself in the part of Willy Loman. Scott is an actor of such power that his Willy acquired a strength of character somewhat at odds with his other weaknesses—a contradiction reminiscent of Richard Burton's Hamlet of a few years back and with its same audience-shaking strength taking up some of the strain it placed on the play. The 1976 series of revivals by this Theodore Mann-Paul Libin group began with O'Neill in his front-porch, Fourth-of-July mood of nostalgic Americana in *Ah, Wilderness!* under the direction of the Long Wharf Theater's exceptionally accomplished Arvin Brown, who lent himself generously to Broadway projects this season. Mann himself directed a luminescent revival of *The Glass Menagerie* with Maureen Stapleton as Amanda, Pamela Payton-Wright as her daughter, Paul Rudd as the gentleman caller and Rip Torn playing son and brother with a wild-animal ferocity that brought a new and perfectly appropriate cutting-edge to his role in this wonderful, enduring play. The Circle in the Square season then provided the mystery and glamor of Vanessa Redgrave as Ibsen's *The Lady From the Sea* in the atmosphere of Rouben Ter-Arutunian's craggily spare Norwegian-fjord design. At season's end, this group was struggling forward toward a late-June premiere of a problematical effort to revive the Rodgers-Hart musical *Pal Joey,* with a successful season already emblazoned in the record, whatever might happen next.

Arvin Brown's directorial mastery was at work again on behalf of T. Edward Hambleton's Phoenix Theater in its outstanding program of two hardy one-acters: Tennessee Williams's *27 Wagons Full of Cotton,* with Meryl Streep in an unforgettable portrayal of a bored and seduceable wife, and Arthur Miller's *A Memory of Two Mondays,* with John Lithgow, Roy Poole and others rising painfully above the depressing anonymity of the daily grind in an auto-parts warehouse. The Phoenix's *They Knew What They Wanted* was another standout 1976 revival, with Barry Bostwick (Joe), Louis Zorich (Tony) and Lois Nettleton as the emotionally storm-tossed trio, with Stephen Porter directing. The second half of the Phoenix's schedule was of lighter weight, with William Gillette's *Secret Service* playing in repertory with Sam and Bella Spewack's *Boy Meets Girl.*

In addition to the new musical *The Robber Bridegroom,* John Houseman's Acting Company presented a varied revival repertory. Besides *Three Sisters* and *The Time of Your Life,* they did Christopher Marlowe's seldom-seen *Edward II,* about a politically and sexually troubled English king who met a violent end at the hands of brutal subjects. This was Ellis Rabb's second distinguished directorial stint of the season, with the first professional New York production of record of this challenging play.

Finally in group production of Broadway revivals there was London's visiting D'Oyly Carte Opera Company with its meticulous, historically correct versions of Gilbert and Sullivan operettas. Among individual productions, Ben Gazzara and Colleen Dewhurst delivered the powerful impact of Edward Albee's *Who's Afraid of Virginia Woolf?* with full force under the author's own direction. Pearl Bailey returned for what she said was a farewell to Broadway in a limited engagement of *Hello, Dolly! Angel Street* brought back its melodrama, with Dina Merrill and Michael Allinson as husband and wife and Christine Andreas playing the maid Nancy just prior to her taking on the title role of *My Fair Lady.*

Off Broadway, the revival scene was important, but not yet quite predominant, with 29 revivals (a total somewhat inflated this year by the inclusion of nine Light Opera of Manhattan and four Classic Stage Company productions, two groups not listed in previous seasons) as compared with 32 new American plays and musicals. Among producing organizations the standout was Gene Feist's and Michael Fried's Roundabout, a going and ongoing New York theater concern now expanded into two theaters and broadening the scope not only of its production but its very name from Roundabout Theater Company to Roundabout Theater Center. The eclectic, high-quality programs of this, its tenth, season included a Bicentennial re-viewing of Booth Tarkington's *Clarence* (about a wounded World War I soldier's romantic conquests upon his return), as well as *Summer and Smoke, The Cherry Orchard* and the Roundabout's customary one new play, *Dear Mr. G,* a gangland comedy by Donna de Matteo.

The Classic Stage Company (CSC), like the Circle, moved up this season from OOB to full professional status, bringing with it the expertise with which Christopher Martin has put on so many programs over the past few years. Its 1975–76 repertory consisted of *Measure for Measure, Hedda Gabler, A Country Scandal* and Anouilh's *Antigone* (a list which provides some idea of its versatility and grasp), plus a new adaptation of *The Hound of the Baskervilles* and a few other productions which were mounted in the course of the CSC's season but were withdrawn before being formally presented to critics and public.

The Light Opera of Manhattan was and is firmly established at the Eastside Playhouse on East 74th St. Under the direction of William Mount-Burke, this company of gifted enthusiasts offered a musical repertory of six perennial Gilbert and Sullivan favorites, plus three operettas from the golden romantic age: Victor Herbert's *Naughty Marietta,* Rudolf Friml's *The Vagabond King* and Sigmund Romberg's *The Student Prince,* thereby assuring New York theatergoers a close and immensely rewarding acquaintance with what is probably the sweetest segment of its theater heritage.

The Brooklyn Academy of Music played host to the Royal Shakespeare Company's *Henry V* and *The Hollow Crown.* At the Delacorte in Central Park, Joseph Papp put on the summer *Hamlet,* later moved to winter quarters at the Beaumont, plus a production of *The Comedy of Errors;* and downtown he provided house room for Shaliko's version of *Woyzeck.* Of independent revival production off Broadway there was less than a smattering this season: a 7-performance production of J. B. Fagan's 1926 play about Samuel Pepys *And So to Bed* and a 9-performance *The Homecoming* brought up from OOB.

The most important function of New York's broad 1975–76 spectrum of 28 revival productions on Broadway and 29 off is to provide new insights into our theater's past and deepen our perspective. This it has done, to an extent which no single repertory company anywhere in the world could possibly aspire.

Offstage

The 1975–76 New York theater season was just beginning to take on its autumn momentum when the Broadway musicians struck, darkening all the big musicals. Local 802 was contending for an increase in pay, plus various other benefits. The strike started Sept. 18, and its issues were soon obscured as far as the public was concerned by its impact on New York City's already hard-pressed restaurants, hotels and other entertainment support facilities whose health depends on the theater much more than they know or realize in ordinary times. When the strike was settled (it lasted Sept. 18-Oct. 12, inclusive) the musicians had won a raise from $290 a week to $350-380. The estimated cost to the New York City economy was $1 million a day for the duration of the strike, proof expensive and positive of the theater's huge importance to the community's economic as well as cultural life.

A summer controversy over the Equity showcase code had lesser economic but perhaps greater artistic ramifications. With the rising importance of off off Broadway, Equity leadership proposed new rules that would have mandated a vested interest for actors in the future of workshop scripts in whose experimental productions they appeared: 2 per cent of profits from all subsequent productions if they rehearsed four weeks, 8 per cent if they rehearsed longer, with the showcase producer and author responsible for future reimbursements. It should be pointed out that actors more often than not receive no pay for showcase appearances and sometimes not even carfare; on the other hand the author gets no return either except the attention of critics, agents and producers to his work—and a showcase for the author is a showcase for the actor too. In any case, the Dramatists Guild (the professional association of stage authors) and the Off-Off-Broadway Association vigorously opposed the Equity Showcase Committee's proposed new code, the Guild circularizing its members and some other dramatists advising them not to sign any such agreement to share future royalties. Many Equity members also disagreed with their leadership's proposals, on the grounds that they would curtail the very OOB activity which offers a major, ongoing opportunity for training and exposure. At a special Equity membership meeting Aug. 25, a motion was adopted recommending to the Equity Council that the old code be reinstated pending further discussions. This was done, ending the acute phase of this controversy at least for the duration of the season. The New York *Times* commented in an editorial: "The off-off-Broadway scene is a remarkable phenomenon. It is home for innovation, for trying new wings and themes, for learning and dreaming. Equity's members have done their union and the community a service by recognizing that this delicate blossom could be killed by too much regimentation."

The year's only audible critical hassle took place in hottest midsummer over the right to review the performance of a temporary replacement for an ailing star. When Gwen Verdon had to leave *Chicago* for a few weeks for a throat operation, Liza Minnelli was brought in to replace her so that the show would have a continuity of star quality at its center. The show's producers didn't want the critics to review Miss Minnelli's performance, however, on the grounds that comparisons between her and Miss Verdon could only be odious whichever way they pointed. Clive Barnes and the New York *Times* editors insisted that the appearance of Miss Minnelli on a New York stage was a news event demanding coverage as soon as her performance was set. The *Times* won its point. The critics came to praise Miss Minnelli without any consequent reflection on Miss Verdon, whose performance was later nominated for a Tony. Other replacement "events" such as the uptown move of *A Chorus Line,* Richard Burton for Anthony Perkins in *Equus* and the new cast and direction of *Knock Knock* were routinely covered, without objection.

The importance of subsidy to the live performing arts was increasing faster than the sums allotted to it in 1975–76. The White House asked Congress for $82 million for the National Endowment for the Arts and was lucky to get $79.5 million ($6.3 million of which was the portion of theater groups in the form of matching funds), almost $5 million more than in 1974–75. The New York State Council on the Arts, under its new chairman, Joan K. Davidson, had its subsidy reduced slightly in 1976 to $33 million from $34.1 million the year before and is expected to be cut again to $27.3 million in 1977. Discouraging as this trend may be, New York is still way ahead of the rest of the country in supporting its arts institutions, according to a state-by-state estimate published by *Variety* early in the year. New York's arts allotment is incomparably (and perhaps not surprisingly) the largest; Michigan is in second place with a mere $2.3 million for the year. New York's per capita contribution from state revenues is also tops: $1.96 per person. Only Alaska ($1.47), Hawaii ($1.30) and maybe Colorado ($.86) are in the same ball park. Sample per capita arts subsidies by other large states are California $.05, Illinois $.08, Pennsylvania $.13, Texas $.01, Connecticut $.13, Massachusetts $.28, New Jersey $.11, Ohio $.09.

At these pitiful levels of support, government aid to the arts in this richest and among the most creative of all countries is more promise than performance, a mere token of things we hope are soon to come. The money itself was of real help as far as it went ($121,000 to Chelsea, $125,000 to Negro Ensemble, $150,000 to New York Shakespeare Festival at the Public and the same at the Beaumont, $125,000 to Theater Development Fund, etc., etc.) which was nevertheless only a very short distance on the long, long uphill road stretching in front of the live performing arts through the end of the 1970s on into the 1980s.

So the 1975–76 theater season in New York can take any number of curtain calls for its performance—its illusion of a booming year—in which, to be sure, superb entertainment was sometimes a reality.

No, we didn't come up with a musical as popular as *A Chorus Line* in 1975–76, but we had *A Chorus Line* itself on Broadway all year, plus the popular *Chicago,* the brilliantly innovative *Pacific Overtures,* the smashing

Threepenny Opera and a glorious *My Fair Lady*. We didn't come up with a well-made play as entertaining as a new vintage Simon, but *The Norman Conquests* came triply close; we didn't have a stunner like *Equus*, but we did have one like *Streamers*.

One memorable event of the 1975–76 New York season wasn't visible on any stage except by reflection: the venturing into theater sponsorship of two large corporations scarcely connected with show business. Xerox gave American Bicentennial Theater its initial impetus with a grant of $400,000 and Coca-Cola backed *1600 Pennsylvania Avenue* for $1 million plus or minus, events whose importance towers above their immediate results.

In the former case, outstanding productions of *The Royal Family* and *Sweet Bird of Youth* reflect great credit, prestige and *attention* upon Xerox, just as the TV episodes of *Upstairs, Downstairs* have made many if not most of us aware for the first time in our lives that there is such a thing as Mobil Oil Corporation. As for the expensive demise of *1600 Pennsylvania Avenue*, even though the show fell far short of hopes and expectations the Coca-Cola Company deserves our most hearty applause for helping bring it into being. We commiserate with Coca-Cola on the insidious uncertainties of show business which, like a football, is of a peculiar shape and can bounce in any direction no matter how skillfully it is set into motion—by an Alan Jay Lerner or a Leonard Bernstein or even, ideally, an Alan Jay Lerner *and* a Leonard Bernstein.

We believe that in the case of the professional theater the game is worth the candle, however, and our personal respect and admiration goes out to anyone like Coca-Cola who dares to play it. The subsidy of first-class stage productions by non-entertainment corporate institutions is an idea whose time is long overdue. The possible advantages are obvious and so are the possible disadvantages—you can't win them all, and in the theater not even half of them. We hope and believe that both Coca-Cola and Xerox will discern that the former outweigh the latter in the long run, which is the only run that should concern the institutions of American arts and economics. They are made for each other, and the times are pushing them closer and closer together, in the live performing arts' need for additional sources of support and the corporations' need for some kind of public-service identity to sweeten the public's perception of their ever-increasing profitability. We expect that other large corporations will avail themselves of this new opportunity, now that Xerox and Coca-Cola have blazed the trail.

In 1975–76, the New York theater paid little attention to its country's Bicentennial celebrations of the past. Thanks to the efforts of unnamed corporate deciders, though, it may have started something this season that will materially brighten its future.

The Orphans in their "It's the Hard-Knock Life" number in the musical *Annie,* book by Thomas Meehan, music by Charles Strouse, lyrics by Martin Charnin.

PHOTO BY MARTHA SWOPE

1976-77

"WE ARE LIVING in a vulgar, brutal time and audiences go to the theater and movies to relieve their anxieties. Today, it's a theater of shock," Dore Schary remarked at a theater forum, going to the heart of the matter of the 1976-77 theater season in New York. Mr. Schary was not speaking of *all* audiences, any more than a New York *Times* Sunday article was speaking of all playwrights when it mentioned a group of newcomers who "are not afraid of offending, even alienating, an audience." But certainly the cutting edge of the theater year was sharpened with shock and alienation, whatever crowd-pleasers may have come along behind.

The year's most powerful script was a clinically detailed study of a painful, bloody miscarriage — David Rudkin's *Ashes* — a parable of our disturbed times and an almost unbearable theatergoing experience for all but the case-hardened and anxiety-ridden (but exactly how the latter might derive some relief from this experience is beyond my understanding). A one-acter by a promising new playwright — Albert Innaurato's *The Transfiguration of Benno Blimpie* — raised the audience's gorge with images of an emotional defective fattening himself for an ultimate goal of self-cannibalism and suicide by meat cleaver. Next to these 1976-77 shock and alienation pace-setters, the contemplation of death looming over three terminal patients and their families in Michael Cristofer's Pulitzer Prize-winning Broadway play *The Shadow Box* was a laff-riot.

An artistic current as strong as this one inevitably generates its own back-eddies and counter-currents; the reaction of warm-hearted optimism in *Annie*, self-indulgent farce in *Sly Fox*, nostalgia in a series of revivals like *Fiddler on the Roof* and *The King and I*. But it was shock that was making the history this year from the bleeding aristocrats in *Comedians* to the foul language of the Critics Award-winning *American Buffalo*, along with the icy alienation of another Critics Award-winner *Otherwise Engaged*, making the apparently masochistic audience's heart beat faster and drawing its attention away from such offerings as Dore Schary's literate but disappointingly short-lived biography of the founder of Zionism, *Herzl*, or Preston Jones's *A Texas Trilogy*, the latter popular everywhere else but quickly outcast in New York.

There was 18 per cent more action along Broadway in 1976-77 than in the previous season and the money was fabulous on a scale of Ali Baba's cave — but the best news of all was the encouraging increase in the number of new American playscripts in Broadway production. We count 65 new shows this season, the same number as last, but 17 of them were new American plays compared with only ten last year (see the one-page summary accompanying this report). Unhappily, there was a big slump in musical production to only six this year from 13 last — but three of the six seem to be hits at this writing and some of the slack was taken up by outstanding musical revivals. The best measure of Broadway activity is its playing-week total (if ten shows play ten weeks, that's 100 playing weeks) which rose to 1,347 in 1976-77 from 1,136 last year, continuing its climb from the historic low of 852 in 1973-74.

"Legit Posts Its Greatest Season" was the way *Variety* put it in a banner page

The 1976-77 Season on Broadway

PLAYS (17)

CALIFORNIA SUITE
Checking Out
A Texas Trilogy:
Lu Ann Hampton
Laverty Oberlander
THE LAST MEETING OF
THE KNIGHTS OF THE
WHITE MAGNOLIA
THE OLDEST LIVING
GRADUATE
Wheelbarrow Closers
Best Friend
Herzl
SLY FOX
Something Old,
Something New
The Trip Back Down
AMERICAN BUFFALO
Unexpected Guests
THE SHADOW BOX
Ladies at the Alamo
Gemini (transfer)
Vieux Carré

MUSICALS (6)

Godspell (transfer)
The Robber Bridegroom
(return engagement)
Music Is
*Your Arms Too Short
to Box With God*
I Love My Wife
ANNIE

REVUES (2)

Let My People Come
(transfer)
*Side by Side by
Sondheim*

FOREIGN PLAYS
IN ENGLISH (8)

Days in the Trees
Poor Murderer
Siamsa
Don't Step on My
Olive Branch
No Man's Land
COMEDIANS
*Dirty Linen &
New-Found-Land*
OTHERWISE ENGAGED

FOREIGN-LANGUAGE
PLAYS (4)

Nat'l Theater of Greece:
Oedipus at Colonus
Knights
Ipi-Tombi
La Guerre de Troie
N'Aura Pas Lieu

REVIVALS (17)

Circle in Square 1976:
Pal Joey
Guys and Dolls
Going Up
Oh! Calcutta!
Porgy and Bess
Circle in Square 1977:
Night of the Iguana
Romeo and Juliet
The Innocents
The Eccentricities of
a Nightingale
Fiddler on the Roof
Vivian Beaumont:
The Cherry Orchard
Agamemnon
Caesar and Cleopatra
Anna Christie
*The Basic Training
of Pavlo Hummel*
The King and I
Happy End (transfer)

SPECIALTIES (11)

An Evening With
Diana Ross
Shirley MacLaine
For Colored Girls, etc.
(transfer)
Debbie
I Have a Dream
A Party With Betty Comden
and Adolph Green
Piaf . . . a Remembrance
Mark Twain Tonight!
(return engagement)
*Lily Tomlin in Appearing
Nitely*
Mummenschanz
*Toller Cranston's
The Ice Show*

HOLDOVERS WHICH
BECAME HITS
IN 1976-77

The Belle of Amherst
Chicago
Me and Bessie

Plays listed in CAPITAL LETTERS have been designated Best Plays of 1976-77.
Plays listed in *italics* were still running June 1, 1977.
Plays listed in **bold face type** were classified as established or likely hits in *Variety's* annual estimate published June 8, 1977.

one headline over a story announcing that its estimate for the total Broadway gross during the 52 weeks of the 1976-77 season was a whopping $93,406,082, 31.85 per cent higher than last year's all-time record $70.8 million, towering above the previous historical high of $58.9 million in the season of 1967-68. Broadway shows on the road also enjoyed huge prosperity, grossing what *Variety* called a "sensational" $82,627,309, bringing the 1976-77 combined total for Broadway shows to $176,033,391, 42.62 per cent over last year's all-time record — right out of the ball park.

Taking these long figures apart to see what really glues them together, we remember that the price of a top ticket broke through the $15 barrier last season and reached upward through $17.50 to touch the inevitable $20 at *Fiddler on the Roof* — but this accounts for only a drop in the season's enormous bucket. There were a few high-grossing newcomers like *For Colored Girls, Sly Fox* and the late-opening musicals *Annie, I Love My Wife* and *Side by Side by Sondheim*, but they don't account for the season-long boom in ticket sales.

It would seem from the facts that an increase in the theatergoing audience or attendance (estimated by *Variety* to be 8,815,095, 22.57 per cent more than last season), not in the number or quality of new shows, produced that $93 million record gross. Certainly 1976-77 was no circus parade of gala new offerings trooping through town — not, at least, until the musicals followed each other on in April, trunk to tail. Broadway was more like an investment portfolio of gilt-edged capital assets — the long-run holdovers and attractive revivals — generating something like two-thirds of the theater's box office by attracting new audiences to a gilt-edged backlog of entertainments like *Grease* and *Fiddler on the Roof.* These new audiences may be observed any evening, rain or shine, freeze or swelter, lined up for last-minute cut-rate admissions at the TKTS booth at Duffy Square (TKTS sold more than three quarters of a million such tickets this season for Broadway and off-Broadway shows). As the 1976-77 record shows, these new audiences like what they see and are coming back at full prices and bringing their friends.

Audiences are plentiful, but not yet adventurous; the hit syndrome still troubles the outwardly thriving commercial theater. The number of 1976-77 shows estimated by *Variety* to be hits or likely-to-become hits was an enormous eighteen — count 'em, 18 — but any individual show was apt to starve in the midst of this plenty unless it could establish itself with some fancy-capturing advantage, like shock voltage. Quality alone was no guarantee of success — c.f. the short run of Jones's Texas plays or the $100,000 estimated loss of the Critics Award-winning *American Buffalo*. The exotic enticement of foreign origin didn't always help, either — the distinguished British play *Comedians* dropped its original investment of $300,000 plus $50,000 more during its Broadway run, according to *Variety* estimate.

The most spectacular losses took place out of town, however, where David Merrick's musical *The Baker's Wife* folded in Washington for an estimated $1 million and Alexander H. Cohen's updated *Hellzapoppin*, with Jerry Lewis, collapsed in Boston for an estimated $500,000 more than its original cost of $750,000.

On the good-news side of the box office, *Sly Fox* recouped its $300,000 cost by the end of the season according to *Variety* estimate, and the three April musicals were headed in the same direction. *For Colored Girls,* etc. was transferred to Broadway in mid-September and was still playing to SRO, 102 per centof capacity, at the end of May. *Same Time, Next Year* was in its third year with a

$2.2 million-plus profit on its initial $230,000 investment already in its backers' pockets. Among the older shows, *Fiddler* had returned 1,308 per cent (and came back for another dip), *Hello, Dolly!* 1,298 per cent, *Gypsy* 182 per cent, while *Pippin* had returned $1,659,207 on its $500,000 investment and road grosses of *Raisin* had mounted up to more than $5 million — etc., etc., in sufficient volume to keep the hopes and dreams of backers alive, and a respectable number of new shows coming.

If you judge a book not by its cover but by its best chapter, then the theater season in New York should be viewed through the rose-colored glasses of its Best Plays, be they theater of shock, theater of alienation, theater of nostalgia, theater of the obscure and whatever else it was — and indeed it *was* — in 1976-77. Our list of the year's ten Best Plays is a stylistic kaleidoscope, with David Rudkin's powerful antithesis of entertainment, *Ashes,* alongside Neil Simon's multiply entertaining *California Suite* and Larry Gelbart's well-made farce *Sly Fox.* The classic differences between "comedy" and "serious" drama have all but disappeared in the whirlpools and cross-currents of modern playwriting: Trevor Griffiths' *Comedians* is a shocker full of laughs, while Michael Cristofer's *The Shadow Box* is a reassuring play about death. Alienation by illiteracy is a major thrust of David Mamet's *American Buffalo,* as is alienation by literacy in Simon Gray's *Otherwise Engaged. Annie* by Thomas Meehan, Charles Strouse and Martin Charnin is in a class by itself in more ways than the most obvious one of being the only musical on the list. And also there are two of Preston Jones's appealing and revealing reconstructions of Southwest Americana, *The Oldest Living Graduate* and *The Last Meeting of the Knights of the White Magnolia.*

Only one of the above — *Sly Fox* — was an original Broadway production. Three — *Comedians, Otherwise Engaged* and *Ashes* — originated on the London stage. The other six were first produced in regional theater — demonstrating its great importance as an incubator of American theater in the 1970s.

Broadway

It was a playwrights' season on Broadway in 1976-77. Neil Simon enhanced the whole year with a new script, Tennessee Williams and Paul Zindel came in from the cold for brief visits and Arthur Miller got as far as Washington. They found themselves in the thick of new talent cropping up all over the place, flowering in purple and orange hues of shock and alienation, or in some cases softer colors.

Most promising of the Broadway debuts was one of the latter kind: Preston Jones's with his three Texas plays compassionately chronicling the agonies of slowly-dying pride and prejudice in a small Southwest Texas town. His *The Last Meeting of the Knights of the White Magnolia* uncovered the last vestiges of racism, become almost as pitiful as contemptible, in the events of a tacky lodge meeting. His *The Oldest Living Graduate* saw new money clashing with old values. His *Lu Ann Hampton Laverty Oberlander* watched a cheerleading beauty queen become a lonely barfly, amid fading social standards. This last and least of Jones's three plays was stretching a one-act point into three acts, a weakness which even a strong performance by Diane Ladd in the title role couldn't redeem. But the first two were well-made plays about victims of cultural transition clinging to remnants of the past, but drowning nevertheless —

well-made with a structure and mobility of events as well as of emotional bias. In these two Best Plays Fred Gwynne found a rich character in an aged, half-senile — but absolutely undefeated — Texas patriarch and World War I veteran whose proudest boast is that the great Black Jack Pershing once spoke to him and told him to shut up. Patrick Hines's redneck booze-seller, Red Grover, also made an indelible impression. Preston Jones is an actor and a writer-in-residence at the Dallas Theater Center, where the plays of *A Texas Trilogy* were first produced. But that's not all — Jones is a play-maker, too. His works seem native-born to the stage where they are sure to prosper mightily, their weak New York reception to the contrary notwithstanding.

Another actor-playwright made his New York debut this season: Michael Cristofer whose *The Shadow Box* won the Pulitzer Prize and the Tony best-play award at the same time he was making his New York acting debut in *The Cherry Orchard* at Lincoln Center. In contrast to Jones, Cristofer is a scene-writer. His play is remarkable more for texture and tone than momentum, as it shares its attention among three terminally ill patients and the relatives and friends keeping them company in separate versions of the same situation, interlocked in the play without touching each other (no one in one group ever says so much as "hello" to anybody in another). One of the patients is a family man (Simon Oakland) insisting that his wife set aside her fear so that they can enjoy these last days together. Another is an intellectual bisexual (Laurence Luckinbill) who hopes that his still-fond ex-wife (Patricia Elliott) and his male lover (Mandy Patinkin) won't sour this last of the wine by picking a quarrel with each other. The third is an old woman (Geraldine Fitzgerald) clinging painfully to life while an unappreciated daughter (Rose Gregorio) helps her pretend her favorite, long-dead daughter is still alive. Cristofer handled his subject — not death itself, but life before death — with emotional maturity, with a touch of gallows humor but no trace of morbidity. Like Preston Jones, he has a regional theater writing-acting affiliation — the special Tony Award-winning Mark Taper Forum in Los Angeles whose artistic director, Gordon Davidson, staged this difficult piece in all its versions from the Taper to Broadway and won this year's play-directing Tony.

Jones is a play-maker; Cristofer a scene-writer; and a third 1976-77 new-comer, David Mamet, is a dialogue-writer whose ear for contemporary speech distinguishes his work. His professional New York debut had a sort of preview last season with off-off-Broadway productions at St. Clements of *American Buffalo* and *Sexual Perversity in Chicago* which won him an Obie Award as the best new playwright. Both plays made the debut official in commercial productions this season. *Sexual Perversity,* a juggling act of comic sexual cliches, was a season-long success off Broadway on a bill with Mamet's short *Duck Variations,* an exercise in making mountains of character out of molehills of conversation between two old men sitting on a park bench. Mamet's more substantial work, *American Buffalo,* came all the way up to Broadway, winning the Critics Award for best American play and a Best Play citation as an outstanding — if certainly not flawless — new theater work. In it, two over-the-hill petty crooks and their young stooge plan to steal a coin collection — planning and planning, reacting to each other but never taking action, until it becomes obvious that like the arrival of Godot, this crime will never take place.

In the opening scenes of *American Buffalo* Mamet surely intended to shock and alienate his audience with some of the foulest language ever heard on a stage. The language cools off a bit finally (or seems to). The dialogue is like a violin finely tuned to the vibrations of a junk-shop owner (Kenneth McMillan) and his small-time hoodlum friend (Robert Duvall), the words in perfect pitch at each delicate touch of the excellent acting and the direction by Ulu Grosbard, who coped brilliantly with this difficult play. Santo Loquasto's junk-shop setting, surely the year's most imaginative design, was a sight to make sore eyes much sorer, and indeed "entertainment" is a word not easily applicable to *American Buffalo.* Virtuosity, yes — Mamet has mastered a verbal instrument of high quality, and we can expect that his next number will carry a more rewarding tune.

Highly promising and performing new playwriting growth wasn't limited to the Best Plays list either on or off Broadway. Like David Mamet, Albert Innaurato came heavily upon the professional theater scene this season with two startlingly effective plays: the one-acter *The Transfiguration of Benno Blimpie* off Broadway and *Gemini* both off and on. The interrelation of emotional and physical distortion is the preoccupation of both works. The former, one of the season's premier shockers, is a study of a misfit child unloved even by his mother (Rosemary De Angelis in a mesmerizing performance) who stuffs and smears food into his mouth in compensation, fattening himself for ritual slaughter like a suicidal pig. Poor Benno was played to disgusting and pitiable perfection by James Coco under Robert Drivas's remorseless direction.

The latter, *Gemini,* which began off Broadway at Circle Repertory Company and moved uptown in late spring, played out a double-twin motif in a Philadelphia backyard setting: a brother and sister both feel a sexual attraction for a college chum who in turn feels some sexual attraction for both of them. The play's air is full of Italian family warmth (notably provided by Danny Aiello and Anne DeSalvo), somewhat counterbalanced by the presence of another Benno Blimpie, an awkwardly fat youth (Jonathan Hadary) driven to weird excesses. Innaurato's concepts were often so far out of human scale in both plays that they tended to acquire the shortcomings as well as the advantages of a cartoon.

Another newcomer, John Bishop, made the journey from the boondocks of OOB to the bright lights of Broadway with his first professionally-produced script, *The Trip Back Down,* about a racing car driver whose career has reached its peak — or never peaked very conspicuously — and is now on the downslide. As played by John Cullum, the driver was appealingly devoid of self-delusions on a visit to family and friends in his old home town, trying to renew his energy for another go-round of the tracks. His victory over his own doubts takes place very slowly and somewhat monotonously at first, but it picks up momentum for a touching scene in which the driver invites his daughter to come along with him on the auto-racing circuit but advises her "I never win" with a shy sort of pride. Like Jones, Cristofer, Mamet and Innaurato, Bishop is a name to be remembered among the extraordinary new playwriting talent that surfaced in the professional theater this season.

The happiest 1976-77 results among the previously-established dramatists were achieved by Larry Gelbart in his adaptation of Ben Jonson's durably comic *Volpone* into Broadway's richly comic *Sly Fox.* Gelbart re-entered the territory fenced off by Jonson and made it over into a gag-filled playground for the kind of one-dimensional but unforgettable characters to be found in his TV series *M.A.S.H.;* characters a director like Arthur Penn could juggle hilariously and actors could bounce off all three walls of the auditorium. The latter included, memorably, George C. Scott as the fox tricking the greedy with promises of riches in his will, Hector Elizondo as his henchman (the Mosca character in *Volpone*), Jack Gilford as a scabrous old money-lender and Bob Dishy as an insanely jealous but even more avaricious husband.

Another Best Play by an experienced hand was *California Suite* by Neil Simon, a matched set of four hotel-room episodes. Simon is what Jean Kerr has called the master of the garde play, and he makes doing his thing seem so easy that new Simon hits are not only taken for granted, they're an obligatory part of any Broadway season in the 1970s. In his latest, in the manner of *Plaza Suite,* four different sets of people follow each other into the same hotel accommodations and lift up a corner of their lives to reveal themselves. The ensemble under Gene Saks's sure direction consisted of Barbara Barrie, Tammy Grimes, George Grizzard and Jack Weston moving in and out of the four playlets as (1) an acerbically articulate and divorced New York couple (Grimes and Grizzard), (2) a Philadelphia family man caught by his wife *in delictu* so *flagrante* as to be forgivable (Weston and Barrie), (3) a conveniently married British movie star and antique dealer in town for the Academy Awards (Grizzard and Grimes again) and (4) two Chicago couples at each other's throats at the end of a shared vacation (all four). After *God's Favorite* in 1974-75, Neil Simon took a well-documented powder to California, so that he neglected to supply Broadway with its annual Simon treat last season. As the season of 1976-77 began (his new play opened in June) it was certainly good to have him back.

Tennessee Williams also returned to town this season with a new script, *Vieux Carré,* his first professional New York production since his unhappy attempt at absurdism in *Out Cry* four years ago. The style was as fondly remembered in his best work: moody, poetic, with sexual obsessions and deprivations of the inhabitants of a run-down New Orleans boarding house viewed through a gauze of memory. It was indeed a shadowy play, episodic and incoherent, informed by the author's insights but not his craft. Paul Zindel had better luck with *Ladies at the Alamo,* a clash of tigresses in a take-over attempt behind the scenes of a major Texas regional theater operation (is Alamo an intentionally alliterative suggestion of Alley?). Frank Perry directed it like an animal trainer cracking his whip over an ensemble of five intensely striving actresses led by Estelle Parsons. It was effective, and it might have made a stronger impression outside this season's theater-of-shock context.

This year of 17 new American plays was like a new beginning for Broadway, but it repeatedly contemplated endings in scripts like Allen Swift's *Checking Out,* with an aged Yiddish actor stage-managing his own death; and Louis La Russo II's *Wheelbarrow Closers,* with Danny Aiello as a vigorous wheeler-dealer kicking against the pricks of his own inevitable retirement. Also on the playbill were Michael Sawyer's study of a malevolent woman in *Best Friend* and Jordan Crittenden's of a problematical marriage in *Unexpected Guests.*

British authors were well represented but didn't dominate the season or its best lists as has sometimes happened in the past. The best of their Broadway offerings was *Comedians* by Trevor Griffiths, in his American playwriting debut with an abrasive play about aspiring comics sweating through a tryout engagement at a third-rate social club and then analyzing their performances after the show. Mike Nichols directed its changes of key back and forth between standup gags and painful introspection with perfect timing. The performances had to be very good, and they were — none better than Jonathan Pryce's conscientious clown determined to pursue the truth at all costs, exacerbating class hatreds in his routine as a bully harrassing a pair of papier-mache dummies in evening dress.

The other British Best Play on Broadway this season was Simon Gray's Critics Award-winning *Otherwise Engaged,* like his previous Best Play *Butley* a meticulous study of disintegration. It isn't the personality of the protagonist that is coming apart here (as in *Butley*), but his connections with other members of the human race. He is at the center of a gathering storm of relationships with friends and family, at the calm center where he insists on remaining. He maintains a cool, rational detachment when others expect heated involvement, and therefore he is increasingly incapable or unwilling to share in others' lives or permit others a share in his. Tom Courtenay played the central role in a performance precision-engineered under Harold Pinter's direction.

Pinter's other major contribution to the 1976-77 Broadway season was his play *No Man's Land*, providing a vehicle for two of the most accomplished heavyweights in the business: John Gielgud and Ralph Richardson. The tilt of Richardson's chin and the slant of Gielgud's eyebrow sufficed to send shock waves to the farthest reaches of the balcony, as they performed a strange encounter of two writers chatting over drinks and cigars, while menacing servants enter and exit on unexplained errands. The performances had to suffice, because the play itself was an enigma, an audience do-it-yourself project with either a few pieces or a few lines of instruction missing, or both. Finally from Britain there was Tom Stoppard's *Dirty Linen,* an evanescent gag farce about a Parliamentary committee investigating sex scandals. It was so vaporous that in fact it vanished altogether at one point to make room for a long monologue inset (delivered earnestly by Jacob Brooke), *New-Found-Land,* describing a journey across North America in cartoon images of tourist attractions.

On the darker side, the Czechoslovakian play *Poor Murderer,* by Pavel Kohout, appeared in English translation in an absolutely first-rate production with Laurence Luckinbill (in one of his two important performances this season), Maria Schell, Kevin McCarthy, Ruth Ford, Larry Gates and others under Herbert Berghof's direction. This play concentrated intensely on the interrogation of an actor, a prisoner in an insane asylum, who is prepared to believe he has actually killed the actor playing Polonius while playing Hamlet in the bedroom scene. This script is said to have political overtones, and its New York production took place at a time when Kohout and some of his fellow-writers were suffering a wave of oppression in their native land. In a program note in *Playbill* Kohout explained that his own country refused him permission to come to the United States to see his play.

A translation from the French of *Days in the Trees* by Marguerite Duras was the leadoff production of Circle in the Square's season, with Mildred Dunnock playing a mother with a special affection for her ne'er-do-well son — "one son in reserve for when the bad times come" — affirming their kinship even as they clash over the details of their lives. The 1976-77 program of foreign works in English also included visits from the National Folk Theater of Ireland (*Siamsa*) in an evening of emerald-green folklore and an Israeli musical revue of satiric and patriotic comment, *Don't Step on My Olive Branch.*

Broadway's visiting foreign-language productions ranged from the imposing National Theater of Greece repertory of Sophocles's *Oedipus at Colonus* and Aristophanes's *Knights* (the first professional New York production of record of this comedy in any language), through Tréteau de Paris's *La Guerre de Troie N'Aura Pas Lieu* (known in English as *Tiger at the Gates*), to the somewhat controversial South African musical *Ipi-Tombi,* a colorful and rhythmic expression of the black South African spirit in various village, tribal and even big-city rituals and celebrations.

On our own musical stages, it was as though invention had evaporated and the production of new shows had come to a standstill, until April 17 when presto! the West Forties came alive with the sound of music. *I Love My Wife* appeared on that date, followed the next night by *Side by Side by Sondheim* and three nights later by *Annie* — and about a week later the Chelsea production of the Brecht-Weill *Happy End* moved over to Manhattan to add a fourth part to this late-season harmony of shows. Granted that *Happy End* is a revival and the revue assemblage of Stephen Sondheim numbers is a new collection but not new work; still, the freshness of their approach and presentation contributed importantly to this late-season musical bonanza.

Annie immediately drew the longest lines at the box office, together with a faint echo of scorn drifting downwind, for its manner and substance even more simplistic, possibly, than the *Little Orphan Annie* comic strip from which the show was derived. We're convinced that *Annie* was the musical of the year, with a consistent soft-sell style of music, performance, design and humor that for once wasn't so over-seasoned with gags that it lost the taste of wit (remember, Mike Nichols produced this show for Broadway). When Dorothy Loudon as the keeper of an orphanage comes in to rouse her little girls as roughly as possible with a police whistle, blows it, and nearly takes the top of her own head off because of a hangover she's forgotten she has, you know that *Annie* is going to be all right: it isn't going to be sentimental about either victims or villains, it is never going to reach for the sugar when the salt is handy. When poor little Annie (Andrea McArdle, a cheerful and forthright young personality) arrives as a Christmas charity guest at the grand mansion of Daddy Warbucks (Reid Shelton), is asked ingratiatingly, "Now, Annie, what do you want to do first?" and replies, "The floors. I'll scrub them, then I'll get to the windows," you wonder where you'd find a more satisfying line than that these days, however far upwind.

Dorothy Loudon was wonderful as the orphans' harsh mistress, a function which until *Annie* has remained an unappealing stereotype, even in cartoons; Sandy was wonderful; Robert Fitch danced up a breeze as a small-time con man; David Mitchell's New York skyline sets and Theoni V. Aldredge's costumes were as stylish as the staging and choreography by Martin Charnin and Peter Gennaro. Charles Strouse's music was eminently hummable as well as singable (notably in "Tomorrow" and "Easy Street"). For those who insist on profound social comment in the framework of the musical stage, well, *Annie* is a statement of values in total revolt from the present conventional theater of shock and alienation. *Annie* dares to be different. It insists that a child has a right to its innocence as it stares with wide eyes upon such ugliness as a Depression; that blank pupils may perceive subtle purposes that hard glares are sure to miss. It further insists that once in a while even the New York audiences of the 1970s deserve the unashamed relief of shiny entertainment, a proposition with which the editor of this volume joyfully agrees.

I Love My Wife was vastly entertaining, too, in a more conventional 1970s package. It explored the obligatory 1970s subject — sexual adventure — and the show was for it, sort of, in a book about two Trenton, N.J. couples determined to celebrate Christmas Eve with a wife-swapping orgy. The title was a tipoff to the outcome; in the meantime, the one joke was worked and reworked, wrung out, rinsed off and wrung out again under Gene Saks's resourceful Tony-winning direction. The performance of Lenny Baker as the most eager and least skillful of the quartet stood out in good company. The jazzy Michael Stewart-Cy Coleman score was the year's best. It was played by four musicians right on the stage, taking little direct part in the action but serving as a sort of Greek-chorus commentary as they came on in different costumes playing different instruments and harmonies reflecting the events and mood of the show at the moment. Their Act II opening number "Hey There, Good Times" was a show-stopper.

A rousing Gospel musical *Your Arms* (sic) *Too Short to Box With God*, conceived by Vinnette Carroll from the Book of Matthew and developed in her Urban Arts Corps via a Washington tryout with music and lyrics by Alex Bradford and Micki Grant, was for many, many weeks the only new musical game in town. The season's other early-opening new show, George Abbott's effort to make another modern musical out of Shakespeare's *Twelfth Night* in *Music Is*, was a very brief candle.

Broadway's musical program was augmented with revivals, with the transfer of the marathon-running *Godspell* (another inspiration from the Book of Matthew) from off Broadway, and with the return engagement of last year's *The Robber Bridegroom* with Barry Bostwick making another of his strong impressions and winning the Tony Award in the title role. The sex-centered off-Broadway cabaret revue *Let My People Come* also transferred for a moment in the Broadway limelight, where it had more of a negative impact on the League of New York Theaters and Producers, who regarded it as "antithetical," than a positive impact on theater audiences. A late-coming but major element of the musical season's enjoyment was the revue *Side by Side by Sondheim* brought over from London with its indefatigable and inimitable British cast singing up a storm of memorable Sondheim lyrics and tunes by himself and other composers with whom he has collaborated.

Specialties, like revivals, were numerically and artistically important this season. Ntozake Shangé's touching "choreopoem" *For Colored Girls Who Have Considered Suicide/When the Rainbow Is Enuf* was a major adornment after it transferred uptown from the Public Theater in September. It was categorized as a "play" on the Tony nominations list, but that is a courtesy title — it is an original theatrical entity of dance, poetry and performance which created its own category and made a big space for itself on Broadway.

A Party With Betty Comden and Adolph Green brightened up the place for weeks with a new version of the performers' popular two-person show. Martin Luther King Jr. was warmly remembered in his own words and Billy Dee Williams's performance in *I Have a Dream*, as was Edith Piaf in song and Juliette Koka's performance in *Piaf . . . a Remembrance*, and as was Mark Twain in a return engagement of Hal Holbrook's celebrated one-man impersonation *Mark Twain Tonight!* The Swiss *Mummenschanz* pantomine-and-mask show paid Broadway a visit, and the Palace became a winter wonderland in May, housing a Canadian skater's spectacle, *Toller Cranston's The Ice Show*.

The comedienne Lily Tomlin captivated Broadway audiences with a repertory of characterizations ranging from wide-eyed schoolgirl to drug-addicted babe, in a solo show called *Lily Tomlin in "Appearing Nitely."* Many other solo bookings were spotlighted on 1976-77 Broadway scene, some of them billed as "revues" and some as "concerts" in Broadway theaters, attracting fans to join and mingle with the crowds of theatergoers at curtain time. For the record, Diana Ross, Debbie Reynolds and Shirley MacLaine appeared in one-woman "shows." Somewhat differently presented but equally popular in "concert" were Bing Crosby, Barry Manilow, Nana Mouskouri, Al Green and many other pop stars and combos — as well as two entire musicals, *She Loves Me* and *Knicker-*

bocker Holiday, performed in concert versions at Town Hall by such stars as Madeline Kahn, Rita Moreno, George Rose and Richard Kiley. There was even a new Robert Wilson theatrical what-is-it, *Einstein on the Beach,* presented for a couple of special, unclassifiable performances at the Metropolitan Opera House.

Off Broadway

Off Broadway in 1976-77 the program was loaded with revivals as usual, what with the Roundabout, CSC, LOOM and other organizations concentrating heavily in this area of production. The numbers yielded ground grudgingly in the vital category of new American shows, plays and musicals: 22 and 9 in 1976-77 (see the one-page summary accompanying this report), only one down from last year's total of 26 and 6, but well off the pace of 30 and 12 the year before. A rise in the number of foreign plays in English from three last year to nine this year additionally shores up the total. Institutional production dominated independent more than ever, especially in the huge output of revivals and in the new-play category.

Only one off-Broadway script, *Ashes,* made the Best Plays list this season, as compared with last season's record-breaking five — not because of diminishing quality but because of the marked numerical and qualitative increase in the Broadway competition. Off-Broadway plays like *G.R. Point, The Brownsville Raid, The Transfiguration of Benno Blimpie, A Tribute to Lili Lamont, Gemini,* and *Cold Storage* might well have made the list in other seasons.

Ashes was the New York playwriting debut of its British author, David Rudkin, as it progressed from OOB production at the Manhattan Theater Club to its commercial booking under the sponsorship of Joseph Papp and his New York Shakespeare Festival Public Theater. *Ashes* was the peak of the off-Broadway season and the spearpoint of the theater of shock (not quite as disgusting as *Monsters,* but more penetrating), in a parable of the Northern Irish political tragedy reflected in the personal agonies, both mental and physical, of a childless husband and wife trying to preserve their heritage at all costs, no matter the clinical indignities, no matter the blood and pain of their heroic but miscarrying efforts. It is hard to imagine how the acting of Brian Murray and Roberta Maxwell as the couple and the brutally direct staging by Lynne Meadow could have been bettered. It was effective to the point where it risked shattering the audience's suspension of disbelief with theater of *unendurable* shock, that dangerous esthetic territory where even the ancient Greeks feared to tread.

Also on Papp's schedule at the Public was another tell-it-like-it-is closeup, this one of a shelter for emotionally disturbed teen-agers, *Hagar's Children,* written in changing keys of violence and compassion by Ernest Joselovitz, a onetime staff member of just such a haven. Papp's downtown schedule was additionally filled out with *On the Lock-In,* a musical about prison life by David Langston Smyrl; *Marco Polo Sings a Solo,* a melange of absurdist comment and characterization in John Guare's individualistic comic style; and revivals of the Strindberg one-acters *The Stronger,* and *Creditors,* plus workshop activity.

If Papp came up with the best off-Broadway play this season, Marshall W. Mason's Circle Repertory Company came up with the most interesting group of shows. Like New York Shakespeare, Circle mined gold out of peripheral

The 1976-77 Season off Broadway

PLAYS (22)

Negro Ensemble 1976:
  Livin' Fat
Beware the Jubjub Bird
Sexual Perversity in
  Chicago & Duck
  Variations
Circle Repertory 1976:
  Mrs. Murray's Farm
American Place:
  Jack Gelber's New
  Play: Rehearsal
Comanche Cafe
  & Domino Courts
Isadora Duncan Sleeps
  With the Russian
  Navy
Cold Storage
Does Anybody Here Do
  the Peabody?
Circle Repertory 1977:
  A Tribute to Lili
  Lamont
My Life
Gemini
Phoenix Theater:
  Ladyhouse Blues
Marco Polo
G.R. Point
Lincoln
The Brownsville Raid

Public Theater:
  Marco Polo Sings
  a Solo
Hagar's Children
Monsters
Jockeys
I Was Sitting on My
  Patio This Guy
  Appeared I Thought I
  Was Hallucinating

FOREIGN PLAYS IN ENGLISH (11)

The Farm
Bingo
The Prince of Homberg
Canadian Gothic
  & American Modern
A Sorrow Beyond Dreams
The Crazy Locomotive
ASHES
The Perfect Mollusc
Curtains
The Sunday Promenade
Scribes

MUSICALS (9)

Becoming
The Club
Joseph and the Amazing
  Technicolor Dreamcoat
The Cockeyed Tiger
Castaways
Movie Buff
On the Lock-In
*Der Ring Gott
  Farblonjet*
New York City Street
  Show

REVUES (5)

Lovesong
2 by 5
Nightclub Cantata
Jules Feiffer's Hold Me!
*Starting Here, Starting
  Now*

SPECIALTIES (3)

Dylan Thomas Growing Up
Davy Jones' Locker
In My Father's Time

REVIVALS (34)

Roundabout 1976:
  The World of Sholom
  Aleichem
Actors' Alliance:
  The Tavern
Lullaby
Hay Fever
Delacorte:
  Henry V
  Measure for Measure
Light Opera Manhattan:
  H.M.S. Pinafore
  The Mikado
  The Pirates of Penzance
  Ruddigore
  Princess Ida
  The Merry Widow
  Naughty Marietta
  The Vagabond King
  The Yeomen of the
    Guard
Utopia, Limited

Roundabout 1977:
  The Philanderer
  The Rehearsal
  John Gabriel Borkman
  Endgame
  Dear Liar
Classic Stage Company:
  Heartbreak House
  The Homecoming
  Tartuffe
  The Balcony
  The Plough and the Stars
  All the Way Home
  Happy End
BAM Theater:
  The New York Idea
  Three Sisters
  The Great Macdaddy
  *Creditors
    & The Stronger*
  Peg o' My Heart
  Exiles

FOREIGN-LANGUAGE PLAYS (3)

Kraljevo
Rodogune
Waiting for Godot

production in bringing Albert Innaurato's *Gemini* (described in the previous chapter of this report) from the PAF Playhouse in Huntington, L.I., into the off-Broadway and finally the Broadway limelight. Also at the Circle, Arthur Whitney's *A Tribute to Lili Lamont* (his second professionally-produced script) reminded us in an encounter of a once-was movie star (Leueen MacGrath) with the remnants of her last surviving fan club that fan-ism is a two-way street — fans need identification with their idol to bolster their self-esteem every bit as much as the star needs their adoration to feed her ego.

Mason also imported for Circle production a brooding David Storey play about a craggy Yorkshire farmer and his self-possessed daughters, *The Farm;* and he brought in Corinne Jacker's *My Life,* an exploration of motives in one man's memories of his past. Mason also filled out his 1976-77 schedule with a revival, *Exiles,* James Joyce's only play. Season after season, production after production, Circle Repertory has consistently rivalled the best in town, and this year was no exception.

T. Edward Hambleton's Phoenix Theater did its usual number of rising from the flames with a refreshed identity and came on with an international show-casing program of six new scripts. Kevin O'Morrison's *Ladyhouse Blues* was a backward glance at an America that once was in 1919 but is no more, with a cast of five women waiting for their men to come home from World War I and take up a life that is immediately going to suffer radical change. This sensitive play had been selected by American Playwrights Theater for production by its member university, regional and community theaters across the United States. Equally effective in more somber colors at the Phoenix was a backward glance at a corner of America's participation in the Vietnam War, David Berry's *G.R. Point,* about members of a Graves Registration unit adapting each in his own way to the presence of death confronted in battle and storehoused in green plastic body bags. John Heard (a recruit) and Lori Tan Chinn (a Vietnamese maid-of-all-work) led a fine ensemble under the direction of Tony Giordano. From other lands the Phoenix offered a translation from the German of Peter Handke's *A Sorrow Beyond Dreams,* a dramatic monologue with Len Cariou as a writer expressing the many ways of his grief and bewilderment over his mother's suicide; a program of one-acters, *Canadian Gothic* and *American Modern,* by Canada's Joanna M. Glass; and *Scribes* by Barrie Keeffe, about the tribulations of a small-town British newspaper. A *Marco Polo* for children completed the Phoenix's season.

American Place was a new-play haven as usual under Wynn Handman's supervision. Its season began well with a script self-described in the title — *Jack Gelber's New Play: Rehearsal.* This one turned inward to examine the personalities and processes of the theater itself in a rehearsal-within-a-play depicting actors, director, author, producer at work. The group went on to a program of William Hauptman one-acters, *Comanche Cafe* and *Domino Courts;* played host to the Tréteau de Paris's production of Corneille's *Rodogune* for a week's visit; offered Jeff Wanshel's fanciful and semi-biographical *Isadora Duncan Sleeps With the Russian Navy;* and ended the season on a high note in a key of contemplative drama, Ronald Ribman's *Cold Storage,* with Martin Balsam and Michael Lipton as a pair of wheel chair-bound patients on a hospital rooftop contemplating death in some of its past and ever-present forms. The popular success of American Place's season came out of its American Humorists series in the Subplot Cafe, where Caymichael Patten staged a revue collection of Jules Feiffer cartoon characters that went out to a commercial run at the Chelsea

Westside Cabaret Theater under the title *Jules Feiffer's Hold Me!*

Chelsea itself was attracted to English translations of foreign material this season, including the American professional premiere of Von Kleist's *The Prince of Homberg,* a 165-year-old German political conundrum about a prince in moral conflict with the state he serves heroically; and Witkiewicz's *The Crazy Locomotive,* a between-World-Wars Polish play about the imminent demise of civilization. Chelsea's 1976-77 popular success was a new adaptation by Michael Feingold of the Bertolt Brecht-Kurt Weill musical *Happy End* (classified by the Tony Nominations Committee as a "new" musical but viewed here as an extraordinarily skillful and imaginative revival) which leapt from Brooklyn to Broadway. An interesting anomaly on the 1976-77 Chelsea program was Saul Levitt's multimedia *Lincoln,* a one-performer (Fritz Weaver) show with multiple sound and visual effects built up around the character of the great Civil War president. Chelsea made it a regular policy this season to bring its programs across the river to Theater Four for midtown Manhattan bookings, following their Brooklyn engagements.

Season after season Negro Ensemble Company comes up with an outstanding new work. This year's was *The Brownsville Raid* by Charles Fuller, a historical drama of a 1906 incident in which a black Army regiment stationed in Texas was falsely and racistically accused of participating in a violent public disturbance, for which the whole regiment was unjustly punished with a dishonorable discharge, with the collusion of authorities including President Theodore Roosevelt. Directed by Israel Hicks and performed by Douglas Turner Ward at the head of an NEC ensemble, this was an eloquent re-examination of history in the form of first-rate theater. For the second offering of its season, the group revived its own previously-produced symbolical drama, *The Great Macdaddy.*

Two emergent ex-OOB groups came up with new work on their 1976-77 schedules. T. Schreiber Theater presented Enid Rudd's *Does Anybody Here Do the Peabody?,* a nostalgic 1930s movie-style romance of a poor, sweet widow and an attractive scoundrel, as well as the American premiere of the British play *Curtains* by Tom Mallin about a couple's disintegrating relationship. Christopher Martin's Classic Stage Company (CSC) slipped the New York professional premiere of Edward Bond's *Bingo,* the pessimistic portrait of a disillusioned Shakespeare nearing the end of the line, into its schedule of revivals.

Individual production of off-Broadway shows was a rarity in 1976-77, and sometimes of great value. For example, David Mamet's professional New York theater debut took place off Broadway in June at the Cherry Lane with the Lawrence Goossen-Jeffrey Wachtel production of two short Mamet works, *Sexual Perversity in Chicago* and *Duck Variations,* described in the previous chapter of this report. And in this season of alienation, no program was more forbidding (or horribly fascinating, to put a positive face on it) than Adela Holzer's off-Broadway production *Monsters.* This consisted of the two one-acters *Side Show* by William Dews, with Drivas (who directed the whole program) and Richard De Fabees as Siamese twins who have just slaughtered the hated parents who first abhorred and then exploited them; and the more substantial *The Transfiguration of Benno Blimpie* by Albert Innaurato, described with his other work in the previous chapter of this report. Also among independent productions there appeared another of Robert Wilson's perplexing divertissements, laboriously and comma-lessly entitled *I Was Sitting on My Patio This Guy Appeared I Thought I Was Hallucinating,* produced off Broadway by Richard Barr for some reason in the season's final week.

In off-Broadway musical production, it was a cheerful and fruitful year. Circle in the Square (Downtown) brought Eve Merriam's *The Club* in from the Lenox, Mass. Arts Center. The show satirized male attitudes and vanities with a cast of women playing turn-of-the-century clubmen in consummate style under Tommy Tune's direction, carrying the joke even so far as to bill themselves in the program by sexless initials in place of first names (example: G. Hodes instead of Gloria Hodes), with a score of selected songs of the period. Still another off-Broadway musical hit imported from Lenox's Music-Theater Performing Group (overseen by Lyn Austin and Mary D. Silverman) was Elizabeth Swados's *Nightclub Cantata* at the Top of the Gate, a rich cabaret assortment of musical commentary varied in subject but consistent in skill and imagination (this was a fruitful year for Miss Swados, who also wrote the exceptionally effective background music for *The Cherry Orchard* and *Agamemnon* at Lincoln Center). The year's off-Broadway program of revues also took in two notable collections of show tunes: *2 by 5*, a John Kander-Fred Ebb medley, and *Starting Here, Starting Now*, an OOB-originated collage by Richard Maltby Jr. and David Shire.

The *Jesus Christ Superstar* authors, Tim Rice and Andrew Lloyd Webber, turned to the Old Testament for their *Joseph and the Amazing Technicolor Dreamcoat*, produced with considerable success by London's Old Vic under the direction of Frank Dunlop, who came across the Atlantic to stage this musical at Brooklyn Academy of Music and remained to help set up the new BAM Theater Company. The 1976-77 off-Broadway musical program also included *Movie Buff*, one of this season's several reminiscences of 1930s movies; a Charles Ludlam-Ridiculous Theatrical Company burlesque of Wagnerian opera *Der Ring Gott Farblonjet;* and Peter Copani's street musical *New York City Street Show*.

A special event of the off-Broadway year was the limited engagement at BAM of the German-language *Waiting for Godot*, directed by Samuel Beckett himself in the Schiller Theater production. Other visitors from abroad were the Gavella Theater of Zagreb, Yugoslavia in a Croation play *Kraljevo* (The Kermess); the Abbey Theater troupe in O'Casey's *The Plough and the Stars;* and Emlyn Williams and Eamon Kelly in their one-man shows, *Dylan Thomas Growing Up* and *In My Father's Time,* respectively. Our home-grown, perennial and cherished specialty, the Bil Baird Marionettes, presented the Mary Rodgers-Waldo Salt-Arthur Birnkrant musical *Davy Jones' Locker* throughout the season.

As a whole, 1976-77 was a busy and productive year off Broadway in every category of shows, but mostly grouped together in one category of production: organizational. Off Broadway helped introduce outstanding new playwrights and provided a showcase for small-scale, innovative musicals. Its costs may have been creeping in the direction of Broadway, but the perceptions of its most impressive work were not. It was doing its own thing, offering an alternative New York theater at a professional level for both artists and audiences.

Revivals

The New York revival scene has broadened in this decade like a wide-angle lens, until in 1975-76 revivals outnumbered the total of new American plays and musicals on Broadway and nearly reached it off. In 1976-77 their presence on

Broadway attenuated somewhat, with "only" 17 as opposed to 28 the previous year, but they predominated off Broadway with a grand total of 34. In both areas they were a Presence with a capital P, making a world festival of our stages.

The Broadway revival season was distinguished by the number and high quality of life-sized copies of musicals which, far from laying on any veneer of newness, strove mightily to recapture the exact thrust and glamor of the original. The Gershwins' *Porgy and Bess* came to town in a Houston Grand Opera production that was larger than life-size, in that it presented the work in its seldom-seen original version, uncut, with operatic recitatives in place of conventional dialogue. Gifted singers (including Clamma Dale and Larry Marshall, nominated for Tonys) alternated in the leads. The show itself won the Tony for "most innovative revival" and was indeed one of the most rewarding events of the musical season, which also took in a snappy *Guys and Dolls* with an all-black cast headed by Robert Guillaume as Nathan Detroit; Zero Mostel and Yul Brynner recreating their towering original roles for *Fiddler on the Roof* and *The King and I*, as well as regroupings of *Pal Joey* (at Circle in the Square) and even *Oh! Calcutta!* In a class by itself as usual was Light Opera of Manhattan (LOOM) which put on a repertory of ten operetta revivals under William Mount-Burke's direction including well-loved works by Lehar, Friml, Herbert and a cluster of Gilbert & Sullivan from *H.M.S. Pinafore* to the seldom-produced collector's item *Utopia, Limited*.

Topping the list of revivals which strove for a kind of newness was Chelsea's *Happy End*, a Bertolt Brecht-Kurt Weill musical shaped so imaginatively that it almost seemed like a new work. *Almost*, we repeat, because we consider *Happy End* a revival even though it was nominated for a Tony in the new-musical category after it moved from Brooklyn to Broadway. It is "new" by virtue of the fact that it has never been professionally produced in New York, though its material, written in 1929, has been excerpted in at least two Broadway shows. We agree that a *Sly Fox* becomes a new play in *total* adaptation of setting, characters, dialogue, style, etc., retaining only the original concept, the Holinshed of the matter; but we don't accept a technicality by which ancient Greek plays which have never received a professional New York production would qualify as "new" — and we did not consider the revamped *Candide* of a few seasons back a "new" musical.

If not a new work, this *Happy End* was certainly a creative one, particularly in Michael Feingold's free adaptation of the book and lyrics. A scholarly note in the Chelsea program informs us that the book was credited to Elisabeth Hauptmann, Brecht's secretary, who had supposedly based it on a play by a non-existent "Dorothy Lane." Feingold's book was more than a translation; Weill's and Brecht's "The Bilbao Song" would stop any show; and Meryl Streep (a competent singer as well as a consummate actress) and Christopher Lloyd played a Salvation Army lass and a gangster of the 1920s as though they'd never met before, not even in *Guys and Dolls*.

Another musical work revised in the direction of newness for modern audiences was *Going Up*, a 1917 musical with a Louis Hirsch-Otto Harbach score and several ice cream flavors in its adventure of a daring young man showing off to a maiden fair by going aloft solo in an airplane, though he's never flown one before. These days, even revivals have cross-country origins: *Going Up*, like the equally innocent *Annie*, was first launched at the Goodspeed Opera House in East Haddam, Conn.; and *Happy End* tried out in Yale Repertory

Theater before coming to New York.

In the straight-play category, Joseph Papp turned Andrei Serban loose on *The Cherry Orchard* (in a new English adaptation by Jean-Claude van Itallie which, it was reported, the Tony Eligibility Committee had considered classifying a "new" play) and Aeschylus's mighty *Agamemnon* at the Vivian Beaumont. In both cases, but most lucidly in the former, Serban achieved imposing and startling effects of ritualistic theater, with Irene Worth leading the intricate ensemble measures of the Chekhov play. Papp recruited Michael Moriarty and Paul Rudd for *Henry V* and Sam Waterston and Meryl Streep for *Measure for Measure* in his outdoor summer season in Central Park and ended his indoor winter season with a program of Strindberg one-acters.

The Broadway revival as star vehicle was much in evidence. Liv Ullmann gave us an *Anna Christie* clear as glass, shining through every detail of the Eugene O'Neill character under José Quintero's direction. Al Pacino reshaped the role of the nonentity caught in the tide rip of the Vietnam War in David Rabe's *The Basic Training of Pavlo Hummel* and made it his own. Rex Harrison and Elizabeth Ashley did Shaw's *Caesar and Cleopatra* conspicuously but briefly. Claire Bloom moved gracefully through *The Innocents* (based on Henry James's *The Turn of the Screw*) under Harold Pinter's direction, and Paul Rudd and Pamela Payton-Wright concentrated on the love story in Theodore Mann's abridged version of *Romeo and Juliet*. Tennessee Williams added less to his reputation with his new play than he did with his Broadway revivals this season: *The Eccentricities of a Nightingale,* the rewrite of *Summer and Smoke* previously produced in London, off Broadway and in the present, still further rewritten version first produced at Studio Arena in Buffalo; and *The Night of the Iguana,* revived under Joseph Hardy's direction and Circle in the Square's unfailingly competent production auspices.

Shaw's *The Philanderer* and Ibsen's *John Gabriel Borkman,* with Gale Sondergaard, were highlights of the Gene Feist-Michael Fried Roundabout Theater Center's 1976-77 schedule on its busy stages. Christopher Martin's Classic Stage Company (CSC) put on the first New York production of Jean Genet's full script of *The Balcony,* in a repertory that ranged from Pinter's *The Homecoming* to Molière's *Tartuffe*. A new group, the BAM Theater Company, was formed at the Academy of Music with the help of Frank Dunlop of London's Old Vic, attracting a number of stellar performers to do *Three Sisters* and a 1906 Langdon Mitchell comedy, *The New York Idea,* under Dunlop's intercontinentally renowned direction. Various OOB groups were making the effort to emerge at the commercial level with revival productions, including Actors' Alliance *(The Tavern, Lullaby* and *Hay Fever),* T. Schreiber Theater *(All the Way Home)* and Lion Theater Company *(Peg o' My Heart)*.

The whole of the New York Theater revival festival of 1976-77 was greater than the sum of its parts. As entertaining, as revealing, as stimulating as many of the individual attractions were, there was a greater service to the theatergoer in making *all* of them available in the same place within the same short time frame. This informal but impressive festival took in not only Shakespeare, Shaw, Ibsen and Chekhov, but Coward, Beckett, O'Neill and O'Casey — and Pinter, Rabe, Anouilh and Williams — and Gershwin, Loesser, Rodgers and Harbach. From *Agamemnon* to *The Basic Training of Pavlo Hummel,* from *Tartuffe* to *Waiting for Godot* is a world of theater not too wide for the New York stage to encompass.

Offstage

The clinking of coins and the clicking of credit cards at the Broadway box offices was the most conspicuous offstage activity of the 1976-77 season, but the second most conspicuous was the downward slide of the neighborhood — slowed a bit, perhaps, but unchanged in direction. Boarded-up stores, half-lit hotel foyers uncleaned in this century and trash-filled doorways lined the approaches to Broadway. The best that can be said for the Sixth Avenue-to-Broadway blocks these days is that they provide audiences with a suitable preparation for a theater of shock and alienation.

Thanks to the persistent efforts of New York City departments, who are perfectly aware of the theater's enormous value to both the economy and lifestyle of the city, Broadway and its approaches were at least kept safe for theatergoers. The neighborhood isn't inviting, but its only negative impact during theater hours is esthetic.

Competing with the theater for public attention in the Broadway area, and having far outstripped the movies there, is the blatant marketing of sex, an intrusive presence which both theater and city oppose at every level, apparently unavailingly. In June, 1976 Gov. Hugh Carey of New York State signed an anti-loitering bill designed to keep prostitutes off certain streets. Broadway's sidewalks nevertheless teem with their annoying shills with their massage-parlor handouts and their cries of "Check it out!" which has replaced the newsboy's "Whatdya read?" as Broadway's background noise (it's hard to find a place to buy a newspaper there these days). The unceasing efforts of the League of New York Theaters and Producers to inhibit and shut off the porno traffic boomeranged when Lester Osterman, a League member, booked off Broadway's self-styled "sexual musical" *Let My People Come* into the Morosco. A special meeting of the League's Board of Governors declared this action "antithetical" to their policies. The show's producer, Phil Oesterman (no relation to the theater operator) immediately branded the League's action as censorship. The show went into the Morosco for a short and uneventful run and the controversy died down; but the League remains on record in its Aug. 31 resolution that "a cause for dismissal from membership in the League shall be deemed to exist when . . . . . a League member shall be found to have produced and/or presented and/or booked a play which shall be antithetical to the programs of the League seeking to upgrade the physical appearance of ths theatrical district; to eliminate sex-related businesses, such as massage parlors, peep shows, prostitution hotels, street prostitution, topless bars and pornographic motion picture theaters from the theater district; and to generally improve the urban environment in the midtown area."

Later in the season, a revival production of the erotic revue *Oh! Calcutta!* slid quietly into the smallish Edison Theater on West 47th Street, alternating performances with *Me and Bessie* and then staying on alone after *Bessie* closed, without raising any objections, a sort of if-you-can't-lick-'em-join-'em response to the theater's present environmental predicament.

Joseph Papp announced a theater-refurbishing program for the Vivian Beaumont; and then, just as everyone was beginning to speculate where he was going to get the $6.5 million he wanted to do this, he threw in the towel entirely and gave up on the Lincoln Center operation. Papp never found his feet uptown; he tried new plays, toyed with the idea of Shakespeare repertory, grudgingly lowered his sights to take aim at the subscription audience with a series of first-rate revival productions he hoped might be crowd-pleasers. Still, Papp's dedication to excellence emerged through all the problems; and whatever happens to the Beaumont now, it will be a long time before it matches Papp's finest hour there last season with the new adaptation of *Threepenny Opera* in the big theater and *Streamers* in the little Newhouse Theater in the basement.

The theater season's loudest street quarrel took place over the arrival in New York of the South African musical *Ipi-Tombi* for a booking at the Harkness Theater, following its long and successful London engagement. Well-organized protesters gathered under the marquee trying to make a political issue of the show, passing out literature which argued, "*Ipi-Tombi* is not simply an African musical symbolical of 'happiness.' If anything other than another cultural ripoff, *Ipi-Tombi* represents just the opposite: a sad and dangerous burlesque of the very real day-to-day victimization of our brothers and sisters in Azania (South Africa)."

Pickets castigated the show as a subliminally racist indoctrination of audiences with "a bogus air of happiness" and an exploitation of the performers for this purpose. The producers maintained that it was a non-political entertainment and a tribute to its participants' cultural achievements. The cast cried out that, far from being exploited, they were being very well paid indeed and wanted to keep on doing their thing in New York. None of the protesters we questioned had actually seen the show, which indeed ignored any white presence in South Africa (except for the starkly inhuman atmosphere of a city scene) and indeed showed great respect for the tribal arts of music and dance. In any case, the show wasn't a strong enough attraction, and it soon closed without any help from the pickets. The lyrics made one reverberating comment in the line, "I smile, but is this my face?" — but nothing could have impressed protesters who objected to begin with that the musical didn't spell its title, meaning "Where are the girls?", in a fashion more respectful of its language of origin: "Iphi-Ntombi."

In September, a group of producers instituted a court challenge to United Scenic Artists, Local 829 over its status — union or illegal combination in restraint of trade — in much the same way that the Dramatists Guild and the Society of Stage Directors and Choreographers have been challenged previously. In another part of the forest, the producers and stagehands settled on a new three-year contract with built-in raises of 10 per cent the first year and 8 per cent for each of the next two years (by which time, no doubt, the $20 ticket will be an ubiquitous Broadway reality).

Major changes of personnel taking place in theater circles this season included a changing of the guard in the powerful position of daily drama critic of the New York *Times*. The paper announced that Clive Barnes's occupancy of this post would come to an end with the 1976-77 season, and that he would concentrate on his duties as dance critic while Richard Eder, a 44-year-old former foreign correspondent and present member of the *Times* amusement staff, would take over in drama (while Walter Kerr remains as Sunday drama critic).

Still another of the longtime Critics Circle regulars, Henry Hewes, resigned as drama critic of the *Saturday Review*. In another major theater personnel change, Kitty Carlisle (Mrs. Moss) Hart was named by Gov. Carey to succeed Joan Davidson in the important and prestigious post of chairman of the New York State Council on the Arts.

One last backward glance at the 1976-77 theater season in New York: shock and alienation were its dominant tones, yes, but it was as diverse as perverse. The 180-degree opposition of lifestyles portrayed in *Annie* and *I Love My Wife,* its two best musicals, is a point-counterpoint symbol of this season, together with the foul language of *American Buffalo* opposite the meticulously weighed-up phrases of *Otherwise Engaged,* the bloody tissues of *Ashes* opposite the tennis rackets of *California Suite.* The award-giving at season's end reflected the diverse more than the perverse nature of the season, with the Pulitzer Prize and Tony Award going to *The Shadow Box* and the Critics Awards to *Otherwise Engaged* and *American Buffalo.* The Circle's significant first ballot of *first* choices for best play was so diversified that there was a four-way tie for second place.

Jessica Tandy and Hume Cronyn in *The Gin Game* by D. L. Coburn.

PHOTO BY MARTHA SWOPE

1977-78

THE 1977-78 season in New York was a castle built on sand, an arresting demonstration of how to succeed in show business without really trying. To call it average would be kind to its whole but unkind to its parts — the average show is as hard to find as the average man, with always an exceptional emotion, laugh, idea, performance, tune or piece of business even in the shortest-lived efforts (like Stuart Ostrow's *Stages* or Gus Weill's *The November People*, which lasted only one performance on Broadway, or the musical *Angel*, which lasted only five). To call it memorable would be true in the sense that Broadway shattered all previous box-office records with a year's gross of more than $100 million but untrue in the sense that production was off, with a total of only one effective new musical in the traditional Broadway style (*On the Twentieth Century*), in a used-car-lot atmosphere of shows borrowed from other centers of stage activity and from the past. To fill the musical void, memorable scripts and scores and even performances were awakened like Sleeping Beauty to arouse the affections of a recently-metamorphosed audience which never saw live theater before the days of *Grease, Pippin* and *The Wiz* and therefore look upon *Hello Dolly, Man of La Mancha* and *The King and I* as fresh experiences, or at least as something they've seen before only in the movies.

To dwell upon the season's brightest aspect — its ten Best Plays — Broadway and off Broadway were in balance with five Bests each (last season only one appeared off and nine on). Broadway offered two indelible geriatric studies, Hugh Leonard's soft-focus *"Da"* and D.L. Coburn's sharp-focus *The Gin Game;* Ira Levin's intriguing murder game, *Deathtrap;* a new Neil Simon, *Chapter Two,* raising the emotional questions of second marriage; and a new Bernard Slade, *Tribute,* weighing contrasting values of pleasure-seeking and commitment. Off Broadway played more than a supporting role, providing the best musical comedy of the season, the cheerful and high-spirited *The Best Little Whorehouse in Texas* by Larry L. King, Peter Masterson and Carol Hall. Independent off-Broadway production took over the center ring for a change with David Mamet's parable of youth and age, *A Life in the Theater,* and Dick Goldberg's chess game of family hostility, *Family Business.* The cream of the organizationally-produced crop was Thomas Babe's police-station drama *A Prayer for My Daughter* at New York Shakespeare Festival Public Theater and Lanford Wilson's assortment of character studies in *The 5th of July* at Circle Repertory Company.

New growth? *The Gin Game* is its author's first play, and the circumstances of his deciding to write it are the stuff of fantasy. *Family Business* is Dick Goldberg's New York playwriting debut. *The Best Little Whorehouse in Texas* is the first produced play of its book authors, King and Masterson, and the professional stage debut of its composer-lyricist, Carol Hall.

To turn from the sublime subject of esthetic accomplishment to the ridiculous economics of today's theater, these were boom times in New York both on and offstage. The city played host to an all-time-high 16,500,000 visitors during the year. They spent an estimated $1,600,000,000 and "generated" another $4,800,-

The 1977-78 Season on Broadway

PLAYS (13)

THE GIN GAME
Some of My Best
  Friends
An Almost Perfect
  Person
Golda
CHAPTER TWO
The November People
Cheaters
DEATHTRAP
The Water Engine
  (transfer) & Mr.
  Happiness
Stages
Patio/Porch
The Mighty Gents
TRIBUTE

MUSICALS (5)

The Act
On the Twentieth
  Century
Angel
Runaways
  (transfer)
Working

REVUES (4)

Beatlemania
Dancin'
A History of the
  American Film
Ain't Misbehavin'

FOREIGN PLAYS
IN ENGLISH (4)

The Night of the
  Tribades
The Merchant
Do You Turn
  Somersaults?
"*DA*"

FOREIGN-LANGUAGE
PLAYS (1)

Estrada

REVIVALS (14)

Circle in the Square 1977:
  The Importance of Being
    Earnest
The Cherry Orchard
  (transfer)
Circle in the Square 1978:
  Tartuffe
Saint Joan
13 Rue de l'Amour
Man of La Mancha
Hair
Dracula
Jesus Christ Superstar
A Touch of the Poet
Cold Storage
  (revision)
Timbuktu (Kismet)
Hello, Dolly
The Effect of Gamma Rays
  on Man-in-the-Moon
    Marigolds

SPECIALTIES (5)

Miss Margarida's Way
  (Transfer)
Comedy With Music
Bully
Paul Robeson
Diversions & Delights

HOLDOVERS WHICH
BECAME HITS
IN 1977-78 (2)

Side by Side
  by Sondheim
Your Arms Too Short
  to Box With God

Plays listed in CAPITAL LETTERS have been designated Best Plays of 1977-78.
Plays listed in *italics* were still running June 1, 1978.
Plays listed in **bold face type** were classified as hits in *Variety*'s annual estimate published May 31, 1978.

000,000, a fair portion of this at theater box offices. For the third straight
season, according to *Variety's* figures, the total Broadway gross was an all-time
record high. In 1976-77 it was $93.4 million, 31.8 per cent above the previous
year's $70.8 million, in a different world from the previous historical high of
$58.9 million in 1967-68. This season it climbed again by 11 per cent to $103,-
846,494 — jumping over the $100 million moon for the first time and, in com-
bination with the grosses of Broadway shows on the road, jumping twice as high
as that to a galactic combined gross of $209,543,379.

As we fill our lungs to rejoice at this good news, we're arrested in mid-breath
by other, doubt-casting numbers: Broadway production had thinned from 54 to
41 productions (not counting specialties). Playing weeks (if ten shows play ten
weeks, that's 100 playing weeks) were up only slightly to 1,360 from 1,348 last
season and attendance was down from 8.8 to 8.6 million, per *Variety's* figures.
This leads us to the conclusion that the record gross was at least as much the
result of inflation (see our report on the $25 ticket in the "Offstage" chapter of
this report) as of popularity — plus a little bit of unexpected luck with massively
successful revivals led by the $12 million-grossing *The King and I*. Among the
1977-78 shows, there were only four new works and three revivals established as
hits as of the end of the season, according to *Variety* estimate, and only two
holdovers had become hits since the end of 1976-77.

In the ebb and flow of box office activity, *A Chorus Line* was bringing in
$475,000 a week from its Broadway and two touring companies. *Pippin* finally
closed after 1,944 performances and a $1,659,207 profit so far on its $500,000
investment, but a long run was no guarantee of long numbers in the bank account — *Shenandoah* had recouped only about 80 per cent of its cost after 1,050
performances. Broadway producers looked enviously at their opposite numbers
in the concert field, some of whom were using Broadway theaters for conspicuously lucrative rock concerts and solo shows.

Attempts to showcase acting stars didn't usually come off so well. Liv
Ullmann's adventure in *Anna Christie* last season turned an estimated $150,000
profit, but the effort to bring Mary Martin back to Broadway with Anthony
Quayle in a Russian comedy about middle-aged romance, *Do You Turn Somersaults?*, dropped all of its $400,000 cost. So did the Ted Knight vehicle *Some of
My Best Friends*, a comedy in which the TV star played a disenchanted business
man looking for happiness and escape from the rat race by opening up a
dialogue with plants and animals. This one lost its entire $250,000. So did *The
Night of the Tribades*, a dark study of Strindberg's emotional life translated
from the Swedish, with Max Von Sydow, losing its comparatively modest $225,-
000 stake.

The most conspicous characteristic of the Broadway year as a whole was its
very great scarcity of musical inspiration. It's possible that the Broadway
musical as we have known it is an endangered species suffering the environmental impact of rising production costs and dwindling esthetic nourishment. There
are at least four contemporary concentrations of effort to shelter and nurture the
stage musical in special circumstances outside New York until it finds its feet
again: the Musical Theater Lab in Washington, D.C., the Lenox, Mass. Arts
Center/Music-Theater Performing Group, the American Musical Theater
Center at Duke University, Durham, N.C. and the Goodspeed Opera House,
East Haddam, Conn. In the meantime, we were making do in 1977-78 with a
transferred off-off-Broadway cabaret revue, *Ain't Misbehavin'*, which won the
Critics and Tony best-musical citations; another cabaret turn, *The Act*, tailored

for a star; a tour de force of design and atmosphere in *On the Twentieth Century;* Bob Fosse's revue-like celebration of *Dancin';* Studs Terkel's ditto of *Working;* and a bushel basket full of revivals. What more could we have wished back there in the mid-1960s than Carol Channing in *Hello, Dolly!* or Richard Kiley in *Man of La Mancha* — or a revival of what was then a venerated old 1950s musical, *The King and I,* with Yul Brynner repeating his memorable performance as the King of Siam? It wasn't wishing that made it so all over again, more than a decade later in the season of 1977-78.

Glancing over our shoulder at the off-Broadway season, we see that the Joseph Papp skyrocket reached a point in its trajectory where it exploded in a dazzling shower of productions. His season began with Central Park engagements of his own previously-acclaimed *Threepenny Opera* and *Agamemnon,* and he put on three more revivals — *The Mandrake, The Dybbuk* and a musicalized *The Misanthrope* — among his fourteen 1977-78 offerings downtown in the nooks and crannies of the Public Theater. These comprised a half dozen new plays, two "poemplays," two musicals and a specialty, the while he was also setting up a cabaret theater under his roof and sponsoring odds and ends of guest production and workshop activity. In the damp and woundy theater climate of today, part of Papp's 1977-78 fireworks display fizzled, of course, but it achieved some spectacular bursts, notably the Best Play *A Prayer for My Daughter,* the ground-breaking musical *Runaways* and the striking novelty *Miss Margarida's Way.*

Also off Broadway, Lynne Meadow's Manhattan Theater Club finally put its toe in the water of the commercial theater with a series of five-week runs of foreign plays new to New York audiences. MTC has previously confined itself to the off-off-Broadway arena, where it has achieved mightily (for example, *Ain't Misbehavin'* was developed in its cabaret). Probably MTC will now plunge in and sink or swim — at least part-time — with the rest of off-Broadway's distinguished organizational producers: Circle, Roundabout, Chelsea, Negro Ensemble, Phoenix, LOOM and the aforementioned Joseph Papp.

Broadway

The development of the so-called musical comedy — or latterly, just the musical — has been traced by Stanley Green and other theater historians from its roots back beyond Gilbert & Sullivan through Victor Herbert and Jerome Kern, through Cole Porter and George Gershwin, through Rodgers & Hammerstein to Stephen Sondheim and . . . beyond? Aye, there's the rub, because not since *Company* has there been significant development (the music itself excepted) in the concept of what we have come to think of as the "Broadway musical." It has taken interesting tangents like *Pacific Overtures* and *I Love My Wife,* but mutation? — not really. Maybe the nearest thing to it was *A Chorus Line,* with setpieces of dancing and character monologues strung like beads along a single theme, making a kind of connection between the book musical and the revue (*Ain't Misbehavin'*) or concert (*Beatlemania*) form. *Runaways* and *Working* went along this same line this season. Theirs is an entertainment form which is neither book musical nor revue but a *theme* musical, a little less than kin but more than kind in its resemblance to the traditional Broadway show.

Elizabeth Swados's *Runaways* was an imaginative, disciplined musical-theater image of the runaway child, the battered casualty in flight from the family battleground. There was pity and terror in its music and dance rhythms, in the tone of its frightened young voices, in the solemnity of its performances by a part-professional, part-real-runaway cast. Accusation is its theme: accusation of parents for their selfishness and insensitivity, of society for exploiting or punishing instead of comforting the runaways (though exploitation and comfort sometimes go hand in hand, as is the case with a child prostitute who feels warmly protected by her pimp). The subject was thoroughly researched by Miss Swados and developed in workshop at Joseph Papp's Public Theater before being presented first off Broadway and then on. There was no lack of emotional contact between characters and audience in *Runaways* — what was lacking was any developmental change or progress as the show began, continued and ended on its one pounding note of helpless despair, varying little even in intensity, until you longed for an exceptional insight to break the surface. For all its poetic nature, the succession of scenes and musical numbers in *Runaways* didn't build on the image created in the opening number.

Likewise, Stephen Schwartz turned a set of Studs Terkel sketches of working people into a theme musical in *Working*. There was as much continuity of style in this series of snapshots of masons, secretaries, etc. as in the anecdotes of the dancers in *A Chorus Line,* but no such common purpose to give it momentum, other than statement and re-statement of admiration for those whose devotion to small duties often demands more endurance and self-sacrifice than is expected of those with more conspicuous responsibilities.

In *Working,* as in *Runaways,* there was again no developmental progress in the course of — or as the result of — the events/influences of the material. This is the sticking point of the theme musical at the 1978 stage of its evolution, if indeed it is an advancing musical mutation. It's highly probable that our theater artists will soon come up with a book-less show that rings profound emotional changes with the variations on its theme. It hasn't happened yet, though, and until it does we'll continue to regard the full-fledged book-musical concept like *The Best Little Whorehouse in Texas* or *On the Twentieth Century* as the co-stars of the passing show together with the unalloyed and exceptional revue like *Ain't Misbehavin'.*

There's mileage in the old form yet (*Grease, Annie*) but it is footsore from repetition. With the cost of a Broadway-sized musical now in the forbidding neighborhood of $1 million, and with the expenses of an out-of-town shakedown now so high that it's getting to be impossible to take a big show out on a tryout tour, it's safest to rely on a proven classic or a proven star or a musicalized play, novel or even movie that seems to have a built-in audience appeal. Even with the bets hedged, the action this year was pitiful. Only *On the Twentieth Century* succeeded in developing a concept into a full-fledged Broadway musical with book, music, lyrics and (seemingly) cast of thousands. This Betty Comden-Adolph Green adaptation took a firm hold on the era as well as the material of its Hecht-MacArthur source, and nostalgia proved to be its best and winning bet. The train itself stole the show, dazzlingly represented onstage in Robin Wagner's chromium plated art deco designs, a vestige of the 1930s as it powered sleekly from New York to Chicago by means of turntables, miniatures, cutaways and other stage devices, and with the Cy Coleman score pounding out the rhythm of the rails.

On the Twentieth Century could run a train onstage, but it didn't — perhaps couldn't — quite evoke the overwhelming glamor that a top-ranking movie star radiated with her mere presence in those days. Consequently the activities of the passengers, in particular the Broadway impresario trying to change his bad luck by signing a movie actress to star in his next play, lost much of their comic pressure; and no amount of arm-waving by John Cullum as the producer, of posing by Madeline Kahn as the star or of acrobatics by Kevin Kline as her lover could restore it. Imogene Coca added a dash of flavoring as a religious fanatic in a manic phase. But the train was the best part. Those closest to it — namely, Keith Davis, Quitman Fludd III, Ray Stephens and Joseph Wise as four self-satisfied porters — fared best of all.

The *Shenandoah* team (Philip Rose, Gary Geld and Peter Udell) put together the only other book musical that got as far as Broadway this season: *Angel,* adapted from the Ketti Frings play and Thomas Wolfe novel *Look Homeward, Angel.* They had only slightly more success (5 performances) than the producers of *The Prince of Grand Street, Nefertiti* and *Spotlight,* which folded out of town.

Others had better luck whipping up entertainments which avoided some of the challenges of the traditional Broadway musical. For example, *Beatlemania,* a concert-style rock musical recreating and imitating the Beatles' performance of their best-liked numbers, grossed more than $7 million during the season at the Winter Garden. Liza Minnelli also won applause on Broadway in a tailor-made wrap-around called *The Act,* about how a night club singer makes it to the top (Las Vegas) — thus giving the singer, Miss Minnelli, her cue to do her thing continuously, almost concert-style, to the outer limits of her colorful stage presence and voice, with Barry Nelson coming on and off once in a while as her mentor in a barely discernable shadow of a book. Musical or concert, *The Act* was an entertainment that drew the crowds to see Miss Minnelli in what was clearly the year's standout performance by an actress in a musical.

Likewise, *Ain't Misbehavin'* celebrated the works of Thomas "Fats" Waller in a concert-style revue (almost no dialogue; song number following song number) that originated in the mind's ear of Richard Maltby Jr., was put on by him as a Manhattan Theater Club cabaret and then brought to Broadway. This toe-tapping compendium of about 30 numbers written or made famous in performance by Waller differed from the idea of *Beatlemania* in that it attempted no impersonation of its honored subject. But it certainly recreated the ebullient Waller spirit up on that stage with a minimum of fuss and a maximum of talent embodied by the singing ensemble — squeaky Nell Carter, buxom Armelia McQueen, zany Charlaine Woodard, stylish Andre De Shields and the cut-up Ken Page — with Hank Jones playing Fats Waller piano and conducting a fine jazz combo. *Ain't Misbehavin'* riffled up and down the whole keyboard of moods from the haunting "Black and Blue" in the bass to the outburst of "Your Feet's Too Big" in the high treble. It was a huge success, deservedly, and ran away with the Critics and Tony Awards for best musical. We agree — *Ain't Misbehavin'* certainly was the best "musical" of the New York year, though obviously not a "play" in any sense.

And then there was *Dancin',* still another kaleidoscope with choreographer Bob Fosse demonstrating what he could do with a Broadway show if he could push such extraneous distractions as book, music and lyrics out of the way and concentrate on the dance numbers. His cast of sixteen human bodies (including that of Ann Reinking) expressed themselves eloquently in line, gesture, motion and rhythm, singly and in groups, with background music chosen from the works of about two dozen composers including such tunesmiths as George M. Cohan, John Philip Sousa, Cat Stevens and Johann Sebastian Bach. *Dancin'* was uniquely a soaring celebration of the dance, if not — again — a Broadway musical in the full sense of the term.

In a similar construction there was Christopher Durang's well-traveled *A History of the American Film,* which had four regional theater productions before arriving on Broadway as its author's New York playwriting debut. It was a kaleidoscope of Hollywood movies from the silents to the disaster epics, part satire and part sweet nostalgia. It had a great deal of musical energy in scene after scene written to be recognized as reflections of past glories of James Cagney, Henry Fonda, Gary Cooper, Bette Davis, Loretta Young and other favorites. The director, David Chambers, kept it moving along in style, but it was not finally going anywhere.

Over on the straight-play side of Broadway, the traumas of aging and impending death preoccupied some of the best work of 1978 as it did in 1977. Last year it was *The Last Meeting of the Knights of the White Magnolia* and *The Shadow Box* on Broadway and *Cold Storage* off (the latter moving around the corner to Times Square this season for revival in a version revised by its author, Ronald Ribman, with Martin Balsam repeating his role of the terminal patient *vis à vis* Len Cariou as a newcomer to the hospital). This year it was *"Da," The Gin Game* and *Tribute* leading the parade, with intimations of mortality making themselves felt in other works all the way down the line.

"Da," the Critics and Tony best-play winner, is every inch an Irish play, with an Irish author (Hugh Leonard, veteran Dublin dramatist and director of the 1978 Dublin Festival); Irish characters played by a multi-national ensemble headed by Barnard Hughes as a crusty patriarch, Brian Murray as his adopted son, Sylvia O'Brien as his wife and Lester Rawlins as a prosperous neighbor; an Irish setting in the kitchen of a humble cottage with a view of the Mountains of Mourne; and an Irish flavor of life endured and death accepted. (Irish as it may be, it world premiered at Olney, Md.) "Da," as the son always called his father, has died as the play opens, after a life of hard work as an underpaid gardener on a nearby estate, with the compensation of solid family and community relationships. But Da has been such a strong influence that his son can't put him out of mind and memory, however hard he tries; and so Da is very much with us as scene follows vivid scene in the son's remembered growing-up with love, anger, pride, failure, hope, frustration and fulfillment. Directed by Melvin Bernhardt and acted with full power; lilting in its emotional rhythms as the brogue in which all its characters speak; never very far from either laughter or tears, *"Da"* was a shade the best of the year's Best Plays.

This season's Pulitzer Prize winner, *The Gin Game,* was more than a shade its best American play. Its two characters are welfare cases in a home for the aged. They begin to find a little solace in getting together over a game of gin rummy, only to have the game's aberrations expose the worst side of their natures, until they lose their last pitiful vestiges of both mutual and self respect. *The Gin Game* is full of sympathy but devoid of comfort, a first play by an author — D.L. Coburn — who has only just turned 40 but seems to have as unerring an instinct for the *terra incognita* of creeping senility as he does of playwriting. Hume Cronyn and Jessica Tandy played the couple in what will surely go down as one of the theater's memorable dual performances, the equal of their married couple in *The Fourposter.* They are strangers who meet, make connections through a ritual of card-playing which turns out to be a no-win game, and finally part as strangers returning to their no-win lives. Under the combined power of the spare but effective script and the Cronyns' performance, the play is unnerving, not depressing. When Mike Nichols, who directed it, was reminded during the out-of-town tryout that it had "only" two characters, he replied, "Who counts characters?" It's true, in *The Gin Game* these two uncommunicating old people are, finally, almost everybody.

The season's overcast of somber preoccupation darkened even Neil Simon's newest comedy, *Chapter Two,* as it posed the question: is there life for a devoted husband after the untimely death of his beloved wife? The widower (Judd Hirsch) is besieged by well-meaning but ill-advised efforts to find a new someone for him; then he discovers to his own astonishment that he's willing to try again with a young divorcee (Anita Gillette) as balky and bright as himself; and then he plunges them both into a maze of despair and recrimination, which they will escape some day only if they hold tight to each other's hands and refuse to yield to panic. The dialogue flashes with emotional gallows humor, the mood is as contemporary as tomorrow and the insights are something special and probably a bit personal. Simon, recently a widower, is now married to Marsha Mason, and some of his *Chapter Two* strains and stresses were certainly autobiographical.

In *Tribute,* Bernard Slade, author of the long-run comedy hit *Same Time, Next Year,* also underlined his humor with a black streak of mortality, in his study of a modern-day jester battling leukemia and forced to take a long look at himself and his past life, in particular his relationship with his only son, in a strange new twilight. A towering performance by Jack Lemmon as a pleasure-loving sort who has plenty of talent but always goes for the laugh instead of the achievement — and therefore has a great many friends but few medals — dominated and informed this somewhat flawed script with total conviction and endless nuance.

Slade has seen fit to offer up his play with a tacky frame around it: it begins with and keeps returning to a testimonial gathering, the "tribute" of the title, while the play flashes back to key incidents in the guest of honor's recent past. But performances like Lemmon's cannot hold up, as it did, without solid members beneath them; and Slade's play is buttressed firmly with wit and feeling in the important scenes, whatever its structural flaws may be. Jack Lemmon's performance and Bernard Slade's play were a jackpot-winning entertainment combination.

Another Best Play, Ira Levin's *Deathtrap,* had a great deal to do with mortality but nothing whatever to do with geriatrics or sympathy for those who are about to suffer it somewhere in the coils of its sardonic murder-game involvements. This comedy thriller was like an elaborately constructed apparatus for an exceptionally gifted circus acrobat: you couldn't imagine how all the trapezes and taut wires are to be used, but you were certain they would be because they were there. A deathtrap is indeed hidden somewhere in the relationship of a middle-aged playwright envious of his student's work. Discovering the exact nature of the trap was as difficult as it should be in a first-rate mystery, and being fooled time after time was part of the fun of seeing how it came out. John Wood gave a brilliant circus performance as the playwright, timing his comedy inflections and angular movements with the play so that trapeze met hand at exactly the right instant, time after time. Much of the credit belongs to Robert Moore's concise direction, more to Levin's clever script, but even more to Wood in one of the acting gems of his sparkling career.

Among new Broadway scripts with a fairly serious thrust was William Gibson's docu-drama *Golda,* a review of events in Israel's 1973 Yom Kippur War and in the life of its great prime minister, Golda Meir. The play benefited hugely from Anne Bancroft's presence in the title role. Head thrust aggressively forward, snapping a verbal whip at the savageries of statecraft, Miss Bancroft combined imitation, admiration and insight into to the subject in a commanding performance. The author has announced that the script produced on Broadway isn't the version of his heart's desire, so that when *Golda* reappears on world stages it will be in different, but official, form.

Richard Wesley's *The Mighty Gents* was another work of considerable power, reflecting the contemporary undersociety in characterizations of grown-up members of a one-time Newark, N.J. black youth gang who can now find or make no place for themselves, no identity in the grownup world. The performances of Dorian Harewood as a former youth gang leader, Howard E. Rollins Jr. as a gangster and Morgan Freeman as a derelict wino who refuses to be ignored as a non-person were scathing setpieces. Their rage was convincing, their fate pitiable but their play lacked a spine to make it stand up straight, even though it was tried out twice off off Broadway, at Manhattan Theater Club and Urban Arts Corps. In this form it was more polemic than play.

David Mamet's second New York playwriting year consisted of two show-biz stories: the Best Play *A Life in the Theater* off Broadway and *The Water Engine* which began off and was brought uptown. The latter is a radio-play-within-a-staged-play about a vulnerable inventor up against ruthless business interests, staged as if in a Chicago radio station in the 1930s (and consequently more memento than drama), on a bill with a curtain raiser, *Mr. Happiness,* a Mamet monologue for an offensively cheerful radio announcer. Among other on-balance-comic matters this year were the romantic vagaries of a hard-hitting female politician (Colleen Dewhurst), in *An Almost Perfect Person;* spouse-swapping with all the devious opportunities it offers to performers like Lou Jacobi and Jack Weston, in *Cheaters;* and the manners and conversational styles of Texas women in Jack Heifner's chatty one-acters, *Patio/Porch.*

On the list of the year's imports along with *"Da," The Night of the Tribades* and *Do You Turn Somersaults?* was an effort by Arnold Wesker to place the people and events of Shakespeare's *The Merchant of Venice* in a new stage perspective entitled *The Merchant* — new but not especially revealing. The only foreign-language visitor to Broadway was *Estrada,* a Russian variety show which stopped by for a week of circus and musical numbers.

The specialty productions were certainly something special this year. Hard-driving Estelle Parsons gave the season's outstanding female performance as a totally self-centered and fanatically domineering schoolteacher in *Miss Margarida's Way,* Roberto Athayde's play which drafted the audience in the role of Miss Margarida's classroom full of browbeaten pupils. Joseph Papp brought this extraordinary tour de force of acting, writing and direction (also by Athayde) uptown to Broadway after a run at the Public. Papp also sheltered Phillip Hayes Dean's biographical study *Paul Robeson,* starring James Earl Jones, by putting it into repertory with the long-running *For Colored Girls,* etc. when it otherwise would have closed after only a short Broadway run and a longer siege of controversy (see the "Offstage" section of this report).

James Whitmore brought Theodore Roosevelt into characterization in Jerome Alden's *Bully!,* as did Vincent Price with Oscar Wilde in John Gay's *Diversions & Delights.* And then there was Victor Borge, uniquely inimitable in still another welcome *Comedy With Music* sojourn on Broadway.

The 1977-78 Season Off Broadway

PLAYS (28)

Public Theater:
Landscape of the Body
The Water Engine
A PRAYER FOR MY
  DAUGHTER
Museum
Curse of the
  Starving Class
The Passion of Dracula
American Place:
Cockfight
Passing Game
Fefu and Her Friends
Conjuring an Event
Circle Repertory:
Feedlot
Ulysses in Traction
Two From the Late Show
THE 5TH OF JULY
Old Man Joseph and His
  Family
A LIFE IN THE THEATER
The Running of the Deer
Phoenix:
Uncommon Women and
  Others
The Elusive Angel
Esther

NEC:

The Offering
Black Body Blues
The Twilight Dinner
The Contessa of
  Mulberry Street
FAMILY BUSINESS
The Neon Woman
International Stud
The Ventriloquist's Wife

SPECIALTIES (13)

The 2d Greatest
  Entertainer in the
  Whole Wide World
The Square Root of Soul
Public Theater:
Miss Margarida's Way
Tales of the Hasidim
A Photograph
Mango Tango
The Grand Kabuki
Housewife! Superstar!
  I
A Man and His Women
Joe Masiell Not at the
  Palace
My Astonishing Self
23 Skiddoo

MUSICALS (6)

Public Theater:
Runaways
*I'm Getting My Act
  Together and Taking
  It on the Road*
Hot Grog
Green Pond
A Bistro Car on the CNR
*THE BEST LITTLE
  WHOREHOUSE IN
  TEXAS*

FOREIGN PLAYS
IN ENGLISH (9)

Survival
Rum an Coca Cola
Manhattan Theater Club:
Chez Nous
Play and Other Plays
Statements After an
  Arrest Under the
  Immorality Act &
  Scenes From Soweto
Catsplay
Strawberry Fields
One Crack Out
The Biko Inquest

REVUES (6)

Unsung Cole
Children of Adam
The Present Tense
Nightsong
By Strouse
The Proposition

REVIVALS (45)

Delacorte:
Threepenny Opera
Agamemnon
LOOM:
H.M.S. Pinafore
The Pirates of
  Penzance
The Merry Widow
Naughty Marietta
The Vagabond King
Ruddigore
The Mikado
The Sorcerer
Iolanthe
Mlle. Modiste
The Grand Duchess
  of Gerolstein
Patience
The Gondoliers
Stage Blood
Public Theater:
The Misanthrope
The Mandrake
The Dybbuk
Counsellor-at-Law

Roundabout:
Naked
You Never Can Tell
Othello
The Promise
The Show-Off
Pins and Needles
Lulu
CSC:
A Midsummer Night's
  Dream
Rosmersholm
Serjeant Musgrave's Dance
The Maids
The Madwoman of
  Chaillot
Joseph and the Amazing
  Technicolor Dreamcoat
The Beard
BAM:
The Devil's Disciple
The Play's the Thing
Julius Caesar
Waiting for Godot
P.S. Your Cat Is Dead
Acting Company:
Mother Courage
King Lear
Duck Variations
Life of Galileo
Ludlam Repertory:
Stage Blood
Camille

Plays listed in CAPITAL LETTERS have been designated Best Plays of 1977-78.
Plays listed in *italics* were still running June 1, 1978.

Off Broadway

To get a close look at the seething ferment of 1977-78 theater activity on the fringes of Broadway and beyond, you have to follow the action to the ends of narrow alleys undisturbed since Peter Stuyvesant's day; to lofts reachable only up multiple flights of stairs that would tax the stamina of a Sherpa guide; even across bridges to the *terra incognita* that Brooklyn has become since the Dodgers left. It's been many years since one "off" sufficed to identify this bubbling cauldron of theater; and now "off off" scarcely suffices to cover all the contingencies of stage production in New York.

At the tributary theater's highest professional level, where most of the bubbles are, is what we call "off Broadway" (hyphenated when used as an adjective, not so when used as a noun). By the lights of these *Best Plays* volumes, an off-Broadway production is defined as one (a) with an Equity cast (b) giving 8 performances a week (c) in an off-Broadway theater (d) after inviting public comment by critics on an opening night or nights. And according to Paul Libin, president of the League of Off-Broadway Theaters, an off-Broadway theater is a house seating 499 or fewer and situated in Manhattan *outside* the area bounded by Fifth and Ninth avenues between 34th and 56th Streets, and by Fifth Avenue and the Hudson River between 56th and 72d Streets.

Obviously there are exceptions to each of these rules. No dimension of off Broadway can be applied exactly. In each *Best Plays* volume we stretch these definitions somewhat in the direction of inclusion — never of exclusion. For example, the word "Manhattan" means what we want it to mean, *Alice in Wonderland*-wise, when we include Brooklyn's Chelsea Theater Center and Academy of Music programs. Casts are sometimes only part-Equity and schedules sometimes take in 7 and in rare cases 6 performances a week (but we don't knowingly list 5-a-weekers, which are distinctly off off Broadway).

The point is that off Broadway isn't an exact location, it's a state of the art (generally advanced), a structure of production costs (generally reduced, but climbing), a level of expertise and effort. The point we must make with increasing emphasis as the seasons pass is that the borderline between professional off-Broadway and semi-professional off off Broadway (OOB for short) has all but disappeared. OOB groups often use part-Equity casts under special showcase arrangements, while off-Broadway groups do not always meet all the off-Broadway standards in all their shows. As for the level of professional quality in the finished work, consider that this year's best-of-bests, *"Da,"* came directly into the limelight from OOB in a Hudson Guild Theater production brought to Broadway virtually intact, as did the best musical, *Ain't Misbehavin',* reaching the Broadway pinnacle with its Manhattan Theater Club cabaret OOB production.

With all measurement blurring, the New York *Times* has ceased trying to categorize off Broadway in its annual summary, and *Variety* has all but given up trying to keep a complete count. We'll continue making the distinction between off and off off here in our year-by-year reports however, as long as it seems useful to do so for the record, while reminding all who read these lines that formal distinctions are no longer as clear as they were and we tend to include rather than exclude.

This said, let's immediately welcome Manhattan Theater Club into the off-Broadway ranks. That 73d Street OOB group has established a commanding presence in the New York Theater under the artistic direction of Lynne Meadow. This season for the first time a part of its multiple production activity — its Downstage schedule of five scripts from abroad — was produced with off-Broadway contracts. The importation from Hungary of Istvan Orkeny's *Catsplay* in the Clara Gyorgyey translation was the standout offering of MTC's first off-Broadway year. The script is a vehicle for a wide-ranging performance by an actress (in this case the admirable Helen Burns) playing a woman in her mid-60s writing letters to her sister — and speaking them aloud in the long descriptive monologues which comprise much of the play — about her life as a widow alone in Budapest and her ongoing romance with a has-been opera singer who was once her lover and is now her hedge against loneliness. Full of laughter and sympathy in good measure, this production was moved from MTC to another off-Broadway theater for a second run into the summer under independent auspices.

MTC's 1978 Downstage schedule also took in Peter Nichols's *Chez Nous*, about a British couple experimenting with sex and lifestyles; Athol Fugard's *Statements After an Arrest Under the Immorality Act*, about regulations of sexual apartheid in South Africa on a double bill with *Scenes From Soweto;* the British *Strawberry Fields* by Stephen Poliakoff, a clash between right-wing activists and a hitchhiker they take into their van as they move along a British turnpike; and the first New York productions of Samuel Beckett's *That Time* and *Footfalls* on a one-act play program with his *Play*. It's typical of today's shifting boundaries that MTC's most prominent 1977-78 show was *not* on this off-Broadway list, but its OOB production *Ain't Misbehavin'* which went from MTC cabaret to its Critics and Tony Award-winning Broadway engagement.

In the midst of rivals like MTC and Circle Repertory, and divested of his Lincoln Center responsibilities, Joseph Papp is still the king of the off-Broadway hill with his Public Theater complex, his Delacorte schedule, his workshops, cabarets and Broadway hits — and especially his instinct for challenging theater. Tops on his schedule of new work this season was Thomas Babe's *A Prayer for My Daughter* a Best Play which — like Babe's previous Best Play about Southern women in confrontation with General Sherman in his march to the sea — traps its characters in a situation not of their choosing and rubs their skin off until flesh and nerves are exposed. In *A Prayer for My Daughter* they are two police officers who have taken into custody two suspects in a particularly callous murder and are going to extract confessions from them if it takes all night (and it happens to be the small hours of the morning of July 4). Identities become somewhat confused in the heat of the night, with overlapping streaks of brutality and sexual involvement, as one of the policemen insists on staying to do his duty and beat up the prisoners even though his daughter is in trouble and has threatened to kill herself, and as one of the criminals fingers the other for the murder. The performances by Laurence Luckinbill (killer) and George Dzundza (cop) and the direction by Robert Allan Ackerman were as strong as the play.

Another particularly striking 1978 offering at the Public was Sam Shepard's *Curse of the Starving Class*, a metaphor of the human condition and of the way *not* to go, in its study of hunger physical and hunger spiritual as both a blight and a weapon of the exploiters against the exploited. In addition, Papp's downtown 1978 kaleidoscope of innovative off-Broadway theater comprised three more new plays, an Improvisational Theater offering, three revivals, two musicals, two "poemplays", a one-woman-performance specialty *Miss*

Margarida's Way which made it to Broadway, plus all kinds of experimental activity. The new work in this imposing total of 14 off-Broadway productions included, besides the Babe and Shepard scripts, John Guare's widely-admired *Landscape of the Body* about a young woman under stress in the big city; Paul Sills's improvisations and Martin Buber dramatizations in *Tales of the Hasidim;* Ntozake Shangé's "poemplay" study of cruelty, *A Photograph,* and Jessica Hagedorn's of growing up in Manila, *Mango Tango;* David Mamet's 1930s radio-play-within-a-stage-play, *The Water Engine,* which also made it to Broadway; Tina Howe's *Museum* in which paintings were watching people; and the musicals *Runaways* and *I'm Getting My Act Together and Taking It on the Road,* the latter an energetic Gretchen Cryer-Nancy Ford show celebrating the status of the liberated woman on the threshold of middle age, emotional adjustments and all.

Papp never found his feet at Lincoln Center, but his stance at the Public is ever more firm on a foundation of new scripts of dramatic quality — but not *just* quality. They also tend to be innovative but not *just* innovative; sensitive but not just sensitive; courageous but not just courageous; socially concerned but not just concerned. Papp's downtown 1978 season had something of all of these, in a concept of theater unmatched in its inborn respect for striving artists and adventurous audiences.

Another invariably stimulating and highly successful producing group is Marshall W. Mason's Circle Repertory Company which, sure enough, came up with a Best Play this season: Lanford Wilson's *The 5th of July,* a group of characters in search of themselves, youngish folk who were the right age to take part in the uproar of the 1960s and who now, in the 1970s, are trying to get to the bottom of their identities. They've come together for a holiday weekend visit (the actual date has as little importance here as it does in *A Prayer for My Daughter)* at a Missouri country place owned by a Vietnam veteran who lost both his legs in the war and so must rely on his male lover for both physical and emotional support. His guests are his sister and her fatherless and obnoxious sub-teen-age daughter, two former high school chums (an heiress who'd rather be a pop singer and her ambitious husband), a Nashville-bound guitar player and a widowed aunt who is as cool as any of the younger members of the house party. *The 5th of July* is closer to its author's *The Hot l Baltimore* than to his more recent Best Play *Serenading Louie* (both produced by Circle Rep under Mason's direction), in that it is a not-very-tightly structured study of the human spirit in the aftermath of stress. In *The Hot l Baltimore* they are perhaps going to lose the hotel; here they're perhaps going to give up the old family place, and that's about it as far as plot is concerned. But with Wilson's insights, Mason's stagecraft and the coordination of a first-rate acting ensemble, this was one of the year's best entertainments.

Another standout on the Circle's schedule was Patrick Meyers's *Feedlot,* a drama of love/hate relationships among men in the long hours of the night while tending a large cattle-fattening operation, directed by Terry Schreiber of off-off-Broadway fame. Circle Rep's schedule of new scripts also took in an allegorical play by Albert Innaurato, *Ulysses in Traction,* about students rehearsing a play while a riot is going on outdoors, not exactly a laughing matter but hilarious in its overtones; and a pair of one-acters, *Brontosaurus* by Lanford Wilson and *Cabin 12* by John Bishop.

The Phoenix Theater rose again on schedule under the managing directorship of T. Edward Hambleton, offering a sampling of new scripts including Wendy

Wasserstein's reflections on bright "Seven Sisters" college years, *Uncommon Women and Others;* Jack Gilhooley's *The Elusive Angel* about a childless couple trying for an adoption; a Canadian version of the pool hustler vs. gamblers conflict in David French's *One Crack Out;* and *Hot Grog,* a Jim Wann-Bland Simpson musical about the pirate Blackbeard, developed at the Musical Theater Lab in Washington, D.C.

American Place, under Wynn Handman's direction, frequently occupied itself with guest productions like the Acting Company's repertory of revivals. It also came up with four challenging new scripts: Elaine Jackson's *Cockfight,* about the macho pose when there is naught behind it; Steve Tesich's *Passing Game,* a deadly one played by two wife-abusers, one black and one white; Maria Irene Fornes's *Fefu and Her Friends,* a gathering of women staged by the author so that the action (and the audience) sometimes broke into several parts in separate sections of the theater; and Richard Nelson's *Conjuring an Event,* examining the power of journalism to cause as well as report an action.

Over in Brooklyn, Robert Kalfin's Chelsea Theater Center continued to explore byways of theater and share its findings with Manhattan audiences by bringing its productions across the river to the Westside Theater following their Brooklyn runs. These included *Rum an Coca Cola,* a study of a Trinidadian Calypso artist and his young pupil, by the much-admired London playwright Mustapha Matura; *Green Pond,* the Robert Montgomery-Mel Marvin musical of 1970s attitudes, first produced by Stage South, S.C.; and Biblical Joseph's childhood presented as a folk tale in Romulus Linney's *Old Man Joseph and His Family.*

Douglas Turner Ward and Robert Hooks steered their Negro Ensemble Company into three dramatic examinations of the black experience, two of them by Gus Edwards: *The Offering,* a confrontation of the generations, and *Black Body Blues,* a clash of lifestyles, both giving off showers of sparks under Ward's direction. NEC's season concluded with Lennox Brown's *The Twilight Dinner,* a confrontation of two black friends of the 1960s from different countries, now discovering new problems in their relationship. And Charles Ludlam's Ridiculous Theatrical Company brought his *The Ventriloquist's Wife* up from OOB in a late-season Ludlam repertory, the rest of which were revivals.

David Mamet's *A Life in the Theater* is an opposite of his last season's Best Play, *American Buffalo:* light with personality where the other was darkly repressed, buoyed with aspiration where the other was weighed down with ignorance and failure. The new work uses a backstage setting with two actors (Ellis Rabb and Peter Evans) as a metaphor of life and its irresistible passage of time. The elder actor is accomplished but on the downhill slant, the younger with a lot of talent and a lot to learn on the way up, communicating now and again but not as clearly as they should in this shared experience of the youth-age relationship. Little scraps of their "performances" in plays they're doing out front (burlesquing theater cliches like war melodrama or drawing-room comedy) are sometimes visible. More often, though, these two are seen in dressing-room encounters, adjusting to each other and to the changing circumstances of their lives and careers, in a comic coat-of-many-colors.

Also in independent production was Dick Goldberg's *Family Business,* a very well-made and deeply-considered play about four brothers trying to settle their lives as they settle their father's estate. The patriarch's death throws them off balance (they were already teetering), and they grab at each other trying to maintain their equilibrium: the plodding storekeeper, the profligate psychiatrist, the wild one and the mama's boy who'd like to keep them all together under the old roof, whatever compromise and/or forgiveness is necessary to do so. As played by Richard Greene, David Rosenbaum, Joel Polis and David Garfield (in the order of the characters named above) under the direction of John Stix, their emotional abrasion gave off showers of sparks with its steady, grinding pressure.

The best book musical of 1978 has at least two things in common with *Grease:* it originated off Broadway in the theater at the corner of 12th Street and Second Avenue now called Entermedia, and it has an unappetizing title. *The Best Little Whorehouse in Texas* was certainly the best little new musical play in town this this season, but it was not, as its name suggests, an exploitation of sex or a thinly-disguised burlesque show. There may be one or two bits of business or dialogue that would offend your Aunt Minnie, but probably not if she had a glass of wine with dinner before the show. The moralists are the villains, yes, in this book by Larry L. King and Peter Masterson about do-gooders using TV as a means of publicizing and closing down a beloved rural institution devoted to sexual pleasures. But this place is strictly and decorously overseen by all-seeing, all-knowing, handsome Madam Mona (Carlin Glynn) who runs the kind of place you can take the whole football team to after the homecoming game.

The character themes in both book and score had a way of suddenly going deeper than you expected; for example in the case of a shy young hayseed (Joan Ellis) who has left home to escape her father's advances, or a hamburg-joint waitress (Susan Mansur) who stopped the show with a song about her frustrated dreams, "Doatsey Mae." Carol Hall's music and lyrics aren't showy, but they are vigorous, with echoes of country rock; the book's tone ranged all the way from touching to hilarious; and Tommy Tune's musical staging was as imaginative as it was energetic. Henderson Forsythe's performance as a fire-breathing Texas sheriff provided the finishing touch, throwing the temple of femininity into full masculine perspective. *The Best Little Whorehouse in Texas* maintained its balance of taste on its tightrope of a subject and added a generous portion of entertainment to the season, both downtown where it began and uptown where it followed *Grease* to Broadway in June.

The additional conglomeration of independent production off Broadway evinced no marked trend or fad. It roamed free through revue-style commentaries on contemporary life and events in shows like *Children of Adam, The Present Tense, Nightsong, The Proposition* and, from Canada, the musical *A Bistro Car on the CNR*. It offered a delightful medley of once and future Charles Strouse numbers in the revue *By Strouse;* a collection of unjustly obscure Cole Porter numbers in *Unsung Cole;* a popular new rendition of the Dracula tale by Bob Hall and David Richmond, *The Passion of Dracula*, off Broadway's long-run contribution to this Dracula season; A Tom Eyen-style, far-out burlesque of mystery plays in *The Neon Woman*. It provided an outlet for two more cries of South African pain, *The Biko Inquest*, dramatized by Norman Fenton and Jon Blair from transcripts of the inquest into the death of Stephen Biko, and *Survival*, a set of prison episodes created by the cast and director. It viewed the life, times and emotions of a drag queen in Harvey Fierstein's *International Stud* and the legendary Queen of Persia in C.K. Mack's *Esther.* Among its variety of subjects were family life in Little Italy in Nicholas D. Bellitto's *The Contessa of Mulberry Street* (emergent from OOB's Gene Frankel Workshop) and the last months of 1776 in America in Karen Sunde's *The Running of the Deer*, which grew out of activity at CSC, of which she is a member, and which attests to the internal vitality of that repertory company otherwise devoted to the production of revivals.

The off-Broadway specialties this season included visits from two foreign troupes: Japan's world-renowned national treasure, The Grand Kabuki, with a program of two Kabuki plays; and a Belgian multimedia group, *23 Skiddoo,* a series of extravagant audio-visual comments on the perplexing present and dark future. Performers who came on in solo showcases were Dick Shawn (*The 2nd Greatest Entertainer in the Whole Wide World*), Adolph Caesar (*The Square Root of Soul*), Anne West (*I*), Barry Humphries (*Housewife! Superstar!*), Craig Russell (*A Man and His Women*), Joe Masiell (*Joe Masiell Not at the Palace*) and Donal Donnelly (as Shaw in *My Astonishing Self*).

The time when the off-Broadway plateau was a fertile field for experimental theater has long passed (except occasionally, in the shelter of a producing institution like New York Shakespeare, Circle Repertory or American Place), what with ever more stringent contractual obligations and costs, within the continuing outside limitation of a 499-seat house (and most are nowhere near that large). But venture is still possible even though raw experiment generally is not; and off Broadway ventured widely in 1977-78. Viewed in perspective, its season also rated high in results, with five of the Best Plays; and in versatility, since three of these top-notch shows appeared in independent production. While Broadway was racing forward, widening its lead in pursuit of the $25 ticket, and off off Broadway was treading on its heels, off Broadway seemed to be settling into a steady stride for a long race.

Revivals

The attenuation in the number of Broadway revivals from 28 in 1975-76 to 17 in 1976-77 continued into 1977-78, when a mere 14 oldies were displayed in Broadway showcases — but their importance on the theater scene had attenuated not one bit. As previously noted, *Man of La Mancha* with Richard Kiley in his original role of the impossible dreamer Don Quixote, *Hello, Dolly!* with Carol Channing in her original role of Dolly Gallagher Levi dazzling the waiters with that entrance and even *Hair* and *Jesus Christ Superstar* padded the slender musical season in all the right places. Also, the colorful and romantically tuneful *Kismet,* in a rendition entitled *Timbuktu!* and transposed from Bagdad to an African setting, demonstrated some of the enduring possibilities waiting on the American musical library shelf. With an arresting Eartha Kitt performance, fanciful costumes, choreography and direction by Geoffrey Holder and the twice-familiar Borodin airs which became "Baubles, Bangles and Beads," "Stranger in Paradise," "Night of My Nights" and "This Is My Beloved" in passing through the hands of Robert Wright and George Forrest, this was a handsomely refinished antique, the most innovative musical revival of the season.

The same distinction in the straight-play category belongs to *Dracula,* the old Hamilton Deane-John L. Balderston dramatization of Bram Stoker's novel. Here again was a triumph of style and design in Edward Gorey's bat-winged scenery and elegant costumes, in a superbly molded and modulated performance by Frank Langella in the title role. It was the show's vampirish concept under Dennis Rosa's direction that it settle down to play *Dracula* with 100 per cent conviction, letting the baroque curlicues of the ghostly story move the audience to chills or laughter when and where it pleased. The result was a show that actually chilled more than it chuckled.

Then there was the José Quintero *A Touch of the Poet*, with Jason Robards in a landmark performance of Con Melody. Robards had already played a number of major O'Neill roles with major distinction, but never this one until now, when he made it his own in one of the season's several first-rate acting achievements. In other revival production, a somewhat revised version of Ronald Ribman's *Cold Storage* gave Martin Balsam a chance to repeat on Broadway his outstanding performance of a terminal patient talking out an ending, offered last year off Broadway at American Place opposite Michael Lipton as his companion patient and this year opposite Len Cariou. John Wood's *Tartuffe* and Lynn Redgrave's *Saint Joan* at Circle in the Square also were major ornaments of the Broadway year.

Elsewhere in its schedule Circle in the Square mounted an attractive Feydeau farce, *13 Rue de l'Amour*, adapted and translated by Mawby Green and Ed Feilbert from *Monsieur Chasse;* and, in June 1977, *The Importance of Being Earnest* as last season's caboose production (this season's was a revival of *Once in a Lifetime* in June 1978).

In early 1977 summer, Joseph Papp brought Andrei Serban's production of *The Cherry Orchard* back for his swan-song offering at the Vivian Beaumont in Lincoln Center. At the other end of the season, Paul Zindel's *The Effect of Gamma Rays on Man-in-the-Moon Marigolds* spent a moment or two in the Broadway limelight.

Off Broadway, where established organizations provide whole seasons of shows from the theater library shelves, there was an imposing total of 45 revivals in 1977-78. Joseph Papp opened the season with a pair of return engagements in Central Park of his own acclaimed Lincoln Center productions — *Threepenny Opera* and *Agamemnon* — and salted his Public Theater schedule with a musical *The Misanthrope* and new looks at *The Mandrake* (Machiavelli's *Mandragola*) and *The Dybbuk*. William Mount-Burke's Light Opera of Manhattan played right around the calendar in a 13-operetta revival year, mixing golden oldies of Victor Herbert, Rudolf Friml, Franz Lehar, etc. with Gilbert & Sullivan, and adding three new productions to their repertory: Victor Herbert's Parisian hat-shop idyll *Mlle. Modiste* (with Alfred Simon consulting in the production), Jacques Offenbach's send-up of war and other human vanities, *The Grand Duchess of Gerolstein*, and G & S's *The Sorcerer* (on a bill with *Trial by Jury*).

In eclectic revival production, the senior group is Gene Feist's and Michael Fried's Roundabout Theater Company, a midtown fixture now operating out of two theaters in a season-long series of dance and other entertainments in addition to its major effort of producing a whole range of playscripts, classic to only-yesterday nostalgic, many of them long forgotten by other New York producers. Roundabout's five-play season took in Pirandello's *Naked*, Shaw's *You Never Can Tell*, Shakespeare's *Othello* directed by Gene Feist on a bare stage, the Russian play *The Promise* of a few Broadway seasons back, directed by Michael Fried, Kelly's *The Show-Off* and, for a caboose production, Harold Rome's *Pins and Needles*, the famous garment-center revue originally produced by the ILGWU and never before revived on the New York professional stage, with Philip Campanella, an accomplished actor who has doubled for many seasons as the Roundabout's music man, serving the show as musical director and performer at one of the twin pianos which constituted its pit orchestra.

Another revival-producing organization with an eclectic policy is Classic Stage Company (CSC), only three seasons old in off-Broadway status but with a wide grasp in its repertory schedule. This year the CSC put on a new play by one of the members of its acting company (Karen Sunde, as mentioned previously in the off-Broadway section of this report) and a new English version of Ibsen's *Rosmersholm* written and directed by the group's artistic director, Christopher Martin. There was a Shakespeare in its season — *A Midsummer Night's Dream* — and there was also a John Arden (*Serjeant Musgrave's Dance*), a Jean Genet (*The Maids* with an all-male cast) and the Jean Giraudoux-Maurice Valency *The Madwoman of Chaillot.*

Over in Brooklyn, Frank Dunlop's BAM Theater Company went into its second season with a Shaw (*The Devil's Disciple*) a Molnar (*The Play's the Thing*) a Shakespeare (*Julius Caesar* with George Rose in the title role, Rene Auberjonois as Brutus and Austin Pendleton as Marc Anthony) and Samuel Beckett's own English version of *Waiting for Godot* (which he had staged at Berlin's Schiller Theater) with Sam Waterston and Austin Pendleton as Didi and Gogo.

John Houseman's Acting Company was a guest of American Place for a repertory of a Brecht (*Mother Courage and Her Children*), a Shakespeare (*King Lear*) and a second look at David Mamet's *Duck Variations* which was produced off Broadway last season. Charles Ludlam's Ridiculous Theatrical Company revived *Stage Blood* twice, in July and later in May in a repertory of Ludlam plays including his version of *Camille*. And a new group, the New York Actors' Theater, arose at Columbia's Havemeyer Hall, with Laurence Luckinbill as one of the artistic directors, making a wholly creditable first effort with Brecht's *Life of Galileo.*

The only revival in independent off-Broadway production was a revision by James Kirkwood of his *P.S. Your Cat Is Dead*. This play about a trapped burglar attempting the homosexual seduction of his intended victim was first produced at the Arena Stage in Buffalo, then came to Broadway in the 1975 season for only 16 performances. As of the end of the 1978 season off Broadway it had already played more than five times that long and was still running strong.

Elmer Rice and Michael McClure (*Counselor-at-Law* and *The Beard* at the Quaigh), Frank Wedekind (*Lulu* at Circle Repertory) and Tim Rice and Andrew Lloyd Webber (*Joseph and the Amazing Technicolor Dreamcoat* at BAM) were also among those present in 1977-78 New York revival production, Its breadth in time from Aeschylus to David Mamet and in character from Dracula to Dolly was enormous; and its value to a versatile, well-balanced season was the same.

Offstage

Driven by its own internal dynamism or merely following the crowd up the inflation spiral, the New York theater was subject to ever-rising costs in 1977-78 (a $1 million price tag for a full-fledged Broadway musical would be a commonplace, if full-fledged Broadway musicals were still commonplace; and some producers, notably The Shubert Organization have now decided that it's too expensive to take a big show out of town for a trial run). The box office was presenting the theatergoing public with prices to match. The double-sawbuck barrier had scarcely been leaned on by last year's revival of *Fiddler on the Roof,* when it collapsed under *The Act's* announcement of a $22.50 top on weekend evenings ($20 weeknights) to hear Liza Minnelli in a show which at that time was admittedly in pre-Broadway trouble and had only just brought in Gower Champion to help spruce it up.

That announcement proved to be an underestimate. By the time anyone could get to the box office, *The Act* was asking and getting a $25 top for Saturday night. Upward went prices at other Broadway shows until, at season's end, the price of a top ticket was $22.50 at *Dancin'* and *On the Twentieth Century,* $20 at *Ain't Misbehavin'* and $19.50 at *Annie* and *Timbuktu* — and a $17.50 top was routine at the more attractive straight plays. Successful off-Broadway productions operating outside subsidy were asking and getting $9.95 for some tickets, while *The Best Little Whorehouse in Texas* was wall-to-wall with customers at an $11.50 top ($19.50 after it moved uptown to Broadway). If there are any forces at work to prevent Broadway from becoming a $25-$30 theater and off Broadway a $10-$15 theater, they aren't visible at this time.

It was a restive year for critics. Richard Eder replaced Clive Barnes in his play-reviewing function at the New York *Times,* and then Barnes departed the *Times* to become play and dance reviewer for the New York *Post,* where Martin Gottfried's services were less and less in demand until he began doing pieces for *Cue,* where Marilyn Stasio had resigned her play-reviewing post to join the *Trib,* which suspended publication before she could get started.

No one threw anything at John Simon, critic of *New York* magazine, as far as we know, but a number of producers voted to take his name off their first night list after he'd been heard to use a four-letter word to describe *The Shadow Box* on a TV talk show (and many were incensed by his derogatory description of Liza Minnelli's physical appearance in *The Act*). The New York Drama Critics Circle voted 13-4 at its annual meeting in October to protest this action to the League of New York Theaters and Producers as a form of censorship. Members of the League argued that it was not censorship because Simon was free to buy tickets to their shows if he chose; rather, they said, it was a fair protest against Simon's caustic style of reviewing. Not all members of the League supported this Simon-censuring action taken by a majority of those members who responded to a recommendation of the League's Media Committee. It turned out to be pretty much a token protest, with many producers sending first-night tickets to the magazine rather than its critic, and with Simon re-acquiring his freebies to most shows by season's end.

In an atmosphere of steeply rising costs and prices, Actors' Equity and the producers negotiated a new three-year contract in efficient fashion, the new actors' minimum being $355 weekly the first and second years and $400 for the third (the old minimum was $285), with the road minimums going to $547.50, $582.50 and $645 expenses included (the old road minimum was $395) and with stage managers' fees rising proportionately from a former $500 to $900 at musicals and from $420 to $805 at plays. Among other provisions: actors will not be required to wear other actors' shoes; and nude performances are forbidden except with the actors' written consent and control over the release and use of photos.

The Dramatists Guild, an organization of playwrights, composers, lyricists and librettists, was in the process of exploring with the League the possibilities for changes in the Minimum Basic Agreement between them, a script-leasing arrangement of royalty percentages and provisions that has defined the author-producer relationship since the 1920s.

The Dramatists Guild also took a position in the case of Phillip Hayes Dean's *Paul Robeson,* which prior to its Broadway opening, came under attack by an *ad hoc* committee in newspaper ads and elsewhere for supposedly misinterpreting some of the facts and goals of its title character's life, in a group pre-judgment by signatories some of whom hadn't seen or read the play. In an open letter over the signatures of 33 leading dramatists including all the Guild officers (Stephen Sondheim president, Richard Lewine vice president, Dore Schary treasurer, Sheldon Harnick secretary) and Edward Albee, Lillian Hellman, Arthur Miller and Richard Rodgers among others, the Guild agreed that "a playwright must be prepared to accept criticism, no matter how bitter or even unfair," but "group censorship of a play violates the principles of the First Amendment," in this case by an action which "assailed the accuracy and integrity of the play in an attempt to pre-judge it for theatergoers . . . . . If the practise of group censorship takes root in the American theater, freedom of expression will be gravely imperiled."

For the third time in Broadway history, all the marquees went dark at the same time on purpose, in the absence of any blackout, on Aug. 5. The occasion was an observance of the death of Alfred Lunt at 84 two days previously — or rather, not so much to mark his death as to express the whole theater's deep admiration of his life, so much of which was lived with such great distinction on Broadway. The two previous marquee blackouts took place in honor of Gertrude Lawrence and Oscar Hammerstein II. An entertainment era which had long since passed away was buried in 1978 with Alfred Lunt — and, in other media, with Bing Crosby and Charles Chaplin.

All the mighty institutions of government were at the theater's service — to the usual feeble extent. The National Endowment for the Arts found $6,004,160 to aid the theater in fiscal 1977-78, a brave $102,000 more than the previous year and many millions less than any other civilized country in the Western World. The New York State Council on the Arts, considerably more aware (under the chairmanship of Kitty Carlisle Hart) of the importance and value of the theater as a regional and national arts treasure, spread $3 million over 150 theater organizations in 34 counties.

We began this offstage report with Liza Minnelli's $25 top and we'll end it by noting the Nov. 9 *Variety* headline: "Liza's Lip-Synch in *The Act* Shocks Purists." Miss Minnelli's performance was a strenuous one — dancing, singing and dancing *while* singing — so that at certain places in the show it would be physically impossible to summon enough breath to project the notes distinctly, let alone the lyrics. The obvious measure was taken, therefore, for brief intervals, of synchronizing the star's recorded voice over the theater's loud speakers with the movement of her lips and gestures — "lip-synching" it's called, the staple of every movie musical and a number of rock shows.

The *Variety* story called those who object to using such a device in live theater "purists" and concluded: "Maybe they should be sentenced to attend a special performance of *The Act* without lip-synching. That would sink 'em."

We'd go much farther than that. We'd suggest that such purists keep their $25 in their pockets. We'd suggest that they be entirely deprived of *The Act* and all shows like it, which deserve the warm welcome of Las Vegas and/or Radio City Music Hall, where they belong, and equally deserve a cold shoulder from our demanding, puristic legitimate stage, where they do not. We aren't ignorant of the fact that all Broadway musicals are now more or less heavily electronic both onstage and in the pit (we had to hold our hands over our ears, for example, at moments in *The Best Little Whorehouse in Texas* and *Ain't Misbehavin'*) and maybe that's one reason why there are so few of them around these days. Electronic gimmickry is all too obtrusive in the present show biz environment —

and where did all those fabulous dinosaurs go?

Live contact and close relationship between performer and audience are the vital signs of living theater, and *anything* interposed between them is unhealthy in the long run. The $25 Broadway ticket top is only a damned nuisance compared to the life-threatening symptom of electronic faking of live performance (no reflection on Miss Minnelli, who when she catches her breath can belt a song out into the middle of 45th Street). Let the star sing *or* dance with her own breath; we'll be satisfied, maybe even $25 worth. Let the theater's illusions be electric in the cosmic sense, not electronic. Let it use all available devices to enhance, not replace, the uniquely warm-blooded illusions of what the purists hope is to remain the eternally warm-blooded living stage.

Len Cariou and Angela Lansbury in the musical *Sweeney Todd, the Demon Barber of Fleet Street,* book by Hugh Wheeler, music and lyrics by Stephen Sondheim.

1978-79

THE 1978-79 SEASON in New York was a broad success. It had just about everything from a masterpiece of musical theater, *Sweeney Todd, the Demon Barber of Fleet Street,* to the new-rich affluence of a record Broadway gross. It had a sufficient number of hits, thanks partly to the British playwrights. It had a spate of musicals, 13, reversing last year's drought of only 5. It had heart (*On Golden Pond*), insight (*Wings*) and/or both in the same package (*First Monday in October*). What it *didn't* have was the audience-busting play or musical, the equivalent of the home run in baseball, the attraction that lines them up on the street outside the box office and lifts them out of their seats cheering with that special, universal four-bagger appeal. 1978-79's hottest tickets were *Annie* (1977) and *A Chorus Line* (1975), while *Grease* (1972) kept tilting its cap and trotting around the bases again and again, undaunted by the competition of a movie version, the second-longest running musical in Broadway history.

If the season waited in vain for a box office homer, it didn't lack for a shattering climax in the unique *Sweeney Todd,* the Stephen Sondheim-Harold Prince-Hugh Wheeler musical about a mad barber and his mad mistress cutting throats and baking the corpses into meat pies in 19th century London. The provenance of this material from a popular 1847 melodrama through numerous stage versions to the present monumental musical version is outlined elsewhere in this volume, but there's no way of explaining exactly how the collaborators, Sondheim in particular, managed to turn this base metal — at best Grand Guignol, at worst disgusting — into purest gold. Prince's staging is absolutely explicit, no pussyfooting here as throats are cut in full frontal view, stage center, and the blood flows red. The Sondheim score is absolutely commanding, no dawdling tunes, and his lyrics make every kind of assault upon the sensibilities — whiplash, witticism, slashing, appealing, bludgeoning — with hardly a wasted syllable. The performances are hammered out to perfection by Len Cariou as Sweeney brutalized into brutishness and Angela Lansbury trailing clouds of lethal innocence, Cockney-style, as Mrs. Lovett the piemaker extraordinary. Even the Eugene Lee set is forbidding, with its structure of steel girders so huge that it intrudes beyond the proscenium and beggars all human beings under its influence, in the auditorium as well as on the stage.

These are some of the parts of this best of 1978-79 Best Plays, and the whole is a good deal greater. *Sweeney Todd* is subtitled "A musical thriller," which it is — but pity redeems its terror. Sondheim and his colleagues have superimposed a theme which, incredibly, not only survives but dominates the shock of the subject matter (in a summer Q & A session with dramatists, Sondheim said that the central metaphor of *Sweeney Todd* is "obsession," Prince that it is "impotence," and both are right). As in Camus's *Caligula,* so in *Sweeney Todd:* if inhumanity (in this case of industrial-revolution London) is permitted as public policy, then anything is permitted. If the powerful may feed off the weak at their figurative pleasure, then the literal, ghastly reverse becomes almost . . . almost thinkable. As Sweeney and Mrs. Lovett dare to act out this ghastly image, they are perceived not merely as grotesques but also as victims. Their wickedness is bearable because in this environment it is ironic, an impossible nightmare made

The 1978-79 Season on Broadway

PLAYS (15)

The Crucifer of Blood
FIRST MONDAY IN OCTOBER
Gorey Stories
Taxi Tales
WINGS (transfer)
Trick
Are You Now or Have you Ever Been (transfer)
ON GOLDEN POND (transfer)
Zoot Suit
A Meeting by the River
Manny
Break a Leg
Bosoms and Neglect
Knockout
Murder at the Howard Johnson's

MUSICALS (13)

The Best Little Whorehouse in Texas (transfer)
King of Hearts
Platinum
Ballroom
A Broadway Musical
The Grand Tour
Sarava
They're Playing Our Song
SWEENEY TODD, THE DEMON BARBER OF FLEET STREET
Carmelina
My Old Friends (transfer)
The Utter Glory of Morrissey Hall
I Remember Mama

REVUES (2)

The American Dance Machine
Eubie!

FOREIGN PLAYS IN ENGLISH (7)

Players
Spokesong
The Kingfisher
BEDROOM FARCE
Faith Healer
WHOSE LIFE IS IT ANYWAY?
THE ELEPHANT MAN (transfer)

FOREIGN-LANGUAGE PLAYS (1)

Coquelico

REVIVALS (11)

Circle in the Square 1978:
Once in a Lifetime
D'Oyly Carte:
Iolanthe
The Mikado
H.M.S. Pinafore
The Pirates of Penzance
Stop the World — I Want to Get Off
Circle in the Square 1979:
The Inspector General
Man and Superman
Whoopee
G.R. Point
The Goodbye People

SPECIALTIES (5)

St. Mark's Gospel
The Playboy of the Weekend World
Monteith and Rand
Peter Allen Up in One
A New York Summer

HOLDOVER WHICH BECAME A HIT IN 1978-79 (1)

Tribute

Plays listed in CAPITAL LETTERS have been designated Best Plays of 1978-79.
Plays listed in *italics* were still running June 1, 1979.
Plays listed in **bold face type** were classified as hits in *Variety's* annual estimate published June 9, 1979.

possible on the living stage by Stephen Sondheim and his colleagues in a remarkable work for which, if for nothing else, 1978-79 deserves to be a well-remembered season.

With the musical ticket widely priced at $20 and pushing toward $25; with straight plays reaching toward and finally touching a $20 top (with *First Monday*), and with attendance on the rise, a record Broadway gross for fiscal 1978-79 was anticipated as far back as early autumn when there was a mini-booking jam of incoming shows, and when it became apparent that not even a prolonged strike of the daily newspapers was going to slow down the action in the West Forties this year. That strike began Aug. 9 and lasted into November before all the papers came back on line, but the theater was virtually unscathed. "No immediate box office impact . . . . . negligible," said *Variety*. Richard Barr, president of the League of New York Theaters and Producers (and co-producer of *Sweeney Todd*) declared, "Even the new shows haven't been seriously affected. We were prepared, and we went all out in keeping the public informed through other available media. The result is, we haven't been disturbed seriously."

When the dust finally settled and all the numbers were counted at the end of the season May 31, Broadway had racked up an all-time record gross of $128,-105,764 according to *Variety* estimate, the second $100 million gross in its history, better than 20 per cent up from last year's $103 million. Attendance was up, too, from last year's 8.6 million to 9.1 million, and so were playing weeks (if ten shows play ten weeks that's 100 playing weeks), a more sensitive barometer of success than box office receipts in these inflationary times: 1,472 Broadway playing weeks as compared with 1,360 last season. Total production was up from 40 shows last year to 48 (not counting specialties and foreign-language works), with a healthy rise among new plays, musicals and revues from 26 to 37. And the road was "a bonanza" in *Variety's* estimation, with Broadway shows taking in more than they did at home base, $143 million in 1,192 playing weeks, bringing the grand total of Broadway's 1978-79 income to more than $271 million. (Parenthetically, the League of New York Theaters issued a summary which had Broadway grossing $136 million with a 9.8 million attendance and 1,571 playing weeks in 1978-79, slightly different numbers but the same story.)

This affluence was a front behind which very few offerings were individually, dynamically successful. As of season's end, only four of the 1978-79 productions were clearly definable as economic successes by *Variety* (see the one-page summary of the season at the beginning of this report), with perhaps half a dozen more still having a realistic chance to end up in the black. The rest were "flops" in the economic sense, unlikely ever to pay off their cost — and these included no less than eight full-blown musicals such as *Ballroom* which danced away $2,400,000 and *Carmelina* which cost $1,062,500, as well as *Alice* and *Home Again* which folded out of town for $1,050,000 and $1,250,000 respectively. A distinguished 1977-78 Broadway musical, *On the Twentieth Century*, was still in the red for 85 per cent of its $1,100,000 cost when it closed after a year's run, *Variety* reported. At the straight-play level, the tab for *Broadway, Broadway*, which closed in tryout, was $300,000; for a painstaking off-Broadway revival of *The Diary of Anne Frank*, $46,000; for *A Meeting by the River* which survived for only one performance at the Palace, $250,000.

These days a record gross signifies an accumulation of hits from past seasons still running. The big-winning holdovers continued to win big, with *A Chorus Line* establishing itself as a legitimate stage box office champion owning a $22,000,000 *profit* so far (not including the $5,500,000-plus-percentage movie sale) from an audience estimated at 2 million in New York and 4 million on the road. The 1977 Broadway revival of *The King and I* ran through December 1978, taking in a $1,200,000 profit on its $600,000 investment. The popular *Annie* had returned $2,500,000 on $800,000. *Same Time, Next Year* was estimated a winner by nearly $4 million so far. *Deathtrap* had made $600,000 on its $200,-000 investment, and *"Da"* $240,000 on $200,000, both still counting. On tour, *A Matter of Gravity* pulled in $1,049,000 profit on its $160,000 investment. And, providing extra bounce for the eternal-springing hope of the show biz investor was *Variety's* notation that the profits of *Fiddler on the Roof* have now reached 1,378 per cent and *Hello, Dolly!* 1,307 per cent of their original costs.

Performers? Well, last season Hume Cronyn, Henderson Forsythe, Barnard Hughes, Jack Lemmon and Jason Robards made it an actors' year. This season turnabout was superb playing by Constance Cummings in the bewildering haze of *Wings;* Frances Sternhagen coping cheerfully in *On Golden Pond;* Angela Lansbury saucily doing the unspeakable in *Sweeney Todd.* Then there were Carole Shelley as the Elephant Man's friend; Meryl Streep and the *Taken in Marriage* ensemble; Jane Alexander as a U.S. Supreme Court Justess; Dorothy Loudon middle-aged and lonely in *Ballroom.* Among other standout 1978-79 performances by members of both sexes were the *Bedroom Farce* ensemble . . . Philip Anglim anguished in body and Kevin Conway anguished in mind as patient and doctor in *The Elephant Man* . . . Tom Conti (*Whose Life Is It Anyway?*) and Graham Brown (*Nevis Mountain Dew*) in variations on the theme "To be or not to be?" in circumstances of hopeless paralysis . . . Rex Harrison, George Rose and a glowing Claudette Colbert in the romantic minuet of *The Kingfisher* . . . Edward James Olmos strutting in *Zoot Suit* . . . Susan Kingsley, a spare, determined Arlene in *Getting Out* . . . Robert Klein, Len Cariou, Joel Grey and Vincent Gardenia in their musicals and Tom Aldredge, James Mason and Michael Moriarty in their plays .

Broadway

That native-born supernova the Broadway musical burst forth in abundance in 1978-79. There were 13 — count 'em — 13 where last season there were only five. Unfortunately, there was no safety in this unlucky number. As we have noted, the Messrs. Sondheim, Prince and Wheeler broke the mold in memorable style with *Sweeney Todd,* but other renowned authors of musical hits such as Richard Rodgers, Alan Jay Lerner, Jerry Herman, Joseph Stein, Lee Adams and Clark Gesner failed to make it work this time around.

The popular musical success of the season was Neil Simon's first libretto since *Promises, Promises* combined with Marvin Hamlisch's and Carole Bayer Sager's score and attractive performances by Robert Klein and Lucie Arnaz (Desi and Lucy's daughter) in the two-character *They're Playing Our Song.* It was a prize package of Simon one-liners plus at least one irresistible tune (the title number), directed by Robert Moore into a light-hearted boy-composer-meets-girl-lyricist romance. Theirs is a happy amorous and professional pairing in all the old familiar places of Manhattan and Long Island expressed in Douglas W. Schmidt's imaginative designs projected as black and white sketches. Our only reservation about this show is that most of the game was played out early, in the first act.

A pair of transfers from off Broadway fared better than most of the natives: *The Best Little Whorehouse in Texas,* a Best Play of last season and a deserving favorite among this season's Broadway showgoers; and the newer *My Old Friends* presenting a group of retirees pledged to the continued enjoyment of life in each other's pleasant company, with Maxine Sullivan as a show-stopping senior citizen who alternates belting out songs with hammering away at elected officials for their incompetence. Following an experimental staging at La Mama and a well-received professional one at the Orpheum, *My Old Friends* lit out for Broadway and received a temporary welcome at a theater known as 22 Steps, former the Latin Quarter night club, which also housed the National Theater of Prague's multimedia extravaganza *Coquelico* this season.

A musical which never settled on an opening night but nevertheless drew a greater portion of the audience than most other shows was *Sarava,* an N. Richard Nash-Mitch Leigh collaboration based on a South American novel about a widow, Dona Flor (played by Tovah Feldshuh), who finds herself with two husbands when her first rejoins her as a ghost after she marries again. *Sarava* began giving New York performances at full prices Jan. 11 (the opening date recorded in this volume) but kept postponing a formal debut until the press decided to declare it open and review it. The New York *Times* did so in its Feb. 12 issue, *Variety* on Feb. 14.

Among this season's shorter-lived musicals, the Alan Jay Lerner show *Carmelina* deserved a better fate. It was a cheerful, sprightly telling of a previously-told tale (in an Italian film) about a resourceful Italian woman who convinces each of three American soldiers that he was the father of her daughter. She lives comfortably off the triple-subsistence for nearly 20 years. The scam is perfect until the three Americans — genially personalized by Gordon Ramsey, Howard Ross and John Michael King — visit the village together on a sentimental journey down World War II memory lane, accompanied by their three American wives. It was a snugly, predictably, even tritely entertaining piece, for which there is a place on the Broadway agenda. We regret that *Carmelina* was unable to find it in time to survive the blast it received from most of the critics.

Joseph Stein collaborated with Lerner on the book of *Carmelina* and was the sole author of the book of *King of Hearts,* a World War I tale based on a French film about an American soldier who occupies a small French town after enemy withdrawal, to find it inhabited only by eccentrically carefree escapees from a local asylum. This one struggled on for a few weeks, but 1979 was a doubly disappointing season for the distinguished co-author of *Fiddler on the Roof.* It was the same, singly, for the co-author of *Hello, Dolly!,* Jerry Herman, whose *The Grand Tour,* starring Joel Grey as Jacobowsky in a musicalization of *Jacobowsky and the Colonel,* was a major effort with some fine instances of composition and performance which somehow went awry.

Likewise, Michael Bennett's *Ballroom* had many attractive qualities in a musical study of loneliness relieved in the action and romance of middle-aged dance hall regulars. Dorothy Loudon and Vincent Gardenia acted out a touching relationship while those around them accented it with dancing under the kind of Michael Bennett direction that made a piece of show business history out of *A Chorus Line.* The audience wasn't intrigued this time around, however; nor did it respond in any great numbers to the commandingly attractive presence of Alexis Smith as a movie star looking for new worlds to conquer in *Platinum.*

The last big musical theater event of the year was the arrival on the season's last day of the Richard Rodgers-Martin Charnin show based on the John van

Druten hit *I Remember Mama,* with Liv Ullmann stretching her awesome talent to include musical comedy stardom, singing and all. Her voice was breathy and her dancing tentative, in a crossover experiment that fell short of success. The Rodgers score was uplifting in the wonderful way all Rodgers scores are, but by the time of its arrival on Broadway, this show had been so worked-over by so many people in so many departments that it looked like a couple of bright eyes staring out from behind a mass of bandages.

Two other musicals made quick exits from the Broadway scene after only one performance each. *A Broadway Musical,* with a show business book about the production of a black author's script and a Charles Strouse-Lee Adams score, came to the Lunt-Fontanne Theater after careful preparation including 26 performances in an off-Broadway production, but it was a Broadway musical for only one. Also, Clark Gesner's *The Utter Glory of Morrissey Hall,* about a girl's school, failed to emulate the success of its author's *You're a Good Man Charlie Brown* and was withdrawn after its premiere.

On the straight-play side, six Broadway productions made the Best Plays list this season, not one of them a native-born Broadway play (the musical *Sweeney Todd* was the only such on the list). Of these plays, three came from the West End, two from regional theater and one originated off Broadway. The most impressive of the American scripts, all things considered, was Arthur Kopit's *Wings,* a closeup of the reeling, groping mind of a stroke victim played by Constance Cummings in a memorable, Tony Award-winning performance. From the onset of the disease to its inevitable victory, fragmented images of past and present are collected in the mind of the sufferer, sorted, jumbled and sorted again into a highly subjective and pitiful experience. The play was first developed at Yale Repertory Theater, then brought to Joseph Papp's Public Theater for a limited off-Broadway engagement, and finally to Broadway as a major event of the 1978-79 New York season.

The newest Jerome Lawrence-Robert E. Lee collaboration *First Monday in October* was also meticulously groomed before making its Broadway bow, at the Cleveland Play House and at the Eisenhower Theater in Washington. Like other Lawrence-Lee works, this one had strong overtones of social import in a nevertheless intensely personal drama set a few steps down the line into the future when the first woman will be appointed to the U.S. Supreme Court. In *First Monday,* the playwrights imagine that she will be a gracefully self-confident conservative (Jane Alexander) whose views madden but whose person attracts the Court's most outspoken and most liberal member (Henry Fonda). This is a well-made play, in contrast to the sloppy craftsmanship of too many contemporary efforts, and it didn't disdain to please its audiences with a rationally developed dramatic line, staged with force and clarity by Edwin Sherin, one of the happier events of the season.

A warm welcome is also claimed for Ernest Thompson's Best Play *On Golden Pond,* a playwriting debut transferred from an off-Broadway production directed by Craig Anderson at the Hudson Guild Theater to the uptown limelight, virtually intact (the same origin and course taken by last season's Best Play *"Da"*). This is a charming, winning account of an octogenarian and his wife sampling the pleasures of their 48th summer in a cottage on a Maine lake; she (Frances Sternhagen) embracing the experience with sheer exuberance, he (Tom Aldredge) always prepared for the worst and skeptical when it turns out for the best. Many of this season's Best Plays were edged with geriatric and/or clinical complications, but this one glowed in the darkness of the contemporary theater, a brave beacon of insistence that life is for living and worth the candle.

Also prominent among the American plays on Broadway this season was Paul Giovanni's *The Crucifer of Blood,* with Sherlock Holmes (Paxton Whitehead) and Dr. Watson (Timothy Landfield) as young men delving into one of their first adventures, a crime deep-rooted in the blood-red rubies and violence of Imperial India. This was a flamboyantly — and successfully — romanticized thriller whose remarkable stagecraft included a Gothically menacing thunderstorm and a scene on the foggy Thames with boats moving out of the mists, designed by the play's co-producer, John Wulp.

A vaunted West Coast endeavor entitled *Zoot Suit* put up a bold front with its narrator, Edward James Olmos, slinking through the play in drape-shape get-up, cynically confronting anti-Chicano prejudice. The play was brought to New York in an effort to attract the attention of the city's Hispanic-oriented population. But its Luis Valdez script, based on California's Zoot Suit Riots of 1943 and consequent injustices and oppressions, was dramatically too weak to stir interest among hip New Yorkers, whatever their cultural bias. Its heart was in the right place, in sympathy with Chicano victims of establishment attitudes, but except for the graphic symbolism of the Olmos character its concentration was uncertain.

Eric Bentley's study of prejudice and injustice, *Are You Now or Have You Ever Been,* fared better, with its off-Broadway production moving to Broadway for the latter parts of its run. This is the script taken from the transcript of the testimony at hearings of the House Un-American Activities Committee, with actors playing such beleaguered witnesses as Edward Dmytryk, Ring Lardner Jr., Larry Parks, Abe Burrows, Arthur Miller, Elia Kazan, Lionel Stander, Paul Robeson and Lillian Hellman — the latter played by a succession of stars in cameo appearances reading the famous letter she wrote to the Committee declining to appear in person.

Louis La Russo II brought in a forceful play, *Knockout,* with Danny Aiello as a boxer with a soft heart and a mean left hook, and with a prizefight as its climax. Edward Gorey's fanciful prose was adapted to the stage in the short-lived *Gorey Stories,* while Leonard Melfi brought forth five vignettes of New York living in *Taxi Tales.* Larry Cohen's thriller *Trick* about the murder of a BBC announcer's wife; Raymond Serra's dramatized biography of Edward G. Robinson, *Manny;* Ira Levin's *Break a Leg,* a comedy of Middle European theater folk; John Guare's popular (in Chicago) but rejected (in New York) *Bosoms and Neglect,* a comedy about a maladjusted couple talking out their problems; and, finally, the Ron Clark-Sam Bobrick comedy *Murder at the Howard Johnson's,* a combination of playful behavior and lethal intent the shortness of whose 4-performance run was deplored by several observers who enjoyed it, completed this Broadway season's list of new American plays.

This year Broadway could scarcely have gotten along without its three commanding British Best Plays, *The Elephant Man, Whose Life Is It Anyway?* and *Bedroom Farce.* The former, describing the life and Victorian times and death of a hideously deformed freak-show exhibit who finds refuge at London Hospital under the wing of a sympathetic doctor, received the New York Drama Critics Circle Award for the year's best-of-bests as well as the Tony and is our own choice as the best foreign play of the year. In this connection it's worth noting that in the 1970s the New York critics have been overwhelmingly Anglophile, chosing a British play as their best-of-bests in every year from 1970 on (*Borstal Boy, Home, The Changing Room, The Contractor, Equus,*

Travesties, Otherwise Engaged, "Da" and now *The Elephant Man*), except only for *That Championship Season* intervening as best-of-Critics-bests in 1971-72. Reflecting on our own record, we find that the *Best Plays* selection of best-of-bests in the 1970s preferred American scripts in a couple of instances: *Indians* to *Borstal Boy, The Last Meeting of the Knights of the White Magnolia* to *Otherwise Engaged*. But in others, we picked *another* British play in place of the one chosen by the Critics: *Sleuth* instead of *Home, Noel Coward in Two Keys* instead of *The Contractor, The Norman Conquests* instead of *Travesties*.

The point of this reflection is not only that difference of opinion is as much a part of drama criticism as of horse racing, but also that the British dramatist has been dominating our theater for a decade, reaching not only those whose tastes run along the conventional lines of a *"Da"* or a *Sleuth* but also those of the avant garde with its Pinters, its Stoppards, its Storeys. In the meantime, we are expending our own creative energy in a spate of "interesting" experimentation which probably reached some extreme or other with Robert Wilson's *The Life and Times of Joseph Stalin,* which had a 12-hour running time. The discipline and craftsmanship of an Edward Albee, an Arthur Kopit or a David Mamet (in *American Buffalo*), the polished style of a Neil Simon or a Preston Jones don't seem to exert the influence they should, inducing and inspiring some kind of emulation in the ranks of American dramatists, swelling in numbers as they are weakening in impact. We do not insist on a monotonous artistic diet of "the well-made play," but for imagination's sake let us have the *made* play in whatever style, crafted with care and with the express purpose of communication in something other than code.

There is a minor extenuating circumstance this year in that the New York critics categorized *The Elephant Man* as an American play because its author, Bernard Pomerance, was born in New York City. We consider it a British conception notwithstanding: the author now resides in England, the play was written about British events for British audiences and was twice produced in England before appearing this season in the Richmond Crinkley-produced (for ANTA), Jack Hofsiss-directed on and off-Broadway Best Play. This "elephant man" of hideously twisted and scarred body and poetically lucid mind, a duality portrayed clearly by Philip Anglim, is a symbol of somewhat the same Victorian predicament as Stephen Sondheim's Sweeney Todd: society's victimization of him calls into question that society's values. In the play, these doubts drive the well-meaning doctor (Kevin Conway), who befriends the elephant man, to the edge of hysteria. Even the pitying ministrations of royalty taking an interest in the unfortunate case seem a form of self-serving exploitation in an essentially unpitying social order. Only an actress, played by Carole Shelley, sympathizes profoundly with the elephant man's inability to shed his hideous illusion, to take off his makeup when the show is over. The skill of presentation and performing matched the emotional richness of content in *The Elephant Man,* a striking dramatic success.

Another very strong foreign Best Play was *Whose Life Is It Anyway?* by Brian Clark, a prolific TV author making his American stage debut with this powerfully ironic comedy about the victim of an auto crash who, incurably paralyzed from the neck down, longs to discontinue the treatments keeping him alive but inert in his hospital bed. He bears his helplessness with gallows humor, and with no slackening of his demand that the law free him from the well-meaning but unyielding clutches of medicine. The force of his personality and depth of his feelings were projected by Tom Conti with head and voice alone.

The director, Michael Lindsay-Hogg, carefully balanced the mobile performances of Philip Bosco and Jean Marsh as doctors in orbit around the talking, suffering head, as the play itself balances the bitter humor and the aching pity, the needs of an orderly, ethical society on the one hand and of a human being on the other. This Clark script was an intense theater experience and a major embellishment of the season.

Also on the Best Plays list from England was Alan Ayckbourn's *Bedroom Farce,* another of his space-time continuums like *How the Other Half Loves* and *The Norman Conquests,* an intricately devised but workable pattern of comedy. The action of *Bedroom Farce* takes place along a single time line but in three bedrooms simultaneously, as a left-footed, self-absorbed young married couple criss-cross the fairly circumspect lives of three other couples one zany Saturday evening, turning the others over and over and leaving them in turmoil while themselves ending exactly where they started. A marvellously adept British ensemble (replaced after the first few weeks by an American cast), fresh from the National Theater production, played their personality themes like members of a well-rehearsed orchestra under the direction of the author and Peter Hall. The title refers to the setting, not the action, which included none of that which usually takes place in bedrooms when farce is in the air. Rather, the bumblers (Stephen Moore and Delia Lindsay) manage to upset the decorum of old fogies (Michael Gough and Joan Dickson), the cool of a pair of smooth moderns (Michael Stroud and Polly Adams) and the pretensions of two young party-givers (Derek Newark and Susan Littler) without resorting to sexual leverage in a non-stop free-for-all of innocent fun.

Circle in the Square paused in its series of distinguished revival productions to present the American premiere of a charming Irish play, *Spokesong, or The Common Wheel* by Stewart Parker, with the bicycle a symbol of innocence and peace in murderously strife-torn modern Ireland. The Circle's arena stage became an elliptical track for cyclists, while in the center John Lithgow as a bike shop owner pleaded the cause of the "common wheel," the simple, innocent, unpolluting, personal bicycle, as a cure-all for the confusion, mechanization and consequent depersonalization of the 20th century. With Joseph Maher as a trick rider and Josef Sommer and Maria Tucci as memory figures of the shop owner's parents, and staged by Kenneth Frankel with earnest attention to its central metaphor, the piece filled the Circle's arena with the warmth of its presence.

Another noteworthy work by an Irish author (but making its world premiere in this American production) was Brian Friel's *Faith Healer,* with James Mason, his wife Clarissa Kaye and Donal Donnelly delivering the monologues of which the script is constructed, exploring in considerable depth the life and death of an itinerant mystic. It was a power play of writing and solo acting, but not of theater per se. William Douglas Home's *The Kingfisher,* too, was a showcase for performances in style, with Rex Harrison and Claudette Colbert as onetime lovers finding each other again in later life, plus George Rose in an inimitably abrasive portrayal of a manservant set in his boss's bachelor ways and resentful of the intrusion of romance. Finally on the foreign list there was an Australian visitor, *Players* by David Williamson, a soccer contest not on the field but in the board room where the goal is control of the franchise.

In the revue category, the popular *Eubie* adorned the whole season with the music of the great Eubie Blake, 23 numbers including ten from *Shuffle Along.* And *The American Dance Machine* offered what it described as "a living archive of Broadway theater dance" in a sampling of outstanding dance selections from 13 great musicals of the past.

The specialty attractions ranked among the most appealing events of the Broadway year. Alec McCowen visited New York twice, both on and off Broadway, with his absorbing delivery of the entire Gospel according to St. Mark, one of the season's most ambitiously conceived and adroitly fulfilled achievements and one of its finest performances. Emlyn Williams too was a welcome visitor in his *The Playboy of the Weekend World,* a solo-performed interpretation of more than a dozen Saki tales and vignettes. The improvisational comedy of John Monteith and Suzanne Rand in a program of sketches, some prepared and some devised on the spot, was very well received, as was Peter Allen's self-designed showcase for his revue act, *Peter Allen Up in One.* And the Showplace of the Nation, Radio City Music Hall, took on new life with a musical extravaganza, *A New York Summer,* with 18 numbers designed to display its fabled stagecraft with orchestra, scenery and cast — including 36 Rockettes — moving all over the 144-foot wide stage. The theater has been polished up with new carpeting, etc., and renamed the Radio City Music Hall Entertainment Center, situated as everyone knows on the Avenue of the Americas — the Music Hall on Sixth Avenue, a going concern once more.

Off Broadway

Off Broadway was once a haven for the Broadway script that couldn't find an audience uptown (Tennessee Williams's *Summer and Smoke,* Arthur Miller's *The Crucible*) but kept them coming for a long second look in a smaller playhouse. Today, the traffic goes in the opposite direction, with off Broadway feeding the larger playhouses with its finest. The outstanding example is *A Chorus Line,* still selling out in the fourth year of its run, its $22,000,000 gross underwriting much of the activity of its off-Broadway producer, Joseph Papp's New York Shakespeare Festival. More recently, *The Best Little Whorehouse in Texas* moved from off to on Broadway in mid-June and held the lists for the whole season as the most entertaining musical in town.

More than half of this season's Best Plays made their first New York appearance off Broadway: *Gimme Shelter, Nevis Mountain Dew, Getting Out, Wings, On Golden Pond* and *The Elephant Man.* Half of these, the latter three, then moved uptown for major accolades including across-the-board Tony nominations and the Critics Award. (And it's worth noting in passing that, like Broadway, off Broadway suckles from foster mothers. Two of the abovementioned bests originated in regional theater and two in England.)

Broadway in an annual summary, and *Variety* has all but given up. We'll continue making distinctions between off and off off here in the *Best Plays* volumes, however, as long as it seems useful to do so for the record, while reminding those who read these lines that formal distinctions are no longer as clear as they were and we tend to include rather than exclude — and that elsewhere in this volume we publish the most comprehensive list of 1978-79 OOB productions anywhere.

New scripts totaled 64 in 1978-79 (see the one-page summary accompanying this report). There were 38 new American plays, 15 foreign scripts in English and 11 musicals compared with 28-9-6 last season and 22-11-9 the season before, with off-Broadway productions crowding the Best Plays list and the Broadway limelight, as we have noted.

Like *Wings, On Golden Pond* and *The Elephant Man* described in the previous chapter of this report, *Getting Out* moved from its original off-Broadway base to a more conspicuous position during the season; not to Broadway like the others but from a limited-engagement Phoenix Theater production to an open-ended independent production at the Theater de Lys, where it was still running as the season ended. This script by Marsha Norman is a drama of a woman's struggle to shed the destructive impulses within her personality and to make a new life for herself as a parolee from prison. It was launched at the Actors' Theater of Louisville in November 1977 under Jon Jory's direction. After another staging at the Mark Taper Forum in February 1978, it was cited by the American Theater Critics Association as an outstanding new play of its season and was thus presented in synopsis at the beginning of "The Season Around the United States" section of *The Best Plays of 1977-78*. This season it arrived off Broadway on the two occasions, both under Jory's concise direction, with Susan Kingsley as a gaunt Arlene, the ex-convict freed in law but imprisoned still by her fearful memories, determined nevertheless to make a decent go of her life on the outside, in a script both strongly constructed and deeply felt.

Institutional production is the name of the off-Broadway game these days and identifies most of the action. With very few exceptions, new scripts like *Getting Out* are chosen by partly-subsidized (at least through subscriptions) organizations which present the work either in workshop or in some professional context, often in limited engagements as on the Phoenix Theater's schedule. The latter provided for 22-performance runs of *Getting Out* and another new American play (Corinne Jacker's *Later,* about a mother and daughters in a revelatory family reunion) and two foreign scripts: the Irish *Says I, Says He,* a parable of the current troubles, and in translation the German *Big and Little,* a study of a middle-aged woman staged (as was *Later*) by Daniel Freudenberger, the Phoenix partner of T. Edward Hambleton.

Negro Ensemble Company functioned under the artistic directorship of Douglas Turner Ward as a limited-engagement showcase for works by black dramatists, one of them — *Nevis Mountain Dew* by Steve Carter, the director of NEC's playwrights' workshop — a 1978-79 Best Play. Call it bitter comedy or ironic drama, *Nevis* was a candid but respectful family portrait of a Queens household of West Indian background, with the man of the family confined to an iron lung and his sisters, wife and friends attempting doggedly to create a party mood for his 50th birthday celebration. NEC regulars filled the roles under Horacena J. Taylor's direction, including Frances Foster, Arthur French, Samm-Art Williams and Graham Brown as the invalid wishing he could exit the life he sees only as passing reflections in his mirror, like an inhabitant of Plato's cave. *Nevis Mountain Dew* of course invites comparison with this season's British script on much the same subject, *Whose Life Is It Anyway?,* and the NEC variation on this theme holds its own. It doesn't confront its invalid's question "To be or not to be?" as polemically as its British counterpart, but it takes a similar stand and a closer look at the effects of such a prolongued calamity on those surrounding the victim. Other works by black dramatists on this season's NEC schedule were Judi Ann Mason's *The Daughters of the Mock,* a tale of witchcraft in a Cajun family; Alexis De Veaux's *A Season to Unravel,* a psychological-philosophical exercise taking place in the mind of the protagonist; and *Plays From Africa,* a pair of Nigerian folk tales.

The Chelsea Theater too had an outstanding season, its split personality notwithstanding. Its directing colleagues, Robert Kalfin and Michael David,

The 1978-79 Season off Broadway

PLAYS (38)

Bleacher Bums
WINGS
Just the Immediate Family
Quaigh:
  Momma's Little Angels
  Victim
Hudson Guild
ON GOLDEN POND
Winning Isn't Everything
A Lovely Sunday for Creve Coeur
Ride a Cock Horse
Devour the Snow
Game Plan
American Place:
  The Grinding Machine
  Touching Bottom
Seduced
Tunnel Fever, or The Sheep Is Out
Are You Now or Have You Ever Been
White Pelicans
Phoenix
GETTING OUT
Later

Circle Rep:
  Glorious Morning
  In the Recovery Lounge
  Winter Signs
  Talley's Folly
  Artichoke
Public Theater:
  Drinks Before Dinner
  Taken in Marriage
  The Woods
  Buried Child
Negro Ensemble:
  NEVIS MOUNTAIN DEW
  The Daughters of the Mock
A Season to Unravel
Old Phantoms
Porno Stars at Home
The Wait
Say Goodnight, Gracie
People in Show Business Make Long Goodbyes
Last Days at the Dixie Girl Cafe
Saints Alive!

MUSICALS (11)

Piano Bar
The Coolest Cat in Town
A Broadway Musical
Jimmy & Billy
My Old Friends
Public Theater:
  The Umbrellas of Cherbourg
  Sancocho
  Dispatches
  Wake Up, It's Time to Go to Bed
Telecast
Festival

REVUES (1)

Sterling Silver

FOREIGN-LANGUAGE PLAYS (4)

Grand Kabuki:
  Shunkan
  Renjishi
Comédie Française:
  Le Misanthrope
  La Puce à l'Oreille

FOREIGN PLAYS IN ENGLISH (15)

City Sugar
MTC:
  The Rear Column
  Grand Magic
  Don Juan Comes Back From the War
  Plays From Africa
Dodger Theater:
  GIMME SHELTER
  On Mount Chimborazo
THE ELEPHANT MAN
Phoenix Theater:
  Says I, Says He
  Big and Little
  Chinchilla
Funeral Games & The Ruffian on the Stair
Good Lads at Heart
Chelsea:
  Biography: A Game
  Strider: The Story of a Horse

REVIVALS (35)

Sganarelle
Delacorte:
  All's Well That Ends Well
  The Taming of the Shrew
  Spring Awakening
LOOM:
  (16 operettas in repertory)

CSC:
  Richard II
  Henry IV, Part 1
  Henry IV, Part 2
  Wild Oats
  The Marquis of Keith
Clurman:
  The Lesson
  The Price
Roundabout:
  Candida
  Awake and Sing
  The Diary of Anne Frank
  The Runner Stumbles
Public Theater:
  Julius Caesar
  Coriolanus
  The Coach With the Six Insides
  Tip-Toes

SPECIALTIES (7)

Crimes Against Nature
St. Mark's Gospel
An Evening With Quentin Crisp
Street Songs
The Elocution of Benjamin
Albert Einstein: The Practical Bohemian
A Woman Without a Man Is . . . .

Plays listed in CAPITAL LETTERS have been designated Best Plays of 1978-79.
Plays listed in *italics* were still running June 1, 1979.

parted ways and created two separately functioning groups where there was only one before. David remained in Brooklyn at the Academy of Music but adopted a new name — the Dodger Theater. He offered two new foreign scripts, the first of which, *Gimme Shelter* by Barrie Keeffe, was one of the season's Best Plays. This British work is a youthful outcry from the disaffected chaos of the welfare state in the form of three connected one-acters whose characters, lower middle class youths, are embarking upon lives which as far as they can see ahead are to be spent in hopeless, identityless doldrums. The authority figures don't care that these youths, and perhaps everybody in the welfare society except sports stars and a privileged few, are facing a bleak future, but *Gimme Shelter* is a powerful, at times violent, protest that this should be so. The second offering of the Dodger season was the much less imposing *On Mount Chimborazo,* a murky Tankred Dorst comedy.

Robert Kalfin retained the name Chelsea Theater Center but moved to the group's Manhattan base, the Westside. He brought in two formidable foreign scripts, the first being Max Frisch's 1967 play *Biography: A Game,* an imaginative premise of a professor's opportunity to relive parts of his life, directed by Arne Zaslove. The second was equally effective — *Strider: The Story of a Horse,* an adaptation of the Tolstoy allegory of similar title using a piebald horse as a stand-in for outcasts and underdogs, co-authored and directed by Kalfin himself. With a Best Play by one group and two exceptionally interesting productions by the other, the Dodger-Chelsea split seems to have taken place with both halves remaining fully alive.

The most active of all the producing groups, as usual, was Joseph Papp's New York Shakespeare Festival Theater, which sponsored a dozen productions in 1978-79 — not counting workshops, music festivals and Papp's performance as a singer in a night club for a couple of weeks (he got good notices). Among the three new American playscripts produced at the Public, Thomas Babe's *Taken in Marriage* was a polished exercise, a closeup of five women gathered for a wedding rehearsal which never takes place because the men never show up. The women are the bride (Kathleen Quinlan), her sister (Meryl Streep), her mother (Colleen Dewhurst and later Nancy Marchand), her aunt (Elizabeth Wilson) and an entertainer (Dixie Carter) hired to perform at the festivities. Instead of a rehearsal (or a drama) there is an exchange of recrimination and other hostilities among the women in an ensemble performance, under Robert Allan Ackerman's direction, to rival the best, with Miss Streep putting on an amazing show with her light acting palette. Papp's new-play schedule was additionally laden with E.L. Doctorow's *Drinks Before Dinner,* with Christopher Plummer leading a discussion of impending doom under the direction of Mike Nichols, and David Mamet's latest, *The Woods,* also a discussion, this one a dualogue between lovers whose weekend in a cabin wears thin and finally wears out.

Papp's off-Broadway production schedule was balanced with four musicals, first the Sheldon Harnick adaptation of the French movie *The Umbrellas of Cherbourg,* a warm-hearted and pleasant romance staged by Andrei Serban in a limpid setting of mobile plastic screens by Michael Yeargan. Then there was *Sancocho,* reflecting Papp's current interest in Hispanic artistry in a revue-style presentation of Puerto Ricans finding ways to settle into New York City life. And then there was *Dispatches,* Elizabeth Swados's effort to translate stark episodes and attitudes of the Vietnam War into rock musical idioms. Finally there was *Wake Up, It's Time to Go to Bed,* fanciful musical variations on the Orpheus theme, conceived by Carson Kievman. What remained of Papp's busy schedule was filled out with revivals (of which more in the next section of this report) and the co-sponsorship of the Yale Repertory Theater's *Wings*.

The off-Broadway season's highest standard was maintained at the Hudson Guild Theater, an erstwhile OOB group that raised its head this season and instantly seemed ten feet tall. Its opening 1978-79 offering was the Best Play *On Golden Pond* under the direction of Craig Anderson, the company's artistic director, who left the group and moved on elsewhere after the season ended. The second Hudson Guild production was a George Abbott-staged political election in Lee Kalcheim's *Winning Isn't Everything*. It was followed by Tennessee Williams's latest, typically a shimmering mood piece about four lonely spinsters, entitled *A Lovely Sunday for Creve Coeur*, and then by an introspective British script about a man and his women, *Ride a Cock Horse*. Finally the Hudson Guild rescaled the heights with *Devour the Snow*, a grainy account of the ghastly Donner party adventure in which snowbound survivors lapsed into cannibalism, a potent script by Abe Polsky constructed in the form of a trial for libel (a trial which actually took place but of which there is no record), directed by Terry Schreiber.

Marshall W. Mason's Circle Repertory Company had a busy year as usual but saved its best for last: Lanford Wilson's *Talley's Folly*, with Judd Hirsch filling the stage and the play with his portrayal of an irrepressible and irresistible first-generation American from middle Europe who would not be cowed by bigotry and tyranny and isn't going to take no for an answer from the woman he is now wooing. Those who saw Wilson's *The 5th of July* last season at the Circle will remember the Talley family and Aunt Sally, a widow who was carrying her husband Matt's ashes around in a candy box, looking for a place to bury them. Well, *Talley's Folly* describes the courtship of Sally and Matt 33 years before in an ornate and decrepit old boathouse (designed by John Lee Beatty) on the Talley place. It is a box full of roses, thorns and all; a one-act sketch imaginatively enlarged and sustained by its author and filled out by Mason's direction and the acting of Hirsch as Matt and Trish Hawkins as Sally, whose mating is as much duel as love affair. The Circle's 1978-79 schedule was a continuous quest for better and more provocative theater in three other new scripts: *Glorious Morning* by Patrick Meyers, about a family contending with incurable illness; *In the Recovery Lounge* by James Farrell, the lighter side of convalescence in a hospital; and John Bishop's *Winter Signs*, the troubled reunion of a middle-aged Broadway stage director with old friends in Minnesota.

In early summer, American Place made its facilities available to a visiting troupe, the Organic Theater of Chicago, with *Bleacher Bums*, an affectionate group portrait of diehard baseball fans, written by the performers after careful study of this subject in the bleachers at Cubs games. The next most entertaining event at American Place this season was a Bruce Jay Friedman evening in the American Humorists series in the Subplot Cafe; and the most penetrating was Rip Torn's personification of Howard Hughes in his last, straggle-haired, drug-ridden stages of decay, a prisoner of his own indulgences attempting one last fling in a reunion with two former loves, in Sam Shepard's *Seduced*. The group also produced a triptych of two-character one-acters, *Touching Bottom*, by Steve Tesich, an American Place regular, and a satiric fantasy about the escape of a professor and student from a strange university, *Tunnel Fever, or The Sheep Is Out*, by Jonathan Reynolds, whose *Yanks 3 Detroit 0 Top of the Seventh* was an American Place hit a few seasons back.

The continuous activity at Lynne Meadow's Manhattan Theater Club included a group of five productions with off-Broadway qualifications. One of these was a new Simon Gray script, *The Rear Column,* about a lost patrol of Victorian empire-builders in Africa, reverting in their isolation to forms of savagery, like grown-up *Lord of the Flies* children. The MTC schedule also took in Joanna M. Glass's *Artichoke,* a droll tale of a farmer's wife and an affectionate poetry professor, with a Canadian background; and Italian and Austrian works. MTC was not exactly a haven for American dramaturgy in its main efforts of 1978-79, nor was this one of their vintage years in other departments.

Among other off-Broadway groups, the Quaigh Theater, a Queens-based organization, twice visited Manhattan with creditable new scripts. One of these was the work of the author of *Knockout* on Broadway, Louis La Russo II, this time probing hatreds arising within a family after the matriarch's death in *Momma's Little Angels.* The other Quaigh offering was Mario Fratti's *Victim,* a mystery thriller with menace at each of the three corners of wife, husband and intruder. And the South Street Theater Company presented an off-Broadway program of two short Joe Orton works: one, *The Ruffian on the Stair,* about a couple who permit an insolent stranger to invade their lives, originally written for radio; the other, *Funeral Games,* a satire with murderous impulses, originally written for TV. The Brooklyn Academy of Music gave the National Youth Theater of Great Britain a platform for their performance of *Good Lads at Heart,* a tale of reform-school inmates written by Peter Terson especially for this talented young troupe.

If most of the action off Broadway in 1978-79 took place under organizational umbrellas, a goodly share of the applause was stolen by independent productions. Sam Shepard's *Buried Child* carried off the Pulitzer Prize. The ANTA-sponsored but finally independent *The Elephant Man* took the Critics and Tony Awards. Eric Bentley's *Are You Now or Have You Ever Been,* previously seen in New York in 1973 in a meticulous staging OOB at Theater of the Riverside Church, played a long engagement off Broadway and then moved up to Broadway, as noted in a previous section of this report.

Other independent highlights were Jay Broad's *White Pelicans,* with José Ferrer and Morgan Freeman as prospectors crying in the wilderness; Leonard Melfi's amusing *Porno Stars at Home,* about blue-movie actors in their off-duty hours at a birthday party; *Say Goodnight, Gracie,* a conversation among members of the television-oriented generation, written by Ralph Pape and staged by Austin Pendleton; and *Last Days at the Dixie Girl Cafe* by Robin Swicord, a slice of local-colored life in a rural Georgia hashhouse, with flavors of bigotry and romance.

Of the six musicals in independent production, only two attracted more than fleeting attention. These were *Piano Bar* by Doris Willens and Rob Fremont, a 21-number musical visit to a pub near Grand Central, and *The Coolest Cat in Town,* by William Gleason and Diane Leslie, stirring up a high school with the return of an alumnus who, 20 years before, was an Elvis Presley-type rock star. On the very bottom of the musical scale was *Jimmy & Billy,* about the Carter brothers, which vanished into the mists after only a single performance.

Specialty shows played a prominent role all over town in the 1978-79 season. Alec McCowen's *St. Mark's Gospel* was first presented off Broadway before returning for a second run on. *An Evening With Quentin Crisp* was one man's review of his life as a homosexual over the past seven decades; and *Crimes Against Nature* acted out concerns and conflicts in the same area. *The Elocution of Benjamin* was an enactment by Gordon Chater of the emotional life of a transvestite, dramatized as a one-character play. Other solo stints were offered by Geraldine Fitzgerald in a program of songs; by Martha Schlamme in a program of songs and poetry; and by Ed Metzger in a philosophical impersonation of Albert Einstein. Japan's Grand Kabuki brought two of its uniquely stylized programs to town for a limited visit. The antique jewel of the French theater, the Comédie Française, showed local audiences how Molière's *Le Misanthrope* and Feydeau's *La Puce à l'Oreille* (A Flea in her Ear) should be done.

And speaking of audiences, if there was any general impression left by the twelve variegated months of off-Broadway theater ending May 31, 1979, it was of self-absorption; inner-directedness. A healthy streak of extrovertism to generate a force of communication was conspicuously lacking. Most of the work offered off Broadway this season seemed to have appeared out of some special compulsion of an author or artistic director, not because of any probability — or even possibility — of gratifying an emotional, entertainment or other need of the audience. There were a few obvious exceptions, of course, but more often than not they were inspirations shaped elsewhere and brought in like visiting dignitaries to tone things up. For all its rising expectations and costs, off Broadway still retains much of its original avant garde character. This could be all to the good if in some glorious future there occur breakouts in new directions of creative theater. In the meantime, audiences should be advised that their concerns seem to be no part of off-Broadway's, although they are cordially invited to share the growing pains.

Revivals

Revival production on Broadway reached a numerical peak in 1975-76 and, in that and subsequent seasons, artistic peaks like *The Royal Family,* the Houston Grand Opera *Porgy and Bess,* the Joseph Papp *Threepenny Opera* and the current *Dracula.* The numbers have been diminishing, however, from 28 back then to 17 in 1976-77, 14 last season and 11 this year. Off Broadway, where organizations devote entire schedules to the theater library shelf, the numerical trend has been the reverse — 29, 35, 45 — until this year, when the total dropped back to 35. Shrinking though revival production may seem to be, it is still imposing as of 1978-79, with 49 offerings on and off Broadway up and down the scale from *Babes in Toyland* to *The Diary of Anne Frank,* from *Whoopee* to *Coriolanus,* making New York one of the great repertory theaters of all time.

On Broadway, Circle in the Square is annually a treasure trove of past masterpieces — our own recent past in a June presentation of the Moss Hart-George S. Kaufman comedy *Once in a Lifetime* with John Lithgow and George S. Irving; and Europe's in their two later-season offerings: Nikolai Gogol's *The Inspector General* in a translation by Betsy Hulick staged by Liviu Ciulei (one of the group who will be running the Vivian Beaumont at Lincoln Center), and, under Stephen Porter's direction, Shaw's *Man and Superman.* This was the same version of the work offered in 1964 by the Association of Producing Artists (APA) which included the *Don Juan in Hell* section, frequently omitted in performance, and abridged the earlier part of the play. With the outstanding *Spokesong* also on their schedule and with the new Michael Weller script *Loose Ends* in preparation in June, Theodore Mann and Paul Libin were offering the best of both theaters, old and new, for their subscribers at Circle in the Square, which nevertheless found itself in a state of acute financial crisis as the season drew to a close.

Providing a second look at possibly disadvantaged works of the recent past was once a special function of the off-Broadway theater. It remains a function of the New York revival stage as a whole. David Berry's Vietnam War play *G.R. Point,* a close contender for the Best Plays list when it was first produced by the Phoenix in 1977, was restaged for Broadway audiences by William Devane, with Michael Moriarty in the leading role of the recruit in a graves registration unit coping with emotions, conscience and body bags. It was a valid production but added little to the recent memory of the Phoenix's version. The same was true of another second viewing, Herb Gardner's extraordinarily eloquent and amusing *The Goodbye People,* about a long-retired Coney Island purveyor of hot dogs who sees that his children, his friends and the world in general have deteriorated to the point at which the only thing that can rescue it all is for him to reopen his old stand on the boardwalk in the middle of February. Milton Berle played it to perfection in 1968 (but for a run of only 7 performances). Herschel Bernardi played it this time with more manner, less feeling and for only 1 performance.

Two full-scale musical revivals helped add meat to the bones of the Broadway season: *Stop the World — I Want to Get Off* exhibiting Sammy Davis Jr. in full cry in the role of Littlechap; and the latest in the parade of antique musicals shined up at the Goodspeed Opera House in East Haddam, Conn. for the trip back to Broadway, *Whoopee,* with Charles Repole in the lead. A welcome visit from the D'Oyly Carte in four of the best-loved works in the Gilbert and Sullivan repertory — *Iolanthe, The Mikado, H.M.S. Pinafore* and the *The Pirates of Penzance* — added its fanfare and flourish to the Broadway revival season. These same operettas were also presented off Broadway in Light Opera of Manhattan's twelve-month bonanza of 16 musical revivals, which included new (for LOOM) productions of Gilbert and Sullivan's *The Grand Duke* and Victor Herbert's *Babes in Toyland,* with new book and lyrics by Alice Hammerstein Mathias and William Mount-Burke, LOOM's artistic director.

Off Broadway, Joseph Papp stood as tall in revival as in new-play production, playing host to Andrei Serban's evening of Molière farces, *Sganarelle,* brought in from New Haven, and the Juilliard production of Wedekind's *Spring Awakening;* then presenting Shakespeare as usual in the Central Park summer nights, *All's Well That Ends Well* and *The Taming of the Shrew* (with Meryl Streep as Katharina and Raul Julia as Petruchio). One of Papp's major midseason accomplishments was the assembling of a Black and Hispanic Acting Ensemble in productions of *Julius Caesar* and the much more problematical *Coriolanus* (with Morgan Freeman in the lead) under Michael Langham's direction. The Ensemble included such notable performers as Arthur French, Sonny Jim Gaines, Gloria Foster and Jaime Sanchez and will presumably be seen again in similar contexts.

The new Harold Clurman Theater on 42d Street's renovated Theater Row distinguished itself in its first season with a revival of Arthur Miller's *The Price* staged by John Stix with Fritz Weaver in the lead, scheduled for a June move to Broadway. The 1978-79 highlight of Roundabout's short schedule was a *Candida* directed by the resourceful Harold J. Kennedy. Circle Repertory interrupted its schedule of new plays to give its audiences a new look at *The Runner Stumbles,* the 1976 Best Play by Milan Stitt, now the Circle's dramaturg. The Theater of the Open Eye rose to one off-Broadway occasion, the revival of Jean Erdman's *Finnegans Wake*-inspired, 1963 Obie-winning *The Coach With the Six Insides.* The Classic Stage Company presented an interesting and provocative season under Christopher Martin's artistic directorship, with the Hollow Crown trilogy (*Richard II* and the two *Henry IV*s), an 18th Century Irish play, *Wild Oats,* and Martin's own adaptation of Wedekind's *The Marquis of Keith.* Across the river, the Brooklyn Academy of Music sponsored a revival of George Gershwin's musical *Tip-Toes,* a Florida revel with scene descriptions like "The deck of Steve's yacht, the next evening."

The single example of independent off-Broadway revival production was *The Diary of Anne Frank.* It too was organizational in the sense that it was a family affair for the acting Wallachs: Eli (Mr. Frank), Anne Jackson (Mrs. Frank), Katherine (Margot Frank) and Roberta in the title role of the young heroine of this wartime tragedy, movingly revisited.

That was the revival year on the New York stage — eclectic and partisan, dramatic and merry, above all respectful of the theater's heritage in its 49 productions spread across town and across just about every conceivable audience curiosity about the theatrical past.

Offstage

The Broadway theater's brightening prospects of record grosses in a gradually improving neighborhood were summed up late in the year by Gerald Schoenfeld, board chairman of the Shubert Organization, in a landmark address to the New York City Chamber of Commerce and Industry. His company, owners of 16½ playhouses and other enterprises, has the single biggest financial stake in the Broadway theater which, Schoenfeld said, began in 1969-70 to slide downhill into economic recession (only 5.4 million admissions and a $45.3 million gross by 1972-73) and porno infestation (430 installations between 30th and 60th Streets). "We couldn't move away — we couldn't afford to," Schoenfeld told his audience. "Faced with these conditions and having no friends or allies in government or in the other areas of the performing arts, we had to look to ourselves to get things done . . . . . We commenced our campaign for survival.

"The success of the joint effort of improving the urban environment was reflected in the 1977-78 New York theatrical season, when 9.6 million tickets to Broadway shows were sold — more than the combined sales for all the metropolitan area's professional sports teams: the Yankees, Mets, Knicks, Giants, Jets, Rangers, Islanders and Cosmos," Schoenfeld told the gathering of New York businessmen. 1978-79 was even bigger, and that's not all: "The effect of the sale of 9.6 million tickets costing $141 million during the 1977-78 season was the generation of related expenditures by theatergoers for restaurants, transportation, parking and so on, of an additional $123 million. The economic impact of the Broadway theater on the economy of the New York metropolitan area amounted to $379 million. And since Broadway theater is performed throughout the United States, as witness outside-of-Broadway ticket sales last season of $106 million, the total contribution of the Broadway theater to the United States economy, including that $106 million, was $1.138 billion."

Today's high ticket prices contributed in some measure to the expanding grosses, and Schoenfeld faced this fact with the claim that the Broadway ticket is merely going with the flow of the economy: "The average top musical price in 1968-69, ten years ago, was $12. This compares to the average top ticket price for Broadway musicals in December 1978 of $20. The increase is 68 per cent, which on its face appears to be quite high. This is at a 30 per cent lower rate, however, than the cost-of-living index in New York, which rose 88.3 per cent in the same ten-year period . . . . . Compared to the increase in prices of all other goods, ticket prices to Broadway musicals are 30 per cent cheaper than they were ten years ago."

To sum up Schoenfeld's state-of-the-theater address, by dint of special effort Broadway's downward slide has been reversed, and the situation both inside and outside the theaters is good and getting better. "I look forward to Times Square and midtown New York being the prime example of something New Yorkers can be proud about not too far into the future," he finished.

However the "average top ticket price" may be calculated, the top itself continued to move upward in 1978-79. Among straight plays the season before, *Golda* commanded the highest top price of $18. By October 1978, both *First Monday in October* and *The Gin Game* were asking $20 for weekend evenings. Few dared to keep pace with these front-runners, but at season's end the top at *Whose Life Is It Anyway?* was $18.50, with the field strung out behind. Among musicals, by January 1979 *Ballroom* and *Dancin'* were topping off at $25, *A Chorus Line* at $24. *I Remember Mama* came in late at the $25 level, while *Sweeney Todd* was making it on $22.50 and *Annie* was selling out at $19.50.

In 1978-79 the legitimate stage was gaining playhouses. The Billy Rose Theater on West 41st Street, dark for most of recent seasons, was purchased by James M. Nederlander and two British partners, renamed the Trafalgar, brightly lit up again with the successful *Whose Life Is It Anyway?* and now is destined, according to plan, as a New York showcase for a string of London imports.

A block uptown in the bilges of the Times Square district, in the forbidden city block of 42d Street just west of Broadway, the Apollo Theater was refurbished with a new marquee and entrance across 43d Street from the *Times*. It got its second wind as a legit house Feb. 28 with *On Golden Pond*. This 1,163-seat single-balcony theater opened in 1910 as the Bryant, a movie-and-vaudeville showplace. It converted to legit once before, in 1920, and continued with such productions as Lionel Barrymore's *Macbeth*, W.C. Fields's *Poppy*, several editions of *George White's Scandals* and other shows starring Ed Wynn, Bert Lahr, Kate Smith and Ethel Merman.

Likewise the Vivian Beaumont and Mitzi E. Newhouse Theaters at Lincoln Center, abandoned to darkness 18 months ago by Joseph Papp, showed signs of lighting up again soon. They are to be managed, it was announced, by a five-person directorate whose disciplines overlap from theater into opera and movies, with Richmond Crinkley as executive producer, with Edward Albee as in-house playwright and with a 1980 start in prospect as we went to press.

One of the new OOB theaters on 42d Street was named in honor of a critic — Harold Clurman. Other good news for critics included the reinstatement of John Simon on the first night list after a season of official (but not *de facto*) banishment after some blunt comments on *The Shadow Box* on a TV show and on Liza Minnelli in print. Mel Gussow of the *Times* was elected to membership in the New York Drama Critics Circle, joining Walter Kerr in *Times* representation on that body.

The controversy over when a Broadway show is reviewable was running hot all season long. When is a show not yet a show but just a work in progress in a prolongued series of previews? This was the question raised about *Sarava*, a musical which opened (as far as this volume is concerned) on Jan. 11 but kept postponing its premiere until finally in mid-February both *Variety* and the *Times* declared it open and sent their reviewers to cover it. In our view, a show is open on the day it begins to charge full price for admission up and down the ticket scale, and from that date on the public should be served with information about what they're being asked to pay full price *for,* sight unseen. *Sarava* was still running at season's end (which was more than could be said for most 1978-79 musicals), had not yet named an official opening night but, according to a spokesman for its producer, has no objection to Jan. 11 as its opening date of record.

Joseph Papp confronted the critics on a similar matter but in entirely different circumstances: at the request of his stars, he asked that the reviews of his Central Park revival of *The Taming of the Shrew* (which charged no admission whatever) be withheld from publication until after the show was to close Sept. 3. The *Times* replied that it would insist on covering the show at the previously-announced opening performance, however. This was to be Aug. 16; but by an ironic turn of the wheel, the *Times* went on strike Aug. 9 and the problem vanished. With his next production, *Drinks Before Dinner,* Papp tore the critics from the bosom of their families by scheduling his premiere on Thanksgiving night, after a long month of pre-opening performances.

As the season came to a close, the New York *Post* laid down a brand new rule governing the practise of quoting its critic in advertisements to promote shows. The *Post's* distinguished critic, Clive Barnes, formerly of the *Times,* turns the kind of phrases that make good ad quotes, and sometimes his entire review is reprinted as an ad, sometimes in the *Times,* by producers who want a widened readership to experience the thrust of Barnes's more enthusiastic judgements. The trouble is that a quote ad in the *Times* butters no parsnips for the *Post,* which in June announced a new policy: henceforth, permission for producers to quote Barnes in other publications will not be given unless said producers buy equal space in the *Post.*

In other parts of this forest, an agreement between the Society of Stage Directors and Choreographers and the League of New York Theaters and Producers established a minimum fee for Broadway and its touring companies: $4,410 for directors, $3,570 for choreographers. The designers also had a meeting of minds with the League in an agreement with an extraordinarily long life span — 11½ years with minimums reviewable in 1984 and 1987 — setting minimums for scene designs from $2,750 (for a single-set straight play) to $9,000 (for a multi-set musical), for costume designs from $1,500 (for a modern-dress show with one to three characters) to $9,000 (for a musical with more than 36 characters) and lighting from $1,700 to $4,500.

The Dramatists Guild, not a union but a craft organization of playwrights, composers, lyricists and librettists, whose Minimum Basic Agreement with the League has changed very little since George Bernard Shaw helped get it by the Shuberts, was in the process of re-thinking the dramatist's economic relationship with the modern theater. Dramatists aren't employees of the producer, but owners of their scripts whose use they rent out for a royalty. Up to now, they receive little "front money" but are paid from a percentage of the box office receipts when — and if — these begin to come in. *Variety* reported in mid-season that "serious talks" between the Guild and the League were taking place, talks directed at changing the agreement so that dramatists might receive a substantial pre-payment in exchange for modifying their royalty position until their show has paid back its cost. The Dramatists Guild re-elected all its incumbent officers including its president, Stephen Sondheim, named to his fourth two-year term.

Another dispute between Guild and League over the televised 1978 Tony Award ceremonies, at which the winning authors and composers — founders of this feast — were relegated to a place not even at the foot of the table but out in the pantry receiving their awards off-camera, was amicably adjusted. The televised 1979 Tony Awards, masterminded so adroitly by Alexander H. Cohen and his wife Hildy Parks, went off with great eclat and without a hitch. And the world did not come to an end when participants were obliged to speak THAT word out loud, distinctly, on national television, nine times, in announcing each of the nine nominations for *The Best Little Whorehouse in Texas.*

The Theater Development Fund's TKTS booths in Duffy Square and lower Manhattan continued to buttress the commercial theater with *Variety*-estimated sales for the year of $10,783,334 worth of half-price tickets to Broadway shows, $426,192 to off-Broadway shows. TDF also dispensed more than $300,000 in the purchase of tickets to selected Broadway shows to help prime the pump in the early days of the run. Among other friends of the theater, the New York State Legislature made available $34,713,400 to its Council on the Arts for 1979, an increase of 6 per cent over 1978 (the theater's share is about 10 per cent of that, with another $6 million distributed by the National Endowment in Washington). And a gift of $1.25 million by the Billy Rose Foundation to the theater collection of the New York Public Library at Lincoln Center benefited that noted theater archive so handsomely that it was formally re-named the Billy Rose Theater Collection. This is all the more appropriate because Billy Rose himself spent many hours at the Library analyzing the popular music of his time, aiming to become a successful song writer. He concluded that hits fell into four distinct categories, one of which was the song built around a silly sound or syllable, with "oo" the most promising. On the basis of this Collection-gleaned information, Rose put together his first song hit, "Barney Google With the Goo-Goo-Googly Eyes."

Such was the New York theater season of 1978-79 — active, impressive and varied but, as we noted in the opening paragraphs of this report, without a smash hit. Those of us who view the theater through the rose-colored glasses of art for art's sake — which is to say the vast majority of the audience — would call any season a success for bringing out a *Sweeney Todd,* and damn the economic torpedoes which are somebody else's emergency. The trouble is, our New York theater is one of the very few live performing-arts operations that is expected to pay its own way like a circus or a basketball team. Its performance at the box office affects its performance on the stage, which is why we annually devote a portion of this summary to the theater's economics.

So it's particularly encouraging to learn from the address (summarized at the beginning of this section) by Gerald Schoenfeld of the Shubert Organization that somebody up there who owns half the neighborhood looks upon the theater not only as a dollar factory but also as an arts institution worthy of our deepest civic and national pride — and trying to persuade others in government, the theater and the business world to give it the same special place in their esteem. The more of us who insist that the theater is a going concern and not an invalid, however fabulous, the more likely the concern is to go. In the Schoenfeld report and elsewhere, the New York theater is being perceived not as somebody else's business but as a public asset to be cared for as lovingly as possible in every aspect of our social and economic as well as artistic lives. As an art form, the theater is a vital organ of evolved mankind, indivisible from man's civilized existence on this planet. As a functional entity, the New York theater as we know it in 1978-79 is being strengthened by positive attitudes and actions which for the first time in many years seem to be trying to repair it to last.

1987 PERSPECTIVE: And so the 1970s ended on an upbeat with a bunch of huge musicals in the playhouses, a record gross in the till and the New York theater turning the corner into the sunlight—where its problems were ever more glaringly visible. A lousy million dollars might no longer be half enough to finance one of those musicals, and in a soaring real estate market a lousy billion dollars was only a fraction of the beckoning profit in tearing down the theaters and developing the Times Square area. Joseph Papp stated in the darkest days of the mid-1970s that, owing to economic conditions, off Broadway was "d-e-a-d" (fortunately he was wrong and soon relieved by the phenomenal success of "A Chorus Line," which he'd only just produced). But not even Maestro Papp could make a go of Lincoln Center, as he lapsed into revivals at the Vivian Beaumont and then closed down his operation in both theaters. The decade ended optimistically with a consortium including Richmond Crinkley, Liviu Ciulei and Edward Albee set to operate there, but we now know that little came of their short-lived efforts.

Speaking of predictions, our 1976-77 report observed in passing that "Oh! Calcutta!", off Broadway's breakthrough of sexual humor, "slid quietly" into revival in a small house in the Broadway area. Quietly indeed; almost a decade later it's still going strong in the second-longest run in Broadway history, second only to "A Chorus Line" which we now confidently predict will run forever.

The most significant loss to the New York theater in the 1970s was the dramatist's "chance to fail," the vitally important opportunity for the theater's creative artists to learn from doing. The formal, expensive, union-contracted, eight-performances-a-week context of Broadway and even off Broadway became so expensive and at the same time so perilously dependent for survival on the opinion of one person—the New York Times play reviewer, whoever he might be—that anything like tryout or experimentation in those areas became no longer possible. The playwright's "chance to fail" and to learn his craft from his mistakes—vital to a vital theater—disappeared from Broadway and off Broadway in the 1970s. The continuous creative impulse caused it to resurface in what is called "off off Broadway" and in some of the Chicago, Los Angeles and other regionals. But before the 1970s came to an end, the theatrical unions were moving in on the New York workshop activities, and by 1986 costs here too were becoming worrisome.

The emerging "bests" of OOB and the regionals invariably migrate eventually to Broadway and/or off Broadway, because these are still the display windows of American theater. But if the 1985-86 New York theater program was a sample of the best that our authors and producers can put on display, then something is draining their energy and weakening their impact. Very likely it is their disappearing "chance to fail" without any greater consequences than a lesson learned. In this situation, like a pro team taking the field without practice or trial games, they face their challenges resolutely but without the training they deserve and require in order to win.

O.L.G. Jr.

PART IV:
THE
EIGHTIES

Shirley MacLaine in *Shirley MacLaine on Broadway*

Mickey Rooney and Ann Miller in the burlesque musical *Sugar Babies,* sketches by Ralph G. Allen based on traditional material.
PHOTO BY MARTHA SWOPE

1979-80

ONE OF THE NEW YORK THEATER'S specialties is embarrassing nay-sayers. Season after season, it teases them, like a bird doing a broken-wing bit, into the most pessimistic pronouncements—and then confounds them by coming on strong, often in its apparently weakest mode.

The season of 1979–80 was no exception. Is the "star system" only a memory? Mickey Rooney of *Sugar Babies* and Mary Tyler Moore of *Whose Life Is It Anyway?* would be interested to hear it. Is the book musical disappearing from popular favor? Not so as the potent revivals of *West Side Story, Peter Pan* and *Oklahoma!* would notice it.

Is traditional American theater sinking beneath the treacherous surface of the avant garde like a doomed character in a Beckett one-acter? Well, Harold Pinter's *Betrayal* was certainly different (its succession of scenes moved backwards in time) and so was Tom Stoppard's *Dogg's Hamlet, Cahoot's Macbeth* (it invented a new language), but it was *they* who were up to their ears in conventional dramaturgy. Nostalgia was one of the season's most conspicuous elements (c.f. the big theme musicals *Sugar Babies, Barnum* and *A Day in Hollywood/A Night in the Ukraine*), while Arthur Miller told a *U.S. News & World Report* interviewer, "That brand of theater (absurdist) has run its course. Today, people want to identify with what they're looking at. In the theater, younger people want shape again. They want to trace out relationships again."

The theater on and off Broadway in 1979–80 got a crick in its neck looking backward at Scott and Zelda, Hemingway, Gertrude Stein and other literary expatriates of the 1920s, in their own words and even in Tennessee Williams's. And Stoppard himself brought to Broadway a conventionally-structured play, *Night and Day*. And, yes, Neil Simon *could* do it again, maintaining his steady pace of crowd pleasers (1977 *California Suite,* 1978 *They're Playing Our Song,* 1979 *Chapter Two*) with yet another comedy of eccentric modern manners, *I Ought To Be in Pictures*.

Will the good old days of the powerhouse musicals never return? The record shows that *these* are the good old days, with the longest running New York show of all time, *The Fantasticks,* entering its 21st year (it opened May 3, 1960) and its 9th set of 1,000 performances; with *Grease,* the longest-running show in Broadway history, overtaking the old champ, *Fiddler on the Roof,* and setting a new record of 3,388 performances before calling it a run; and with the durable hits *A Chorus Line* and *Annie* beginning to count in the thousands too.

Did off Broadway have a so-so season? Yes, but it stole the show on Broadway, where Lanford Wilson's 1979 play *Talley's Folly* carried off two of the three major best-play awards, while Samm-Art Williams's *Home* made it all the way from St. Marks Place to the Best Plays and Tony nominations list. And just as it was being given up for lost, it ended with the triple bang of *Mass Appeal, Mecca* and *A Coupla White Chicks Sitting Around Talking*.

And could anyone forsee that Paul Osborn's *Morning's at Seven,* a 40-year-old back-porch family comedy lasting only 44 performances in its original 1939 Broadway run, could be rejuvenated in revival as one of the hits of 1980? Yes—

The 1979–80 Season on Broadway

PLAYS (22)

LOOSE ENDS
Lone Star and Pvt. Wars
On Golden Pond (return engagement)
Devour the Snow (transfer)
Romantic Comedy
Last Licks
Strider (transfer)
BENT
Teibele and Her Demon
THE LADY FROM DUBUQUE
Harold and Maude
TALLEY'S FOLLY (transfer)
Clothes for a Summer Hotel
CHILDREN OF A LESSER GOD
Horowitz and Mrs. Washington
I OUGHT TO BE IN PICTURES
Goodbye Fidel
Past Tense
NUTS
Hide and Seek
HOME (transfer)
The Roast

MUSICALS (13)

The Madwoman of Central Park West
Got Tu Go Disco
But Never Jam Today
Evita
The 1940s Radio Hour
SUGAR BABIES
King of Schnorrers (transfer)
Comin' Uptown
Reggae
Happy New Year
Barnum
A Day in Hollywood/A Night in the Ukraine
Musical Chairs

REVUES (2)

Live From New York
A Kurt Weill Cabaret

FOREIGN PLAYS IN ENGLISH (10)

Dogg's Hamlet, Cahoot's Macbeth
Once a Catholic
Night and Day
BETRAYAL
Filumena
Whose Life Is It Anyway? (return engagement)
Charlotte
Censored Scenes From King Kong
Heartaches of a Pussycat
Of the Fields, Lately

REVIVALS (11)

Richard III
The Price (transfer)
Father's Day
Peter Pan
The Most Happy Fella
Oklahoma!
Watch on the Rhine
Canterbury Tales
West Side Story
Major Barbara
Morning's at Seven

SPECIALTIES (8)

Every Good Boy Deserves Favour
Radio City Music Hall: Snow White and the Seven Dwarfs
The Magnificent Christmas Spectacular
A Rockette Spectacular
Mister Lincoln
Black Broadway
Blackstone
Billy Bishop Goes to War

HOLDOVER WHICH BECAME A HIT IN 1979–80

The Elephant Man

Plays listed in CAPITAL LETTERS have been designated Best Plays of 1979–80.
Plays listed in *italics* were still running after June 1, 1980.
Plays listed in **bold face type** were classified as hits in *Variety's* annual estimate published June 4, 1980.

someone could. We point with pride to Burns Mantle's perception of it as one of his Best Plays of that season.

Innovation? Well, there was no *Sweeney Todd* or *Wings* on the 1980 Best Plays list, but James Lapine certainly found a new angle of vision to examine family relationships in *Table Settings,* as did Samm-Art Williams with the black experience in *Home,* the adventures of a good-humored survivor. 1979–80 plays tended to be traditional in form and approach, or at least characteristic of well-established authors, but that isn't to say that they were short on power or high spirits or distinction. The year's most heavily muscled play, *Bent,* was as repugnant as an execution (and as undeniably affecting) with its searing blasts of Nazi hate and grotesque redemptions of love—and what's more, it represents new growth as the American theater debut of its author, Martin Sherman.

This year's book musicals failed to challenge the plays for a place among the script-oriented Best Plays, but we unhesitatingly single out *Sugar Babies* with a special Best Play citation for the manner in which its sketches by Ralph G. Allen celebrate and re-create the burlesque-show style and material, heaped up in golden kernels in Allen's clever adaptation of the old routines, evoking the past of baggy pants and bump-and-grind (being a nostalgic show, it had to be better than the original, and it was, with a good selection of period show tunes and a blazing performance by Mickey Rooney as the top banana).

In the Broadway box offices the grosses mounted inexorably and predictably toward another all-time record season, the fifth in a row which began with 1975–76. Ticket prices inevitably inflated, along with just about everything else in the world, in a trend that has raised them 48 per cent in the last five years, according to *Variety* estimate. The double sawbuck top for straight plays, first touched in the fall of 1978 by *First Monday in October,* held for only a little more than a year. By early 1980 *Whose Life Is It Anyway?* and *The Lady From Dubuque* were asking as much as $22.50 and *Strider* $25 while calling itself a musical. In May *The Roast* made the $25 top for straight plays a little more official, lasting for only 4 performances but certainly a portent of things to come. Among musicals, in November *Dancin'* set what *Variety* called "a new high for legit tickets" of $26. By the end of the season this had become $27.50 at *Dancin', A Chorus Line* and *They're Playing Our Song*—and if $27.50 comes, can $30 be far behind?

We should note that attendance for the 12 Broadway months ending June 1, 1980 was up too, by almost 6 per cent according to *Variety* estimate, from 8.9 million last year to 9.3 million this year. Therefore the record 1979–80 Broadway total gross of $143,430,673 included some hard as well as some inflationary gain. The League of New York Theaters and Producers, which counts a little differently from *Variety,* figured the year's Broadway gross at $146 million, but both agreed that this was a record, the third $100 million-plus year in succession. *Variety's* figures show an increase of 11 per cent over the previous record $128 million in 1978–79. On the road, Broadway shows took in another $181 million, a huge $40 million increase over last year, bringing the combined total of the 1979–80 Broadway production take to a previously unthought-of $324,631,828.

Even more encouragingly, the volume of Broadway production and playing time has risen along with the box office receipts during these three $100 million seasons (see the one-page summary in the Broadway section of this report). The 40 shows of 1978 (not counting specialties and foreign-language works) became 48 in 1979 and a big, big 58 in 1980, with a healthy rise in the production of new plays, musicals and revues from 26 to 37 to 47 (which included two return engagements and five transfers from off Broadway). The total of playing weeks (if ten shows play ten weeks, that's 100 playing weeks) is probably a more accurate measure of growth than the balance sheet in these inflationary times. According to *Variety's* calculations, Broadway put together 1,541 playing weeks during the twelve months of 1979–80 as compared with 1,472 last season and 1,360 the season before, with an additional 1,351 (about 200 more than the previous year) on the road.

Amid all this action and cash flow, only three shows *(Romantic Comedy, Sugar Babies* and *Evita)* had achieved official hit status and were thus operating in the black as of season's end June 1, according to *Variety* estimate, leading to the conclusion that either a) individual shows were doing only moderately well even though there were a lot of them or b) production and operating costs were so high that it was taking longer than ever to get off the nut. It was easy to lose $1 million in show business in 1979–80—at least *Daddy Goodness* made it look easy, folding on the road for at least that *(Variety* reported). A moderate-sized, modestly successful Broadway musical like *The 1940s Radio Hour* could and did lose more than its initial $700,000 cost, while a bigger one like *Comin' Uptown* went for more than $1.4 million. A respectable three-character straight play like *Last Licks* could make $350,000 vanish like magic; likewise *Clothes for a Summer Hotel,* Tennessee Williams notwithstanding, with $400,000. Even an artistic landmark like *Sweeney Todd* could and did (by *Variety* estimate) end its memorable New York run in the red, $400,000 worth of an investment of about $1.2 million. So did the Best Play *Betrayal* with a loss of $100,000 of $300,000.

Yet the large sums of money needed to finance new production seemed possible to raise, $1.1 million for *Barnum* and $1.9 million for *42nd Street,* the musical David Merrick was preparing for an August premiere as we went to press. Angels are still on the wing because, for example (and by *Variety* estimate), *Death-trap* was running at a $1 million-plus profit, 256 per cent on its original $200,000 investment; *Hello, Dolly!* has passed the 1,300 per cent profit level, and still counting. The little *The Elephant Man* was at almost 100 per cent over cost; the dubious *A Matter of Gravity* was reporting $1 million plus on $160,000; *They're Playing Our Song* $1.2 million on $800,000; the Broadway *Dracula* revival $2 million on $300,000; *Same Time, Next Year* $3.2 million (695 per cent) on $230,000; *Ain't Misbehavin'* $2.4 million on $375,000; *Annie* $6.3 million on $800,000. One of this year's hits, *Sugar Babies* had returned its initial $1.3 million and was earning its backers $70,000 a week at the season's end.

The ultimate insignia of New York professional theater achievement (we insist) are the Best Play citations in these volumes, designations which are 16 years older than the Critics Awards and only three years younger than the Pulitzer Prize. Each Best Play selection is made by the present editor with the script itself as the first consideration, for the compelling reason that the script is not only the quintessence of the present, it is most of what endures into the future. So the Best Plays are the best scripts, with as little weight as humanly possible given to comparative production values. The choice is made without any regard whatever to a play's type—musical, comedy or drama—or origin on or off Broadway, or popularity at the box office, or lack of same.

If a script of above-average quality influences the very character of a season, or by some function of consensus wins the Critics, Pulitzer or Tony Awards, we take into account its future historical as well as present esthetic importance to the season as a whole *(Talley's Folly* is an example). This is the only special consideration we give, and we don't always tilt in its direction, as the record shows.

We don't take scripts of other eras into consideration for Best Play citation in this one, whatever their technical status as American or New York "premieres" which don't happen to have had a previous production of record. We draw a line between adaptations and revivals, the former eligible for Best Play selection but the latter not, on a case-by-case basis. We likewise consider the eligibility of borderline examples of limited-engagement and showcase production one at a time, ascertaining that they are "frozen" in final script version, and no longer changeable works-in-progress, before they are considered for Best Play citation (and in the case of a late-season off-Broadway arrival like *Talley's Folly,* the final decision may await a determination the following year).

Broadway

Tennessee Williams made the scene in 1979–80 with a new script, *Clothes for a Summer Hotel,* fantasizing the talent-haunted, doomed world of Scott and Zelda (and Ernest) in a work he described as "a ghost play"—a will o' the wisp with flashes of light but little or no heat. So did Arthur Miller with an off-Broadway-to-Broadway revival of *The Price,* and with the first little steps of a new work, *The American Clock,* a play of the 1920s–1930s Depression, mounted in unreviewed previews at the Harold Clurman Theater prior to its world premiere at the Spoleto-in-Charleston Festival in late May. So did Tom Stoppard with three—count 'em, three—new works, two predictably far-out but one surprisingly conventional. It was a scene dotted with off-Broadway transfers like *Devour the Snow, Talley's Folly* and *Strider;* with the return engagements of *On Golden Pond* and *Whose Life Is It Anyway?;* with one- two- and three-character plays such as *Mister Lincoln* (with Roy Dotrice impersonating the great President with a studiously mid-Western accent), *Charlotte* (with Uta Hagen as a provincial German housewife recounting her affair with Goethe to her silent husband, played by Charles Nelson Reilly with only one word to speak at the very end of the show), *Past Tense* by Jack Zeman (with Laurence Luckinbill and Barbara Feldon cauterizing the deep wounds of a failed marriage) and of course *Talley's Folly, Betrayal, I Ought To Be in Pictures,* Frank D. Gilroy's *Last Licks*—but not *Billy Bishop Goes to War* which may have had only two *actors* but called forth a large group of well-defined characters.

Edward Albee, Neil Simon, Harold Pinter, Mark Medoff and a good many others also made the scene, in company with a newcomer named Martin Sherman who stood beside them with *Bent,* the strongest (if not the most pleasing) work of the year. Its overt acts of homosexual affection in the violent context of Nazism constituted, not a horror show (though it seemed like one at times) but a sort of discordant paean to love, to its redeeming and restorative powers even in the most destructive of circumstances. Love is absolutely essential to the integrity of the human spirit and the survival of person and personality (Sherman contends in his drama); with love, both spiritual and physical survival are possible even in a Nazi concentration camp where, this play avers, the pink-triangled homosexual was treated even more despicably than the yellow-starred Jew. A dissolute young man arrested as a homosexual but posing as a Jew to obtain better treatment (Richard Gere) and his defiantly uncloseted friend (David Dukes) spoke in dramatic language sometimes so strong it threatened to cut audience's connections to the play with the force of shock. *Bent* was hard to take straight but compelling to reflect upon; a powerfully written and directed (by Robert Allan Ackerman) bleeding piece of raw theater.

Mark Medoff's *Children of a Lesser God,* the Tony best play award winner, took up the cudgels for still another misrepresented minority—the deaf—in a play of softer but extremely attractive hue. In it, the privacy of a born-deaf woman who wants to be left alone to live in her silent world is invaded by a well-meaning speech therapist who insists that she must learn to lip-read and speak (and incidentally love and marry him) if she is to achieve first-class citizenship in the hearing, speaking world. The actress portraying the deaf woman, Phyllis Frelich, didn't need to learn the mannerisms of the deaf and their eloquent language of signs—she is in reality a born-deaf person. Her vivid projection of the fierce emotions and frustrations of her role was matched by an ardent, insistent performance of the teacher by John Rubinstein under Gordon Davidson's precise direction. With the rationale that he is trying to teach her to lip read, he repeated aloud everything she signed, thus communicating to the audience what the deaf character was "saying" with her flying fingers. There was none of your "By George, I think she's got it!" payoffs here—the point of this play is her refusal to "get it." The play is an outcry for a group which, it insists, speaks more eloquently for itself in signs than hearing people are able to manage with mere words and therefore should never be condescendingly forced to adopt such a mannerism as speech, merely to conform to a hearing person's image of what a deaf person should be.

Three more Broadway dramas at the top of the list this season were Michael Weller's *Loose Ends,* Edward Albee's *The Lady From Dubuque* and Tom Topor's *Nuts.* Weller's play makes the strongest theatrical statement yet about the self-preoccupation of the so-called "me" generation with its flimsy front of cliches, in the example of two young people within reach of their goals and of each other, but star-crossed by selfishness. To the ambitious and basically unloving woman of this play (acted with detestable "cool" by Roxanne Hart), life is not to be lived, it is something you "deal with" to keep it at arm's length, to avoid commitment. Neither her husband (Kevin Kline) nor her unborn child are immune from being "dealt with," though she is, finally, the principal victim of her narcissistic ways. *Loose Ends* is the script that was chosen last season by the American Theater Critics Association as an outstanding cross-country work and appeared in synopsis in last year's *Best Plays* volume. Its New York production by Circle in the Square under Alan Schneider's direction fully realized its values.

Schneider's direction certainly evoked an ensemble-like expertise from the performers of the difficult *The Lady From Dubuque,* vintage Albee in its perplexing characters and unique manner of speaking in his special voice, in few words but many mysterious overtones. Who was the lady from Dubuque who entered this troubled suburban house unbidden, pretending to be its mistress's mother come in the nick of time to ease her daughter's pain of dying, offering a consolation that neither her real mother, her self-centered friends nor her panicking husband were able to give? Irene Worth, playing the lady as though totally convinced she is exactly who she says she is, wasn't telling; neither was the lady's companion (Earle Hyman), as unflappable as Death himself; neither was the agonized victim (Frances Conroy), who knows a mother when she needs one. Friends and husband remain bewildered, and the author was not moved to explain his unfathomable metaphor of ineffable comfort. Its abrasions both physical and spiritual were moodily enhanced in Schneider's direction and Rouben

Ter-Arutunian's spare geometry of a setting. *The Lady From Dubuque* echoes elements of Albee's *Tiny Alice* and *All Over* in an even more subtle confrontation of mortality than either. The fact that it lasted for only 12 performances on Broadway this season was a reflection on the system, not on this distinguished and durable play.

Tom Topor's *Nuts* was for two of its acts the most gripping courtroom session in years and a survivor of its weaker third. Gaunt, aggressively chip-on-shouldered Anne Twomey played the subject of a sanity hearing in a Bellevue Hospital case, with the presiding judge (Ed Van Nuys in a take-charge performance) asked to decide whether she is a victim of her doctors' and her parents' prejudices, or whether she is indeed a paranoid threat to society who should be hospitalized indefinitely. This defendant is not an unflawed victim; if found sane, she will have to then stand trial for a killing she claims was justifiable homicide, under circumstances reflecting on her character and morals. Her unhappy—and gradually sympathy-inspiring—tale was told in the recollections of witnesses (including herself and Hansford Rowe and Lenka Peterson as her appalled parents) and the recriminations of lawyers (notably Richard Zobel as her attorney) within a Tom Schwinn setting and concise Stephen Zuckerman direction that seemed just right for this play. The author's final disposition of the defendant's emotions and case had a little bit the look of a neatly-tied ribbon, inappropriate but only very slightly demeaning to his otherwise solid and abrasive play.

Among other American dramas in the unusually large number of new plays produced on Broadway this season was Frank D. Gilroy's *Last Licks,* with a son trying to get his widowed father settled (and also settle some of the longstanding disturbances in their relationship) before moving out of town, and with Susan Kellermann in notable support as the father's longtime mistress. In the thriller genre, Lezley Havard's *Hide and Seek* provided the achingly suspense-provoking kind of heroine (Elizabeth Ashley) who, left alone in a haunted house at midnight, is determined to explore the cellar. Howard Sackler's *Goodbye Fidel* was a chronicle of displacement, following a set of upper-class Cubans from their pleasures under the pre-Castro regime into helpless and purposeless exile.

The New York Drama Critics Circle, which voted *Talley's Folly* their best of bests in 1980, decided informally not to consider it last season (though it opened before the date of their meeting) but wait until this year when their membership would have had a better chance to have seen and to consider it. In these reports we also will take a second look at distinguished limited-engagement scripts which reappear the following season in, perhaps, somewhat revised form; but that isn't the reason *Talley's Folly* did not appear as a Best Play in our 1978-79 overview. We ranked it last year as first runner-up, calling it as we saw it: an excellent but rather slight script magnificently augmented in production. We still see it that way, but we include it now among the Best Plays of 1979–80 for journalistic reasons stated previously in this report — but with unreserved admiration for the work.

Neil Simon's 17th Broadway production, *I Ought To Be in Pictures,* was a warmly amusing father-and-daughter game played by Ron Leibman as a faltering screen writer who abandoned his family in New York years before and now receives a surprise visit from his grown-up, 19-year-old daughter (Dinah Manoff) who has hitch-hiked across the country in denim shorts. She has a mind of her own—subject to frequent consultation with her dead grandmother—and is equal to any challenge, including rebuilding decrepit old automobiles and her father's decrepit old personality. Habitually, this screen writer is able to hold life at bay with one-liners, but he is penetrated to the heart by this daughter for whom he has done so little and finally cares so much. David Jenkins's design was a convincing rendition of a downward-mobile batchelor's quarters, Western style, and Herbert Ross's directorial timing of the play seemed exactly right for maximum savoring of its progression from laughter to sweet sorrow. Simon is by far our most consistently effective contemporary dramatist, and *I Ought To Be in Pictures,* his 11th Best Play, was very definitely up to his usual admirable standard.

Not parenthood but romance assails the inner bastions of another apparently unassailable writer, played by Anthony Perkins, in Bernard Slade's hit *Romantic Comedy.* He is a playwright with the world by the tail, but the tail wags him as he marries one woman and courts another (Mia Farrow) in a loosely-fastened series of comeuppances that finally bring him to his knees. Another effective comedy idea whose brief Broadway run (4 performances) was an inaccurate measure of its quality was *The Roast* by Jerry Belson and Garry Marshall, an enactment of one of those banquet tributes at which comedians insult the guest of honor to demonstrate how much they love him. Skillfully staged by Carl Reiner to individualize each of its large group of colorful male characters, it was well served by an ensemble which included Peter Boyle (looking like Bob Hope) as the target, Joe Silver as a gravel-voiced toastmaster, Bill Macy with a dirty mouth, Arny Freeman tottering about in Groucho Marx-like beret, Doug McClure as a fish out of water (a straight man), Antonio Vargas as the black delegate and Rob Reiner as the situation's tactless problem child. That's all the play was—a situation going nowhere after dessert, but in the meantime richly concocted.

Also on the season's agenda of American comedies were *Lone Star* and *Pvt. Wars,* a pair of James McLure one-acts united in a theme of the Vietnam experience; the Isaac Bashevis Singer-Eve Friedman fairy tale *Teibele and Her Demon,* with F. Murray Abraham as a lover persuading a pretty widow that he is not a person but a demon, and therefore unbound by human moral taboos; *Harold and Maude* by Colin Higgins, based on his 1971 movie about an attachment between an octogenarian and a teen-ager, with Janet Gaynor making a stage appearance as the former; and Henry Denker's *Horowitz and Mrs. Washington,* with Sam Levene as a patient who, after suffering violence at the hands of blacks, finds himself in the care of a black nurse, played by Esther Rolle.

This was a season when foreign plays were present but seldom conspicuously so—except for Harold Pinter's meticulous *Betrayal,* a tightly interlocked triangle of wife (Blythe Danner), husband (Roy Scheider) and lover (Raul Julia, also the husband's best friend). Their betrayals in this Best Play take the form of mutual sexual infidelity, and Pinter sauced the dish by playing the affair backwards from its cooling ashes to its irresistible kindling in the final episode of the play. Since the audience does not know in the beginning what has happened (is going to happen), the device was somewhat counterproductive in the opening scenes but made its points in the closing scenes in which the audience (but not the characters) knows the important consequences which will result (have resulted) from the smallest developments. A husband-wife confrontation at midpoint in a Venice hotel room is chillingly and achingly understated—Pinter to perfection. Miss Danner's every movement as a careless wife but not uncaring lover took marvelous effect. The same cannot be said for the Messrs. Scheider and Julia who, adroit and courageous performers as they are, tackled these indelibly British roles with the best will in the world but with their Western Hemisphere showing like the roots of a dye job. As we understand it, American and British Equity employment rules caused the producers to seek American actors for these roles so that, if the play was a long-run hit, they wouldn't have to replace British actors with American ones after the permitted period of employment (which apparently was the case last season with Tom Conti in *Whose Life Is It Anyway?*).

If Pinter's work was riding point for the 1979–80 season of foreign plays on Broadway, Tom Stoppard's was ranging all over the place, beginning with a novelty co-authored with André Previn and entitled *Every Good Boy Deserves Favour* (i.e., the musical phrase E-G-B-D-F) which required a full symphony orchestra (as the leading character, a dreamer, imagines that he is conducting one) and room for it to perform. The show played the Metropolitan Opera House for a limited 8-performance engagement staged by Stoppard himself.

Then there was the Stoppard program of two one-acts *(Dogg's Hamlet, Cahoot's Macbeth)* which literally spoke its own language. In the first, schoolboys invent a language by giving new meanings to common English words. It is not slang or gibberish, but the words have new equivalents: "Cretinous pig-faced twit" means "What time is it?", while "Afternoon, Squire" is a schoolboy's insult. Anyhow, they played *Hamlet* highlights in this "language," which after a while took on a weird eloquence of its own. The second piece, *Cahoot's Macbeth* was a play-within-a-play, dedicated to the Czechoslovakian dramatist Pavel Kohout. It is about a government raid on a Czech Living Room Theater troupe's performance of *Macbeth*. These theater folk, forbidden to work in public, offer their services for performances in private homes.

Thirdly, Stoppard brought to these shores his *Night and Day,* a conventional melodrama in conventional English about the press coverage of an African uprising, with a diplomat (Joseph Maher) and a newsman in confrontation with an impulsive black leader (ClarenceWilliams III), observed by the diplomat's wife (Maggie Smith) in a role curiously detached from the main business of the play. As Pinter chose to reverse time in *Betrayal,* Stoppard chose to reverse style in *Night and Day,* a unique straightforward play from a notorious curve-ball artist.

Another import that resists categorizing was the Canadian *Billy Bishop Goes to War*—is it a play, is it a musical, is it a virtuoso specialty act? Well in either or all cases it was certainly Superman, with Eric Peterson giving a superhuman performance in 17 roles ranging from the quick sketch of a female night club singer to the fully developed characterization of Billy Bishop. Bishop was in life and onstage the World War I flying ace who entered the fray as a prank, like a naughty boy, and emerged a 72-kill ace, seen here as shaken by the conflicting emotions aroused by the horrible excitement of man-to-man combat in the air. The script by John Gray (who also provided the piano accompaniment for his own musical numbers and an occasional comment on events) is so constructed that it didn't absolutely have to be, as it is, almost a one-man show. Other actors could have played some of the characters in confrontation with Billy Bishop, but certainly no better than Peterson played all of them, male and female, pompous and frightened, in a dazzling display.

Brian Clark's effort to change his *Whose Life Is It Anyway?* from a play about a male victim who prefers easeful death to a life of permanent total paralysis, to a play about a female victim, ditto, was entirely successful. So was Mary Tyler Moore's valiant, special Tony Award-winning performance in it, as she adventured out from behind that TV screen into live theater. She conveyed a shade less bitterness but a shade more agony than Tom Conti in his memorable performance in the same part last season. Miss Moore's conquest of this new world was undeniable, and the play proved as moving as before with the sexes of the victim, the sympathetic doctor (here a male played by James Naughton) and the lawyer (here a woman played by Susan Kellermann) reversed under the direction, again, of Michael Lindsay-Hogg.

With Laurence Olivier's direction, Franco Zeffirelli's design, Joan Plowright in the lead and a successful London run behind it, Eduardo de Filippo's *Filumena* aroused a great many more expectations than it could fulfill with a series of situation-comedy episodes in the life of a domineering Italian family man (Frank Finlay) whose mistress of long standing has decided it's time he married her. This was in a sense the second time around for the de Filippo comedy, which appeared on Broadway in an F. Hugh Herbert adaptation entitled *The Best House in Naples* for 3 performances the season of 1956–57.

The Argentinian production of the French script *Heartaches of a Pussycat* was good to look at, with characters (in an archly stylized memoir of a mid-19th century femme fatale) dressed as animals in imaginative costumes and masks, the former designed by Claudio Gastine, the latter by Rostislav Doboujinsky after an 1843 work of the French illustrator J.J. Grandville. A Canadian play *Of the Fields, Lately* by David French presented the kind of father-son relationship recently seen in *"Da"*, but to only moderate effect. Two British scripts, *Once a Catholic* (about a girls' school) and *Censored Scenes From King Kong* (a sort of pastiche of the famous movie) made visits to Broadway that were appropriately brief.

On the musical scene, an import from the London stage, *A Day in Hollywood/A Night in the Ukraine,* was right up there with *Sugar Babies* at the top of the heap of a dozen productions. Both of these were heavily overlaid with show-biz nostalgia, *Sugar Babies* recreating some of the old burlesque routines with Mickey Rooney and Ann Miller in the foreground, *Hollywood/Ukraine* with an ensemble cast in a two-parter, the first part paying homage to old movies and the second imitating a Marx Brothers comedy's situations, characters and style. Tommy Tune's direction of *Hollywood/Ukraine* in this American production (particularly in its first segment, an intricate intercutting of old-movie memories, with a Graumann's Chinese Theater theme) and Ernest Flatt's of the saucy and ebullient girlie and baggy pants routines were more than impeccable; they were inspired. So were the script treatments of the burlesque material by Ralph G. Allen and the Nelson Eddy screen era by Dick Vosburgh. So were the performances by Mickey Rooney—proving once again, as if he needed to, that he is one of the very best actor-performers of our time—and by the *Hollywood/Ukraine* ensemble, in particular Priscilla Lopez as Harpo and Stephen James in various guises. Both *Sugar Babies* and *Hollywood/Ukraine* built their scores upon the solid rock of old numbers of their eras and genres, the latter salted with some new ones composed by Frank Lazarus. Give *Sugar Babies* a shade of superiority for script, *Hollywood/Ukraine* for direction, and you have an approximation of their relative delights. Otherwise, we wouldn't dare to choose between them as evenings of exceptionally entertaining Broadway musical theater.

The 1940s Radio Hour, written and directed by Walton Jones, was another nostalgic re-run, also with a score of fondly remembered numbers, and also a standout of the season. Here again was a fine ensemble re-enacting without intermission and almost within its own actual time one of those radio variety programs beamed enthusiastically from the Hotel Astor. Stanley Lebowsky supervised and directed the music and played the leader of the orchestra onstage. Josef Sommer as the host ran to and fro collecting his performers including Jeff Keller (playing a crooner who reminded us a lot of young Frank what's-his-name) and Dee Dee Bridgewater. Arny Freeman played the stage doorman with whom it all began and ended—the radio show right on time, the Broadway run of this superior production much too soon.

Jim Dale in the title role of *Barnum* and Gregory Hines as Scrooge in the shorter-lived *Comin' Uptown* were two of the musical season's prime attractions. Both their shows were production-heavy, the former with carnival scenes in a musical biography of the famous impresario, the latter with a brightly-colored Robin Wagner stage representation of Harlem in an adaptation of *A Christmas Carol* casting Scrooge as a Harlem slumlord. Both leading players leapt upon the stage and played as though celebrating the sheer vitality of their vehicles, which in the case of both scores (*Barnum* by Cy Coleman and Michael Stewart, *Comin' Uptown* by Garry Sherman and Peter Udell) was justified. Not so in the case of both books, but the winning ways of the Messrs. Dale and Hines went a long way to make up for any deficiencies. So did those of Patti LuPone as Eva Peron in the Critics and Tony Award winner, *Evita,* with ferocity seething under the surface of her playing of the Argentine dictator's mistress, and with the show also owing much to the tightly-fastened Harold Prince direction and the choreography by Larry Fuller.

Performing and design were very much in harmony with the material in *King of Schnorrers,* a musical transfer from off Broadway, a folk tale of 18th century Sephardic beggars in London adapted and musicalized by Judd Woldin. Lloyd Battista as the king of the beggars and Sophie Schwab as his pretty daughter led the measures, appropriately costumed by Patricia Adshead, in compact but versatile Ed Wittstein settings. Phyllis Newman held the stage in the one-woman musical *The Madwoman of Central Park West,* playing a modern folk character, the housewife who would be a career woman (or vice versa), coping staunchly with life in New York as described in the book by Miss Newman and Arthur Laurents and as reflected in a dozen or so songs by a number of major composers and lyricists.

Style was a principal element of Burt Shevelove's effort to transform Philip Barry's *Holiday* into the musical *Happy New Year* with a polished book about life and love in a Fifth Avenue mansion, with the interpolation of Cole Porter songs, and with narrative comment by John McMartin detached from the action but giving it an extra dimension with wry observation. This show didn't quite succeed in its intentions; nor did Vinnette Carroll's *But Never Jam Today,* nor the special-interest shows *Got Tu Go Disco* and *Reggae,* nor *Musical Chairs,* in which the cast was an "audience" watching the show.

Joining the throng in memory lane this season were several Bertolt Brecht and Kurt Weill retrospectives on and off Broadway, the most tenacious being *A Kurt Weill Cabaret,* a revue with Martha Schlamme and Alvin Epstein presenting many Berlin and a few Broadway songs. It began as a kind of late show at the Bijou Theater after performances of *Mummenschanz* and then returned in May for a limited run on its own. Another revue, *Live From New York,* was tailored by and for Gilda Radner in a series of her characterizations. In the spring, Harry Blackstone evoked the memory of his magical father, recreating his stage effects in *Blackstone,* billed as a "Magnificent Musical Magic Show." Personal appearances on the other side of the thin line between the revue and the concert included record-smashing stints by Frank Sinatra at the Metropolitan Opera House and Carnegie Hall; Bette Midler in a context called *Bette! Divine Madness* at the Majestic in December; Bruce Forsyth for 6 performances at the Winter Garden in June; and Grand Ol' Opry at the St. James for 2 performances in August.

Both the Radio City Music Hall Entertainment Center (a.k.a. the Music Hall) and Town Hall edged into the Broadway act this season. The Music Hall offered a king-sized stage version of the Walt Disney movie *Snow White and the Seven Dwarfs,* followed by *A Magnificent Christmas Spectacular* and then a full-length tribute to its longtime star performers, *A Rockette Spectacular,* with Ginger Rogers as a guest star. Town Hall came on stream with *Black Broadway,* a backward look at great show-biz moments of its title in a revue-concert form. It also found room for the booking of the Yiddish musical comedy *Rebecca—the Rabbi's Daughter* with book by William Siegel, music by Alexander Lustig and Abraham Ellstein and lyrics by Lustig and Jacob Alperin.

Off Broadway

More than three dozen new American playscripts, fewer than a double handful of musicals, solid blocks of foreign plays in English, revues and specialities, a mountainous heap of revivals—that was the off-Broadway season of 1979–80 (see the one-page summary accompanying this report). With its organized repertory and new-play production, in some instances stimulated by subsidies along the blurring edge of the line dividing its professional activities from off off Broadway's "showcasing" (also often professional, but invariably experimental), an off-Broadway season is sometimes more activity than productivity. This was certainly the case this season. Judging by its successes rather than by its volume (and it is the successes, the transfers to Broadway and other hits, by which an off-Broadway season is judged these days), it was a year of slim pickings until the eleventh hour, of only two Best Plays, *Home* and *Table Settings,* compared with six last year and five the year before. It is true that an off-Broadway upstart, Lanford Wilson's *Talley's Folly,* stole the Broadway show including the Critics Circle and Pulitzer awards—but that was a leftover from last year when another transfer from off Broadway, *The Elephant Man,* also dominated the scene.

The record reveals that 1979-80 production of new scripts did not quite equal last year's bumper crop but was certainly a voluminous harvest: 58 productions including 39 American straight plays, 7 musicals and 12 foreign works in English, as compared with 38-15-11 last year and 28-9-6 and 22-11-9 in the seasons immediately preceding. The production of revues off Broadway soared from one in 1978–79 to 11 in 1979–80, among which there were several palpable hits. Revival production edged up from 35 to 44, counting the 12-month LOOM operetta season.

Samm-Art Williams's *Home* was the year's banner new script, not only for the organization that produced it, The Negro Ensemble Company, but also for off-Broadway as a whole. The play was mostly in the first person singular, the person being Cephus Miles, a black and beautiful character beautifully played by Charles Brown, who loves his life on a Southern farm with his Godfearing family and pleasure-loving friends. When events begin to overwhelm Cephus, first plucking him out of his cocoon for the Vietnam War draft (which he refuses and so is sent to prison) and then exposing his unarmed personality to the slings and arrows of big city life up North, Cephus doesn't suspect God of abandoning him, he merely assumes that He must be on vacation in, say, Miami. The various women in Cephus's life were personified by two actresses, L. Scott Caldwell and Michele Shay, while the men he encounters are pictured in his mind's eye, as are the locales in the appropriately malleable setting by Felix E. Cochren. Under the direction of Dean Irby downtown and Douglas Turner Ward (NEC's artistic director) when the play moved uptown for a Broadway run and a Tony nomination, *Home* was small in size but big in scope, a statement of love, courage, faith and good humor. NEC devoted the remainder of its season to a pair of scripts by Dan Owens, *The Michigan* and *Lagrima Del Diablo,* one-acts by Ali Wadud and Roy R. Kuljian and a series of readings of works in progress by members of its playwrights' workshop.

Off-Broadway's other 1979–80 Best Play, the independent production (arisen from the Playwrights Horizons OOB workshop) *Table Settings* also used the stage in an unconventional manner to put the commonplace in a new perspective. James Lapine both wrote and directed this extraordinary play, which was as one-track-minded in centering its attention on a single object, the dining table, as *Home* was in its attention to a single character. *Table Settings* related all the emotional tangles of three generations of a family, from Jewish matriarch to hip sub-teen ager, to the eating rituals at home and in restaurants, exaggerating them for the comedy effect of a perceptive cartoon strip. Where *Home* called for an overpowering central performance, *Table Settings* called for an ensemble to work like a carefully rehearsed acrobatic team on the author's startling fancies, under his agile direction. This they did, bringing each and every character into full focus, in one of the truly imaginative and redeeming entertainments of the off-Broadway year.

Dennis McIntyre's *Modigliani* was another strong script in independent production, with Jeffrey De Munn as the painter in his last year, discouraged and in surrender to his own and his Montparnasse friends' sensual impulses. A standout foreign script in independent production was *Class Enemy* from the London stage, a Nigel Williams drama of unruly students further agitated by an unregenerate ringleader in a state school in a problem section of South London. Further to independent off-Broadway's credit was a new John Ford Noonan play about a prim Westchester housewife whose already disintegrating life is invaded by a pushy, flamboyant new neighbor just moved in from Texas. *A Coupla White Chicks Sitting Around Talking* is its perplexing title. Why white? They are, but why the racist identification? And why the sexist "chicks"? There's nothing of racism or sexism in the play, which explores the characters of the two women, clearly delineated on the stage by Eileen Brennan (the Texan) and Susan Sarandon (the housewife) under Dorothy Lyman's direction. The husbands never appear, but exert an important influence on the play's emotional tides. These run strong through what is certainly a fully developed two-character script, with the accent on character.

Other independent straight-play efforts of note off Broadway this season included Ken Eulo's *The Frankenstein Affair,* paralleling events in Mary Shelley's marriage with those in her celebrated novel; the limited engagement in English translation of the modern Chinese play *Peking Man* by Cao Yu, presenting a family trying to preserve some of China's old ways in the new era; Louis La Russo II's *Marlon Brando Sat Right Here,* a moody slice of life in a Hoboken bar *after* all the excitement of filming *On the Waterfront* was over and the movie captains and kings had departed; and a collision of generations and attitudes

The 1979–80 Season off Broadway

PLAYS (39)

Buried Child
(return engagement)
Public Theater:
Spell #7
Mercier & Camier
Tongues & Savage/Love
The Art of Dining
Sorrows of Stephen
Salt Lake City Skyline
Marie and Bruce
After the Rise
Manhattan Theater Club:
Losing Time
Mass Appeal
The Office Murders
American Place:
Letters Home
Rumstick Road
Ladyhouse Blues
Circle Repertory:
Reunion
Innocent Thoughts,
Harmless Intentions
Back in the Race
Phoenix:
The Winter Dancers
The Trouble With Europe
Save Grand Central
Second Avenue Rag
Modigliani

The Frankenstein Affair
Negro Ensemble:
The Michigan
HOME
Lagrima del Diablo
Companions of the Fire
& Big City Blues
Altar Boys
Holeville
Fugue in a Nursery
TABLE SETTINGS
These Men
My Great Dead Sister
The Man in 605
Marlon Brando Sat Right
Here
*A Coupla White Chicks
Sitting Around Talking*
Crimes and Dreams
News Boy

MUSICALS (7)

Not Tonight, Benvenuto
King of Schnorrers
God Bless You, Mr.
Rosewater
The Housewives' Cantata
Changes
Fourtune
It's Wilde

REVUES (11)

Sky High
Scrambled Feet
Big Bad Burlesque
The All Night Strut
Potholes
One Mo' Time
Paris Lights
Shakespeare's Cabaret
Blues in the Night
Song Night in the City
Tintypes

SPECIALTIES (8)

*Gertrude Stein Gertrude
Stein Gertrude Stein*
B.B.
Woody Guthrie
Paris Was Yesterday
Ah! Or the First
Washerwoman Cantata
Jane White Who . . . ?
An Evening With W.S.
Gilbert
The Haggadah

FOREIGN PLAYS IN ENGLISH (12)

Wine Untouched
Emigrés
The Jail Diary of Albie
Sachs
Flying Blind
Class Enemy
Shout Across the River
Chelsea:
Monsieur Amilcar
Dona Rosita: While She
Waits
Peking Man
BAM:
Barbarians
The Marriage Dance
Mecca

REVIVALS (44)

Roundabout:
Family Business
Little Eyolf
The Dark at the Top of
the Stairs
A Month in the Country
The Blood Knot
Heartbreak House
LOOM:
(9 Gilbert & Sullivan
operettas in repertory)
Ten Nights in a Barroom
Mlle. Modiste
The Merry Widow
Babes in Toyland

LOOM (cont'd):
The Fortune Teller
Naughty Marietta
Happy Days
The Days Between
Delacorte:
Coriolanus
Othello
CSC:
Cuchulain
The Cavern
Doctor Faustus
Don Juan
The Merchant of Venice
Circle Repertory:
Hamlet
Mary Stuart
Manhattan Theater Club:
Endgame
Biography
Production Company:
Hosanna
The Guardsman
BAM:
The Winter's Tale
Johnny on a Spot
He & She
The Irish Hebrew Lesson &
Guests of the Nation
Journey's End
Acting Company:
Elizabeth I
The White Devil
*Mother Courage
and Her Children*

Plays listed in CAPITAL LETTERS have been designated Best Plays of 1979–80.
Plays listed in *italics* were still running after June 1, 1980.

personified by a garrulous old writer and an aspiring young poet in Alan Gross's *The Man in 605.*

It was easy to spot the peaks in the range of 1979–80 organizational productions. The Manhattan Theater Club's *Mass Appeal* by Bill C. Davis was a two-character encounter between a wine-sipping, rather self-satisfied priest (charmingly portrayed with the wisp of an Irish brogue by Milo O'Shea) and a young would-be priest (Eric Roberts) moved by a sincerely inquiring, rebellious spirit to upset his elders and indeed the whole diocese. The dramatic pattern is similar to *A Coupla White Chicks*—a forceful personality intrudes into the ordered existence of another and upsets its precarious equilibrium—and it worked as well here in Davis's play about church matters as it did in Noonan's about housewifery, under the accomplished direction of the accomplished actress Geraldine Fitzgerald.

Another organizational standout this season was the Quaigh Theater's *Mecca* by British playwright Ted (who formerly billed himself as E.A.) Whitehead, also directed by an accomplished actor, Kevin Conway. Conflict between East and West was only one of the confrontations in this tale of tourists on Morocco holiday; sexual, economic and age differences also came under this play's caustic scrutiny. The Theater Guild picked up the Quaigh's OOB showcase and test-ran it this season in a 32-performance limited off-Broadway engagement, to be followed next season by a Broadway production. The other major offering on the Quaigh's 1980 schedule was *The Office Murders,* a melodrama by Martin Fox.

Under the ANTA umbrella, with Richmond Crinkley as producer, the sun was still shining on the organization that last year gave us *The Elephant Man.* This year it provided another look at Kevin O'Morrison's touching *Ladyhouse Blues* (previously produced off Broadway in a limited engagement), a highly-charged study of a household full of women awaiting a loved one's return from the wars, with an admirable five-actress ensemble under Tony Giordano's direction. And ANTA's finale was another of the season's glowingly nostalgic events: *Tintypes,* a charming assembly of songs and sketches of the Theodore Roosevelt era.

Downtown, Joseph Papp's Public Theater bubbled with experimentation and high hopes, with few of the latter fully realized in a long list of productions including *Sorrows of Stephen* by Peter Parnell (the contemporary life and loves of a not very persuasive young man), *Marie and Bruce* by Wallace Shawn (starring Louise Lasser, with the distinguished cartoonist Frank Modell in his acting debut, in a slice of modern New York liberated life), a new Ntozake Shangé choreopoem *(Spell #7),* a new Sam Shepard *(Tongues),* a new Thomas Babe *(Salt Lake City Skyline)* and a new Elizabeth Swados *(The Haggadah).* Uptown, American Place called it a season with Rose Leiman Goldemberg's adaptation of Sylvia Plath's *Letters Home* and two musicals, one *(Paris Lights)* a revue adapted from the writings of the American-in-Paris celebrities of the 1920s. The Phoenix devoted itself to a five-play program of new American and foreign scripts, among them the theater debut of still another distinguished *New Yorker* cartoonist, William Hamilton, as the author of still another script about the lives and loves of the modern young partygoing set, *Save Grand Central.* Circle Repertory kept its franchise with revivals, with David Mamet's program of one-act plays *Reunion* and with Milan Stitt's new full-length *Back in the Race,* a confrontation of old-fashioned Puritan philosophies with modern values and imperatives. Chelsea Theater Center sent its distinguished *Strider* over to Broadway and meanwhile continued to do its thing on West 43d Street with limited engagements of two adaptations of scripts by foreign authors: the French play *Monsieur Amilcar* and Garcia Lorca's *Dona Rosita: While She Waits.* The Dodger Theater's short limited-engagement season at the Brooklyn Academy of Music included a translation of Slawomir Mrozek's *Emigrés;* a sinister cartoon of terror in modern America by Jeff Wanshel, *Holeville;* and a Bread and Puppet Theater production, *Ah! Or the First Washerwoman Cantata.*

The season at the Harold Clurman Theater on 42d Street's Theater Row was headlined by a non-event: the production in previews only of Arthur Miller's new play about Depression trauma, *The American Clock,* The Clurman also mounted an Irish play about the current troubles, Bill Morrison's *Flying Blind,* and two other entries which were right in step with the 1979–80 crowd: a one-woman rendition by Celeste Holm of Janet Flanner's nostalgic reminiscence *Paris Was Yesterday* (adapted by Paul Shyre) and a two-character comedy of female confidences, Mayo Simon's *These Men*, staged by the distinguished acress Zoe Caldwell. A group new to the off-Broadway scene, The Production Company, with Norman René as artistic director, presented a variegated schedule of revivals—*The Guardsman* and the Canadian play *Hosanna*—plus a new comedy of family relationships, *My Great Dead Sister* by Arthur Bicknell, and a musical revue, *Blues in the Night,* a reverie of two women and their blue memories in a sleazy hotel room.

Off Broadway had little luck in finding an audience for its book musicals this season, with the single exception of *King of Schnorrers,* in which Judd Woldin assembled an attractive musical package for his tale of a masterful Sephardic beggar (Lloyd Battista), his pretty but willful daughter (Sophie Schwab in a particularly appealing performance) and the persistent and resourceful youth who woos her. Grover Dale's direction and choreography were as outgiving as Patricia Adshead's colorful costumes, in a show which merited more attention that it received when it moved to Broadway for a short visit. The year's other passing book-musical fancies included a version of Kurt Vonnegut's *God Bless You, Mr. Rosewater;* a tale of three sisters in *The Housewives' Cantata,* with book by William Holtzman, music by Mira J. Spektor and lyrics by June Siegel; a tale of two couples coming together and breaking up in a Danny Apolinar-Addy Fieger effort entitled *Changes;* a tale of two couples juggling their sexual identities while singing four-part harmonies in *Fourtune;* and a pair of backward glances at the lives of Benvenuto Cellini and Oscar Wilde.

It was a great year for revues off Broadway, with a high success ratio in a generous group of 11 productions. In one part of the Village Gate, the John Driver-Jeffrey Haddow show *Scrambled Feet* was giving show business a going over, while in another part of the same establishment Vernel Bagneris's black vaudeville *One Mo' Time* was holding forth in style. As previously noted, Richmond Crinkley brought in a bounteous collection of at least 50 numbers of the ragtime era in the sprightly and melodic Mary Kyte conception *Tintypes.* The Colonnades came up with *Shakespeare's Cabaret,* a successful revue concept with selections from the Bard's lyrics set to music by Lance Mulcahy. Elinor Guggenheimer, former Commissioner of Consumer Affairs for New York City, aired some pet peeves in a revue called *Potholes*, while Fran Charnas's *The All Night Strut*, a collection of songs from the era between the big wars, found adherents in a brief visit. Music *(Sky High),* burlesque *(Big Bad Burlesque),* the blues *(Blues in the Night)* and romance *(Song Night in the City)* were other subjects under revue treatment off Broadway this year.

The specialty list provided one of the most effective 1979–80 theater evenings in New York: *Gertrude Stein Gertrude Stein Gertrude Stein,* with Pat Carroll invoking the person and spirit of the great writer in an outstanding one-woman performance of what was billed as "a one-character play" by Marty Martin. The great British operetta author was impersonated songs and all by John Wolfson in his *An Evening With W.S. Gilbert,* while on other stages Tom Taylor put together a one-man portrait of Woody Guthrie, and Jane White simply presented her versatile self in the musical autobiography called *Jane White Who? . . .*

As usual in recent years, the 1979–80 off-Broadway season was hugely and admirably augmented by a spate of revival productions, taken up in the next chapter of this report. Among the new works there seemed to be an inordinately large amount of wasted effort even for an experimental arena, particularly in the area of organizational production. Artistic directors were distracted, perhaps, by offstage economic and/or social problems, or were simply having an off year. What 1979–80 *did* achieve, however, was first-time or added recognition for the group of authors who provided us with *Home, Table Settings, Modigliani, Class Enemy, A Coupla White Chicks Sitting Around Talking, Mass Appeal* and *Mecca.* Their game was worth the candle, sputtering and all.

Revivals on and off Broadway

The 1979–80 theater season in New York was a parade of revivals as good or better than their original productions—or so it seemed. Certainly Paul Osborn's 1939 play *Morning's at Seven* was one of the biggest hits of the Broadway season, with an immensely appealing ensemble cast under the warmth-and-humor-laden, Tony Award-winning direction of Vivian Matalon. Making a marvelously detailed and harmonious group portrait of four sisters and their families leading their closely interknit but sometimes troubled lives in adjoining back yards were these nine wonderful performers: Nancy Marchand, Maureen O'-Sullivan, Elizabeth Wilson, Teresa Wright (the four sisters), Maurice Copeland, Richard Hamilton, Gary Merrill (husbands), David Rounds (son and nephew) and Lois de Banzie (fiancee). In this version, the play's period was moved backward from its own time (1939) to the 1920s, increasing its advantages of nostalgia in the style not only of the performances but also in the look of the show: the double back porch environment designed by William Ritman and the Linda Fisher costumes. *Morning's at Seven* is an ode to human nature and some of its ways of love. It had the stature of a new play not only in respect to the skill with which it was revived but also in reality, because very few theatergoers even noticed it during its short original run. One of those who did was Burns Mantle, who selected it as one of the Best Plays of the 1939–40 volume and noted in his review of the season that it "made many friends but was not sturdy enough to meet the musical comedy competition. The play is herein included to prove how sensitively written it is, and how pleasant its gentle character humor."

Another Best Plays commentator, Garrison P. Sherwood, seemed a bit taken by surprise when he wrote of its only previous New York revival in the 1955–56 volume: "Proscenium Productions did remarkably well with a revival of *Morning's at Seven.*" Now, in 1979–80, we were all taken by one of the pleasantest surprises of this or any New York theater season.

Another comedy which received even less attention on Broadway (4 performances) at about the same time (1942) was *Johnny on a Spot*, revived this year in BAM Theater Company repertory, in a production that made New York theater audiences sit up and take notice. A Charles MacArthur script about political chicanery, in a style reminiscent of the same author's *The Front Page*, it was directed by Edward Cornell for apparently more than it was worth in the original. This Brooklyn acting company under the artistic direction of David Jones and Arthur Penn planted both feet firmly on the scene in its first repertory season with the MacArthur play, plus new looks at Shakespeare's seldom-seen *The Winter's Tale* and Rachel Crothers's 1920 play *He & She*, plus the first New York productions of record of Maxim Gorky's 1905 *Barbarians* (about the effect of the coming of the railroad to a small Russian community) and short works by Bertolt Brecht *(The Wedding)* and Georges Feydeau *(The Purging)* under the portmanteau title *The Marriage Dance*.

Shaw's caricature of an armaments manufacturer and his family in *Major Barbara* received a precisely calibrated staging by Stephen Porter, in exact degrees of irony portrayed by Circle in the Square's outstanding cast including Philip Bosco as the debonair and persistent merchant of death, Laurie Kennedy and Nicolas Surovy as the pair of young do-gooders and Jon De Vries in a grimy personification of the undeserving poor. *Watch on the Rhine* was redone at the Long Wharf in New Haven under Arvin Brown's direction and then brought to Broadway, with Harris Yulin and George Hearn acting out Lillian Hellman's famous living room confrontation between rightist and anti-Nazi. In a Broadway production housed in an off-Broadway theater, American Place, Oliver Hailey's eight-year-old *Father's Day* was one of the scripts that gained strength in revival with its orchestrated attitudes of three divorced women and the husbands who rejoin them for a special holiday occasion, including an indelible caricature by Susan Tyrrell of the most outspoken of the three.

All the way off Broadway, Gene Feist and Michael Fried mounted their customary season of first-rate revivals at the Roundabout, including a rendering of William Inge's *The Dark at the Top of the Stairs* by John Stix (who also staged an original-cast return engagement of *Family Business* for Roundabout and the revival of Arthur Miller's *The Price* starring Fritz Weaver); Turgenev's *A Month in the Country* with Tammy Grimes and Farley Granger, and Ibsen's seldom-seen *Little Eyolf*.

In a quite different vein, Light Opera of Manhattan also did its tuneful thing again and again in 15 operetta revival programs from *Ten Nights in a Barroom* through Gilbert and Sullivan to a new LOOM production of Victor Herbert's *The Fortune Teller*. Shakespeare was perhaps not as conspicuously present as in recent seasons, but he was present in Central Park with *Coriolanus* and *Othello*; in Classic Stage Company's repertory with *The Merchant of Venice*; in BAM repertory with *The Winter's Tale* (as previously mentioned); in a Circle Repertory production of *Hamlet*, directed by Marshall W. Mason with William Hurt in the title role (in tandem with a Mason-directed production of Schiller's *Mary Stuart*); and on Broadway with *Richard III* as a vehicle for Al Pacino. A feature of the abovementioned CSC's repertory season under Christopher Martin's direction was the presentation in toto of Yeats's five-play study of the Celtic hero Cuchulain, an American first. Anouilh's *The Cavern* in the Lucienne Hill translation, Marlowe's *Doctor Faustus* and Molière's *Don Juan* completed the CSC season.

Among modern playwrights, Samuel Beckett was well represented by New York Shakespeare Festival productions of *Happy Days* and the Frederick Neumann adaptation of the novel *Mercier & Camier*, plus a Manhattan Theater Club staging of *Endgame*; Athol Fugard by the Roundabout's *The Blood Knot*; Robert Anderson by the New York premiere of his 1965 play *The Days Between*; Paul Foster by the Acting Company's *Elizabeth I*. S.N. Behrman's blithe *Biography* was done by Manhattan Theater Club, Bertolt Brecht's brooding *Mother Courage and Her Children* by New York Shakespeare Festival, adapted by Ntozake Shangé as a post-American-Civil-War sociological study with an ex-slave heroine and a black cast. Remembrance of battles past a continent away was provided by an off-Broadway revival of R.C. Sherriff's touching World War I drama *Journey's End*, the first since 1939, as well as the Colonnades' program of two one-act dramatizations of the 1921 Irish troubles, *The Irish Hebrew Lesson* by Wolf Mankowitz and *Guests of the Nation* by Neil McKenzie from a Frank O'Connor story.

Last and most in point of conspicuous presence there was the elephantine march of the Broadway musical revivals, beginning with an elaborate *Peter Pan* designed by Peter Wolf (scenery) and Bill Hargate (costumes), with an appealing Sandy Dennis performance in the title role—and, of course, flying by Foy. Frank Loesser's *The Most Happy Fella* made its stately way across the Broadway stage with the opera star Giorgio Tozzi projecting the songs in a Tony-nominated starring performance. *Oklahoma!* played the Palace all season in an attractive copy of the original staged by William Hammerstein, and an elegantly costumed (by Sigrid Insull) *Canterbury Tales* had but a short life at the Rialto, the movie house newly reclaimed for legit shows. Best of the musical reincarnations was *West Side Story,* still vibrating with its Shakespearean undertones and its modern street-smart overtones, still a prize package of high drama crammed with unforgettable musical numbers, cast rather too blandly (with the exception of Debbie Allen and Hector Jaime Mercado) but directed by Jerome Robbins and Gerald Freedman striving for a spirited duplication of the original.

Such was the revival year of 1979–80—a bounty of more than 50 productions on and off Broadway, adding up to the theatergoing opportunity of, say, a dozen regional theaters, making New York far and away the greatest repertory town, not merely of them all, but of a lot of them put together.

Offstage

All year long, actors were in the limelight offstage as well as on, through the actions of their union, Actors' Equity Association. Equity was at odds with the 50-theater Off-Off Broadway Alliance (OOBA) over the remuneration of actors in this constantly fermenting (even without Equity's yeasty behavior) area of experimental stage production. Equity actors are permitted to take roles in OOBA's non-Equity productions for limited periods of time in what have come to be known as "showcases," under exactly specified circumstances by special arrangement between the theaters and the union.

As the fall came around, the time for the quickening of OOBA stages was at hand. But many of the planned showcases (the "showcase" being the top of OOBA's production line) were postponed pending some resolution of the dispute with Equity. This was now centering on OOBA's insistence on a flat rate of pay for Equity actors, and Equity asking for a percentage of the theaters' total gross in an employment code declared in effect (though resisted by many OOBA managements) as of Sept. 1.

In January, the dispute still unresolved, OOBA appealed to Equity's rank and file to ask their executive secretary, Donald Grody, and others in the Equity leadership to hold a special meeting to settle the matter. A special Equity membership meeting to consider Equity-OOBA relations was scheduled for May 16.

Meanwhile, an equally serious and possibly even more consequential dispute was growing between Equity and the playwrights who license their new scripts for OOBA showcases. The so-called "showcase code," unilaterally recognized by Equity without any formal discussion or negotiation with the authors, provided that Equity actors creating roles in these showcase productions were entitled either to employment in future productions of the same script (in movies and TV as well as onstage) or, if not, some sort of financial compensation. Playwrights were asked to sign this showcase code as a prerequisite for the appearance of Equity actors in their works, and they were to be held responsible for seeing to it (even to the point of paying out of their own usually empty pockets) that this lien against their script was indeed honored.

Authors who signed the Equity showcase code discovered that, for example, a regional theater producer who wished to put on a previously-showcased script might decide not to do so when he found that he would be committed to employing a specific set of actors, paying their salaries and travel expenses, or a comparable indemnity if he insisted on casting his own people. Under the Equity showcase code, authors were thus placed in peril of losing productions; and obviously, OOBA producers would be affected, as authors became more and more reluctant to license their scripts for showcases—and this could mean less employment for actors.

The authors (whose Dramatists Guild is *not* a union but a craft guild, and therefore cannot behave with the aggressive collectivism of a union under the laws of the land) protested in individual outcries and warnings to each other against signing the Equity showcase code. Dramatists Guild President Stephen Sondheim summed up the dramatists' attitude in the Spring issue of their intercom, the *Dramatists Guild Quarterly*, when he characterized Equity's unilateral effort to impose the code as "dictatorial intimidation."

When the prearranged May 16 meeting of Equity's membership took place, the playwrights issue overshadowed the Equity-OOBA issue. According to *Variety*'s report of the meeting, the actors "recommended overwhelmingly that the union's showcase and non-profit funded theater codes be amended to state categorically that playwrights are not to be held accountable for payments to showcase casts when their plays are subsequently produced." With producers presumably continuing to be obligated by a showcase lien, it seemed likely that future production of showcased work would continue to be inhibited, and authors would continue to resist signing the Equity showcase code.

As for the flat rate vs. percentage dispute with OOBA, *Variety* reported that there was "a strong sense of support for the council-staff position that Equity deserves a 'fair share' of the income of these off-off-Broadway theaters, which rely primarily on public funding." After a whole year's controversy, it looked at season's end as though neither OOBA's nor the authors' differences with the actors' union were likely to be resolved any time soon. As of the end of May, Equity was taking up still another cudgel against unpaid staged readings by its members at the level above OOBA, in the off-Broadway theater.

Other problems with the employment of actors (a National Endowment survey concluded that one-third of all actors were unemployed during 1979) made offstage news this season. The largely non-Hispanic casting of 17 Hispanic characters in *Goodbye Fidel* raised the ire of minority actors, who picketed the theater and circulated handbills stating in part: "Originally no Hispanics were cast. After Actors' Equity forced management to reopen auditions, four Hispanics were cast in tiny roles," calling these "merely cosmetic changes" and arguing that "Every minority actor should be considered for every role" and "The artistic freedom of a director to cast according to his taste is unchallengeable *as long as it is moral*" (emphasis theirs). The show's management countered with its own handbill statement: "In casting *Goodbye Fidel,* we have excluded only actors whose talent, experience and suitability could not allow us to consider them." The controversy disappeared, unresolved, with the untimely end of the show.

Organizational determination expressed itself this season in a new three-year agreement between IATSE Local 1 (the stagehands) and the League of New York Theaters and Producers (the producers) calling for raises of 9, 8 and 7 per cent in succeeding years, with no material changes in the regulations governing the number of stagehands in each crew. ATPAM (the press agents and managers) also came to agreement with the League on a new three-year contract trading extra Sunday pay for salary increases of from $597 to $651 weekly, about 9 per cent, to be followed by raises of 9 and 10 per cent in subsequent years. ATPAM members re-elected Merle Debuskey their president and returned all other officers including Shirley Herz as chairman of the press agents' chapter. At Equity, all incumbent officers were re-elected, Theodore Bikel to his third term as president of the actors' union.

A major individual change in critics' assignments took place in midsummer, as the New York *Times* announced that Walter Kerr would move from Sunday back to his old job of daily reviewer, replacing Richard Eder in that influential post. In this new setup, Kerr avoids writing to a first-night deadline, covering in previews not more than two (or in exceptional circumstances three) shows a week, in self-made assignments, with the other *Times* theater reviews allotted to Mel Gussow and others. How does Kerr decide in advance which shows to cover? "I'll try to figure out which ones interest the reader most," he answered. "It's obviously a journalistic decision, but it's still guesswork. It's not just a matter of covering Broadway first—what the reader's interested in, or thinks he's interested in, comes first. I want to keep my eye on off Broadway too."

And then, there was a *Times* report that the poison of miking was continuing to spread through the body of the living theater, with this antithetical practise no longer largely confined to musicals but extending to straight plays in what is euphemistically labeled "sound reinforcement" at *I Ought To Be in Pictures*, *Romantic Comedy* and *Clothes for a Summer Hotel*. The prevailing attitude, according to one sound engineer, is "forget the purity and let the people hear," taking some of the pressure off the actors' historic obligation to make this happen. And in the matter of Federal subsidy for the arts the trend continues upward from microscopic to minuscule (compared to other civilized nations) at a snail's pace, the requested 1981 total arts endowment being $167,960,000, an increase of 8.8 per cent over the 1980 funding.

In the matter of prizegiving, a suggestion published by Dan Sullivan in the Los Angeles *Times* urged Pulitzer Prize people to take a new look at their venue. Sullivan points out that new-play production is no longer a local New York exclusive but has spread countrywide—"the energy is national"—and therefore the Pulitzer judges should consider new cross-country as well as New York plays for their prize. Sullivan found nothing in the Pulitzer rules to forbid this and declares: "Change is possible and necessary if it wants to become an American award and not just a local one."

Looking back on a theater season which itself placed so much of its emphasis on looking backward, we perceive an aura of self-satisfaction, of having run a good course under precarious circumstances, of a self-confident readiness to face whatever may come in 1980–81. Some seasons crash onto the shore like a breaking wave, exploding with imagination, thrusting the boundary higher and higher. One like 1979–80 is given to the recessive but no less essential phase of action, drawing in the creative forces, building up and up on itself until its own potential energy is ready to drive it forward once more. With new hits added to the holdovers, new talents to the old, and all that money flowing through the box offices, the 1979–80 theater season in New York was a good one, no doubt of that. The next pulsation of time and the next, as we see what grows from its accomplishments, will tell whether, if at all, it touched greatness.

Lee Roy Reams and ensemble in the Gower Champion dance number "We're in the Money!" in the musical *42nd Street*.

PHOTO BY MARTHA SWOPE

1980-81

FOR SOME MYSTERIOUS REASON, the New York theater took its first steps into the new decade in uncertain stride and with a ragged profile in the large and small playhouses alike. Did the inflationary surge in the price of theater tickets alter the mix of the audience? Did the damming-up of a creative tributary, off off Broadway, by playwrights' resistance to Equity's enforcement of a showcase code, result in a drying-up of the mainstream? Did a coincidence of mediocrity suddenly enervate a significant proportion of authors old and young, producers angeled and unangeled? Were any or all of these the underlying reason why the 1980–81 theater season in New York was one in which vigor was remarkably scarce and experience no warranty of success? We can only guess, but we know for certain that in 1980–81 some climatic influence was altering the very personality of the New York stage, and not for the better.

To consider these factors one at a time, the price of a top ticket to a Broadway show broke the double sawbuck barrier in 1980 and did not even pause respectfully at the $25 mark in 1981 on its way to the $35 top ($50 for house seats) at David Merrick's musical *42nd Street* and $30 at the straight play *Amadeus*—both Best Plays, to be sure. Inflation kept flooding the box office at every level, as Broadway attracted an all-time record week's gross of $4,886,970 on a 244,323 attendance the week of Jan. 3. By the end of the season, there was no ongoing new 1980–81 Broadway production that *wasn't* asking at least $25 for third row center on Saturday night. $30 was no longer unusual, *Woman of the Year* was venturing to join *42nd Street* up there at $35, and the *average* price of a Broadway ticket had risen from $15.49 in 1979–80 to $19.72 in 1980–81 according to *Variety's* estimate—about 27.5 per cent.

At those prices, a holdover like *Deathtrap* was a real bargain at a $17.50 top; and at those prices, it's not surprising that *Variety's* annual estimate of the total twelve-month Broadway gross soared to an unbelievable $194,481,091 for 1980–81, dwarfing last year's all-time record high of $143 million and wiping out of memory the seasons not so long ago when $50 million seemed an impossible dream. An additional 1980–81 road gross of almost $219 million brought the year's total income of Broadway productions to more than $413 million. At the same time, playing weeks (if ten shows play ten weeks, that's 100 playing weeks) climbed to a record 1,545, just topping last year's 1,541, and 1,472 the year before, with an additional 1,343 (almost the same as last year) on the road. What's importantly more, *Variety* estimated that Broadway attendance took a healthy jump this year to 10,822,324 from about 9.4 million and 9.1 million in the past two seasons, sharply reinforcing the upward trend.

There were slightly fewer new shows to attract these paying customers (see the one-page summary accompanying the next chapter of this report). Not counting specialties, there were 51 new Broadway productions in 1980–81, as compared with 58 last year. These included 14 revivals, so that the total number of new plays, musicals and revues amounted to 37 (including two return engagements and two transfers), as compared with 47 and 37 in the past two seasons. In the strange circumstances, a running show developed irresistable momentum, so that of the 14 longest-running Broadway shows as of June 1, 1980, 12 were still going

The 1980–81 Season on Broadway

PLAYS (18)

Passione
Division Street
Fifth of July
  (return engagement)
Tricks of the Trade
LUNCH HOUR
The American Clock
Mixed Couples
Frankenstein
To Grandmother's House
  We Go
Heartland
The Survivor
Lolita
Fools
Animals
THE FLOATING LIGHT
  BULB
Inacent Black
I Won't Dance
It Had To Be You

MUSICALS (11)

Your Arms Too Short to
  Box With God
  (return engagement)
It's So Nice To Be Civilized
Fearless Frank
42ND STREET
Charlie and Algernon
Perfectly Frank
Onward Victoria
Bring Back Birdie
Woman of the Year
Copperfield
The Moony Shapiro
  Songbook

REVUES (2)

Tintypes (transfer)
Sophisticated Ladies

FOREIGN PLAYS IN
ENGLISH (6)

The Suicide
A LIFE
A LESSON FROM ALOES
AMADEUS
Piaf
Rose

REVIVALS (14)

The Music Man
Circle in Square 1980:
  The Man Who Came to
  Dinner
Camelot
Circle in Square 1981:
  The Bacchae
John Gabriel Borkman
The Father
Brigadoon
Lincoln Center:
  The Philadelphia Story
  Macbeth
The Pirates of Penzance
  (transfer)
The Five O'Clock Girl
Jacques Brel
Can-Can
The Little Foxes

SPECIALTIES (12)

Radio City Music Hall:
  Manhattan Showboat
  America
Insideoutandallaround
  Shelley Berman
Banjo Dancing
Quick Change
Emlyn Williams as Charles
  Dickens
  (return engagement)
Shakespeare's Cabaret
  (transfer)
Broadway Follies
Aaah Oui Genty!
Passionate Ladies
Lena Horne
St. Mark's Gospel

HOLDOVERS WHICH
BECAME HITS IN
1980–81

Barnum
Children of a Lesser God
A Day in Hollywood/A
  Night in the Ukraine
Evita
I Ought To Be in Pictures
Peter Pan

Plays listed in CAPITAL LETTERS have been designated Best Plays of 1980–81.
Plays listed in *italics* were still running after May 31, 1981.
Plays listed in **bold face type** were classified as hits in *Variety*'s annual estimate published June 3, 1981.

a year later. And six of the holdovers—a very large number compared to recent seasons—achieved hit status and began making a profit during the twelve-month period.

$194 million gross . . . $50 top . . . to some extent this is mere numerology, not the prosperity it might appear to be. At these prices, a large part of the New York theater audience is transformed from theater-lovers to occasion-seekers. This makes a difference, affecting the kind of material that can be profitably produced. The splashy musical (*42nd Street*), the big star vehicle (*Woman of the Year* or *The Little Foxes*), the out-and-out comedy (*Lunch Hour*), the trumpeted revival (*The Pirates of Penzance*), the vaunted prizewinner (*Amadeus*) provide an *occasion* along with an evening of theater. They manage to attract celebrants and thrill-seekers at any price, while a finely-tuned instrument like *A Life,* written, acted and directed to perfection, dies of neglect where a few seasons ago it might have flourished, because mere theater-lovers can no longer afford often to attend a Broadway show unless they manage to arrive there by the reduced-price route of the TKTS booth in Duffy Square (and a good many of those near-capacity throngs at the $27.50 shows are there thanks to TKTS and other twofer arrangements).

Equity's attempt to establish and enforce an actor-favoring policy for showcase productions in New York and around the country (for which neither the actor nor the dramatist receives any pay) was inhibiting dramatists from offering their works for production off off Broadway because of conditions which might be placed upon their scripts in future, larger productions. The status of this confrontation as of season's end is outlined in the Offstage chapter of this report. We mention it here because it seems to have affected materially the quality of the whole theater season, like a plant whose roots are parched. We cannot of course point to any specific group of scripts witheld in 1980 or 1981 from experimental production because of the showcase code and which otherwise would have enhanced the season with their presence. We know, however, that many scripts *have* been withheld by their authors, inhibiting the creative flow at its source and most certainly affecting the quality of theater seeping up through the production levels toward Broadway.

Established dramatists experienced less competition from the upstarts than usual this season, but for the most part they appeared only at their second best, with all too many of them suffering the fate of the mighty Casey in *his* moment of greatest opportunity. An exception was Peter Shaffer with the first-rate play *Amadeus,* a drama of envy, imported from the London stage, very much the best play of the 1980–81 season. Hugh Leonard was also at the top of his form with *A Life,* a warm and winning elaboration of the character of Drumm, the Irish civil servant introduced in the previous Leonard Best Play *Da*. Others who kept the faith were Athol Fugard with a study of South African interracial friendship, *A Lesson from Aloes;* Jean Kerr with a merry marital whimsy, *Lunch Hour;* Brian Friel with yet another sensitive and mournful study of Irish character and endurance in *Translations;* and Woody Allen with Brooklyn variations on the theme of a domineering mother in *The Floating Light Bulb.*

While these authors did not fail us, many of them did not surprise us with their best, either. There were plenty of surprises at the other end of the scale among so-called "established" dramatists. High hopes for Arthur Miller's *The American Clock,* Edward Albee's *Lolita* and Neil Simon's *Fools* were unfulfilled, while elsewhere there was a succession of indifferent offerings by the otherwise promising likes of Albert Innaurato, Steve Tesich, Sidney Michaels, Joanna M.

Glass, Sam Shepard, Samm-Art Williams and Simon Gray.

Much the same was true of the musical side of New York production which took on momentum in August with David Merrick's admittedly fabulous *42nd Street,* adapted by Michael Stewart and Mark Bramble from the same source as the famous 1933 movie. At season's end it was still leading the parade, easily the best musical of 1980–81 and of course a Best Play selection. Especially disappointing was the failure of Michael Stewart's second effort, *Bring Back Birdie,* in collaboration with the distinguished Messrs. Lee Adams and Charles Strouse (the latter suffering the double jeopardy of the score for the short-lived *Charlie and Algernon*). *Woman of the Year,* the Lauren Bacall vehicle based by Peter Stone on the 1942 Katharine Hepburn-Spencer Tracy movie, with a John Kander-Fred Ebb score, was a creditable effort with some good results. Off Broadway, Stephen Sondheim's trunk songs were collected with distinction in *Marry Me a Little,* and James Lapine's ardent direction almost managed to make something resembling a silk purse out of the emotional postures in *March of the Falsettos.* With Broadway's two shiniest new musicals based on old movies, and with heavy reliance on hit revivals like *Camelot* and *The Pirates of Penzance,* the adventurous spirit was in notably short supply on the musical scene, even while money poured into some of the box offices.

Whatever it is that the theater lacks today, it doesn't seem to be backing. $2 million no longer sounded exorbitant for the production cost of a musical star vehicle like *Woman of the Year* or *Camelot*, nor did David Merrick balk at spending $2.5 million (*Variety* reported) to mount his nonesuch. A straight play in 1980–81 could easily cost more than $800,000 to put on, and the lavishly electrical production of *Frankenstein* failed to electrify the audience and closed after its opening night performance which reportedly cost its backers $2 million. While we're on the subject of costs, we should note that off Broadway too was raising its sights materially. It cost a hefty $175,000 to get *Cloud 9* on at the Theater de Lys, and as spring turned into summer it was playing there at an $18.50 top, a level achieved at the same time by the Al Pacino revival of *American Buffalo.*

Ongoing success stories kept backers interested in the New York theater, however. For example, according to *Variety* estimate, *Sugar Babies* had gilded its angels' haloes in the amount of $1-2 million and was earning a steady $70,000 a week on Broadway (but its road company dropped $1 million while folding in Boston). *Annie*'s various companies topped $100 million total gross (once an impossible dream for an entire Broadway season) and the show has paid a profit of going on $10 million on an $800,000 investment. *Deathtrap* has earned 355 per cent profit ($1,340,000 on $200,000), *They're Playing Our Song* $3.6 million on $800,000, *Children of a Lesser God* $865,000 on $400,000. The revival of *The Pirates of Penzance* was earning back its $1.3 million cost at the rate of $50,000 a week (and the movie rights to this conception of the golden Gilbert & Sullivan oldie were sold for $1.5 million).

Remember the 1967 off-Broadway musical *You're a Good Man Charlie Brown*? It has paid its backers $58 for every dollar invested, and still counting. Such sensational statistics provide a glossy facade for the theater's economic structure; but behind them, shows of quality struggle to survive. For example, the operating loss of the Broadway *Fifth of July* stood at $135,000 at season's end, and the two productions of the recent *Whose Life Is It Anyway?* totaled a $132,000 Broadway loss.

Broadway

The opening number of *42nd Street* is called "Audition." As the orchestra came to the end of its overture and the house lights dimmed to black, a sound like tapping feet penetrated the heavy curtain. Tapping feet? . . . Innocent rhythms of the 1930s musical theater? The curtain rose on the lighted stage, and the muffled tapping became the compelling unison beat of 40—count 'em—40 tap dancers "rehearsing" the musical-within-the-musical that is the subject of this book by Michael Stewart and Mark Bramble, subtitled "The Song and Dance Fable of Broadway." The fable began to revolve like a spinning wheel in a fairy tale, and the audience was soon lost in its enchantment.

This Broadway *42nd Street* was based on the same Bradford Ropes novel from which the well-remembered 1933 Dick Powell-Ruby Keeler-Warner Baxter-Beebe Daniels movie was taken, and it spins the same yarn. Producer-director Julian Marsh (Jerry Orbach) is trying to make a much-needed comeback with a show called *Pretty Lady* in New York rehearsal and Philadelphia tryout, aiming toward a big opening night at the "42nd Street Theater." Julian's difficulties are compounded by the economic strictures of the Depression and the temperament of his star Dorothy Brock (Tammy Grimes), who has persuaded an admirer to angel her show. The worst happens: the star breaks her ankle, so that neither she nor the show can go on. Philadelphia is now the graveyard of hopes and dreams: the sets are struck, Julian is broke, all the kids are out of work, the train is headed back to New York—but wait! That little chorus girl Peggy Sawyer (Wanda Richert), who was fired from the cast the other day, knows all the star's numbers. She can dance up a storm and sing back the blue sky, and her looks and personality are as naturally refreshing as a lilac bush in June. Perhaps . . . perhaps Julian can persuade her to come back and take over the leading role ("Come on along and listen to/The lullaby of Broadway"). The show could go one after all—on and on and on, as a new star is born together with a new smash hit.

This oft-told tale developed a kind of gee-whiz show-biz glamor and bravado on the silver screen in 1933, and it stood up to a clever satirical treatment in the 1960s off-Broadway musical *Dames at Sea*. Searching for a niche somewhere in between, *42nd Street* was reported to be in worse trouble during its tryout tour than the troubled show it was about, so that it seemed for a while that not even a Gower Champion (its director-choreographer and certainly its artistic mentor) or a David Merrick (its producer, a comeback story in himself) could find a way to save it. Their persistence paid off, however. The show found its place, not in awe or mockery, but in a dreamland combination of nostalgic affection and spectacular musical comedy technique: Broadway as fable, embellished by masters. It relished every wishful thought of its larger-than-life Broadway, where ambition knows no shame, talent is triumphant and the production numbers overflow the stage.

From the 40 tap dancers in the opening scene to the "42nd Street" finale, these numbers were a glorious procession of musical comedy entertainment devised by Gower Champion, a choreographic masterpiece of hoofing, left as a legacy after Champion's untimely death from leukemia on the afternoon of the show's debut. The director-choreographer's airborne cast glided through a shadow waltz, capered on a double staircase, shuffled off to Buffalo in a cutaway railroad car right out of a Busby Berkeley film and tapped on to the crescendo of the "42nd Street" finale, rivalling in imaginative movement just about anything in the modern musical theater including Champion's own *Bye Bye Birdie* and *Hello, Dolly.*

The Harry Warren-Al Dubin score from their movie *42nd Street,* augmented with other notable Warren-Dubin songs, included such golden oldies as "Young and Healthy," "I Know Now," "You're Getting To Be a Habit With Me," "We're in the Money," "Lullaby of Broadway," "Shuffle Off to Buffalo" and the title number. The show was large physically, with scenery by Robin Wagner and costumes by Theoni V. Aldredge, but all elements of this superbly designed unit are in proportion and tune with the whole, with even the star performances obedient to Champion's staging of the piece not as a joke but always in fun in its romantic, nostalgic way. Orbach's Julian was a take-charge guy who wore his gratifications and disappointments on his sleeve, never leaving the audience in doubt about what it should feel. In the performances of the Misses Grimes and Richert, the star's acid and the chorus girl's sugar were diluted to avoid any dominating flavor in the blend of straight musical talents, simplistic drives, engaging harmonies and compelling rhythms.

Woman of the Year also tells a tale previously told in the movies (in the 1942 Katharine Hepburn-Spencer Tracy comedy of the same title, written by Ring Lardner Jr. and Michael Kanin), thoroughly modernized in a book by Peter Stone (instead of a sports writer and a quiz-show whiz, the ill-matched couple in the stage version are a cartoonist and a TV talk-show hostess) and embellished with an attractive score by John Kander and Fred Ebb. Lauren Bacall is not a singer, but she *is* a Star with a capital S, and in the title role she commanded the stage with every gesture, while Harry Guardino played the cartoonist as a mere mortal wooing the intellectual lady in congenial fashion. Roderick Cook was a suitably self-possessed male secretary, while Marilyn Cooper made the most of her only scene as a kitchen-bound housewife with hair in curlers, standing up to her glamorous house guest, Miss Bacall, in the number "The Grass Is Always Greener." Robert Moore's direction and the designs by Tony Walton and Theoni V. Aldredge served the purposes of this prototypical Broadway musical.

Vinnette Carroll's Gospel musical *Your Arms Too Short to Box with God* payed Broadway a return visit for 149 summer performances, while Micki Grant's early-June effort to celebrate a city neighborhood in song, *It's So Nice to Be Civilized,* came a fast cropper. Then there were the Franks, Fearless and Perfectly: *Fearless Frank,* a short-lived attempt to set the life and loves of Frank Harris in a musical context, and *Perfectly Frank,* a vehicle strained to carry its collection of more than 60 numbers by the late, great Frank Loesser. A Charles Strouse score was the principal ingredient of *Charlie and Algernon*, based on the novel about a medical experiment on a brain-damaged subject which was also the basis for the movie *Charly,* but it could not carry the day. Much more disappointing because it aroused higher expectations was Strouse's second 1980–81 effort, *Bring Back Birdie,* a two-decades-later sequel to *Bye Bye Birdie,* starring Donald O'Connor in a Michael Stewart book (speaking of second efforts) and with Lee Adams lyrics, surviving for only 4 performances in the cruel world of the modern musical theater. The latter was also inhospitable to two other major efforts with 19th century scenes: *Onward Victoria,* about the feminist Victoria Woodhull, closing after its opening performance; and *Copperfield,* with George S. Irving as Mr. Micawber, in a musicalization of the Dickens novel.

The musical theater season was greatly enhanced in the revue section by *Sophisticated Ladies,* with Gregory Hines leading the cast through a selection of Duke Ellington songs in one of his uniquely and inimitably energetic song-and-dance performances under the direction and with the choreography of Michael

Smuin and Donald McKayle. In this revue category, it was perplexing that *Tintypes*, a show that proved itself inimitable in its own Gay-Nineties-turn-of-the-century way off Broadway last season, couldn't attract an audience to sustain a run of more than 93 performances in transfer. In effect, nostalgia seemed to be a thread running through the few popular new musical offerings of the season—*42nd Street*, *Woman of the Year* and *Sophisticated Ladies*—and among the musical revivals *Camelot* and *The Pirates of Penzance* (of which more in a later section of this report)—but it was no absolute guarantee of popularity.

There can seldom have been a New York theater season in which foreign plays dominated the scene as they did in this one. On Broadway, each and every one of the half-dozen foreign scripts showed some credentials of craft and vision, in marked comparison to the halting American efforts, three times as numerous and less than a third as effective. Far and away the year's best play was Peter Shaffer's *Amadeus*, an import from the National Theater which set Broadway aflame with the warmth of its dramatization of the nature of genius—its over-whelming superiority to mere talent. Shaffer himself is a genius at summoning up in his plays a sort of Platonic ideal looming behind the reality of his subject: the ideal of Horse in *Equus*, the very spirit of Music in *Amadeus*. *Amadeus* is told in monologue, to an even greater extent than *Equus*, by the character upon whom the events of the play are having the most profound intellectual as well as emotional impact: in *Equus* not the frantic boy but his doctor, in *Amadeus* not the genius Mozart but his jealous rival Salieri. The latter, played in high style by Ian McKellen, recalled all too well in aching detail how it was when brash, uncouth, ill-mannered but gloriously gifted young Mozart (Tim Curry) arrived at the Austrian court, where Salieri was the Emperor's musical mentor, but where Mozart proceeded to overshadow the older man with his heart-stopping concert and opera works.

In his own youth, Salieri had made a bargain with God, a vow of a lifetime of service and obeisance in exchange for the talent to become renowned in the world of music. God seemed to have kept his bargain with Salieri until "Ama-deus" intruded upon the scene—Wolfgang Amadeus Mozart who is apparently heedless of God's will but is so entirely, unfairly beloved of God that the divine harmonies pouring out of him (Mozart doesn't find it necessary even to rewrite his scores) expose the most intense musical efforts of all others, including Salieri's, as earthbound mechanical compositions. Salieri's resentment of God's unfairness finally grows out of control; emotions darken while the music becomes more sublime. The play's grand design was most sensitively realized in Peter Hall's direction of Shaffer's brilliant script, in the manipulation of the musical back-ground, in the tastefully gilded John Bury sets and costumes and in the supporting performances including Nicholas Kepros's philistine Emperor Joseph. *Ama-deus* would be a peak of dramatic accomplishment in any season; in this one, rising from the valley floor, its presence was immense.

The Irish play *A Life* by Hugh Leonard, a sort of companion piece to his popular *Da,* was the year's chief rival to its English competitor in every depart-ment except audience response. For reasons suggested earlier in this report, Leonard's fine play couldn't find acceptance on Broadway, where it remained for a scant 72 performances but left glowing embers of warmth in the memory of theatergoers who were lucky enough to have seen it. In *Da*, the crusty Irish civil servant Drumm was a colorful minor character; *A Life* moved in for a closeup of this intellectually dominant but emotionally forbidding fellow. The rich characterization takes Drumm from ambitious youth to disillusioned age, from half-realized love to half-appreciated wedlock, in a dual performance by Roy Dotrice as Old Drumm and Adam Redfield as Young Drumm, as these two actors uncannily reflected each other's mannerisms and even general appearance. The supporting performances by Pat Hingle (Drumm's pal), Helen Stenborg (Drumm's wife) and Aideen O'Kelly (Drumm's youthful infatuation), the Peter Coe direction and the ingenious Robert Fletcher multilevel setting were all worthy of a script that ranked among the very best the theater had to offer this season.

The inbred ability of the aloe to flourish and bloom in a desert climate became a metaphor of the human spirit in the searing sociological climate of South Africa, in yet another distinguished 1980–81 script from abroad. Athol Fugard's *A Lesson from Aloes* celebrated the friendship between two South Africans, one white and the other black, just as it is coming to an end because the black has decided, after a prison term for a political offense, that he's had enough of trying to survive in this forbidding environment and is taking himself and his family away to resettle in England. Like other notable Fugard works (*The Blood Knot*, *Boesman and Lena*, *Sizwe Banzi Is Dead*, *The Island*), this one was a cry of despair echoed by hope for his beloved country. Harris Yulin as the doggedly enduring white Afrikaner, the "aloe;" Maria Tucci as his wife, who has already broken down once and is probably not going to be able to stay the course; and James Earl Jones as the black friend were directed by the author as the work was written, in steady and determined progress through somber measures. In the consensus voting of the New York Drama Critics Circle, *A Lesson from Aloes* was cited as the best-of-bests for 1980-81, an award to which it certainly does honor.

Two other British plays provided platforms for outstanding performances by their leading ladies: *Piaf* by Pam Gems, with Jane Lapotaire recreating the entertainment style and the street-wise, doomed personality of the famous French singer Edith Piaf, in a Tony Award-winning performance; and *Rose* by Andrew Davies, a less flamboyant but more complex portrait of an enlightened Midlands school teacher trying achingly hard to reshape both her humdrum marriage and the inadequate education system into more satisfactory form. As played by Glenda Jackson, with Jessica Tandy as her mother and confidante, Rose was a raw-boned, close-cropped mass of contradictions: masculine and feminine, arrogant and vulnerable, repellant and appealing, in one of the year's strongest performances.

Also on the distinguished visitors list was *The Suicide*, a 1920s Russian play by Nikolai Erdman satirizing the drawbacks of collectivism, denied production in Russia and now rescued from oblivion in translation, first in England in 1979 and then in a regional theater production here in 1980. The play considers in comedic terms the plight of an unemployed worker brushed off by his closest neighbors as well as by the state until he attracts attention by announcing that he is going to shoot himself. This production was stretched well beyond the limits of its content by excesses of style, but the show did boast an engaging performance in the leading role by the British actor Derek Jacobi, and by John Heffernan in support as a tatterdemalion intellectual.

Easily the best American play on Broadway this season was Jean Kerr's effervescent *Lunch Hour*, about wife-swapping in the Hamptons, staged by Mike Nichols, with one member of the quartet (a marriage counselor played by Sam Waterston) at the extreme of sophistication in these matters, another (the wide-eyed Gilda Radner, dangerously innocent) at the opposite extreme, and with their spouses caught and manipulated in the middle. The point of *Lunch Hour* isn't that it explored profound truths, but that like all other Jean Kerr plays it was a lark. Her very stylishly constructed comedy found its laughter in fellow-feeling for the characters rather than in jokes at their expense—and with any luck there may after all be something like a profound truth lurking there among the witticisms.

Woody Allen's *The Floating Light Bulb*, another American Best Play on Broadway this season, sets a *Glass Menagerie*-type mother upon her achingly shy son (Brian Backer), whose favorite magic trick gives the play its title. In the indomitable person of Beatrice Arthur, the mother pushes the boy into auditioning for a theatrical manager (Jack Weston), the equivalent of a gentleman caller in these variations on a theme similar to Tennessee Williams's, with a similar resolution: Williams's crippled girl will never find a suitor, and Allen's terrified youth will never make it in public as a magician. In the latter case, the caller is perceived as both a professional opportunity for the son and a romantic refuge for the mother, in a touching encounter (delicately performed under Ulu Grosbard's direction) between two people who are long past their prime and almost past hoping for the best, but still in possession of courage and self-respect.

The equal of this year's best in any category was Lanford Wilson's *Fifth of July*, which was named a Best Play in its off-Broadway production at Circle Rep three years ago. This was the first of Wilson's Talley family plays, but a generation later in time than *Talley's Folly*, with a widowed Aunt Sally watching a new Talley generation trying to get over the aftereffects of Vietnam shock. This new Broadway production could not be called a "transfer" from off-Broadway (though Jeff Daniels as Ken Talley's loving attendant, Jonathan Hogan as his friend, Joyce Reehling as his sister and Amy Wright as her daughter remain from the original cast), nor a "revival" (directed by Marshall W. Mason, like the original), nor a "new play" (though somewhat rewritten), and of course we cannot re-include it in the Best Plays list, where it would certainly belong had it not appeared there previously. For want of a better term we've classified this as a "return engagement," certainly an illustrious one, in which both Christopher Reeve and his successor, Richard Thomas, made an impression in the role of Ken Talley.

Here and there among the other new American offerings on Broadway was a script which, though falling short of success this first time around, seems likely to find a new life elsewhere. The romantic adventures of Renee Taylor as a TV actress and Joseph Bologna as a producer of TV commercials in their *It Had To Be You* worked up quite a comic froth under Robert Drivas's direction and should prove to be a cheerful and durable item on the road. Edward Albee's *Lolita* succumbed quickly to critical overkill, but among its admittedly sometimes offensive clutter there lurked sequences of intensely powerful theater. In this dramatization of Vladimir Nabokov's sardonic tale of the professor (Donald Sutherland), his nymphet and his nemesis (Clive Revill in a weirdly colorful performance), emotional electricity went out of control, but this is not to say that this project is forever impossible—nor was it, like so much else on this year's schedule, narrow in vision or weak in effect.

We also have to believe that Neil Simon may some day find a way to twist the controls of *Fools* and get it going as a properly stylized farce of the intellect, in its tale of a Russian village mysteriously cursed with stupidity; that Arthur Miller will finally get his feelings about the Depression across to the audience in some future version of his *The American Clock*; that Albert Innaurato will write another play about an Italian family, possibly including a segment of this year's *Passione*; that Steve Tesich's *Division Street*, about the mellowing of 1960s radicals, will have a life after its mere 21 Broadway performances, as it did before them at Mark Taper Forum in this Gordon Davidson-directed production; that James Prideaux (*Mixed Couples*, about wife-swappers meeting 25 years later) and Joanna M. Glass (*To Grandmother's House We Go*, with Eva Le Gallienne as the matriarch of a troubled family) will be heard from more eloquently in future, and the sooner the better.

Other short-lived American scripts, whose very existence on Broadway was proof that some producers considered them sufficiently vibrant to make a go of it in the biggest time of all, included *Heartland* about homicidal mania, *The Survivor* about Nazi persecution in the Warsaw ghetto and *Inacent Black*, the name of an angel (Melba Moore) who comes down to earth to help out with the problems of an upper middle class black family in Westbury, L.I. Certainly no work considered deserving of Broadway production deserves to feel the hook after only one performance, but this debacle happens more often than it should, this season to *Frankenstein*, *Onward Victoria*, *Broadway Follies* and to Sidney Michaels's spy melodrama *Tricks of the Trade* and the trio of short comedies entitled *Animals*. The only import to suffer this fate this season was *The Moony Shapiro Songbook*, a British musical satirizing anthology shows of famous composers' works, which opened and closed after only one Broadway performance—and was nominated for a Tony in the best-book category. David Merrick, who began the season with the fireworks display of *42nd Street* made another kind of spectacle as he withdrew Oliver Hailey's *I Won't Dance*, a dark and violent play about the emotions of a paraplegic in a wheelchair, after only one Sunday afternoon performance, thus running the gamut of production experience in a single season. He made his entrance, after a long absence, onto the Broadway scene both with his shield and on it, in the highest triumph and the most attenuated defeat.

Specialty productions were both numerous and conspicuous in the Broadway environs this season. Lena Horne knocked them dead in a one-woman show as musically enthralling as the star herself. Radio City Music Hall launched two of its extravaganzas—*Manhattan Showboat* and *America*, a salute to all the 50 states —in which the Rockettes were and always will be the prime attraction. At the other end of the scale, the theater district is scheduled to lose the little Bijou Theater on 45th Street if the developers have their way, at a time when its importance to the area has never been more apparent. Its intimate proportions provided a comfortable fit for one-performer shows by Shelley Berman, Michael McGiveney (portraying 30 different characters in *Quick Change*) and Barbara Perry (playing five specially chosen *Passionate Ladies*), as well as for the French marionette show *Aaah Oui Genty!* and the revue *Shakespeare's Cabaret*, transferred from the Colonnades and setting many of the Bard's songs, poems and lyrical passages to music by Lance Mulcahy. In other parts of the specialty forest were *Banjo Dancing*, a one-man instrumental concert by Stephen Wade; Emlyn Williams returning in his memorable stage portrait of Charles Dickens; Alec McCowen also returning in his rendition of the Gospel according to St. Mark; and *Broadway Follies*, a comeback of vaudeville to the big time—but only for one performance.

Off Broadway

In the smaller playhouses, the tail wagged the dog. The plays arousing the most enthusiasm among New York theatergoers came from that area called "off off

Broadway," or OOB—paradoxically, in a season which starved OOB for new scripts because of the dispute between Equity and the dramatists over showcase commitments. Only one American play in full-fledged off-Broadway production (*Zooman and the Sign*) and two scripts from abroad (*Translations* and *Cloud 9*) rivaled the mighty OOB mites who stole the passing show: *How I Got That Story, Crimes of the Heart* (the Pulitzer and Critics Award winner and a Best Play) and *March of the Falsettos*, which moved up to full off-Broadway status after first appearing as an OOB offering. Certainly all three of them will continue to make ever-widening circles, with plans afoot to present them in expanded productions.

We have no intention of drawing indelible lines across the off-Broadway programming to divide it absolutely into professional and experimental categories; but we must make some distinction between what is possibly a work-in-progress and what is probably a "frozen" script ready to face the world as a completed work in publication or production. Only the latter is regularly considered for Best Play designation. All the new Off-Broadway plays and musicals are eligible for Best Play selection on the same terms as those listed under the Broadway heading, whereas works-in-progress are not.

This said, let us note that 1980–81 production of new scripts off Broadway dwindled somewhat for the third straight year: 55 productions including 33 American straight plays, 14 musicals and 8 foreign plays in English, as compared with 58 (39-7-12) last year and 64 (38-15-11) the previous season. The number of revues dropped dramatically from 11 last year to only one this year (see the one-page summary accompanying this report), while the revival total held at 44 for the second straight season.

Foreign playwrights stole the show off Broadway as they did on, leading the long parade with the exceptionally effective works produced by Lynne Meadow and Barry Grove at Manhattan Theater Club. Brian Friel's *Translations* was a shade the best of the entire off-Broadway year, with an affectionate, caring dramatization of an 1833 episode in the English-Irish struggle of character and policy. Friel's Best Play recalls a time when there was a formidable language as well as an emotional barrier between the two factions, with Barnard Hughes as the principal of a one-room "Hedge School" teaching all subjects including Latin and Greek to Gaelic-speaking country folk. The British presence is symbolized by Army personnel come to occupy, map and Anglicize the country. Daniel Gerroll as a young lieutenant who falls in love with Irish ways and an Irish lass, Jarlath Conroy as a bilingual Irish intellectual, Stephen Burleigh as one inclined to collaboration and Jake Dengel as a boozy old classicist led the skillful ensemble through these measures, directed by Joe Dowling. The play was sometimes irresolute but never unfeeling, squeezing out every drop of compassion for both sides of the conflict.

Another very bright spot on the MTC program was Stephen Poliakoff's *American Days*, a brash and kookie treatment of the rock music scene, previously produced in London. Its aspiring performers slaver for the limelight, as they try to attract the attention of a bored record publisher with eccentricities of dress and behavior reminiscent of TV quiz show contestants. Pippa Pearthree gave a stunning performance as the least likely but finally most successful of the aspirants, in a play that was remarkable for both intensity and style under Jacques Levy's direction. The MTC's exceptionally distinguished 1980–81 schedule also included *Close of Play*, an enigmatic rummaging among family frictions by the

The 1980–81 Season Off Broadway

PLAYS (33)

American Place 1980:
Killings on the Last Line
Knitters in the Sun
Circle Rep 1980:
The Woolgatherer
Public Theater 1980:
FOB
Cassatt
A Sleepless Night With an Honest Man
An Act of Kindness
Transcendental Love
Album
Richie
Circle Rep 1981:
The Diviners
Childe Byron
In Connecticut
Negro Ensemble:
The Sixteenth Round
ZOOMAN AND THE SIGN
Weep Not for Me
In an Upstate Motel
Home (return engagement)
Vikings
Judgement
Bohemian Heaven
Moma
Coming Attractions
The One Act Play Festival

Last Summer at Bluefish Cove
Public Theater 1981:
True West
Phoenix:
Beyond Therapy
The Captivity of Pixie Shedman
Memory of Whiteness
The Legendary Stardust Boys
Marching to Georgia
Black Elk Lives
The Buddy System

SPECIALTIES (8)

Macready
American Place 1981:
The Impossible H.L Mencken
The Amazin' Casey Stengel
Public Theater 1981:
Dead End Kids
Penguin Touquet
The Haggadah (return engagement)
Truman Capote at Lincoln Center
It's Me, Sylvia

MUSICALS (14)

Chase a Rainbow
Billy Bishop Goes to War (transfer)
A Matter of Opinion
Public Theater 1981:
Girls, Girls, Girls
Alice in Concert
Really Rosie
Frimbo
Ka-Boom!
Trixie True, Teen Detective
Hijinks
An Evening with Joan Crawford
Marry Me a Little
I Can't Keep Running in Place
March of the Falsettos

REVUE (1)

Ah, Men

FOREIGN PLAYS IN ENGLISH (8)

Phoenix:
Bonjour, Là, Bonjour
Meetings
Manhattan Theater Club:
American Days
Close of Play
TRANSLATIONS
We Won't Pay! We Won't Pay!
Glasshouse
CLOUD 9

REVIVALS (44)

The Cocktail Party
Roundabout 1980:
Look Back in Anger
Fallen Angels
To Bury a Cousin
LOOM:
Trial by Jury, The Zoo and Cox & Box
The Desert Song
(11 operettas in running repertory)
Public Theater 1981:
The Pirates of Penzance
The Sea Gull
Mary Stuart
Long Day's Journey Into Night

Circle Rep:
Twelfth Night
The Beaver Coat
Roundabout 1981:
The Winslow Boy
Don Juan in Hell
Inadmissible Evidence
A Taste of Honey
Hedda Gabler
CSC:
Oedipus Rex
Oedipus at Colonus
Antigone
Gilles de Rais
Woyzeck and Leonce and Lena
The Chekhov Sketchbook
Naomi Court
BAM:
A Midsummer Night's Dream
The Recruiting Officer
The Wild Duck
Jungle of Cities
Oedipus the King
Veronica's Room
Acting Company:
Il Campiello
Waiting for Godot
A Midsummer Night's Dream

Plays listed in CAPITAL LETTERS have been designated Best Plays of 1980–81.
Plays listed in *italics* were still running after May 31, 1981.

British playwright Simon Gray, and Steve Metcalfe's *Vikings*, about craftsmen coping with this era of mass production—not to mention MTC's program of productions in the OOB category in its UpStage Theater.

In independent off-Broadway production, a British playwright, Caryl Churchill, carried off top honors with a farce of sexual identity and preference, *Cloud 9*, masterfully staged by Tommy Tune. Its characters—father, mother, son, daughter, servant, family friends—were seen first as an assemblage of 1880 Empire Victorians in Africa. Under their facade of decorum, their sexual activity covers just about the whole spectrum of possibility—and then some, because the characters are cast transsexually. It was the author's fancy that some of this group appear 100 years later (but only 25 years older) in the second act, in sexually liberated 1980, with a whole new set of preferences and personae. It was never entirely clear who was doing what to whom in *Cloud 9*, and it scarcely ever mattered; as in a Feydeau farce, it is the contest and not the order of finish that provides the hilarity, with a cast who gave a new meaning to the term "ensemble." Pitfalls of vulgarity which gape on either side of an enterprise like this weren't even visible from the perspective of *Cloud 9*, styled, paced and performed as it was to outlandish perfection under Tommy Tune's adventurous guidance.

T. Edward Hambleton's Phoenix Theater, too, offered a 1980–81 schedule of scripts consistent in superior quality, among them the world premiere of the Trinidadian dramatist Mustapha Matura's *Meetings*, with a gleaming but food-less kitchen symbolizing the flaws of upward mobility among its Trinidadian characters. The Phoenix also offered a translation of French Canadian playwright Michel Tremblay's *Bonjour, Là, Bonjour*, about a troubled family, as well as new works by two of our accomplished younger dramatists: *Beyond Therapy* by Christopher Durang, a stirred mixture of sex and psychiatry, and *The Captivity of Pixie Shedman* by Romulus Linney, a Southerner's evocation of his past. Linney himself had a two-play season off Broadway, as his *Childe Byron* examined the relationship between the poet and his daughter in strong performances by Lindsay Crouse and William Hurt, the outstanding 1980–81 production at Circle Repertory.

Along with the Phoenix and MTC offerings of foreign scripts, there were three in independent production: Dario Fo's comedy of Italians coping with inflation, *We Won't Pay! We Won't Pay!*, which managed a respectable 120 off-Broadway performances; Fatima Dike's short-lived *Glasshouse*, about an interracial friendship; and the aforementioned *Cloud 9*.

Among American scripts produced off Broadway this season, Charles Fuller's Best Play *Zooman and the Sign* at The Negro Ensemble Company was the standout. Under Douglas Turner Ward's direction, it brought into sharply antipathetic focus a teen-aged punk whose criminal violence causes the death of a child in a black Philadelphia neighborhood. The child's father (Ray Aranha) becomes a nonviolent nemesis of this "Zooman" (played by Giancarlo Esposito in a repusively telling performance) when he sees that his neighbors in the community want no part of testifying against the killer or helping in any way to bring him to justice. Fuller's play points the finger at everybody and has some compassion for everybody—Zooman included. Other subjects dramatized in works put on by the NEC this season were the plight of a has-been prize fighter hiding from gangsters (*The Sixteenth Round* by Samm-Art Williams, whose 1980 Best Play *Home* was brought back on this year's NEC schedule), multiple murder in the black ghetto (*Weep Not for Me* by Gus Edwards) and big-city violence in which victim is also perpetrator (*In an Upstate Motel* by Larry Neal).

In other 1980–81 institutional production, Joseph Papp's busy (with musicals, revivals and guest productions) New York Shakespeare Festival Public Theater came up with only one new play in its 1981 season: *True West*, Sam Shepard's latest, not a Western but a clash of siblings, one of whom is a screen writer and the other a vagrant ne'er-do-well—symbolizing, as in other Shepard plays, the decay of American life and spirit. The Public's finest hours took place in June 1980 with *FOB*, a play by David Henry Hwang about the difficulties of Chinese immigrants adjusting to America, directed by Mako; and, much later in the season, as it gave over its stage to the Mabou Mines anti-nuclear diatribe *Dead End Kids*, an inventive company led by JoAnne Akalaitis in acting out warnings by famous scientists re the perils of unleashed radiation. Richard Foreman's Ontological-Hysteric Theater production of *Penguin Touquet*, a kaleidoscope of stage imagery; Jean-Claude van Itallie's version of *The Sea Gull* directed by Andrei Serban; Elizabeth Swados's musical rearrangement of Lewis Carroll, *Alice in Concert*, with Joseph Papp directing and Meryl Streep in the title role; the Dodger Theater's *Mary Stuart*; and *Long Day's Journey Into Night* played by an all-black cast under Geraldine Fitzgerald's direction were also on the Public's varied guest and house program this season.

Circle Repertory began with William Mastrosimone's *The Woolgatherer*, a two-character encounter between a truck driver and a salesgirl, which opened in June 1980 and was later joined in repertory by Frank Barrie's impersonation of the famous actor William Charles Macready. Circle Rep then proceeded to the American College Theater Festival winner, *The Diviners* by Jim Leonard Jr., which looked at life in a small Indiana town through the eyes of a child with a gift for dowsing, a retired preacher and other such individuals. After revivals of *Twelfth Night* and Gerhart Hauptmann's 1893 German comedy *The Beaver Coat*, Circle Rep came up with *Childe Byron*, followed by *In Connecticut* by Roy London, a play developed in Circle Rep workshop and in production at GeVa in Rochester, N.Y., about the tribulations of moving from the suburbs to a New York apartment. As the 1980–81 season ended, this group was aiming toward a June production of Lanford Wilson's *A Tale Told*, the third in its author's series of plays about the Talley family, the subject of his previous *Fifth of July* and *Talley's Folly*.

American Place had little luck this year, either with its presentations of single characters onstage (*The Impossible H.L. Mencken* with John Rothman and *The Amazin' Casey Stengel* with Paul Dooley) or with its more extensive dramatizations *Memory of Whiteness*, a family conflict play by Richard Hamburger, or, just across the border in June 1981, *The Fuehrer Bunker*, a dramatization by W.D. Snodgrass of the last days of the Hitler gang, with music by Richard Peaslee. Lincoln Center made an effort to launch its small Newhouse Theater as an off-Broadway showcase with a personal appearance during the Christmas holidays by Truman Capote reading from his own works, and later with a program of one-acters by Jeffrey Sweet, John Guare and Percy Granger. The arrangement by which Edward Albee served as artistic director of this enterprise, produced by Richmond Crinkley, probably will not continue, nor is there an ongoing program for the Newhouse firmed up at this writing.

Within the broad pipeline of independent play production off Broadway, there was scarcely a trickle of real interest. David Rimmer's *Album* was one noteworthy arrival, with the mid-1960s growing pains of a quartet of teen-agers intimately dramatized, directed (by Joan Micklin Silver) and performed. This script emerged from a previous OOB production at the WPA Theater and is perhaps a measure of what might have been had not this year's flow been somewhat stemmed by the Equity showcase controversy. Also emergent from OOB in The Glines production was Jane Chambers's *Last Summer at Bluefish Cove*, a strong script about the summer loves of single women, who happen in this case to be lesbians. Other subjects raised in the new scripts in their numbers were the painters Mary Cassatt and Degas (*Cassatt*), Benedict Arnold (*A Sleepless Night With an Honest Man*); Ralph Waldo Emerson (*Transcendental Love*), cannibalism (*Judgement*), economics (*Bohemian Heaven*), Vietnam (*Moma*), the Sioux (*Black Elk Lives*) and an array of domestic and marital conflicts, forgettable as speedily as their departure from the scene after very short runs.

The production of book musicals off Broadway doubled from 7 in 1980 to 14 in 1981, and they were generally more substantial than the straight plays. Playwrights Horizons established a presence off Broadway this season with upward-mobile OOB productions: *Coming Attractions* (a Ted Tally melodrama about a terrorist and the media), and much more firmly with *March of the Falsettos*, a musical by William Finn describing the emotional stresses of husband, wife and child when the former takes off with a homosexual lover and the family psychiatrist takes his place in the bed. The show had no spoken dialogue but was made up of 20 songs, without intermission. James Lapine's direction was an irresistible driving force adding voltage to the material and propelling an energetic cast headed by Michael Rupert as the father torn between passion and parenthood.

Another of the off-Broadway year's musical attractions was *Marry Me a Little*, a bundle of Stephen Sondheim trunk songs (written for shows but dropped in production, often for reasons other than quality) and numbers from *Saturday Night*, which never reached the New York stage. Two young performers—Suzanne Henry and Craig Lucas (who collaborated with the director Norman René on the development of the show itself)—acted out a love story implied by the succession of Sondheim lyrics, previously unheard but now, fortunately, embedded in the record of the New York stage. That a leading composer's trunk songs are not necessarily, or even probably, inferior work was proven again in *Marry Me a Little*. There was nothing second-rate about the Sondheim numbers or the show.

The multi-character Canadian musical *Billy Bishop Goes to War* by and with Eric Peterson and John Gray reversed the usual flow of traffic by moving down from Broadway to off-Broadway for an extended summer visit. Maurice Sendak's *Really Rosie*, with music by Carole King, setting forth the adventures of the Nutshell Kids and their alligator friend, made it past indifferent reviews and cheered up the off-Broadway season in a long run. Unhappily, *Frimbo*, a musical adaptation of *New Yorker* stories about an avid railroad buff, lasted for only one performance, even though staged in the ultra-realistic setting of Tracks 39 to 42 at Grand Central Terminal, where the coming and going of a real railroad train was no problem for the technical crew.

The title of *Ka-boom!* said it all, or almost all, in a musical comedy fantasy about what it might be like, after a nuclear holocaust, to put on a show. *Trixie True, Teen Detective*, with book, music and lyrics by Kelly Hamilton, parodied its genre of detective adventure to some effect, in a tale of a novelist (Gene Lindsey) trying to kill off his popular, but by him unwanted, teen-aged detective heroine. The Chelsea Theater Center's *Hijinks!*, a musical adaptation by Robert Kalfin, Steve Brown and John McKinney of *Captain Jinks of the Horse Ma-*

rines, was a highlight of the off-Broadway season, though it didn't develop an audience to keep it on for any length of time—or to encourage the Chelsea group, which had decided to call it quits after this year, to try for another season of off-Broadway production.

Barbara Schottenfeld's *I Can't Keep Running in Place*, with Marcia Rodd as a psychiatrist in workshop sessions with the sextet of woman patients, and with a decidedly feminist orientation, advanced its cause ardently in a musical context. In the revue catgory, *Ah, Men*, a series of reflections on "the male experience," was assembled by Paul Shyre from the works of a couple of dozen savants from Jean-Jacques Rousseau to Groucho Marx, with songs by Will Holt—a tingling entertainment. It very likely signifies nothing but coincidence that only this one revue appeared off Broadway this year as compared with 11 in 1980. A corresponding rise in the production of book shows in 1981 almost balanced out the shortfall.

The ebb and flow of indifferent material off Broadway this season cannot demean its accomplishments: the three Best Plays *Translations*, *Cloud 9* and *Zooman and the Sign*, the best moments of its musicals, the stimulating revivals which are considered in the next chapter. If its vision narrowed and its creativity attenuated in 1981, off Broadway shared those failings with the whole expanse of New York theater. It could not escape the widespread epidemic of mediocrity for which there is no cure except a new and better season and renewed resolve.

Revivals

This was the year that Joseph Papp pulled a rabbit out of his hat and made the Messrs. Gilbert and Sullivan hit musical authors of 1981 with a smashing revival of *The Pirates of Penzance*. In athletic style under the direction of Wilford Leach; in rock-star magnetism with the presence of Linda Ronstadt as Mabel and Rex Smith as Frederic; in show-biz flair with the casting of Kevin Kline as the Pirate King and Patricia Routledge (and later Estelle Parsons) as Ruth; in ineffable G & S humor with George Rose as a very model of a Major-General; in design, melody and general allure, this was a first-rate entertainment, removed from the shelf of 19th century theater and brought first to Central Park and then to Broadway without a speck of dust upon its silvery surface. Joseph Papp waved some kind of wand over these pirates and general's daughters and brought forth the revival of the New York theater year.

Much newer, and still shining brightly in reproduction, was *Camelot*, with Richard Burton recreating his role of King Arthur in the Lerner-Loewe musical theater adaptation of this folk tale as told by T.H. White in *The Once and Future King*. Burton commanded the stage so completely it was hard to believe that Guenevere would look elsewhere for excitement; nevertheless this production regenerated the original's emotional and melodic appeal. This wasn't true of other full-scale Broadway musical revivals this year. Shows that came and went without attracting the new audience to whom it had been presumed they would appeal were *Brigadoon*, *The Music Man* with Dick Van Dyke, Cole Porter's *Can-can* (revised by Abe Burrows) with Zizi Jeanmaire, a Goodspeed Opera House revamping of *The Five O'clock Girl* and the Jacques Brel musical on a visit to Broadway. On the other hand, Light Opera of Manhattan (LOOM) demonstrated its usual staying power, going its tuneful way through a 52-week season in its small East Side theater with its extensive Gilbert and Sullivan repertory, plus the operetta likes of *The Desert Song*, *The Vagabond King*, *The Student Prince* and *The Merry Widow*.

Among straight-play revivals it was no contest for the limelight, as Elizabeth Taylor and company swept New York's audiences (if not its drama critics) off their feet in *The Little Foxes*. It was the glittering international movie star's stage debut they came to see, not so much Lillian Hellman's acerbic play about greed and family abrasions. Miss Taylor gave them a vivid presence as Regina, leaving to other members of the cast—most notably Maureen Stapleton as Birdie—to fill in the subtler tones. Miss Taylor's effort was so conspicuously whole-hearted, holding nothing back that she had to offer, that it overshadowed any minor shortcomings in the esthetics of the enterprise.

Uniformly the best of Broadway's 1980–81 straight play revivals was Philip Barry's *The Philadelphia Story* as staged by Ellis Rabb, with Blythe Danner as Tracy, Edward Herrmann as Mike and Frank Converse as Dexter. The enduring charm of this comedy of Main Line manners was brought to full flower in all departments of the show, which reopened the Vivian Beaumont Theater at Lincoln Center under Richmond Crinkley's production supervision, following the dark seasons since its abandonment by Joseph Papp. After this attractive beginning, the Beaumont survived a difficult *Macbeth* staged by opera impresario Sarah Caldwell and went on to a new work of Best Play dimensions, Woody Allen's *The Floating Light Bulb*. Mr. Crinkley and his colleagues have of course not yet charted the Beaumont's destiny, but at least they made their presence felt after they turned the lights back on.

Another major function of a New York revival season, apart from dusting off classics or remounting hits for a new audience, is the second look at a contemporary script, perhaps from an angle somewhat different from the original. A success in this category this season was the off-Broadway revival of Ira Levin's *Veronica's Room*, a thriller of impersonation and its consequences which first played Broadway in 1973 and was reshaped somewhat in a 1978 Hasty Pudding production in Boston, the blueprint for this one. Similar efforts to try again with Gus Weill's *To Bury a Cousin* and Michael Sawyer's *Naomi Court* met with little acceptance; but in one of the OOB byways, the Richard Allen Center for Culture and Art, Eugene O'Neill's *Long Day's Journey Into Night* was put on by a distinguished all-black cast under the direction of Geraldine Fitzgerald, in an experiment so felicitous that it was soon invited into Joseph Papp's Public Theater to settle down for an extended run.

After closing its 1980 schedule in summer with the Kaufman-Hart comedy *The Man Who Came to Dinner* starring Ellis Rabb, Theodore Mann's and Paul Libin's Circle in the Square moved through reported financial problems into its 30th anniversary season. It was one of sturdy classical selections: Euripides's *The Bacchae*, Ibsen's *John Gabriel Borkman* and Strindberg's *The Father*. Off Broadway, the Classic Stage Company (CSC) followed Sophocles's *Oedipus Rex*, *Oedipus at Colonus* and *Antigone* (in repertory, but including 4 marathon performances of the three-play cycle) with the first English-language presentation of Roger Planchon's play about Bluebeard, *Gilles de Rais*, plus adaptations by and with the company's artistic director, Christopher Martin, of Büchner's *Woyzeck* and *Leonce and Lena*.

John Houseman's Acting Company was invited by Joseph Papp to the Public Theater for 10 guest performances of plays by Goldoni, Beckett and Shakespeare. Over in Brooklyn, the BAM Theater Company put on a repertory of five revivals: yet another version of Sophocles's *Oedipus*, plus works of Shakespeare, George Farquhar, Ibsen and Brecht. After this formidably eclectic season, BAM announced that it would cease to function after this, its second year at the Brooklyn Academy of Music. The demise of any theater organization as professionally accomplished as BAM is regrettable, but hope springs eternal that another way may be found to use the Academy for the continuing benefit of New York legitimate theater audiences.

Of all the revival producing organizations, Gene Feist's and Michael Fried's Roundabout Theater Company seems to have the surest sense of theater on its two stages, usually selecting fairly modern works ready to be seen again, like last summer's *Look Back in Anger* or, later in the season, *The Winslow Boy* and *A Taste of Honey*, the latter following the path beaten by Joseph Papp and Circle Rep by transferring to Broadway after its run at the Roundabout. This group often casts its shows aggressively, as with Arlene Francis, Paul Sparer and Philip Bosco in *Don Juan in Hell* or Nicol Williamson in his original role in *Inadmissible Evidence* or Susannah York as *Hedda Gabler*, always producing with care and insight. The Roundabout is a perennial star of the huge New York revival show, which is surely a precious and unique cultural asset, covering as it always does the whole spectrum of theater from the starkest nightmare of the ancient Greeks to the frothiest operetta of the mauve decade. As the song says, "That's entertainment . . . It could be *Oedipus Rex*/Where a chap kills his father/And causes a lot of bother." On the 1980–81 New York revival scene, it actually was—twice.

Offstage

Occupying a major portion of the New York theater's offstage attention this season were the feast-or-famine economy and the Equity showcase controversy, both rooted in the past and carrying over into the seemingly ever-more-problematical future. The rising cost of everything from production costs at one end to theater tickets at the other was resulting in outlandish grosses at the Broadway hits and severe penury elsewhere. Inflation was a contributing cause of the demise of two important off-Broadway producing groups, Chelsea Theater Center and BAM Theater Company (whose expenses this season exceeded its $1 million income and $700,000 subsidy by about $1 million, according to *Variety* estimate). A 1980s economy in which a $200,000 off-Broadway production cost no longer seemed impossible, and an $18.50 ticket had become a reality, would very likely stifle the activity of other groups before very long.

Meanwhile, in the governmental part of the forest, Little Red Riding Hood arrived at Grandmother's door hoping for a warm welcome and a goodly $175 million from the National Endowment on the Arts, only to be confronted by wolfish teeth and a proposed 50 per cent slash in the 1982 Federal arts subsidy penciled in by the previous administration. This severe reduction at a time when the partially subsidized sector was already hurting moved Joseph Papp (whose New York Shakespeare Festival receives subsidies but is also heavily self-endowed with a share of the Broadway profits from *A Chorus Line* and now *The Pirates of Penzance*) to declare publicly that the National Endowment should be abolished, thereby saving $10 million in administration expenses, and any Federal arts allotment be distributed directly to the state arts councils. "I do not believe that an agency for the arts needs to exist in Washington," Papp stated, "I don't think it's proper for people in Washington to make decisions about the arts in New York City." They will continue to do so, however, and no doubt there will be a large reduction in the 1982 arts subsidy by the Federal budget-cutters.

The drying-up of adventurous new scripts in the area of off-off-Broadway production because of Equity's insistence on a showcase code of future commitment to participating actors was the second major offstage preoccupation this season. The majority of working dramatists continued to feel that the conditions of the proposed showcase code would inhibit future productions of their scripts, and therefore they continued reluctant to release them for presentation in showcases, the staple of the OOB diet. Back in June 1980 the Equity Council accepted a recommendation from its members that the proposed code's wording be changed to assure the author that his or her "only obligation, both morally and financially, is to give notice in writing to any future producer and Equity, prior to bonding, that the play was done in showcase" (so that, under certain circumstances, Equity could oblige sponsors of a new production to hire or indemnify actors who contributed their services to the showcase). While this freed the author from personal financial obligation (to indemnify such actors not hired), it did not free his work from the risk of being turned down for possible production because of the albatross of obligation tied round its neck by the terms of the Equity code.

This change in wording had little effect upon the dramatists' determination not to obligate their scripts under this code. Neither did the Equity Council's vote in August not to renew the contract of Executive Secretary Donald Grody, one of the chief proponents of the code. Michael Weller and other authors brought a suit against Equity in Federal court in October charging the actors' union with violating sections of the Sherman Antitrust Act and the National Labor Relations Act, after Equity had ordered its actors to cease performing in Weller's OOB production *Split* when Weller refused to sign the code. The complaint, as quoted in *Variety,* also alleges that "a provision of Equity's contract with the League of Resident Theaters requiring LORT managements to hire or compensate earlier showcase casts is also illegal and should be nullified." As of June 1981 no resolution of this case had been announced.

Meanwhile, as bargaining agent for the actors, Equity won from the League of Off-Broadway Theaters a 10.6 per cent pay increase for performers in off-Broadway productions, in a new contract to remain in effect until October 1984. New weekly minimums for the five categories of off-Broadway shows range from $169 to $351. And Equity members contributing their services in showcase productions are to receive three weeks' salary in lieu of an offer to repeat the role, if the show moves to the off-Broadway level from OOB.

An important change in the personnel of New York theater critics took place in September with the New York *Times's* announcement that Frank Rich would replace Walter Kerr in the daily reviewing spot, with Kerr returning to that role of unhurried observer of the passing theater scene in the Sunday paper which he prefers. Rich, 31, a native of Washington, D.C., served his reviewing apprenticeship on the Harvard *Crimson, Time* and other publications before joining the *Times* in April 1980. Rich called theater "a dominant passion" from his early childhood, "*before* I made the discovery of movies and TV." In his first season of reviewing he proved to be neither a crowd follower nor an iconoclast, calling them as he saw them but without often raising his voice, with sensitivities that seemed more personal than Olympian.

The ceremony of announcing and presenting the Tony Awards for Broadway's bests has become an annual TV fiesta. This year it certainly symbolized the twelve months of New York theater which it was trying to celebrate. Three of its four nominees for best play were foreign scripts, the other a return engagement from a previous off-Broadway season. All of its musicals were retreads of old material. One of its best-book nominees had survived for only one performance. Three of its best-score nominees had been palpable flops. The number of producers who nowadays huddle in groups to put on a single show was so large that it defeated the efforts of an admittedly slow reader, Elizabeth Taylor, to handle all their names in the cumbersome list of nominees. And yet . . . and yet there were the shining individual achievements of a Gower Champion, a Peter Shaffer. There was even one producer who was able to put on a show all by himself, David Merrick, who, as he accepted the best-musical award, posed the rhetorical question, "What would the musical season have been without *42nd Street*?" We shudder to think what this or any other theater season would have been without those special inspirations for which the theater of any time is remembered. We are more than usually grateful for the very few which brightened the 1980–81 season in New York and hope for a brighter cluster in the year to come.

Roger Rees, *center, in Romeo costume,* in the title role, David Threlfall as Smike, *center in robe,* and the Royal Shakespeare Company in *The Life & Adventures of Nicholas Nickleby,* adapted by David Edgar from Charles Dickens.

PHOTO BY MARTHA SWOPE

1981-82

THIS WAS THE SEASON that the Royal Shakespeare Company's production of *The Life & Adventures of Nicholas Nickleby* came to Broadway for a 49-performance visit in which it changed some of our ideas about modern theater, reaffirmed others and was so far outstandingly 1981–82's best play that some of its rivals grumbled about its eligibility for consideration in the Tony Award nominations—which it swept.

The adaptor of the Charles Dickens novel, David Edgar, described some of his and the company's intentions to a group of New York theater people: from the outset, they determined to dramatize *all* of *Nicholas Nickleby*. No subplot was to be cut, though incidents here and there could be dropped (and sometimes the status of "subplot" vs. "incident" was hotly debated during production). Much of the Dickens dialogue was used verbatim onstage, but in places Dickens's purposes were better served by invented dialogue—for example, when characters have an important presence in the novel but little to say. Requiring an eight-and-one-half-hour running time to tell its whole tale, *Nicholas Nickleby* changed, first, our estimate of how long an audience will tolerate a single sitting (broken three times for intermissions, plus an hour-long interval between Parts I and II) and end up shouting for more. Because of its extraordinary length, its adaptor tried to make material cuts in his initial working script but found that the threatened passages suddenly developed more importance than expected, taking on so much weight of continuity that most turned out to be unexcisable.

Nicholas Nickleby also changed, and probably not for the better in the long run, our notion of how much the audience might be induced to pay for a ticket to a unique experience of live theater. The impetus didn't come from the reviews, some of which were lukewarm. *Nicholas Nickleby* started slowly, but word of mouth worked its magic until theatergoers were eager to pay $100 (or $50 at the performances which offered only one part at a time) for any seat anywhere in the house during this limited engagement. "It would have been a bargain at $1,000 a ticket," declared one noted Dickens authority—hinting at unimaginable economic terrors lying in wait for the theater of the future.

What made this *Nicholas Nickleby* a bargain at $100 and up, captivating for all of its eight and one-half hours, was its reaffirmation of basic stage values: insightful faith in its source and purpose; clear-cut conflicts of good and evil, love and hate; superbly imaginative design, direction and performing. For example, we could swear that we saw a stagecoach loaded, hitched and setting out on its journey with passengers, including Nicholas, perched on its roof—but on second thought it must have been merely an illusion created with a few common objects and a group of uncommon actors under the direction of Trevor Nunn and John Caird. The design by John Napier and Dermot Hayes reached out with both arms to embrace the stage on several levels and parts of the auditorium for its travels, carnivals, duels, etc.—big enough to contain *Nicholas Nickleby* in its multifarious entirety, at the same time permitting the most intimate exchange. Here were infamous Dotheboys Hall and the preposterous Crummles troup of Shakespearean players; rakes at their insidious seduction of innocent maidens, climbers flattering a rich relative with attentions; fashion houses and counting houses

The 1981–82 Season on Broadway

PLAYS (18)

Wally's Cafe
Scenes and Revelations
The Supporting Cast
A Talent for Murder
Einstein and the Polar Bear
Crimes of the Heart (transfer)
Ned and Jack
MASS APPEAL (transfer)
The West Side Waltz
Grown Ups
Kingdoms
The Curse of an Aching Heart
Special Occasions
Come Back to the 5 & Dime Jimmy Dean, Jimmy Dean
Eminent Domain
AGNES OF GOD
Solomon's Child
Beyond Therapy (revised version)

MUSICALS (10)

Marlowe
Oh, Brother!
Merrily We Roll Along
The First
Dreamgirls
Waltz of the Stork
Pump Boys and Dinettes (transfer)
Is There Life After High School?
NINE
Do Black Patent Leather Shoes Really Reflect Up?

FOREIGN PLAYS IN ENGLISH (5)

THE LIFE & ADVENTURES OF NICHOLAS NICKLEBY
THE DRESSER
Duet for One
"MASTER HAROLD" . . . AND THE BOYS
The Hothouse

REVIVALS (12)

A Taste of Honey (transfer)
Fiddler on the Roof
My Fair Lady
Circle in the Square:
Candida
Macbeth
Camelot
Little Me (revised version)
Joseph and the Amazing Technicolor Dreamcoat (transfer)
Othello
The World of Sholom Aleichem
Little Johnny Jones
Medea

SPECIALTIES (3)

This Was Burlesque (return engagement)
An Evening With Dave Allen
Encore

HOLDOVERS WHICH PROBABLY BECAME HITS in 1981–82

42nd Street
Sophisticated Ladies
The Little Foxes
Lena Horne

Plays listed in CAPITAL LETTERS have been designated Best Plays of 1981–82.
Plays listed in *italics* were still running after May 31, 1982.
Plays listed in **bold face type** were classified as hits in *Variety*'s annual estimate published June 2, 1982.

whose financiers occupied no middle ground but were either so charitable as to be almost saintly (the Cheerybles) or so ruthless as to be almost demonic (Ralph Nickleby). The saga of young Nicholas trying to support his widowed mother and sister in the largely uncaring 19th century world was not what kept the audience on the edge of their seats hour after hour—after all, the general direction and final outcome of a Dickens plot could hold little mystery even for the majority who had never read this novel. The suspense was not in what was to happen, but in how it happened in episode after episode whose every detail was worth watching carefully.

Forty-two Royal Shakespeare Company performers appeared in 138 speaking roles in an ensemble display that brought to mind for comparison the same group's great *Marat/Sade* in 1965—and not to the disadvantage of *Nicholas Nickleby*. The quality of the acting varied only in length and prominence of role, the standouts being Roger Rees (the Tony winner) as Nicholas, Edward Petherbridge as humane and tipsy Newman Noggs and David Threlfall as the unfortunate Smike (Tony nominees); and, on another level, Emily Richard as Nicholas's sister Kate, John Woodvine as his sinister uncle Ralph, Alun Armstrong as the abusive schoolmaster Squeers, Patrick Godfrey as Mr. Kenwigs the paterfamilias, Christopher Benjamin and Lila Kaye as the performing Crummles's, Bob Peck as vicious Sir Mulberry Hawk, David Lloyd Meredith and Hubert Rees as the Cheerybles—and many, many others who took part in this triumph. Certainly *Nicholas Nickleby* was not merely the best play of New York's 1981–82 season, winning both the Tony and the New York Drama Critics Circle Awards, it was a stage achievement to be remembered for many years to come.

The 1981–82 theater season in New York was additionally and vividly memorable for a banner off-Broadway year. Four off-Broadway productions are Best Plays: Charles Fuller's Pulitzer Prize and Critics Award-winning drama of hatred and murder in a World War II barracks of black soldiers, *A Soldier's Play;* David Henry Hwang's enchanting two-character tribute to 19th century Chinese immigrant laborers, *The Dance and the Railroad;* Harvey Fierstein's touchingly sympathetic presentation of the life and times of a drag queen, *Torch Song Trilogy;* and A.R. Gurney Jr.'s emotionally and comically needling variations on a theme of WASP family life and times, *The Dining Room*. Furthermore, these off-Broadway bests were backed in depth by other scripts of considerable note: Jonathan Reynolds's *Geniuses,* David Pownall's *Livingstone and Sechele,* Christopher Durang's *Sister Mary Ignatius Explains It All for You* and Amlin Gray's *How I Got That Story,* to name the standouts.

Taking a few paces backward to view the Broadway season as an economic whole, the box office gross continued to expand like a gas under steadily reducing pressure. During the early part of the season this one rising-gross statistic tended to conceal the truth about prosperity, which was attenuating along Broadway as it was in almost every other area of American life. The first sign of trouble was noticed in attendance figures, which began to sink below comparable 1980–81 levels and had shrunk 500,000 admissions by mid-season. "B'way Season Looms as Worst in Years," decried *Variety* in midwinter, in a story that deplored the shortage of original musicals and of the "capacity smash" amid "a substantially lower total of new productions." About a month later, *Business Week* echoed the gloomy conclusion that "the lights are dimmer on Broadway," with falling admissions and rising ticket prices and production costs, in a crisis in which "virtually every Broadway play and musical . . . . . is trying to lure patrons with half-price tickets." Twofers were lying about on counters all over town, and the TKTS booth in Times Square, purveyors of cut-rate theater tickets to last-minute show-shoppers, was doing a business amounting to more than 10 per cent of Broadway's total gross.

Looking back at the 12 months as the dust settled on June 1, *Variety* finally concluded that 1981–82 was a "nervous" Broadway theater season which grossed a record $221,234,791 in New York (over $200 million for the first time, compared with $194, $143, $128 and $103 million in the past four years) and a "staggering" $249,531,109 on the road. An important proportion, if not all, of this 13.7 per cent increase over 1980–81 was caused by inflation, with the Broadway top (not counting *Nicholas Nickleby*) rising to $40, with $35 becoming commonplace, and with the *average* Broadway ticket price at $23.08 by June 1 as compared with $19.72 a year before.

Further evidence that this phenomenal gross was mere inflation is provided by the general falling-off of activity elsewhere in *Variety*'s final 1981–82 count. Attendance was down to just over 10 million as compared with 10.8 million in 1980–81 (but handsomely above the 9.4, 9.1 and 8.6 million attendance of the three previous years). And playing weeks (if ten shows play ten weeks, that's 100 playing weeks) took a dive to 1,461, reversing the upward movement of the recent past: 1,360, 1,472, 1,541 to the record 1,545 in 1980–81. As the season ended, there were only 26 shows playing on Broadway, compared to 30 at the same time the previous year—but again, handsomely above the 23 a decade and 21 two decades ago.

By our own count, there has been a continuing decline in the volume of Broadway production during recent seasons, becoming sharply steeper in this one. Not counting specialties, 1981–82 provided only 45 new Broadway productions, compared with 51 last year and 58 at a 1979–80 peak. This year's 45 included 12 revivals, so that the total number of new plays and musicals amounted to 33 (four fewer than last season) including three transfers and a revision. The hits were running longer (14 of the shows playing June 1, 1981 were still playing a year later), and it was taking considerably longer for a show to pay off its cost and thereby achieve hit status, and no wonder: the capitalization tab for the musical *Nine* was an estimated $2,750,000, and straight plays were lucky to get on at $500,000. As of the end of the year, only three Broadway productions other than *Nicholas Nickleby* were deemed by *Variety* to have reached the black: the off-Broadway transfer *Crimes of the Heart,* the revival of *Othello* and Katharine Hepburn's vehicle *The West Side Waltz.*

Under these conditions, a failed musical, *The First,* cost its backers $3 million (according to a *Wall Street Journal* estimate). *Colette* dropped $1,500,000 in tryout without ever reaching Broadway. *Barnum* recouped its $1.2 million Broadway cost but dropped $2 million in a Paris production and folded on the road. The popular *Woman of the Year* was still in the red, and the celebrated *Piaf* was estimated to have lost $670,000 of its $725,000 cost as of the end of its run.

Nevertheless, it was still possible to make a bundle with the right Broadway show, though accurate prediction of which show would be "right" still eluded the vast majority of investors. With 30 productions running in Broadway theaters and playing to 89.8 per cent of capacity the last week in December, the total week's gross rose over $6 million for the first time to a record $6,477,866 according to *Variety* estimate. Among the holdovers in 1981–82, *Deathtrap* had paid its backers $1,460,000 (365 per cent) on their $200,000 investment and *Children of a*

Lesser God $2,500,000 (237 per cent) on $400,000. Off Broadway, *Cloud 9* had paid off its $175,000 cost and was earning $5,000 weekly. *Ain't Misbehavin'* had brought in $3,028,500 (403 per cent) for its $375,000 cost, and one of the all-time box office champs, *Fiddler on the Roof,* had reached $10,889,500 profit (1,452 per cent) on its original $375,000—and still counting.

Broadway

Nicholas Nickleby arrived early in the season to light up the midtown sky and left early, as the year turned, at the end of its limited engagement, with its Royal Shakespeare troupe physically exhausted and its producers breathing sighs of relief that this supremely distinguished undertaking managed to break even on the balance sheets. Ronald Harwood's *The Dresser* remained, however, to demonstrate all season long the power of British theater at its best. This script concerned itself with the last day in the life of a provincial Shakespeare touring-company star (Paul Rogers), and more particularly with this star's close relationship with the admiring dresser (Tom Courtenay) who fusses over him, catering to his every need and seeing that he is ready to go on at curtain time. Courtenay's finicky performance of this mannered, single-minded creature stood at the center of a bustling play, busy with the backstage activity before, during and after a provincial performance of *King Lear.* The dresser's bewildered grief at the death of his master, his *raison d'etre,* even more acute than that of the star's wife (Rachel Gurney), climaxed this extremely skillfully acted, directed (by Michael Elliott) and designed (by Laurie Dennett and Stephen Doncaster) piece of introverted theater.

For the second year in succession, Athol Fugard provided a hard-hitting script for the Best Plays list. Like last season's *A Lesson From Aloes,* Fugard's *"MASTER HAROLD"* . . . *and the boys* was a harsh reflection of racial attitudes in his apartheid-plagued native land of South Africa, viewed in this case through the friendship, almost to the point of father-and-son kinship, between a white youth (Lonny Price) and the older black man (Zakes Mokae) who has served his family for many years. A third character, a black man (Danny Glover) menially employed in the white family's tea room, acts and reacts as a kind of Greek chorus accenting the values of the play. Under its author's direction, and with this superbly coordinated acting trio, *Master Harold* subjects the white youth to gradually increasing emotional stress until, like a skunk at bay, the boy releases his inbred racism on his longsuffering friend. The play, performed without intermission, is essentially a one-acter stretched to carry more weight that it can comfortably bear in the opening stages, but it finally arrives at a shattering collision. Whereas Fugard's *A Lesson From Aloes* was indigenously South African in its characters and situation, *"MASTER HAROLD"* . . . *and the boys* is a universal, potent variation on the theme of racism in general, anywhere, any time, and may well prove as durable as anything ever written for the stage on this subject.

Two days after *Master Harold* arrived on Broadway in its regional (Yale Repertory Theater) production, still another notable foreign script, Harold Pinter's *The Hothouse,* came to Broadway in its American premiere production by the Trinity Square Repertory Company in Providence, R.I. *The Hothouse* (written in 1958 between Pinter's *The Birthday Party* and *The Caretaker* but put away in his drawer until now) was a classic example of absurdist comedy trimmed with black at the edges. It was set in a madhouse ruled by the Establishment (a penetrable metaphor), and it ridiculed the excesses and shortcomings of bureaucracy and other conceits cherished by everyone from the director down to his lowliest eager-beaver employee (the inmates never put in an appearance). As usual in vintage Pinter, least menacing is most dangerous (remember the glass of water in *The Homecoming?*), with Richard Kavanaugh perfectly portraying the director's impeccable assistant—correct, straightforward and therefore the square backdrop against which all the ragged-edged absurdity is silhouetted, as well as the detonating device which increasingly threatens to touch everything off. The "Pinter pauses"—those beats of silence punctuating the dialogue—were carefully observed in the direction by Adrian Hall. *The Hothouse* made only a brief appearance on Broadway, but it left long memories. Not so another import from London, Tom Kempinski's *Duet for One*, about a psychiatrist treating a musician whose career is ended prematurely by a crippling disease, despite the formidable acting services of Max von Sydow in the former and Anne Bancroft in the latter roles.

Economic and social conditions being what they are in the 1980s, no longer can the state of American playwriting be appraised by its Broadway experience. Of this year's 18 new American scripts on Broadway, fewer than a handful possessed the right stuff—whatever it is—to survive even modestly in an artistically forbidding environment beset by enormous costs, discouraging ticket prices and audience tastes that are narrowing as the audience shrinks. The American script most comfortable under these conditions was Bill C. Davis's Best Play *Mass Appeal*, well polished under Geraldine Fitzgerald's direction in this and a previous production at Manhattan Theater Club and having the very great advantage of a memorable performance by Milo O'Shea of a good-natured, easygoing, middle-aged Catholic priest brought face-to-face with his own compromises by the penetrating comments of a young seminarian. For this once, Broadway audiences settled for charm and intelligence and kept *Mass Appeal* going all season long.

The theme of *Mass Appeal*—an examination of aspects of Roman Catholic style and dogma—recurred on and off Broadway in such scripts as *Sister Mary Ignatius Explains It All for You, Catholic School Girls* and even in a short-lived musical set in a Parochial School and antically entitled *Do Black Patent Leather Shoes Really Reflect Up?* On Broadway, *Agnes of God* by John Pielmeier was an emotionally violent study of a young nun who has been convicted of killing her own infant immediately after its birth. Under pressure from a court-appointed psychiatrist (Elizabeth Ashley) and under the wing of a Mother Superior (Geraldine Page), the nun gradually reveals an ascetic, child-of-God nature that transcends the most dreadful reality with sublime spiritual, even miraculous interpretations. This duality—sublime cause and brutal effect—was beautifully handled in Amanda Plummer's acting of the nun, who may be possessed by the Holy Ghost, or the devil, or merely a pathetically wracked slip of humanity, or a combination of all three. Miss Plummer's interpretation was the season's female acting peak.

Another accomplished American script with a forceful theme—stated to more effect in individual scenes than as a structural unit—was Jules Feiffer's *Grown Ups*, in which Bob Dishy played a family man fighting simultaneous battles against his demanding parents, his self-centered child and his abrasive wife, with diminishing hope of victory. Percy Granger's *Eminent Domain*, about a college professor at a critical stage of his career and his family relationships, was given a solidly satisfying production by Circle in the Square under the direction of Paul Austin, with Philip Bosco as the professor and Betty Miller as his ex-alcoholic wife. Beth Henley's *Crimes of the Heart* transferred to Broadway this season, and Mary Beth Hurt and company repeated their celebrated off-Broadway performance of family members in crisis over a wife's attempted murder of her husband. The writing-acting team of the 1966 Best Play *Hogan's Goat* was reunited with Faye Dunaway playing a Brooklyn Irish woman looking back over the tribulations of her life and pronouncing it a triumph in William Alfred's *The Curse of an Aching Heart.* The year's further stage contemplations of rather serious matters included Elan Garonzik's *Scenes and Revelations* (19th century family strife in Lancaster, Pa.), Edward Sheehan's *Kingdoms* (ideological confrontation between Napoleon and Pope Pius VII), Tom Dulack's *Solomon's Child* (deprogramming a youngster who has been brainwashed by a religious cult) and Sheldon's Rosen's *Ned and Jack* (Edward Sheldon and John Barrymore on the brink of hitting the skids)—which last, with Bernard Slade's *Special Occasions* (the ongoing love affair between a divorced husband and wife) and an updated revival of George M. Cohan's *Little Johnny Jones* starring Donny Osmond shared the harsh experience of closing after their opening performance.

On the lighter side, Ernest Thompson's vehicle for Katharine Hepburn, *The West Side Waltz,* costarred with *Mass Appeal* in this year's Broadway parade. Thompson's is a play of spirit in the ascendancy, with Miss Hepburn as a pianist who manages to keep her fingers on the keys and her good-humored wits about her even as the aging process lays upon her one infirmity after another. We have seen this gifted actress play women of indomitable courage before, and now we have seen her do it again, in full Hepburn style and with the help of Dorothy Loudon as a friend who provides the pianist with disbelieving encouragement as well as competent violin accompaniment. George Furth's *The Supporting Cast* benefited from its casting of an accomplished ensemble (Hope Lange, Betty Garrett, Sandy Dennis, Jack Gilford and Joyce Van Patten) playing the subjects of an author's embarrassingly tattle-tale memoirs, under Gene Saks's direction in an attractive Malibu beach house set designed by William Ritman.

The latest Broadway effort of Sam Bobrick and Ron Clark, *Wally's Cafe,* with Rita Moreno, James Coco and Sally Struthers hanging out in a Las Vegas roadside cafe, was a nonentity on Broadway, like most of their other work—and like it may also go on to wide international popularity. Audiences around the world dig Bobrick & Clark, Broadway to the contrary notwithstanding. Still another pair of renowned comedy writers, Jerome Chodorov and Norman Panama, missed their step with a comic murder intrigue, *A Talent for Murder,* about a mystery writer (Claudette Colbert) confined to a wheelchair in the midst of a multi-million-dollar art collection and a bunch of acquisitive relatives. *Einstein and the Polar Bear* (eager beaver young female reporter thrusts herself upon a reclusive novelist played by Peter Strauss) greatly disappointed its regional theater partisans, as did *Come Back to the 5 & Dime Jimmy Dean, Jimmy Dean* (the fan club 20 years after Dean's *Giant,* with Cher on parade among a sizeable cast). Christopher Durang scored a resounding hit off Broadway with his one-acter *Sister Mary Ignatius Explains It All for You,* but his effort to whip his *Beyond Therapy* (which played 30 performances at the Phoenix last season) into Broadway shape in a revised version, a farcical treatment of sexuality, psychiatry and an assortment of other foibles, divided his audience into pros and cons.

Chagrin at the faltering step of the 1981–82 Broadway musicals (including three major efforts, *Say Hello to Harvey, The Little Prince and the Aviator* and *Colette,* which closed out of town or in previews) was relieved at the last possible moment, on the day before the Tony nominations closed in May, by the arrival of the exciting *Nine,* staged by Tommy Tune in determination to try anything once—and imagining an abundant number of new things to try in a musical theater context. The Arthur Kopit book was based on a Mario Fratti translation of his own Italian version, apparently taking off (though unbilled in the program) from Federico Fellini's celebrated movie *8 ½* about an internationally renowned director gone dry of ideas but struggling to make one more "film." Raul Julia played the director in *Nine,* the only other male characters being children (the movie director at age 9 and several of his Parochial School classmates). A harem of females is grouped around the introspective hero, however, each doing her own thing, mostly with sexual overtones. The patient forbearance of a wife (Karen Akers), the hilariously overblown seductions of a mistress (Anita Morris), the sleek and savage attentions of a movie producer (Liliane Montevecchi) are a few of the enticements found here, where every musical number in Maury Yeston's compelling score stopped the show. The design (scenery by Lawrence Miller, costumes by William Ivey Long) was literally out of this world, relentlessly confined to black and white except for one sequence depicting the filming of a movie scene, when the colors spilled out into pastel in a romantic insert bringing to mind the Valentine sequence in the otherwise stark *Follies.* The black-clad silhouettes of the performers were sharply defined within the shiny, sanitary white surroundings of this Venetian spa setting, with Venice itself a mirage glimpsed in the far distance. This whole show, a Best Play, was a triumph of imagination in every department. No wonder *Nine* collected so many of the Tony Awards for which it arrived just barely in time to contend.

Dreamgirls, too, had its moments; it was a burst of color and energy with Michael Bennett staging, designs by Robin Wagner (sets) and Theoni V. Aldredge (costumes) and most conspicuously with the performance of Jennifer Holliday as the lead singer of a female rock trio. Miss Holliday's violent protest when she is both professionally and emotionally jilted at the end of Act I in the number "And I Am Telling You I'm Not Going" was a powerful outburst on a scale seldom realized outside grand opera—a performing moment to remember. The musical itself explored narrow passageways of the personal-appearance and recording entertainment world, with Ben Harney in major support as a selfish impresario. It was reverberantly loud in every sense, and, except for Miss Holliday and Mr. Harney, mostly forgettable.

A young, bright and cheerful exception to this year's rule of faltering musicals was *Pump Boys and Dinettes,* not a Broadway native but a transfer from off Broadway. Conceived and written by Jim Wann and other members of the cast, it packaged a group of country music numbers in a modern highway setting, the girls being waitresses in the diner on one side of the road and the boys gas jockeys on the other side. Also among the strivers was *Waltz of the Stork,* a "comedy with music" that sprang full-grown from the brain of Melvin Van Peebles and then walked around in his shoes. He wrote, directed, produced and starred in this series of autobiographical monologues joined by musical elaborations.

A disappointment to remember was *Merrily We Roll Along*—first, because it occupied a season of one of our theater's most valued musical artists, Stephen Sondheim; and second, because after all was said and done it didn't seem to be worth even the time required to play or watch it in the theater. It goes without saying that Harold Prince's staging of the piece was in precise control, or that there were numbers in the Sondheim score that sent his fans running out to acquire the original cast album. The Kaufman-Hart play from which the musical was adapted by George Furth travels backwards in time to show how its idealistic young hero ruined his life. This version moves back from 1980 to 1955, as a young stage hopeful on the threshold of success decides to abandon a difficult wife, an irritatingly dogmatic collaborator and the hellish strictures of the theater itself to follow the evil gleam of the recording industry.

Also on the disappointing side was the economically massive failure of a large-scale musical about Jackie Robinson's entry into professional baseball, *The First,* with David Alan Grier impersonating the famous Brooklyn Dodger first baseman. *Marlowe* (a rock musical imposition on the Elizabethan dramatist), *Oh, Brother!* (a modernized spinoff from *The Comedy of Errors*), *Is There Life After High School?* (growing up can be half the fun) and *Do Black Patent Leather Shoes Really Reflect Up?* (antics at the Parochial School) fell even farther short of inspiration.

This year's specialty shows included a new production at Radio City Music Hall, *Encore,* celebrating that theater's golden jubilee with re-enactments by the Rockettes and others of noble Music Hall stage-show numbers of the past 50 years. Ann Corio's *This Was Burlesque* paid Broadway a return-engagement visit. The only straight specialty was *An Evening With Dave Allen,* with the BBC-TV star presenting his comedy monologues at the Booth Theater.

Off Broadway

In the smaller New York playhouses in 1981–82, there was a perception that the status of what we call "off Broadway" was evolving—not exactly changing, not exactly increasing in stature, but in the process of evolving from a tributary theater into what could become the main event of the New York stage in this decade.

The narrowing circumstances of Broadway acceptance (the smash musical, the popular comedy, the shock-treatment drama) are causing the creative baton to be passed elsewhere. It could be argued, for example, that a finely-drawn script like Charles Fuller's Pulitzer Prize and Critics Award-winning Best Play *A Soldier's Play* wouldn't find an economically sustaining audience in a Broadway production, any more than Samm-Art Williams's *Home* was able to do so a season ago. What to do, then? A theater that cannot support *Home* or *A Soldier's Play* doesn't deserve the name of a national art form; and the New York theater is certainly that, even if Broadway isn't any more. At this point, an alternative seems to lie in evolving off Broadway into the principal bearer of creative theater, raising the price of the top ticket to more than $20 and pushing the production cost well up into six figures, hoping it will become economically feasible to maintain such a theater in the dozens of smaller auditoriums scattered throughout the city. If this sounds like past Broadway mistakes—raise prices and costs and hope for the best—it should serve as a warning to off Broadway against playing follow-the-leader over the same cliff. Right now, good plays and willing audiences exist in abundance off Broadway, even at $14 to $20 a seat. Whether this will enable off Broadway to establish an economically stable outlet for its creative energies is still very much an ongoing question.

The 1981–82 Season Off Broadway

PLAYS (45)

The Fuehrer Bunker
Isn't It Romantic
The Butler Did It
A Tale Told
The Diviners
  (return engagement)
How It All Began
Zooman and the Sign
  (return engagement)
Key Exchange
Public Theater:
THE DANCE AND THE RAILROAD
Family Devotions
Twelve Dreams
Red and Blue
Sea Marks
Particular Friendships
Grace
2 by South
Manhattan Theater Club:
Crossing Niagara
Sally and Marsha
Gardenia
Playwrights Horizons:
Sister Mary Ignatius & The Actor's Nightmare
THE DINING ROOM
Geniuses

Fighting Bob
Circle Repertory:
Threads
Confluence
Snow Orchid
The Great Grandson of Jedediah Kohler
Young Playwrights Festival
  (three programs)
Negro Ensemble:
A SOLDIER'S PLAY
Colored People's Time
The Good Parts
TORCH SONG TRILOGY
Clownmaker
Chucky's Hunch
How I Got That Story
Lydie Breeze
Weekends Like Other People
Poor Little Lambs
Scenes Dedicated to My Brother, etc.
Catholic School Girls
The Six O'Clock Boys
The Freak

MUSICALS (9)

El Bravo!
The Heebie Jeebies
Pump Boys and Dinettes
Double Feature
Head Over Heels
Francis
Oh, Johnny
Lullabye and Goodnight
T.N.T.

FOREIGN PLAYS IN ENGLISH (7)

Hunting Scenes From Lower Bavaria
Maggie & Pierre
After the Prize
No End of Blame
Zastrozzi
Three Acts of Recognition
Livingstone and Sechele

REVUES (4)

The Laundry Hour
Pigiazz, II
Tomfoolery
Maybe I'm Doing It Wrong

SPECIALTIES (12)

"No"
Shay Duffin as Brendan Behan
Oscar Remembered
Everybody's Gettin' Into the Act
The Ballad of Dexter Creed
Behind the Broken Words
My Own Stranger
Cotton Patch Gospel
Whistler
Kaufman at Large
Cast of Characters
The Regard of Flight

REVIVALS (40)

American Buffalo
Entertaining Mr. Sloane
Misalliance
Delacorte:
The Tempest
Henry IV, Part 1
What the Butler Saw
Chekhov on the Lawn
Roundabout:
Miss Julie & Playing With Fire
The Caretaker

Roundabout (cont'd):
The Browning Version
The Chalk Garden
The Broken Pitcher
LOOM:
The Red Mill
H.M.S. Pinafore
A Night in Venice
  (13 operettas in running repertory)
Taken in Marriage
Classic Stage:
Peer Gynt I
Peer Gynt II
The Cherry Orchard
King Lear
Ghost Sonata
Joseph and the Amazing Technicolor Dreamcoat
The Unseen Hand & Killer's Head
Birdbath & Crossing the Crab Nebula
Acting Company:
Twelfth Night
The Country Wife
Antigone

Plays listed in CAPITAL LETTERS have been designated Best Plays of 1981–82.
Plays listed in *italics* were still running off Broadway after May 31, 1982.

This said, let us note that 1981–82 production of new scripts off Broadway was on the rise after a three-year falloff. There were 60 productions including 45 American straight plays (of which two were return engagements), 9 musicals and 7 foreign plays in English. This compares favorably with the totals of the past two seasons, 55 (33-14-8) in 1981 and 58 (39-7-12) in 1980, and is gaining on the 64 (38-15-11) of 1979; and the large number of American straight play productions last season indicates where the action was. In addition to the above, there were 4 revues and 40 revival productions off Broadway in 1981–82, a number which is not significantly out of line with other recent seasons.

Last year in summing up we wrote, "Foreign playwrights stole the show off Broadway," but this year the American dramatists overwhelmed the list with outstanding scripts. The aforementioned prizewinning Best Play *A Soldier's Play* made a distinguished name for itself as the opening production of The Negro Ensemble Company's tenth anniversary season, becoming virtually the whole NEC season in itself, held over all year in the group's Theater Four just west of the Broadway area. NEC wisely decided not to move this Charles Fuller hit to Broadway, where it couldn't possibly have grown any bigger than it already was, in any important way. In form it was a whodunit, with the murder of a spit-and-polish black sergeant (Adolph Caesar) in a World War II training camp for black recruits. The murder is investigated by a black captain (Charles Brown) assigned by the adjutant general's office over the strong objections and prejudice of the black soldiers' white officers. The working script (but not the playbill) carries the notation that the play is based on Herman Melville's *Billy Budd,* a fact which is not self-evident in Fuller's development of theme and situation. There is indeed an exemplary young recruit, vulnerable but extremely popular except with the tough sergeant, who views the recruit's accommodating nature as a handicap to the rapid wartime advancement of the black race and promptly makes a victim out of the lad. But there are many other antagonisms to be resolved as they orbit in flashback around the murder under Douglas Turner Ward's impeccable direction, in Felix E. Cochren's serviceable set—was it a race killing (by white officers), a revenge killing (by resentful recruits) or just a brawl? And will the white officer elite permit the black lawyer to uncover the truth? *A Soldier's Play* answered these questions by means of first-rate theater in a production perfectly suited to its off-Broadway environment. NEC had to use another theater, the Cherry Lane, for its second production of the season, Leslie Lee's *Colored People's Time,* directed by Horacena J. Taylor and outlining black American history from the Civil War to the 1960s civil rights movement.

Another standout of the off-Broadway year was Harvey Fierstein's *Torch Song Trilogy,* in which homosexuality is flaunted in the form of transvestism and then profoundly and movingly empathized in a network of family relationships. This Best Play is in fact three one-acters firmly connected by the central character (played with passionate conviction by the author), introduced as a drag queen who tires of hectic promiscuity and manages to form a meaningful attachment but suffers agonies when his lover leaves him for a woman (in the first one-acter, *The International Stud*); savors some of the pleasures of a more stable existence in tandem with another lover (in the second, *Fugue in a Nursery*); and finally reaches out to help a gay teen-ager in a cruelly hostile world, acting as both mother and father (in the third and intensely affecting *Widows and Children First!*). The theme was carried forward with a good deal of gay sexual gallows humor, but physical details of the experience were few and, except for one incident, restrained. What mattered in *Torch Song Trilogy* was not sexuality but common humanity, or its absence in the treatment of some homosexuals in some circumstances—with consequent tragic emotions rising in the midst of comedy in this outstanding play. It moved to Broadway shortly after it closed off Broadway in May.

Then there was the exceptionally successful season on the mainstage of Playwrights Horizons on 42d Street's Theater Row, where artistic director Andre Bishop and managing director Paul Daniels put every other organization in the shade with a schedule made up of *Sister Mary Ignatius Explains It All for You, The Dining Room* and *Geniuses,* all three of them still running in June when the old New York theater season faded out and the new one faded in. The most meticulously shaped and deeply penetrating of these three fine comedies was *The Dining Room,* firmly positioned on the 1981–82 Best Plays list. This production of A.R. Gurney Jr.'s play, set in that disappearing facility which in our day is used mainly for family warfare, office space and everything else except dining, was a triple threat of playwriting, acting and direction. The play is constructed as a series of events with changing sets of characters of all ages flowing in and out, but with each event a silhouetted unit of personal or family crisis, poignant or funny, alternately and in combination. These vignettes, disconnected except by the central theme of fading WASP glory symbolized by the fading function of the dining room, were clearly and compellingly staged by David Trainer. The ensemble led by Remak Ramsay (appearing now as a grandfather, now as a child at a birthday party) and Pippa Pearthree defined each of the many characters stylishly and harmoniously. Like a well-planned feast, *The Dining Room* was sometimes tart, sometimes sweet, always generously portioned and served with undeniable flair.

As the record at Playwrights Horizons so eloquently demonstrates, it wasn't only the headlining Best Plays that made this off-Broadway season such a rewarding one, it was a depth of excellent productions which might easily have made the Best Plays list themselves in a less competitive year. Jonathan Reynolds's *Geniuses* was a comedy in the boisterous tradition: literate, bawdy, hyperactive and irreverent about both New York and Los Angeles lifestyles. With Joanne Camp as a sexy movie star stirring libidos and egos, this three-acter played games with some American movie makers trapped indoors by a monsoon in the Philippines and beginning to give off steam. In the end, Superego (an epic movie director played by David Garrison) is a god who comes down from the sky in his machine (a helicopter) to set everybody back on proper course. Gerald Gutierrez swung his direction like a battleaxe (no needles here) in the spirit of good mean fun.

Likewise, Christopher Durang's *Sister Mary Ignatius Explains It All for You* made a strong impact on Playwrights Horizons audiences with Elizabeth Franz as a teaching nun whose devotion to her faith and dogma has crossed the border of fanaticism, so that instead of inspiring her students she rouses them to resentment and suffers their vengeance. Durang's satire was powerful acid, preceded on the program by a more frivolous one-acter, *The Actor's Nightmare,* about a player finding himself onstage in a leading role for which he has had no rehearsal.

Downtown at Joseph Papp's New York Shakespeare Public Theater there was a busy season of new plays both foreign and domestic, but it never re-attained the stature of the opening presentation, David Henry Hwang's *The Dance and the Railroad.* This was an utterly charming and subtly realized character portrait of a 19th century Chinese immigrant railroad laborer fighting the dehumanizing erosion of his daily task by practising dance steps and pantomime for a role in traditional Chinese opera. John Lone directed Hwang's piece, choreographed it, wrote the score and played the leading role, supported by Tzi Ma as a youthful laborer eager to learn opera performing too. This Best Play was a unique combination of dance movement, sound and dramatic insight, a very large entertainment in a small package. While *The Dance and the Railroad* was still running, a second play by this same author, *Family Devotions,* was produced at the Public. Its reach was broader as it compared the ways of modern Chinese Americans with those of a visiting relative from Communist China, but its grasp was far less sure.

Another leading dramatist represented on the Public Theater's schedule was James Lapine, whose *Twelve Dreams* under his own direction was a painful probing of the dreams and the sanity of a troubled 10-year-old. David Rabe too had a play at the Public this season, the gangster comedy *Goose and Tomtom,* but he can't be said to have been "represented" there, since he disavowed the production of his play before it opened. *Zastrozzi* by the Canadian George F. Walker also dealt with crime in a clash of good and evil symbols under Andrei Serban's direction, while the personal stresses of 16 characters were exposed in an art-exhibition setting in Botho Strauss's 1977 German play *Three Acts of Recognition,* staged by Richard Foreman in flamboyant style. Also mixed into the Public Theater potpourri this season were a topical revue *The Laundry Hour;* Michael Moriarty's counterattack against the critics, *The Ballad of Dexter Creed; Antigone* staged by Joseph Chaikin; a new Elizabeth Swados musical *Lullabye and Goodnight,* surveying the world of the prostitute; a pair of colored light bulbs flashing in beat with offstage conversation in *Red and Blue,* directed by JoAnne Akalaitis; plus a return engagement of Miss Swados's Old Testament-oriented *The Haggadah,* which promises to be an annual event at the Joseph Papp theater complex.

The off-Broadway year's best foreign play was first produced in showcase at the Quaigh Theater, then moved up to full professional status there. *Livingstone and Sechele* by David Pownall, previously produced at the Edinburgh Festival and in London, yielded very little to its contemporaries on the Best Plays list and had the advantage of a striking portrayal of a 19th century African chieftain by Afemo, an actor who, according to the Quaigh's program notes, "considers himself a child of the Yoruba culture in Nigeria." The Livingstone of the title is the one once presumed by the explorer Stanley; and the chieftain, Sechele, was the only convert achieved by the Scottish doctor's African evangelizing. The half-naked savage is more than a match, in shrewdness as well as in strength, for the Scots Presbyterian as they attempt to join their two disparate cultures by means of Christian faith and ethic. Afemo's open-eyed, indomitable Sechele was one of four strong performances, the others being by Mike Champagne as the born loser Livingstone, Prudence Wright Holmes as his wife with twice his resilience and twenty times his strength, and Esther Ryvlin as the most alluring and intractable of Sechele's wives. Directed by Will Lieberson, the Quaigh's artistic director, *Livingstone and Sechele* was one of the major contributions to this notable off-Broadway season.

Amlin Gray's *How I Got That Story* made a big splash off off Broadway a season ago and was likewise one of this year's premier events in transfer to full off-Broadway production. In the framework of an American journalist's adventures while trying to cover the Vietnam War, and in farcical style, it exposed the futilities and frustrations of that national misstep in a series of encounters with military and non-military persons on both sides. All of the latter appeared under the single character name "The Historical Event," and all were played by Bob Gunton in a virtuoso display of comedic skill. The same was said by some observers of Kevin Wade's *Key Exchange* in its WPA Theater production's season-long run at the Orpheum Theater, with three eager young people making believe that their relationships and commitments were of comic consequence— a belief we were not able to share.

Gardner McKay's *Sea Marks,* the romance of an Irish fisherman touched with the gift of poetry and the Liverpool woman who loves, encourages and exploits him—a script often produced and highly respected in regional theater— made its professional New York debut early in the season under John Stix's direction. In another part of the forest, Casey Kurtti's *Catholic School Girls* was an amusing series of incidents in a Catholic school for girls, Grades One to Eight, cleverly compressed into a small package under Burry Fredrik's direction, with four well-chosen actresses playing both the students as they grow up and the teachers who cherish or bully them. This play inaugurated a new playhouse on 42d Street's Theater Row, the Douglas Fairbanks Theater, a comfortable auditorium set back from the street behind a courtyard. Other off-Broadway plays of more than fleeting interest were Paul Rudnick's *Poor Little Lambs,* a comedy imagining that a mere woman would attempt to join the celebrated all-male Yale singing group, the Whiffenpoofs; the comedy whodunit *The Butler Did It* by Walter and Peter Marks; the Juilliard School's *How It All Began,* dramatizing the origins of West German terrorism; *Chucky's Hunch* by Rochelle Owens, with Kevin O'Connor as a disillusioned artist unburdening himself in letters to a former wife; a pair of Joel Homer one-acters at the South Street Theater; Sidney Morris's *The Six O'Clock Boys* about a middle-aged woman and the youthful visitors to her room in a Columbus Avenue welfare hotel; and *The Freak* by Granville Wyche Burgess, looking into the early life of Edgar Cayce, a faith healer.

American Place's 1981 season carried over into June with W.D. Snodgrass's own dramatization of his cycle of poems, *The Fuehrer Bunker,* with Robert Stattel as Hitler in the last days of the Third Reich. The group's 1982 season was meager in both size and scope, consisting of only one play, Jane Stanton Hitchcock's character study of the unpleasantly outspoken female operator of an Oklahoma laundromat, *Grace* (moved up from American Place workshop), plus two exceptionally attractive specialties: *Behind the Broken Words,* with Roscoe Lee Browne and Anthony Zerbe in a collection of poetry excerpts, and *The Regard of Flight,* a comic vaudeville with Bill Irwin clowning and carrying on in pantomime routines and verbal send-ups written by himself.

The Phoenix rounded out its 1981 season with Wendy Wasserstein's *Isn't It Romantic,* about women in the big city, then went on to a pair of foreign plays: the Canadian *Maggie & Pierre* with Linda Griffiths playing both the Trudeaus and Eric Peterson as an interviewer, and the world premiere of Fay Weldon's *After the Prize,* a British script about the aftereffects of the Nobel on the emotional life of a woman laureate. The Phoenix ended 1982 with an American overview of the life of the blue collar worker, *Weekends Like Other People.*

Inevitably, there were those 1981–82 off-Broadway entries which promised much more than they were finally able to perform. For example, Lanford Wilson's attempt to round off his Talley family series (*The 5th of July, Talley's Folly*) with *A Tale Told* at Circle Repertory met with far less than the enthusiasm accorded to the two former Best Plays. The new one dealt with family frictions up in the house on the same night as the Matt Friedman-Sally Talley rendezvous down in the boathouse in *Talley's Folly*. Circle Rep continued its season's activities with two more family plays—Jonathan Bolt's *Threads* and Joe Pintauro's *Snow Orchid*—and another Lanford Wilson play, *Thymus Vulgaris*, on a program of one-acters named for its John Bishop script, *Confluence*, and including Beth Henley's *Am I Blue*. Bishop's *The Great Grandson of Jedediah Kohler*, about the descendant of a gun-totin' frontier marshal and his search for his own identity as a modern hero, was also produced by Circle in repertory with a revival of *Richard II* which closed after previews. Another 1981–82 Circle project was the production in conjunction with the Dramatists Guild Fund, Inc. of ten new plays on three programs written by children age 8 to 18, winners of the Dramatists Guild Young People's Playwriting Contest. The young people's plays were staged and performed by professionals at the Circle and were admiringly received by reviewers.

Another fully promising effort was made by John Guare with two plays in his series set in 19th century Nantucket and dealing with several generations of Americans groping for values within the rapidly-changing context of a young but maturing country. The two plays were *Lydie Breeze* (produced independently and directed by Louis Malle) taking place in the 1890s and bringing in venereal disease as a symbol of the spreading consequences of individual behavior, and *Gardenia* (produced by Manhattan Theater Club and directed by Karel Reisz) taking place after the Civil War, with the characters trying to get a running start into the new era. The plays were sensitive and eloquent, like all Guare works, but unstructured and confusing in both style and intent. Another challenging script at Manhattan Theater Club was the British *No End of Blame* by Howard Barker, subtitled "Scenes of Overcoming" chronicling the troubled career of a Middle European political cartoonist subjected to forms of censorship and suppression on both sides of the Iron Curtain. Back in June, MTC had also raised the question of the pervasiveness of Nazi evil in the 1966 German play *Hunting Scenes From Lower Bavaria*. The MTC also presented Alonso Alegria's *Crossing Niagara* about the French tightrope walker Blondin, and Sybille Peterson's *Sally and Marsha*, a sturdy vehicle for the exceptional performances of Bernadette Peters and Christine Baranski as New York and South Dakota housewives meeting across a New York City apartment hallway.

The off-Broadway straight-play season was enhanced by return engagements of *The Diviners* by Jim Leonard Jr. and last season's Best Play *Zooman and the Sign* by Charles Fuller. Israel Horovitz ventured once more briefly onto the scene with a new play about mid-life crisis *The Good Parts*. Other subjects under scrutiny in short-lived appearances off Broadway were the actress and the homosexual (*Particular Friendships*), rape (*Precious Blood* in *2 by South*), the career of Robert M. La Follette (*Fighting Bob*) and the Diaghilev-Nijinsky relationship (*Clownmaker*).

On the musical side, off Broadway came up with the cheerful and charming *Pump Boys and Dinettes*, a loose-jointed creation by its cast including Jim Wann, with gas jockeys and diner waitresses singing to each other across the highway in an assortment of country music styles and moods. Dodger Productions offered it at the Colonnades for 112 performances and then moved it to Broadway where it brightened its corner and the whole musical season. Zev Bufman took a similar route with his hit revival of the Andrew Lloyd Webber-Tim Rice Old Testament musical *Joseph and the Amazing Technicolor Dreamcoat*, running it up to Broadway after a spell downtown. Both these off-Broadway interlopers stole a significant part of the uptown show, between them winning nine Tony nominations including Best Musical in both cases.

Among those off-Broadway musicals that did not make it to the big time were *El Bravo!* (the Robin Hood legend transposed to a New York barrio), *The Heebie Jeebies* (homage to the singing Boswell Sisters of the 1930s) and *Francis* (the life and works of St. Francis of Assisi). In the revue category, off Broadway offered a new edition of the topical, satirical *Pigjazz;* an adaptation of Tom Lehrer numbers from the 1950s and 1960s, *Tomfoolery;* and a Randy Newman pop concert entitled *Maybe I'm Doing It Wrong.*

The specialty list was crowded with historical reminiscences and nostalgia such as *Shay Duffin as Brendan Behan,* John Cullum as (James McNeill) *Whistler, Oscar* (Wilde) *Remembered,* excerpts from Anne Sexton's works (*My Own Stranger*), Bible stories set to music (*Cotton Patch Gospel*), John Lithgow in his own adaptation of (George S.) *Kaufman at Large,* a Bob Ost vaudeville revue *Everybody's Gettin' Into the Act* and Patrizia Norcia recreating Ruth Draper's character sketches in *Cast of Characters.*

Such were the individual parts of off-Broadway's contribution to the 1981–82 theater season in New York, whose whole was much greater than their sum. Off Broadway was the principal repository of American playwriting, with four very strong Best Plays—*The Dance and the Railroad, A Soldier's Play, Torch Song Trilogy* and *The Dining Room*—backed up by a dozen or more standouts. And it was the source, two seasons ago, of one of Broadway's two American plays on this year's Best Plays list, *Mass Appeal.* Its two transferred musicals supplied Broadway with half its Tony nominees for Best Musical, while the titles of its transferred holdovers were blazoned all over the Broadway marquees: *A Chorus Line, Crimes of the Heart, Oh! Calcutta!, The Pirates of Penzance, The Best Little Whorehouse in Texas.* With Broadway becoming more a display case than a production facility, off Broadway was making moves to take over. Certainly it was where most of the action and substance was in 1981–82.

Revivals

New York is a year-round celebration of living theater in retrospect, from Euripides to Orton, from Shakespeare to Shepard. The former's *Medea* in the Robinson Jeffers version under Robert Whitehead's direction was one of the season's lightning bolts, with Zoe Caldwell painstakingly physical in the title role made famous in the 1940s (in a production co-produced by this same Mr. Whitehead) by Judith Anderson, who herself appeared in this production as the gauntly misgiving Nurse. In revival, Sam Shepard's *The Unseen Hand,* a manipulation of time bringing together the Old West and outer space, embellished the last half of the off-Broadway season, as did a pair of black Joe Orton comedies, *Entertaining Mr. Sloane* and *What the Butler Saw,* in the first half. As usual, Shakespeare reappeared all over the place on and off Broadway: *Othello* with Darth Vader-voiced James Earl Jones as secure in the title role as though it had been written for him, and with Christopher Plummer as a sharp-edged Iago with nerves exposed; the *Macbeth* of Nicol Williamson at Circle in the Square; *The Tempest* and *Henry IV, Part 1* (Kenneth McMillan as Falstaff) at the Delacorte in Central Park; the *King Lear* of Robert Stattel in Classic Stage Company repertory; the Acting

Company's *Twelfth Night;* not to mention an aborted *Richard II* and fun-house-mirror distortions of segments of *Romeo and Juliet* and *King Lear* as plays-within-plays of *Nicholas Nickleby* and *The Dresser,* respectively.

As in other recent seasons, major undertakings to redo big Broadway musicals for the new generation that didn't see them the first time around were elegantly achieved—but they met with precious little enthusiasm this year. Herschel Bernardi as Tevye in *Fiddler on the Roof,* Rex Harrison as Professor Henry Higgins in *My Fair Lady* and Richard Harris as King Arthur in *Camelot* were all in fine fettle but failed to draw crowds. A reworked version of Neil Simon's 20-year-old musical *Little Me* made a brief reappearance with James Coco in some of the roles originally played on Broadway by Sid Caesar. As mentioned previously in this report, only *Joseph and the Amazing Technicolor Dreamcoat* among this season's musical revivals really caught on.

Chekhov? Yes, of course—the Classic Stage Company (CSC) did *The Cherry Orchard,* and the Russian dramatist also appeared as a character onstage reading and discussing his works in *Chekhov on the Lawn* by Elihu Winer, a one-man show performed by William Shust. The major achievement of CSC's season, though, was the presentation of the full text of Henrik Ibsen's *Peer Gynt* in two alternating evenings. It was translated by Rolf Fjelde, directed and designed by CSC's artistic director, Christopher Martin, and billed as the American premiere of the complete text of the play, previously presented only in abridged versions such as the Public Theater's in Central Park in 1969. Characterized by Mel Gussow as "One of our basic repositories of classics," CSC rounded off its season with Strindberg's *Ghost Sonata.*

One of the highlights of the Broadway revival year was Amanda Plummer's Tony-nominated performance in a Roundabout Theater Company revival of Shelagh Delaney's *A Taste of Honey* moved up from its off-Broadway origins. If Miss Plummer's double Tony nomination in this and the featured-actress category, which she won for her Agnes in *Agnes of God,* is not a first, surely the added fact that her father Christopher's Iago was also nominated makes it a unique family triple. Joanne Woodward played Shaw's *Candida* for Circle in the Square uptown, and Jack Gilford and Joe Silver appeared in a revived series of Arnold Perl sketches based on stories by various authors and entitled *The World of Sholom Aleichem,* who was one of them.

In addition to *A Taste of Honey,* Gene Feist's and Michael Fried's Roundabout had a fruitful and stimulating twelve months, ending their 1981 season in late June with Shaw's *Misalliance,* beginning again in September with Strindberg's *Miss Julie* and *Playing With Fire* and ending their 1982 season in full stride with Irene Worth and Constance Cummings sweeping through the leading roles of Enid Bagnold's *The Chalk Garden.* In between, this active and steadily achieving organization kept its two playhouses attractively filled with Harold Pinter's *The Caretaker* (not seen here in a major production since the Roundabout did it nine years ago) and Terence Rattigan's *The Browning Version,* with Lee Richardson as the aging misfit schoolteacher, in its first major New York revival, with J.M. Barrie's *The Twelve-Pound Look* as a curtain raiser. Revival may be the name of the Roundabout's game, but it is not now and never has been a follower.

Uptown at the Light Opera of Manhattan (LOOM), melody was in fashion as usual, heavily accented with Gilbert & Sullivan but frequently branching into Romberg, Friml, Herbert and Lehar. Three new productions were inserted in the group's broad operetta repertory this season. LOOM did over its versions of *H.M.S. Pinafore* and *The Red Mill,* then in May mounted a production of Johann Strauss's 1883 comic opera *A Night in Venice,* the romance of a street singer and a senator's daughter. Remembered like so many operettas more fondly for its score than for its book, *A Night in Venice* was freely adapted in this version by LOOM's producer-director, William Mount-Burke, in collaboration with Alice Hammerstein Mathias, who also supplied new lyrics.

Wycherley? Certainly, with the Acting Company's *The Country Wife.* Scattered elsewhere among off Broadway's 1981–82 revival offerings were Leonard Melfi's *Birdbath;* Heinrich von Kleist's 1808 German comedy *The Broken Pitcher* (originally *Jug*) in a Jon Swan translation produced by Goethe House; the Public Theater's new translation of Sophocles's *Antigone* (which, theater historian Thomas T. Foose reminded us, has been produced in New York in three major adaptions—by Jean Cocteau, Bertolt Brecht and Jean Anouilh, which was actually named a Best Play in the 1946 volume—and at least 12 minor ones); and Thomas Babe's *Taken in Marriage* revived by The Woman's Ensemble.

And finally, among the first of the 1981–82 revivals in importance as well as in point of time was the June 3 reappearance of David Mamet's Best Play *American Buffalo* in a production directed by Arvin Brown at the Long Wharf Theater in New Haven, Conn. and brought into town by Elliot Martin. Al Pacino vividly recreated the leading role of Teach done on Broadway by Robert Duvall. The show suspended performances in midwinter but returned and was still a prominent feature of New York City's multi-theater revival program as the season ended. From Mamet to Sophocles off Broadway, from Delaney to Euripides on, our revival year was eclectic as usual and sparkled across an impressive proportion of its broad surface.

Offstage

All year the battle over the block on the west side of Broadway between 45th and 46th Streets was joined in court and committee, and then the inevitable happened. A final rejection in Federal and New York State courts of the organized efforts of theater folk to save the Morosco, Helen Hayes and Bijou Theaters was handed down. At the end of March, with tearful actresses and angry playwrights sounding their last-minute objections, and in a society which has come to value a sweet real estate deal more than a cultural treasure, the bulldozers had their way. Steel bent and buckled; brick and plaster fell; and soon, where noble theaters once stood, there was only a level plain of rubble to be occupied in the fulness of time-and-a-half-for-overtime by a huge new hotel tower.

Granted that the Morosco and the Hayes were run down and economically inconvenient in design (with second balconies, unsellable to today's audiences); granted that a new theater will be built like a sentient Jonah in the digestive system of the juggernaut; granted that even though other recently-built theaters like the Uris and the Minskoff have proven uncomfortable for most legitimate stage productions, we ought not to prejudge the potential of this one. Such reasoning convinced committees, mayors and judges that these theaters should fall that a hotel might rise; but it is not reason that prevails when a theater lover stares at the ropes hanging from the bared flies like the entrails of a cadaver. The emotional shock of coming upon the empty place where a legitimate theater was destroyed is a function of the body's warning system against danger—real danger. Whatever the economics, it is viscerally appalling to lose theaters to a glass-faced monster that will certainly distort the scale of the whole district, let alone exacerbate all the logistic problems of the area. We must remember, not *why* it happened, but how it *felt,* and be instinctively, politically, emotionally on guard against it ever happening again.

Now for the good news: in May, the New York City Board of Estimate beefed up the zoning regulations to place a prohibition against the demolishing of Broadway theaters for a period of one year, during which the Planning Commission is to draw up new regulations concerning them. And in line with the apparently expanding popularity of the Broadway stage in the early 1980s, there is movement afoot to bring some or all of nine former legitimate theaters, now grind houses, on 42d Street in the Broadway-to-Eighth-Avenue block, back into the fold. The Shuberts, the Nederlanders and the Brandts are looking closely at the possibilities there, with the 1,500-seat New Amsterdam Theater, former home of some of the New York stage's most effulgent glories, seemingly the most desirable. The Brandts have already refurbished their Apollo and Rialto for Broadway and own the Selwyn, Victory, Times Square, Lyric (in process of refurbishing), Empire and Liberty Theaters in that area. The Nederlanders are set to begin conversion of the New Amsterdam and Harris Theaters, and no doubt there will soon be further developments (excuse the expression) of this nature.

In negotiations with the musicians (Local 802 of the American Federation of Musicians) the League granted a $50-a-week increase for each musician working in a Broadway show each year for three years, which will raise the pay scale from the present $470 a week to $620 a week by 1985. Fringe benefits include an additional $10 a week for instrument maintenance ($40 for harpists) and a premium of $50 for first-chair trumpeters. Musicians appearing onstage get $30 extra and $20 more if in costume. Requirements for employment minimums attached to theaters remained in effect and caused a controversy over the continuing run of *The Best Little Whorehouse in Texas.* According to *Variety,* this show uses nine musicians but was required to pay 16 additional "walkers" (who are not contractually required to attend a performance) at the 46th Street Theater, because that theater calls for the employment of 25 musicians. The management of the show stated its intention of moving to the Music Box, a nine-musician house; the union insisted on continued enforcement of a 25-musician run-of-the-play agreement, with its $6,000-a-week extra cost. *Whorehouse* suspended New York performances in March, moved to Boston, then moved back to Broadway May 31, still obligated to pay 16 "walkers" in yet another nine-musician house, and with both union and producer still adamant.

Among organizations, the Off Off Broadway Alliance (OOBA) of 94 tributary-theater producing organizations moved into a new headquarters on Spring Street under the new executive directorship of Jane S. Moss and adopted a new name: Alliance of Resident Theaters/New York, abbreviated as ART/NY. Volume 1, Number 1 of a new ART/NY bimonthly, *Theater Times,* stated two principal aims: "First, expanded management and marketing services must be developed and new strategies for their implementation explored. Second, state-of-the-art issues must be addressed." Across the forest at the leading edge of the trees, The Shubert Organization was partially freed from the restrictions of the Federal consent decree which has limited its operations for the past 25 years. A Federal judge ruled that the Shubert group can begin acquiring additional theaters outside

New York immediately and will be free of the decree's other restrictions as of Jan. 1, 1985.

In the largest voting turnout in its history, Actors' Equity Association elected its first woman president: Ellen Burstyn, the choice of the nominating committee, who defeated her independently-nominated rival by a three-to-one margin. Merle Debuskey also swept away all opposition and was re-elected to yet another two-year term as president of the Association of Theatrical Press Agents and Managers.

Turbulence is the first word that comes to mind as we glance back for a last look at the twelve months of the 1981–82 New York theater season on and off Broadway; economic turbulence tossing the biggest pretenses in an unaccustomed chaos of inflation; social turbulence forcing the experimental fringe to rechannel its efforts and reconsider its context; esthetic turbulence seemingly draining creative energy from both the top and bottom of the scale and concentrating it in the center, in the theatrical halfway house we call off Broadway. And there is new turbulence on the way in the sure-to-be-irresistable influence of cable TV and its possibilities for the afterlife of stage productions. The cloud no larger than a man's hand has already passed overhead in Home Box Office's purchase of the cable rights to *Camelot* for $1.2 million and the first taping of a live play on Broadway, *It Had To Be You*. The theater has weathered other storms as well and even better than could reasonably have been expected, and it is getting ready for another one surely on the way. While it prepares for the worst, it hopes for the best: that the turbulence to come will prove to be a storm of technical advantages, new opportunities and stimulating challenges.

Anne Pitoniak and Kathy Bates in *'night, Mother* by Marsha Norman.

PHOTO BY MARTHA SWOPE

1982-83

FOR the second season in a row, British playwrights dominated the New York stages. In 1981–82 they did it by standing especially tall with the towering, multi-award-winning *The Life & Adventures of Nicholas Nickleby*. In 1982–83 they did it with the force of numbers, pervading every production area with new scripts of major distinction.

The Best Plays list for 1982–83 records this transatlantic triumph with five of the ten from British dramatists: the musical *Cats* and the plays *Good* and *Foxfire* on Broadway, *Quartermaine's Terms* off Broadway and *Plenty* both off and on. And behind these loomed a backup contingent of strong 1982–83 British offerings in all shapes and sizes: *Slab Boys*, *Top Girls*, *Passion*, *Whodunnit*, *Steaming*, *Skirmishes*, plus the Royal Shakespeare Company's production of *All's Well That Ends Well*, in a humbling display of energy and virtuosity.

It's some consolation that the season's best-of-bests was the stark *'night, Mother*, Marsha Norman's piteously detailed study of suicidal despair; and that the American musical stage finally—*finally*—provided *My One and Only* to share the limelight with *Cats*, but it took a Gershwin score, Peter Stone co-authorship of the book and Tommy Tune dances to do it. Other American dramatists who made this year's Best Plays list were William Mastrosimone, in whose *Extremities* a victim of an attempted rape turns on her attacker; Patrick Meyers with his implacably cliff-hanging *K2*; and Lanford Wilson exposing various strong-minded individuals to a possible nuclear accident in *Angels Fall*.

A funny thing happened to the Broadway theater on the way to seemingly infinite riches: the price of a ticket was rising steadily toward the impossible dream of $50, with the $45 musical becoming a commonplace and *Cats* determined to go higher at the turn of the year, when the whole hydraulically inflationary process ran out of power. *Cats* never did make it to $50, at least not as of the end of the 1982–83 theater season on May 31. According to *Variety* estimate, the *average* paid Broadway admission had risen during the twelve months to $27.69 from $23.08 (which it had reached from $19.72 the year before); even so, the total overall Broadway gross fell off, failing to establish a new record for the first time in many seasons. It fell from $221 million last year to $203,126,127 in 1982–83, while the road receipts dropped from a record $249 million to $184,-321,475. These were still the second-highest New York and third-highest road grosses in theater history; but with production costs finding it possible to reach $4 million for a full-scale musical and $1 million for a straight play, these receding totals put the Broadway theater right in the middle of the 1980s recession along with everything else. Its most vital statistic—total paid attendance—fell off from about 10.7 million in 1981–82 to 8,102,262 in 1982–83, or about 73 per cent of capacity on the average, a level at which few Broadway productions could even hold their own, let alone ever make it into the black. This may account for the fact that of the 1982–83 Broadway offerings, only *Plenty* had paid off its investment as of the end of the season, according to *Variety*.

Now for the good news: production activity held up pretty well during the past year, both on and off Broadway. Not counting specialties, Broadway housed 49

The 1982–83 Season on Broadway

PLAYS (15)

Torch Song Trilogy
  (transfer)
The Wake of Jamey Foster
Twice Around the Park
84 Charing Cross Road
Monday After the Miracle
A Little Family Business
Almost an Eagle
ANGELS FALL
  (transfer)
Moose Murders
Brighton Beach Memoirs
K2
'NIGHT, MOTHER
The Man Who Had Three
  Arms
Total Abandon
*Breakfast With Les and
  Bess*

MUSICALS (10)

Blues in the Night
Cleavage
Play Me a Country Song
Seven Brides for Seven
  Brothers
Your Arms Too Short to
  Box With God
  (return engagement)
A Doll's Life
CATS
Merlin
MY ONE AND ONLY
Dance a Little Closer

FOREIGN PLAYS IN ENGLISH (8)

GOOD
FOXFIRE
Steaming
Whodunnit
PLENTY
Slab Boys
Teaneck Tanzi: The Venus
  Flytrap
Passion

REVUES (2)

Rock 'n Roll: The First
  5,000 Years
*The Flying Karamazov
  Brothers*

REVIVALS (14)

Circle in the Square:
  Present Laughter
  The Queen and the Rebels
  The Misanthrope
  *The Caine Mutiny
    Court-Martial*
Ghosts
Alice in Wonderland
A View From the Bridge
On Your Toes
*You Can't Take It With
  You*
Porgy and Bess
All's Well That Ends Well
Show Boat
The Ritz
Private Lives

SPECIALTIES (3)

Herman van Veen: All of
  Him
Marcel Marceau on
  Broadway
Aznavour

HOLDOVERS WHICH BECAME HITS IN 1982–83

Dreamgirls
Nine

Plays listed in CAPITAL LETTERS have been designated Best Plays of 1982–83.
Plays listed in *italics* were still running after May 31, 1983.
Plays listed in **bold face type** were classified as hits in *Variety's* annual estimate published June 1, 1983.

new productions as compared with only 45 in 1981–82, 51 the year before that and 58 at a 1979–80 peak. This year's 49 included 14 revivals, so that the total number of new Broadway plays, musicals and revues amounted to 35, two more than last year, including three transfers and a return engagement. Musicals held their level of ten new shows (plus three important, full-scale revival productions), and while new American plays fell off a bit, British imports took up the slack. The bad activity news was the continuing drop in Broadway playing weeks (if ten shows play ten weeks, that's 100 playing weeks) from the record 1,545 in 1980–81 to 1,461 in 1981–82 to 1,259 in 1982–83.

Off Broadway, the production of new plays and musicals (routinely at a $14–16 top but rising above $20 on occasion) also held steady, reaching 59 in 1982–83 after 60 last year. The pinch was felt most strongly off Broadway in the demise of the Phoenix Theater, which called it quits after 30 years of distinguished contribution to the New York stage; and in the wavering of some groups moving their productions up and down across the boundary between off and off off Broadway, with their differing commitments, at the mercy of the ebb and flow of financial tides. Only Manhattan Theater Club and Circle Repertory Company seemed to strengthen in 1982–83, the former bringing all of its Upstage offerings (previously OOB) up to off-Broadway status equal to its Downstage productions, and the latter mounting a remarkable parade of new scripts by American dramatists.

Financial data on individual shows didn't seem to be disseminated as freely as in past seasons, but there were inklings of both triumph and disaster in what few press reports were available. In these random *Variety* citations of recent figures on a series of hit musicals, note the rising production costs: *Company* (1970), $245,000 profit on an original investment of $530,000; *Nine* (1982), $546,000 profit on $2,750,000; *A Doll's Life* (1982), a clean loss at $4 million; *My One and Only* (1983), capitalized at $2,750,000 but reported to have cost over $4 million. And the March 1983 West Coast production of *Dreamgirls* cost almost as much to put on ($3 million) as the original 1981 Broadway version ($3.6 million)—but *Dreamgirls* paid off its huge nut in 34 weeks, by August 1982, something of a modern record.

Under such conditions, it can come as a surprise to few that producing shows in the New York theater of 1982–83 has evolved from an impresario to a team effort, with numbers that rival a baseball aggregation, the bench included (i.e., it took nine producers to put on the musical *Nine* a year ago, and five *organizations* plus four producers for *All's Well That Ends Well* this season). As a corollary, an active producing unit was apt to make the team of a goodly number of shows (gone were the days when one impresario laid one egg, golden or otherwise, or nursed one chicken to maturity). By our count—and it's possible that we've overlooked one or more at bats—Kennedy Center and/or Roger L. Stevens were most active, participating in ten (*Ghosts, Twice Around the Park, Monday After the Miracle, Angels Fall, On Your Toes, Dance a Little Closer, Show Boat, The Caine Mutiny Court-Martial* and the two Broadway-bound plays that closed out of town, *Outrage* and *Make and Break*). Slightly less active but even more conspicuous was The Shubert Organization with eight, four of them Best Plays (*Cats, Good, Angels Fall;* '*night, Mother; Marcel Marceau* and *All's Well That Ends Well* on Broadway and *The Middle Ages* and *Little Shop of Horrors* off).

Broadway

In the vanguard of this season's British parade was the vivacious and imaginative *Cats*, in which Andrew Lloyd Webber set portions of T.S. Eliot's *Old Possum's Book of Practical Cats* to music, with additional material based on Eliot works adapted by Trevor Nunn and Richard Stilgoe. To begin, Eliot's verses are irresistible. The cast acted them out in high spirits, tails up and costumed by John Napier to appear uniformly feline in individualistic ways. Napier's deliberately overblown set represented a cat-scale garbage dump—that is, the simulated trash on the Winter Garden's stage was enlarged so that the size of strewn objects was in the same proportion to the human actors as those in a real dump would be to real cats. A whispered suggestion of "plot" was superimposed on the Eliot sketches: an aged puss named Grizabella (Betty Buckley), mourning past possibilities in her hapless present with the haunting ballad "Memory," is magically endowed with new life by sage Old Deuteronomy (Ken Page) in another sphere beyond the Heaviside Layer. But the main business of this theme musical was to fill its theater with essence of Cat with a capital C (the word is always capitalized in the Eliot poems) in the many personalities of the agile ensemble featuring such as Timothy Scott (Mistoffolees), Terrence V. Mann (Rum Tum Tugger), Stephen Hanan (Growltiger) and Bonnie Simmons (Jellylorum). Under Nunn's direction, *Cats* was a live wire crackling with cat-fur electricity of humor and style.

The *Cats* company barely had time to read its notices before the arrival from London of another British Best Play: the late C.P. Taylor's *Good* in the Royal Shakespeare Company's production, starring Alan Howard under the direction of Howard Davies in the role of a German university professor, a veteran of World War I, who temporizes little by little the Nazi encroachment upon his life and ideals, until finally he out-Himmlers Himmler. As the playwright saw it, the act of becoming a Nazi was a bitterly comedic act, however ghastly its effect. The professor has a mother who is succumbing to senility in a nursing home, which she detests; he writes a book in which the case for euthanasia is considered; he is recruited by Eichmann to make reports in this field; then, inadvertently but inevitably, he loses himself forever in the smoke of burning books, the sound of breaking glass, the smell of escaping gas. The professor's one clear obsession is music, and Taylor used snatches of songs, symphonies, etc. to set the mood for each sequence of *Good* (a title making reference to "good" Germans), which was itself like a musical composition of briefly experienced notes of character (Hitler, Goebbels, etc.), some recurring and some not. All these notes found their place in a scheme which brought Howard's portrayal of intellectual-turned-viper to its climax: a black-uniformed SS officer with pinched features under the peaked cap, pulling on his leather gloves preparatory to going to see how he can improve efficiency at Auschwitz. In Howard's memorable performance, he is the principal victim of his own venomous progress, the clownish point of a horror story.

Still another 1982–83 British Best Play came to Broadway the long way round, from London's National Theater to Chicago to New York Shakespeare Festival downtown, and finally under the same auspices uptown. *Plenty* was the star of Joseph Papp's season, and Kate Nelligan was the dark star of *Plenty* in the role of an English Anywoman who, after rising to the demanding occasion of World War II, disintegrates in parallel with what she sees as her country's decay in the post-war period into crass commercial, political and social expediency.

Hers is a slow-motion tantrum of selfishness, with Miss Nelligan turning herself and her character into a thoroughly reprehensible person, and with Edward Herrmann as her diplomat-husband trying to cope with his wife's mental and emotional disintegration, symbolizing that of her country. Written and directed by David Hare, *Plenty* was not so much a requiem for the England that was, as a head-on confrontation of what England might become, in a play that was both arresting and repellent.

The inimitable *Foxfire* must also be credited to this category of foreign plays, though it doesn't comfortably fit there. Its authors, though U.S. residents, are British (Susan Cooper) and Canadian (Hume Cronyn). Its subject—the life and times of a hardscrabble Georgia hillbilly farm couple—is as American as its production here on Broadway (but it *did* have its first production in Toronto). One thing is perfectly clear, however: it belongs on the 1982–83 Best Plays list with a script, adapted from material on Appalachia edited by Eliot Wigginton, that captures and gently celebrates the rough-hewn, indomitable character of these mountain folk. Yes, there were shining performances: Jessica Tandy as an aging farm widow clinging to her mountain home and her memories of her ornery husband (Hume Cronyn), while trying to understand her guitar-playing son (Keith Carradine). David Trainer's direction maintained the clarity of scenes which shifted through the present in reality, the present in imagination and various points of past time, and David Mitchell's mountain-view set was most appealing. Intercraft and international collaboration was the open secret of *Foxfire*'s success, with writing, performances, direction and design serving each other with conspicuously heartwarming results.

Foxfire and *Good* and probably even *Plenty* are comedies in the broadest sense of that term. In the simple dimension of laughter, however, nothing this season exceeded *Slab Boys*, another foreign visitor traveling the long way from Edinburgh, London, regional theater and off off Broadway to a small house in the West Forties. The boys of this John Byrne script's title are wage slaves mixing pigments in the battered back room of a studio for designers of carpets and wall paper. Social and educational discards, they are out of reach of even the bottom rung of any ladder, but they have developed a style of their own and the imagination to relieve the drudgery and monotony by splashing their walls with color and their lives with an irrepressible comic spirit expressed in arrogance toward their superiors and an infinite variety of pranks played on each other. Under Robert Allan Ackerman's open-throttle direction, in a paint-spattered set designed by the play's author, the back-room types—bully, gaffer, victim, tea lady, even sex object —were led through their energetic paces by Sean Penn as the head boy looking as though he had been born working at his slab. The comedic form was familiar and the message obvious (youth against the demeaning world), but the laughter was plentiful in this Scottish version of the tale.

Peter Nichols's *Passion* (known in London as *Passion Play*) also concentrated on the winsome notes at the lighter end of the scale, exploring comic possibilities of love among characters who are not only of two minds but in some cases also of two embodiments. In this play by the author of *Joe Egg*, husband and wife have been virtually faithful to each other in long and respectable wedlock. The wife has had one minor fling but is now ready to settle for home and husband, at precisely the moment that the husband, who has never strayed, is ready to surrender to the charms of a cheerful young blonde (Roxanne Hart) swinging a tantalizing miniskirt. Husband and wife were each played by two performers dressed alike and working in tandem but not in unison, representing different aspects of each personality in each circumstance. Bob Gunton and Cathryn Damon were the long-married couple keeping up appearances, while Frank Langella and E. Katherine Kerr moved about more freely as the adventurous side of their natures, acting out impulses which the sedate pair might never even dare express in words. Inevitably, *Passion* ran down into sitcom after a while; but certainly in its first half it was subtly and amusingly insightful into some of the ways of affection.

Other British imports to Broadway represented the London stage in an even more frivolous mood. Nell Dunn's *Steaming* featured a group of women skinny-dipping in an onstage swimming pool; but it was more remarkable for the engaging performance of Judith Ivey as an open-hearted, man-loving Cockney lass than for its dialogue about sex and sexism. Anthony Shaffer's *Whodunnit* (previously seen in London as *The Case of the Oily Levantine*) was a takeoff of the country-house murder mystery, with a gloomily paneled set by Andrew Jackness and deceitful costumes by Patricia Zipprodt for a set of duplicitous Agatha-Christie-type characters confronting one another with chicanery and menace. The caricature was almost too perfect—right down to the identity of the killer—for *Whodunnit* to achieve the full maturity as a work of theater reached by the author's previous *Sleuth*. As for a third comic entry from Britain, *Teaneck Tanzi: The Venus Flytrap* (staging the battle of the sexes as a wrestling match with its theater, the Nederlander, temporarily converted into a wrestling arena), it visited Broadway for only a single performance, the only foreign play so short-lived this season (American authors suffered the same fate with two plays—*Moose Murders* and *Total Abandon*—one revival—*The Ritz*—and three musicals—*Cleavage*, *Play Me a Country Song* and *Dance a Little Closer*).

American playwrights kept part of this season's franchise by dominating the drama category both on and off Broadway, most notably with the Pulitzer Prize-winning (on the basis of its Boston production) Best Play (in Broadway production) *'night, Mother* by Marsha Norman, a closeup of a suicide—not the act itself, but its motivation. A clock on the wall of an appropriately nondescript living-room-kitchen set (the work of Heidi Landesman) marked time running out without intermission or faltering of purpose for a daughter (Kathy Bates) who informs her mother (Anne Pitoniak) that she has made all the necessary arrangements for her carefully considered and planned suicide, which she intends to effect by pistol shot this very evening. After the older woman's reflexive "No!" came the pleading "Why?", the question which lay at the heart of this play's paralyzing matter. Is the intended suicide agonized by disease? (No, but she has had epilepsy, now under control.) Is she suffering unrequited love? (No, but her husband has long since left her, and so has her son, a flagrant delinquent.) Is she a lonely outcast? (No, but she is not "good company" either.) Is she insane? (No, it is her very inward-probing intelligence which has brought her to this brink.) She is simply an unremarkable human being who, perhaps through little fault of her own, was unable to realize any of her modest dreams and now finds her existence devoid of any pleasure, opportunity or meaning, or the prospect of any. Her life is empty, and she says "No" to hope. Inside, there remains to her the resolve to be master of her fate and to make an efficient exit. She asks herself "Why not?", and the terror of this play took the form of gradually dawning awareness that all the mother's arguments (and all the reassurances that came most quickly to mind as we listened to the daughter's conclusions) would be inadequate to deflect her inexorable purpose. Miss Bates's starring performance was excruciatingly matter-of-fact in contrast to the subject, while Miss Pitoniak's encompassed both fear and pity with scarcely a trace of love. Tom Moore's direction earned its share of applause, maintaining an even texture and total concentration on Miss Norman's moving, disturbing, perplexing theme, in a play which was certainly the best-of-bests of this 1982–83 New York season.

The standard of drama was also held high by Patrick Meyers in *K2*, a literally cliff-hanging adventure of two climbers whose place in history has been assured because they have just scaled the Himalayas' second-highest peak, but whose lives are in extreme jeopardy because of an accident that has taken place on the way back, exacerbated by a careless omission in preparing for the expedition. The two men are trapped on a ledge indenting the sheer ice wall. The team leader (Jeffrey De Munn), a macho district attorney in civilian life, has neglected to include in his pack the spare length of rope essential for lowering his teammate (Jay Patterson), a physicist and liberal humanist, who cannot climb down because he has broken his leg in a fall to this ledge. The former will have to climb back up to retrieve discarded rope, if they are both to survive. Ming Cho Lee designed a shockingly bleak and forbidding mountain soaring out of sight above the rim of the proscenium. De Munn (and director Terry Schreiber) devised agile means of climbing it that created a compelling illusion within the compact, intermissionless running time. An ongoing right-vs.-left discussion between the two men established an emotional context for their adventure in this Best Play, which was just about as theatrical as the theater can get.

Lanford Wilson turned his attention from the Talley family (*Fifth of July*, *Talley's Folly*, *A Tale Told*) to the more pressing question of 20th-century reaction to the ever-present possibility of nuclear holocaust. Wilson's Best Play *Angels Fall* (transferred to Broadway after its premiere at Circle Repertory) imagines a nuclear emergency in New Mexico, with the Army hovering overhead in helicopters, sounding the alarm and sending people in the area to shelter. A random assortment of folks take cover in a mission: a renegade professor (Fritz Weaver), his supportive wife (Nancy Snyder), a patroness of art (Tanya Berezin) and her tennis-champ consort (Brian Tarantina), an aggressively promising young Indian doctor (Danton Stone) and a jocular mission priest (Barnard Hughes) maintaining Catholicism in the desert, even if it means conducting the Mass in Navaho. On the whole, their individual convictions (the professor's that his own teaching has lacked validity, the doctor's to become a researcher instead of a local M.D., the priest's faith in God and man) hold up under the weight of the emergency. No major detonation takes place, of course (New Mexico is still there, even in imagination), but there were plenty of bursts of irony and provocation among the characters, whose development in this dramatic process was given sharp outlines in Wilson's writing and Marshall W. Mason's direction.

In a lighter vein of domestic playwriting was Murray Schisgal's *Twice Around the Park*, a pair of one-act two-character comedies written, acted (by the Wallachs, Eli and Anne Jackson) and directed (by Arthur Storch) as episodes in the ongoing identity clash between men and women, so painful to experience, so amusing to observe. In the first, he was an actor and she was a female cop who lives upstairs and comes down to give him a summons for disturbing the peace with his noisy rehearsing—but the lady is distracted by his romantic ploys. In the second, they were a modern middle-aged couple trying to juice up their drab marriage with a tape-recording of instructions by a cultist sex guru. Masterfully constructed and executed, Schisgal's concept resembled those which Neil

Simon has handled so very adroitly in the past, but which eluded Simon's grasp in this season's *Brighton Beach Memoirs*, a series of crayon-colored caricatures of puberty and other matters in a Brooklyn boyhood, reputedly based somewhat on the author's own, received by many theatergoers with laughtrack enthusiasm but leaving others cold. Its major asset was the ingenious performance of the youth by Matthew Broderick, who appeared off Broadway last season as the teen-ager in the final segment of Harvey Fierstein's *Torch Song Trilogy*. In early June 1982, Fierstein transferred this 1981–82 Best Play (on the basis of its off-Broadway showing) and his own outstanding performance as the drag queen in it to Broadway, flavoring the uptown season with its bittersweet comedy and collecting the 1983 Tonys for both best play and best performance. Young Broderick, who won the 1983 featured-actor Tony for his performance in Simon's play, had long since left the cast of Fierstein's.

A real charmer was *84 Charing Cross Road*, the true story of pen-pal affection blossoming between a book-loving New Yorker and the manager of a London second-hand-book store supplying her literary needs by mail over a period of 32 years, adapted and directed by James Roose-Evans from Helene Hanff's book. Joseph Maher's restrained, sensitive portrayal of the London bookman, opposite Ellen Burstyn as Miss Hanff, was one of the season's acting gems. In the play as in reality, the two never met; by the time she was able to travel to England, her bookdealer friend had died. For all its virtues, *84 Charing Cross Road* suffered from its determination to remain true to the original, so that an obligatory scene—a face-to-face meeting, at last, between the two transatlantic friends—was missing.

William Gibson took another look at his *The Miracle Worker* pair in a 16-years-after sequel, *Monday After the Miracle*, with the relationship between now world-famous Helen Keller (Karen Allen) and her mentor Annie Sullivan (Jane Alexander) disturbed by the presence and personality of a man (William Converse-Roberts) who arrives on the scene as a literary advisor for Helen and stays to marry Annie. This emotionally searching play, directed by Arthur Penn who also did *Miracle Worker*, was abruptly withdrawn after only 7 performances but inspired minority partisanship and looks like making a place for itself on the international theater scene. A less promising future might be predicted for Edward Albee's 1983 effort *The Man Who Had Three Arms*, a diatribe about celebrity delivered in lecture form by Robert Drivas as "Himself" under the author's own direction. Beth Henley followed her prizewinning *Crimes of the Heart* with *The Wake of Jamey Foster*, about another small-town family in crisis but lacking the deadly aim of her previous work. Jay Presson Allen entered the lists again with the adaptation of a French comedy by Pierre Barillet and Jean-Pierre Gredy, *A Little Family Business*, with Angela Lansbury as a wife taking over her ailing husband's affairs, this time without the success of the collaborators' previous *Forty Carats*. Lee Kalcheim's *Breakfast With Les and Bess* brought the tribulations of a radio talk show couple all the way from OOB to a Broadway production. Another entry, *Almost an Eagle*, sputtered briefly with Boy Scout adventures, while *Moose Murders* attempted a spoof of murder mysteries for only a single performance, a fate shared by *Total Abandon*, with Richard Dreyfuss as a divorced father who violently abuses his infant son.

If a disastrous musical season can be redeemed at the 11th hour by a single show, then 1982–83 on Broadway can be said to have achieved success through the arrival in May of *My One and Only*—but except for the borrowed finery of *Cats*, magicianship and revivals, it was a disaster on all other counts. Full-scale musical productions folded one after another, on occasion after only 1 performance lambasted by the reviewers, with single-show losses estimated in the millions.

Three modest theme-musical pot pourris started things off inauspiciously in June: *Blues in the Night*, a compendium of 24 mostly blues numbers by various authors; plus *Cleavage* and *Play Me a Country Song*, haplessly folding after only 1 performance each. Next came the disappointing full-scale production of a stage version of the M-G-M musical *Seven Brides for Seven Brothers* for a mere 5 performances. A limited return engagement of Vinnette Carroll's inspiring *Your Arms Too Short to Box With God* lifted spirits which were destined soon to be dashed by another disappointing major musical effort, *A Doll's Life* by Betty Comden, Adolph Green and Larry Grossman, which imagined Nora's struggle to survive on her own in the male chauvinistic 19th century after she walked out on her husband and slammed the door in Ibsen's play *A Doll's House*. Co-produced and directed by Harold Prince, this show was a smoothly crafted failure of expertise, dismally skillful, vanishing into the mists after only 5 performances despite its gilt-edged credentials.

The distinguished visitor *Cats* then lit the lights in the New York musical theater in October and kept them burning and beckoning. Except for some handsome revivals, the only response was *Merlin*, a Doug Henning magic show in a musical wrapper, with Henning's spectacular illusions coming off far more believably than his efforts to portray King Arthur's wizard as a young man in a book and score crammed into the interstices between his magic tricks.

Then in May, to nearly everyone's delighted astonishment, there arrived what could rationally be labeled a "new" Gershwin musical, *My One and Only*, taking its place beside *Cats* on our list of 1982–83 Best Plays on the basis of its charming book by Peter Stone and Timothy S. Mayer (parenthetically, the Tony eligibility committee declared both musicals eligible for nomination in all "new" categories, excepting only the Gershwin score of *My One and Only* because it had been previously used in shows, but not excepting the Eliot verses of *Cats* because they hadn't). The musical's joyful presence was all the more uplifting because it was so unexpected. When *My One and Only* began its tryout engagement in Boston in February, it was billed as "a new production of George and Ira Gershwin's *Funny Face*," with a new book and appropriate numbers from other shows augmenting the *Funny Face* score. Initial reaction was mixed, but instead of saying die the participants went to work to develop their show. The supremely accomplished librettist Peter Stone came in to work on the book about the romance between a boyish 1920s aviator (who is going to fly the Atlantic non-stop solo in what looks like a Ryan monoplane) and a wide-eyed flapper celebrated for having swum the English Channel. The star and co-choreographer Tommy Tune, whose current credits include no less than the direction of the long-run hits *Nine* and *Cloud 9*, took over the staging with his colleague Thommie Walsh, and other show business friends-in-need like Mike Nichols were said to have been helpful.

Thirteen weeks and an estimated $4.5 million later, *My One and Only* opened on Broadway—a spectacular surprise hit, remarkable not only in that each and every department was worthy of the exhilarating Gershwin tunes, but also that the many individual contributions had been brought together into a seamlessly unified whole. As the gangling aviator, Tommy Tune was an engaging presence, and of course an absolutely superb dancer. Twiggy showed herself capable of playing Ginger Rogers to his Astaire in both song and dance, with a twinkle in her eye that would have excused much, had there been anything to excuse. The

Stone-Mayer book was a musical comedy masterpiece—not a developed theme, or a "play with music," or an opera manqué, but a *musical comedy* honoring its glorious form like *42nd Street*, stylishly warm and lighthearted, unselfconscious except in the service of wit, tongue sometimes inimitably in cheek but taking pains to avoid pastiche, all in fun and quite a trick if you can make it work. The Tune-Walsh dances, showing off Tune's limber limbs and the close-order work of a lively chorus, were also masterful. The attractive cardboard-cutout scenery by Adrianne Lobel and flapper-era costumes of Rita Ryack contributed to the merriment, as did the supporting performances in every instance, particularly those of Charles "Honi" Coles matching wits and taps with Tommy Tune, Denny Dillon as a slangy but cherubic grease monkey, Bruce McGill as a deep-dyed villain, the New Rhythm Boys (David Jackson, Ken Leigh Rogers and Ronald Dennis) setting the show's pace and the Ritz Quartette echoing its spirit with sweet harmonies. Tommy Tune's entire cohort put *My One and Only* right up there alongside other memorable Gershwin musical comedies, and they looked for all the world as though they were having fun doing it.

But before the month of May and the season ended, Broadway was to suffer still another major musical disappointment. Much was expected of *Dance a Little Closer*, an updated musical version of Robert E. Sherwood's *Idiot's Delight*, with book, lyrics and direction by Alan Jay Lerner. The Charles Strouse score seemed perfectly adequate, and Len Cariou played Harry, the American hoofer, as though he were testing the tensile strength of the character, but the show around him could not find its feet or settle on an approach to its tale of the international set awaiting the beginning of a new World War in a luxury Austrian resort hotel. At any rate, *Dance a Little Closer* closed after only 1 performance, an expensive (in wasted talent as well as cost) debacle.

The revue form made its appearance twice this season on Broadway, in *Rock 'n Roll: The First 5,000 Years*, a show which promoted that musical genre with 60—count 'em, 60—musical numbers; and *The Flying Karamazov Brothers*, a variety show of juggling, comedy and other displays at the Ritz Theater, newly refurbished for legitimate stage use. Broadway theaters also housed a number of one-man concert-style shows during the year, among them those of Barry Manilow, the pop singer; Charles Aznavour, the French balladeer; and Herman van Veen, the Dutch comedian. And internationally renowned Marcel Marceau paid Broadway a visit with a program which included half a dozen new pantomimes among the Bip and other characterizations in his famed repertory.

Off Broadway

It's a good thing that Joseph Papp and his New York Shakespeare Festival took part in welcoming the British visitors to the smaller New York playhouses, because it resulted in his having a lion's share—what else—of the off-Broadway year's major achievements. First he brought in David Hare's *Plenty* (described in the previous section of this report) which had been produced at London's National Theater and went on to Broadway after its Public Theater engagement. He then made an exchange agreement with the Royal Court Theater which brought over their production of Caryl Churchill's *Top Girls* and sent over New York Shakespeare's subsequent production of a new Thomas Babe play. Miss Churchill is the author of the long-running Best Play *Cloud 9*, a comedy of sexual sleight-of-hand, and it's clear in her subsequent *Top*

Girls that she is a player of games onstage. The game in the first act of this new one is an all-female dinner party brimming with philosophical observations among guests including famous women of history like Pope Joan and Dull Gret. But the name of the game in her second act is Theater with a capital T in a confrontation between two sisters, one of whom has risen to high-gloss success as the head of an employment agency in London, the other remaining a country drudge cleaning other people's houses for a living. These women are electrifyingly symbolic of major social currents, with neither given an edge by the author. The ambitious sister has earned her success and has a right to it, but the drudge and the admittedly unpromising child she is raising are also human beings—and as in the case of Willy Loman, some attention must be paid. An American cast replaced the Royal Court cast in *Top Girls* in mid-season, without loss of momentum. Once past its forgettable dinner party, this Churchill script rivaled anything in *Plenty* and the other off-Broadway British Best Play, Simon Gray's independently-produced *Quartermaine's Terms*.

Furthermore, Joseph Papp punctuated his highly successful season in late May by bringing over the London production of Miss Churchill's *Fen*, another play of strong imagination and socioeconomic convictions, telling of the hard lives of rural folk in an outlying district and conferring on its author the very rare, if not unique, distinction of having three off-Broadway productions running simultaneously.

Simon Gray's *Quartermaine's Terms* (the "terms" of the title are boys' school terms) is a worthy successor to its author's other two Best Plays, *Butley* and *Otherwise Engaged*. Also like them, it puts forward a central character whose most conspicuous trait is his failure (as in *Butley*), or refusal (as in *Otherwise Engaged*), or inability (as in *Quartermaine's Terms*) to maintain connections with the world around him. As expressed in an understated style of contemporary playwriting also practised with great success by Harold Pinter, this mysterious detachment produces an emotional tension within the most mundane events in all three plays.

St. John Quartermaine of *Quartermaine's Terms* is the opposite of arrogant and suffers from no evident trauma but is equally detachable from the circumstances in which the author places him. We first see Quartermaine taking his ease in the faculty room of the school which he has served from its beginning, apparently a comfortable member of a well-defined, close-knit group—and then we watch him being slowly torn from this environment and discarded like an irrelevant page in a notebook. If the connections Butley was able to maintain destroyed him; if Hench did everything possible to avoid connections, Quartermaine (played in various keys of apology by Remak Ramsay) does everything he can to keep physical and emotional contact with the only outside world he knows. His efforts are obvious, unceasing, pathetic, courteous—and failing, as his colleagues put him at further and further distance, like a herd of animals shrinking from a dying member. Quartermaine is going to suffer the same wound as Butley and Hench, and in his case it will be as near mortal as makes no difference.

And now, let us record that 1982-83 production of new scripts off Broadway continued at about last year's level (see the one-page summary of the off-Broadway season accompanying this report). There were 59 as compared with 58 and 2 return engagements in 1981–82. The 1982–83 contingent comprised 39 American straight-play programs, 7 musicals and 13 foreign plays, as compared with 45-9-7, 33-14-8, 39-7-12 in the past three seasons and the peak 38-15-12 of 1979. In addition to the 59 abovementioned, there were 5 revues, 36 revivals and 8

The 1982–83 Season Off Broadway

PLAYS (39)

Booth
Looking-Glass
Divine Hysteria
Jane Avril
Negro Ensemble:
Abercrombie Apocalypse
Sons and Fathers of Sons
About Heaven and Earth
Manhattan Made Me
Circle Repertory:
A Think Piece
ANGELS FALL
Black Angel
What I Did Last Summer
Young Playwrights
Festival
Fool for Love
Herringbone
The Fox
Inserts
Manhattan Theater Club:
Talking With
Standing on My Knees
Triple Feature
Elba
Early Warnings
The Price of Genius

Baseball Wives
Greater Tuna
Edmond
Some Men Need Help
Penelope
EXTREMITIES
Balloon
Hannah
Goodnight, Grandpa
Buck
The Middle Ages
Win/Lose/Draw
Wild Life
Buried Inside Extra
Out of the Night

REVUES (5)

Forbidden Broadway (transfer)
R.S.V.P.
Upstairs at O'Neals'
A Bundle of Nerves
It's Better With a Band

MUSICALS (7)

A Drifter, the Grifter & Heather McBride
Life Is Not a Doris Day Movie
Broken Toys
The Death of Von Richtofen as Witnessed From Earth
Little Shop of Horrors
Charlotte Sweet
Snoopy

FOREIGN PLAYS IN ENGLISH (13)

Manhattan Theater Club:
The Singular Life of Albert Nobbs
Skirmishes
Summer
Lennon
N.Y. Shakespeare:
PLENTY
Top Girls
Fen
Two Fish in the Sky
Nurse Jane Goes to Hawaii
Poppie Nongena

QUARTERMAINE'S TERMS
The Other Side of the Swamp
Welcome Home Jacko

REVIVALS (36)

Roundabout:
The Learned Ladies
The Holly and the Ivy
The Entertainer
Duet for One
Winners & How He Lied to Her Husband
Delacorte:
Don Juan
A Midsummer Night's Dream
Three Sisters
True West
CSC:
Faust Part One
Faust Part Two
Ghost Sonata
Wild Oats
Danton's Death

LOOM:
H.M.S. Pinafore
The Gondoliers
Rose Marie
(12 operettas in running repertory)
Hamlet
Acting Company:
Pericles
Tartuffe
Play and Other Plays
My Astonishing Self
The Cradle Will Rock
Jacques Brel Is Alive and Well and Living in Paris

SPECIALTIES (8)

With Love and Laughter
Johnny Got His Gun
a/k/a/ Tennessee
Anthem for Doomed Youth
Do Lord Remember Me
A Christmas Carol
Egyptology: My Head Was a Sledgehammer
Jeeves Takes Charge

Plays listed in CAPITAL LETTERS have been designated Best Plays of 1982–83.
Plays listed in *italics* were still running off Broadway after May 31, 1983.

specialties, making a grand total of 108 programs presented off Broadway during the past twelve months.

The standard-bearer for domestic playwriting was William Mastrosimone's Best Play *Extremities*, with Susan Sarandon as a winsome blonde who manages to overpower a would-be rapist (James Russo), trusses him up and coolly considers torturing and destroying him. Tautly directed by Robert Allan Ackerman, Mastrosimone's second New York production (his first was *The Woolgatherers*) raised provocative questions within the melodrama, questions about the failure of the intended victim's friends to offer appropriate support and sympathy, distrust of the law's ability to dish out punishment, fear of letting the attacker go, unwarranted shame and warranted fury at being demeaned as a woman and as a human being.

Extremities stood taller than other American scripts off Broadway this season, but it did not stand alone. David Mamet's *Edmond* examined in even more varied detail the dark side of human nature, in the decline and fall of a middle-class family man who wilfully immolates himself in the nighttime evils of Manhattan streets, participating finally in brutal murder and sodomy. Also in independent production, John Ford Noonan's *Some Men Need Help* described an attachment between two ill-matched men (as the women were ill-matched in the author's previous *A Coupla White Chicks Sitting Around Talking*), with the older (Philip Bosco) helping the younger (Treat Williams) fight alcoholism. On the lighter side, A.R. Gurney Jr.'s *The Middle Ages* reviewed the past few decades of WASP high life in a country club setting through the antics of a black sheep (Jack Gilpin) getting his kicks from disrupting family rituals. And the tour de force *Greater Tuna* by Jaston Williams, Joe Sears and Ed Howard took an affectionate view of a small Texas town with a host of local characters all played by the Messrs. Williams and Sears.

Among off Broadway's producing organizations, Circle Repertory Company turned its season into an opportunity for some of the contemporary theater's clearest voices to be heard. Jules Feiffer's *A Think Piece*, about a family's subsurface stresses, played the Circle in June and July; then in October a new cycle of plays began with Lanford Wilson's Best Play *Angels Fall* (described in the previous section of this report) which later moved uptown for further acclaim including a Tony nomination. The cycle continued with Michael Cristofer's *Black Angel*, a probe of Nazi war guilt; A.R. Gurney Jr.'s *What I Did Last Summer*, about a youth constrained by his WASP environment; Corinne Jacker's *Domestic Issues*, taking another look at the 1960s radicals in today's light; and Sam Shepard's *Fool for Love*, an abrasively comic lovers' meeting that was more of a collision than an embrace. And Circle Rep articulated the works not only of these veteran American playwrights but also of the young people's one-actors chosen by the Dramatists Guild Foundation in its second annual Young Playwrights Festival, a contest which brings to light and encourages writing talent among teens and sub-teens. This Circle Rep-Dramatists Guild program received a special citation from the New York Drama Critics Circle in the annual voting for the season's bests.

Manhattan Theater Club's recent concentration on the works of foreign authors lapped over from last season with the presentation in June of Simone Benmussa's *The Singular Life of Albert Nobbs*, based on a George Moore tale of a woman posing as a man in order to make something of herself in the sexually restrictive Ireland of the 1860s. There followed at MTC a season weighted with

American playwrights, beginning with *Talking With,* several striking character monologues written under the nom de plume "Jane Martin," with a truly remarkable ensemble of actresses (including Anne Pitoniak) repeating the roles they created in the original Actors Theater of Louisville production. MTC continued with a new Jean-Claude van Itallie version of Chekhov's *Three Sisters* and later a showcase of van Itallie one-acters, *Early Warnings*; Vaughn McBride's *Elba,* about the plight of the elderly; John Olive's *Standing on My Knees,* telling of a poet's schizophrenia; and three one-act showcases for playwrights and directors, *Triple Feature.* Also embedded in the MTC schedule were the British plays *Summer,* Edward Bond's reflections on the Nazi occupation of the Balkans, and Catherine Hayes's *Skirmishes,* a stark conflict between two sisters quarreling over their duty to their dying mother. This season the MTC raised its Upstage presentations from off-off-Broadway to off-Broadway status equal to those in its Downstage facility, thereby considerably increasing the scope of its major activities.

In the wake of its memorable 1981–82 Best Play and Critics and Pulitzer Prizewinning *A Soldier's Play,* The Negro Ensemble Company busied itself with a one-act play program, *About Heaven and Earth,* staged by the group's artistic director, Douglas Turner Ward, and including a work of Ward's own, *Redeemer,* in which an assortment of individuals prepares for Judgment Day, each in his or her own fashion. The NEC schedule also took in Paul Carter Harrison's *Abercrombie Apocalypse,* pitting the black caretaker of a vacated mansion against the son of its late owner, an allegory of evil; and Ray Aranha's *Sons and Fathers of Sons,* about the travails of student, professor and sharecropper's son in a small Mississippi town from 1943 to 1960. NEC peaked in May with Gus Edwards's *Manhattan Made Me,* the adventures of an out-of-work art director (played by Eugene Lee) in the Big Apple, directed by Ward and viewed through a comic lens.

Playwrights Horizons, which last season came up with three outstanding off-Broadway offerings including a Best Play, barely got into the game this year with Tom Cone's *Herringbone* (a play with songs, with David Rounds playing all ten roles), the co-production of Ronald Ribman's *Buck* (with Priscilla Lopez in an indictment of cable TV as an exploiter of violence) and a William Finn musical that didn't get past its previews.

In July, as a sort of afterthought to 1981–82, Joseph Papp presented the interesting Des McAnuff musical *The Death of Von Richtofen as Witnessed From Earth,* the Red Baron's life and times presaging the yearning for a larger-than-life-sized leader. Besides the aforementioned British entries, Papp's eclectic schedule also took in a revival of *Hamlet* with an actress, Diane Venora, in the title role, and the new Thomas Babe comedy—*Buried Inside Extra*—with an all-star cast under Papp's direction playing newsroom types in the twilight of their paper, the show which was exported to the Royal Court in London for six weeks in exchange for *Top Girls.*

Aside from its cabaret and Women's Project programs American Place made the scene this season only with the co-production of *Buck,* plus James DeJongh's *Do Lord Remember Me,* whose cast headed by Frances Foster repeated a 1930s Federal Theater project recording first-hand memories of slavery in the United States. T. Edward Hambleton's Phoenix Theater, alas, made a final exit, cutting short its projected three-play season—and ceasing to function altogether —after the short run of *Two Fish in the Sky,* a British play about a wily Jamaican thwarting the authorities' efforts to deport him from England.

Among highlights in independent off-Broadway production were *Baseball Wives* by Grubb Graebner, looking at the tribulations of three wives of baseball superstars from opening day through the World Series; and *Poppie Nongena*, with an imported cast interpreting a Sandra Kotze-Elsa Joubert play with songs based on the latter's book about a South African girl progressing with dignity from age 13 to age 36 through the pitfalls of apartheid. An English play with music, *Lennon*, celebrated the person and accomplishments of that widely admired member of the Beatles, while Canadian sources contributed a farce about a female author of romantic novels, *Nurse Jane Goes to Hawaii*. Other subjects under scrutiny on the off-Broadway circuit this season included the Booth brothers and the Lincoln assasination (*Booth*), the life of Lewis Carroll (*Looking-Glass*), doomsday in New York (*Divine Hysteria*), Toulouse-Lautrec and friends (*Jane Avril*), a D.H. Lawrence novella, adapted by Allan Miller, about a young man's impact on the lives of two women (*The Fox*, presented on the Roundabout's schedule), blue movies (*Inserts*), a 17th century Mexican playwright-poet (*The Price of Genius*), Benjamin Franklin (in Karen Sunde's *Balloon* on CSC's schedule), a 1930s stage star (*Penelope*), the actual heroics of a Jewish woman battling the Nazis (*Hannah*), a centenarian (played by Milton Berle in *Goodnight, Grandpa*), Communist disillusionment (*Out of the Night*), a sendup of big-time TV (in Shel Silverstein's *Wild Life*, a program of one-acts whose centerpiece, *The Lady or the Tiger Show*, reenacted that timeless cliff-hanger as a Houston Astrodome spectacular with full TV coverage); and, again from London, homosexual men in love (Royce Ryton's *The Other Side of the Swamp*) and the club life of London's black youths (Mustapha Matura's *Welcome Home Jacko* in the Quaigh Theater's imported Black Theater Cooperative production).

Off Broadway enjoyed a substantial musical season. *Little Shop of Horrors* opened early, stayed on and carried off the Critics Award for best musical, the first such they have voted in three years in their exotic system of proportional consensus. With book and lyrics by Howard Ashman and music by Alan Menken, this show was based on a Roger Corman horror film about a flytrap-type plant which grows so formidably large that it's finally able to ingest a whole human being. The score and performances (led by Lee Wilkof as the florist's assistant who grows the monstrous plant) were amiable in definite contrast, under Ashman's direction, to the plant itself, "Audrey II," the bloodthirsty star of this outrageous tale. Audrey II was designed (we presume) and manipulated by puppeteer Martin P. Robinson to gobble up everything that comes near it, including the inoffensive heroine of the piece (Ellen Greene), the "Audrey" after whom this fatal foliage is named. *Little Shop of Horrors* was a very good thing in a small package, snapping up the Critics Award like Audrey II devouring a juicy dentist, under the very noses of the two large-package musicals uptown.

A heartwarming echo of the music hall in turn-of-the-century England also found a place on the off-Broadway musical scene in *Charlotte Sweet* (book and lyrics by Michael Colby, music by Gerald Jay Markoe). *Snoopy*, a musical with Charles M. Schulz's "Peanuts" comic strip characters, a score by Larry Grossman and Hal Hackady and David Garrison playing Charley Brown's quixotic pet, charmed audiences all season long, though not with the irresistible force of its Clark Gesner predecessor and Best Play *You're a Good Man Charlie Brown*. And as previously mentioned, *The Death of Von Richtofen as Witnessed From Earth* was a stimulating musical fantasy. Three other 1982–83 off-Broadway musicals—*A Drifter, the Grifter & Heather McBride* (a romantic triangle),

Life Is Not a Doris Day Movie (performers seeking that first big break) and *Broken Toys* (love brings a toy soldier to life)—failed to make the grade. But four out of seven wasn't bad, especially when you added in Martin Charnin's hit cabaret musical *Upstairs at O'Neals'*, a grab bag of witty and acerbic musical comments written by a multitude of contributors and performed by an energetically talented cast; plus the cabaret musical *Forbidden Broadway* at Palsson's, a send-up of past and present pretensions in the big theaters, which opened as an OOB offering last year but soon raised its status and settled in for a long off-Broadway run.

The specialty programs, always an important element of an off-Broadway season, ranged through an evening of recitation by Celeste Holm, Wesley Addy and Gordon Connell of excerpts from the works of stage authors (*With Love and Laughter*); Jeff Daniels as the quadriplegic in an adaptation of Dalton Trumbo's famous *Johnny Got His Gun*; a one-man portrait gallery by Edward Duke of Bertie Wooster, his gentleman's gentleman and ten other P.G. Wodehouse characters in *Jeeves Takes Charge*; Tennessee Williams excerpts (*a/k/a Tennessee*) and Wilfred Owen excerpts (*Anthem for Doomed Youth*). It included the sublime (Orson Bean's adaptation of *A Christmas Carol*) and ended with the absurd (in a non-pejorative sense) in another of Richard Foreman's assemblage of stage effects—dramatic, comic and musical—in this case expressing some of his ideas about different cultures, as boisterous as its title *Egyptology: My Head Was a Sledgehammer*.

Viewed in twelve-month perspective, the 1982–83 off-Broadway season was eminently rewarding. There was no dog-wagging in the smaller playhouses as in some previous seasons, but the tail end of the professional New York theater was in continuous and vigorous action, resulting in four Best Plays—*Plenty*, *Extremities*, *Angels Fall* and *Quartermaine's Terms*—and the clever *Little Shop of Horrors*. For good measure, there were *Top Girls*, *Edmond*, *Talking With*, *The Middle Ages*, *Greater Tuna*, *Upstairs at O'Neals'* and Circle Rep's barrage of American scripts—a measure in which entertainment was mixed generously with accomplishment.

Revivals

Arthur Miller, George Abbott, Richard Rodgers and Lorenz Hart, George and Ira Gershwin, Noel Coward, George S. Kaufman and Moss Hart, Oscar Hammerstein II and Jerome Kern—these were some of the authors featured prominently on the marquees around New York this season, together with—of course —William Shakespeare, Molière, Ibsen, Chekhov and Gilbert and Sullivan. In the protracted 1982–83 scarcity of new musical get-up-and-go, Abbott himself directed a spirited reincarnation of his and Rodgers and Hart's *On Your Toes*, a Tony Award-winning revival starring Tony Award-winning Natalia Makarova as the prima ballerina in that show's choreography by the late, great George Balanchine, including the famous "Slaughter on Tenth Avenue." This outstanding show, whose company included George S. Irving and Dina Merrill, overrode an unfavorable New York *Times* review, demonstrating that it could be done, and went on to fame and fortune at a $40 top. Abbott is in his middle 90s with at least 110 shows on his list of author's and director's credits (and this year he received Kennedy Center Honors for "lifetime achievement in the theater," which is putting it mildly). Here he enjoyed the help of younger men like 88-year-old Hans Spialek, who recreated his original orchestrations and arrangements. This ebullient *On Your Toes* was indeed a multifaceted triumph.

The Gershwins also made Broadway this season—thrice, each time in a big way. Their immortal *Porgy and Bess* came to Radio City Music Hall in its uncut version, in a production so impressively suited to the dimensions of the Music Hall stage that it may have been bigger (it was observed) than the real Catfish Row locale for this folk opera. With a host of gifted performers sharing the responsibilities of the leading roles in a huge cast, this *Porgy and Bess* was a resounding Gershwin spectacle, followed a month later by the musical phenomenon *My One and Only*, the "new" Gershwin musical described in a previous section of this report.

The Gershwins also provided the theme music for the 1983 Tony Awards ceremonies, at which they received an additional fanfare with the changing of the name of Broadway's vast Uris Theater, home of the Theater Hall of Fame, henceforth to be called the Gershwin Theater. At the time of its renaming, Jerome Kern and Oscar Hammerstein II were also being honored within the Gershwin Theater's walls with a lavish production of their own renowned *Show Boat*, revived full-scale under the direction of Michael Kahn in the Houston Grand Opera production imported to Broadway, with Donald O'Connor presiding as Cap'n Andy. The sweetest of memories was awakened with such songs as "Only Make Believe," "Why Do I Love You," "Bill" (with its P.G. Wodehouse lyric) and the organ timbre of "Ol' Man River" sung by Bruce Hubbard.

On the straight-play side of the revival season, Arthur Miller's *A View From the Bridge* regenerated its power in an Arvin Brown-staged Long Wharf Theater production brought to Broadway with Tony Lo Bianco in a dynamic portrayal of the Brooklyn longshoreman passionately obsessed by the niece he and his wife have raised like a child of their own. This Miller work appeared originally in September 1955 as a one-acter and Best Play of its season, then was expanded to full length to be produced first by Peter Brook in London the following year and then by Ulu Grosbard off Broadway with Robert Duvall in January 1965 for 780 performances. This season's *A View From the Bridge* was billed in some of its promotion as "a new play," and in some ways indeed it was: new to Broadway, staged and acted with new insights, yielding not merely a reproduction but new values of compressed emotion.

Herman Wouk's *The Caine Mutiny Court-Martial* also rekindled its dramatic fires in revival under Arthur Sherman's direction at Circle in the Square, with Michael Moriarty as the arrogant, crumbling Lt. Cmdr. Queeg so indelibly branded in memory by Lloyd Nolan, who created the role onstage, and Humphrey Bogart, who took it to the screen. Perhaps there was little that Moriarty could add to their portrayals, but he did not disappoint, nor did John Rubinstein in the Henry Fonda role of attorney for the defense.

The Broadway revival schedule for 1982–83 also included, on the drama side, a new Arthur Kopit adaptation of Ibsen's *Ghosts*, starring Liv Ullmann. On the lighter end of the scale, Noel Coward won one and lost one this season. George C. Scott's interpretation, both as actor and director, of the life and loves of a matinee idol in a Circle in the Square revival of *Present Laughter* was one of the year's major assets, opening in July and so tenaciously popular that it forced the Circle to open its fall season at the Plymouth while its own house was so pleasantly occupied. On the other hand, the widely-promoted revival of *Private Lives*, starring those two vividly public-lived personalities Richard Burton and Elizabeth Taylor, was unable to get into step with the style and mood of this brilliant Coward duologue, though as a kind of romp it attracted star-struck, curiosity-seeking customers at a $45 top.

Kaufman and Hart were much better served by a high-spirited, star-studded reproduction of *You Can't Take It With You* directed by Ellis Rabb (who did the same for the 1965 hit revival of this play), with Jason Robards at the head of an exceptionally gifted company in the many individualistic roles of this engaging, stimulating and durable comedy. Shakespeare was also exceptionally well served by his home-town devotees, the Royal Shakespeare Company of Stratford-on-Avon and London, in a highly developed and polished production of *All's Well That Ends Well*, presented as though the action of this 1603 comedy were taking place in the Edwardian era, and staged by Trevor Nunn, Royal Shakespeare's joint artistic director, whose *Cats* was already a bright fixture of the season. Molière too found a place on the sunny side of Broadway with Circle in the Square's *The Misanthrope* with Brian Bedford, Carole Shelley and Mary Beth Hurt under Stephen Porter's direction. Elsewhere, Broadway revival production took in Ugo Betti's *The Queen and the Rebels*, with Colleen Dewhurst, about a group of travellers detained by a revolution in a small country; and the Eva Le Gallienne-Florida Friebus 1932 *Alice in Wonderland* with Miss Le Gallienne directing and playing the White Queen, and with John Lee Beatty's scenery and Patricia Zipprodt's Tony-nominated costumes recreating the Tenniel-drawing "look." And a restaging of Terrence McNally's Turkish-bath farce *The Ritz* survived for only one performance as an adjunct of the disco Xenon, formerly Henry Miller's Theater.

The revival-producing organizations, which year after year make off Broadway a treasure trove of the theatrical past, hardly broke stride along the rocky financial paths of 1982–83. "The high point of the 1982–83 season as to stage history," theater historian Thomas T. Foose informs us, "was in the summer of 1982 when one found playing concurrently fully professional productions of two rare plays by Molière. At the Delacorte was the Public Theater production of *Don Juan* (or as purists have it, *Dom Juan*). At about the same time, the Roundabout was offering *The Learned Ladies* (*Les Femmes Savantes*). Richard Wilbur's 1977 translation as *The Learned Ladies* sparked interest in a Molière play long neglected in English.

"As to United States stagings of the Molière *Don Juan*, the most important prior to the Delacorte production was that at the Guthrie Theater in Minneapolis in June of 1981, from which stemmed the Delacorte staging just one year later. The Donald M. Frame translation, the Richard Foreman direction and settings and the Patricia Zipprodt costumes were all the same, with modifications, of course, for the out-of-doors."

Furthermore, John Seitz as Don Juan and Roy Brocksmith as Sganarelle repeated their Guthrie Theater performances in the Central Park cast. Thus, even in the area of revivals our cross-country theater plays its vital part.

Gene Feist's hardy Roundabout Theater Company maintained its customary high standards, following up *The Learned Ladies* with a series of works of 20th century theater, beginning with Wynyard Browne's *The Holly and the Ivy* (the American premiere of the 1948 London play about a village minister's troubled family) directed by Lindsay Anderson. Nicol Williamson colored with his own brush the Laurence Olivier role of the British music hall comedian in John Osborne's *The Entertainer*. And the Roundabout did Brian Friel's 1968 *Winners* about a loving but ill-fated young Irish couple, and Tom Kempinski's two-character *Duet for One* with Eva Marie Saint in the role of the concert violinist crippled by disease, played on Broadway only last season by Anne Bancroft. Roundabout Producing Director Feist's former colleague, Michael Fried, left the group this season, and Todd Haimes joined it as managing director.

The classic mode was well represented on other stages around town. Joseph Papp's season included *A Midsummer Night's Dream* in Central Park and *Hamlet* at the Public Theater, while Manhattan Theater Club inserted a *Three Sisters* in its schedule. Christopher Martin's Classic Stage Company (CSC) distinguished itself and its artistic director with Goethe's complete *Faust* (reputedly the American premiere of *Faust* unabridged) translated by Philip Wayne and directed and designed by Martin in two parts, each of which was presented as a full-length play. Strindberg (*Ghost Sonata*), O'Keeffe (*Wild Oats*) and Buechner (*Danton's Death*) were also honored in CSC production.

William Mount-Burke's Light Opera of Manhattan (LOOM) provided its uptown patrons with new productions of *H.M.S. Pinafore*, *The Gondoliers* and Rudolf Friml's *Rose Marie*, meanwhile keeping up its 12-month schedule of Gilbert and Sullivan, Victor Herbert and other operettas. And this year's Acting Company repertory included *Tartuffe* along with Shakespeare's seldom-seen *Pericles, Prince of Tyre*, plus Samuel Beckett's *Come and Go* on a one-act program with his *Play* and *Krapp's Last Tape*. As an extra added attraction, the Acting Company assembled a group of its alumni for a special production of Marc Blitzstein's *The Cradle Will Rock* under the direction of John Houseman, the group's producing artistic director, who also took center stage to deliver a short introductory talk at each performance, detailing the colorful origins of this musical satire on the labor movement which he himself co-produced at the Mercury Theater in 1938.

Independent production of revivals off-Broadway virtually ground to a halt this season. A repeat of Donal Donnelly's one-man portrait of George Bernard Shaw in *My Astonishing Self*, the 15th anniversary revival of the Jacques Brel revue at First City and Sam Shepard's *True West* were the only ones offered outside organizational shelter—and Shepard's play was in one sense more of a premiere than a revival. Its first production at the Public Theater in January 1981 was repudiated by its author, who is said to have considered this 1982–83 one the authentic representation of his script about a loathesome desert rat (repellently personified by John Malkovich) moving in on his respectable screenwriting brother (Gary Sinise, who also directed this version) and forcing him into an exchange of personalities. Like other Shepard plays, it managed powerfully ironic and emotional moments within a showoff kind of theater which thumbs (and in this case picked) its nose at the audience with a jumble of shock effects and harsh words.

Anyhow, the off-Broadway revival season provided Shepard, one of our most prolific and generally admired contemporary dramatists, with a second hearing for a problematical work, as it has in the past for Tennessee Williams, Arthur Miller and many others. This is a hugely important asset, nearly equal in long-term value to the celebration of the recognized historical glories of Shakespeare, Molière, Chekhov, Ibsen and company. Fortunately, our revival stages remained alert to both these functions in the season of 1982–83.

Offstage

An atmosphere of hard economic times pervaded all areas of the theater in

1982–83. The rumbles of distant financial thunder persisted in news reports of the drying-up of support from economizing government, foundation and private sources; of the curtailing of festival and other production schedules at home and abroad; of the growing scarcity of middle-income backers; of regional theater shrinkage and the Guthrie Theater's first deficit ($632,000) in 13 years; of the disappointing audience response to pay-TV's first-ever live broadcast Nov. 5 of a Broadway show, *Sophisticated Ladies*, which attracted a mere 60,000 viewers at $15 apiece from a pool potentially more than ten times that size.

Closer to home and more specifically damaging to the New York theater, T. Edward Hambleton's noted Phoenix Theater called it quits after 30 years and more than 100 productions which enlarged the scope of the contemporary stage in all dimensions. The Phoenix had been a major presence in the not-for-profit theater with its schedules of mind-expanding imports and important revivals, sprinkled with new scripts by American dramatists, including Marsha Norman's first play, *Getting Out*. The Phoenix production of Tolstoi's massive *War and Peace* on a tiny uptown stage was a feat of imagination to match Shakespeare's Battle of Agincourt at the old Globe, as unforgettable as such other Phoenix highlights as Ionesco's *Exit the King*, Mary Rodgers's *Once Upon a Mattress*, Arthur Kopit's *Oh, Dad, Poor Dad*, etc., Daniel Berrigan's *The Trial of the Catonsville Nine*, Conor Cruise O'Brien's *Murderous Angels* and David Berry's *G.R. Point*, not to mention eloquent homage to Shakespeare, Shaw, Eliot, Brecht, Chekhov, Ibsen, Marlowe, Molière, even Boucicault, Goldsmith and Richard Brinsley Sheridan. The Phoenix was a casualty of general economic conditions: cuts in its funding from all sectors had stripped it to the bone, when a seemingly unrelated Wall Street problem caused the cancellation of an expected corporate grant, a last straw which broke its three-decades-long spine of production. After only one offering, the Phoenix's 1982–83 season was cancelled with a finality that included the dissolving of its charter, so that no ashes remained from which it could rise. Its passing leaves a distressingly empty space on the New York stage.

As we were going to press with last year's *Best Plays* volume, a reported rift between producers and authors widened into a chasm of lawsuits unbridged by season-long efforts to negotiate the differences, still yawning as we sent this volume to the printer. The men and women who write the plays and musicals, most of them members of the Dramatists Guild, *lease* their work for a percentage of the box office gross laid down in a Minimum Basic Agreement drawn up in the 1920s: for plays, 5 per cent of the first $5,000, 7.5 per cent of the next $2,000 and 10 per cent thereafter; and for musicals, 6 per cent divided among the authors. Ownership of the work remains in the hands of the dramatist (unlike that, say, of the screen writer, who sells his work to the producer outright), who may continue to lease it again and again for other productions in other places and circumstances.

For several years in the recent past, representatives of the League of New York Theaters and Producers (the producers' organization) and the Dramatists Guild have explored the possibility of modernizing the old agreement in line with changed conditions of the contemporary theater; but, according to *Variety*, their discussions ended in an impasse and were broken off in the fall of 1981. Then, on July 7, 1982, the League filed an anti-trust suit against the Dramatists Guild in the Federal Court in New York, seeking "injunctive relief to enable producers to negotiate freely with authors, and to prohibit the Guild from requiring the use of contracts containing minimum terms and conditions, or involving itself in any way, directly or indirectly, in negotiations between an author and a producer concerning the terms and conditions for the rights to produce any author's works." The suit was filed in the name of Richard Barr, president of the League, and in *Variety's* estimation "is expected to be prolonged over a number of years."

The Dramatists Guild "vigorously denied" allegations of anti-trust practises; and then, in October, League and Guild representatives resumed the discussions broken off a year earlier, in a new effort to settle their differences, with *Variety* reporting that "Many producers and playwrights are unhappy with the lawsuit, which is seen as a divisive and costly development at a time when existing economic conditions in legit are heading out of control." These talks broke off again in February, with no agreement reached and the League suit being pressed. And then on April 29 the Dramatists Guild's answering volley came: a counter-suit charging anti-trust violations, filed in Federal Court in New York, naming as defendants the League, The Shubert Organization, the Shubert Foundation, the Nederlander Organization and, as individuals, Gerald Schoenfeld and Bernard B. Jacobs (Shubert officers) and James M. Nederlander (but not Richard Barr, in whose name the League suit had been filed). This counterclaim stated that the Shubert group (owners of 16½ Broadway theaters) and the Nederlander group (owners of 12 Broadway theaters, two of them in process of renovation) "have control of every facet of theatrical production, and are able to dictate the positions which the League takes with the Guild in dealing with playwrights" and have tried to force dramatists to accept "artificially low and non-competitive levels" of payment for the use of their scripts. A New York *Times* article reported that "The Guild, in its counterclaim, takes the position that . . . it is in fact the League and the Shubert and Nederlander organizations who are guilty of anti-trust violations because they have been bargaining with the Guild for years." At season's end, this cloud of internecine dissension seemed at its darkest, hovering low over the New York theater and showing no signs of disappearing any time soon.

Among the theater's other organizations, the Society of Stage Directors and Choreographers reached an agreement with the League which runs through October 1984, granting a small rise in minimum fees to $6,800 for directors and $5,500 for choreographers, plus non-returnable advances against royalties of $4,700 and $4,000. Local One of IATSE (the stagehands) negotiated 5, 6 and 7 per cent raises over a period of three years, with weekly wages topping out at $475.43 to $621.63 for department heads. Actors' Equity Association negotiated a 21.4 per cent raise in the performers' minimum salaries over a three-year period, bringing actors' base pay from $575 to $610 weekly in the first year of the new contract, with a corresponding rise in the $385 weekly living expense allotment for those on tour.

Taking a last long look over our shoulder at the 1982–83 season in New York, we are left with the impression that it was a year of growing fiscal concern over such developments as declining attendance, the $45 Broadway and $22 off-Broadway ticket, the $4 million musical, the confrontation of authors and producers over the distribution of box office receipts. It's sometimes hard to remember that what we call "theater" in one word doesn't stand or fall, suffer or enjoy, as a unit. We must continuously remind ourselves that even "Broadway" isn't a single big business with a lot of branch offices, it is an assembly of separate parts whose individual condition is of greater importance to the well-being of what we call "theater" than the sum total of achievement or average condition of the whole.

As we look back on 1982–83, we can see clearly that *Cats* and *Torch Song Trilogy* and *My One and Only* and *'night, Mother* have joined the dance with *Amadeus* and *42nd Street* and *Nine*, while off Broadway *Extremities* and *Little Shop of Horrors* and *Quartermaine's Terms* have come into step with *Cloud 9* and *The Dining Room*—at least for a goodly part of a season, and not forgetting *The Fantasticks* way, way out there at the head of the cotillion. We conclude that, whatever its shortcomings and continuing problems, 1982–83 succeeded in bringing forth for the audience's enjoyment and stimulation a number of impressive shows—and there's little in "theater" of greater value than that.

Gene Barry and George Hearn in the musical *La Cage aux Folles,*
book by Harvey Fierstein, music and lyrics by Jerry Herman.

1983-84

MUSICALS, musicals, long-running musicals (*A Chorus Line* in the longest run in Broadway history and *The Fantasticks* in its 25th year off Broadway, the longest New York run of all time) . . . musicals, musicals, musicals about musicals (*La Cage aux Folles*, *The Tap Dance Kid*) . . . musicals, musicals, musicals everywhere dominating the 1983–84 theater season in New York. From the off-Broadway hit *Taking My Turn* in early June 1983 to the thrilling Broadway crescendo of *Sunday in the Park With George* in May 1984, this was a conspicuously musical year, with the likes of *La Cage aux Folles*, *The Human Comedy*, *Zorba*, *La Tragédie de Carmen*, *Doonesbury*, *Baby* and *The Tap Dance Kid* marching shoulder to shoulder behind the band and the holdovers *Cats*, *Dreamgirls*, *42nd Street*, *Nine*, *My One and Only*, *Little Shop of Horrors* and *On Your Toes* (the latter, at 505 performances, second only to *Pal Joey* as Rodgers & Hart's longest-running hit).

No wonder, therefore, that our list of the ten Best Plays is weighted with musicals, two out of the ten for the second year in a row: *La Cage aux Folles*, with a Jerry Herman score and a Harvey Fierstein book based on the French movie and stage comedy, and the innovative *Sunday in the Park With George*, with book by James Lapine and score by Stephen Sondheim, plus a special eleventh Best Play citation to *La Tragédie de Carmen*, Peter Brook's creative remodeling of the Bizet classic.

"The shortest distance between two points is a hit review in London," observed the playwright Louis Phillips recently, and certainly it was the road taken by the two towering straight plays of 1983–84: Tom Stoppard's *The Real Thing* and David Mamet's *Glengarry Glen Ross*. Both started as London hits, Stoppard's a native product, Mamet's an American import at the National Theater. So did the hilarious *Noises Off* by Michael Frayn and the touching *And a Nightingale Sang . . .* by the late C.P. Taylor. The Samuel Beckett one-acts cited in this volume's list of Best Plays were produced in Europe, often in London, before appearing in New York, while *Carmen* was originally staged in Paris, in French, with a later English translation having been provided in New York by Sheldon Harnick.

One of the more dramatic developments on Broadway in 1983–84 was the precipitous drop in the production of new plays, diminished by almost half from last year: 8 American playscripts where there were 15, 4 foreign ones where there were 8. Even revivals dropped off, from 14 to 11, and there was only one revue in place of two (only specialties showed a rise, from 3 to 4). With musicals holding steady at 10 shows for the third straight year, total Broadway production (not counting specialties) amounted to only 34 offerings, a new low, off from 49 last year, 45 in 1981–82, 51 the year before that, 58 in 1979–80 and the previous nadir, 47 in 1978–79.

Because of a sustained high level of quality among the recent shows, leading to longer runs, or continuing inflation, or a combination of the two, the year's total Broadway box office gross, was *up* from $203 million last year to a record $226,507,518 in 1983–84, according to *Variety* estimate (the League of New York Theaters and Producers estimate differed slightly but not materially). The road

The 1983–84 Season on Broadway

PLAYS (8)

The Guys in the Truck
Brothers
Open Admissions
GLENGARRY GLEN ROSS
The Golden Age
Play Memory
A Woman of Independent Means
End of the World

MUSICALS (10)

LA CAGE AUX FOLLES
Amen Corner
LA TRAGEDIE DE CARMEN
Marilyn
Doonesbury
Baby
The Tap Dance Kid
The Rink
The Human Comedy (transfer)
SUNDAY IN THE PARK WITH GEORGE

FOREIGN PLAYS IN ENGLISH (4)

Edmund Kean
NOISES OFF
THE REAL THING
Beethoven's Tenth

REVUE (1)

Five-Six-Seven-Eight . . . . Dance!

REVIVALS (11)

Mame
The Corn Is Green
Zorba
American Buffalo
The Glass Menagerie
Circle in the Square:
Heartbreak House
Awake and Sing!
Death of a Salesman
Oliver!
A Moon for the Misbegotten
The Wiz

SPECIALTIES (4)

Peg
Ian McKellen Acting Shakespeare
Shirley MacLaine on Broadway
The Babe

HOLDOVERS WHICH BECAME HITS IN 1983–84

Brighton Beach Memoirs
Cats
My One and Only
Torch Song Trilogy

Plays listed in CAPITAL LETTERS have been designated Best Plays of 1983–84.
Plays listed in *italics* were still running after May 31, 1984.
Plays listed in **bold face type** were classified as successes in *Variety*'s annual estimate published June 6, 1984.

gross was up too, to $206 million from $184 million, and so was the average price of the Broadway admission, $29.75 in June 1984 as compared with $27.69 the year before. On the down side were total attendance, 7.9 million, declining from 8.1 million last year and 10.7 the year before, and playing weeks (if ten shows play ten weeks, that's 100 playing weeks), off sharply from 1,259 in 1982–83 to 1,119 in 1983–84. We should add that because of a calendar anomaly, these *Variety* totals were derived from a 53-week season.

Production costs were up—of course. The price tag on each of the ten musicals didn't always reach $5 million, but it did at *La Cage aux Folles*, which began to recoup rapidly at a $45 top (pretty much the going rate for a musical this year but expected to be headed toward an inevitable $50), bringing in a *Variety*-estimated $130,000 weekly profit from a $450,000 weekly gross. *La Tragédie de Carmen* came in from Paris for a mere $1.5 million, and the short-lived Marilyn Monroe musical, *Marilyn*, was estimated to have cost its backers about $3 million. Among the long runners the Broadway champ, *A Chorus Line*, is now estimated by *Variety* to have earned a net profit of $37 million, $16 million from the Broadway company. The marathon run of *The Fantasticks* off Broadway has profited those who put up the $16,500 to produce it $2.5 million so far, which is even more impressive when expressed as 7,674 per cent. But the Babe Ruth of this league is David Merrick who "hit a Broadway homer," as *Variety* put it, when he put up all the money for *42nd Street* and was collecting an estimated $500,000 weekly net profit from the Broadway and two touring companies.

The level of straight-play production costs and ticket prices in 1983–84 was more modest than that of the musicals, but still forbidding. $32.50 was a commonplace top-of-the-scale ticket, with $37.50 not unknown. At these prices, *The Real Thing*, an $825,000 hit, was estimated to be profiting $135,000 out of its $250,000 weekly gross. This year's $850,000 hit revival of *Death of a Salesman* came into town with a $1.8 million advance sale. *Torch Song Trilogy*, brought uptown at $400,000, was off the nut and making a profit in the second year of its run in a smallish house. On the road, a company of *Master Harold . . . and the Boys*, assembled for $200,000, collected a $300,000 profit on that investment.

At the economic levels illustrated by these examples, it wasn't surprising to find 1983–84 legitimate stage production spreading out over a group of producers widening to share the heavy risks, increasing in size as rapidly as the costs. A head count adds up to 90 producing individuals and organizations (not counting associates) billed above the titles of the 34 Broadway shows. *La Cage*, for example, listed seven, but in this respect, we believe, *Marilyn* topped them all with 12 producers and one associate, plus three more associates named in the below-title credits.

Broadway

Sandy Duncan and the Rockettes tided Broadway over the summer with *Five-Six-Seven-Eight . . . Dance!*, a spectacular melange of musical and comedy numbers, Ron Field choreography and wide-stage showmanship at Radio City Music Hall. Before the end of August, however, more good musical news was being made with the arrival of *La Cage aux Folles*, based on the same Jean Poiret play about a homosexual couple and their Riviera night club as the popular French movie comedy. Harvey Fierstein, author of the long-running Best Play

Torch Song Trilogy, wrote the book about the cabaret owner and his lover, the glamorous star of his floor show, who have raised a son (the result of a single heterosexual adventure in the cabaret owner's youth). The son, grown up, now wishes to marry the daughter of a notoriously prudish politician. The French-farcical possibilities of that situation were roundly realized in the script and in Arthur Laurents's direction, but as Fierstein remarked to someone while his show was in the crucible of preparation in its Boston tryout, "It's really about 'Honor thy father and mother.' " There is an undertow of feeling beneath the laughter in *La Cage* that tugs irresistibly at the audience's sympathy for Georges (Gene Barry) and his drag-queen lover Albin (George Hearn in his Tony-winning performance), a respectable couple with the same sensibilities as any middle-aged married pair trying to adjust to their son's choice of a bride. Sexual identity was the running gag of this musical comedy, but it was family affection that was finally put to the test.

The embellishments were superb. Jerry Herman's score was loaded with shining take-home melodies ("Song on the Sand," "I Am What I Am," "Look Over There") and refreshingly singable, articulate lyrics. Theoni V. Aldredge's costumes were as outlandishly colorful as the drag chorus line they dressed. So was Scott Salmon's choreography featuring an athletic can-can performed by the mostly-male "Les Cagelles" dressed as female dancers. David Mitchell's sets were able to evoke St. Tropez, though most of them were home and night club interiors. Laurents's direction dominated the production with taste, style and wit, and the performances were impeccable—Barry's in a conspicuously masculine key of self-respect, Hearn's in that of proud effeminacy. Even in a busy year for musicals, *La Cage* stood far out as musical theater entertainment.

At the other end of the season, Stephen Sondheim ventured once more into musical *terra incognita*, this time in company with James Lapine, and they returned to place marvels on display in their *Sunday in the Park With George*. "George" is the painter Georges Seurat; the "park" is described in a Sondheim lyric as "a small suburban park" on an island in the Seine, the island named in Seurat's impressionist masterpiece "A Sunday Afternoon on the Island of La Grande Jatte." Strollers, fisher folk, picnickers, lovers, even the dogs in that painting are characterized and set in motion by Lapine's book and direction and Sondheim's music and lyrics. The painter himself (played by Mandy Patinkin) is seen as an artist so obsessed by his vision of a new approach to color and composition that he can't even look up from his drawing pad to see his newborn daughter by his mistress "Dot" (Bernadette Peters). His painting gradually comes together, though, and it is beautifully consummated in Act I, even as the lovers are being pulled apart. But their great grandson, the *raison d'etre* of Act II, is also an artist exploring new ground with light itself (the laser beam). He is helped to find his way by the example of his ancestor.

A *Sunday in the Park* program note stated that all the characters were "products of the authors' imagination," though "suggested" by the life of Georges Seurat. This musical was a show of many parts: Sondheim's pointillist arpeggios timed to the tip of Seurat's dotting paint brush, the notes then coming together in the ear of the audience (like Seurat's solid-color dots blending into subtle shades on the retina of the beholder) in aria-like harmonies for the singers, soaring mightily in the act finales entitled "Sunday"; the endless versatility of Sondheim's dynamic lyrics, expressing the highest aims of the artist or amusing themselves and the audience by imitating the yapping of a small dog; Lapine's staccato book, making up somewhat in variety for what it lacked in dramatic tension, and his staging of the stylized movements, gestures and poses of the bustle era; the Tony Straiges scenery with its clever use of cutouts; the Seurat-colored costumes by Patricia Zipprodt and Ann Hould-Ward; the spectacular laser effect in Act II by Bran Ferren; and of course the performances by and around Miss Peters, a three-dimensional presence within this musical tribute to two-dimensional art. Each of these contributions to *Sunday in the Park* was a remarkable example of its kind. They combined in the form and perspective of the musical stage in an effect even more remarkable than the sum of its parts, a Best Play and the Critics Award winner as best musical.

Another original and compelling musical theater concept was *La Tragédie de Carmen* as reshaped by Peter Brook, as though he had not already given us more than enough to think about with his *Marat/Sade* and his unique *A Midsummer Night's Dream*. His *Carmen* was very different from the opera, though in it Brook retained a goodly share of Bizet. It was a "written" work, so to speak, though not exactly in the words of the French libretto (translated into an English version by Sheldon Harnick during its New York run). Brook "writes" in stage-craft, a medium of expression and dramatization of which he is a master. To say that he "directed" this *Carmen* wouldn't adequately define his creative function. With the art of stagecraft, Brook "rewrote" *A Midsummer Night's Dream* without much altering Shakespeare's words, and he has similarly "rewritten" *Carmen*, realizing the drama in a magical series of stage images (carried out in Jean-Guy Lecat's design) and including highlights from Bizet's haunting score.

A remarkable book by Charles Blackwell was in large measure responsible for the success of *The Tap Dance Kid*, which was not at first received with unbridled enthusiasm. By season's end, however, it was managing to make a run of it in the vasty Minskoff Theater. This musical richly deserved and finally found an audience for its family drama of a black lawyer (Samuel E. Wright, taut as a tuned violin string) who has struggled desperately to pull his family up into the middle class, only to find his sub-teen-age son reverting to stereotype, possessed with ambition to become a dancer like his uncle (Hinton Battle) and maternal grandfather. The emotional structure, as family members lined up one by one on the side of the child against his formidable father, was strong enough to carry a straight play, directed by Vivian Matalon for all it was worth in intensity.

The score was a fuller participant in two other appealing musicals, *The Rink* and *Baby*. In the former, John Kander and Fred Ebb provided an emotionalized group of songs to be sung by Liza Minnelli as a prodigal daughter and Chita Rivera as her skeptical mother, belting their animosities and affections out to each other. A spectacular Peter Larkin set depicting a run-down roller-skating rink next to the roller coaster at an Eastern amusement park was a metaphor for the drama of a deteriorated mother-daughter relationship moving painfully toward crisis in the book by Terrence McNally. Likewise, the David Shire-Richard Maltby Jr. score of *Baby* was a prime attraction of this musical celebration of childbirth in a book by Sybille Pearson dividing its attention among three college-town couples: a pair of undergraduate posslq's who face imminent parentage with chin up and thumbs down on marriage; a middle-aged faculty pair who, following an evening of too-careless rapture, find themselves becoming parents *again* just as they are breathing a sigh of relief that their children are grown and fled and they can settle down to easeful retirement; and an athletic pair trying so hard to have a baby (and failing) that they're willing to suffer the indignities of a clinical approach to their problem. Joy and wonder abounded onstage in *Baby*, both in the performances of the ensemble under Maltby's direction and in the matching score.

Even more of a *tour de force* of music was *The Human Comedy*, with William Saroyan's novel about a California family of the 1940s set hauntingly to music by Galt MacDermot. In a libretto (truly a libretto, all singing, no dialogue) by William Dumaresq, Bonnie Koloc dominated her scenes as a widow who never quits trying to keep her family going, even after she loses her oldest son to World War II. A large cast of neighbors served as a Greek chorus for the individuals who stepped forward out of concert-style groupings to play their parts under Wilford Leach's direction, which harmonized the performances, the sentimentality of the score and the episodes of family life and death into a unified paean to the faith and endurance of small-town America. *The Human Comedy* originated off Broadway at New York Shakespeare Festival, where it was conspicuously popular. It didn't find much of an audience in transfer to Broadway but seems certain to be headed for future success elsewhere.

We also suspect that *Doonesbury*, with Garry Trudeau's famous cartoon characters doing their socially satirical thing in book and lyrics by Trudeau himself and score by Elizabeth Swados, will have another life. The season's agenda also included two other large-scale musicals: *Marilyn*, musicalizing Marilyn Monroe's life, with Alyson Reed in the title role, and *Amen Corner*, the Philip Rose-Peter Udell-Garry Sherman musical version of James Baldwin's play about the lady pastor of a Harlem storefront church.

The number of new straight plays presented on Broadway this year was pathetically and historically small, but among them were scripts of the first quality. Tom Stoppard's *The Real Thing*, for example, the Critics Award best-of-bests winner, glittered in language like his *Travesties* and sometimes shivered in despair like his *Rosencrantz and Guildenstern Are Dead*. The play explored the ways of sexual infidelity under the direction of Mike Nichols and as performed by Jeremy Irons as a playwright who knows very well how a flippant husband-wife scene should be written for the stage, but not how to make a game out of the agonies of "the real thing" when his own beloved goes astray. Tony Walton's set accommodated this play comfortably, even though it moved around a lot in space and time. The play in turn challenged its audience with wit and moved it to pity and dismay.

Another British Best Play, Michael Frayn's *Noises Off*, was a masterpiece of its farcical genre, masterfully directed by Michael Blakemore and played by a team of thespian athletes who must have broken the all-time record for exits and entrances within the limit of three acts. The play depicted the antics on and offstage of the members of a touring troupe performing a kinetic farce in a country-house setting with eight doors and a window; and, simultaneously, hammering at each other backstage in a tangle of jealous personal rages. The Michael Annals sets and costumes were marvels of engineering to fit this cleverly engineered script's special needs of comings and goings, of wrapping-on and ripping-off of clothing. The play-within-the-play being "performed" by these "actors" was also a farce, about trysts in a supposedly empty house. Its first act was seen being "rehearsed" in Act I of *Noises Off*, "played" in Act II but observed from the "actors'" point of view behind the scenes, and then "played" again in Act III (and become an absolute shambles of missed cues and careless improvisations) again from the audience's point of frontal view, all the while amusing itself with the slings, arrows and egos of the backstage personnel. Playing together with the precise timing of a baseball infield, and with as much physical energy, the ensemble led by Dorothy Loudon, Paxton Whitehead and Brian Murray were champions at their hilarious game.

Another import from the London stage, Raymund Fitzsimons's *Edmund Kean*, was a showcase for a Ben Kingsley performance of that gifted, harried 19th century tragedian in the great Shakespearean roles. Though this was a one-man performance alternating excerpts from the plays and from Kean's life, it was billed as a "play," and certainly Kingsley made it seem so, filling the stage with his characterization. And Shakespearean roles also came under scrutiny in the portrayals and comments by Ian McKellen in his one-man show *Ian McKellen Acting Shakespeare*, also imported. Finally, Peter Ustinov's comedy *Beethoven's Tenth*, starring the author as the composer come back to earth to advise and succor a music critic played by George Rose, could not repeat on Broadway the popular success it had enjoyed on the London stage before its appearance here.

An American playscript arriving—triumphantly—on Broadway by way of London was David Mamet's stinging *Glengarry Glen Ross*, a life-of-a-salesman comedy of real estate hustlers conniving their way through another day. When Mamet considered his completed script, he feared that its halves might be somewhat mismatched in style (Act I is a series of three two-man conversations in a Chinese restaurant, Act II sends the balloon up in the real estate office with the whole cast), and he took this problem to his friend Harold Pinter who read it, decided the only thing wrong with it was that it hadn't yet been produced and handed it to Peter Hall of the National Theater who promptly produced it. This wasn't a case, therefore, of an American play turned down by American producers until it was put on in London (which has happened). *Glengarry Glen Ross* won the best-play award of the Society of West End Theaters and was still running in London when it opened in Chicago and New York.

Mamet is a resident playwright of Chicago's Goodman Theater whose artistic director, Gregory Mosher, produced and directed the play there in January. When this Chicago production was brought to New York in March, it had already been seen by the 1984 Pulitzer Prize committee and won that award as a regional theater offering, just as *'night, Mother* won it last year in Boston. Mamet's play, cited by the New York Drama Critics Circle as the best American play of the season, was as broad-shouldered as the city which first produced it in America. As in Mamet's *American Buffalo*, its language is a painfully perfect expression of lower middle class characters who are more shrewd than articulate, ambitious beyond their education, and therefore have learned to express themselves by imaginative inflections and combinations of the few words they know and trust. For example, their copious repetition of four-letter obscenities shades every other word and phrase with a little more or less meaning than its dictionary definition. Mamet has made the most of this form of communication, as John O'Hara did with upper middle class speech forms, to express the simple but ferocious intentions of an ensemble of hungry real estate salesman vying and cheating each other for hot leads in a sales competition with a Cadillac as the prize. Mosher's direction made a frontal assault on the audience's cool, in particular with the performances of Joe Mantegna, the champion salesman, a sleek go-getter with an answer for everything, and Robert Prosky, old, tired, wily and trying desperately to keep his hold on the bottom rung. The play's construction *is* a bit uneven, but there was nothing shaky about this immensely successful collaboration of acting, directing and writing.

It's worth adding that it wasn't London origin but Chicago momentum that helped define the 1983–84 theater season in New York. This was a Chicago year in Manhattan, with *Glengarry Glen Ross* at the head of a parade of Chicago-originated productions and personalities including another Best Play (*And a Nightingale Sang . . .*, with Joan Allen in the season's outstanding performance by an actress); the first fully professional production of Lanford Wilson's 1965 off-off-Broadway play *Balm in Gilead*, brought to Circle Rep by Chicago's Steppenwolf Ensemble; the Second City troupe in their revue *Orwell That Ends Well*; and a number of other performers from Chicago in casts all over town.

It was a long time between the appearances of the few other new American playscripts making it to Broadway this season, and short shrift for all of them once they arrived. Shirley Lauro's *Open Admissions* dramatized the shortcomings of the well-intentioned policy of extending the opportunity of higher education to all comers, whether or not the system is equipped to deal with them or the student is qualified to profit from the experience. This candid and timely script, previously produced successfully OOB and in regional theater, survived only 17 performances on Broadway. A new A.R. Gurney Jr. play, *The Golden Age*, suggested by Henry James's *The Aspern Papers*, with Irene Worth as an elderly dowager in possession of a valuable manuscript coveted by a young scholar (Jeff Daniels), lasted for only 29. Arthur Kopit's *End of the World* (one of two straight plays staged by Harold Prince this season) confronted the menace of nuclear holocaust in a whimsical context but at a length too great for its breadth, though it had the advantage of performances by Barnard Hughes as a mystery millionaire commissioning a play to arouse the public to its danger, John Shea as the playwright who accepts this challenge and Linda Hunt as his tiny but formidable agent, an affectionate caricature of Audrey Wood. Miss Hunt was nominated for a best-supporting-performance Tony, an accolade which carried this May production no farther than the ides of June. The other play staged by Harold Prince was Joanna M. Glass's *Play Memory*, scenes of family decline and disintegration, nominated for a best-play Tony even after it had departed after less than a week's run. Applause was muted, however, at the other short-lived American entries: *The Guys in the Truck*, about sports broadcasting; *Brothers*, with Carroll O'Connor as a tough union leader dominating his offspring (it opened and closed in only one performance); and *A Woman of Independent Means*, a one-performer play with Barbara Rush as a Texas matriarch of this century reviewing the events of her life.

Among the specialties, *Shirley MacLaine on Broadway* drew cheers late in the season with this year's Academy Award-winning star in a personalized, solo (with backup dancers) song-and-dance show. Earlier in the season, Peggy Lee's solo performance recalling events from her life and reprising songs from her glittering career, *Peg*, found no such support and closed after a brief run. Likewise, an attempt to memorialize Babe Ruth with a one-character play about his life and career, *The Babe*, with Max Gail playing the 1920s Sultan of Swat, couldn't draw his fans to 1984 Broadway in any significant numbers.

Off Broadway

Musicals also burgeoned off Broadway this season, their production total nearly doubling from 7 a year ago to 13, and in revue form growing from 5 to

7. There was some erosion in the total of straight-play production, but considering the shrinkage taking place uptown, off Broadway made an admirable showing in 1983–84 (see the one-page summary of the off-Broadway season accompanying this report). There were 57 new plays and musicals (including one extended engagement, one transfer and one revised version) produced off Broadway in 1983–84, as compared with 59 in 1982–83 and 58 in 1981–82. This season's contingent comprised 32 American straight-play programs, the 13 abovementioned musicals and 12 foreign plays as compared with the 39-7-13, 45-9-7, 33-14-8 and 39-7-12 in the past four seasons and the peak 38-15-12 of 1979. In addition to this year's 57, there were the 7 revues, plus 35 revivals and 11 specialties, making a grand total of 110 programs presented off Broadway during the past twelve months.

Not a New York season in the 1970s and 1980s has gone by without something from Samuel Beckett—a revival of *Waiting for Godot* here, a new one-acter or an excerpt of a program of collected highlights there. This season we were treated to six new-to-New-York Beckett one-acters on two separate programs directed by the late Alan Schneider, an incomparable interpreter of Beckett's work, who met an untimely death in a London street accident this spring. This tragic event removed much of our pleasure but doubled our resolve, taken before the accident, to cite Beckett as a 1983–84 Best Play author. This we do with profound admiration for the work and profound regret that it is the last to be staged by Mr. Schneider.

In making this citation, we don't single out the first program of one-acters offered in June 1983 under the title *Samuel Beckett's Ohio Impromptu, Catastrophe, What Where*, nor the second one in February under the title of *Rockaby*, comprising *Enough, Footfalls* and the title play, and presenting Billie Whitelaw from the London stage in three aspects of womanhood. Each of these six works encompassed infinite riches of Beckett insight and imagery in the most compact and sparsely furnished room he could devise for his purposes, which ranged from an object lesson in tyrannous government to the last gasps of a dying crone. We should emphasize that it is the whole collection of his six Schneider-directed presentations that we salute with this 1983–84 Best Play citation.

Another off-Broadway Best Play from abroad was *And a Nightingale Sang . . .*, an affectionate study of a British family during World War II, written by the late C.P. Taylor whose *Good* was one of last season's Best Plays. This family is in no way heroic, nor does it cringe from events: Dad is an air raid warden, Mom places her trust in her church, Grandpa accepts his transient status of being shuttled between the households of his children, and younger daughter is a sweetheart of the armed forces. But it was the luminous performance of Joan Allen as the plain-Jane older daughter that lit the corners of this play with a growing brightness as the character gradually responds to the opportunity of romance offered by a soldier (Peter Friedman) stationed nearby. In her ugly duckling phase there is no hint of the swan to come, nor much of the duckling finally left at the end of the play, in a performance which seemed uncannily effortless and yet solidly true. Miss Allen came on from Chicago, where *And a Nightingale Sang . . .* had previously been produced, to provide New York with the year's best performance by an actress in one of its Best Plays.

The translation of a Polish play, *Cinders* (previously produced in London) by Janusz Glowacki, was a major achievement of Joseph Papp's New York Shakespeare Festival season. The play is set in a Polish reform school for girls, some of

The 1983–84 Season Off Broadway

PLAYS (32)

Circle Rep:
FOOL FOR LOVE
  (extended run)
Full Hookup
Levitation
The Harvesting
American Place:
Great Days
The Danube
Terra Nova
Yellow Fever
A Weekend Near Madison
Basement Tapes
A Little Madness
Public Theater:
Sound and Beauty
Young Playwrights
Playwrights Horizons:
Baby With the Bathwater
Isn't It Romantic
Fables for Friends
PAINTING CHURCHES
Negro Ensemble:
Puppetplay
American Dreams
The Lady and the Clarinet
Manhattan Theater Club:
Friends
THE MISS
FIRECRACKER
CONTEST

Living Theater:
The Archeology of Sleep
The Yellow Methuselah
Street Theater:
To Gillian on Her 37th
  Birthday
The Flight of the Earls
The Actors' Delicatessen
A Hell of a Town
The Vampires
'night, Mother
  (transfer)
Spookhouse

MUSICALS (13)

Taking My Turn
Non Pasquale
Public Theater:
Lenny and the
  Heartbreakers
The Human Comedy
American Passion
Dogs
The Brooklyn Bridge
Preppies
Blue Plate Special
Weekend
Tallulah
Love
Nite Club Confidential

REVUES (7)

Serious Bizness
Sunset
Leftovers
One More Song/One More
  Dance
Babalooney
A . . . My Name Is Alice
Orwell That Ends Well

FOREIGN PLAYS IN ENGLISH (12)

Greek
BECKETT ONE-ACTS
Manhattan Theater Club:
Mensch Meier
Other Places
Big Maggie
Big and Little
Public Theater:
A Private View
Cinders
AND A NIGHTINGALE
  SANG . . .
ROCKABY
Woza Albert!
Dracula

REVIVALS (35)

LOOM:
Rose Marie
  (extended run)
(12 operettas in running
  repertory)
Roundabout
Ah, Wilderness!
The Knack
The Master Builder
The Killing of Sister
  George
Old Times
On Approval
King Richard III
Fen
The Philanthropist
CSC:
Hamlet
Dance of Death
Circle Rep:
The Sea Gull
Balm in Gilead
Mirror Theater:
Paradise Lost
Inheritors
Rain
Ghosts
The Hasty Heart

Living Theater:
The Antigone of
  Sophokles
The One and the Many
Pieces of Eight
The Shadow of a Gunman

SPECIALTIES (11)

Public Theater:
Goodnight Ladies!
Orgasmo Adulto Escapes
  From the Zoo
My Uncle Sam
An Evening With Quentin
  Crisp
Fun House
American Place:
The Vi-Ton-Ka Medicine
  Show
Do Lord Remember Me
  (return engagement)
Secret Honor
Dinah! Queen of the Blues
Nostalgic for the Future
Hey, Ma . . . Kaye Ballard

Plays listed in CAPITAL LETTERS have been designated Best Plays of 1983–84.
Plays listed in *italics* were still running off Broadway after May 31, 1984.

whom are staging their version of the Cinderella tale while a government deputy and TV crew eavesdrop on their project. All the TV reporter (Christopher Walken) cares about is getting a sensational story, and all the deputy (Robin Gammell) cares about is political obeisance, and neither cares much what he has to do to get it. The principal (George Guidall) is sensitive to the needs of of the girls in his charge; but in the end this doesn't do any of them much good, neither victimized Cinderella (Lucinda Jenney) nor the Prince (Dori Hartley), a survivor and reform-school ringleader. Under John Madden's direction the play developed a momentum that brought it very close to the inner circle of the Best Plays list.

Another important element of the New York Shakespeare Festival season was a group of three Czechoslovakian one-acters by Vaclav Havel offered in translation. The title, *A Private View*, suggested that these autobiographical sketches were written to be played in private homes because they were banned from public view in an authoritarian society which had once jailed their author for human rights activities and which was the butt of the injustices and failings portrayed and protested in these plays. The Papp organization also revived Caryl Churchill's *Fen*, an episodic drama of English farmers being dispossessed by big-capital conglomerates, with a marvelous set by Annie Smart featuring rows and rows of richly fertile potato-field soil pointing out at the audience like accusing fingers.

Manhattan Theater Club found room in its full season for two productions of new foreign works: *Other Places*, three Harold Pinter one-acts directed by the late Alan Schneider, and *Mensch Meier*, the translation of a German play by Franz Xaver Kroetz depicting workers on the West side of the wall as blue-collar slaves (Kroetz had three plays produced in New York this year, the two others OOB). MTC also presented a revival of a British script, Christopher Hampton's 1971 Best Play *The Philanthropist*.

The humor and skill of the performers, Percy Mtwa and Mbongeni Ngema (who had also helped develop the material), in the independently-produced *Woza Albert!* didn't lessen the impact of their two-man show's statements about the injustices, absurdities and cruelties of apartheid in their South African homeland. CSC (formerly Classic, now City Stage Company) mounted a Christopher Martin translation from the German of Botho Strauss's 1978 comment on modern society under the title of *Big and Little/scenes*. Other importations of this off-Broadway season were a British re-working of the Oedipus tragedy, *Greek* by Steven Berkoff; an Irish play about a resourceful widow, *Big Maggie* by John B. Keane; and a British version of the Dracula tale facetiously entitled *Dracula, or A Pain in the Neck*.

Among the best of the American scripts off Broadway was Tina Howe's *Painting Churches*, stepping up from a prizewinning off-off-Broadway production the season before at Second Stage, whose Carole Rothman also directed this version. The play's subject wasn't architectural refurbishment, as the title might imply, but the Church family of Boston: father (George N. Martin), a famous poet, lovable but on the edge of senility and becoming a problem; mother (Marian Seldes), bravely, competently and wittily making the best of increasingly difficult circumstances; and daughter (Elizabeth McGovern), a successful artist who has come home to help her parents in their hour of need and, incidentally, to paint their portrait. The father's decline and the daughter's memories of how hard it was to get started in her career were played in counterpoint on the sensitive instrument of the mother, in Tina Howe's first Best Play.

"Abrasively comic" and "more of a collision than an embrace," we noted of Sam Shepard's *Fool for Love* in the 1982–83 Best Plays volume. In further consideration of this 1984 Obie Award-winner and 1983–84 Best Play, we find ourselves going back to those phrases to describe this kinetic script, in which a half-brother and half-sister practise emotional and physical violence on one another, as though punishing each other for their incestuous but irresistible love. They are hopelessly locked in a lifelong affair that began at first sight, before they knew they were related, and cannot be severed even by this knowledge. Their father observes and comments from the sidelines like a disembodied spirit, and an outsider intrudes on the lovers in a final scene that emphasizes both the black-comic and the passionate aspects of their relationship. Shepard directed his own script with total perception of its powerful content, while the cast served him boldly throughout the bruising action. Shepard is one of his generation's most prolific and successful American playwrights (his *Buried Child* won the Pulitzer Prize and his *True West* ran off Broadway for more than a year). *Fool for Love*, his first Best Play, is the equal in impact and the superior in style and depth of vision of any of his other work that we have seen.

Circle Rep brought the Shepard play to New York in the Magic Theater of San Francisco (where it originated) production, in what was to be a limited engagement; but, as the play gathered momentum, it was upped in status to an open-ended off-Broadway run, with the show moved to Theater Row uptown, to make room for the new season at the downtown facility. When Circle Rep resumed play-producing in November, it presented new American scripts in a revival sandwich. Warming up with a Jean-Claude van Itallie translation of Chekhov, the group proceeded to *Full Hookup* by Conrad Bishop and Elizabeth Fuller, another drama of violence between the sexes; *Levitation* by Timothy Mason, in which an aspiring playwright tries to heal his wounds in a homecoming visit to the Midwest; and *The Harvesting*, a detective drama written and directed by John Bishop. Circle Rep then put the finishing touches on its 1983–84 season with an important revival of Lanford Wilson's 1965 comedy *Balm in Gilead*, of which more in the next chapter of this report.

Beth Henley's *The Miss Firecracker Contest*, a comedy about very un-average small-town Mississippi folk, was one of only two American scripts to make it to opening night at Manhattan Theater Club this season, but it was a Best Play and a triumph of teamwork of authorship and production in MTC's small UpStage space. Like its author's previous Best Play *Crimes of the Heart*, this one boldly silhouetted with eccentricities the kind of Southern characters Miss Henley either knows so well or invents so vividly: a competent, attractive young woman come home to take refuge and seemingly able to manage everything but her own life (an almost exact equivalent of one of the *Crimes of the Heart* sisters); a wild young female spirit trying to break loose and make her mark in a local beauty contest, paying a price at every turn (another close equivalent); the young man of the family who, judging from his aimless past, ought to be a wimp, but isn't; a family friend (in an outstanding performance by Belita Moreno) whose honesty is a delight as she plays the unpromising cards life dealt her and, suprisingly, wins almost every hand. With the help of Stephen Tobolowsky's hyperactive direction, Miss Henley stirs these people up with a small-town beauty contest. They are irresistibly—but not consistently—charming, and there are real horrors lurking at the edges of their lives. Miss Henley put a backspin on these follies that made them all the more entertaining, from an opening blast of super-patriotism to a curtain line that tops the comedy. The other American play offered by MTC was Lee Kalcheim's *Friends*, a reunion of two college pals in midlife crisis.

The good times in American playwriting off Broadway in 1983–84 didn't end where it was necessary to draw the line on Best Plays selections. R.A. Shiomi's *Yellow Fever* delightfully converted Humphrey Bogart-type private-eye cliches for a cast of orientals in a Vancouver setting, with Donald Li and later Mako turning up the collar of the trenchcoat in the leading role. A more poetic approach and style was successfully taken by David Henry Hwang in two one-acters with Japanese locales and characters directed by John Lone. The first, *The House of Sleeping Beauties*, introduced an aging novelist into a strange brothel where the girls are maintained in a state of drugged insensibility—an effort, a program note states, to create a fantasy around the suicide of the Japanese writer Yasunari Kawabata. The second play, *The Sound of a Voice*, featured Lone himself as a Samurai in a fateful love affair with a bewitched creature of the forest. This program of outstanding one-acters by an outstanding playwright, offered under the title *Sound and Beauty*, was the only new American straight play produced this season at Joseph Papp's Public Theater complex, other than the special Young Playwrights Festival of one-acters by teen-agers selected in the Foundation of the Dramatists Guild's third annual contest encouraging young people to write scripts.

Playwrights Horizons, on the other hand, expended all its energies in the American-play category. This Andre Bishop-Paul Daniels group's schedule included a new Christopher Durang comedy, *Baby With the Bathwater*, slashing at the immediate and long-term results of parental incompetence; and Mark O'Donnell's *Fables for Friends*, an assemblage of nine comedy sketches of friendship. A revised version of Wendy Wasserstein's comedy *Isn't It Romantic*, with Cristine Rose as a girl managing to cope with the big city despite the attentions of her indulgent mother (Betty Comden), proved solidly popular with Theater Row audiences. Playwrights Horizons also helped bring in Ted Tally's South Pole adventure play, *Terra Nova* (much applauded in regional theater productions), with Robert Foxworth and Anthony Zerbe as the explorers Scott and Amundsen, in partnership with American Place. As for American Place itself, the Wynn Handman organization also offered on its schedule *Great Days* by Donald Barthelme, a cluster of conversations about our life and times; a Maria Irene Fornes play about a romance in the shadow of nuclear holocaust, *The Danube*; and a recreation of a famed old American entertainment form in *The Vi-Ton-Ka Medicine Show*, complete with down-home music combo, a bullwhip and six-shooter artist and the hawking of bottles of "tonic" to the members of an audience who, to an even greater degree than usual, permitted themselves a willing suspension of disbelief.

The Negro Ensemble Company presented Pearl Cleage's *Puppetplay*, contemplating a world in which people are turned into puppets, and *American Dreams* by Velina Houston, a drama of black vs. Asian racial frictions. And the Julian Beck-Judith Malina Living Theater of 1950s and 1960s fame made a brief return visit with a repertory schedule which included Beck's *The Archeology of Sleep*, directed by Malina, a series of dramatic images and comments on its title subject, with the performers moving into the aisles and making contact with members of the audience in the renowned but not always appreciated style of *Paradise Now* and other Living Theater presentations.

A worthwhile effort in independent production was *A Weekend Near Madison* by Kathleen Tolan on a subject recurring on our stages: the reunion of 1960s activists 20 years later, with a reassessment of their ideals. Later in the season, Michael Brady's *To Gillian on Her 37th Birthday* mixed contrasting colors of family conflict and undying family love in the retrospections of a widower grieving over his wife's death. And Michael Cristofer's *The Lady and the Clarinet* came in from California with high hopes, destined to be dashed, for a Gordon Davidson-directed play starring Stockard Channing as a lady reminiscing about her past loves for a clarinet player hired to play background music for her dinner date.

Since Harvey Fierstein, the author of two current Broadway hits, was unable to repeat his success with the black comedy *Spookhouse* (set in an apartment above the Coney Island horror show and starring Anne Meara), it's no wonder that a number of other 1983–84 efforts also fell far short of acclaim. Evocation of the Nixon era was twice attepted, once in the form of satire (*Basement Tapes*, an imaginary meeting of G. Gordon Liddy with the Messrs. Ford and Nixon) and once as a monologue with the former President telling his side of the Watergate story to a tape recorder in *Secret Honor*. Other subjects raised briefly in new American scripts off Broadway were a son placing his family in crisis by dabbling in the sale of armaments (*A Little Madness*), the 1959 Christopher Street gay bar riot (*Street Theater*), the present tragedies in Ireland (*The Flight of the Earls*), the days of vaudeville (*The Actors' Delicatessen*), survival of nuclear disaster (*A Hell of a Town*) and suburban family eccentricity (*The Vampires*).

The very first offering of the off-Broadway musical year, *Taking My Turn*, proved to be its star attraction all season. Conceived and directed by Robert H. Livingston, with a score by Gary William Friedman and Will Holt, it was a comforting review of growing old, a theme musical with a great deal to say on the subject of "the golden years," all of it basically upbeat and entertaining. New York Shakespeare Festival soon followed suit with a warm-hearted musical version of Saroyan's *The Human Comedy* which later moved to Broadway. Joseph Papp's group also offered (at the Delacorte in Central Park) a pop opera called *Non Pasquale*, based on *Don Pasquale* and starring Ron Leibman under Wilford Leach's direction; and (at the Public Theater) a rock musical, *Lenny and the Heartbreakers*. Also in organizational production was a country-Western musical comedy soap opera, *Blue Plate Special*, at Manhattan Theater Club.

An early off-Broadway musical entry, *American Passion*, came and went after a single performance. The notion of having the Mayor of New York City adopt a dog from the city pound in *Dogs* didn't last much longer, nor did musical homage to the massive *The Brooklyn Bridge* in its 100th anniversary year, nor prep school quirks and culture in *Preppies*, nor young love in Manhattan in *Weekend*. The Tony Lang-Arthur Siegel-Mae Richard musical *Tallulah* was a little more substantial, with Helen Gallagher and Russell Nype in its cast and Tallulah Bankhead as its subject. The late-arriving musical *Love*, based on Murray Schisgal's comedy with the same title spelled in three letters, stepped forward with an Outer Critics Award book by Jeffrey Sweet. Sweet's skillful adaptation kept faith with the style and the humor of the Schisgal work, and the show also had the advantage of an appealing score by Howard Marren and Susan Birkenhead. Finally, there was *Nite Club Confidential*, an arrival from OOB written and directed by Dennis Deal, with old and new musical numbers in night club settings from Sutton Place to the Village, from Hollywood to Paris.

The revue form was alive and well off Broadway this season. While *Forbidden Broadway* continued at Palsson's with revisions bringing its satire up-to-date with developments in the big theaters, O'Neals'/43d Street brought *Serious Bizness*, a collection of sketches on the contemporary scene staged by Phyllis Newman, from American Place (where it began in the American Humorists series) to the cabaret scene for a season-long run. Musical revues built around the life of the entertainer (*Sunset*), compulsive eating (*Leftovers*), ballet (*One More Song/One More Dance*) and company-developed music and comedy numbers (*Babalooney*) proved short-lived. Not so the subjects of feminism and society's eccentricities in the season's two final revue offerings, *A . . . My Name Is Alice* (which began as an American Place Women's Project and continued in full off-Broadway status, both as a theater and as a cabaret offering) and *Orwell That Ends Well* created and performed by Chicago's famed Second City troupe.

The highlights of the season's specialty programs off Broadway usually came from the reflected glow of their stars: Estelle Parsons in *Orgasmo Adulto Escapes From the Zoo*, a two-part new English version of Italian political satire by Franca Rame and Dario Fo; Quentin Crisp in one of his evenings; Eric Bogosian in sinister characterizations facetiously entitled *Fun House*; and Kaye Ballard in the story and songs of her life and career, *Hey Ma . . . Kaye Ballard*.

In April, Marsha Norman's 1982–83 Best Play and Pulitzer Prize drama *'night, Mother* was transferred from Broadway to off Broadway, intact, with its renowned performances by Anne Pitoniak and Kathy Bates. While there has always been considerable Broadway-to-off-Broadway traffic in *scripts* in revival or second productions, the traffic in whole *productions* like *A Chorus Line*, *Torch Song Trilogy*, etc., has been a one-way flow uptown, making this a most unusual, if not unique, occurrence. While Broadway was struggling like Laocoön to get new plays produced in its strangling 1983–84 circumstances, off Broadway gave a hearing to dozens of new playscripts and found room for *'night, Mother* too.

Revivals on and off Broadway

The commercially appealing promise of Broadway musical hit potential inspired four attempts this season to do it all over again. Of the four, however, only *Zorba* attracted a sizeable audience, thanks in large measure to Anthony Quinn's starring portrayal of Nikos Kazantzakis's ebullient Greek. True, this Joseph Stein-Fred Ebb-John Kander show proved durable (remember the songs "No Boom Boom" and "Happy Birthday"?) as staged by Michael Cacoyannis and choreographed by Graciela Daniele. But it was Quinn's lusty characterization, fitting him as perfectly on the musical stage as it did when he played it in the straight screen version *Zorba the Greek*, that electrified this handsome revival.

The same might have been expected of Angela Lansbury's Mame in a revival of the show of that title. Indeed, Miss Lansbury owns the part if anyone does and operates it flawlessly—but without popular success this time in a full-scale 1983–84 Broadway incarnation. Patti LuPone fared no better as Nancy in a re-run of *Oliver!*, nor did a Geoffrey Holder-directed ensemble in a revival of *The Wiz*. Off Broadway, Light Opera of Manhattan was alone on the musical revival scene and enhanced it as usual with Gilbert & Sullivan, Friml, Herbert, Strauss et al—though for LOOM this was a tight-belt season, in that they mounted no new productions in their repertory; and, finally, a sad one punctuated by the death of their noted producer-director and inspiring mentor, William Mount-Burke.

Over on the straight-play side, notes our corresponding theater historian Thomas T. Foose, "A distinction of 1983–84 was the number of revivals of modern classics on Broadway itself." Most conspicuous of these was the Robert Whitehead-Roger L. Stevens production of Arthur Miller's *Death of a Salesman* with Dustin Hoffman as Willy Loman and John Malkovich, a gifted alumnus of Chicago's Steppenwolf troupe, as Biff, under the direction of Michael Rudman. In the Ben Edwards set, shadowy high-rises in the background threatened to engulf the Loman home with the very forces that built it—an accurate reflection of the play itself. Hoffman's performance was intelligently detailed, a young man masterfully assuming an old man's persona, with fury showing underneath and through his despair. Hoffman's Willy Loman was an acting *tour de force* certainly worthy of the support of an excellent cast in this first-rate revival of Miller's masterpiece.

The large group of Broadway revivals of modern classics also took in a Eugene O'Neill play, the difficult *A Moon for the Misbegotten*, with Kate Nelligan in a powerful portrayal of Josie under the direction of James Leveaux. In fact, stars shone everywhere in this reflection of Broadway's recent past in Broadway's busy present: Cicely Tyson as Miss Moffat, the Ethel Barrymore role, in Emlyn Williams's *The Corn Is Green*; Al Pacino bringing his justly renowned Teach to Broadway this season as he did off Broadway in 1982, in David Mamet's *American Buffalo* (nominated for a best-revival Tony, as was Mamet's *Glengarry Glen Ross* in the best-play category—probably the first time any playwright has been nominated for two plays in the same year); Jessica Tandy as Mother, the Laurette Taylor role, in Tennessee Williams's *The Glass Menagerie*; Rex Harrison and Rosemary Harris in George Bernard Shaw's *Heartbreak House*; and Nancy Marchand in Clifford Odets's *Awake and Sing!*, the latter two revivals comprising the entire season at Circle in the Square.

Modern classics were also abundantly available off Broadway in 1983–84. O'Neill was well represented by a John Stix-directed *Ah, Wilderness!* at Gene Feist's two-theater Roundabout company, whose programs were a major attraction of the season both in the appropriateness of the selections and the quality of their presentation. The Roundabout's 1983–84 schedule, honored by a special Outer Critics Circle Award, took in *The Knack* by Ann Jellicoe, *The Killing of Sister George* by Frank Marcus, *Old Times* by Harold Pinter, *On Approval* by Frederick Lonsdale (its first major New York revival since its original 1926 Broadway production), plus Ibsen's *The Master Builder* and the abovementioned O'Neill.

Circle Repertory probably didn't consider *Balm in Gilead* by Lanford Wilson (one of its playwriting regulars) a modern classic when the company decided to mount a revival of the play, but they may have turned it into one with the magic of a masterful production. The script looks into the lives and personalities of a number of patrons of a seedy all-night Upper Broadway coffee shop of the kind to be found on a corner near Wilson's "Hot 1 Baltimore" and catering to about the same trade. *Balm in Gilead* was Wilson's first full-length play, produced in 1965 at Cafe La Mama in the early days of OOB but never in major New York revival until the last day of this season, when it appeared with a large cast of Circle Rep regulars and aspirants under the direction of the abovementioned John Malkovich of Steppenwolf (who revived it in Chicago in 1980). It was well worth waiting for; the vitality built into the script was fully realized in a presentation that opened on the last day of the season and gave a new meaning to the old expression "last but not least."

The season also witnessed a promising—and much-performing—attempt to establish a repertory company in New York, as the Mirror Theater under the artistic directorship of Sabra Jones came onto the scene with the stated purpose "To create an alternating company and to develop a formula of operation economically and artistically possible" and the stated goals "To play in alternating repertory, to return the artist to management and to preserve the art of acting through the development of an ensemble and the stylistic variety of repertory: actors both skilled and feelingful," the latter being a word we've never encountered before but which could be applied usefully to any number of this year's New York stage performances. The Mirror Theater expects to be searching for material of all periods, including new plays, in seasons designed to "provoke active thought" and "celebrate life." We earnestly hope they will succeed where so many other repertory efforts have found it impossible to make it in New York City. They have begun well with a quartet of modern classics—Susan Glaspell's *Inheritors* (1921), John Colton's *Rain* (1923), Clifford Odets's *Paradise Lost* (1935), John Patrick's *The Hasty Heart* (1945)—plus the Eva Le Gallienne translation of Ibsen's *Ghosts*.

The off-Broadway year's "modern classic" repertory also took in the Irish Arts Center's revival of Sean O'Casey's *The Shadow of a Gunman*, directed by Jim Sheridan and transferred from OOB; a collection of modern one-acters presented by the Acting Company in a brief guest appearance at the Public Theater; and a translation of Ernest Toller's 1920 expressionist German drama, *The One and the Many*, in Living Theater repertory. The historically classical canon was also represented on the latter group's schedule with *The Antigone of Sophokles*. New York Shakespeare Festival produced a *King Richard III* with Kevin Kline in the title role at the Delacorte; and Christopher Martin's City Stage Company (CSC) presented a free adaptation by Martin and Karen Sunde of *Hamlet*, with Noble Shropshire as the prince, and an English version by Martin of Strindberg's *Dance of Death*.

As in the other categories, the revival numbers were down slightly this year both on and off Broadway, but not the quality of the entertainment. With big musicals lumbering onto Broadway side by side with the "feelingful" star turns in *Buffalo*, *Salesman* and *Misbegotten*; with Circle in the Square, LOOM, Roundabout, CSC and even Circle Rep in full revival feather; and with the new Mirror Theater planting its feet on the scene, New York City in 1983–84, as in other seasons, was in and of itself an ambitious repertory of revivals of great theater of many eras and nations.

Offstage

A very large camel thrust its nose into the tent sheltering copyrighted legitimate stage material when, in January, the U.S. Supreme Court decided in the Sony Betamax case that the increasingly common practise of home videotaping for private use was not illegal, as a lower court had ruled. The 5-to-4 decision stated in part: "One may search the Copyright Act in vain for any sign that the elected representatives of the millions of people who watch television every day have made it unlawful to copy a program for later viewing at home."

This would not seem materially to affect the stage until one remembers the huge body of the beast behind that nose: the many other videotaping uses which threaten to erode authors' ownership of the material they themselves have created, and which take reflected encouragement from the Supreme Court decision in this particular case. "Piracy is the enemy," declared a prominent composer on the subject of videotaping in the Spring 1984 issue of *The Dramatists Guild Quarterly,* the stage authors' intercom. He had recently examined a mail order catalogue of taped musicals offered for sale at a post office box address. Two of the tapes on that list were of shows he himself had produced on TV. No deal for selling their tapes had been sought or permission obtained.

"Once a tape of show is made, there is no possibility of control of its production in whatever quantity, for whatever purpose," he concluded. Whether in private hands or in the most carefully negotiated contract, as soon as songs, dramatizations, film versions, etc. are recorded in the laboratory, the possibility—even the certainty, some believe—exists that copies will be made and *circulated,* let alone those that are made off the air by individuals for their own libraries.

The opposite point of view—that videotaping of stage material broadens its potential use and will therefore be of long-range benefit to authors—was expressed by a leading theatrical agent, who stated, "What it boils down to is, you don't have effective protection of the material. But if you can make a very good deal up front, and if you want a record of your show, I really think that the good balances out the bad." The recording companies will continue to explore possibilities of safeguarding product by means of new technologies, and it is expected that the U.S. Congress will eventually write laws to define the dos and don'ts of taping. In any case, the camel has settled in and is likely to remain for a very long time.

On Broadway, in modern times, the expression "The show must go on" has meant that it must be played eight times a week by the star as well as the supporting cast—especially the star in, say, a revival production linking audience interest to his/her presence in the leading role. In the case of an exceptionally demanding role, physically, it has become acceptable for a player to substitute for the star at matinees (as in the title role of *Evita* or the *Torch Song Trilogy* lead), but not as a rule. This season, however, according to a Richard Hummler article in *Variety,* "The tendency is increasing among legit stars in demanding roles to play fewer than the conventional 8 performances a week." The article cited the cases of Kate Nelligan, who was excused from playing the *A Moon for the Misbegotten* matinees during the first weeks of the run; Al Pacino, who played only 7 and later 6 performances of *American Buffalo*; and Dustin Hoffman, who played only 7 performances of *Death of a Salesman* during the last weeks of its spring run.

Federal antitrust lawsuits between the Dramatists Guild (the organization of playwrights, composers, lyricists and librettists) and the League of New York Theaters and Producers (the organization of Broadway producers and theater owners) in a controversy reported in this section in the two previous *Best Plays* volumes, dragged on, unsettled and unlitigated, through another season, though it did not seem greatly to affect the working relationship between these two inseparable groups of the collaborative theater art. In its June survey of the 1983–84 season, *Variety* reported that "Many productions are operating under new royalty formulas which obviously are agreeable to both producers and authors."

In other organizational developments, the Association of Theatrical Press Agents and Managers came to terms with the League which called for pay hikes rising over a three-year period to 7 per cent and a new minimum of $893 weekly for managers and 6 per cent and $1,018 for press agents. The Society of Stage Directors and Choreographers reached a new agreement with the off-Broadway League by which the flat fees of $1,300 for directors and $1,050 for choreographers were changed to a scale sliding in proportion to the seating capacity of the small theaters and rising to $3,250 and $2,600 in a 351-to-499-seat house, with 20 per cent royalty minimum for directors and 1.5 per cent for choreographers remaining unchanged.

The tenth anniversary of the Theater Development Fund's TKTS half-price ticket booth in Duffy Square was celebrated in style with Joseph Papp as master of ceremonies, Colleen Dewhurst and Eddie Albert as greeters and New York City Mayor Edward Koch congratulating TDF President Anna E. Crouse on this popular and valuable support project.

Both the administrators of the Tony Awards and the members of the New York Drama Critics Circle altered somewhat the rules for selection of their annual bests. Only a few years ago, almost all the members of the Tony nominating committee were regularly published working critics (including the editor of the Best Plays volumes). By 1983, the panel comprised about half working critics and half bureaucrats, educators and retired critics. In 1984, it was decided to eliminate working critics entirely from this committee because, as a statement from the administration put it, it would "burden them with an obligation that might place them in a position of conflict," particularly with respect to other awards. It was also decided that the panel would meet and confer, whereas in recent years they had filed their ballots of nomination without consulting one another. Variety speculated that both these changes in Tony nominating procedure "may be related to" lack of a best-play nomination for Neil Simon's popular Brighton Beach Memoirs last year.

A major change in New York's critical personnel was the retirement after last season and his 70th birthday of Walter Kerr from regular duty as drama critic of the Sunday New York Times. Starting in the 1950s when he first came to new York on the Herald Tribune after a stint as critic for the Roman Catholic bi-weekly Commonweal, Kerr's penetrating insights have influenced every aspect of theater—especially criticism itself—with his conscientious, informed, superbly articulate play-reviewing and general criticism. Kerr moved over to the Times in 1966 for one season as its daily and subsequent seasons as its Sunday critic, maintaining throughout his career a combination of expertise and stylistic skill that none in his generation of critics could equal.

Work continued apace on refurbishing 42d Street theaters and the building of a 1,500-seat house, to be known as the Marquis Theater, within the huge new Marriott Marquis Hotel structure which is replacing the Morosco, Helen Hayes and Bijou Theaters on 45th-46th Streets (and the Little Theater on 44th Street was renamed the Helen Hayes to keep that distinguished lady's name glowing in Broadway lights). And in an effort to forestall any future demolition of theaters, New York City's Theater Advisory Council has outlined a plan for making real estate concessions to the owners of 44 legitimate playhouses, permitting them to increase the scale of nearby development projects, provided they promise to maintain. their theaters.

Off Broadway, the new Playhouse 91 was busy with *Quartermaine's Terms* most of the season. The renovated 384-seat Promenade Theater at Broadway and 76th Street came into off-Broadway action, and the new, $1.8 million, 420-seat Minetta Lane Theater in Greenwich Village was getting ready for a summer 1984 debut under the same ownership as the Orpheum Theater on lower Second Avenue. Gene Feist's distinguished Roundabout Theater Company lost its West 23d Street home but found another 499-seat theater at Park Avenue and 17th Street which is being readied for the group's first fall production Oct. 10.

In a last, long look backward over our shoulder at the 1983–84 theater season on and off Broadway before it disappears over the horizon of history, we can't help the sinking feeling that rising production and ticket costs and changing public entertainment habits are slowly strangling the theater as we have known it for several generations. Broadway is settling deeper and deeper into the role of an "occasion," worth at least $50 a ticket for a big musical, a major award-winner or a star vehicle, but incapable of maintaining at those prices even admittedly superior plays like Shirley Lauro's *Open Admissions* (17 performances) or Joanna M. Glass's Tony-nominated *Play Memory* (5 performances).

Out of these threatening flames, however, there have arisen at least two plans for a vital living-theater future, one from Joseph Papp of the New York Shakespeare Festival and the other from Roger L. Stevens of Broadway and Kennedy Center, putting forward two concepts of the same entity: a national theater. Papp suggested that a fund be established—$10 million to start with, rising to $50 million later—to finance subsidized non-profit productions on Broadway side by side with the commercial ones, thus broadening the base of quality attractions. The monies, Papp suggested, should come from sources having the greatest obligation to a healthy, creative, imaginative theater: "The City of New York, developers, builders and the theater industry. Additional financing should be sought from the state, the Federal government, the film and television industries, foundations, corporations and individuals."

Stevens's concept of a national theater, *Variety* commented, "is somewhat more tangible but still in the early planning stages." It calls for a joint formation by Kennedy Center and the American National Theater and Academy (ANTA) of an American National Theater Company funded by outlays of $1 million a year for five years by ANTA from monies received from the sale of its New York theater, and $1 million a year starting the second year by Kennedy Center, to stimulate a continuing series of productions originating at the Eisenhower Theater in Washington, with touring potential. By the end of the season, ANTA-Kennedy Center had already taken "the first steps toward the foundation and development of an American national theater company" by naming Peter Sellars, a 26-year-old who has already made a name for himself as a director of theater and opera, to the post of artistic director and chief operating officer of the venture.

The Messrs. Papp and Stevens have long since established themselves on the theater scene as Titans of their era by more than usually imaginative and resourceful means: Papp by stubbornly putting on admission-free performances of Shakespeare, Stevens by producing a string of Broadway hits after selling the Empire State Building to somebody. Things being as they are on the threshold of 1984–85, perhaps the time has finally come to implement their bold suggestions for continuing achievement in our theater's less and less promising commercial circumstances.

Brian Delate, Richard Chaves, Vincent Caristi, *in background,* and
Jim Tracy use an M-16 rifle as a limbo stick in the Vietnam War
drama *Tracers,* conceived by John DiFusco.

PHOTO BY SUSAN COOK

1984-85

THAT conspicuous ingredient in all reflections on the 1984–85 theater season on and off Broadway—disappointment—wasn't universally deserved. The glaring multi-million-dollar failure of large-scale Broadway musicals accounted for most of that sinking feeling, in the absence of a blockbusting new musical hit. Production costs were another downer (even off Broadway they were edging ever-closer to the $500,000 line), influencing dramatists to think and write small (two characters, one set preferred) if they wanted to be produced, thus aggravating the shortage of scripts with potentially broad audience appeal. And Broadway's shortcomings were further exposed in the Tony ceremonies summing up a season which offered so little in three of the musical categories (leading actor, leading actress, choreography) that they were dropped from consideration.

On the other hand, the Tony TV show sparkled with past musical glories of Jule Styne, Andrew Lloyd Webber and Cy Coleman, with enticing samples of new ones to come from all three, and it achieved a couple of important firsts: the first best-play Tony to Neil Simon and the first best-scenery award to a woman, Heidi Landesman, for *Big River*. And 1984–85 *did* find the New York theater's creative and interpretive artists in their usual dynamic mode, generating enough excitement to make the rounds of every special taste. And if shows of broad appeal were few, they weren't entirely lacking. No season which treated its audiences to a new Neil Simon comedy like *Biloxi Blues*, with the author remembering his World War II basic training in full comedic power, can be entirely discounted; nor did Hugh Whitemore's spy drama *Pack of Lies*, a visitor from the London stage, deserve anything but cheers. And in a living theater whose wonders never cease, the past rallied to support the present with the triumphant return engagement of Yul Brynner in his memorable character of the King of Siam in *The King and I* (it showed what might have been in store for a new musical hit by grossing $605,546 in its final week, a new record for a single Broadway week, topping its own previous record of $553,245, according to *Variety*). And a series of stunning straight-play revivals—*Much Ado About Nothing*, *Cyrano de Bergerac*, *Strange Interlude* and *Aren't We All?* from London and *Joe Egg* from the Roundabout off Broadway—were the arenas for some of the year's outstanding individual achievements.

And yes, there were many more than ten good plays around the town in 1984–85 and certainly ten Best Plays including David Rabe's *Hurlyburly*, a comedy-drama of modern societal decadence directed by Mike Nichols and emerging from off Broadway to be received by Broadway audiences as the year's major new American drama by an "established" playwright. August Wilson's Critics Award-winning *Ma Rainey's Black Bottom*, depicting a recording session by a 1927 blues singer and her accompanists under the direction of Lloyd Richards, was the outstanding Broadway playwriting debut. The only one of the Best Plays produced originally and directly for Broadway—and "middle Broadway" at that—was David Wiltse's *Doubles*, a comedy of male friendship. Off Broadway chimed in with Larry Shue's *The Foreigner*, which ran where the brave

The 1984–85 Season on Broadway

PLAYS (10)	MUSICALS (6)	FOREIGN PLAYS IN ENGLISH (2)	REVUES (2)	REVIVALS (12)	SPECIALTIES (3)
HURLYBURLY (transfer)	Gotta Getaway!	Accidental Death of an Anarchist	Haarlem Nocturne	Circle in the Square: Design for Living	Kipling
MA RAINEY'S BLACK BOTTOM	Quilters	PACK OF LIES	Streetheat	The Loves of Anatol	Whoopi Goldberg
Alone Together	Harrigan 'n Hart			Arms and the Man	Doug Henning and His World of Magic
Home Front	Leader of the Pack			Oedipus Rex	
Dancing in the End Zone	Grind			Royal Shakespeare: Much Ado About Nothing	HOLDOVER WHICH BECAME A HIT IN 1984-85
The Octette Bridge Club	Big River			Cyrano de Bergerac	La Cage aux Folles
Requiem for a Heavyweight				The Three Musketeers	
BILOXI BLUES				The King and I	
AS IS (transfer)				Strange Interlude	
DOUBLES				Joe Egg (transfer)	
				Take Me Along	
				Aren't We All?	

Plays listed in CAPITAL LETTERS have been designated Best Plays of 1984–85.
Plays listed in italics were still running after June 2, 1985.
Plays listed in bold face type were classified as successes in Variety's annual estimate published June 5, 1985.

dare not go into the perilous realms of situation farce and was nothing but funny; with Dennis McIntyre's *Split Second*, the guilt-haunted dilemma of a black policeman who shoots a taunting white suspect in a fit of justifiable anger; with William M. Hoffman's *As Is*, a tribute to a lover's loyalty to an AIDS sufferer, transferred from Circle Repertory to Broadway; with a collective reminiscence of Vietnam agonies, *Tracers*, created by John DiFusco and other members of its Vietnam Veterans Ensemble Theater Company original cast (Vincent Caristi, Richard Chaves, Eric E. Emerson, Rick Gallavan, Merlin Marston, Harry Stephens and a writer, Sheldon Lettich), now "frozen" as a scripted show imported to New York by New York Shakespeare Festival and exported by them to London in their exchange arrangement with the Royal Court; and with Christopher Durang's acerbic commentary on the stresses of family life and ties, *The Marriage of Bette and Boo*.

The precipitous 1983–84 drop in Broadway production reported in last year's *Best Plays* volume leveled off in 1984–85. A year ago there were 34 Broadway productions (including 8 new American plays, 4 new foreign plays, 10 new musicals), while this year there were 35 Broadway productions (including 10 new American plays of which two were transfers, two new foreign plays, 6 new musicals). Two large-scale cabaret revues and three specialties padded the list. So did the 12 revivals (there were 11 the season before), including three massive musical revivals which in a sense stood in for the missing "new" musical productions. Broadway production in 1984–85 was indeed down from the historical and even the recent past, which recorded 58 shows in 1979–80, 51 in 1980–81, 45 in 1981–82 and 49 in 1982–83. 1984–85 certainly held to 1983–84's slower pace.

The extent to which the 35 Broadway shows of 1984–85 were audience-pleasers is another matter, possibly reflected in *Variety's* statistical summary, which estimated that the season's total gross for the 52 weeks was $208,006,181 (down from 1983–84's $226 million gross for a "53-week" year owing to a calendar anomaly, but still well ahead of the $203 million the year before). The 1984–85 road gross of touring Broadway shows was almost $226 million, way ahead of the previous year's $206 million, bringing the combined take to almost $444 million, the highest in Broadway history. The *average* Broadway admission price was $29.75 in June 1984, but it had *fallen* to a *Variety*-estimated $27.33 as of June 1985 (owing in part to the proliferation of twofers), so that the sustained high grosses cannot be entirely credited to inflation. The 1984–85 decline in the overall Broadway gross was matched by a decline in playing weeks from 1,097 in 1983–84 to 1,062 (if ten shows play ten weeks, that's 100 playing weeks) and in total paid attendance from 7.9 million to 7.1 million. All of this amounts to a warning signal, perhaps, that the year's shows didn't run as long and didn't pull audiences as they should, and that the theater must resolve to redouble its creative efforts in the coming year; but it is so far from a chronicle of disaster that those who are looking for sensational bad news to report should look elsewhere than at the state of our legitimate theater.

The year's big losers were the failed Broadway musicals including *Grind* which lost its entire capitalization of $4,750,000 and the Goodspeed Opera House production of *Take Me Along*, which folded after its opening night. The big winner was *The King and I*; or perhaps it was *La Cage aux Folles*, which had recouped its $5 million cost and was grossing more than $1.5 million weekly from the combination of its New York, West Coast and national companies; or perhaps it was the Broadway long-run champ *A Chorus Line*, whose eight-figure profit was augmented this year by a $2 million advance for its stock and amateur rights. *Cats* was still selling out and had accumulated a *Variety*-estimated $8 million on its $5 million cost, while another British holdover, *Noises Off*, recouped its $850,000 cost and was netting $30,000 weekly before it left town. The only 1984–85 shows to have paid off by the end of this season, according to *Variety*, were *The King and I*, the Whoopi Goldberg specialty and *Hurlyburly*, which was showing a $550,000 profit on the original $400,000 investment for its off-Broadway production.

This $400,000 cost level wasn't uncommon off Broadway in 1984–85, though of course many shows came in for much less and a few like the musical *3 Guys Naked From the Waist Down* for more (estimated at $500,000 but would have been twice that uptown). The Broadway revival of *Strange Interlude* came in from London at $900,000 but could take in $150,000 for its weekly 6 performances at a $50 top. A guesstimate for the production cost of a frugally-mounted straight play on Broadway would be somewhere around $600,000, with musicals in seven figures as high as they would dare to go (but one of the losers, *Home Front*, was estimated by *Variety* to have gotten onto the Broadway stage this season for an astonishingly small $313,000). One of 1984–85's mightier economic struggles was waged by *The Tap Dance Kid*, which opened last year for $2.8 million, upped to $4 million when the show changed theaters in mid-run, and had returned about $1.9 to its backers on the eve of its national tour.

Broadway

Comedy was king this season, where once musical comedy reigned. The laughter was crowned on Broadway by Neil Simon's new *Biloxi Blues* and richly caparisoned by David Wiltse's *Doubles*, Lawrence Roman's *Alone Together* and the reappearance of masterworks by Noel Coward (*Design for Living*), William Shakespeare (*Much Ado About Nothing*), Frederick Lonsdale (*Aren't We All?*) and George Bernard Shaw (*Arms and the Man*).

The Neil Simon of his 12th Best Play, *Biloxi Blues*, is the Neil Simon of *Brighton Beach Memoirs*, with an added dynamic that pulls the play up through its sitcom levels into Simon's tickling (and sometimes stabbing) insights into human nature and the way we look at life now. Eugene Morris Jerome, the semi-autobiographical Simon figure, painfully adolescent in *Brighton Beach Memoirs*, has grown old enough to be drafted into the World War II army in *Biloxi Blues*. Now he has become a green twig of middle-class innocence being vigorously bent in the basic training program. Played once again by Matthew Broderick with youthful diffidence and the mannerisms of a magician distracting the audience's attention from the mechanics of a trick, Eugene sets out on his odyssey from Brooklyn to Biloxi, determined to 1) lose his virginity, 2) stay alive and 3) become a successful writer. We know the outcome of 2 and 3, and here we watch him pursue 1, in a scene with Randall Edwards as a busy prostitute, directed by Gene Saks on a fine line between prurience and farce. But it is Eugene's preparation to achieve his second goal that provides most of the fun in this play. Yes, the sergeant-vs.-recruit confrontation of ruthless discipline in order to turn civilians into soldiers is an oft-told tale in both comedy and drama (c.f. this season's Best Play *Tracers*). But this time they put the young Neil Simon through it, and he noticed that it was agonizing to obey but very difficult to outwit the sergeant (crisp and indomitable in the performance of Bill Sadler)—difficult but not impossible for a misfit individualist (Barry Miller in his Tony-winning performance) willing to pay any price to retain his identity and dignity. He noticed that the training has little effect on the essential character of the slobs and goof-offs among his barracks mates (Brian Tarantina, Matt Mulhern, Alan Ruck and Geoffrey Sharp). Simon shares his findings with us in a flow of gags and situations, many of them hilarious, toward the ironic conclusion that with all this effort nothing much has been improved or lost, except virginity.

Likewise David Wiltse, whose only other major New York production was *Suggs* at Lincoln Center in 1972, came on strong with *Doubles*, a verbal and sight gag-loaded locker room farce about the ways of friendship among men, the paradox of commitment even when they may actually not like each other all that much. Their occasion in this Best Play is a weekly tennis foursome of a grocer (Ron Leibman, a bull in a china shop), a tennis reporter (John Cullum), a lawyer (Austin Pendleton) and a stockbroker (Tony Roberts) in the well-scrubbed, stylish locker room setting designed by Robert Fletcher. However these four may perform on the court (we never see that), under Morton Da Costa's direction their affectionate/abrasive relationships hilariously expose the conceits and finally the fears of the male animal in the 1980s jungle. This *Doubles* was a canny script well served in design and direction and superbly in its four-star acting, one of the very pleasant surprises of the Broadway year.

Lawrence Roman's *Alone Together* was another comedy of contemporary manners, with Kevin McCarthy and Janis Paige as a Los Angeles couple breathing a deep sight of relief when the last son goes off to college, only to soon find all three sons drifting back home. The nest mom and dad hoped could now be exclusively devoted to champagne for two and other delights of a well-earned rest is bulging instead with full-grown fledglings, refugees from the real world. This timely theme was sympathetically and amusingly spun out, in an ideal Broadway comedy which deserved a wider audience than it managed to attract this time around.

The human comedy was also a strong element in two bittersweet Best Plays, August Wilson's *Ma Rainey's Black Bottom* and David Rabe's *Hurlyburly*. The former, whose title refers to a popular dance of the 1920s, the decade in which it was set, depicted a Chicago recording session of a blues pioneer, Ma Rainey (who could give Bessie Smith lessons), with her black accompanists and hangers-on and the white managers of the record company in attendance. Ma Rainey's proudly tyrannous attitude, the musicians' shop talk and the fawning of the satellite characters were strongly comedic elements under the direction of Lloyd Richards, who staged this play at Yale first and then on Broadway. The heart—or rather, the black bottom—of this matter, however, was the downhearted echo of racial injustice in the all-too-vivid memories of the jazz musicians portrayed by Joe Seneca, Robert Judd, Leonard Jackson and Charles S. Dutton, and in the chip-on-the-shoulder strut of Theresa Merritt as Ma. The play ends in a tragedy not quite as believable as the humor plastered over the scars, or as the very adroit synchronization of action with a recorded sound track which created a perfect illusion that the actors playing the musicians were also really playing their instruments in the sequences of music.

Hurlyburly was the season's dominant American play, appearing off Broadway in June, then transferring to Broadway in August for a run that carried it right to the end of the theater year. As directed by Mike Nichols in both venues, Rabe's newest Best Play was an account of the "me" generation in fading flower in the Hollywood hills, living on the borders of show business and from moment to cocaine-enhanced, sex-troubled moment. William Hurt and Judith Ivey received Tony nominations for their portrayals of two of the seven characters blended into an ensemble of self-destruction so wanton that it was hard to develop strong allegiance to any of them. But even to that segment of the audience which remained emotionally distant from it, *Hurlyburly* offered rewards of writing and stagecraft.

Another American Best Play transferred triumphantly from off Broadway was William M. Hoffman's *As Is*, one of two scripts coming to grips with the subject of the deadly Acquired Immune Deficiency Syndrome (AIDS) this season (the other was Larry Kramer's hard-hitting *The Normal Heart*, of which more in the off-Broadway chapter of this report). With a marvellous economy of means and imaginative direction by Marshall W. Mason in production at his Circle Repertory, this fine play viewed the subject from the perspective of a discarded but still faithful lover (Jonathan Hadary) who stands by his former lover (Tony-nominated Jonathan Hogan), though the latter has jilted him, caught AIDS and then drifted back to the only person who will instantly accept him "as is" (his family, his partner and others shy away when they learn of the illness). *As Is* dwelt upon loyalty and commitment rather than the horrors or sociological implications of the disease itself, relieving the compression of its relentless, intermissionless sequence of events with a sort of gallows humor. The broader consequences of AIDS are sketched in around the intense personal drama of failing health and unfailing affection, one of the season's major achievements of writing, acting and direction.

Another major social strain—the distress of an American family trying to reassimilate a son home from the Vietnam war but unable to relieve his trauma —was the concern of James Duff's *Home Front*, with Carroll O'Connor in an exceptionally strong performance as the father. O'Connor buried Archie Bunker, his TV series character, invisibly deep inside his portrayal of a parent who is less than perfect but doing his determined best to understand and help. The father finally reaches the point of no more putting up with a son who goes out of his way to upset and hurt and finally exhausts the audience's profound sympathy along with the father's.

Also a more effective stage instrument than its short run would indicate was *Dancing in the End Zone* by Bill C. Davis, about a football coach (Laurence Luckinbill) who takes a fatherly interest in his star quarterback but pushes him to risk permanent injury in order to win games. Douglas W. Schmidt's flexible setting suggesting anything from a classroom to a football stadium was one of the play's considerable assets. Two other American plays which made the Broadway scene this year were P.J. Barry's *The Octette Bridge Club*, with a star-studded cast playing eight sisters in family reunions ten years apart, and the Arvin Brown-directed stage version of the late Rod Serling's 1956 television play about a has-been boxer, *Requiem for a Heavyweight*, with John Lithgow in a Tony-nominated performance of the title role that is now memorable to all too few members of the Broadway audience.

Among foreign plays in English (or rather, between them, because there were only two this season), Dario Fo's *Accidental Death of an Anarchist* travelled no better than a very fragile regional wine in transit from the Italian stage to Richard

Nelson's Broadway adaptation, even with Jonathan Pryce giving another of his shrewd comic performances as The Fool, the butt of the authorities. Hugh Whitemore's spy drama *Pack of Lies* travelled admirably, however, from the London stage to Broadway and Best Play status. Like much of its author's work, it was based on real events and persons, in this case a suburban family's reactions to having a counterespionage team borrow their house as an observation post to keep watch on suspected neighbors—and not merely neighbors, but the householders' (Rosemary Harris, George N. Martin and Tracy Pollan as their daughter) best friends (Dana Ivey and Colin Fox). With Patrick McGoohan as an unflappable and coldly efficient government agent nearly freezing the warm blood of this gentle family, the play gave out its secrets liberally and soon (this caper was part of Gordon Lonsdale's 1960–61 spying activities in Britain) while dramatizing the effects of all this duplicity on the nonprofessionals caught up in it. Rosemary Harris as the mother was most deeply affected and effective under the direction of Clifford Williams, in the obligatory annual major attraction borrowed from the London stage.

The bad news about Broadway's bad 1984–85 musical season was widely broadcast and has to do with the absence of any sign of a successful new show for most of the year, in the midst of failing large-scale efforts. The good news was that *Big River: The Adventures of Huckleberry Finn* finally showed up at the end of April and turned some of the lights back on with an entertaining and sometimes touching book adapted by William Hauptman from Mark Twain's novel. It also enjoyed a strong visual personality in the designs of Heidi Landesman (scenery, with Huck and Jim's raft moving freely downstage while the Mississippi winds back into the distance) and Patricia McGourty (costumes of the homespun era). The inner strength of character of the runaway slave Jim was stressed and forcefully projected in action and song by Ron Richardson, and on occasions by his capable understudy Elmore James, under Des McAnuff's conscientiously stylized direction. Rene Auberjonois sank his teeth and everything else into the role of the Duke, clown as well as villain. Roger Miller's score with simplistic, repetitive, rock-style lyrics had the grace to keep its decibels at a painless level so that its melodious moments came over the footlights handsomely, helping to establish *Big River* as a positive and welcome asset in the Broadway balance.

There is no questioning the effort and expertise that was poured into *Grind*, the Harold Prince-directed, Lester Wilson-choreographed, Clarke Dunham and Florence Klotz-designed, Ben Vereen, Stubby Kaye and Leilani Jones-acted period musical trying to depict a slice of burlesque life in 1933 Chicago. What they were driving at was sometimes unclear, as in its tale of a remorseful IRA killer converted into a burlesque performer; but that they were indeed driving was obvious in every energetic moment. Certainly the Vereen song-and-dance solos and the backstage spectacle of comedians, strippers, etc., were diverting in a vaudeville kind of way, while missing the collective payoff of a Broadway musical. Another musical backward glance, *Harrigan 'n Hart*, celebrated the careers of the renowned pair of 19th century musical stage stars, but not even with a Michael Stewart book under Joe Layton's direction could it find the handle to musicalize its subject effectively.

Radio City Music Hall's summer musical was *Gotta Getaway!*, with Liliane Montevecchi and Tony Azito front and center and with the perpetually amazing

Rockettes, taking audiences around the world on a luxury cruise as directed and choreographed by Larry Fuller. *Quilters*, extrapolating the lives of pioneer women from the patterns in their quilts, was a charming concept born and raised in regional theater, with score and direction by Barbara Damashek and book co-authored by her, and with Lenka Peterson as prototype and narrator. The more boisterous rock musical *Leader of the Pack* was more comfortable on Broadway, with Ellie Greenwich recapitulating the life and songs of Ellie Greenwich, herself as herself in the 1980s and Dinah Manoff as her younger self, directed and choreographed by Michael Peters. The musical season was further embellished by a pair of cabaret-style revues: *Haarlem Nocturne*, conceived by and with Andre De Shields, and *Streetheat*, devised by Michele Asaf and Rick Atwell around New York's "now" culture. It was the revival sector, however, which provided New York's musical year with its only solid hit, *The King and I*, its most dramatic misstep, the closing of *Take Me Along* after only one performance, and perhaps its greatest disappointment, the faltering of *The Three Musketeers* despite a new book.

In the specialty category, Mike Nichols supervised the meteoric rise to Broadway stardom and acclaim of Whoopi Goldberg in her solo presentation of character sketches, all sharply pointed and generally loaded with humor. Doug Henning also stopped off in New York for one of his mystifying sessions of magic, and Alec McCowen recreated the personality and explored some of the works of Rudyard Kipling in a one-man reminiscence.

Off Broadway

In the season of 1984–85, off Broadway was looking more and more like the major creative stimulus in the New York theater, holding a virtual monopoly on innovation and generating a vigor essential to the survival of the fiercely commercial theater uptown. This was a year in which off Broadway supplied Broadway with three of its major attractions in transfer: *Hurlyburly*, *As Is* and the memorable revival of *Joe Egg*. Its institutions and independents produced on their own or brought up from OOB six Best Plays and an outstanding musical, *Kuni-Leml*. Of course, overcommercialization is an insidious penalty of success like this. With its over-$20 ticket and six-figure production costs, off Broadway is certainly sailing on the edge of the troubled waters in which storm-tossed Broadway is barely managing to keep afloat. As of this season, though, the applause was much louder than the warnings.

Production volume of musicals was off sharply to only 4 as compared with 13 a year ago, but the production of new American plays was up, and there were works of remarkably high quality in all categories. Off Broadway produced 52 new plays and musicals (including one return engagement) compared to 57 a year ago and 59 in 1982–83. This season's new-play contingent comprised 39 American straight-play programs, the 4 abovementioned musicals and 9 foreign plays, as compared with last year's 32-13-12 and the 39-7-13, 45-9-7, 33-14-8 and 39-7-12 of the previous four seasons. In addition to this year's 52 new-scripted productions, there were 7 revues, 10 specialties and 40 revivals (see the one-page summary of the season accompanying this report), making a grand total of 109 programs—only one fewer than last year's total—presented off Broadway during the past 12 months.

The New York theater season was only a week old in June when off Broadway's first 1984–85 Best Play, Dennis McIntyre's *Split Second*, appeared in independent production. Here a black policeman (John Danelle) is goaded by the racial taunting of a white car-thief to such fury that he draws his gun and shoots his handcuffed prisoner dead. This wasn't a melodrama, however, but an inner conflict: does the policeman tell the truth like a good officer and take the consequences, or does he arrange the details of his unwitnessed act to look like self-defense?—the latter not only in self-interest but to avoid a charge of racist violence which might rub off onto all the other black officers. His best friend and his wife (Peter Jay Fernandez and Michele Shay) pull him toward coverup; his father (Norman Matlock), a retired policeman of some renown, pushes him toward full confession, a conflict which was dramatically stated and fully explored under Samuel P. Barton's direction, building toward the play's final lesser-of-two-evils choice.

And the season was less than a month old when *Hurlyburly*, discussed in the previous chapter, made its appearance with Mike Nichols and company using off Broadway as a tryout town in transit to Broadway. And the autumn leaves had hardly turned when a third Best Play appeared in independent off-Broadway production: *The Foreigner*, a situation farce in which a painfully shy Englishman (Anthony Heald), in order to avoid conversation, arranges to have the inhabitants of a Georgia fishing lodge believe he is an exotic who speaks no English. The author, Larry Shue, played a take-charge character who sets up the situation, goes away and then comes back to mop up after it boils over with really boisterous skullduggery flavored with a dash of romance. Under the direction of Jerry Zaks, the deception and its hilarious consequences came off splendidly.

The early part of the season provided yet another highlight of independent production which slipped into a commercial run from its off-off-Broadway origin: Craig Lucas's *Blue Window*, an imaginatively conceived and constructed examination of one evening in the lives of a group of Manhattanites preparing for a dinner party. Under Norman Rene's direction, it broke up space and time to serve its special purpose of exposing the emotions and ambitions of the characters one by one and two by two. This comedy-drama, which won the newly-established George and Elisabeth Marton Award to encourage a new American playwright, first appeared in June as an offering of Rene's off-off-Broadway Production Company and was raised to full off-Broadway status without moving from its original theater, a process that is being repeated these days, as it holds down some of the original production cost until it's clear that a new work is going to succeed.

Another standout in independent off-Broadway production was Laurence Carr's exceptionally theatrical *Kennedy at Colonus*, directed by Stephen Zuckerman. It was an ensemble rendering of major events in the life and career of Robert F. Kennedy, with Christopher Curry playing the late Senator, beginning on, flashing back from and finally ending on the day of his assassination in California in 1968. In the course of the season, the independents also came up with a return engagement of Beth Henley's 1983–84 Best Play *The Miss Firecracker Contest* and a modern Russian play about the 1941 friendship of two Kiev families, one Christian and one Jewish, entitled *Before the Dawn* and adapted by Joseph Stein from an English translation. Other American scripts in independent off-Broadway production concerned themselves with a straight young man pretending to be gay in order to approach closer to a desirable young woman (*The*

The 1984–85 Season Off Broadway

PLAYS (39)

Danny and the Deep Blue Sea
SPLIT SECOND
Playwrights Horizons:
Elm Circle
Romance Language
Life and Limb
Young Playwrights Festival
Kennedy at Colonus
Public Theater:
Found a Peanut
Ice Bridge
The Ballad of Soapy Smith
TRACERS
Coming of Age in Soho
The Normal Heart
THE MARRIAGE OF BETTE AND BOO
HURLYBURLY
Blue Window
Circle Rep:
Bing and Walker
Dysan
AS IS
Medea and the Doll
The Miss Firecracker Contest (return engagement)

Manhattan Theater Club:
Husbandry
Messiah
Digby
California Dog Fight
The Pretender
THE FOREIGNER
Losing It
Negro Ensemble:
District Line
Henrietta
Two Can Play
Cliffhanger
The Mugger
Orphans
Eden Court
Rommel's Garden
Man Enough
The Return of Herbert Bracewell

MUSICALS (4)

Kuni-Leml
3 Guys Naked From the Waist Down
In Trousers
Mayor

FOREIGN PLAYS IN ENGLISH (9)

Public Theater:
The Nest of the Wood Grouse
Tom and Viv
Virginia
Salonika
Rat in the Skull
All Strange Away
In Celebration
Before the Dawn
Childhood & For No Good Reason

SPECIALTIES (10)

An Evening With Ekkehard Schall
The Chinese Magic Revue
Elvis Mania
Viva Vittorio!
Avner the Eccentric
Zelda
Between Rails
Hannah Senesh
The Singular Dorothy Parker
Penn & Teller

REVUES (7)

Shades of Harlem
Rap Master Ronnie
I Hear Music
Hang on to the Good Times
Diamonds
Ann Reinking . . . Music Moves Me
Lies & Legends

REVIVALS (40)

Delacorte:
Henry V
The Golem
Harold Clurman:
Endgame
A Kurt Weill Cabaret
Roundabout:
Come Back, Little Sheba
She Stoops to Conquer
Joe Egg
The Playboy of the Western World
An Enemy of the People
The Voice of the Turtle
After the Fall

LOOM:
The New Moon
(12 operettas in running repertory)
Love's Labor's Lost
The Country Girl
Pacific Overtures
La Boheme
CSC:
Agamemnon
Elektra/Orestes
George Dandin
The Underpants
Total Eclipse
Mirror Rep:
The Madwoman of Chaillot
Clarence
Vivat! Vivat! Regina!
Ceremonies in Dark Old Men
Acting Company:
A New Way to Pay Old Debts
As You Like It
The Skin of Our Teeth

Plays listed in CAPITAL LETTERS have been designated Best Plays of 1984-85.
Plays listed in *italics* were still running off Broadway after June 2, 1985.

Pretender); rustics philosophizing over their beers (*Losing It*); a college professor, played by Henderson Forsythe, weaving a tangled web of murder around a particularly irritating female colleague (*Cliffhanger*); street crime as an occupation for the unemployed (*The Mugger*); the life and times of tavern owners (*Crossing the Bar*); marital problems among the mobile-home set (*Eden Court*); a lovable turn-of-the-century character actor and his actress-wife (Milo O'Shea and Frances Sternhagen in *The Return of Herbert Bracewell*) and a well-made study of a family reassessing its values under the influence of a handicapped member (Patty Gideon Sloan's *Man Enough*).

On the institutional side of 1984–85 off-Broadway production, it seemed that Joseph Papp's New York Shakespeare Festival was coming up with a challenging new theater piece every week. In fact, he lit up the Manhattan sky more often than once a month with two Central Park revivals, five foreign imports (including two in an exchange program with London's Royal Court Theater), one musical revival (*La Boheme* with a new English libretto, new English lyrics by David Spencer and with Patti Cohenour, Linda Ronstadt and Caroline Peyton alternating as Mimi under Wilford Leach's direction) seven new American plays (including two Best Plays), making an imposing total of 15 productions by the Lafayette Street group. One of the Best Plays was a Los Angeles visitor to the Public Theater, *Tracers*, a tattoo of incidents of training and combat in the Vietnam war, with a pre-recorded rock score giving it sometimes the extra dimension of a musical. It was conceived, directed and co-developed by John DiFusco and six other members of its original Vietnam Veterans Ensemble Theater Company cast, plus one writer—all of them having lived through real experiences of Vietnam training and combat. It had a smell of blood and powder in its battle scenes and a whiff of resentment in its reflections from a present-day perspective. Three of the original cast (DiFusco, Vincent Caristi and Richard Chaves) appeared in the New York production, a controlled explosion of ensemble performance.

The large number of Papp's 1984–85 programs included some like *Tracers* which were not materially developed at the Public Theater. Others like Christopher Durang's provocative *The Marriage of Bette and Boo*, a black comedy about an ill-starred marriage and its emotional consequences, were what might be termed Public Theater originals (*Marriage* had been performed elsewhere, but in a much shorter version). In fact, originality was a long suit of this Best Play— not structure or appeal but originality in the conception, expression and staging of its ironies of husband-wife hostility, interfamily scorn, flippant attitudes toward death and emotional disaster, etc., glittering like a polished knife blade and often cutting to the bone. Joan Allen played a forbiddingly unsympathetic wife and mother obsessed with bearing babies doomed to die from RH factor and overburdening her only living child with fulsome sentimentality and guilt. The latter, the only really heartstruck and heartstriking character in the play, served as a narrator to link the many episodes not always in time sequence. He was played by the author in a touching portrayal of the real victim of these ironic fantasies. Only a highly skilled ensemble under strong direction by Jerry Zaks in Loren Sherman's wonderfully adaptable setting of sliding screens could have maintained the style and concentration of this work, which was a sort of random conversation suddenly become all too revealing.

Albert Innaurato also swelled the Public Theater's 1984–85 agenda with *Coming of Age in Soho*, with John Procaccino as a bisexual ex-husband and father whose solitude is continually disturbed by a flow of children, women and even gangsters through his spacious loft—a diffuse but substantial play directed by its author. Larry Kramer's *The Normal Heart* was another of the Public's important contributions to the season, a polemical but dramatic protest against government and other organizational indifference to the growing threat of AIDS. It exposed societal foot-dragging with relentless determination and in rather more depth than the year's other AIDS drama, but without achieving its personal intensity. Michael Weller's *The Ballad of Soapy Smith* was a wide-angle saga of a con man's adventures during the Alaska gold rush, intriguing enough to attract a best-play vote in the Critics' balloting. Donald Margulies examined some of the conflicts of childhood with adults playing characters age 5 to 12 in *Found a Peanut*, while the abovementioned Vietnam Veterans Ensemble Theater Company made an early-season appearance, seven months prior to their *Tracers*, as troops guarding an Arctic nuclear installation in *Ice Bridge*.

Papp himself helped to focus his organization's attention on scripts from abroad early in the season by directing a translation of Victor Rozov's *The Nest of the Wood Grouse*, a Russian family comedy so contemporary that it was playing at the Satire Theater in Moscow while the New York version was being offered at the Public. Later in the year, stars shone downtown in foreign scripts as an exchange program with the Royal Court Theater brought over their production of *Tom and Viv* by Michael Hastings, a closeup of T.S. Eliot's home life with Edward Herrmann playing the poet. Jessica Tandy brightened Louise Page's *Salonika* (a script also previously produced at the Royal Court) as an octogenarian widow visiting the seaside grave of her soldier-husband killed decades before in World War I, still finding pleasure and identity in life while her resentful daughter (Elizabeth Wilson) cannot. This was a play made like a patchwork quilt of small conflicts between flesh and spirit, with the flesh graphically symbolized onstage by a sunbathing youth whose stark nakedness is taken in stride by the other characters. Another British import, *Virginia*, provided Kate Nelligan with the opportunity of appearing as Virginia Woolf in a character study based on the Woolfs' writings.

Papp's 1984–85 New York Shakespeare Festival season at the Public Theater closed with another exchange production from the Royal Court, a sledghammer political tract by Ron Hutchinson entitled *Rat in the Skull* (a metaphor for the gnawing intrusion of doubt into a fanatic's thoughts), with a would-be bombthrowing IRA terrorist (Colum Convey) arrested by British police officers in London (Philip Jackson and Gerard Horan) and interrogated by an Ulster policeman (Brian Cox), a protestant, with shattering insistence that their north-south Irish brotherhood is stronger than their religious and political enmity, however deeply rooted in bloody history. This was powerful punctuation for the Public Theater season, directed by Max Stafford-Clark and acted with total conviction by an astonishingly practised and perfected Royal Court cast.

Viewed in 12-month perspective, Papp's season was as exceptionally distinguished as it was active—and profitable, if that word can be applied to a not-for-profit, semi-subsidized theater group. The box office, which normally provides 10 to 12 per cent of the New York Shakespeare Festival's annual income, brought in almost 25 per cent with the successes of 1984–85. It might not be unreasonable to wish that this wonderfully versatile Lafayette Street facility, with its many theaters built into the former Astor Library, could have been filled more often for developmental and less often for hospitable purposes of housing work prefabricated elsewhere. But it would be unreasonable to lean too heavily on this point, especially in a year when Papp gave Herrmann, Nelligan and Tandy vehicles for major performance, brought in the timely and vivid reminder *Tracers* and offered Durang, Innaurato, Weller and Margulies—four of America's leading younger playwrights—the opportunity to develop and display their latest work.

Marshall W. Mason's Circle Repertory Company also reached the Best Play peak with one of their new American plays, *As Is*, which moved uptown and was discussed in the previous chapter of this report. The Circle season included two more new American scripts—James Paul Farrell's *Bing and Walker*, with a self-sacrificing spinster trembling on the brink of happiness, and Patrick Meyers's *Dysan*, a chronicle of enduring love—plus a revival of *Love's Labor's Lost*. Lynne Meadow's and Barry Grove's Manhattan Theater Club expanded this season into the City Center Theater space, while maintaining some operations on 73d Street. The standout on their schedule was David Storey's 1969 play *In Celebration* in its first major New York production, directed by Lindsay Anderson—a British drama of family strife, as three sons come home to Yorkshire to celebrate their parents' wedding anniversary and settle a few old scores. The new American plays at MTC on both sides of town were a Martin Sherman script, *Messiah*, in which a 17th century village of Polish Jews fantasizes a hero to relieve them from oppression; plus three others taking up the plight of the American farmer (*Husbandry*), platonic romance (*Digby*) and the pitting oï bull terriers (*California Dog Fight*). MTC also offered a Richard Maltby Jr.-directed revue of Gretchen Cryer-Nancy Ford songs, *Hang on to the Good Times*.

A visiting organization, Chicago's Steppenwolf Theater Company, brought in *Orphans*, a Lyle Kessler dark comedy explosively dramatizing the changing relationships among two brothers—one a criminal and one a shut-in—and their kidnap victim, similar in tone to the group's previous version of Sam Shepard's *True West* and as flamboyantly acted (by Kevin Anderson and Terry Kinney as the brothers and John Mahoney as the victim who turns the tables on them). *Orphans* was directed in Steppenwolf's acrobatic, irresistably theatrical style by Gary Sinise, who won an Obie for *True West*. Steppenwolf was recognized as one of America's major theatrical forces by a special Tony Award this year, voted by the members of the American Theater Critics Association, and it was further importantly represented in this New York season by its member Joan Allen's performance in *The Marriage of Bette and Boo* and its member John Malkovich's direction of the Circle in the Square revival of *Arms and the Man*.

The Andre Bishop-Paul Daniels group Playwrights Horizons put on an ambitious fantasy-panorama of events of the American past, *Romance Language* by Peter Parnell, and an expose of the American lifestyle in the return to his family of a Korean War veteran, *Life and Limb* by Keith Reddin, directed by Thomas Babe. They also allied themselves with Dramatists Guild projects this season, presenting Mick Casale's *Elm Circle* as part of the Foundation of the Dramatists Guild/CBS New Plays Program and, later in the season, the Young Playwrights Festival of new plays by authors up to 18 years of age, selected in the Guild's annual contest designed to encourage young people to write plays.

The Negro Ensemble Company began its season later than any of the other major groups and also paid homage to its distinguished past with a revival of

Lonne Elder III's *Ceremonies in Dark Old Men* with Douglas Turner Ward, the group's artistic director, re-creating under his own direction his original performance as an ex-vaudevillian living with his daughter in the Harlem of the 1950s. The new plays offered at NEC this year concerned themselves with cab drivers on the Washington-Maryland border (*District Line* by Joseph A. Walker), a Harlem bag lady graphically portrayed by Frances Foster (*Henrietta*) and a two-character anti-male-chauvinism farce (*Two Can Play*). In other off-Broadway group activity, the Barbara Barondess Theater Lab brought in a drama of a psychiatrist dealing with an instance of child abuse, *Medea and the Doll*. Both the Circles—the Square and the Rep—joined in an early-season co-production of John Patrick Shanley's *Danny and the Deep Blue Sea*, a drama of violence-prone lovers previously produced at Actors Theater of Louisville and presented at Circle in the Square's downtown facility. In a season it devoted mostly to revivals and showcases for foreign artists (including *Childhood*, a Simone Benmussa adaptation of a childhood memoir by Nathalie Sarraute), Jack Garfein's Harold Clurman Theater offered a one-character stage version of a 1976 Samuel Beckett prose piece, *All Strange Away*, and a two-character World War II cliffhanger under Garfein's direction, *Rommel's Garden*. And the American Place Theater was given over this season to guest productions and OOB activities including its ongoing Women's Project.

On the musical side, off Broadway provided two of the year's three best new musicals, plus an important revival of *Pacific Overtures*, plus a collection of high-quality revues. *Kuni-Leml*, the operetta-like romance of an heiress and her two suitors, one an ill-favored rabbi-to-be and one a handsome but impecunious student, began as an OOB project of the Jewish Repertory Theater and was brought uptown for a season-long commercial run. It was based on a popular 19th century Yiddish Theater farce and was played with the earnest and charming suspension of disbelief of a fairy tale under Ran Avni's direction. The Raphael Crystal music and Richard Engquist lyrics, the Nahma Sandrow book and the high spirits of an appealing ensemble fitted together smoothly and brought off the season's most uniformly beguiling musical.

On the other hand, another durable off-Broadway musical, *3 Guys Naked From the Waist Down*, sputtered with brilliant comedy within a smothering score. The title is backstage argot for a stand-up comic, not a porno reference, and the show concerned three such performers aspiring to the Johnny Carson-sized big time. The humor was at its most penetrating in the dark-edged clowning and miming of John Kassir, reminiscent of Jonathan Pryce in *Comedians*, but with the sound of its rock numbers turned up to assault the eardrums and smash the lyrics to smithereens.

Warren Leight (book) and Charles Strouse (music and lyrics) took up the subject of New York Mayor Edward I. Koch and his administration as reported in his autobiography *Mayor*. The cabaret musical of that title was produced by a consortium at the Top of the Gate and was well received as what might be called a tart and tuneful topical revue, except that its songs and sketches concentrated on a single topic, the colorful Mayor of New York and satellite personalities: Carol Bellamy, the Helmsleys, Donald Trump, Harrison Goldin and ex-Mayors Lindsay and Beame. And another 1984–85 off-Broadway musical, *In Trousers*, was written by William Finn of *March of the Falsettos* but could not find much of an audience for its examination of confused sexuality in a husband and father who finds himself increasingly attracted to members of his own sex.

Revues too were an important part of the off-Broadway scene. In addition to MTC's abovemmentioned Cryer-Ford session, the 1984–85 program consisted of a revisit by *A Kurt Weill Cabaret* at the Harold Clurman Theater, with Martha Schlamme and Alvin Epstein in this 15-year-old touring pot pourri of Weill numbers; *Shades of Harlem*, a Cotton Club cabaret with music of the 1920s mingled with new songs; the politically satirical *Rap Master Ronnie* with music by Elizabeth Swados, lyrics by Garry Trudeau and with Reathel Bean as the President (it closed shortly after Election Day, when the Reagan run was extended); Jo Sullivan in a recapitulation of her career (*I Hear Music . . . of Frank Loesser and Friends*) with songs of major Broadway composers; the Harold Prince-directed, multi-authored collection of baseball songs and episodes, *Diamonds*; the song-and-dance session *Ann Reinking . . . Music Moves Me*, made to order for its star; and the "story songs" of the late Harry Chapin in a revue at the Village Gate.

Among the specialty attractions, while Broadway was enjoying its Whoopi Goldberg, off Broadway was relishing the carryings-on of Avner Eisenberg in *Avner the Eccentric*, a one-man extravaganza of clowning, juggling and other engaging accomplishments. The off-Broadway program also included one-performer studies of Elvis Presley (*Elvis Mania*) performed by Johnny Seaton, Zelda Fitzgerald (William Luce's *Zelda*) by Olga Ballin, a renowned Hungarian Jewish heroine (*Hannah Senesh*) by Lori Wilner, Dorothy Parker (*The Singular Dorothy Parker*) by Jane Connell, as well as an anonymous black housekeeper reviewing the events of her life (*Between Rails*) by Thelma Louise Carter. The distinguished Berliner Ensemble actor Ekkehard Schall visited New York with a one-man program of excerpts from the works of his distinguished father-in-law, Bertolt Brecht, performed in the original German. The distinguished Italian actor Vittorio Gassman brought to town his internationally-performed showcase of sketches. And a stopover by *The Chinese Magic Revue* represented still another culture and continent among the year's off-Broadway speciality programs, while native talent was conspicuously and ably represented by the two title stars of the magic-and-comedy show *Penn & Teller*.

With its spate of revivals as reported in the next chapter, off Broadway provided three times the action of Broadway on its stages during the season of 1984–85; stages that were smaller than Broadway's but big enough to hold more than half the Best Plays and other major excitements of the theater year. It shares to some extent Broadway's increasingly prominent characteristics as a showcase for material developed in less demanding economic circumstances, i.e. OOB or regional theater, areas in which *Blue Window*, *Tracers*, *Hurlyburly*, *Kuni-Leml*, *The Foreigner* and other outstanding off-Broadway programs were first produced. But as of this season off Broadway continued also to function as a proving ground, for better or for worse, for relative newcomers like the authors of *As Is* and *3 Guys Naked From the Waist Down*, as well as for such treasured talents as David Storey, Michael Weller, Joseph A. Walker, William Finn, Patrick Meyers, Martin Sherman, Christopher Durang and Albert Innaurato, not to mention fresh looks at the work of an Arthur Miller, a Stephen Sondheim. No such proving-ground function was really viable in 1984–85 on Broadway, with its ballooning costs; but for another year, at least, in the face of the growing menace of similar commercialization, it still stood on a broad base in the narrower byways of New York professional theater.

Revivals on and off Broadway

The history of the theater is measured in millenia, and nothing so convincingly demonstrates its immortality as a season like this one, in which the past came forward to bolster the present in revivals all over town. Our corresponding historian, Thomas T. Foose, observes that "1984–85 will be remembered for three classics staged on Broadway, and not off as is usually the case, which three were among the principal artistic successes of the season." He was speaking of *Cyrano de Bergerac* in an Anthony Burgess translation (the 13th New York stage production of the Rostand work, by Mr. Foose's calculations), *Much Ado About Nothing* ("highly popular in New York during the entire 19th century, but for the first four decades of the present century there was little interest in this work") and *Strange Interlude* (Lynn Fontanne opened in the original 1927–28 New York production of "this taxing play" and was later replaced by Judith Anderson). And Broadway produced 9 other revivals this season, making a total of 12 to off Broadway's 40, or a grand New York revival total of 52. If dramatists enjoyed temporary reincarnation along with their works, in 1984–85 we could have seen Shakespeare catching up on the news of O'Neill and Ibsen, Molière smiling at the pleasantries of Goldsmith, Coward or Shaw, Aeschylus marveling at the lyric imagination of Puccini, Victor Herbert, Franz Lehar and of course the Messrs. Gilbert and Sullivan.

It was the late great team of Rodgers and Hammerstein who scored the season's biggest Broadway hit with the revival of *The King and I*, billed as Yul Brynner's farewell appearance in the role of the King of Siam (June 30 was the date of his final performance) which he created so vividly opposite Gertrude Lawrence in the original 1951 production. Its enormous success, including setting a new all-time record for a week's Broadway gross ($605,546) was achieved in the absence of new musical hits, but not merely so, *faute de mieux*. It was a combination of glorious, untarnished script and score and performance that would have succeeded in any competition.

Likewise, the Jim Dale-Stockard Channing performance of Peter Nichols's *Joe Egg* under Arvin Brown's direction did credit to both major areas of New York theater production, originating off Broadway on the Roundabout schedule. This American production of the British play soon moved up to Broadway to share its spotlight with an English production of an American play, Eugene O'Neill's abovementioned *Strange Interlude* starring Glenda Jackson under Keith Hack's direction. The British stage didn't send over as many potent new scripts as in some seasons past, but important revivals like those Royal Shakespeare Company versions of *Cyrano* and *Much Ado*, directed by Terry Hands, with Derek Jacobi as Benedick and Cyrano, took their place. Finally from the London stage Broadway welcomed Frederick Lonsdale's 1923 comedy *Aren't We All?* staged by Clifford Williams with Rex Harrison and Claudette Colbert charming audiences in a glittering cast which included Lynn Redgrave, George Rose and Jeremy Brett. Also visiting from Europe this season was the Greek National Theater's Epidaurus production of Sophocles's *Oedipus Rex*, presented at the Vivian Beaumont in the modern Greek language in a translation from the ancient tongue by Minos Volanakis, who also staged the classic.

It was a directors' year at Circle in the Square. There George C. Scott proved that Noel Coward's *Design for Living* is indeed a lively design, as he staged an energetic version with Raul Julia, Frank Langella and Jill Clayburgh in the three-cornered romance. Ellis Rabb followed, directing his own co-adaptation of Arthur Schnitzler's *The Loves of Anatol*. Finally, John Malkovich of last year's *Death of a Salesman* (acting) and *Balm in Gilead* (directing) fame grappled with the ironies of Shaw's *Arms and the Man* performed by a cast headed by Kevin Kline, Raul Julia and Glenne Headly.

A revival-producing equivalent of Broadway's Circle in the Square (as always, under the direction of Theodore Mann and Paul Libin) is off Broadway's Roundabout Theater Company (continuously under the direction of Gene Feist), ingeniously bringing to the New York stage a flowing series of top-drawer productions of scripts which seem almost invariably well-timed for a fresh viewing. This season, the Roundabout acquired and refurbished new quarters at 100 E. 17th Street, signaling its determination not to permit real estate problems to slow the pace of its contribution to our theater. Its 1984–85 program included the electrifying *Joe Egg* which went on to Broadway, the classic Oliver Goldsmith comedy *She Stoops to Conquer*, directed by Daniel Gerroll, with Kaye Ballard and E.G. Marshall, Synge's *The Playboy of the Western World*, Ibsen's *An Enemy of the People* in a new English version, with Roy Dotrice pursuing his American career in the role of Dr. Stockmann, and, just before the season ended, a new look at John van Druten's comedy *The Voice of the Turtle*.

In other parts of the city, the organizations principally devoted to the gems of the theatrical past were doing their thing in stately defiance of current economic difficulties. New York Shakespeare Festival annually justifies its name these days with summer action at the Delacorte in Central Park, this year offering a *Henry V* with Kevin Kline in the title role, and an English translation of the Yiddish melodrama *The Golem* by H. Leivick (our Mr. Foose notes that he is listed as "Halper Levick" in *The Oxford Companion to the Theater*), with Richard Foreman directing a cast headed by F. Murray Abraham, who later in the year won the best-acting Academy Award for his performance of Salieri in the movie version of *Amadeus*. He also figured in the season of Mirror Repertory in a guest appearance for two weeks in their production of *The Madwoman of Chaillot* (that company also offered revivals of Booth Tarkington's *Clarence* and Robert Bolt's *Vivat! Vivat Regina!* this season under the artistic direction of Sabra Jones).

Ancient Greek tragedy was a preoccupation of Christopher Martin's City (formerly Classic) Stage Company, presenting Aeschylus's Oresteia divided into two programs with inserted excerpts from Sophocles and Euripides. CSC also found time for a Molière (*George Dandin*, as adapted by Alex Szogyi), and an Eric Bentley translation of a German comedy *The Underpants*. They also worked on a version of *Frankenstein* intended for the CSC schedule in the fall of 1985. And the John Houseman-Michael Kahn Acting Company, touring under the auspices of Kennedy Center, made a brief but eclectic appearance in New York with a one-week repertory of *A New Way to Pay Old Debts* by Philip Massinger, Shakespeare's *As You Like It* and Thornton Wilder's *The Skin of Our Teeth*.

Much was hoped for in the re-mounting of Rudolf Friml's *The Three Musketeers*, a seven-figure Broadway production with a new book by Mark Bramble. The old melodies marched bravely through the score, but the show remained a weak echo of its former self, like a musketeer in middle age. Another full-blown Broadway musical in its Goodspeed Opera House production, *Take Me Along*, closed after its opening night, so that these two large-scale musical revivals played a combined total of only ten performances. The theater's musical repertory was more effectively represented this season by the aforementioned revamped *La Boheme* at the Public Theater, and most notably by an exceptionally distinguished revival of the Stephen Sondheim-John Weidman-Hugh Wheeler musical *Pacific Overtures* directed by Fran Soeder in independent production off Broadway by The Shubert Organization and McCann & Nugent. The Sondheim score is one of the most haunting in the modern theater, so sophisticated that its flavor seems to improve by repetition. It is eminently revivable, and its presence here this season was both a pleasure and a powerful reminder that we lack an organized facility for sampling such masterworks *every* season, doing for the later part of the 20th century what LOOM has been doing for the earlier part.

The voice of Samuel Beckett was heard at the Harold Clurman, with Alvin Epstein directing and performing in an *Endgame*. Arthur Miller's semi-autobiographical reminiscence of his life and times with Marilyn Monroe, *After the Fall*, with Frank Langella and Dianne Wiest, was staged by John Tillinger, who later put on a revival of Christopher Hampton's *Total Eclipse*, a 1974 play about the attachment between the French poets Verlaine and Rimbaud. Clifford Odets was well represented by his *The Country Girl* as played by Hal Holbrook and Christine Lahti, as was Lonne Elder III in The Negro Ensemble Company's revival of *Ceremonies in Dark Old Men* with Douglas Turner Ward starring and directing.

Sondheim and Romberg, Beckett and Ibsen, Shakespeare, Goldsmith and Molière, Miller and Inge and Odets, and of course, Aeschylus, Sophocles and Euripides—the work of these dramatists speaks to us in revival year after year and certainly spoke with special eloquence in this one, when so many new voices were muted, so many new songs unsung.

Offstage

The playhouses themselves were in the forefront of concern during 1984–85, partly because of a leftover feeling of uneasiness over the destruction of the Morosco, Helen Hayes and Bijou Theaters to make way for a hotel complex looming ever-higher over the Broadway area as the season progressed. A major defensive development at the very beginning in June was an 84-page report by the Theater Advisory Council to the City Planning Commission containing what the New York *Times* called "provisions that would make it difficult for a theater to be demolished unless it was actually deemed unsafe." The Council, consisting of 14 theater professionals including representatives of the Shubert, Nederlander and Jujamcyn holdings, had been appointed in 1982 by New York City Mayor Edward I. Koch to suggest ways to safeguard theaters from further demolition. The report recommended continuing requirement (already in force) of a special permit from the Planning Commission before a theater can be torn down. It also suggested the formation of a theater trust fund to purchase any playhouse threatened with demolition and recommended the banning of further large-scale development from the theater district. Matters of landmark status and air-rights of builders were taken up but not resolved in the report. Orville H. Schell, chairman of the Council, was quoted by the *Times*, "The message to the City of New York is: the theater is worth preserving."

Also on the positive side was the Morton Gottlieb experiment with *Dancing in the End Zone* at Broadway's Ritz Theater, shutting off the balcony and roping off 49 of the 548 orchestra seats to convert the Ritz from a full to a "middle" Broadway house (300 to 499 seats), therefore eligible for materially reduced production and operating costs at lower levels of contractual obligations. For example, under Actors' Equity regulations this procedure reduced the actors' minimum from $650 (Broadway) to $430 (middle Broadway) weekly, with corresponding concessions from other theater unions across the board. The price of a ticket in this arrangement was required to be lowered under $30, whereas $37.50 for straight plays and $45 for musicals was the going Broadway top this season.

Mr. Gottlieb believes that this tradeoff of fewer-seats-at-lower-prices in exchange for materially reduced costs (*Dancing in the End Zone* was estimated by *Variety* to have come in for $450,000) is an economically efficient means of encouraging the Broadway production of straight plays and the utilization of its smaller theaters. Then too, if one of these middle-Broadway offerings proved to be a hit, down could come the artificial barriers and up could go the play's status to full Broadway, raising prices and running expenses together with capacity. This is already done on a smaller scale with successful tributary-theater productions like *Blue Window*, frugally mounted at the off-off-Broadway level and then moved up to full off-Broadway status by a few strokes of the pen, without breaking performance stride or even changing theaters (it's also possible to move *down* a notch from off-Broadway to OOB, as *Man Enough* did this year). *Dancing in the End Zone* wasn't able to attract enough of an audience to provide a full test of this Gottlieb plan at the Ritz, but a later arrival, the Best Play *Doubles*, tried the same arrangement at the same theater. *Variety* estimated that it cost about $400,000 to bring in and could break even at $62,000 weekly under middle-Broadway circumstances, about two-thirds of what its operating cost would be as a full Broadway production in the same theater. *Doubles* was still running at season's end and could eventually prove the advantages of this plan all the way out.

One of the most glaring New York theater vacancies in recent seasons has been that of the Vivian Beaumont at Lincoln Center, a theater designed for repertory but now used all too infrequently for one-at-a-time visiting attractions like the Peter Brook *Carmen* or the Greek National Theater's *Oedipus Rex* or *And a Nightingale Sang . . .* in the little Mitzi E. Newhouse space downstairs. Vivian Beaumont management controversies seem to have been finally smoothed away by the appointment in September of ex-Mayor John V. Lindsay (admittedly no theater person, but an organizational live wire) as chairman of the theater's board. The board's search for an artistic director for the Lincoln Center Theater Company to replace Richmond Crinkley, who resigned, settled on Gregory Mosher, former artistic director of Chicago's Goodman Theater, a 1983–84 Tony nominee for his staging of *Glengarry Glen Ross* and winner this year of the prestigious Margo Jones Award. And Bernard Gersten, a former associate of Joseph Papp, was named executive producer by the Lincoln Center board to handle the business side of the enterprise.

One of the conflicts which have arisen in recent years between branches of the theater profession—exacerbated by the constantly changing nature of the economic environment—was resolved with a new Approved Production Contract between the Dramatists Guild (the playwrights, lyricists, composers and librettists) and the League of New York Theaters and Producers (Broadway producers and theater owners). The statement announcing the settlement of outstanding legal disagreements, as well as the contract, stated in part as follows: "The terms of the new agreements involve meaningful alterations of the royalty structure which will assist the producers and backers of plays and musicals to recoup their production costs more quickly. In return, authors will receive substantial improvements in option and advance payments, and in the sharing of subsidiary uses, thereby offering them the opportunity to spend more time writing exclusively for the theater as well as to enjoy a greater portion of long-range income that dramatists have come to consider their retirement benefits.

"In addition, the Guild and the League have provided for the creation of a Theatrical Conciliation Council, a body comprised of equal numbers of authors and producers, to be convened whenever problems arise with an individual contract and which is empowered to adjudicate such problems."

Relations between dramatists and actors continued strained, however, over the Actors' Equity Association's showcase code provisions requiring job offers or reimbursement for showcase performers in the event that the script they helped to showcase (and which showcased their acting) goes on to commercial production. In the view of authors and their agents, such a lien on a playscript inhibits future productions of it, since it can add to the production cost. Offered the choice between an encumbered and an unencumbered script of equal appeal, producers would tend to select the latter. In several instances during the season, authors were denying production rights to avoid such a lien, or losing production opportunities because of it.

Members of the Society of Stage Directors and Choreographers too were causing concern to dramatists by requesting in some instances a guarantee of first refusal of directing or choreographing assignments for future commercial production of a script they had directed or choreographed at the showcase stage. The Dramatists Guild issued a statement to its members over the signature of its vice president, Terrence McNally, warning against giving such guarantees, as "a play encumbered in writing with the services of a director may have difficulty in finding another director or producer."

In other developments, the League is changing its name from New York Theaters and Producers to American Theaters and Producers, wanting to add to its membership its colleagues in the key road cities. The League also came to an agreement with the musicians' Local 802 on a new three-year contract with annual 5 per cent raises which will bring the weekly Broadway minimum from $620 to $720 in the third year (and from $77.50 to $90 extra for playing a second instrument). The SSDC and the League rolled over the directors' and choreographers' contract for another 18 months; meanwhile the SSDC won substantial increases from the League of Regional Theaters and brought artistic directors into their fold.

Equity reached an impasse over how many non-Equity actors would be permitted in LORT shows but agreed to roll over the existing contract, plus a 4.5 per cent cost-of-living increase, for 14 months of further negotiations (the actors' contract for dinner theaters was also renewed, with allowance for future cost-of-living raises). And Equity and the League of Off-Broadway Theaters and Producers came to terms on a new sliding-scale reimbursement for actors in each of the five off-Broadway categories, with new weekly minimums as follows: Category A (100–199 seats) $225, B (200–250 seats) $275, C (251–299 seats) $320,

D (300–350 seats) $385 and E (351–499 seats) $435, with the percentage of increase weighted toward the lower end of the scale. And Colleen Dewhurst was elected president of Actors' Equity to succeed Ellen Burstyn, who did not run for reelection.

Badmouthing a New York theater season has always been a popular sport, especially in seasons like the one just past. Certainly the first traits visible on the horizon of an overall view of 1984–85 are its shortcomings: attenuation of audience, continued low-volume Broadway production, absence of a new blockbuster musical, hyping of revivals, a general scarcity of glitter and glamor in the personality of the season as a whole. Look a little closer, though, and you will see excellence in the foreground: humor (*Biloxi Blues*, *The Foreigner*, *Doubles*), imagination in writing and staging (*The Marriage of Bette and Boo*, *As Is*, *Blue Window*) and in design (*Big River*), tragedy (*Tracers*), suspense (*Pack of Lies*) and an abundance of social concerns (*Split Second*, *Ma Rainey's Black Bottom*, *Hurlyburly*, *The Normal Heart*, *Rat in the Skull*).

It can be said of 1984–85 that it offered nothing for everyone but something for each, with many offerings limited, not in skill or intensity, but in the scope of their appeal. Too much of our theater today seems directed only to this or that segment of the potential audience. Its economics are so heavily biased in favor of the two-character, one-set idea that we probably shouldn't look for much encouragement or inspiration for the whole-audience kind of show. 1984–85's Best Play authors are a distinguished group of dramatists, but among them only Neil Simon and Hugh Whitemore appeared to be trying to address the broadest possible theater audience. That whole audience won't respond to every good play or musical, nor should all dramatists attempt to write for it all the time. But it is always there, it always will be there, and the best hope for the future is that the theater's creators will continue to keep it in mind.

The New York theater's curtain times proceed onward into the late 1980s with such as Wallace Shawn's *Aunt Dan and Lemon,* played by Linda Hunt, *right,* and Kathryn Pogson.

PHOTO BY MARTHA SWOPE

1986, 1987 AND BEYOND

As the 1980s crossed their center line and proceeded through the last half of the decade, two largely undistinguished theater seasons paraded bravely but somewhat forlornly by. 1985–86 consisted of 42 Broadway and 108 off-Broadway productions and came to a close with a whimper of a Tony Awards ceremony in which the leading musical nominee was the off-Broadway transfer "The Mystery of Edwin Drood" and two of the four nominated plays were good old scripts from the past—"The House of Blue Leaves" and "Blood Knot"—and the off-Broadway past, at that. Fortunately there was also Herb Gardner's "I'm Not Rappaport" emerging from the off-Broadway present to stand tall and alone as the 1985–86 straight-play Tony winner.

And the haunting problems of the 1970s weren't going away, they remained eyeball-to-eyeball with the late-1980s professional stage: fragmented audiences, inhibiting production and ticket costs, menacing real estate interests, uncomfortable theatergoing, drying up of subsidy, etc. Roger L. Stevens's idea for a national theater was sputtering in Washington, while Joseph Papp's was still in the dinner-conversation stage. The season's most vivid image of violence wasn't against people, it was the half-eviscerated Helen Hayes Theater on 46th Street with its privacy violated, its dignity open to the sky, ropes dangling from the flies like entrails of the mortally wounded creature that it was.

Broadway's 12-month attendance in 1985–86 withered by 9 percent to 5,837,725 (down by two-fifths in the past five seasons, the smallest since the early 1970s, Richard Hummler of Variety *observed) and its gross by 8 percent to $190,600,000. Off Broadway wagged the dog in quality as well as quantity, carrying off the Critics Award with Sam Shepard's "A Lie of the Mind" and preempting eight of the ten Best Play citations: "Drood," "Rappaport," "Aunt Dan and Lemon," "The Perfect Party," "It's Only a Play," "Season's Greetings," "Largo Desolato" and "Drinking in America," plus the specially cited "Goblin Market," leaving only two places for Broadway's "Benefactors" and "Execution of Justice."*

The theater's sighs of relief as 1985–86 passed into history soon turned to groans of frustration as 1986–87 plodded through 12 more mostly lackluster months which came to an end as we went to press with this volume. Yes, there was a new Neil Simon ("Broadway

The 1985–86 Season on Broadway

PLAYS (7)

I'M NOT RAPPAPORT
(transfer)
The Boys of Winter
Execution of Justice
Precious Sons
So Long on Lonely Street
Social Security
The Boys in Autumn

MUSICALS (7)

Singin' in the Rain
Song & Dance
Mayor
(transfer)
The News
*THE MYSTERY OF
EDWIN DROOD*
(transfer)
Wind in the Willows
Big Deal

REVUES (3)

Jerry's Girls
Jerome Kern Goes to
Hollywood
Uptown . . . It's Hot!

FOREIGN PLAYS IN
ENGLISH (3)

BENEFACTORS
Corpse
The Petition

FOREIGN-LANGUAGE
PRODUCTIONS (5)

Italy on Stage:
La Gatta Cenerentola
I Due Sergenti
Pipino Il Breve
Il Campiello
Tango Argentino

REVIVALS (11)

The Odd Couple
(revised version)
Follies
(concert version)
The Iceman Cometh
Circle in the Square:
The Marriage of Figaro
The Caretaker
Blood Knot
Hay Fever
Loot
(transfer)
Sweet Charity
*Long Day's Journey
Into Night*
The House of Blue Leaves
(transfer)

SPECIALTIES (6)

The Grand Kabuki
(two programs)
*The Search for Signs of
Intelligent Life in the
Universe.*
The Magnificent Christmas
Spectacular
The Robert Klein Show
Lillian
Juggling and Cheap
Theatrics

HOLDOVER WHICH
BECAME A HIT IN
1985–86

Big River

Plays listed in CAPITAL LETTERS have been designated **Best Plays** of 1985–86.
Plays listed in *italics* were still running after June 1, 1986.
Plays listed in **bold face type** were classified as successes in Variety's annual estimate published June 4, 1986.

Bound"), a new Tina Howe ("Coastal Disturbances"), two new Arthur Miller one-acts ("Danger! Memory"), a new A. R. Gurney Jr. ("Sweet Sue," with Mary Tyler Moore and Lynn Redgrave), plus a new August Wilson (the Pulitzer Prize-winning "Fences") and a new Horton Foote ("The Widow Claire"). All of these were effective stage presentations, but only in the case of the latter two could their authors be said to be equalling and perhaps topping their previous comedic and dramatic insights. The saddest story of 1986–87, however, was the dismal failure of what can only be called a mess of Broadway musicals: "Honky Tonk Nights" (4 performances), "Rags" (4 performances), "Raggedy Ann" (5 performances), "Into the Light" (6 performances) and "Smile" (48—count 'em—48 performances). Even the Mike Nichols (direction)-William Shakespeare (lyrics) collaboration in the revue "Standup Shakespeare" floundered on Broadway for only 2 performances—that's the kind of season it was.

Fortunately for the New York Theater, the old world came to the rescue of the new with the charming London musical revival "Me and My Girl," starring Robert Lindsay, and the monumental Paris-to-London-to-New York, near-operatic, emotionally stirring, brilliantly performed (especially by Colm Wilkinson as Jean Valjean and Terrence Mann as his nemesis Javert) musical version of Victor Hugo's "Les Miserables," a wonderful piece of stagecraft. Foreign authors also nearly stole the straight-play show with the likes of Michael Frayn's "Wild Honey," Christopher Hampton's "Les Liaisons Dangereuses," Steven Berkoff's "Kvetch," Janusz Glowacki's "Hunting Cockroaches" and the collaborative South African "Born in the R.S.A."

So 1986–87 was in some respects a discouraging continuation of 1985–86, and yet . . . and yet, wasn't Broadway attendance rallying back toward the 6 million mark and the gross toward the $200 million mark as this review was going to press? Didn't some of those voices we heard during the two bleak seasons sound like original new voices of stage authorship?—Wallace Shawn ("Aunt Dan and Lemon"), Polly Pen and Peggy Harmon ("Goblin Market"), George C. Wolfe ("The Colored Museum," a revue taking a hard look at the black condition), Eric Bogosian and Lily Tomlin in and out of monologue, a new height for the collaborative creation of stage material in "Born in the R.S.A." And how many readings/workshops/productions of record (let alone the unreported)

The 1985–86 Season Off Broadway

PLAYS (38)

PH 1985:
Fighting International Fat
Raw Youth
I'M NOT RAPPAPORT
In the Belly of the Beast
For Sale
Theater in Limbo:
  *Vampire Lesbians of
    Sodom & Sleeping
    Beauty or Coma*
Times Square Angel
Two Can Play
  (return engagement)
The Custom of the Country
Circle Rep:
  Tomorrow's Monday
  The Beach House
Alice and Fred
NEC:
  Eyes of the American
  House of Shadows
Jonah and the Wonder
  Dog
Louie and Ophelia
Public Theater:
  AUNT DAN AND
    LEMON
Jonin'
Rum and Coke
Cuba and His Teddy Bear

PH 1986:
Anteroom
Little Footsteps
THE PERFECT PARTY
Inside Out
CSC:
  Frankenstein
  A Country Doctor
  A Lie of the Mind
  Prairie du Chien & The
    Shawl
Be Happy for Me
Gertrude Stein and a
  Companion
MTC:
  IT'S ONLY A PLAY
  Principia Scriptoriae
  Women of Manhattan
  Another Paradise
  Daughters
  Orchards
  Smoking Newports, etc.
A Place Called Heartbreak

MUSICALS (11)

Options
THE MYSTERY OF
  EDWIN DROOD
Paradise!
Yours, Anne
Hamelin
Just So
Nunsense
To Whom It May Concern
Halala!
Williams & Walker
GOBLIN MARKET

FOREIGN PLAYS IN ENGLISH (7)

Faulkner's Bicycle
SEASON'S GREETINGS
Public Theater:
  A Map of the World
  LARGO DESOLATO
  Not About Heroes
  Quiet in the Land
  Cheapside

SPECIALTIES (7)

DRINKING IN
  AMERICA
Anais Nin
Elisabeth Welch
Mummenschanz
Spalding Gray
  (three programs)

REVIVALS (36)

Dames at Sea
Measure for Measure
LOOM:
  Sweethearts
  (10 operettas in running
    repertory)
Springtime for Henry
Curse of the Starving Class
Circle Rep:
  Talley & Son
    (revised version)
  The Mound Builders
Caligula
Roundabout:
  The Waltz of the
    Toreadors
  Mrs. Warren's Profession
  Room Service
Tatterdemalion
CSC:
  Brand
  A Medieval Mystery
    Cycle
MTC:
  Oliver Oliver
  Loot
  The Importance of Being
    Earnest
Mirror:
  The Time of Your Life
  Children of the Sun
  The Circle
  El Grande de Coca-Cola
  Hamlet
  The House of Blue Leaves
  The Eden Cinema
  Ten by Tennessee
    (two programs)

REVUES (9)

Ladies and Gentlemen,
  Jerome Kern
What's a Nice Country, etc.
  (revised version)
The Golden Land
Personals
Sweet Will
The Alchemedians
Beehive
*National Lampoon's Class of
  '86*
Professionally Speaking

Plays listed in **CAPITAL LETTERS have been designated Best Plays of 1985–86.**
Plays listed in *italics* were still running after June 1, 1986.

were there OOB in each of the last two seasons?—at least 350, wasn't it, the vast majority of them new scripts?

If theater consists of the proverbial "two planks and a passion," certainly there doesn't seem to be any scarcity of playwriting, composing, directing, acting or design passion as we head toward the 1990s. As for the planks, we cherish the Booth and the St. James (and would even hate to lose the Minskoff, Uris and Marquis) and sincerely hope that ways will be found to sustain our stage establishment. But one way or another, the theater is alive in New York as we go to press; not a repository for literary artifacts—though there were scores of those brought to life on New York Stages in 1986 and 1987—but a living theater of renewing inspiration. And it will be so while that passion abounds.

O.L.G., Jr.

INDEX

Play titles appear in **bold face**.

Otis L. Guernsey Jr., editor of the Best Plays year-book, began his long association with the theater at Yale University, where he wrote three plays that were presented by student groups. For nineteen years he was associated with the *New York Herald Tribune*, beginning as copy boy and then graduating to reporter, film and drama critic, and drama editor. He became a free-lance writer in 1960, authoring two original film stories. He now edits the *Dramatists Guild Quarterly* and is a national popular lecturer on the modern theater. He is a former member of the New York Film Critics (past chairman) and the New York Drama Critics Circle. Mr. Guernsey has also been a member of the panel of critics who selected the Tony Award nominees and served as a member of the advisory committee of the Bicentennial program at Kennedy Center, Washington, D.C. He is a charter member of the newly formed national critics' organization, American Theater Critics Association.